"Higgins's epic work showcases more than two centuries of U.S. financial history, providing helpful context regarding the world's most important capital markets whose impact reverberates across the world to this day. The book will give you all the context you need to understand where we are in financial markets today. A must-read!"

—**Muitheri Wahome**, author, *Building Capital:*
A History of Asset Management in South Africa

"It's very important for investors to have at least a basic grasp of financial history, and Mark's book is an excellent introduction to the subject. It provides readers with valuable context and perspective, as well as practical lessons on how to invest. It's also essential reading for anyone seeking a better understanding of the asset management industry, how it has developed over time, and why it doesn't serve investors as well as it should. I can highly recommend it."

—**Robin Powell**, editor, *The Evidence-Based Investor*

INVESTING *in* U.S. FINANCIAL HISTORY

Understanding the Past to Forecast the Future

MARK J. HIGGINS, CFA, CFP®

GREENLEAF
BOOK GROUP PRESS

Published by Greenleaf Book Group Press
Austin, Texas
www.gbgpress.com

Distributed by Greenleaf Book Group

For ordering information or special discounts for bulk purchases, please contact
Greenleaf Book Group at PO Box 91869, Austin, TX 78709, 512.891.6100.

Design and composition by Greenleaf Book Group and Mimi Bark
Cover design by Greenleaf Book Group and Mimi Bark
Cover image used under license from ©Shutterstock.com/Yosuke Hasegawa

Publisher's Cataloging-in-Publication data is available.

Print ISBN: 979-8-88645-134-4

eBook ISBN: 979-8-88645-135-1

To offset the number of trees consumed in the printing of our books, Greenleaf
donates a portion of the proceeds from each printing to the Arbor Day
Foundation. Greenleaf Book Group has replaced over 50,000 trees since 2007.

Printed in the United States of America on acid-free paper

24 25 26 27 28 29 30 31   10 9 8 7 6 5 4 3 2 1

First Edition

Dedicated to:
Virginia Schwartz Higgins

My mother taught me the power of reading and
self-education. This book was possible only because
of her role modeling and encouragement.

CONTENTS

ACKNOWLEDGMENTS

I have the deepest gratitude and admiration for my wife, Katie Higgins. There were many highs and lows over the past three years, and she was always there to celebrate the highs and coach me through the lows. I am equally grateful for the support of my two inspiring children, Jack Higgins and Lila Higgins. Jack's passion for trains shaped the content of several chapters. The pictures we took during our West Coast train tour appear in the book, and our experience taking them is permanently etched in my memories. Lila's constant support and sense of humor were a reliable breath of fresh air during many tedious moments. Our morning starts at "Starbies" broke bouts of writer's block, and they will remain in my memories forever. My family was a rock throughout this entire process, and this book is as much theirs as it is mine.

I am eternally grateful for the support of my extended family. I am especially appreciative of my mother and father, Virginia Higgins and James Higgins. Their contributions extend well beyond this book, and I am so grateful for their unconditional love and support. I am appreciative of my brother Dan Higgins, whom I admire above all others for his courage and resilience. He also helped collect data used in this book by poring through old newspapers dating back to the mid-1800s. My sister, Laura Hoge, has taught me many psychological principles that prove invaluable both personally and professionally. My brother Mike Higgins helped spread the important message that embracing portfolio simplicity and index funds provide the most powerful competitive advantages to most investors. My in-laws Greg Moore and Linda Moore helped me appreciate that the political divisiveness in this country is more fabricated than real, and it distracts us from much more important problems that this nation must face together. My in-laws Penn Wells and Sally Wells taught me the value of exploring the world outside of one's comfort zone. Our trip to Normandy, France, in the summer of 2022 brought the stories in chapters 19 and 20 to life. I would like to give special thanks to my nephew Jacob Higgins, who helped compile data related to the investment consulting industry. I am grateful for the constant support and positivity of Perla Evans and Josh Evans. I am also grateful for the support of Andy Hoge, Pam Farina, and Shannon Higgins, who provided constant encouragement throughout this arduous process. Finally, I would like to thank my grandmother Agnes Higgins for her inspiring spirit. She passed away at the age of 103 on November 20, 2020. She is one of the few people who lived through much of the history described in this book, and her commitment to her fourteen children, thirty-seven grandchildren, and forty-five great grandchildren is an inspiration to all of us.

I would like to thank numerous academic professionals, industry experts, journalists, and professional investors who provided invaluable feedback. It would have been impossible to assemble a complete history of the U.S. financial system without their extraordinary works on various periods. I am especially grateful for Former Federal Reserve Chairman Ben Bernanke's feedback on the Global Financial Crisis, Richard Sylla's feedback on Alexander Hamilton's financial programs, Casey Whalen's and Dean Takahashi's explanations of the secrets of the Yale University Endowment, Guy Cooper's and Richard Ennis's insights into the history of the investment consulting industry, Winthrop Smith, Jr.'s perspective on the history of Merrill Lynch, Amity Shlaes's input on the Great Society, and Muitheri Wahome's perspective of the financial history of South Africa. I am grateful for the feedback and ongoing relationships with Gregory Zuckerman, Stefan Hofrichter, Michelle Seitz, Spencer Jakab, David Cowen, and Irving Levin.

I am grateful for the opportunities to publish and speak on financial history topics in the run-up to the publication of this book. I am especially grateful for the opportunities provided by Kristin Aguilera, editor of *Financial History* magazine; Paul McCaffrey, editor of *Enterprising Investor* from the CFA Institute; Marina Batliwalla, founder of the *Banking on Girls* podcast; Robin Powell of the *Evidence-Based Investor*; Anita Knotts, founder of the Lotus Women's Institute; Gabby Stranieri, editor of *With Intelligence*; Raphael Palone with Congresso Planejar, and Gene Natali and Jeff Davidek, visiting professors at Carnegie Mellon.

Thank you to the many authors who guided me through the publication process. I am particularly thankful for the assistance provided by Lindsay Pedersen, who helped me understand the pros and cons of different publishing approaches. I am thankful for the tips offered by other authors such as Margaret O'Mara, Stephen Foerster, Clint Greenleaf, Lee A. Craig, Mark Hebner, Richard Ennis, Todd Finkle, James Fok, Matt Hill, and Amity Shlaes. Finally, I am grateful for the entire team at Greenleaf Book Group, especially Tanya Hall, Brian Welch, Mimi Bark, Morgan Robinson, Pam Nordberg, Jen Rios, and David Endris.

I would like to thank my former clients whom I had the privilege to serve for nearly thirteen years as an institutional investment consultant. I always strived to place their interests before all others, and I hope that this book helps them to continue learning and improving their investment performance. I am especially grateful for the support of Dan Villa, Jon Putnam, Cindy Byrd, Betty Lou Morrow, Harry Birdwell, Sarah Green, and Kevin Sanger. Finally, I am especially thankful for the friendship of Elliot Chambers. Not only was he a former client, but his personal research on financial history inspired the chapter covering the Panic of 1819.

I am grateful for the support of several former colleagues. Investment consultants are often trained to build complex and expensive portfolios without questioning whether it is in their clients' best interest. Challenging these practices is difficult because it forces them to confront the paralyzing fear of obsolescence. Several former colleagues had the courage to make this leap. I am especially grateful for the wise counsel and friendship of Eryn Bacewich, as well as support provided by Guy Cooper, Rob Palmeri, Mikaylee O'Connor, Ryan Harvey, Charlie Waibel, and Austin Head-Jones. I am also thankful for the unconditional support of friends, including Doug and Mitzi Harlor, Erin and Adam Storch, Matt and Annie Harad, Mike and Cathy Gay, Wei-Li and Karen Chong, Zac Stillerman, Thad Glavin, Martin Dixon, and Jacob Rothman.

Finally, I am thankful for the many interesting people throughout the world with whom I have interacted over the past several years. Their feedback not only gave me the stamina to persist, but they also made me realize that U.S. financial history has value far beyond America's borders. I am grateful for the feedback and support provided by Désirée Lucchese, Brad Scott, Florian Campuzan, Marco Alfonso, Bahri Haciibrahimoglu, Guan Seng Khoo, Said Mansour, Luciene Miranda, Lily Taft, Leigh Poggio, Mary Ruth Newman, Leah Emkin, Wes Long, Brian Schroeder, Ted Stephenson, Nazneen Motafram, Phoebe Chan, Lance DiLorio, James Watkins, III, Israel Munoz, Georgie Veyccan, Mary Carlson, Betül Kaplan, Wendi Ruschmann, Azam Farooqui, and Vasie Papadopoulos. This book primarily covers the U.S. financial system, but this nation's unique role in the world affects everybody. I hope that revealing America's errors will help other countries to avoid them, while sharing America's strengths inspires other nations to replicate them.

INTRODUCTION

"That's why wise people study history and seek out the original documents. That's why we read biographies of great leaders. And that's why historians say the best way to understand the present is to understand the past and the best way to understand the past is to study what came before and what caused it."[1]

—ANDRÉ PEROLD, professor of finance and economics,
Harvard University (2022)

In March 2020, the global economy came to an abrupt halt after most of the world's inhabitants suddenly realized that the COVID-19 virus had become a deadly global pandemic. Investors panicked, and securities markets throughout the world suffered sharp declines. At the time, I was serving as an investment consultant to U.S. institutional investment plan trustees who collectively oversaw more than $60 billion in assets. With the stock market in free fall, they were getting anxious. I knew that financial panics presented opportunities to rebalance portfolios back into risky assets, but I was hesitant to move too quickly. I recalled that it took nearly two years before the stock market hit bottom during the Global Financial Crisis (GFC), and I assumed that the COVID-19 crisis would be similar. Therefore, I advised clients to use regularly scheduled cash flows to rebalance their portfolios on the margins, but to wait until markets stabilized before fully rebalancing.

I was surprised when markets recovered a few months later after the Federal Reserve and U.S. Congress implemented massive monetary and fiscal stimulus programs. It was the speed of the response that caught me off guard. I figured they would create programs like those used during the GFC, but I thought it would take much longer to implement them. I later realized that I would not have made this assumption if I had been more knowledgeable of financial history. Over the past 230 years, tactics invented during financial crises were often reapplied more rapidly to address subsequent crises.

This was especially true when memories of a prior crisis were still fresh, and in March 2020, recollections of the GFC had not faded. Thus, the Federal Reserve and Congress were preconditioned to enact massive fiscal and monetary stimulus packages in record time. This experience convinced me that I needed to study financial history to be more effective in my job.

As I began casually studying financial history, I also became increasingly concerned about the standard practices employed by institutional investment consultants. Prior to starting my career as a consultant in 2009, I had read David Swensen's book, *Pioneering Portfolio Management*, which explained how the Yale University Endowment generated returns that far exceeded those of the average endowment. I assumed that investment consulting firms could help clients produce returns that were comparable to Yale's. The common assumption was that the key to Yale's success was allocating heavily to alternative asset classes such as venture capital, buyout funds, and hedge funds, as well as selecting the best active managers in traditional asset classes. But after seven years of consulting, it became evident that Yale was the exception rather than the rule. For most other investors, chasing Yale's performance was more likely to reduce portfolio returns, increase fees, and distract clients from more important tasks. I concluded that most clients would be better served by simplifying their portfolios, stabilizing their long-term target allocations, avoiding exotic alternative asset classes, and relying heavily on index funds. Confident that this approach was in their best interest, I gradually shifted them to this strategy. But as I simplified portfolios, I had a nagging fear that clients would fire me because eventually they would conclude that I was no longer needed to manage all the complexity. Nevertheless, as a fiduciary, I was obligated to recommend what was in their best interest, not mine.

Over the next five years, I was both thrilled and relieved by the results. Not only did the strategy reduce fees and improve performance, but it also freed up precious time to focus on more value-added financial and investment activities. I used this time to help clients address challenges that were previously neglected. The irony was that it made my position more valuable rather than less. The paralyzing fear of obsolescence was nothing to fear at all.

Excited by the results, I encouraged colleagues to adopt this strategy, but few were open to it. The strength of their resistance aroused my curiosity about the investment profession itself. I wanted to know why investment consultants entered the rut that is so difficult to escape, and how to inspire the industry to embrace change that promised benefits for all. I knew that to change the status quo, I needed to dive deep into financial history and determine how we had arrived at this place. As fate would have it, the COVID-19 quarantine gave me plenty of time. I no longer had to commute to the office or travel to client meetings, and virtually all social activities were cancelled. So, I began burying myself in books.

Initially, I assumed I could limit myself to recent history, perhaps going as far back as the Great Depression in the 1930s. But after reading a few dozen books, I noticed how people's reactions to past events were always shaped by experiences in the more distant past. So, I traveled further and further back in time until I arrived in 1790, which was the year that Alexander Hamilton created the foundation of the U.S. financial system and restored the nation's damaged credit. This was not the beginning of financial history in the New World, but it was a reasonable place to start.

By December 2020, I had read dozens of books, and I was increasingly using financial history to advise clients. The lessons not only helped contextualize current events but also helped forecast the likely consequences. One notable example was when high levels of inflation persisted in 2021. Having read extensively about the post–World War I/Great Influenza inflation, I immediately noted the similarities to post-COVID-19 inflation. This, in turn, made it possible to predict that the Federal Reserve was highly likely to respond much more aggressively than many people assumed.

A second benefit was gaining a much deeper appreciation for the evolution of the investment profession. Most importantly, I was relieved to discover that many well-respected investors believed that most individual and institutional investors would benefit from less complex allocations and much heavier use of index funds. Examples include William Sharpe, Charles Ellis, Burton Malkiel, Eugene Fama, Ben Graham, Warren Buffett, and even David Swensen himself. I also confirmed that fear of obsolescence was the biggest obstacle that prevented investment professionals from abandoning overly complex strategies that were clearly not optimizing results. Many believed (even if only subconsciously) that if clients adopted simpler, low-cost strategies they would no longer require the services of advisors.

Throughout 2021 and early 2022, I used lessons from the past to help clients understand the present, simplify their portfolios, reduce fees, and improve performance. As I read more books, I also thought how tragic it was that nobody had ever written a book on the full financial history of the United States. I knew that sharing this knowledge could improve the decision-making of professional investors, government policymakers, investment plan trustees, and individuals. I wholeheartedly believed that this book needed to be written, and although I knew it was an ambitious task, I decided to take a shot.

Over the next two years, I read tens of thousands of pages of books, journal articles, old newspapers, government studies, surveys, and original source documents. I watched documentaries on World War I, World War II, and the Vietnam War. I listened to speeches by William Jennings Bryan, Franklin Roosevelt, Ben Bernanke, and Hank Paulson. Every question that I answered raised new questions, but I continued digging until I could piece together a comprehensive financial history of the United States of America.

The book that follows is the product of a nearly four-year endeavor. The knowledge that it yielded has helped demystify current financial events and predict the likely consequences. It has revealed the governing principles of America's financial system and its securities markets. Many principles are visible only when one's knowledge is extended well beyond the maximum human life span. I have found that understanding these principles makes financial manias more recognizable, frauds more predictable, and financial crises less frightening. This experience has also convinced me beyond any doubt that embracing investment strategies with less complexity provides a golden opportunity to enhance the value of the investment profession rather than condemn it to obsolescence. Not a day has passed over the last four years in which I have not read, written, or thought about how to share this story. I have done my best to capture the most important insights on the pages that follow, and I hope that it provides readers with the same feeling of enlightenment that I felt while writing it.

THE VALUE OF STUDYING U.S. FINANCIAL HISTORY

This book was written to help investors, government policymakers, academic researchers, students, and individual Americans to understand key financial, economic, and investment principles by explaining them in the historical context in which they were most relevant. Over the past 233 years, the United States evolved from a colonial territory of Great Britain to become the world's largest economy and dominant financial center. This makes this country an excellent case study to explore many concepts related to economic and financial evolution. The history in this book is U.S. centric, but the insights may prove especially useful to inhabitants of foreign countries. History demonstrates that nations often behave more like regions separated by time rather than space. Therefore, understanding the past and present of one nation can help others appreciate the principles that explain their success and avoid mistakes that impede their progress.

It is impossible to summarize all the insights and lessons in a few pages, but several of the more useful concepts may include:

1. **Government Debt and Creditworthiness**

   - Importance of maintaining a nation's credit and the consequences of abusing it

   - Financial principles of wars, pandemics, natural disasters, and national emergencies

2. **The Benefits and Risks of Fractional Reserve Banking Systems**

   - The origins of fractional reserve banking principles

   - The dynamics of bank runs and strategies to prevent them

   - The critical role and responsibility of central banks

   - The dangers of shadow banking

3. **Principles of Economics and Innovation**

    - Comparative advantage and the benefits of global trade
    - The essential role of capitalism in promoting innovation, competitiveness, and improved standards of living
    - The importance of the proper staging of economic advancement

4. **Depressions, Inflation, and Price Stability**

    - The dangers of deep economic depressions and the counterintuitive solutions to avoid them
    - The role of economic depressions in triggering armed conflicts
    - The benefits of price stability and costs of uncontained inflation

5. **Securities Markets**

    - The broad-based benefits of targeted securities regulations
    - The principles of asset bubble formation and the common early warning signs
    - The laws of market efficiency and the low probability of outmaneuvering efficient markets

6. **Investment Strategy**

    - The benefits of index funds and dangers of active management
    - The problem of excessive diversification and overuse of active managers in institutional investment portfolios
    - The origins and persistence of flawed practices in the investment advisory industry

This is just a small sample of principles that are explored in this book. My hope is that reading this book from cover to cover will help you understand these principles by feeling as if you experienced the conditions in which they were discovered. Additional "Points of Interest" appear in gray boxes throughout the book. These asides are intended to further illustrate concepts, perspectives in time, and key characters both good and bad.

Part 1

Building the Foundation of the U.S. Financial System 1790–1865

"Credit public and private is of the greatest consequence to every Country. Of this, it might be emphatically called the invigorating principle. No well-informed man, can cast a retrospective eye over the progress of the United States, from the infancy to the present period, without being convinced that they owe in a great degree, to the fostering influence of Credit their present mature growth."[1]

—ALEXANDER HAMILTON

The birth of the U.S. financial system occurred soon after the establishment of the nation itself with the ratification of the U.S. Constitution in 1788. To foster economic prosperity, government leaders and private citizens established several institutions and guiding principles that were intended to benefit both current and future generations. **Part 1** covers the first seventy-five years of U.S. financial history. It was a tumultuous period, as the nation struggled to establish a stable financial system and begin the transition from an agrarian to an industrial economy. Embedded in these chapters are multiple concepts that help contextualize challenges that the U.S. continues to grapple with today. Examples include, but are not limited to, the mechanics of fractional reserve banking, the role of central banks in financial systems, the dynamics of asset bubbles, and the financial demands of war.

Chapter 1 begins with Alexander Hamilton's proposals to repair the nation's creditworthiness and modernize its financial system. Hamilton's programs attracted merciless attacks from political opponents, but he persuaded Congress to pass each one. By 1791, the credit of the United States was repaired; the federal government had a reliable revenue stream to support debt payments; and a twenty-year charter was granted to the nation's first central bank, the First Bank of the United States. Hamilton's genius provided the fledgling nation with a sound foundation on which to build more than two centuries of economic prosperity.[2]

Chapter 2 begins with the initial public offering of stock in the First Bank of the United States. Within a matter of weeks, manic trading of subscription rights, referred to as "scrip," created the first asset bubble in U.S. history. Alexander Hamilton's quick reaction deflated the bubble without causing a major financial crisis. But less than a year later, his talents were needed once again when a group of speculators abused the liberal lending practices of the First Bank and attempted to corner the market for U.S. government bonds and two bank stocks. Hamilton broke the corner using several unconventional central banking tactics, but many New Yorkers were financially ruined in the aftermath. Spooked by the fallout, members of the newly formed securities brokerage profession gathered at Corre's Hotel to plot their future in March 1792. Two months later they signed a pledge, referred to as the Buttonwood Agreement, which became the foundation of the New York Stock Exchange.[3]

Chapter 3 begins with the dissolution of the First Bank after Congress failed to renew its twenty-year-charter. Soon thereafter, the financial system devolved into chaos both during and after the War of 1812. Realizing their mistake, many congressmen reversed their opposition to a central bank and voted to approve a charter for the Second Bank of the United States. Soon after the Second Bank became operational in January 1817, it was forced to rein in several years of reckless lending by state-chartered banks. This, in turn, contributed to the Panic of 1819, which caused a deep depression that rivaled the Great Depression.

Chapter 4 begins with the signing of the constitution of the New York Stock Exchange in 1817. Initially considered a secondary market relative to the Philadelphia Stock Exchange, the New York Stock Exchange took center stage by the 1820s due, in part, to its reputation as a venue of choice for speculators. By the 1830s, securities trading in New York surpassed Philadelphia, and the rise of Wall Street accelerated. The chapter ends with the famous Bank War between President Andrew Jackson and the president of the Second Bank, Nicholas Biddle. President Jackson prevailed, and the Second Bank disappeared when its twenty-year charter expired. Its absence contributed to the formation of a massive real estate bubble, which collapsed after the Panic of 1837. A wave of bank failures soon followed, and Americans found themselves mired, once again, in a deep depression. It was only the discovery of gold at Sutter's Mill in 1848 that allowed the U.S. economy to fully recover.

Chapter 5 concludes the Foundational Era. It begins by explaining the divergence of the Northern and Southern economies during the decades that preceded the Civil War. The North pursued a path toward industrialization, while the South remained agrarian. The divergent economic paths brought the conflict over slavery to the forefront, as Northerners sought to constrain its spread westward. The election of Abraham Lincoln in 1860 prompted seven states in the Deep South to secede from the Union, triggering the outbreak of the Civil War in April 1861. The Union prevailed over the Confederacy, thus ending slavery in the United States. The demands of war also prompted several reforms that accelerated the evolution of the U.S. financial system and securities markets. These changes shaped the wild securities markets during the final decades of the nineteenth century, which are commonly referred to as the Gilded Age.

Chapter 1

OVERDUE CREDIT TO AMERICA'S FINANCIAL FOUNDING FATHER

"The honor of a Nation is its life."[1]
—ALEXANDER HAMILTON

The financial system that existed immediately after the formation of the United States was nothing like the one that exists today. After narrowly defeating the British in the Revolutionary War, the U.S. floundered for nearly a decade under a dysfunctional confederation-based system of government and struggled to pay off a mountain of war debt. In 1788, the adoption of a federal system of government under the Constitution stabilized the nation politically, but the financial system remained in disarray. Foreign investors feared an imminent default on America's outstanding debt, and Revolutionary War veterans were outraged by the government's failure to compensate them for their service in the war. Lack of confidence in the nation's financial stability, coupled with growing civil unrest, created an unhealthy economic environment.[2]

A major contributor to the country's troubles was the primitive state of its financial system, which suffered from two deficiencies. The first stemmed from the fact that the economy depended almost exclusively on agriculture. In contrast, many European countries had transitioned long ago to trade and industrial-based economies, which required more sophisticated financial institutions. The second issue was that, prior to the Revolutionary War, the limited capital needs of colonists were often provided by London-based financial institutions. Access to these institutions was limited after the British surrender at Yorktown.[3]

Several Founding Fathers (primarily Federalist Party members) realized that financial reforms were desperately needed, but many others (primarily Democratic-Republican Party members) were hostile toward the introduction of European-like financial institutions. Fortunately, one person possessed sufficient financial expertise and foresight to counter the opposition. Having served in the fast-paced import/ export business as a teenager on the island of St. Croix, the nation's first treasury secretary, Alexander Hamilton, witnessed firsthand how sound credit was an essential catalyst of economic growth. Hamilton supplemented his practical experience with a deep understanding of financial concepts obtained from relentless self-study. While encamped with Washington's armies in harsh locales such as Valley Forge, Hamilton buried himself in obscure books on financial history. He later supplemented these lessons with diligent study of Adam Smith's *The Wealth of Nations* and obsessive reviews of the Bank of England charter.[4]

Hamilton's practical experience and self-education provided him with a unique vision of the nation's potential to transform from a frontier market into an industrial powerhouse. He also realized that his vision was achievable only if the U.S. restored its creditworthiness and modernized its financial institutions. Tasked by President George Washington to make his vision a reality, Hamilton proposed three reforms, shrewdly constructing them to be mutually reinforcing.

1. **Restoration of U.S. Creditworthiness**—Hamilton's most pressing problem was the nation's poor credit. U.S. government bonds were far from "risk-free" in 1790. In fact, outstanding federal and state government bonds regularly traded as low as $0.10 to $0.20 on the dollar. Lack of faith in the nation's credit was justified. Congress had suspended interest payments, and many congressmen wished to renegotiate the principal or even default entirely. Even among congressmen who were committed to honoring the nation's debts, many wished to compensate the original bondholders rather than the actual bondholders (which consisted mostly of foreigners and northern speculators). They reasoned that the patriots who funded the war deserved to be rewarded, as opposed to speculators who stood to profit by buying bonds at distressed prices. In his first report to Congress entitled *First Report on the Public Credit*, Hamilton argued against such proposals, and instead meticulously detailed the benefits of honoring the nation's obligations to current bondholders. Hamilton carefully framed his argument around the benefits to U.S. citizens rather than more abstract moral principles. For example, he emphasized the commercial and trade benefits of having expanded access to credit and lower borrowing

costs. He also emphasized that sound credit was critical to national defense, stating, "Loans in times of public danger, especially from foreign war, are found an indispensable resource, even to the wealthiest of them." Hamilton understood that it was impossible to fight a war without financing it first—a principle that proved instrumental in protecting the Republic several times in future years. Hamilton concluded his proposal by promoting the somewhat radical concept of assumption, which meant that all debt (both federal and state) would be consolidated and paid in full by the federal government. Southern states found this provision especially objectionable, and to get support, Hamilton agreed to move the U.S. center of government from New York City to Washington, DC.[5]

2.   **Establishment of a Central Bank**—Hamilton's second proposal was the creation of a central bank. He modeled it on central banks in countries such as Holland, England, Germany, and France. Hamilton was particularly enamored with the Bank of England, and he often referenced a copy of the charter that he kept in his desk. In his *Second Report on the Further Provision Necessary for Establishing Public Credit*, Hamilton explained to Congress how a national bank would expand access to capital and improve the efficiency of trade. He spent considerable time explaining the mechanics of a fractional reserve banking system, which enables a financial system to increase the amount of currency and credit in circulation to levels that exceed gold and silver reserves.[6] This concept was not well understood at the time, and many politicians feared the potential consequences. Hamilton addressed their fears by explaining how prudent use of a fractional reserve banking system expanded the money supply, which in turn could accelerate the nation's reconstruction and set the stage for future economic growth. Finally, in a stroke of brilliance, Hamilton proposed that 75 percent of the capital provided by private investors could be funded via the exchange of U.S. government bonds. This increased demand for government bonds, thereby bolstering faith in the nation's credit and simultaneously making it easier for existing bondholders to invest in the bank.[7] The establishment of the First Bank of the United States helped fuel the U.S. economic expansion for the next two decades. Banknotes issued by the First Bank (roughly equivalent to Federal Reserve Notes today) were widely used in commerce, and the bank provided vital commercial services, such as issuing loans to citizens and accepting customer deposits. Finally, the First Bank served as the federal government's fiscal agent, handling tasks such as tax collection, management of deposits of the U.S. Treasury, and providing loans to the federal government.[8]

POINT OF INTEREST

Money Isn't What It Used to Be

*"Prices may fluctuate, but few people seriously question whether
a dollar bill—or more and more often, its credit-card
equivalent—is actually worth a dollar."*[9]
—Andrew H. Browning, financial historian

Americans conduct billions of transactions every day without ever questioning the face value of a dollar. But in the late 1700s, currency instability tormented Americans. Multiple paper currencies and banknotes circulated after the Revolutionary War, and none was stable. In fact, the phrase "not worth a Continental" refers to the rapid depreciation of paper currency issued by the Continental Congress and individual colonies to fund the Revolutionary War.[10]

The most reliable stores of value in the late 1700s were gold and silver coins, which were referred to as "specie." The establishment of the First Bank resolved the problem of currency instability. The bank issued "banknotes" that could be redeemed for gold and silver. The bank also served as the primary fiscal agent of the U.S., which provided it with a substantial and stable deposit base. Finally, the bank was well-funded with an initial capitalization of $10 million.[11] In combination, these features ensured that banknotes issued by the First Bank traded at face value, making commerce much more efficient and reliable.

Some financial historians assert that the First Bank was not a true central bank because it lacked many features of a modern central bank. For example, the First Bank lacked authority to regulate other banks, and its ability to manage monetary policy was limited. But if central banking is viewed as an evolutionary process, the First Bank clearly qualified as the first iteration of a central bank in the U.S.

3. **Federal Tariffs**—The final component of Hamilton's plan was the expansion of federal tariffs to support the payment of principal and interest on the nation's debt. Tariff increases were particularly controversial, as the country had just fought a war, in part over the perceived unfairness of British taxes. Nevertheless, Hamilton knew that honoring the nation's debts was impossible without a reliable revenue source. Although politically challenging, Hamilton secured passage of the Tariff of 1790, which increased tariffs on a variety of imported commodities and merchandise.[12]

Figure 1.1 provides a visual illustration of the three components of Hamilton's financial programs and the mutually reinforcing nature of each one.

"Credit is an entire thing. Every part of it has the nicest sympathy with every other part. Wound one limb and the whole tree shrinks and decays."[13]

—ALEXANDER HAMILTON

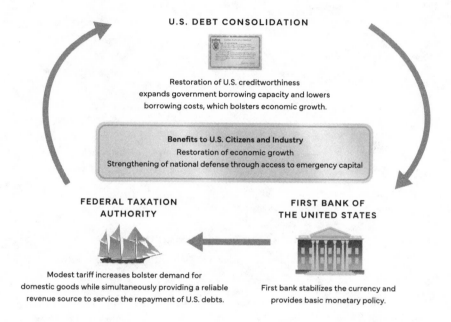

Figure 1.1: Mutually Reinforcing Elements of the Hamiltonian Financial Plan

Congress narrowly approved Hamilton's proposals. In July 1790, the U.S. consolidated all debt issued by the federal government and individual states, and from that moment on, the debt was backed by the full faith and credit of the United States. Principal and interest payments were supported by tariffs, and the First Bank of the United States was chartered on February 25, 1791. The impact of Hamilton's program was almost immediate—U.S. debt securities returned to par value in the secondary market, and borrowing costs for both public and private investors plummeted. A sample of these results are illustrated in the figures on the next page.

Outstanding U.S. debt securities increase in value . . .

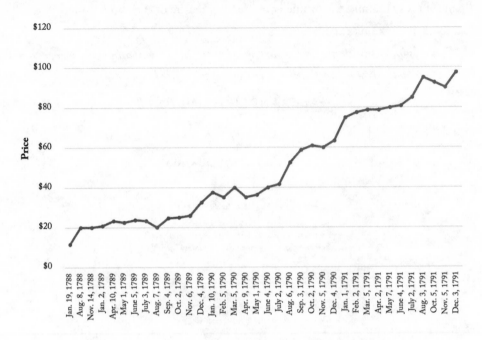

Figure 1.2: Continental Certificates Prices (January 1788–December 1791)[14]

. . . And the economy expands.

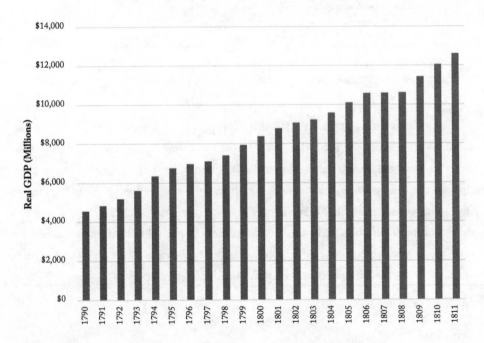

Figure 1.3: Real GDP in 2012 Dollars (Millions) (1790–1811)[15]

Alexander Hamilton's financial programs are rarely discussed in the twenty-first century, yet it is unlikely that the U.S. experiment would have succeeded without them. What makes his accomplishments even more impressive is that he implemented them despite fierce opposition from members of the Democratic-Republican Party, many of whom associated central banks with the same aristocratic oppression from which they had just freed themselves. While serving as treasury secretary, Hamilton suffered relentless personal attacks and persistent efforts to sabotage his reforms. Some of the harsher attacks were attributed to future presidents Thomas Jefferson and James Madison. In fact, convinced that Hamilton was guilty of "blunders and frauds," in the early 1800s, President Jefferson ordered Secretary of the Treasury Albert Gallatin to find evidence of Hamilton's alleged malfeasance. Gallatin, who initially shared Jefferson's suspicions, conducted an exhaustive audit but found no evidence of wrongdoing. When asked by Jefferson to summarize his findings, Gallatin replied: "I have found the most perfect system ever formed. Any change that should be made in it would injure it. Hamilton made no blunders, committed no frauds. He did nothing wrong."[16]

On July 12, 1804, Alexander Hamilton was mortally wounded in a duel with Vice President Aaron Burr. Animosity between them had festered for many years. Some historians believe the fatal rupture in the relationship occurred in 1799 when Burr persuaded Hamilton to support his bid to obtain a state charter to launch a water company. Unbeknownst to Hamilton, Burr planned to use the water company as a vehicle to establish a bank that would compete with the First Bank. When Hamilton discovered Burr's duplicity, he made it his mission to disrupt Burr's political ambitions. His opposition to Burr's bid for governor of New York—along with an alleged slanderous remark—prompted Burr to challenge Hamilton to a duel and fire the fatal shot.[17]

The financial genius of Alexander Hamilton was instrumental in the transformation of the U.S. from a frontier market to a future financial superpower. Hamilton's wisdom is also timeless, and he continues to inspire central bankers, financial professionals, regulators, and politicians to this day. His portrait on the U.S. ten-dollar bill is a just honor for having endured years of abuse from enemies who would reluctantly acknowledge his brilliance after his death. Yet Hamilton himself never claimed to possess superior intelligence; instead, he attributed his achievements to a strong work ethic and endless thirst for knowledge, stating:

> All the genius I have lives in this: when I have a subject in hand, I study it profoundly. Day and night it is before me. My mind becomes pervaded with it. Then the effort that I've made is what people are pleased to call the fruit of genius. It is the fruit of labor and thought.[18]

Chapter 2

SPECULATION ERUPTS
ON WALL STREET

*"As in the August before, and even to-day,
the center of the stock speculation was New York City."*[1]
—JOSEPH STANCLIFFE DAVIS (1917)

I n 1790, New York City was not the financial center of the United States; Philadelphia still held that title. But the first signs of a regime shift appeared after the initial public offering of stock in the First Bank of the United States on July 4, 1791. By the end of the month, intense demand for subscription rights fueled America's first asset bubble. The First Bank headquarters was in Philadelphia, but the speculation was concentrated in New York City. The bubble burst after six weeks, and the masterful response by Alexander Hamilton ensured a soft landing. Less than one year later, however, a much more severe financial crisis struck. Hamilton intervened again, but this time he employed central banking tactics that were decades ahead of his time. The crisis subsided by the summer of 1792, but many New Yorkers were financially ruined. In March 1792, a group of brokers convened a series of meetings to discuss ways to reestablish credibility for their newly formed profession. The meeting resulted in the signing of the Buttonwood Agreement, which became the foundation of the New York Stock and Exchange (NYSE). The remainder of this chapter recounts each of these formative events and explains how they set the stage for the rise of Wall Street.

POINT OF INTEREST

Alexander Hamilton Orchestrates America's First Soft Landing

"I was sufficiently reserved until I perceived the extreme to which bank scrip, and with it other stock, was tending. But when I saw this, I thought it advisable to speak out—for a bubble connected with any operation is, of all the enemies I fear, in my judgment the most formidable . . . to counteract delusions, appears to me to be the only secure foundation on which to stand."[2]

—Alexander Hamilton (1791)

The initial public offering of the First Bank of the United States was held on July 4, 1791. Stock was priced at $400 per share, but payment could be completed in four quarterly installments beginning on January 1, 1792. Purchases of stock were secured with subscription rights—commonly referred to as scrip—which was sold for $25 per share. Scrip was roughly equivalent to a call option.

The IPO was heavily oversubscribed, and the price of scrip soon skyrocketed. By the first week of August, scrip traded as high as $300. The prices of U.S. government bonds—which could be exchanged for First Bank stock—also experienced significant gains. Fearing the formation of a dangerous asset bubble, Hamilton orchestrated a sell-off by publicly opining that prices of scrip and government bonds had risen too high.[3] The subsequent price collapse threatened the nation's creditworthiness. Hamilton reacted by activating the Treasury's sinking fund, which was authorized under the Funding Act of 1790. The sinking fund allowed the Treasury to issue debt to purchase U.S. government bonds in the open market. This was similar to open market purchases that the Federal Reserve regularly uses today to manage interest rates.[4]

Hamilton's actions prevented the bubble from inflating to dangerous levels and then established a solid floor for prices once the bubble burst. His exceptional instincts rescued the nation from its first financial crisis, but he would need to get more creative to tackle a much more dangerous crisis in 1792.

THE BIRTH OF U.S. SECURITIES MARKETS

Securities markets in the U.S. were in the very early stages of development in 1790. The limited trading that occurred involved bonds issued by the states and Continental

Congress to fund the Revolutionary War. These were often traded via informal auctions on the streets of major cities such as Philadelphia, Boston, and New York. On August 4, 1790, U.S. activity in securities markets suddenly exploded after the passage of the Funding Act of 1790, which authorized the issuance of three series of bonds that consolidated federal and state debt accrued during the war. Soon thereafter, merchants, auctioneers, and brokers began trading them. In the summer of 1791, trading accelerated when subscription rights (i.e., scrip) to purchase stock in the First Bank of the United States began trading. Alexander Hamilton intervened to stop the brief scrip bubble. After the crisis subsided, trading continued, but the price volatility witnessed during the summer did not return.[5]

THE PANIC OF 1792

"At length our paper bubble is burst, the failure of Duer in New York soon brought on others, and these still more, like nine pins knocking one another down . . . It is computed there is a dead loss at New York of about 5 millions of dollars, which is reckoned the value of all the buildings of the city: so that if the whole town had been burnt to the ground it would have been just the measure of the present calamity."[6]

—PRESIDENT THOMAS JEFFERSON (April 17, 1792)

The First Bank of the United States opened its doors on December 12, 1791, and immediately began issuing loans. The first month of operations was relatively calm, but by February 1792, Hamilton feared that securities prices were rising too fast and another bubble was forming.

In hindsight, a major contributor to the bubble was the First Bank's liberal lending policies. Hamilton's former assistant treasury secretary, William Duer, then added fuel to the fire by using bank credit to fund a foolish speculative adventure. The details of Duer's plot were never fully documented, but several letters to co-conspirators revealed the basic premise. In one letter, Duer described a plan to "command all the floating Stock, create a scarcity, and oblige deliverers from a want of the stock settle the difference on favorable terms to the receivers." In other words, Duer intended to corner the market for U.S. government bonds and several stocks (later revealed to be the First Bank and Bank of New York). This, in turn, would enable him to demand whatever price he saw fit and "squeeze" short sellers who needed securities to cover their positions. It is also possible that Duer sought to gain control of the Bank of New York by acquiring a majority position.[7]

POINT OF INTEREST

William Duer: The Founding Father of Government Insider Trading

"The public Debt affords the best field in the world of speculation—but it is a field in which strangers may easily be lost. I know no way of making safe speculations but by being associated with people who from their Official situation know all the present & can aid future arrangements either for or against the funds."[8]

—Andrew Craigie (May 1788)

In 1790, Alexander Hamilton appointed William Duer as the assistant secretary of the Treasury. This proved to be a rare lapse of judgment, as Duer was already implicated in several questionable financial activities.

Living up to his reputation, Duer continued concocting financial schemes almost immediately. His first gambit leveraged his advanced knowledge of Hamilton's debt consolidation program. Knowing that it would boost the price of federal and state-issued bonds, Duer and several co-conspirators, such as Andrew Craigie, raced across the country purchasing millions of dollars of bonds from unsuspecting Americans. When Congress approved Hamilton's program, Duer sold the bonds for a substantial profit. Duer's actions clearly met today's definition of insider trading, as he possessed information that was non-public and material. Moreover, even though insider trading was legal for most Americans in the late 1700s, it was specifically outlawed for Treasury employees.[9]

William Duer was probably the first federal employee to engage in insider trading, but he was far from the last. Over the next 233 years, countless politicians engaged in various forms of insider trading, and few were held accountable. In fact, as of the writing of this manuscript, laws do not prevent members of Congress from trading stocks despite having access to material non-public information. It is ironic that insider trading for investment professionals was outlawed with the passage of the Securities Act of 1934, but Congress has yet to apply the same standards to themselves.

Duer's scheme was reckless regardless of credit conditions, but liberal lending by the First Bank made it worse. By January 31, 1792, the First Bank had outstanding loans of approximately $2.68 million. As a percentage of GDP, this is roughly equivalent to $275 billion today.[10] Sensing that lax lending policies were amplifying a

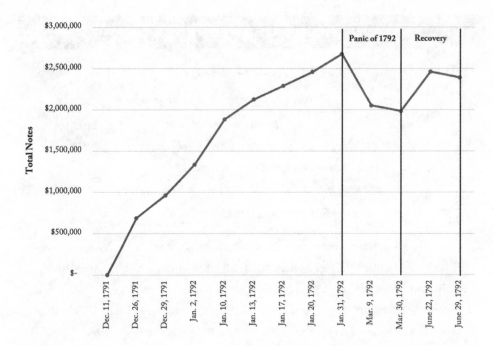

Figure 2.1: Total Bills Discounted by First Bank of the United States (December 11, 1791–June 29, 1792)[11]

dangerous situation, Hamilton advised the First Bank to tighten its lending practices in early February. Between January 31, 1792, and March 9, 1792, total outstanding loans declined by 23.3 percent, and then remained at a lower level for the remainder of the month (Figure 2.1). The contraction of the money supply ruined Duer, as he was unable to renew loans when they matured. On March 9, 1792, Duer defaulted on several loans, sparking a chain reaction of defaults by many New York City residents.[12]

POINT OF INTEREST

Tim Geithner Draws Inspiration from Alexander Hamilton

"It was a sunny day . . . and even though the world was still disintegrating, I felt as light as I had in months. We were going to deploy federal resources in ways Hamilton never imagined but given his advocacy for executive power and a strong financial system, I had to believe he would approve."[13]

—Tim Geithner, chair of the Federal Reserve Bank of New York

On October 11, 2008, Tim Geithner sat beneath a statue of Alexander Hamilton and pondered how the founding father would have responded to the financial crisis that was unfolding. The Federal Reserve and U.S. Treasury planned to introduce multiple unconventional programs, and if they failed, the crisis would likely devolve into a Great Depression–level event. Geithner hoped that Hamilton would have approved their plans, drawing inspiration from an inscription at the base of the statue that stated: "He [Hamilton] touched the dead corpse of the public credit, and it sprang upon its feet."[14]

Any lingering doubts in Geithner's mind likely would have disappeared if he would have taken a full inventory of the unconventional tactics that Hamilton used to end the Panic of 1792. Hamilton's tactics were similar in spirit to the special lending facilities employed by the Federal Reserve in 2008 and 2009. The main difference was that Hamilton's actions were nearly a century ahead of their time. The very concept of a central bank serving as a lender of last resort was purportedly introduced by Walter Bagehot in 1873, yet Hamilton clearly understood it eighty-one years earlier.[15]

Tim Geithner will never know for sure how Hamilton would have responded to the financial crisis in 2008, but it is doubtful that he would have objected to his policies. Sadly, Hamilton probably would have also warned Geithner about the abuse he would likely suffer for his heroism, being that Hamilton suffered the same fate.

By mid-March, panic had seized New York, and Hamilton realized that the integrity of the First Bank was, once again, in jeopardy. Demonstrating instincts that were decades ahead of his time, Hamilton employed several unconventional tactics to prevent the financial system from collapsing. First, he instructed the First Bank to make payments using post notes (a form of credit) rather than cash for the payment of custom duties. This enabled the bank to conserve cash and specie, which panicked customers had withdrawn in large amounts over the prior week. Next, he resumed open market purchases of government bonds using the sinking fund, which created a floor for bond prices. Finally, in his most creative move, Hamilton encouraged bankers at the Bank of New York to continue lending liberally to customers despite their strong inclination to restrict it. To provide aid, Hamilton instructed the bankers to accept U.S. government bonds as collateral. He then reduced the First Bank's risk by agreeing to repurchase 50 percent of the bonds at a stated price when markets calmed.[16]

Hamilton's leadership helped end the Panic in May 1792, but many New Yorkers were financially ruined, nonetheless. William Duer and many of his co-conspirators were arrested and thrown in debtors' prison. The incident terrified members of New York's newly formed securities brokerage profession, and they decided that they needed to act.

THE BIRTH OF THE NEW YORK STOCK EXCHANGE

On March 21, 1792, twenty-four New York City brokers convened at Corre's Hotel for the first of a series of meetings to plot their future. The meeting agendas were never disclosed, but the Panic of 1792 was undoubtedly a major item. The meetings prompted two notable changes on Wall Street. First, the brokers agreed to stop participating in public auctions of securities. These were widely viewed as magnets for unethical behavior, which only encouraged destructive speculation by people like William Duer. Second, they drafted a pledge to charge a fixed-rate commission of 0.25 percent on all securities transactions conducted among members of their group. On May 17, 1792, the group assembled beneath a buttonwood tree located near 68 Wall Street and signed a formal pledge based on their discussions.[17] Henceforth, the pact was known as the Buttonwood Agreement. It made no mention of the avoidance of public auctions, but it did codify the fixed-rate commission. The full text of the Buttonwood Agreement reads:

> We the Subscribers, Brokers for the Purchase and Sale of the Public Stock, do hereby solemnly promise and pledge ourselves to each other, that we will not buy or sell from this day for any person whatsoever, any kind of Public Stock, at a less rate than one quarter percent Commission on the Specie value and that we will give preference to each other in our Negotiations. In Testimony whereof we have set our hands this 17th day of May at New York, 1792.[18]

The Buttonwood Agreement established the foundation of the New York Stock Exchange, but it also marked the beginning of a long lull in trading on Wall Street. The trading of government securities and a handful of stocks resumed but at levels far below those witnessed in 1791 and 1792 (Figure 2.2). Several decades passed before trading volume returned to the highs of 1791. When it did, the brokers would establish a more formal organization.

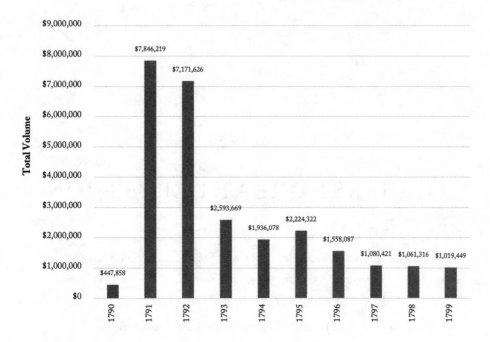

Figure 2.2: Volume of Public Securities Trading in Selected U.S. Markets (1790–1799)[19]

Chapter 3

THE FIRST GREAT DEPRESSION

"The bank bubbles are breaking . . . the merchants are crumbling to ruin, the manufacturers perishing . . . there seems to be no remedy but time and patience, and the changes of events which time affects."[1]

—PRESIDENT JOHN QUINCY ADAMS

After the Panic of 1792 subsided, Americans enjoyed nearly two decades of economic prosperity, and the economy entered an important period of transformation. Americans still depended heavily on agriculture, but manufacturing and trade were also beginning to blossom. The textile industry was especially profitable in New England, as new mills were constructed with design specs stolen from the British.[2] Further, Eli Whitney's invention of the cotton gin made cotton farming profitable in the U.S., which secured a reliable supply of high-quality, domestically produced cotton. State governments supported industry by investing heavily in roads, turnpikes, and steamboat operations to link distant cities. Finally, grassroots entrepreneurship flourished in American homes. Using their spare time, men, women, and children engaged in "outworking," which included light manufacturing tasks to produce simple textiles, shoes, and other low-cost items in their homes.

The economic advancement during the nation's first twenty-five years was a critical first step in America's eventual transformation from a frontier market into an industrial superpower by the turn of the twentieth century. But this progression temporarily stalled in 1819 when a financial panic triggered the nation's first deep depression. Most Americans are familiar with the Great Depression in the 1930s, but few realize that the one that occurred more than one hundred years earlier was comparable.

A theme that repeats throughout the remainder of this book is that people tend to respond to major financial catastrophes by bluntly assigning blame to a small group of individuals. This behavior often hides the more insightful truth that severe financial crises are almost always caused by the convergence of multiple powerful forces. In the case of the Panic of 1819, the mismanagement of the Second Bank of the United States is often cited as the primary cause, but a deeper analysis reveals that this was only one of many factors. The remainder of this chapter explains each of these factors, as well as the devastating consequences that followed.

THE FALL OF THE FIRST BANK

Alexander Hamilton's financial programs restored the nation's credit, and his financial instincts rescued the nation from two financial panics. But after two decades of prosperity, many politicians lost sight of the necessity of his programs. President Thomas Jefferson was especially hostile toward the First Bank. Sensing Jefferson's disdain for the institution, Treasury Secretary Albert Gallatin delayed requesting the renewal of the bank's twenty-year charter for as long as possible. In April 1808, which was the final year of Jefferson's presidency, the First Bank stockholders finally petitioned Congress to renew the charter. After delaying for several years, the House of Representatives rejected the proposal by a single vote in January 1811. One month later, Gallatin encouraged a second attempt in the Senate, but it also failed by a single vote. Gallatin made no further efforts, and the nation's first central bank closed its doors on March 3, 1811.[3]

The disappearance of banknotes issued by the First Bank left a void in the U.S. financial system. The expansion of U.S. commerce required the use of paper currency. Businesses needed to pay laborers; farmers needed cash (and credit) to purchase land; and merchants needed both currency and credit to conduct domestic and foreign trade. To fill the void, state-chartered banks sprouted up throughout the nation and began issuing banknotes aggressively. Figure 3.1 shows the total number of additional state-chartered banks from 1800 to 1819.

In comparison to the First Bank, state-chartered banks were lightly regulated and poorly capitalized. Moreover, as the sheer number of banks increased, it became increasingly difficult to determine the actual worth of their banknotes. The general rule was that the farther Americans traveled from a bank, the less the bank's notes were worth when presented for payment or deposit. The U.S. currency system was, once again, unstable.

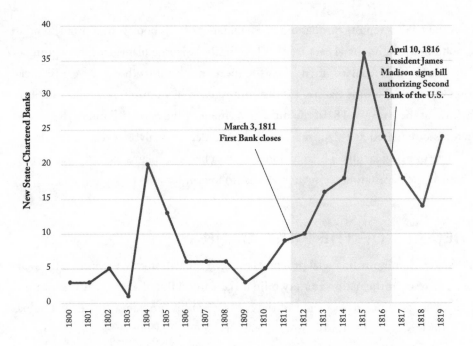

Figure 3.1: Total New State-Chartered Banks (Net of Closures) (1800–1819)[4]

THE WAR OF 1812

POINT OF INTEREST

Fractional Reserve Banks and the Origin of Specie

Understanding the mechanics of a fractional reserve banking system is critical to grasping how and why financial crises occur repeatedly in the United States. Many believe that goldsmiths were the first professionals to employ fractional reserve banking techniques. Charged with safekeeping precious metals for customers, goldsmiths realized that they could lend customer deposits and earn interest on the loans. Such loans were not funded with the gold itself, but rather with "notes" that could be redeemed for gold held in a goldsmith's vaults. Provided that the goldsmith maintained sufficient reserves to satisfy periodic redemptions (and clients did not default in large numbers), goldsmiths made a profit. A fractional reserve banking system employs the same fundamental principles. Banks start with "reserves" provided by investors, and then lend a portion of these funds by issuing banknotes.[5]

The power of a fractional reserve banking system derives from its ability to increase the amount of money in circulation. This happens because when borrowers spend banknotes, the recipients redeposit them into a bank. A portion of these deposits are then lent out again. This process repeats over and over, which significantly expands the money supply. The formula for calculating the total money supply created in a fractional reserve banking system is to divide the total reserves (often referred to as the monetary base) by the reserve requirement. For example, a system that starts with a monetary base of $10 billion and reserve requirement of 10 percent can produce a total money supply of $100 billion.[6]

In the 1800s, the monetary base consisted of "specie," which was a general term that described the commodities for which banknotes could be redeemed. Specie held by U.S. banks at the time consisted of gold and silver coin. Banknotes issued by state-chartered banks were technically redeemable in specie, but during the War of 1812 and the financial crisis that followed, many banks suspended specie redemption. This led to a sharp depreciation in the value of many banknotes, which contributed to high rates of inflation.

Tensions between the U.S. and Great Britain intensified soon after the First Bank disappeared. The dispute centered on harsh trade restrictions imposed by the British during the Napoleonic Wars, as well as Britain's brazen practice of kidnapping crew members of American ships and forcing them to serve on British naval vessels.[7] Unable to arrive at a peaceful resolution, the U.S. declared war on Great Britain on June 18, 1812. The British generally viewed the war as an unwanted distraction from a much bigger conflict with Napoleon Bonaparte in France. Initially, this prevented them from making a full-hearted effort to defeat the Americans. Meanwhile, the U.S. was divided over the need for the war, leaving them open to a graceful exit. After two years of fighting, the War of 1812 ended with the signing of the Treaty of Ghent on December 28, 1814.[8]

The U.S. economy suffered during the war years, but the impact was somewhat lessened by the fact that U.S. exports were already depressed by a preexisting British blockade that sharply reduced trade between the U.S. and European countries. There were also a few unanticipated benefits from the war. For example, the loss of British imports accelerated the development of America's manufacturing industry. Nevertheless, the economic costs were still substantial. One major cost was the deterioration of the federal government's balance sheet. By September 30, 1815, the public debt had nearly tripled to $119.2 million in the span of only three years. Making matters worse, without the assistance of the First Bank, the Madison administration was forced to sell bonds below par value and rely heavily on purchases made by wealthy individuals and bankers, such as Jacob Astor and Stephen Girard. A second cost came in the form of inflation, as unregulated state banks issued banknotes far in excess of their specie reserves. This problem continued long after the war ended.[9]

POST-WAR TRADE DISTORTIONS

"It was well worthwhile to incur a loss upon the first exportation in order by glut to stifle in the cradle those rising manufactures in the United States which the war has forced into existence contrary to the usual course of nature."[10]

—HENRY LORD BROUGHAM, member of British Parliament

The economic impact of the War of 1812 was painful, but the aftermath was even more devastating. Initially, deliberate actions taken by Great Britain were the main problem. After the British defeated Napoleon on June 18, 1815, war-related demand for British manufactured products collapsed. Fearing worker rebellions if unemployment increased, the British encouraged British manufacturers to continue operating at full capacity, thereby minimizing unemployment. Then, manufacturers sold the surplus in the U.S. at fire sale prices to drive American manufacturers out of business. The strategy had a devastating impact on the U.S. textile industry. The most efficient mills survived, but dozens of upstarts failed. The impact was mitigated somewhat by the creation of a protective tariff in 1816, but much of the damage was done before it took effect.[11]

The experience of American farmers was more complex. An act of nature rather than humans was the source of the trouble. On April 10, 1815, Mount Tambora exploded in what was later determined to be the largest volcanic eruption in recorded history. The volcano ejected an estimated thirty-one cubic miles of rock and ash, claiming at least 70,000 lives. But the impact on the climate proved far more deadly and disruptive. The volcano injected an enormous cloud of sulfur dioxide into the upper atmosphere, which repelled sunlight and temporarily cooled global temperatures by an estimated one degree Fahrenheit. The maximum impact hit in the summer of 1816, which was dubbed the "Year without a Summer," and the effects were especially acute in Europe. Crop yields collapsed throughout the world, creating a shortage of agricultural commodities and a sharp rise in prices—especially for wheat and cotton. Figure 3.2 shows the average price of wheat from 1814 to 1817. Wheat shortages were especially severe in Great Britain, forcing the British to temporarily lift import restrictions established under the 1815 Corn Laws. U.S. farmers also suffered poor harvests, but

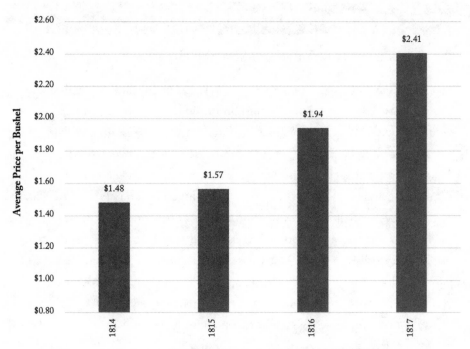

Figure 3.2: U.S. Wheat Prices per Bushel (1814–1817)[12]

the crops that they produced were generally high quality and priced at a premium.[13] The key was planting more, and the U.S. was fortunate to have an abundance of farm-land in the Midwest.

A THUNDERING HERD HEADS WEST

"The demand for lands since the 1st July seems as great as ever; all payments are made in the Mississippi Stock—which is sold at 25 per cent discount . . . the demand for lands is so great I have not time within office hours to attend to my returns or books."[14]

—NICHOLAS GRAY, land office clerk (1816)

In comparison to Europe, the Year without a Summer was less catastrophic in the U.S., but it was still painful. New England was especially hard hit due to the harsher effects of cold weather in the northern latitudes. Thousands of farmers responded by selling their land and heading west. The attraction was twofold. First, they could purchase larger tracts of farmland. Second, crop prices, especially wheat, had risen by nearly 25 percent by the end of 1816. The combination of larger fields and higher prices seemed like the ultimate win-win situation.

The Timeless Temptation of Buying High and Selling Low

The age-old axiom that the key to investing is to buy low and sell high is simple in theory, but most human beings do precisely the opposite. Instead, they tend to buy assets only after witnessing large price increases, hoping that such gains will continue. During the first two decades of the twenty-first century, Americans have engaged in this behavior multiple times and at a massive scale. Examples include dot-com stocks, speculative real estate, and cryptocurrencies.

The stock market barely existed in the early 1800s, but the human instinct to chase returns was as powerful then as it is now. After witnessing the sharp rise in wheat prices in 1816, East Coast farmers moved west where they could purchase larger tracts of farmland, plant wheat, and hope to profit from the bonanza. Few farmers had enough cash to purchase the land they desired, so most financed purchases with loans from state banks and installment plans offered by land offices.

Few farmers considered whether the cold snap that caused worldwide crop failures would persist. Even fewer considered that the aggressive expansion of wheat production alone was bound to cause a glut of supply even if the cold weather continued. By 1818, sulfur dioxide levels returned to normal, global temperatures rebounded, and crop yields improved. The result was a massive global oversupply of wheat. The British government reinstated its import restrictions under its Corn Laws, and American farmers suddenly found themselves stuck with an enormous surplus of wheat. Wheat prices collapsed, and farmers were unable to make payments on enormous debts that they had used to acquire farmland.

In the early 1800s, the federal government was the primary landowner in the Midwest. The Land Act of 1800 provided guidelines for the sale of large tracts of federal land through land offices situated throughout the states. After passage of the act, land sales proceeded at a steady pace but then skyrocketed after the global crop failures in 1815. The federal government sought to increase land sales, but demand was constrained by the inability of most farmers to raise the required capital. This issue was amplified by the Land Act's minimum purchase requirement of 320 acres. The solution was twofold. First, land offices extended credit to farmers and allowed them to pay in multiyear installments. Second, state-chartered banks began lending liberally to farmers. Borrowers not only used bank loans to make installment payments to

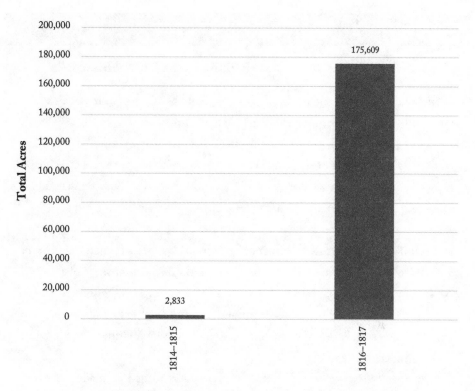

Figure 3.3: Total Washington County Land Sales (1814–1817)[15]

land offices, but many also used them to make down payments. This was perhaps the first large-scale example of Americans purchasing real estate with no money down.[16]

Land sales increased at a feverish pace from 1815 to 1818. The boom was fueled primarily by higher wheat prices in the northern states and higher cotton prices in the southern states. Information on sales volume and prices during the boom is scarce, but the limited data that is available reveals manic buying. Figure 3.3 shows the total acres sold from 1814 to 1817 in the county of Washington, Mississippi. It is a great irony of history that most of the purchases were made with "Mississippi Stock," which was the same name of the securities sold by John Law during the infamous Mississippi Bubble in 1720.[17]

THE CRASH

"There was no single cause of the collapse of America's post-war economy, but among the largest of the contributing factors was the desire to get in on the commodity export boom— and the inability to escape when the boom turned to bust."[18]

—ANDREW H. BROWNING, author of *The Panic of 1819*

POINT OF INTEREST

The Return of Central Banking in the United States

By the end of the War of 1812, many congressmen who had voted against the renewal of the First Bank charter had a change of heart. On April 10, 1816, Congress passed a bill to charter the Second Bank of the United States. The charter resembled that of the First Bank but was much larger in scale. Its initial capitalization was $35 million (versus $10 million for the First Bank), and it eventually operated twenty-six branches (versus only eight for the First Bank).

The goal of the Second Bank was to restore the stability of U.S. currency and stabilize the government's finances by serving as its fiscal agent. The latter goal proved a bit easier than the former. During the five-year absence of a central bank, state-chartered banks issued banknotes recklessly throughout the country. Making matters worse, many of the Second Bank's branches initially engaged in the same behavior. As a result, the value of banknotes circulating in the U.S. far exceeded specie reserves.

By early 1818, the Second Bank was barely able to maintain adequate specie reserves to honor banknote redemptions.[19] The bank sought to strengthen its balance sheet by aggressively redeeming state banknotes for specie, calling in loans, and borrowing specie from abroad. These efforts intensified when the U.S. Treasury demanded $2 million of specie to fund a scheduled payment of principal to holders of Louisiana Purchase bonds issued in 1803. The actions of the Second Bank were equivalent to a sharp tightening of monetary policy during a time in which the U.S. economy was already under intense deflationary pressure.[20]

Global cooling caused by the Mount Tambora eruption was intense but short-lived. Unlike carbon dioxide, sulfur dioxide is naturally removed from the atmosphere within a few years. By 1818, sulfur dioxide levels returned to pre-eruption levels and global temperatures normalized. Owners of Midwestern farmland suddenly found themselves in a dreadful situation. Many had taken on massive loans to purchase land at prices that could only be justified if crops sold at elevated prices for many more years. Instead, the combination of strong harvests and massive expansion of farmland created an enormous global oversupply, which caused prices to plummet. Figure 3.4 shows the sharp drop in wheat prices that began in 1818, and Figure 3.5 shows a similar decline in a broad index of all farming products in the U.S.

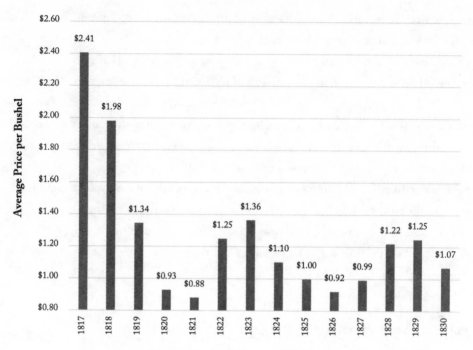

Figure 3.4: U.S. Wheat Prices per Bushel (1817–1830)[21]

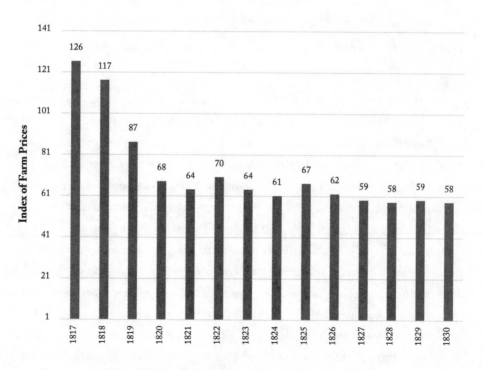

Figure 3.5: Price Index of U.S. Farm Products (1817–1830)[22]

The decline of agricultural commodity prices triggered a collapse in land values as farmers and speculators adjusted their revenue forecasts. At the same time, the Second Bank of the United States, which began operations in 1817, reversed many of its lending policies to stem the erosion of its dwindling specie reserves. The effects were similar to those caused by the Federal Reserve when it tightens monetary policy. State banks responded by suspending specie redemption and calling in loans to strengthen their balance sheets. This caused a sharp reduction in the money supply, which then triggered a severe economic contraction.

The combination of commodity price declines, collapsing land values, tight monetary conditions, and highly indebted landowners was too much for the nation to bear. Unlike most financial panics, there was no single moment that marked the beginning of the Panic of 1819, but the financial misery rivaled anything that the nation had experienced before or since.

THE FIRST GREAT DEPRESSION

"All intelligent writers upon currency agree that where it is decreasing in amount, poverty and misery must prevail. The correctness of the opinion is too manifest to require proof. The united voice of the nation attests to its accuracy."[23]

—**WILLIAM H. CRAWFORD,** secretary of the Treasury (February 1820)

In 1819, the contractionary policies of the Second Bank began driving state banks into insolvency. Statistics from the early 1800s are imprecise, but the estimated rate of bank failures rivaled or exceeded that of the Great Depression in the 1930s. By 1822, more than eighty state banks had closed, and the value of banknotes in circulation contracted by more than 50 percent.[24] Tight monetary conditions triggered a chain reaction that pushed businesses and individuals into insolvency and plunged the nation into a deep depression that lasted until the mid-1820s. Capturing the anguish of the depression is difficult because statistics are scarce, and even figures that are available are difficult to compare to modern times. For example, urban unemployment levels were exceptionally high—several major cities reported unemployment rates exceeding 30 percent—but because a large percentage of Americans were farmers, this data is not directly comparable to modern times. One of the more reliable metrics of standards of living is per capita GDP, and estimates suggest that it was cut by nearly 50 percent between 1814 and 1824.[25]

Qualitative information from the First Great Depression offers better insight into the extraordinary suffering. Records from the early 1820s reveal massive increases in business failures, farm foreclosures, urban unemployment, and homelessness. Perhaps the most heart-wrenching recollections came from debtors' prisons, which were overflowing with inmates. A particularly tragic story circulating at the time was that of Hannah Crispy, who was thrown in debtors' prison with her infant daughter for an unpaid debt of $12. After twenty days, her daughter died, and Hannah was only allowed temporary release to attend the funeral.[26]

FORGOTTEN LESSONS FROM THE PANIC OF 1819

There were many financial lessons from the Panic of 1819, but most were soon forgotten. In fairness, however, many of the financial and economic concepts that explain what happened were yet to be discovered. For example, the relationship between the money supply and economic activity was not broadly understood. Even the term "financial panic" had not yet been coined, although there is some evidence that 1819 was the first year in which the word *panic* was used to describe a financial calamity. Sadly, the panic and depression followed a well-trodden path that Americans would retrace multiple times over the next two hundred years. For this reason, the greatest lesson of the Panic of 1819 may simply be the importance of studying financial history so as to avoid repeating the same mistakes.

Chapter 4

THE RISE OF WALL STREET AND THE PARADOX OF SPECULATION

"He [the American] launches with delight into the ever-moving sea of speculation. One day, the wave raises him to the clouds . . . the next day he disappears between the crests of the billows; he is little troubled by the reversal, he bides his time coolly, and consoles himself with the hope of a better fortune. Some individuals lose, but the country is a gainer; the country is peopled, cleared, cultivated; its resources unfolded; its wealth increased."[1]

—MICHEL CHEVALIER (1836)

Securities trading picked up in New York soon after the Treaty of Ghent ended the War of 1812. The initial public offering of stock in the Second Bank of the United States in July 1816 accelerated trading even further. But unlike the 1790s, investors could choose from a much broader array of stocks and bonds. States had approved corporate charters in greater numbers, and the evolution of limited liability laws made U.S. securities more attractive to domestic and foreign investors. By 1818, thirty-one bonds and twenty-three common stocks were regularly quoted in New York City. Issuance increased steadily each year, suffering only temporary setbacks during economic downturns (Figure 4.1).

In 1817, a group of twenty-seven New York City brokers drafted a formal constitution to establish the New York Stock Exchange. Their goal was to bring order to the market and seize the opportunity to replace Philadelphia as the nation's financial capital. The constitution included standards for the execution of trades and delivery of

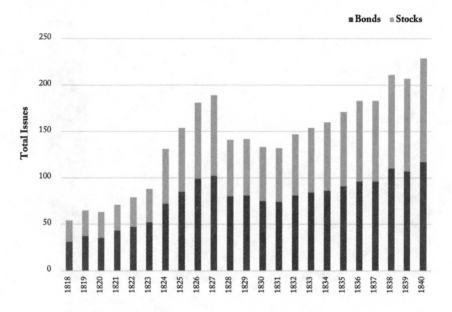

Figure 4.1: Total Stock and Bond Issues Quoted in New York City (1818-1840)[2]

securities, as well as criteria for membership. On March 8, 1817, the New York Stock Exchange constitution was ratified.[3]

The constitution was a key contributor to the rise of the New York Stock Exchange. Although annual trading volume was volatile from year to year, average annual volume increased substantially after the signing of the constitution (Figure 4.2). By 1830, Philadelphia was relegated to a secondary market and never reemerged as a serious threat to Wall Street.

The remainder of this chapter recounts the events that propelled Wall Street into its position as the nation's new financial capital. It then concludes with President Andrew Jackson's fateful veto of a bill to renew the charter of the Second Bank. The depression that followed was even more intense than the one that followed the Panic of 1819.

PROTOINDUSTRIALIZATION AND THE INCORPORATION OF AMERICA

"I weigh my words, when I say that in my judgment the limited liability corporation is the greatest single discovery of modern times . . . Even steam and electricity are far less important than the limited liability corporation and would have been reduced to comparative impotence without it."[4]

—NICHOLAS MURRAY BUTLER, president of Columbia University

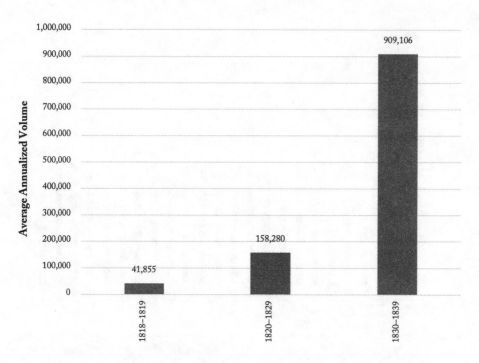

Figure 4.2: Average Annualized Trading Volume on New York Stock Exchange (1818–1839)[5]

POINT OF INTEREST

Economic Time Capsules and American Protoindustrialization

In *The Making of an Economic Superpower*, Federal Reserve economist Yi Wen compares the ongoing industrialization of China to that of the United States and Great Britain in the 1800s and 1900s (see chapter 29). Wen is especially emphatic about the importance of the "protoindustrialization stage," which is a period in which a nation starts expanding beyond subsistence farming and establishes early commercial capabilities that serve as the foundation of an industrialized economy.[6]

The early 1800s was a tumultuous period for the United States. The Panic of 1819 produced suffering that rivaled the Great Depression of the 1930s. But beneath the surface the U.S. was building grassroots commercial enterprises, critical supply chain networks, an entrepreneurial culture, and a rudimentary banking system. It may not have seemed so at the time, but these would serve as the foundation for America's eventual emergence as an economic superpower at the turn of the twentieth century. The critical importance of this phase of economic development is largely forgotten in the 2020s. Even more importantly, many Americans do not see the parallels between the American protoindustrialization in the early 1800s and the Chinese protoindustrialization that began with Deng Xiaoping's reforms in 1978.

The nearly two-hundred-year gulf separating American and Chinese protoindustrialization also creates confusion. Evaluating China by today's standards often leads people to conclude that its economic development lags far behind that of the United States. But when viewed as a function of time, China's advancement is impressive. Further, common claims that China's flaws (i.e., human rights violations, pollution, corruption, financial fraud, etc.) will prevent its continued advancement ignore the fact that America suffered many of the same flaws during comparable phases of development. Therefore, the possibility that China could surpass the U.S. is a threat that may be more serious than people suspect.

Many economists argue that the greatest commercial innovation in the U.S. was not a specific invention, but rather it was the creation and widespread use of the limited liability corporation. In the early 1800s, the U.S. possessed vast potential wealth but had limited capital to exploit it. Many foreign and domestic investors were hesitant to fund entrepreneurs if their liability was unlimited, but once they could limit their losses to the amount of their invested capital, the pool of potential investors increased substantially. The evolution of the U.S. from a regime of unlimited liability in the late 1700s to one dominated by limited liability occurred gradually over several decades, and laws varied within individual states. But by 1830, limited liability was generally recognized as a fundamental component of American business, and it contributed to a surge of new venture formation. Figure 4.3 shows the rapid increase in the number of incorporations that occurred by decade from 1790 to 1839. The leap in 1830 was driven both by wider acceptance of limited liability laws and an increase in speculation that accompanied the return of unregulated banking practices after the demise of the Second Bank of the United States.

Most incorporations captured in Figure 4.3 were small ventures, but the number of listed securities also grew rapidly, as indicated on the prior pages. As trading increased, Philadelphia and New York battled for supremacy, but by 1830, New York was the clear winner.

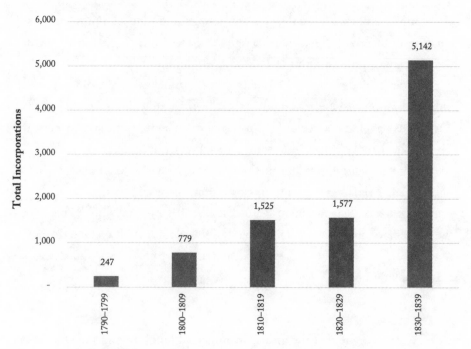

Figure 4.3: Total Incorporations in the United States by Decade (1790–1839)[7]

THE NEW FINANCIAL CAPITAL OF AMERICA

POINT OF INTEREST

The Paradox of Speculation

"Each succeeding era of speculative enthusiasm will leave after its recession the values of honest securities higher than they lay where the preceding wave had flowed and ebbed."[8]

—Edmund C. Stedman, author of *The New York Stock Exchange*

The emergence of Wall Street as the nation's financial capital was aided by the peculiar paradox of speculation. From its very inception, Wall Street was the preferred venue for speculators. In the 1700s, they were called stock jobbers. In the 1800s, they were called stock plungers. In the early 1900s, they were called stock operators. And now they are a mix of analysts, hedge fund managers, and the latest gurus on CNBC.

America has always and likely will always have a love/hate relationship with

Wall Street speculators. Their actions can create great wealth or great misery for those who follow their lead. Yet at the same time, the repetitive process of mania, failure, and renewal has made markets more liquid, efficiently priced, and ultimately more attractive to investors. This, in turn, has enabled American entrepreneurs to acquire funding for countless ventures. Without Wall Street, many of the world's greatest inventions would likely remain locked in the brains of people who have long since passed.

The genius and folly of American speculators could fill several volumes of encyclopedias, and many of their more notable conquests are shared in this book. Each time, you will observe the odd paradox of speculation. For more than 230 years, every mania, bubble, fraud, crash, and depression was followed by renewal and advancement. It is this paradox that has helped drive American progress. The constant battling between bulls and bears also creates a safe, but unappreciated, wake that inspired the greatest financial innovation of the twentieth century: the index fund (see chapter 22).

The New York Stock Exchange caught a big break soon after ratifying its constitution. In the 1820s, Europeans were enamored with canal investments. An initial trickle of foreign capital from more conservative investors, such as the Houses of Barings and Rothschild, soon escalated into a surge of indiscriminate buying. By the mid-1820s, the canal craze peaked, and the issuance of new securities evaporated. Overbuilding and the abandonment of many canal projects contributed to the decline in issuance, but the death blow was the introduction of railroads, which provided more economical transportation—especially over long distances.

By the 1830s, railroad companies replaced canals as the primary recipients of domestic and foreign capital. Although the canal mania was short-lived, the superior performance of canal securities listed on the New York Stock Exchange created the perception that New York was a safer investing venue than Philadelphia. A key driver of the performance dispersion was the large and successful flotation of Erie Canal bonds. The Erie Canal simultaneously played a critical role in establishing New York as the leading commercial center in the United States.

New York's dominance of securities markets continued to strengthen over time. Philadelphia never recovered its former reputation, and to this day the New York Stock Exchange remains the most prestigious securities exchange in the country.

THE FALL OF THE SECOND BANK

"All the evils which the community, in particular parts of the country, has suffered from the sudden decrease in currency, as well as from its depreciation, have been ascribed to the Bank of the United States."[9]

—**WILLIAM H. CRAWFORD,** secretary of the Treasury

In January 1823, the Second Bank's board of directors elected Nicholas Biddle as the bank's new president. Biddle had previously served as a board member for several years. Although he lacked extensive banking experience, his exceptional intellect enabled him to quickly establish a reputation as the most astute board member. Soon after taking the helm at the Second Bank, Biddle reined in the reckless banking practices at several branches and reestablished a sound currency for the nation. The stability provided by the Second Bank fueled economic prosperity for the remainder of the 1820s.

Despite Biddle's reforms, the Second Bank still had many enemies. Farmers who were ruined in the Panic of 1819 blamed the bank for their travails, and state-chartered bank executives resented the ability of the Second Bank to restrict their lending practices. But the most dangerous enemy of all surfaced in 1828. The newly elected president, Andrew Jackson, despised banks and hated the very concept of paper currency. His animosity stemmed from severe financial difficulties that he had experienced earlier in his career, which he blamed on the proliferation of paper currency.

The Bank War

Andrew Jackson openly voiced his desire to curtail the power of the Second Bank during his presidential campaign. After taking office in 1828, his animosity deepened when he heard rumors that representatives of several bank branches had made campaign contributions and issued favorable loans to support opposing candidates. The president challenged Nicholas Biddle to investigate these claims. Biddle's subsequent investigations were deemed to be superficial, and Biddle followed them by issuing staunch defenses of the bank's integrity. This made Jackson even more suspicious that a larger conspiracy was at hand.[10]

Over the next several years both Biddle and Jackson attempted to resolve their differences. Ironically, both men underestimated the willingness of their adversaries to compromise. For example, despite Jackson's awareness of the strong public support for his candidacy in general, he knew that most of the public did not support his opposition to the Second Bank.[11] As a result, he did not wish to make the debate over the renewal of the Second Bank charter an issue in his 1832 reelection campaign. Louis McLane, secretary of the Treasury, informed Biddle that Jackson was open to renewing the Second Bank charter with some modifications, but that he would "reject the Bill if the matter is agitated this session."[12]

In a fateful miscalculation, Biddle ignored Jackson's warning to wait until after the election to resolve the matter. He feared that McLane's assurances that Jackson would renew the charter after the election were unreliable. He was also pressured by Republican Party leaders to make the re-chartering of the bank a key campaign issue. On January 6, 1832, Biddle defied Jackson and submitted a formal application to Congress to renew the Second Bank charter. Biddle knew the bill would easily gain congressional approval. If Jackson followed through on his prior threat to veto it, Biddle believed that the Democrats would suffer in the elections. This would, in turn, provide Biddle with the needed votes to overturn the veto after the election. Alternatively, Jackson might sign the bill and the Second Bank would be granted another twenty-year charter without having to make significant modifications.[13]

The bill comfortably passed both houses of Congress in June 1832, but Jackson followed through on his threat to veto it on July 10. Over the next four months, Democrats and Republicans engaged in vicious campaigns and the bank issue was front and center. Despite broad public support for the bank, popular support for Andrew Jackson proved more powerful. Although Jackson lost some votes in comparison to the 1828 election, he still won a second term in a landslide, and Republicans failed to gain enough seats in Congress to overturn Jackson's veto.

Jackson Pulls the Government's Deposits

Biddle was powerless against Jackson's veto, but he still exercised substantial control over the financial system. This led to a second tragic miscalculation when he decided to use the bank's power to force Jackson to change his policy. In 1833, Biddle ordered the Second Bank to curtail lending and force state banks to redeem the Second Bank's substantial reserves of state banknotes for specie. This triggered a financial panic and recession over the next year, and Biddle hoped that Jackson would be blamed for it. Instead, Biddle was blamed, and congressional support for the Second Bank charter deteriorated even further. Moreover, Biddle's actions enraged Jackson, thus steeling his resolve to destroy the bank entirely.

President Andrew Jackson's character is the subject of endless debate, but most historians acknowledge that one of his more distinguishing traits was his stubborn pursuit of vengeance when he felt wronged. This was a strength in military campaigns but a weakness in the bank war. Jackson was not content to simply let the charter of the Second Bank run out in a few years; he sought to destroy the bank immediately. The first step was to remove the government's deposits and place them with politically friendly state-chartered banks located throughout the country. Despite fierce bipartisan opposition in Congress and even among members of his cabinet, Jackson refused to relent. The federal government began removing its deposits in October 1834, and thereafter the power of the Second Bank withered until its charter expired in 1836.

THE GREAT REAL ESTATE BUBBLE

"Everyone with whom I converse talks of 100 percent as the lowest return on an investment. No one is known ever to have lost anything by purchase and sale of real estate."[14]

—**JOHN M. MORGAN,** Baltimore investor (1836)

Jackson often claimed that the goal of eliminating the Second Bank was to allow experimentation with the use of state-chartered banks as depository institutions. If the experiment failed, he asserted that he was open to the return of a scaled-down version of a central bank. As part of the experiment, Jackson initially ordered the Treasury to pick a handful of state-chartered banks to handle the government's deposits. The number of Jackson's "pet banks" expanded to about twenty as the Second Bank wound down but was soon forced to expand to more than ninety institutions in 1836. This was a function of the Deposit Act of 1836, which placed a cap on the deposits held at any single bank. The sheer number of banks handling government deposits made it impossible to effectively monitor their financial position and lending practices. Further aggravating the situation, the federal government began depositing budget surpluses in state-chartered banks, adding to reserves that were already swollen. Armed with abundant reserves and no longer constrained by the policies of the Second Bank, state banks began lending recklessly just like they had after the First Bank disappeared.[15]

POINT OF INTEREST

The Dangerous Delusion of Ever-Rising Prices

"There is no national price bubble [in real estate].
Never has been; never will be."[16]

—**David Lereah, chief economist, National Association of Realtors (September 2004)**

The formation of asset bubbles requires a large percentage of people to believe that a bubble cannot exist. Usually, widespread acceptance of such narratives depends on heavy promotion by market experts and members of the media. Once the narrative is accepted by a large swath of investors, a bubble is likely to follow.

In the early 2000s, Americans believed that real estate prices had never declined substantially at a national level in all of U.S. history. But not only had a major decline in national real estate prices happened before, it had happened several times. The Hard Times of the 1840s was one such occasion. The Specie Circular (see The Panic of 1837 section below), tight monetary conditions, the collapse of cotton prices, and a wave of bank failures caused real estate prices to collapse.

The misstatement by David Lereah reveals the value of studying financial history. Asset bubbles often repeat because investors' collective memory does not extend far enough back in time to see the repetition. If Lereah had studied the real estate collapses in the early 1820s, 1840s, and even the 1930s, he never would have made his fateful statement in 2004.

The speculative bubble was nearly identical to the one that had occurred twenty years earlier, only this one was more intense. Unconstrained lending fueled feverish speculation in federal land auctions. Figure 4.4 shows the enormous increase in federal revenue from land sales soon after the distribution of the government's deposits to state-chartered banks.[17]

The Panic of 1837

By the spring of 1836, Jackson was disturbed by the real estate speculation and the paper currency that was fueling it. This was precisely the type of scenario that he hoped to prevent by eliminating the Second Bank. Jackson tried to slow the buying frenzy by prohibiting the use of banknotes to purchase federal land. On July 11, 1836, President Jackson issued the Specie Circular. The executive order took effect on December 15, 1836, at which point only gold or silver could be used for the purchase of federal lands. Jackson's actions triggered a surge in demand for gold and silver, which led to a run on the specie reserves of state-chartered banks. By the spring of 1837, many banks were forced to suspend specie redemption.

The Specie Circular was particularly ill-timed because the U.S. economy was already experiencing tremendous pressure from abroad. In 1837, the Bank of England

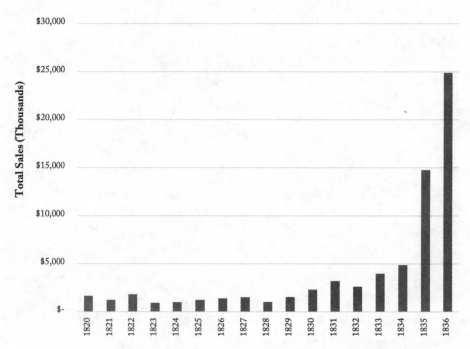

Figure 4.4: Total Revenue from Federal Land Sales (Thousands) (1820–1836)[18]

raised interest rates sharply to stem the outflow of gold.[19] As the British economy weakened, demand for American cotton collapsed. This triggered business and bank failures in the South, which soon spread throughout the country. Over the next several years, the combination of commodity price declines, reckless lending practices by state banks, and a sudden outflow of foreign capital triggered a sharp economic contraction and corresponding decline in asset values. By the time President Martin van Buren took office in January 1837, the economy was trapped in a self-reinforcing downward spiral. For the remainder of the year, the nation suffered a wave of bank failures, and commerce seemed to come to a standstill. By 1838, Americans had suffered a painful economic contraction, but the worst was yet to come.[20]

THE SECOND GREAT DEPRESSION

"The door was still tight shut, however; the same cold, cheerless air prevailed . . . I hastened to inquire its name and purpose, and then my surprise vanished. It was the tomb of many fortunes; the Great Catacomb of investment; the memorable United States Bank."[21]

—CHARLES DICKENS (January 1842)

In 1838, the U.S. economy seemed to have bottomed, and Americans were hopeful that a recovery was forthcoming. Then, the Bank of England raised rates sharply again in 1839, prompting another wave of foreign capital outflows. The second shock proved too much for the U.S. economy to bear. Credit contracted, asset prices collapsed, and bank failures resumed. Even Nathaniel Prime, one of the founders of the New York Stock Exchange, could not escape, and his firm of Prime, Ward & King entered bankruptcy in 1839. In Philadelphia, the last vestige of a U.S. central bank disappeared when the Second Bank of the United States (which was privatized under Nicholas Biddle) failed in 1841. Even state governments could not escape the gravity of the depression. Eight state governments and one U.S. territory defaulted on their debts, prompting outrage among foreign investors.[22]

POINT OF INTEREST

America's Long-Lost Fear of Debt Default

"Now, the Americans have cut themselves off from all resources of credit. Having been as dishonest as they can be, they are prevented from being as foolish as they wish to be. In the whole habitable globe, they cannot borrow a guinea, and they cannot draw the sword because they have not money to buy it."[23]

—Reverend Sydney Smith, British investor in Pennsylvania bonds
(March 8, 1844)

State governments were among the first casualties of the Hard Times. During the 1830s, they had borrowed vast sums from Europeans to build canals, turnpikes, and railroads. Between 1836 and 1838 alone, states borrowed more than $100 million, exceeding the combined national debt of Russia, Prussia, and the Netherlands. The repayment of these loans depended on the ability of these projects to produce revenue. But the Panic of 1837 drastically reduced economic activity, which in turn sharply reduced their revenues.[24]

In July 1841, the state of Michigan became the first U.S. state to default on its debt.[25] Over the next two years, seven more states and one U.S. territory defaulted. The federal government was never at risk of default, but its credit was harmed because many foreign investors did not differentiate the behavior of federal and state governments. In fact, many petitioned the federal government

(continued)

to assume state debts, much like they had in the 1790s. Congress never seriously entertained such proposals.[26]

One hundred years after the Panic of 1837, Congress passed the Public Debt Act of 1939, establishing a limit on the federal debt. Since then, Congress has raised the debt ceiling seventy-nine times. In recent years, the debt ceiling has become a bargaining chip in congressional negotiations, which is a dangerous precedent. Since the passage of the Funding Act of 1790, the federal government has never defaulted on its debt. This track record enables the U.S. to borrow at extremely low rates, which is a luxury in times of prosperity but a necessity in a crisis. The unsustainability of U.S. fiscal deficits is a legitimate concern, and America's procrastination in dealing with it is dangerously short-sighted. However, it is equally reckless to hold the credit of the U.S. hostage. The long-forgotten lessons of the 1840s provide a powerful reminder of the severe consequence of a debt default.

American standards of living plummeted in the 1840s, and the nation's cities looked like dystopian versions of the ones that had thrived ten years earlier. Soup kitchens, bread lines, and overpopulated alms houses were even more prevalent than they were in the 1820s. The final cost of the depression was a frightening breakdown of law and order as Americans desperately competed for scarce resources. Violent uprisings, crime waves, and even outright insurrections erupted throughout the states in the early 1840s.

The most important lesson from the Hard Times is that by far, the greatest risk of an economic depression is the potential unwinding of the fabric of society. In the 1840s, the fabric of American society was frayed, but it fortunately remained intact. Many nations never recover from such events. This risk is revisited in chapter 19, as the final major depression in U.S. history, the Great Depression of the 1930s, triggered the rise of fascism in Europe and militarism in Japan. These toxic ideologies then triggered the outbreak of the worst war in human history.

Chapter 5

THE ECONOMICS OF
THE CIVIL WAR

*"Every day the difference between the North and South is becoming more
prominent and apparent . . . Such a Union is one of interest merely,
a paper bond, to be torn asunder by a burst of passion or to be
deliberately undone whenever interest demands it."*[1]

—SIDNEY GEORGE FISHER (APRIL 1844)

The U.S. economy began a slow recovery by the mid-1840s, but it was the discovery of gold at Sutter's Mill in 1848 that enabled it to achieve escape velocity. The gold itself strengthened the balance sheets of the federal government and banking system, which were bolstered by $50 million in production from 1848–1849 and a total of $555 million over the course of the next decade. The California Gold Rush also boosted the economy by increasing immigration and demand for a variety of supporting industries. As the 1850s commenced, lofty growth expectations once again attracted a deluge of foreign capital, and the U.S. entered a new era of growth and innovation. But beneath the surface, the country was divided, and the cohesiveness of the Union was about to face its greatest test.[2]

The causes and consequences of the American Civil War were complex, and this book does not attempt to address these issues comprehensively. It only seeks to explain the financial consequences of the Civil War. Sadly, this must begin with an uncomfortable analysis of the economics of slavery. It is important to acknowledge up front that describing slavery with financial statistics carries the risk of sanitizing an abhorrent practice. This is neither the intent nor desire of the author. Nevertheless, it is important to describe slavery in financial terms because irrespective of its immorality, the decisions that triggered the Civil War were driven heavily by economic considerations.

After addressing the economic issues of slavery, the chapter shifts to the financial reforms enacted during and immediately after the Civil War. The enormous financial costs of the war prompted the passage of legislation collectively known as the National Banking Acts. These reforms ended the free banking era that began with President Andrew Jackson's veto of the Second Bank charter. The acts created a stable currency and more resilient banking system, but they also introduced new structural flaws that would shape the chaotic securities markets of the Gilded Age.

THE DYSTOPIAN ECONOMICS OF SLAVERY

On November 6, 1860, Abraham Lincoln was elected president of the United States. Lincoln only won 40 percent of the popular vote but achieved a decisive electoral victory because the presidential race included four candidates. Republicans simultaneously won large majorities in the Senate and House of Representatives. Soon after the election, Southern states began seceding from the Union, as they viewed Lincoln and the Republican Party as intolerable threats to the continued enslavement of African Americans.

Over the last 160 years, various myths have circulated regarding the role of slavery in the secession of the Southern states, but historical evidence conclusively reveals that the Northern states' opposition to the westward expansion of slavery was the primary issue that prompted secession. The differences in perspective were heavily influenced by the divergent economic paths of the North and the South. Put simply, the Northern states had proceeded along a path of industrialization, while the Southern states sought to preserve an agricultural economy that depended heavily on cotton. As the U.S. spread westward, Southern states sought to expand the use of slavery to support their economic system, while the Northern states sought to prevent it.

The election of 1860 convinced Southerners that they had not only lost the battle to spread westward, but they were also at risk of losing the right to slavery entirely. They feared that the increased dominance of free states would eventually result in the outlawing of slavery in every state—even if that threat was not yet present.[3] Southerners had many reasons to prevent the end of slavery, but most historians agree that the most powerful one was economic. The economics of slavery were as simple as they were despicable. First, for obvious reasons, the use of free labor was more profitable than paid labor on Southern plantations. Second, because slave labor was profitable, slaves were considered valuable assets. In fact, the value of slaves represented roughly

Table 5.1: Estimated Loss of Income per Capita Due to Abolition of Slavery (1860)[4]

STATE	DATE OF SECESSION	REDUCTION OF INCOME OF FREE CITIZENS	
South Carolina	December 20, 1860	36%	
Mississippi	January 9, 1861	29%	
Florida	January 10, 1860	34%	
Alabama	January 11, 1861	42%	
Georgia	January 19, 1861	29%	
Louisiana	January 26, 1861	24%	
Texas	February 1, 1861	24%	Avg = 31%
CIVIL WAR BEGINS ON APRIL 12, 1861			
North Carolina	May 20, 1861	19%	
Tennessee	June 8, 1861	18%	
Arkansas	May 6, 1861	17%	
Virginia	April 17, 1861	17%	Avg = 18%
CONTESTED OR UNION STATES[5]			
Kentucky	Contested	10%	
Maryland	Union	6%	
Missouri	Contested	5%	Avg = 7%

$4 billion of the total wealth of the Southern states in 1860. If slavery were to end, owners would not only experience a decline in the profitability of their plantations, but they would also lose a large percentage of their wealth. The importance of economics in the decision of Southern states to secede is clearly represented in the timing and contentiousness of their decisions to either join the Confederacy or remain with the Union. Table 5.1 shows the timing of the decision on whether to secede and the estimated reduction in the per capita income of the free population if slavery was abolished in their respective states.[6]

Southerners viewed the continuation of slavery to be a critical component of their way of life—and much of their rationale was economic. As growing political power of Northern states threatened to end the practice, Southerners finally resorted to war to preserve it. On April 12, 1861, Confederate forces opened fire on Fort Sumter, and three days later, the Civil War began when Abraham Lincoln ordered state militias to raise 75,000 troops to quell the rebellion.

FINANCING THE CIVIL WAR

In retrospect, Northerners grossly underestimated the commitment of Southerners to exit the Union and their ability to wage war. Soon after the disastrous First Battle of Bull Run in July 1861, it was apparent that the Civil War was likely to last much longer and cost considerably more than initial estimates. This created two problems for the Union. The first was the instability of the currency. After the disappearance of the Second Bank, paper currency was once again issued by state-chartered banks, and the value of their banknotes varied depending on the strength of the issuing bank. The Union therefore had a difficult time purchasing supplies for troops that were spread across multiple states. The second problem was raising the enormous amount of debt required to fund the war. The U.S. Congress resolved these problems by passing a series of laws between 1862 and 1864.

The Legal Tender Act of 1862

The Union struggled to raise debt soon after the first shots of the Civil War were fired at Fort Sumter. In August 1861, the secretary of the Treasury, Salmon P. Chase, negotiated a deal with New York City bankers to sell $150 million of U.S. government bonds in three tranches. The bankers were required to pay for the bonds in specie, which they expected to quickly recoup after selling the bonds to investors. The first two tranches went smoothly, but the final tranche declined in value before the bankers could sell them. Rather than sell at a loss, the bankers held on to the bonds, but this prevented them from rebuilding their specie reserves, and they suffered a wave of bank runs. Many New York banks responded by suspending specie redemption. Soon thereafter, New York bankers suspended their relationship with the U.S. Treasury when Chase refused to protect them from further financial damage.[7] Without the support of New York bankers, Chase was forced to find other means to raise capital, and the Legal Tender Act of 1862 was the first of several solutions.[8]

On February 25, 1862, Congress approved the Legal Tender Act, which authorized the immediate issuance of $150 million in non-interest-bearing Treasury notes. The notes were soon referred to as "greenbacks" because of the green ink used in their production. Greenbacks were not redeemable for gold and silver, but they were considered "legal tender," which meant that they could be used to satisfy both public and private debts. Greenbacks are regarded as the first fiat currency of the United States, meaning that the value was not based on the ability to redeem the notes for specie, such as gold or silver. The act also authorized the issuance of $500 million in government bonds to ensure adequate funding of the notes.[9]

By July 1863, the U.S. had authorized the issuance of up to $450 million in greenbacks. Nearly the entire authorized amount was in circulation by July 1, 1864. Greenbacks played an important role in the funding of the Civil War, but they were far from sufficient. Instead, most of the funding would come from the issuance of bonds. But with New York bankers no longer willing to underwrite them, the U.S. Treasury was forced to sell bonds directly to individuals.

Jay Cooke and the Rise of the Retail Investor

The issuance of greenbacks was insufficient to address the Union's financial needs. It also set a dangerous precedent, as the printing of currency that was unanchored to gold or silver risked igniting inflation if taken too far. The Union needed to supplement greenbacks with the sale of hundreds of millions of dollars of U.S. government bonds, and they needed to do it without the aid of New York City bankers. Jay Cooke, a Philadelphia-based investment banker, proved instrumental in this effort. In 1861, Cooke was named as a subscription agent for the Treasury, and he began selling U.S. government bonds through his personal network. Cooke was highly successful, but the sheer amount of capital required to fund the Civil War far exceeded the wealth of his connections.

POINT OF INTEREST

The Telegraph Links Main Street, Wall Street, and Washington

"Jay Cooke used the telegraph as no American businessman had ever before used. By means of the wires . . . he kept his eye on military progress in the field, political events in Washington, and the stock and money markets in New York—three strategic points in determining the success or failure of a loan."[10]

—**Henrietta M. Larson, business historian**

In 1837, Samuel Morse submitted a patent for "The American Recording Electro-Magnetic Telegraph." The device used electronic pulses transmitted on wires to distant locations. By the 1860s, telegraph wires connected cities across the nation, allowing the nearly instantaneous communication of vital information related to the Civil War.

The telegraph was one of the early American technological innovations that transformed society. It also played a critical but often unappreciated role in funding the war. Jay Cooke relied on telegraph communications to monitor political activities, battlefield results, and the response of securities markets

(continued)

in New York. These events affected the demand and pricing of bonds, which Cooke used to aid his sales efforts and publicity campaigns.

The telegraph continued to play a vital role on Wall Street after the Civil War ended. But even more revolutionary was the technology that derived from the telegraph. On November 15, 1867, the first "stock ticker" was introduced to Wall Street. The device enabled Americans to track the prices of stocks and bonds trading on securities exchanges in near-real time. The stock ticker would accelerate the growth of securities markets during the Gilded Age.

In 1862, Cooke devised a novel solution. He assembled a network of subagents who sold bonds directly to Americans throughout the Union. At the peak, Cooke had 2,500 subagents under contract. He supported sales efforts with aggressive advertising campaigns that appealed both to Americans' patriotism and the financial benefits of the bonds. Cooke's strategy was extraordinarily successful. In September 1862, the Treasury had sold only $2.5 million of the $500 million of bonds (known as "5-20 bonds") authorized under the Legal Tender Act. By June 30, 1863, the Treasury had raised $175 million. When the sale of the 5-20 bonds ended on January 1, 1864, Cooke had sold approximately $361.95 million, which amounted to more than 70 percent of the total issuance.[11]

Jay Cooke's direct sales strategy was a game changer. During the four fiscal years ending June 30, 1865, the Union raised a total of nearly $2.6 billion, increasing the national debt to $2.68 billion by June 30, 1865 (Figure 5.1). Jay Cooke & Company sold well over $1 billion of bonds. The two biggest loan drives involved bonds known as 5-20s and 7-30s. These constituted more than 50 percent of the total debt issued by the Union, and Cooke sold most of them. Moreover, Cooke charged a commission of less than 0.50 percent. Although this made him a wealthy man, it was a bargain for the U.S. government when considering the value that Cooke created. Finally, Jay Cooke introduced the average American to the concept of investing. After the Civil War ended, this new cohort of investors would attract the attention of Wall Street.[12]

The National Banking Acts of 1863 and 1864

"The percentage of notes of doubtful value which were in circulation in the Western States was so great that the knowledge of an expert was required at every turn to determine what to receive and what to reject."[13]

—ANDREW MCFARLAND DAVIS (1910)

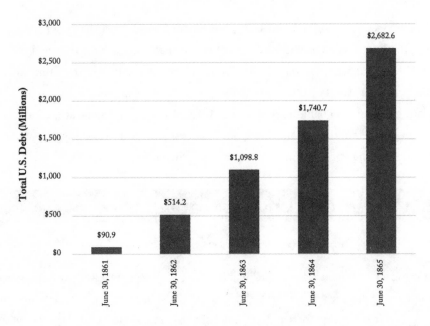

Figure 5.1: Total U.S. National Debt by Fiscal Year End (Millions) (June 30, 1861–June 30, 1865)[14]

The Legal Tender Act, combined with Jay Cooke's bond sales campaigns, enabled the Union to fund the Civil War, but the nation still suffered from currency instability. For three decades, state-chartered banks had proliferated, and many issued banknotes with little regard for their ability to honor specie redemptions. As the sheer variety of banknotes increased, differentiating between high- and low-quality banknotes became nearly impossible. This inefficiency was frustrating during times of peace, but it was intolerable during a time of war. On February 25, 1863, Congress passed the National Currency Act to address this issue. But in addition to establishing a stable, uniform currency, the act also created a national banking system to replace the unreliable system of state-chartered banks. On June 3, 1864, Congress passed the National Bank Act, which made critical adjustments to the National Currency Act to encourage more state-chartered banks, especially those located in New York, to convert to national banks. The National Currency Act of 1863 and National Bank Act of 1864 are now collectively referred to as the National Banking Acts.

The creation of a national banking system provided many benefits to Americans. The National Monetary Commission, which was formed after the Panic of 1907, conducted an exhaustive evaluation of records from the Civil War era to explain the thinking of the politicians who crafted these acts. The Commission's report confirmed that the primary objective was to establish a stable, uniform currency. A secondary benefit was that it increased demand for U.S. government bonds. The reason is because reserves of national banks were secured by holdings of U.S. government bonds rather than gold and silver.[15] This naturally led to increased purchases of government bonds, which helped fund the Civil War. A final benefit of the acts was the creation of the Office of the Comptroller of the Currency (OCC). The OCC was charged with issuing charters of national banks and regulating the national banking system. The OCC was the first federal agency to provide oversight of banks at the national level. State governments had previously provided oversight, but most had been lax in both supervision and enforcement.[16]

POINT OF INTEREST

The Endangered Species of the United States

A critical component of the National Currency Act was the use of U.S. government bonds (rather than gold and silver) as the monetary base of the banking system. This concept was not entirely novel—several states used state-issued bonds as reserves in prior years—but it was a notable difference in comparison to the system employed by the First and Second Banks of the United States.

Under the new system, the U.S. currency remained anchored to gold and silver indirectly because interest and principal of U.S. government bonds was payable in gold. Nevertheless, the use of government bonds as reserves was an important philosophical shift, and it was the first step toward the eventual shift of the U.S. to a fiat currency approximately one hundred years later.

The national banking system took several years to implement. The first challenge was overcoming resistance of state-chartered New York banks, which were the largest financial institutions in the United States. Many of the adjustments introduced by the National Bank Act of 1864 were designed to meet the demands of New York bankers.[17] Momentum for the conversion of state-charted banks to national banks accelerated in March 1865 when Congress passed legislation that levied a 10 percent tax on banknotes issued by state-chartered banks. This tax was a substantial increase to the 2 percent tax that was levied under the National Bank Act of 1864. By 1870, most state-chartered banks had either converted to national banks or closed their doors. Even more importantly, the circulation of banknotes issued by state-chartered banks nearly disappeared. In 1870, state-chartered banknotes had declined by more than 99 percent (Figure 5.2). The U.S. currency was stabilized again, and Americans would never again suffer from uncertainty regarding the value of a banknote, provided it was issued by the national banking system.

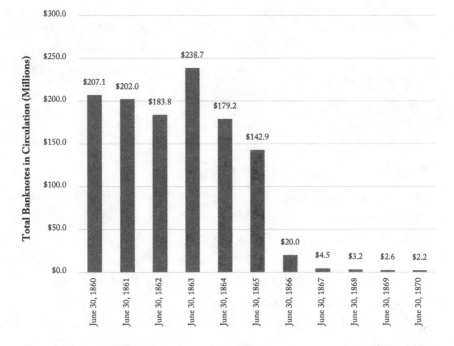

Figure 5.2: Total State-Chartered Banknotes in Circulation (Millions) (June 30, 1860–June 30, 1870)[18]

POINT OF INTEREST

The Pendulum of Financial History: Today's Solutions Create Tomorrow's Problems

Currency instability was conquered once and for all with the passage of the National Banking Acts. The era that followed was a huge improvement over the free banking era that began when Andrew Jackson vetoed the renewal of the Second Bank charter. But the National Banking laws introduced a new structural flaw. The dangers were not obvious in the late 1860s, but they became increasingly costly as the U.S. economy rapidly expanded in the Gilded Age.

The structural flaw was known as currency inelasticity. It referred to the inability of the banking system to adjust the money supply in response to sudden changes in economic conditions. Currency inelasticity was especially problematic during financial panics, and it explains why Americans suffered several preventable financial crises and depressions in the decades to come.

The fact that the National Banking Acts were both a present solution and source of future problems is not a unique phenomenon in financial history. Many financial innovations follow the same pattern. Sometimes unanticipated

(continued)

problems emerge within a few years, but usually they remain hidden for decades. In these latter cases, abandoning well-established solutions is often difficult for people—even when it is obvious that they are no longer useful. Readers will see this pattern repeated multiple times throughout the remainder of this book.

The End of the Foundational Era

On April 9, 1865, General Robert E. Lee surrendered to General Ulysses S. Grant at Appomattox Courthouse. The costs of the Civil War were enormous. A recent study estimated that 750,000 Americans died, which exceeded the combined American fatalities of the Revolutionary War, War of 1812, Mexican War, Spanish-American War, and two World Wars. The U.S. had also amassed approximately $2.0 billion of debt to fund the war. On June 30, 1860, the total public debt was a modest $64.84 million, but on June 30, 1866, it had increased to $2.77 billion. Finally, the reunited country faced the daunting task of Reconstruction. The Southern states were impoverished by the war, and animosity between former African American slaves and white citizens who formerly claimed them as property was hardly pacified by the surrender of Confederate forces.[19]

At the same time, there was also hope for the nation. Slavery was exorcised from the U.S., enabling Americans to bring their laws and ideals into closer alignment. From a financial perspective, the creation of the national banking system provided a much stronger foundation for commerce and created a more attractive destination for foreign capital. Finally, the demands of war itself accelerated multiple industrial advancements that would shape the economic progress of the nation for the remainder of the nineteenth century. Most important was the massive investment in the construction of railroads to connect cities, farms, and eventually the East and West Coasts.

In 1866, a new financial era dawned in the United States. Historians would later refer to the decades that followed as the Gilded Age. Americans enjoyed the benefits of astonishing inventions and extraordinary wealth creation. The wealth of opportunity in America also attracted tremendous inflows of foreign capital, which created insatiable demand for new investment securities. New York City was the focal point for the issuance and trading of securities, but with little regulatory oversight, Gilded Age securities markets were a dangerous place. Part 2 recounts the evolution of the American economy and Wall Street during the Gilded Age. The U.S. remained a shadow of the British Empire after the Civil War, but by the twentieth century, Great Britain's former colony would rise to become its heir apparent.

Part 2

Growth and Grift in the Gilded Age

1866–1895

"What has been true of railroads has been true of other forms of permanent investment. First, high charges and high profits. Then speculative investments in the same line. Next, an overstocked market, and no profit at all. Finally, cut-throat competition and widespread insolvency."[1]

—ARTHUR T. HADLEY, economist (1886)

The end of the Reconstruction era marked the beginning of a new era, which is commonly referred to as the Gilded Age. This period was among the most transformational for the nation's economy and securities markets, but it was also morally confusing. Cognitive dissonance is a term used in psychology to describe the discomfort of holding multiple conflicting beliefs simultaneously. This term perfectly describes the American experience during the Gilded Age. Inventors and entrepreneurs introduced groundbreaking innovations that dramatically improved standards of living, but unscrupulous opportunists engaged in corruption and committed despicable atrocities on vulnerable groups. The Gilded Age was a period in which the best and worst aspects of capitalism were on full display.

The uneven impact of economic advancement during the Gilded Age often makes appreciating the progress that accompanied it difficult. But from a historical perspective, recognizing both the pros and the cons is important. The following chapters seek to strike this balance. The foundation of the stories highlighted in **Part 2** is the rapid acceleration of industrialization in America, which depended heavily on the expansion of a vast network of railroads throughout the nation. The chapters also recount the rapid growth and chaotic trading in U.S. securities markets. These markets enabled companies to raise enormous amounts of capital but often failed to protect the interests of investors and the American public.

Chapter 6 begins by recounting the expansion of America's railroads, which revolutionized American life and triggered the rise of large corporations. Americans enjoyed numerous benefits, but these were often accompanied by undesirable side effects. Chapter 6 focuses on the benefits, which included rapid settlement of western lands, expansion of the nation's communications network, and the advancement of corporate managerial practices.

Chapter 7 addresses the harmful side effects that accompanied the expansion of railroads. Operating under lax governance and little transparency, railroad owners often plundered their companies at the expense of investors. Theft and fraud were often abetted by legislators and judges who happily accepted bribes for their support. But the influence of railroad companies was not just financial. Many companies contributed to the removal of Native Americans from their ancestral lands, and some were complicit in atrocities committed against tribes that resisted. Finally, railroad companies often created harsh and dangerous working conditions for their employees. Deadly workplace accidents and abusive labor practices were common.

Chapter 8 shifts gears back to the positive by recounting the rapid advancement of U.S. manufacturing capabilities. By the mid-1800s, American entrepreneurs and inventors had mastered the elusive art of precision manufacturing. This, in turn, enabled American manufacturers to produce interchangeable parts faster and at a higher quality level than all global competitors. By the turn of the twentieth century, the American System of Manufactures established the U.S. as the world's leading mass manufacturer, thus foreshadowing the end of Great Britain's reign as the world's workshop.

Chapter 9 shifts back to U.S. securities markets, which entered a troubled period of adolescence in the late 1800s. Rapid economic growth attracted massive amounts of capital, and the sheer volume of trading made markets efficient. But the absence of regulation gave unscrupulous stock promoters free rein to raise capital based on exaggerated claims or outright fraud. At the same time, stock plungers, such as Jay Gould, Jim Fisk, and Daniel Drew, manipulated markets at will for their own benefit. Flaws in the banking system only magnified the chaos.[2] The national banking system had stabilized the currency and provided basic regulatory oversight, but the country still lacked several critical central banking capabilities. As a result, financial panics that would be containable today spiraled out of control during the Gilded Age.

Chapter 10 recounts the Panic of 1873. Like all panics, this one resulted from the collision of several economic forces, but the unexpected failure of Jay Cooke & Co. was the trigger that pushed markets over the edge. The depression that followed lasted for most of the remaining decade, but deflationary pressures persisted for more than twenty years. Growing tension between creditors and borrowers prompted the emergence of the free silver movement, which dominated politics for the remainder of the century. The subsequent expansion of the nation's silver reserves initially eased deflationary pressures but eventually led to a currency crisis in 1893.

Chapter 11 concludes the Gilded Age by recounting the Panic of 1893, which was caused by the instability of the nation's bimetallic currency standard based on gold and silver. The overvaluation of silver drove a persistent outflow of gold from the vaults of the U.S. Treasury. The crisis ended when J. Pierpont Morgan orchestrated a private rescue of the nation's gold reserves. In the process, he cemented his position as America's leading financier. After William McKinley defeated William Jennings Bryan in the election of 1896, the nation abandoned silver as a monetary base. This established the gold standard as the basis of the U.S. currency and created a solid foundation on which American commerce would thrive during the subsequent ten-year period known as the American Commercial Invasion.

Chapter 6

RAILS ACROSS AMERICA

*"With the extension of railways over every part of the country, each
industrial organization has the whole land, we might also say the whole
world, before it, as a possible market for its products. It has thus become
possible to mass together much larger industrial organizations than were
possible when each could supply only a limited market."*[1]

—**SIMON NEWCOMB**, mathematician and economist (1880)

The United States always possessed extraordinary economic potential due to its
abundance of natural resources and vast tracts of farmland, but the challenge was
that its resources were scattered across a vast terrain, making it costly to bring them
to market. During the first half of the 1800s, steamships substantially increased speed
and reduced the cost of shipping and travel on large bodies of water, but travel on land
remained slow and expensive. The invention of the steam locomotive in Great Britain
in the early 1800s promised to solve this problem, and the U.S. began aggressively
building its railroad network in the 1830s. By the late 1800s, railroad transportation
was faster, cheaper, and more reliable than transportation on water. This enabled the
U.S. to finally unlock its full economic potential.

The railroad industry also serves as a perfect microcosm of Gilded Age business
activity, as railroad companies almost single-handedly revealed the best and worst
elements of capitalism. Railroads accelerated migration westward, offering rich opportunities for settlers, but enormous federal land grants and brazen treaty violations
simultaneously stripped Native Americans of their ancestral lands and contributed to
unspeakable atrocities against those who resisted. Railroads enabled manufacturing
companies to mass-produce products that were higher quality and more affordable

than those produced in Europe, but owners' insatiable appetite for growth often created harsh working conditions. Finally, railroad companies raised massive amounts of capital, but with few regulatory guardrails, unscrupulous owners often funded their own interests first.

Chapter 6 and chapter 7 provide opposing perspectives on the impact of the railroad industry. Chapter 6 begins with a brief history of the industry, focusing primarily on the post–Civil War period. It explains how railroads accelerated economic growth, westward migration, and corporate innovation. In contrast, chapter 7 highlights the harmful effects of railroads. Taken together, the two chapters illustrate the difficulty of reconciling cognitive dissonance in the Gilded Age.

A BRIEF HISTORY OF RAILROADING

The invention of the steam-powered locomotive is credited to the British mining engineer Richard Trevithick. On February 21, 1804, he successfully tested the first locomotive by pulling five wagons loaded with ten tons of iron and seventy men. On February 28, 1827, the Baltimore and Ohio (B&O) Railroad received the first corporate charter to construct a railroad in the United States. The last surviving signer of the Declaration of Independence laid the first rail on July 4, 1828, and the B&O opened its first route in 1830.[2]

Photograph courtesy of JPH Photography

From March 1827 until December 1848, states issued an additional 1,155 corporate charters to railroad companies. Construction initially proceeded at a brisk pace but then slowed during the deep depression in the 1840s. The discovery of gold at Sutter's Mill triggered a strong economic recovery and added demand for further westward expansion. From January 1849 to December 1860, states granted

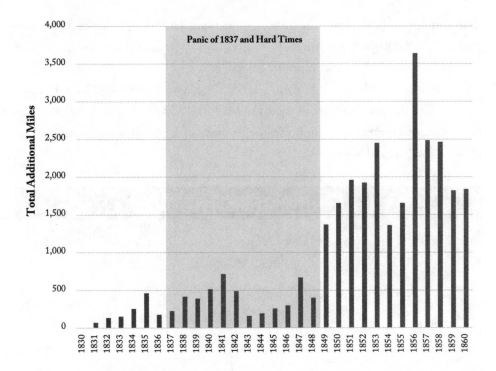

Figure 6.1: Total Annual Increase in U.S. Railroad Mileage (January 1, 1830–December 31, 1860)[3]

another 1,306 railroad company charters with a total authorized capitalization of $2.7 billion. The charters represented only 11.5 percent of all corporate charters issued during this period, but the maximum capitalization of railroad companies was 60.9 percent of the total authorized capitalization of all U.S. companies. From 1849 to 1860, railroad companies added an average of 2,053 miles of track per year, which was more than a sixfold increase over the average during the prior twenty-year period. (Figure 6.1).[4]

POST-CIVIL WAR EXPANSION

In the 1850s, the federal government began exploring an ambitious project to link the East and West Coasts via a transcontinental railroad. Most congressmen supported the idea, but the escalating conflict between Northern and Southern states prevented passage of legislation. However, after the secession of the Southern states in 1861, legislation was no longer impeded by Southern congressmen. In 1862, Congress passed the Pacific Railway Act, which provided enormous federal subsidies for construction, and awarded contracts to the Union Pacific and Central Pacific to complete the work. Progress was slow at first due to restrictions on the use of private capital and resource shortages due to the Civil War. In 1864, Congress accelerated construction by passing a second Pacific Railway Act, which provided much larger land grants and eliminated the restriction against the use of private capital.

When the Civil War ended in April 1865, the Union Pacific and Central Pacific resumed construction at a feverish pace. On May 10, 1869, the tracks of the two companies met at Promontory Summit in the territory of Utah, thus establishing a link between the East and West Coasts.

POINT OF INTEREST

Government Contracts: The Deepest Reservoir of Gilded Age Grift

Photograph courtesy of JPH Photography

On May 10, 1869, the Central Pacific and Union Pacific laid the final tracks at Promontory Summit. After the last railroad tie was secured with a golden spike, the U.S. officially had a railroad network linking the East and West Coasts.

The achievement was extraordinary, but both before and after the laying of the golden spike, the Central Pacific and Union Pacific were the poster children of Gilded Age corruption. The owners of both companies overcharged the federal government by tens of millions of dollars. They routinely extorted villages and cities in exchange for advantageous placement of routes and train stations. And they regularly bribed public officials to serve their own purposes.

The transcontinental railroad was an awe-inspiring project, but it was just one of numerous railroad projects that were linking villages, cities, and farms throughout the nation. Construction waxed and waned during economic booms and busts, but over the three decades following the Civil War, railroads had added nearly 150,000 miles of track, and the total capitalization of U.S. railroad companies was nearly $12 billion. Railroad jobs had become the fastest-growing segment of the U.S. labor force. Between 1860 and 1900, railroad employment increased by 6.6 percent per year, which far exceeded all other industries. This, in turn, contributed to the decline of agriculture as the largest employer of Americans. Between 1860 and 1900, the percentage of the U.S. labor force employed in agriculture declined from 59 percent to 38 percent.[5]

The following series of figures shows several of these trends. Figure 6.2 shows the annual increase in railroad mileage from 1850 to 1899. Figure 6.3 shows the total capitalization of U.S. railroads from 1873 to 1899.[6] Figure 6.4 shows the total percentage of the labor force employed in agriculture.

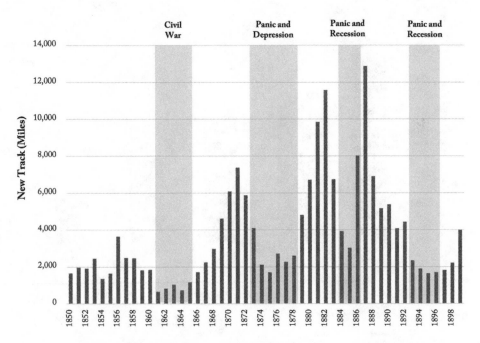

Figure 6.2: Total Annual Increase in U.S. Railroad Mileage (1850–1899)[7]

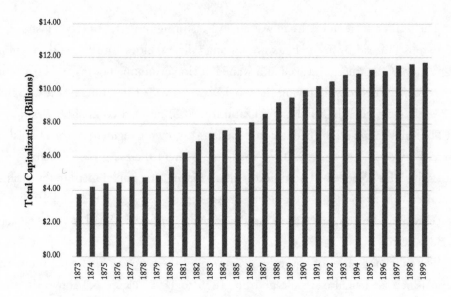

Figure 6.3: Total Capitalization of U.S. Railroad Companies (Billions) (1873–1899)[8]

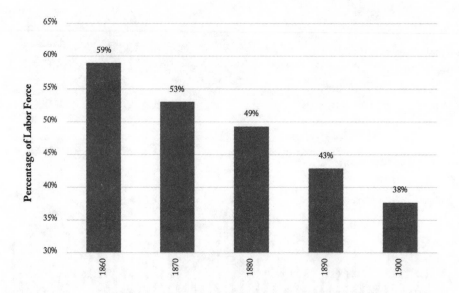

Figure 6.4: Percentage of U.S. Labor Force Employed in Agriculture (1860–1900)[9]

THE BENEFITS OF RAILROADS

Most historical accounts of the Gilded Age focus on the harmful impact of railroad expansion. These are real, and they are covered extensively in chapter 7. But the benefits were also substantial, and a few of the more notable ones are outlined on the following pages.

Strengthening of U.S. Industrial Competitiveness

Railroads dramatically reduced the cost and time required to ship raw materials and manufactured products to both domestic and international markets. Prior to railroads, the dispersion of the nation's population across a vast land was a significant disadvantage relative to global competitors. By eliminating this headwind, American industrial firms thrived by gaining access to affordable raw materials such as coal, iron, and cotton, as well as gaining affordable transportation of products to both domestic and international markets. Combined with advancements in precision manufacturing (covered in chapter 8), railroads positioned the U.S. to become a dominant manufacturing power.

Acceleration of Westward Migration and Immigration

Railroads created many opportunities for Americans migrating westward and new immigrants arriving in the country. Not only did they provide a much safer and faster alternative for travel, but they also expanded the amount of viable farmland due to greater access to affordable transportation. Inexpensive land and an abundance of job opportunities attracted millions of immigrants. From 1865 to 1900, more than 13.5 million immigrants settled in the United States. Annual immigration data is shown in Figure 6.5. Most arrived from the Americas (e.g., Canada and Mexico) and European countries. Many of these immigrants would become leading inventors, scientists, entrepreneurs, and corporate executives.[10]

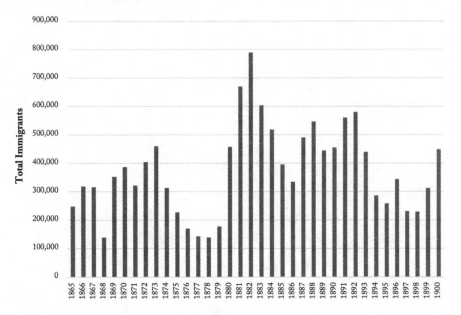

Figure 6.5: Total U.S. Immigration by Year (1865–1900)[11]

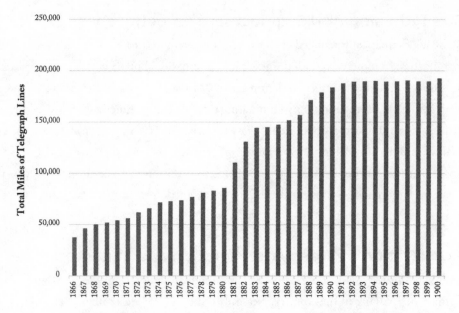

Figure 6.6: Total Miles of Western Union Telegraph Lines (1866–1900)[12]

Expansion of America's Communications Network

The invention of the telegraph in 1837 was fortuitous in that it coincided with the start of the railroad boom. Railroad companies worked alongside telegraph companies to connect major cities. The cost of clearing land and placing telegraph lines would have been considerably higher if not for this symbiotic relationship. The telegraph also proved invaluable to railroad companies, as it enabled them to coordinate construction, operations, and scheduling. Finally, the telegraph infrastructure paid additional dividends during the final two decades of the 1800s. Alexander Graham Bell introduced the telephone in the late 1870s, and telephone lines were added at low cost to the preexisting telegraph infrastructure. Figure 6.6 shows the total telegraph miles of Western Union alone from 1866 to 1900.

Managerial Experimentation and Training

"Successful industry thus requires as never before genius in organization . . . Mill's famous dictum that 'industry is limited by capital' has relatively lost its significance and should be replaced by another, 'industry is limited by the organizing ability of the undertaker.'"[13]

—SIDNEY SHERWOOD, economist (1900)

Railroad construction and operations were highly complex processes. Both required well-coordinated effort among thousands of specialized laborers who were scattered across many states. This forced companies to establish large, hierarchical management structures for the first time, and railroad companies were an ideal training ground for a new managerial profession. Senior managers from the railroad industry often leveraged their experience to lead large industrial companies that thrived in the late 1800s. One notable example was Andrew Carnegie, who gained invaluable experience as a manager at the Pennsylvania Railroad Company in the 1850s. The impact of railroads on corporate operations is difficult to quantify, but it undoubtedly served as a critical source of management innovation that helped fuel America's rise as an industrial superpower.[14]

A Connected Country

By 1900, the U.S. was connected by an expansive network of railroads, telegraph wires, and telephone cables. In the 1840s, settlers heading west on the Oregon Trail faced a grueling five-to-six-month journey in which an average of 10 percent of travelers perished before reaching their destination. In 1870, passengers traveled from New York to San Francisco in approximately one week. As the speed and quality of the tracks improved, travel times and costs declined further with each passing year. Railroads made the U.S. feel much smaller and accessible. It accelerated western settlement, attracted immigrants, opened new markets for agriculture and industry, accelerated construction of the nation's communications network, and provided a training ground for future leaders of America's largest corporations. Nevertheless, the expansion was not without cost. Americans suffered many harmful side effects, the most significant of which are covered in the next chapter.

Chapter 7

THE DARK SIDE OF
THE TRACKS

"So rapid has been the change that men's thoughts have been hardly able to adapt themselves to it; still less has the law been able to keep pace with it. The change has brought evils and dangers, previously unknown, and even now imperfectly understood."[1]

—ARTHUR T. HADLEY, economist (1886)

The growth of railroad corporations came at a cost. Federal and state laws failed to keep pace with their rapid growth, which allowed corruption to flourish. Railroad owners, managers, politicians, and even judges often enriched themselves at the expense of Americans. In the present day, corporate abuse and political corruption still occurs, but the scale is nowhere near that of the Gilded Age. Nevertheless, echoes of this era can still be heard, which makes it important to remember the egregious abuses that follow.

CONSTRUCTION AND FINANCE COMPANIES

Creative forms of grift occurred at every stage of the railroad life cycle. Securities fraud was common on the front end, and price fixing was common on the back end. But the phase that was most prone to abuse was the construction phase because owners were flush with cash from government subsidies and the issuance of new securities. The most lucrative tactic during this phase was the use of construction and finance companies.

The concept of a construction and finance company is rather simple. Prior to breaking ground on a new railroad, a small group of owners created a separately managed company, which would subcontract with the railroad company to handle construction. Investors and members of the public were usually unaware of this relationship. Construction and finance companies then fleeced the railroad company by charging inflated fees for their services. Profits were often obscene. It was not uncommon for construction and finance companies to charge rates that were more than double the fair market rate for labor and materials. In one of the most notorious cases, the Credit Mobilier (the construction and finance company of the Union Pacific) regularly paid dividends of 50–100 percent annually to its shareholders. The misdeeds of the Central Pacific's construction and finance company were allegedly much worse, but the company's books conveniently disappeared when the owners suspected that a congressional investigation was imminent.[2]

Construction and finance companies were also used as currency to bribe politicians. The Credit Mobilier investigation revealed that this practice was widely used to bribe congressmen, even though few were held accountable. It is impossible to quantify the magnitude of waste that passed through construction and finance companies, but if the Credit Mobilier was even remotely representative of the norm, the amounts were quite large. Roughly half of the capital allocated for the construction of the Union Pacific went into the pockets of a handful of owners of the Credit Mobilier.

POINT OF INTEREST

The Credit Mobilier and the Union Pacific

"If reform is to be thorough, it must hold one step across the line of public honor as fatal as if the offender had long forgotten that there was any such boundary."[3]

—*New York Times* editorial (February 1873)

The Credit Mobilier was the construction and finance company used by several owners of the Union Pacific. A congressional investigation that concluded in 1873 revealed that the Credit Mobilier had massively overcharged the Union Pacific for construction costs. This enabled the owners of the Credit Mobilier to enrich themselves at the expense of the government. In total, the Credit Mobilier received $94.65 million to cover costs of construction that amounted to only $50.72 million. The profit of $43.95 million was nearly double the construction costs.[4]

(continued)

Credit Mobilier stock was also used as a currency to bribe members of Congress and influence federal legislation. The ringleader of the scheme was Oakes Ames, a congressman from Massachusetts. Ames sold Credit Mobilier shares to politicians for a significant discount to encourage the passage of legislation and adoption of policies that favored the Union Pacific. Senator James Brooks was identified as the most prolific recipient of these bribes, but he was hardly alone.[5]

Senator Brooks and Representative Ames were censured for their betrayal of the public's trust, but neither was prosecuted criminally. Their fate revealed a stubbornly sad truth regarding the consequences for politicians who violate the public's trust. Although it is undoubtedly true that politicians are more likely to be held accountable for breaking the law today, they still receive a relatively light touch relative to the average American.

BRIBERY

Many of the nation's railroad companies sought assistance from the federal government, state governments, politicians, judges, and law enforcement. Assistance could involve obtaining a charter, securing construction subsidies, or simply looking the other way when the railroad engaged in questionable business practices. The need for government support and/or intervention made bribery an unspoken but essential cost of business. Much like today, many bribes were done carefully to ensure that there was no evidence of a quid pro quo arrangement. Subtle bribes could include offers of contract work, stock tips, and promises of future lobbying contracts upon the expiration of political terms. Railroad owners generally preferred subtlety, but some committed more overt acts of bribery. Examples included gifting shares in highly lucrative construction and finance companies, issuing free passes on future or existing railroads, and even direct cash payments.[6]

The most insidious feature of bribery is that it is difficult to link a bribe to its harmful effects. Bribes enabled railroad owners to overbuild, embezzle, skimp on maintenance, and abuse labor. Many people suffered investment losses as a result, and some even lost their lives. Yet even to this day, few of these bribes were ever directly tied to the traumatic outcomes.

POINT OF INTEREST

"Favors among Friends" in the Twenty-First Century

"The T. and P. Folks are working hard on their bill . . . They offered one M.C. one thousand dollars cash down, five thousand when the Bill passed and ten thousand of the bonds when they got them, if he would vote for the Bill."[7]

—Letter from Collis Huntington to Leland Stanford (1890)

Bribery during the Gilded Age was often referred to euphemistically as "favors among friends." Collis Huntington, cofounder of the Central Pacific, was among the more prolific bribers. He described many of these bribes in six hundred letters sent to the Central Pacific's attorney, David D. Colton. Many letters opened with the phrase "burn after reading," but Colton often ignored these instructions.

Laws to prevent bribery of U.S. public officials have strengthened substantially over the past 150 years, making egregious abuses, such as the acceptance of cash payments, much less common. However, several subtle forms of influence are not all that different. For example, one common "favor among friends" that persists in the 2020s is the promise of high-paying jobs to politicians after they depart Congress. Such offers are rarely memorialized on paper, but verbal hints go a long way. Perhaps even more damaging is the billions spent on lobbying each year. Many financial crises and frauds were made worse because of lobbying. For example, the reckless lending practices of Fannie Mae and Freddie Mac persisted far too long, due in part to Fannie's and Freddie's enormous lobbying budgets. The GFC in the early 2000s was much worse as a result.

CRIMES AGAINST NATIVE AMERICANS

"The train is slowed to a rate of speed about equal to that of the herd; the passengers get out firearms which are provided for the defense of the train against Indians, and open from the windows and platforms of the cars a fire that resembles a brisk skirmish . . . When the hunt is over, the buffaloes which have been killed are secured, and the choice parts placed in the baggage-car, which is at once crowded by passengers, each of whom feels convinced and is ready to assert that his was the shot that brought down the game."[8]

—"BUFFALO HUNTING," *Harper's Weekly*

The westward expansion of railroads often occurred at the expense of Native Americans. Massive federal land grants, which in aggregate exceeded the size of the entire state of Texas, often included land that was protected under formal treaties with Native American tribes. Even more damaging was the railroads' complicity in the extermination of the bison, which Native Americans depended on as a critical food source. The U.S. Army encouraged the slaughter under the theory that if Native Americans were deprived of their food source, it would be easier to clear them from the land. In 1800, an estimated thirty to sixty million bison roamed the Great Plains. In 1884, only 325 remained. Several railroad owners encouraged the slaughter by promoting "hunting by rail" expeditions in which passengers armed with rifles shot buffalo for sport while traveling across the plains.[9]

POINT OF INTEREST

Horrors at Sandy Creek

"It is of no use for me to tell you how the fight was managed, only that I think the Officer in Command [Colonel John Chivington] should be hung . . . women and children were scalped, fingers cut off to get the rings on them . . . little children shot, while begging for their lives."[10]

—Lieutenant Joe A. Cramer, U.S. Army

Battles between Native American tribes and U.S. Army troops, militias, and settlers were often vicious. The list of atrocities is extensive, but a few stand out as particularly unconscionable. Among the worst was the massacre at Sandy Creek in the territory of Colorado.

In October 1864, approximately 750 members of the Arapaho and Cheyenne tribes were encamped about forty miles north of Fort Lyon at Big Sandy Creek. They were instructed by the U.S. Army to temporarily set up camp at this location until negotiations resumed. They were given assurance by the territorial governor, John Evans, and Colonel John Chivington that they would be safe if they went under the protection of the U.S. Army command stationed at Fort Lyon.

In November 1864, Colonel Chivington announced plans to attack the Native American encampment at Sandy Creek. The motive for the unprovoked attack is unclear, but the atrocities committed were unspeakable. The U.S. Army slaughtered an estimated 160 Native Americans, most of whom were women and children. The letters from two soldiers who witnessed the massacre describe brutal killings and the removal of body parts as souvenirs.[11]

In his memoirs, John R. Cook, a prolific buffalo hunter, offered a slight hint of remorse when he wrote, "And at times I asked myself: 'What would you do, John R. Cook, if you had been a child of this wonderfully prolific game region, your ancestors, back through countless ages, according to traditional history, having roamed these vast solitudes as free as the air they breathed? What would you do if some outside interloper should come in and start a ruthless slaughter upon the very soil you had grown upon?"[12]

Sadly, Cook's answer was: "But there are two sides to the question. It is simply a case of the survival of the fittest. Too late to stop and moralize now . . . So at it we went. And Hart, whom we will hereafter call Charlie, started out, and in two hours killed sixty-three bison."[13]

The extermination of bison, which was amplified by the expansion of U.S. railroads, intensified Native American resistance to further construction. Several tribes attacked railroad crews and bison hunting parties. The federal government responded by sending U.S. Army troops, and state governments added reinforcements by raising militias. Many troops received little training and were not screened for character flaws. In addition, many senior officers viewed Native Americans as an enemy unworthy of mercy. This mentality encouraged federal and state troops to commit many horrific atrocities, such as the massacres at Sandy Creek and Wounded Knee. The deep scars from these acts have not yet healed.

LABOR EXPLOITATION

POINT OF INTEREST

The Unsung Heroes of the Transcontinental Railroad

"Without the Chinese it would have been impossible to complete the western portion of the great National highway."[14]

—Leland Stanford, cofounder of the Central Pacific Railroad

Chinese immigrants were treated especially harshly in the late 1800s even though they played a critical role in the construction of the Central Pacific's segment of the transcontinental railroad. From 1865 to 1869, roughly twelve thousand Chinese workers labored on the Central Pacific line, and at least 1,200 perished due to the brutal conditions.[15]

(continued)

Railroad owners were privately awed at the exceptional endurance and skill of Chinese railroad workers, but they often publicly denounced their presence in America. White laborers were even more hostile, as they viewed the Chinese as a threat to their jobs. Periodically, tensions erupted in violence. On October 24, 1871, an especially gruesome attack occurred when a five-hundred-person mob stormed a Chinese neighborhood and killed nineteen people. Hostilities toward Chinese immigrants culminated in the Chinese Exclusion Act, which was signed by President Chester B. Arthur in the spring of 1882. The act placed a ten-year ban on all Chinese laborers immigrating to the United States.[16]

Railroad companies provided many well-paying jobs, but with few labor laws, employees often fell victim to harsh labor practices. In the late 1800s, there was no such thing as unemployment insurance; safety standards were few; and labor unions barely existed.

Labor policies tended to be harshest during economic downturns. A common practice was to reduce the workforce with no notice or severance and/or cut wages of low-level workers. Periodically, tensions devolved into violence. The Great Railroad Strike of 1877 was an especially violent uprising. It began in July when employees of the B&O Railroad locked the engines in the roundhouse and resisted demands by management and state militia to leave. In sympathy for their cause, more than 100,000 railroad workers throughout the nation joined the strike, and clashes with militias and management often turned violent. The violence forced President Rutherford B. Hayes to suppress the strikes with federal troops. After fifty-two days, the strikes ended, but one hundred people were killed. The Great Railroad Strike is often cited as a formative moment for organized labor. More than a decade passed before the American Railway Union became a significant force, but the Great Railroad Strike of 1877 featured prominently in the labor movement.

VILLAGE EXTORTION

"They would go to the most prominent citizens of that village and say 'If you will give us so many thousand dollars we will run through here; if you do not we will run by.' . . . As stated by the gentleman from Los Angeles, General Howard, they have blackmailed Los Angeles County two hundred and thirty thousand dollars as a condition of doing that which the law compelled them to do."[17]

—DAVID S. TERRY, delegate at the 1878–1879 Constitutional Convention of California

Residents and businesses located in towns positioned close to proposed train routes were presented with enormous wealth creation opportunities. A fortuitously placed route or station could increase land values, lower shipping costs for goods, and provide new job opportunities for residents. Alternatively, if the railroad bypassed the town, residents could expect the exact opposite. Railroad owners were well aware of the stakes, and they often exploited it. The Central Pacific was one of the worst offenders, as revealed in the opening quote by David S. Terry.

THE DIFFICULTY OF RECONCILING COGNITIVE DISSONANCE IN THE GILDED AGE

The railroads revealed some of the worst displays of morality in America during the Gilded Age, yet they also established a foundation for the expansion of commerce and improvement of living standards. Many of these benefits would become more dramatic after the turn of the twentieth century. On the other hand, it is undeniable that many less fortunate Americans and courageous immigrants suffered greatly to make these benefits possible. Therein lies the cognitive dissonance. It is difficult to accept that railroads fueled exceptional progress and committed harsh abuses at the same time. American corporate behavior, political standards, and race relations have improved exponentially since the late 1800s, but modern examples of great progress accompanied by corruption can still be found. Thus, gaining exposure to the extreme cognitive dissonance of the Gilded Age may make it easier to tolerate situations that trigger similar discomfort today.

Chapter 8

THE AMERICAN SYSTEM
OF MANUFACTURES

"It is not for a moment denied that the natural resources of the United States are immense, that the products of the soil seem capable of being multiplied and varied to almost any extent . . . The material welfare of the country, however, is largely dependent upon the means adopted for turning its natural resources to the best account, at the same time that the calls made upon human labor are reduced as far as practicable."[1]

—JOSEPH WHITWORTH, British engineer (1854)

On May 1, 1851, Queen Victoria opened a five-month event called the Great Exhibition of Works of Industry of All Nations in London. For nearly one hundred years, the British were at the forefront of the Industrial Revolution, and British entrepreneurs were excited to display their latest innovations once again. British exhibits occupied half of the space in the "Crystal Palace," and the rest of the world shared much smaller spaces in the remaining half. The British welcomed their American cousins even though resentment remained due to the recent debt defaults of many U.S. states in the early 1840s and the persistent lawlessness of U.S. securities markets.[2]

The U.S. exhibitors got off to a rough start, as they had purchased too much space, and several displays arrived late. Even after all displays were in place, the magic of America's industrial products was largely hidden from view. Cyrus McCormick's mechanical reaper and Samuel Colt's revolver were highlighted as intriguing innovations, but the British overlooked the radical advancements in the manufacturing process that produced them. Yet America had quietly achieved the holy grail of manufacturing by creating machinery and processes that enabled manufacturers to produce machine-made products with fully interchangeable parts. These capabilities were refined and improved prior to the Civil War. When the war ended, U.S. manufacturers were equipped with a manufacturing infrastructure that threatened Great Britain's status as the world's workshop.[3]

POINT OF INTEREST

The Holy Grail of Manufacturing: Interchangeable Parts

"I have succeeded in an object that has hitherto completely baffled the endeavors of those who have heretofore attempted it—I have succeeded in establishing the methods for fabricating arms [rifles] exactly alike and with economy."[4]

—John Hall (December 20, 1822)

Beginning in the 1820s, U.S. mechanics introduced multiple innovations that enabled manufacturers to use precision machinery to craft products with interchangeable parts. This achievement may seem relatively inconsequential in the 2020s, but it was groundbreaking in the nineteenth century.

Despite numerous attempts, mechanics had failed for decades to establish a level of precision to manufacture parts that were interchangeable. As a result, manufacturing during the first half of the 1800s was labor intensive and heavily reliant on the use of skilled craftsmen. Finished products consisted of parts that appeared identical to the naked eye but were not interchangeable. This limitation was especially problematic in the U.S. because of the chronic scarcity of skilled labor.[5]

Thomas Blanchard is often regarded as the founder of precision manufacturing. In 1818, he began designing a series of machines to build muskets. Many American engineers subsequently expanded on Blanchard's innovations. John Hall and Samuel Colt are among the more notable. Many of the greatest innovations were created in the armories at Harper's Ferry in West Virginia and the Springfield Armory in Massachusetts.

Prior to the Great Exhibition of 1851, the world was largely unaware of America's rapid advancement in precision manufacturing. After the exhibition, the innovations were collectively referred to as the "American System of Manufactures." The Great Exhibition was a key milestone for the United States. Soon thereafter America became the leading innovator in manufacturing technology, and the American System of Manufactures became the cornerstone of growth of U.S. mass manufacturing in the Gilded Age.[6]

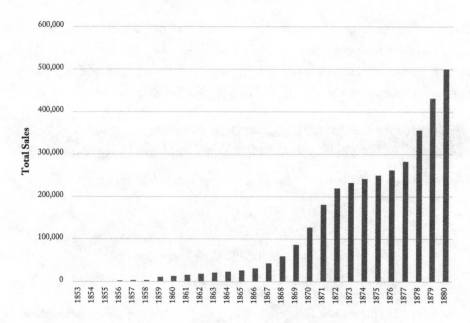

Figure 8.1: Singer Manufacturing Company: Total Sewing Machine Unit Sales (1853–1880)[7]

POST-CIVIL WAR MANUFACTURING

The American System of Manufactures was a game changer, and industrial companies throughout the U.S. soon adopted the principles and hired mechanics familiar with the system. Evidence of its impact can be seen in the production of a wide range of products, such as sewing machines, mechanical reapers, wood furniture, bicycles, clocks, and countless other products.[8] Figure 8.1 provides just a small glimpse of the impact by showing the massive increase in sewing machine sales by the Singer Manufacturing Company. Between 1853 and 1880, unit sales increased at an average annualized rate of 26.9 percent.

AMERICA MOVES INTO HEAVY MANUFACTURING

During the last few decades of the 1800s, a confluence of innovations and fortuitous discoveries of natural resources enabled the U.S. to develop an infrastructure to support heavy manufacturing. First, several discoveries of rich natural resource deposits provided easier and cheaper access to raw materials. In 1859 alone, the U.S. benefitted from the discovery of crude oil in Titusville, Pennsylvania, and a massive deposit of silver, known as the Comstock Lode, in Nevada. With railroads spanning the nation, securing cost-effective transportation to end markets was no longer an impediment.

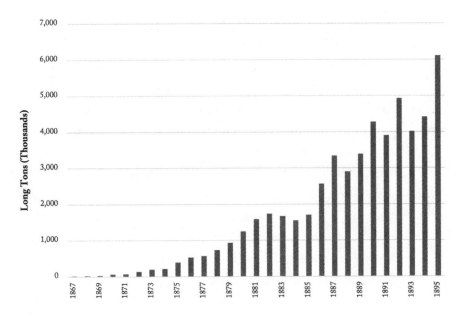

Figure 8.2: U.S. Exports of Steel, Ingots, and Casting (Thousands of Long Tons) (1867-1895)[9]

Second, several inventions increased employee productivity and improved communications across the country. Examples included Alexander Graham Bell's telephone (1876), Edison's incandescent electric light bulb (1879), and Nikola Tesla's alternating current electric motor. Third, American railroad corporations had gained several decades of experience managing large workforces. Many former railroad managers migrated to large industrial companies and applied their skills to accelerate growth and streamline operations. Finally, the American System of Manufactures was a perfect match for companies that pursued mass production.

Many large industrial companies formed during the final decades of the 1800s. Several founders were later referred to derisively as "robber barons."[10] Two of the more notable examples were John D. Rockefeller, founder of Standard Oil, and Andrew Carnegie, founder of Carnegie Steel.[11] One indicator of U.S. advancement in heavy manufacturing was the rapid growth in production of steel-related products (Figure 8.2). Immediately after the Civil War, the U.S. imported most of its steel from Great Britain. But improved production techniques, such as the Bessemer process, combined with rising domestic demand, enabled the U.S. to surpass Britain as a leading producer of steel for the world by the turn of the twentieth century. Consolidation of the railroad industry also contributed heavily to the rise of large corporations. Collectively, the Union Pacific, Northern Pacific, and Southern Pacific employed hundreds of thousands of Americans.

IMPACT ON THE U.S. ECONOMY

The collective decision of American industrialists to pursue mass production and standardization early in the nation's Industrial Revolution explains much of the nation's rapid transformation into an industrial superpower in the twentieth century. For the American strategy to succeed, industrialists were forced to construct large facilities designed for maximum efficiency and run as close as possible at full capacity. This strategy was adopted in many industries, but it was especially noticeable in the steel industry. To this end, while Andrew Carnegie is rightfully credited for establishing a legendary culture of continuous improvement and efficiency, Alexander Holley deserves equal credit for the exceptional quality of his steel plant designs. After constructing his first Bessemer steel plant in 1863, Holley went on to design many of the most productive steel plants in America. The ethos that defined the steel industry spread to other mass manufacturing plants.

In contrast to Americans, European industrialists expressed a bias toward manufacturing products at a relatively small scale and with a higher degree of customization. This difference in philosophy helped the U.S. manufacturing sector outcompete foreign competitors and accelerate the nation's transition from a protoindustrial economy to a mass production industrial economy. The following series of figures show some of the effects. Figure 8.3 shows the growth of manufacturing exports relative to agriculture. Figure 8.4 shows the growth of real GDP per capita during the last thirty-five years of the 1800s versus the prior sixty-five years. Figure 8.5 shows the U.S. balance of trade from 1851 to 1895. Beginning in the 1870s, the U.S. began generating consistent trade surpluses for the first time in its history.[12]

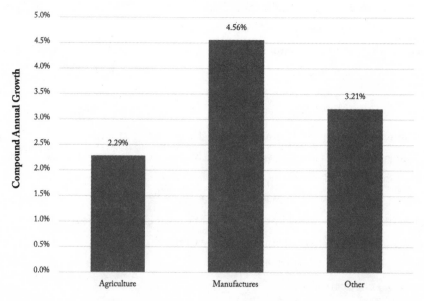

Figure 8.3: Compound Annual Growth of Exports by Sector (1860–1895)[13]

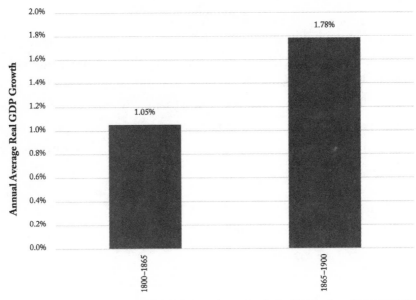

Figure 8.4: Average Annual Real GDP Growth per Capita in 2012 Dollars (1800–1900)[14]

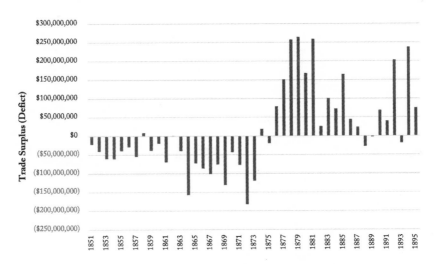

Figure 8.5: Total Trade Surplus (Deficit) in Specie (1851–1895)[15]

A NEW PHASE OF INDUSTRIALIZATION IN AMERICA

The combination of an expansive transportation network, improved communications, and manufacturing innovation significantly strengthened U.S. competitiveness in global markets. By the end of the nineteenth century, U.S. manufacturers were mass producing an impressive array of high-quality, standardized products at competitive prices. In contrast, the reluctance of Europeans to abandon small-scale manufacturing and product customization contributed to declining market share for their manufactured products. As illustrated in the previous chapters, these advancements were not without cost and sacrifice.

The rapid growth of the U.S. economy also required enormous amounts of capital, which dramatically increased activity in U.S. securities markets. After the Civil War, volume on U.S. markets had increased substantially, but similar to the experience in corporate America, laws and regulations failed to keep pace. Chapter 9 reveals the dangers of investing in U.S. securities markets during the chaotic years of the Gilded Age.

Chapter 9

WALL STREET'S TROUBLED ADOLESCENCE

"As fast as a new rule was promulgated by the body of traders [on Wall Street], the shrewdest ones there evolved schemes that were intended to produce fruit for the few and poison for the many."[1]

—HETTY GREEN, the Queen of Wall Street

Trading volume in U.S. securities markets increased substantially during the Gilded Age (Figure 9.1). Volume was temporarily muted in the 1890s but then doubled after the turn of the twentieth century. Investors benefited from higher trading volume by enjoying greater liquidity and market efficiency, but these benefits were often offset by the schemes of insiders and speculators. Higher transaction volume was not matched with a commensurate maturity in terms of regulation.

The New York Stock Exchange solidified its position as the venue of choice for investors, thereby enabling American companies to raise the enormous amounts of capital required to build the nation's infrastructure and manufacturing capabilities. Yet the New York Stock Exchange was also tainted by rampant corruption. Disgusted by the disorder in American markets, Europeans periodically withdrew their capital, and leading financiers became increasingly fearful that one day foreign investors would disappear forever. The fortuitous rise of J. Pierpont Morgan in 1895 temporarily suppressed the worst behaviors on Wall Street, but it was not until the 1930s that federal securities regulations enabled the U.S. to decisively exit this awkward period of adolescence.

Chapter 9 recounts many of the more notable events in Gilded Age securities markets. The American paradox of speculation was in full display. Despite the rampant

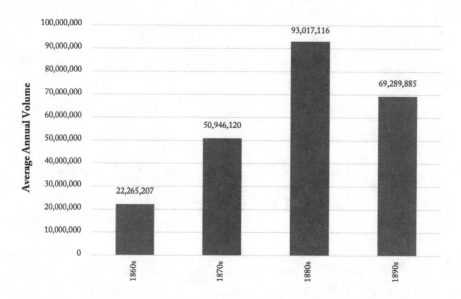

Figure 9.1: New York Stock Exchange Average Annual Volume of Shares Traded (1860–1899)[2]

scheming, corruption, and fleecing of investors, American industry simultaneously raised the capital it needed to fund the eventual dominance of American industry.

Before reviewing these events, it is important to first explain the fundamental principles of securities markets evolution, which helps explain why speculators embraced tactics used to cheat them.

THREE PHASES OF SECURITIES MARKET EVOLUTION

The most important evolutionary development for U.S. securities markets during the mid-1800s was the definitive shift from informal venues to established exchanges such as the New York Stock Exchange. The increase in transaction volume established what is commonly referred to as "market depth."[3] Greater market depth benefited buyers and sellers because they could trade with less fear of impacting securities prices. All else being equal, deeper markets are also more attractive for companies issuing securities because potential investors have more confidence in their ability to resell them at a future date without having to settle for a price that is meaningfully below fair market value. Investors also demand a lower premium to protect themselves from the risk of illiquidity. All else being equal, this enabled companies to issue securities at more attractive prices.

The deepening of U.S. securities markets was not advantageous to all market participants. In fact, it created a particularly vexing challenge for speculators because increased trading volume made securities pricing more efficient. This, in turn, made

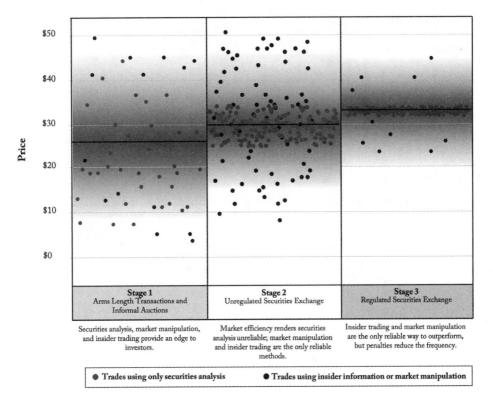

Figure 9.2: Key Stages of Market Maturation

it difficult to profit from mispricing. Instead, the more reliable way to profit on Wall Street was to engage in various forms of insider trading and market manipulation. In other words, speculators preferred to cheat markets rather than outwit them. These tactics have long since been outlawed, but they were legal in the late 1800s.

One way to visualize the governing dynamics of securities markets is to think of their evolution in three stages (Figure 9.2). During the first stage, most securities were sold in private transactions or informal auctions. This described the markets on the streets of New York in the late 1700s and early 1800s. In a Stage One market, investors can profit from skilled securities analysis, as well as insider trading. Market manipulation is possible (especially in auctions) but is generally less effective because there simply is not much of a market to manipulate. As the volume of transactions increases, markets enter a second stage. At this point, formal securities exchanges emerge. Higher trading volume makes securities pricing more efficient, but markets lack strong regulations to prevent abuse by insiders and market manipulators. Because increased pricing efficiency makes it difficult to profit from mere securities analysis and there are few securities laws, market manipulation and insider trading are the optimal strategies. Finally, Stage Three markets introduce regulations that restrict investor abuses in the form of insider trading and market manipulation. Securities markets become even more efficient, and investor abuses become less frequent.[4]

Gilded Age securities markets resided squarely in Stage Two of this framework. In fact, they remained in Stage Two until the passage of the Securities Act of 1933 and Securities Exchange Act of 1934 (chapter 18). In hindsight, the lack of regulation persisted for far too long. It is tempting to criticize the nation's leaders for allowing this to happen, but from the perspective of many Gilded Age Americans, the absence of rules was viewed as one of the nation's most powerful competitive advantages. It probably seemed logical, therefore, that unregulated securities markets promised the best results. Newspapers from the late 1800s clearly reveal that Americans were well aware of the schemes on Wall Street, but they believed that the benefits outweighed the costs. Few feared that corruption would eventually threaten the stability of the financial system, but these truths would become apparent with the passage of more time.

THE GILDED AGE DARK ARTS

"Gambling is a business now, where formerly it was disreputable excitement. Cheating at cards was always disgraceful. Transactions of a similar character under euphemistic names of 'operating,' 'cornering,' and the like were not so regarded."[5]

—TRUMBULL WHITE, journalist (1893)

Unlawful and unethical behavior on Wall Street is by no means uncommon today, but the pervasiveness and audacity of the schemes during the Gilded Age were exponentially worse. The difference is mostly attributable to the fact that markets in the late 1800s were largely unregulated, which allowed stock operators to use a variety of tools that could earn them prison sentences today.[6] Moreover, even when they broke the few existing laws—which they did on many occasions—they had little fear of consequence. Politicians, judges, and law enforcement officers were easily bought.

The other contributing factor was the background of Gilded Age stock operators. In the present day, Wall Street professionals usually have a reasonably strong background in finance and securities analysis. This does not ensure that they provide value to their clients, but most at least attempt to do so by outsmarting the market rather than cheating it. Many of the most powerful Gilded Age stock operators viewed securities markets very differently. To them, it was little more than a game of poker. Lying, backstabbing, and hiding an ace up one's sleeve were just part of the game. Because deception was a key to success, many of the best stock operators had prior experiences that honed this skill. It may seem absurd that Jim Fisk, one of the more notorious stock operators, often boasted about his prior experience working as a traveling circus employee and "peddler."[7] But the circus taught him the importance of theatrics when spreading false information, and his peddling career taught him how to sell anything regardless of its value. Daniel Drew's transition from a cattle drover to a stockbroker seems odd until one considers how this experience allowed him to perfect the art of lying to customers, stealing information from competitors, and committing outright theft when necessary. In fact, Drew allegedly invented the practice of "stock watering," which was a technique used by many railroad owners to siphon off investors' capital for their own personal use. Drew coined the term when he discovered that he could sell cattle for a premium by feeding them salt on the day prior to a sale. Then, a few hours before the transaction, the cattle were given copious amounts of water, which temporarily increased their weight (and their price).

The pages that follow detail the more nefarious tools used by Wall Street speculators. It may not always seem so, but cheating investors in the 2020s is much less common than it was during the Gilded Age. Market manipulation, insider trading, and fraud still occur, but cases are comparatively less common. During the Gilded Age, it was rare to find somebody who abstained from cheating the market when given the opportunity. This is why author Roger Lowenstein once stated, "When folks complain about regulation, as they always have and always will, we must ask whether the good old days were really so good." The pages that follow demonstrate just how dreadful the "good old days" were for the average investor.[8]

Insider Trading

Insider trading simply involves buying or selling a security based on information that is both material and unknown to the public. If an "inside trader" believes the information will cause a security to rise in price, they purchase shares. If they believe it will cause the price to decline, they establish a short position—or at a minimum sell their holdings before the information becomes known.[9] Insider trading occurred regularly during the Gilded Age, and in almost all cases it was perfectly legal. The practice was not broadly outlawed until the passage of the Securities Exchange Act of 1934.

Portrait of a Gilded Age Dark Artist: Daniel Drew

*"After a colorful career as a menagerie flunky, drover, innkeeper, and
loan shark, he [Daniel Drew] had emerged as a steamboat magnate,
expanded to become the presiding desecrator of the Erie Railway,
and found his true genius in gouging the stock market . . . he lived
in a mansion on Union Square, attended church faithfully . . . and
abused grammar whenever he opened his mouth."*[10]

—W. A. Swanberg

Daniel Drew was not the most intelligent speculator, but his utter lack of
conscience often made up for it. Drew claimed to cleanse his conscience by
embracing religion, but many suspect this was, at least in part, to secure a continuous supply of suckers to feed false information to in support of his schemes.[11]

Insider trading and market manipulation were common in the Gilded
Age, but Drew's deceit and utter lack of remorse were exceptional even then.
He orchestrated his most profitable schemes during his ten-year reign as the
treasurer of the Erie Railway. He regularly used insider information, market
manipulation, and brazen embezzlement to profit personally at the expense of
the public and shareholders.

In 1868, Drew's old friend Cornelius Vanderbilt attempted to buy the Erie
Railroad and remove Drew from his position as treasurer. But he soon got a taste
of Drew's treachery. While Vanderbilt aggressively purchased Erie stock, Drew
enlisted the help of Jay Gould and Jim Fisk to illegally print 100,000 shares
and dump them in the market. Vanderbilt purchased nearly $10 million of Erie
stock without increasing his ownership position.[12]

While Drew, Gould, and Fisk were busy robbing Vanderbilt, they neglected
much-needed maintenance on the Erie tracks. On April 15, 1868, the poor conditions of the rails caused a horrific accident in which twenty-four passengers burned
to death. Drew, Fisk, and Gould were never held accountable for their recklessness.[13]

Drew's misdeeds eventually caught up with him—although much later
in life than he deserved. He was forced into bankruptcy soon after the Panic
of 1873 and died a destitute man in 1879. After his death, Drew committed
one last depraved act when the Drew Theological Seminary discovered that the
$250,000 note that Drew had pledged as a charitable gift (but intentionally
withheld) was just worthless paper.

Stock Pools

A stock pool was a technique used to manipulate stock prices. The mechanics were simple. A group of traders pooled their resources and appointed a pool manager to execute transactions on behalf of the entire group. In the case of a "bull pool," the objective was to manipulate the market by increasing the volume of buy orders, thereby raising the price of a security. In the case of a "bear pool," the objective was to increase the volume of sell orders and thereby lower the price. To raise the level of buying or selling as much as possible, pool operators fooled market participants using a variety of techniques. Examples included the use of "wash sales," spreading false rumors, and bribing journalists to write fake stories that were favorable to their positions.[14]

Responding to the hype and/or fictitious spike in volume, members of the public would pile in like lemmings, creating even further upward or downward pressure on the price. At this point, the pool would exit their position, allowing the public to take the loss when the hype dissipated. Like insider trading, pool operations were not outlawed until the passage of the Securities Exchange Act of 1934. Until then, pools were common on Wall Street, and were often used to execute the next two strategies: market corners and bear raids.

Market Corners

A market corner was the most daring feat on Wall Street. For those familiar with the game of hearts, it was akin to "shooting the moon." Speculators attempting a market corner could expect one of two outcomes—either they crushed their opponents, or their opponents crushed them. There was rarely a middle ground.

POINT OF INTEREST

What Is Selling Short?

The concept of "selling short" often confuses investors. Many assume that it is a relatively modern and sophisticated trading technique, but short selling was common in the Gilded Age. The goal of a short seller is to profit from a decline in the price of a stock (as opposed to a rise). The hypothetical scenario below explains the mechanics of a short sale.

Sample Short Sale

1. Short seller borrows 10,000 shares of stock from Investor A.

(continued)

2. Short seller sells the borrowed shares at $100/share in the open market and receives $1 million in cash on Day 1.

3. Short seller repurchases shares on Day 10 and returns the shares to Investor A.

Outcome Resulting in a Gain

Stock declines and short seller repurchases shares at $50/share.

Proceeds from Sale of Stock on Day 1	$1,000,000
Cash to Repurchase Stock on Day 10	- $500,000
Profit to Short Seller:	**$500,000**

Outcome Resulting in a Loss

Stock rises and short seller repurchases shares at $120/share.

Proceeds from Sale of Stock on Day 1	$1,000,000
Cash to Repurchase Stock on Day 2	- $1,200,000
Loss to Short Seller	**($200,000)**

* This is a simplified example to illustrate the fundamental mechanics of a short sale. In reality, short sellers may also pay interest on the borrowed shares, which may be offset by interest earned on the cash they receive after selling the shares.

Market corners were difficult to execute, but the mechanics were simple. The victims were short sellers. The "corner artist" fleeced them by surreptitiously purchasing all available stock circulating in the market before short sellers realized that a corner was underway.[15] If the corner artist succeeded, short sellers unexpectedly found themselves in a desperate situation. They were forced to cover their short position by reacquiring borrowed shares that they had sold, but the only remaining seller was the corner artist. At this point, the corner artist commanded whatever price they saw fit. If short sellers failed to deliver borrowed shares back to the lender upon the due date, the law at the time—known as "the rule"—permitted the lender to purchase shares in the open market and charge the short seller the full cost. If the short seller failed to reimburse the lender, they were forced to declare bankruptcy.[16]

Short sellers were not the only market participants who faced potential financial ruin. Corner artists themselves risked catastrophic losses if the corner failed. Market

Market Corner

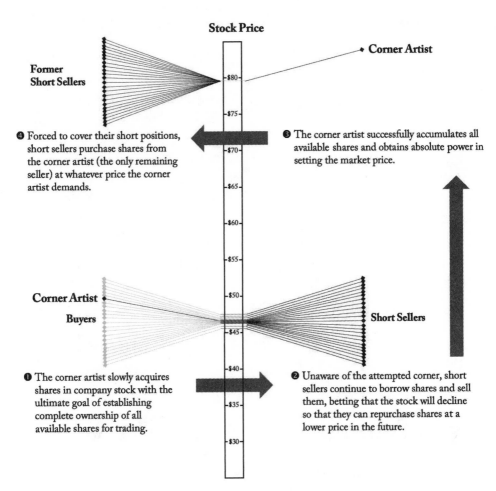

Stock Price

Corner Artist

Former Short Sellers

❹ Forced to cover their short positions, short sellers purchase shares from the corner artist (the only remaining seller) at whatever price the corner artist demands.

❸ The corner artist successfully accumulates all available shares and obtains absolute power in setting the market price.

Corner Artist

Buyers

Short Sellers

❶ The corner artist slowly acquires shares in company stock with the ultimate goal of establishing complete ownership of all available shares for trading.

❷ Unaware of the attempted corner, short sellers continue to borrow shares and sell them, betting that the stock will decline so that they can repurchase shares at a lower price in the future.

Figure 9.3: Mechanics of a Market Corner

corners required large purchases of stock, which usually necessitated heavy borrowing. Loans almost always consisted of short-term debt, referred to as call loans. If the corner artist ran out of money before completing the corner, the stock price would reverse because the primary buyer in the market suddenly disappeared. Short sellers would then intensify the selling pressure, sending the stock into free fall. As the stock fell, the corner artist would receive margin calls, which were often met by selling more stock, thereby creating even more downward pressure on the price. A corner artist's proceeds from sales of a plummeting stock often were insufficient to cover margin debt, forcing them into bankruptcy. This is the scenario that forced William Duer into debtors' prison in 1792. Figure 9.3 provides a visual illustration of the mechanics of a successful market corner.

POINT OF INTEREST

Portrait of a Gilded Age Dark Artist: "Jubilee" Jim Fisk

"If there was one facet of his personality that galled the sedate more than any other, it was his love of notoriety so extravagant that he preferred to be insulted than ignored."[17]

—W. A. Swanberg

Jim Fisk was aptly born on April Fool's Day in Brattleboro, Vermont. He found his calling on Wall Street under the tutelage of Daniel Drew, but his true loyalty was to money and the attention that it garnered. Fisk's specialties were sales and theatrics, which were skills that he likely acquired while working for the circus as a teenager. During the famous Erie War with Cornelius Vanderbilt, Fisk was delighted when Jay Gould granted him the task of signing reams of illegally issued stock certificates. When criticized for this brazen fraud, Fisk claimed he was simply exercising his constitutional right of "freedom of the press."

At the height of the Erie War, Fisk, Drew, and Gould fled to New Jersey to avoid arrest in New York. They holed up in the Taylor Hotel, which Fisk soon referred to as "Fort Taylor." He regularly strolled the hallways donning a military uniform, declaring himself Admiral of the Erie Navy. He even assembled a fleet of four rowboats and staffed them with several dozen men armed with muskets.

Soon after the Erie War ended, Fisk joined Jay Gould's scheme to corner the gold market. Fisk employed his signature theatrics to spread disinformation on the floor of the Gold Room at the New York Stock Exchange. Despite having pushed financial markets to the precipice of collapse and ruining multiple brokers and businessmen, when confronted by a reporter, Fisk simply responded, "Can't a fellow have a little innocent fun without everybody raising a halloo and going wild?"

Fisk's financial exploits produced dramatic ups and downs, but it was a love triangle involving a woman named Josie Mansfield that led to his demise. After multiple heated confrontations, Edward Stokes (Mansfield's second lover) cornered Fisk in a stairwell at the Grand Union Hotel and shot him twice. Jubilee Jim died at the young age of thirty-six—and rumor has it that several of his friends wagered on the hour of his death while he lay mortally wounded.[18]

Throughout the 1800s, stock operators attempted many market corners. The first conquest of note was Jacob Little's cornering of the Morris Canal in 1835. Little purchased the stock at $10/share and exited one month later at $185/share. In 1863, Cornelius Vanderbilt orchestrated several daring corners on the Hudson River and New York and Harlem Railroads, largely to punish corrupt members of the New York Common Council who had shorted stocks prior to enacting legislation unfavorable to these railroads. But the most famous market corner of the Gilded Age was Jay Gould's attempted corner of the gold market in 1869. The climax occurred on September 24, 1869, and is referred to in Wall Street lore as the original "Black Friday." To orchestrate the corner, Gould and several co-conspirators employed a multidimensional strategy, which included bribery of several close associates of President Ulysses S. Grant, a crafty disinformation campaign, and operation of a large stock pool. But when Gould realized the corner would fail after receiving word that President Grant was preparing to break the corner by unleashing the nation's gold reserves, he surreptitiously liquidated his gold holdings, while simultaneously encouraging one of his co-conspirators, Jim Fisk, to keep buying. Fisk was nearly ruined by Gould's treachery. He was only spared by employing some treachery of his own when he refused to honor buy orders communicated verbally to his brokers. Gould also reportedly gave Fisk a charitable payment to reward him for his blind loyalty.[19]

POINT OF INTEREST

Main Street and Wall Street Collide

"According to all contemporary accounts, the Gold Room that morning was less rational than any well-managed madhouse . . . Pickpockets took advantage of the crush, and some dealers were separated from their wallets in addition to their other losses . . . Jay Gould had made eleven million dollars . . . A mob of gamblers, many of them reduced from wealth to penury that same day, burst into the Heath brokerage office with the sincere purpose of murdering him if they could lay hands on him."[20]

—W. A. Swanberg

(continued)

Mayhem in the Gold Room

In September 1869, Jay Gould attempted to corner the market for gold in New York City. Whether he intended to risk a corner from the start is unclear. Gould claimed in congressional testimony that he only intended to raise the price of gold to around $140 to increase demand for American wheat exports. Wheat was priced in gold in London. By raising the price of gold, Gould claimed that he hoped demand for wheat would increase, which, in turn, would increase the volume of eastbound shipments on his Erie Railway.[21]

Regardless of his motive, Gould's manipulation of the gold market was especially disruptive because gold exposure was a critical component of U.S. commercial activities at the time. In 1869, commerce in the U.S. was often conducted in greenbacks, which were a form of fiat currency issued during the Civil War. Unlike most foreign currencies, such as the British pound sterling, greenbacks were not redeemable for gold at a fixed price.[22] Businessmen who engaged in foreign trade often hedged their exposure to fluctuations in the rate of exchange between greenbacks and gold. The Gold Room at the New York Stock Exchange was the primary venue for managing these hedges, and the solvency of many brokers and businessmen depended on the stability of the exchange rate between gold and greenbacks.[23]

On September 24, 1869, Gould's daring attempt to corner the gold market caused the price of gold to shoot up from $130 to $160. This may seem like a modest increase, but it was catastrophic at the time. The reason is because hedges used by businesses were based on the gross value of commercial transactions, which far exceeded their expected profits. For example, a merchant who hedged $10,000 worth of goods could have an expected profit of only $500. If they were on the wrong side of a hedge, a 20 percent move would cost them $2,000, which would wipe out their profit and much more. This is precisely what happened to businessmen who were caught short on gold during Gould's attempted corner. When the price of gold skyrocketed, margin calls exceeded their expected profits and cash reserves, thereby forcing many into bankruptcy. On Black Friday, more than one thousand Americans went bankrupt, fourteen brokerages failed, and several banks shuttered their doors.[24]

The impact of the gold corner extended beyond Wall Street because unlike previous panics, it ruined individuals and businesses that were typically less sensitive to Wall Street speculation. It thus serves as an excellent example of how the integration of Wall Street and Main Street accelerated during the Gilded Age. The strength of this relationship would only intensify with each passing year.

Manipulated Shorts and Bear Raids

Manipulated short sales and bear raids were fundamentally the same tactic at the outset. During the initial phase, the objective was to artificially suppress the price of a stock so that the short seller could cover their short position at a lower price in the future. A manipulated short sale ended when the short seller covered their position. A bear raid, however, continued to a second, more nefarious phase. After covering their short position, the bear raider reversed course and accumulated shares of stock while it remained at a depressed price. In a best-case scenario, the bear raider purchased enough stock to establish a controlling position in the company before the price returned to fair value. Manipulated short sales were common in the 1800s, as they were legal and could be executed on a large or small scale. Daniel Drew was notorious for orchestrating manipulated short sales while serving as the treasurer of the Erie Railroad. Key to Drew's strategy was a secret, illegal stash of convertible bonds that he leaked into the market at will. Bear raids, on the other hand, were less common, as these required more complex planning and a substantial capital base.

Portrait of a Gilded Age Dark Artist: Jay Gould, "The Mephistopheles of Wall Street"

"He had outlived most of his early partners . . . [because he] was shrewd enough to escape both the jail and the assassin . . . If ever a man's gold was 'cankered' it was his. He was throughout his entire financial life not only a gambler on a large scale, but a gambler with marked cards and loaded dice."[25]

—**Reverend Dr. Louis Albert Banks**

To earn the title of "robber baron" on Wall Street, a person required a healthy combination of greed, intelligence, subtlety, disloyalty, and a complete lack of ethics. Jay Gould mastered each of these, making him the most sinister man on Wall Street. Like Drew and Fisk, Gould's loyalty to business partners evaporated as soon as they ceased serving his interests. But what truly differentiated Gould from the ordinary pack of scoundrels was his intelligence, methodical planning, and careful avoidance of public attention. Gould was like an alter ego of Alexander Hamilton. His understanding of fundamental market principles was well ahead of his time, but he used his knowledge to enrich himself rather than his fellow citizens.

Jay Gould quietly pulled the strings on many of the most ambitious Gilded Age schemes. Each conquest was carefully planned and brilliantly disguised. His victims often lamented that they were unaware they were even under attack, much less of who was orchestrating it. If there was a loophole in a contract, Gould would find it. If a contract lacked loopholes, he would create them. To this end, he never hesitated to bribe politicians, judges, police officers, and any other protector of the common good.

Many financial historians consider Gould's attempted corner of the gold market in 1869 to be his grandest act of mischief, but his depravity during the Erie Railway Wars and his six-year reign over the Union Pacific were equally destructive. Unlike that of his former partner in crime, Jim Fisk, Jay Gould's career ended with less drama. In his later years, his influence waned under the shadow of reformers such as J. Pierpont Morgan, Jacob Schiff, James Hill, and Edward Harriman. Suffering from tuberculosis, Gould died in 1892 at the relatively young age of fifty-six. He left his son an inheritance of approximately $100 million, but his true legacy was defined by his notorious schemes. For many financial historians, Jay Gould remains the personification of Gilded Age immorality.[26]

Bear Raid

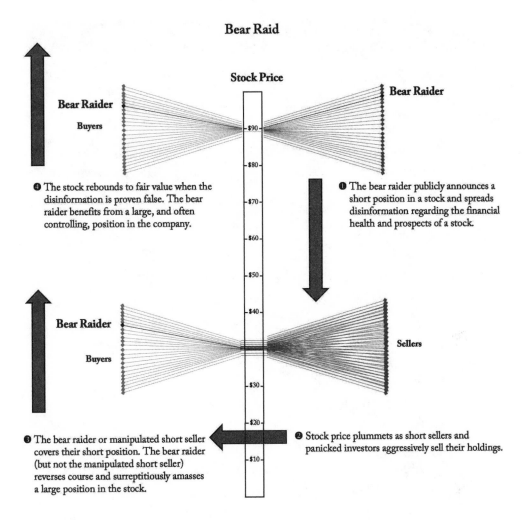

Stock Price

Bear Raider

Buyers

Bear Raider

❶ The stock rebounds to fair value when the disinformation is proven false. The bear raider benefits from a large, and often controlling, position in the company.

❶ The bear raider publicly announces a short position in a stock and spreads disinformation regarding the financial health and prospects of a stock.

Bear Raider

Buyers

Sellers

❸ The bear raider or manipulated short seller covers their short position. The bear raider (but not the manipulated short seller) reverses course and surreptitiously amasses a large position in the stock.

❷ Stock price plummets as short sellers and panicked investors aggressively sell their holdings.

Figure 9.4: Mechanics of a Bear Raid

A successful manipulated short sale or bear raid depended heavily on the ability of the perpetrator to distribute disinformation that was damaging enough to trigger aggressive selling, yet believable enough to ensure that the selling persisted for an extended period. Tactics for creating and distributing such disinformation varied but often included a combination of spreading false rumors on the floors of exchanges, planting fake stories in newspapers owned by the perpetrators, bribing journalists to write fake stories, using wash sales to create an illusion of increased transaction volume, and other devious techniques. The mechanics of manipulated short sales and bear raids are shown in Figure 9.4. The manipulated short seller ended the process by covering their short position, while a bear raider moved on to phase two and began amassing a large position in the stock at artificially depressed levels.

Jay Gould's Bear Raid: The Iron Jaws That Smashed the Pacific Mail

In 1873, Jay Gould gained a controlling interest in the Union Pacific and began devoting his energy toward improving the company's financial performance. Soon after taking the helm, he set his sights on reducing competition with the Pacific Mail steamship company, which was crushing the Union Pacific's margins by engaging in a price war to capture market share for freight traffic along the California coast.

Gould initially approached the Pacific Mail board and suggested that they reinstate a prior pooling agreement, in which the two companies would agree to split traffic and refrain from price competition. The board refused Gould's offer. He responded by conspiring with two owners of the Central Pacific, Collis Huntington and Leland Stanford, to launch a new steamship company to compete with the Pacific Mail. Although suspicious of Gould's intentions, Huntington and Stanford accepted the proposal and began laying the groundwork to form the company. Whether Gould cared much for this project is questionable. More likely, it was simply a ruse to divert the Pacific Mail's attention from the bear raid that he was preparing.[27]

While Huntington and Stanford worked on the steamship company, which they dubbed the Occidental and Oriental Steamship Company, Gould worked in the shadows to create chaos at the Pacific Mail. He first leveraged his relationships with several members of the Pacific Mail board of directors to gather information. After learning of the company's financial challenges and its history of bribing public officials, Gould encouraged his allies to use the information to create divisiveness at the company. His allies proceeded to publicly accuse management and other board members of fraud and mismanagement, which prompted the resignation of the company's president, Russell Sage, and the opening of a congressional investigation into whether the Pacific Mail bribed politicians to receive its charter.

As chaos at the Pacific Mail intensified, the stock plummeted. Gould added to the downward pressure by heavily shorting the stock and publicizing his position. This encouraged short sellers to pile on, placing even more downward pressure on the stock price. As the stock reached its nadir, Gould secretly exited his short positions and began acquiring Pacific Mail stock aggressively. Within a week, he gained control of the Pacific Mail, joined its board of directors, and installed his ally, Sidney Dillon, as president. Soon thereafter, the Pacific Mail reset shipping rates to a level that ensured profitability for both the Union Pacific and Pacific Mail. When the dust settled, Gould walked away with a hefty trading profit and ownership in a new company. It was a perfectly executed bear raid.[28]

HETTY GREEN: THE JEWEL OF THE GILDED AGE

"It has turned out . . . that my life is written down in Wall Street by people who, I assume, do not care to know one iota of the real Hetty Green. I am in earnest; therefore, they picture me heartless. I go my own way, take no partners, risk nobody else's fortune; therefore, I am Madame Ishmael, set against every man."[29]

—HETTY GREEN, the Queen of Wall Street

The Gilded Age dark artists dominated Wall Street in the late 1800s, but there were a few investors who refused to partake in their schemes. The most notable was a woman named Hetty Green. She was the richest woman in America by the end of the 1800s and her wealth exceeded that of most men. Unlike nearly all her contemporaries, however, she acquired it honorably by simply buying low and selling high. Finding a successful Wall Street investor who possesses extraordinary skill, patience, and integrity is rare regardless of the historical period, but they were virtually nonexistent in the Gilded Age. Hetty succeeded by conducting meticulous analysis of securities and real estate properties using only publicly available information. She then demonstrated an exceptional level of discipline and patience, thereby profiting from panics and avoiding getting trapped in the updraft of bubbles. Making her legacy even more exceptional is the fact that she was a woman who had none of the advantages afforded to men. For example, she was not allowed to join the New York Stock Exchange, nor could she serve as a director on corporate boards.[30]

In addition to her investment talents, Hetty served as a reliable lender of last resort to distressed stock operators, companies, and city governments. When money was tight in New York City during the autumn months, she lent liberally at fair rates. Hetty was also the only woman invited to the offices of J. Pierpont Morgan during the Panic of 1907, and she contributed at least $1 million to one of Morgan's hastily orchestrated rescues. Hetty was always well positioned to provide such support because she embraced thrift in her lifestyle and had an uncanny awareness of the ebbs and flows of the money supply.

Hetty Green was usually portrayed as a ruthless miser, but this was a gross distortion of her true character. Her avoidance of extravagance during a period of history in which high living was often celebrated led many to conclude that her thrift was a vice rather than a virtue. Further, her philosophy of "discreet charity" hid many acts of generosity and compassion from public view. Whether it was nursing family members back to health or aiding complete strangers who fell victim to accidents on the street, Hetty instinctively chose empathy over self-interest. That is not to say that she would bow to intimidation. For example, when the notorious scoundrel Collis Huntington threatened to take legal action against her son, Hetty Green gripped a pistol hidden in her rolltop desk and firmly stated, "Up to now, Huntington, you have dealt with Hetty Green the businesswoman. Now you are fighting Hetty Green the mother. Harm one hair of Ned's head and I'll put a bullet through your heart." The balding Huntington promptly fled the scene, leaving his hat for Green to claim as a trophy.[31]

It is a tragedy that the story of Hetty Green is rarely told, and when it is told, it is usually done so inaccurately. Hetty Green's virtues far outnumbered her vices, yet she was often referred to as the "Witch of Wall Street." Neighbors, strangers, financiers, and city officials who benefited from her generosity thought differently, and they often referred to her as the Queen of Wall Street. Her ability to build wealth honestly, outmaneuver multiple market panics, serve as a lender of last resort when the nation lacked a central bank, and display modesty and integrity that were anathema to the time qualify her among the best investors in all of U.S. history. Hetty Green passed away on July 3, 1916, at the age of eighty-three, and her fortune (estimated to be between $100 million and $200 million) was divided equally among her two children. In 1951, the remainder of her estate was distributed to sixty-three charities after the death of her daughter, Sylvia Ann Wilks. Hetty Green's life proves that exceptional investment skill combined with personal integrity could still make an American wealthy in the Gilded Age.[32]

POINT OF INTEREST

Ego and Debt: The Deadly Sins of the Speculator

J. Pierpont Morgan once quipped that "nothing so undermines your financial judgment as the sight of your neighbor getting rich." In other words, fragile egos are often the root cause of reckless financial decisions. Even worse, when investors are in a hurry to inflate their egos, they often use debt to accelerate the process. During the Gilded Age, fragile egos and reckless use of margin debt were commonplace. Countless men acquired and lost fortunes due to their inability to resist these temptations.

In contrast to her contemporaries, Hetty Green had an uncanny immunity to these vices. Although she openly aspired to be the richest woman in America, her objectives were always long term, and she cared little for her *relative* position at any moment. This humility enabled her to ignore her status relative to others, which, in turn, provided her with the fortitude to shun the use of margin debt to accelerate the growth of her financial empire.

To this day, ego and debt remain the bane of many investors. The collapse of overextended financial enterprises and implosion of overly acquisitive businesses are often caused by the timeless combination of hungry egos and excessive use of debt to feed them.[33]

THE GROWING COST OF CORRUPTION

By the early 1870s, European investors were once again disgusted by the corruption in railroad company boardrooms and scheming on the floor of the New York Stock Exchange. At the same time, a flood of new railroad securities exceeded demand, making it difficult to raise capital. The foreign capital cycle in the U.S. had reached another cyclical peak, and memories of the last financial crisis had faded from the nation's collective memory. The consequences of overbuilding, overpromising, underdelivering, and scheming would soon arrive.

POINT OF INTEREST

The Foreign Capital Cycle

"It might be said that the development of American commerce and industry was made possible by natural resources, the unwise investments of Europeans, and the dumb good luck of domestic investors."[34]

—Robert Sobel, financial historian

The canal mania in the 1820s was the first example of a cycle that occurred repeatedly in the nineteenth century. It began with the discovery of a disruptive industrial or technological advancement, such as canals or railroads. Attracted by the potential growth, Europeans invested cautiously at first, but buying

(continued)

inevitably devolved into a frenzy until a bubble was formed. When the bubble burst, Europeans withdrew their capital in a similarly indiscriminate manner and pledged to never touch an American security again. At this point, American investors purchased the securities of the few viable companies that remained for pennies on the dollar.

By the end of the cycle, the U.S. economy benefitted from massive infrastructure investments financed by Europeans, and Americans eventually took ownership of the assets at distressed prices. In other words, Americans ended up owning their infrastructure without having to pay for it, while Europeans were saddled with heavy losses. Despite Europeans' pledges never to fall victim to this cycle again, after the passage of time, it invariably repeated, as they deceived themselves into believing the next opportunity would be different.

A second-order consequence of the foreign capital cycle was chronic overbuilding of U.S. infrastructure. In the later stages of the cycle, companies were forced to engage in brutal price competition to survive. Price wars inspired the formation of collaborative pools to fix prices and/or large-scale industry consolidation. The consolidation process would later be dubbed "Morganization," and it is the reason for the formation of many large trusts at the end of the nineteenth century. Consolidation ultimately provided the country with a formidable competitive advantage in mass-production manufacturing, which enabled the U.S. to outcompete Britain at the dawn of the twentieth century.

Chapter 10

THE PANIC OF 1873 AND THE LONG-WAVE DEPRESSION

"Under no consideration must you allow your pride or interest in the company [Northern Pacific] to place us all in a position of even possible complications with its troubles."[1]

—HARRIS C. FAHNESTOCK, partner in Jay Cooke & Co. (September 1872)

O n September 18, 1873, residents of New York City awoke to the shocking news that Jay Cooke & Co. had closed its doors. The failure was especially disturbing because Jay Cooke was widely regarded as a conservative investor. If Cooke could fail, who was safe? The Cooke failure was also demoralizing because he was highly regarded for his ethical standards. Prior to the Civil War, he was a staunch opponent of slavery, and although he made a fortune selling war bonds, he charged a modest commission of approximately 0.50 percent.

The failure of Jay Cooke's bank triggered a panic on Wall Street. Like many that preceded it, a depression followed. The depression ended by the end of the 1870s, but deflationary pressures persisted for the remainder of the nineteenth century. Deflation was especially painful for farmers, as crop prices declined while their debts remained constant. Financiers experienced the opposite, as the value of their outstanding loans appreciated while the cost of living declined.

Chapter 10 begins with the unexpected failure of Jay Cooke & Co, and then covers the twenty-year period from 1873 to 1893. During this twenty-year stretch the nation was divided on the issue of its bimetallic currency standard based on gold and silver.

The resolution of this debate in the mid-1890s would lead to the rise of J. Pierpont Morgan as the de facto leader of the nation's financial system.

THE FALL OF JAY COOKE

"In one way, and a very significant one, Jay Cooke and many of his contemporaries made a grave error which is not altogether excusable. They forgot that they were bankers and became promoters. They allowed the assets of their houses—even their deposits—to be frozen in advances to and investments in great concerns which gave no promise of immediate returns."[2]

—HENRIETTA M. LARSON, business historian

By the early 1850s, railroads and newly formed industrial companies were raising massive amounts of capital in the United States. Multiple investment banking houses emerged to underwrite securities and sell them to domestic and foreign investors.[3] Many financial institutions that are recognizable today trace their roots to the second half of the 1800s. Examples include Lehman Brothers (1850), Kuhn Loeb (1867), J.P. Morgan & Company (1871), and Goldman Sachs (1869).[4]

POINT OF INTEREST

The Danger of Absentee Board Members and Trustees

"Prior to the Civil War, the directors of American railroads had often been concerned with management . . . The directors of the Northern Pacific were of another kind. They had secured control of the stock with very little invest-ment; their prestige was hardly dependent at all on the success of the Northern Pacific, which was a minor consideration in their business activities; and they were too far removed from the Northern Pacific's roadway and too busy with their own affairs to pay much attention to their duties as directors."[5]

—Henrietta M. Larson, business historian

The gross mismanagement of the Northern Pacific was a major contributing factor to Jay Cooke's bankruptcy. Although corrupt practices in railroad board-rooms was hardly unique in the 1870s, the lack of board director accountability was different in the case of the Northern Pacific. Unlike many railroad companies at the time, many Northern Pacific board members had little financial interest in the company's success and little time to dedicate to oversight of management.

The absence of strong incentives and penalties for corporate directors remains a stubborn problem today. It is also a problem that impairs the performance of institutional investment plans. In the 2020s, many of the nation's largest public pension plans, private pension plans, endowments, and foundations are managed by volunteer trustees who have limited time and incentives to ensure that investment strategies are optimally designed and efficiently executed. Instead, they defer to investment plan staff and investment consultants, whose motives often diverge from those of plan beneficiaries. This often results in the creation of portfolios that are too complex, overinvested in active managers, and inappropriately exposed to alternative investments. This topic is covered in greater detail in chapter 22 and chapter 25.

By the late 1800s the investment banking industry had matured, and bankers had adopted a strict code, which was informally referred to as the "Gentlemen Banker's Code." An important tenet was that investment bankers must refrain from poaching their competitors' clients. This created a challenge for Jay Cooke because he was late entering the railroad business. His fortune derived largely from the conservative business of selling U.S. government bonds. But after the Civil War, the government bond business stagnated. This forced Cooke to pursue business opportunities in other industries, and the railroad industry was by far the largest. In 1869, Cooke identified an opportunity to break into the railroad industry when the Northern Pacific Railway approached him with a proposal to issue a substantial bond offering to fund a northern transcontinental railroad. Despite rejecting the proposal several times in prior years, Cooke expressed interest in 1869.

On January 1, 1870, Cooke signed a contract to sell $100 million of Northern Pacific bonds and serve as the railroad's private banker. Over the next three years, the finances of Jay Cooke & Co. steadily deteriorated because of this decision. Some problems should have been anticipated, but others were simply bad luck. The first problem was that the appetite for Northern Pacific bonds was worse than Cooke had anticipated. Markets were inundated with railroad securities, and distaste for American railroads hardened with each passing year. Meanwhile, the outbreak of the Franco-Prussian War in May 1870 made it virtually impossible to raise capital in Continental Europe. Cooke began selling bonds in mid-1871, but sales were disappointing and only worsened over time. Second, Cooke was reluctantly dragged into multiple ill-advised acquisitions and investments to improve the competitive position of the Northern Pacific. This drained the firm of liquidity. Third, the railroad was poorly managed. Although Jay Cooke & Co. was only contractually obligated to advance up to $500,000 to the Northern Pacific to fund construction, by 1873, chronic misman-agement forced the firm to advance millions of dollars. Finally, the federal government was less willing to provide aid to the Northern Pacific due to the increasing reports of corruption on transcontinental railroads. Opposition in Congress intensified substan-tially after the exposure of the Credit Mobilier scandal in late 1872.[6]

In the spring of 1873, Jay Cooke & Co. was in a precarious position. The firm had $5.2 million in outstanding advances to the Northern Pacific, and outflows of deposits from private banking customers were accelerating. Cooke hoped to solidify the firm's finances by selling a new issuance of U.S. government bonds and a $9 million tranche of Northern Pacific bonds. The government bond sale proceeded much more slowly than anticipated, and the Northern Pacific bond sale failed. Only a stroke of good luck could save Jay Cooke, and 1873 was a horrible year to rely on the whims of fortune.[7]

THE PANIC OF 1873 AND THE LONG-WAVE DEPRESSION

On May 10, 1873, a small blurb appeared on the front page of the *New York Times* announcing the collapse of the Austrian stock market, but it had no noticeable effect in the United States. In August 1873, the annual cycle of withdrawals from New York City banks began as farmers withdrew their deposits from country banks to fund the shipment of crops to market. Country banks, in turn, withdrew capital from New York City banks, creating tight monetary conditions. The combination of a tight money supply, general disgust with railroad securities, and evaporation of foreign capital in the wake of the crisis in Austria triggered a decline in securities prices. Investors and brokerage firms that were caught long and without adequate liquidity began to fail. On September 8, the New York Warehouse and Security Company became the first victim. On September 13, the brokerage firm of Kenyon, Cox & Co. was suspended due to the mischief of Daniel Drew. Then on September 18, the big shockwave hit when Jay Cooke & Co. announced it was unable to meet its financial obligations and was closing its doors.[8]

Panic erupted immediately after the closure of Jay Cooke & Co. Indiscriminate selling and a relentless contraction of the money supply forced twenty-three more brokerages to fail within two days. For the three weeks ending on September 20, aver-age stock prices on the New York Stock Exchange declined by more than 25 percent.

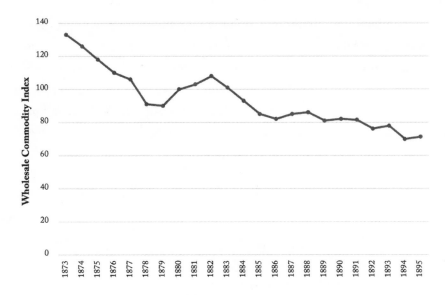

Figure 10.1: Wholesale Commodity Index—All Commodities (1873–1895)[9]

Overwhelmed by selling pressure, the Exchange closed on September 20 for the first time in its history, and it remained closed for ten days. The national banking system held up reasonably well, and by the end of October the most acute phase of the panic had subsided. The crisis, however, was far from over. The root cause of the panic was massive overbuilding of railroads, which was made substantially worse by rampant corruption. Within a few months, twenty-five railroads entered receivership, and the U.S. began a descent into a depression that would last until the end of the decade. By 1877, nearly 20 percent of the railroad mileage in the U.S. was in receivership.[10]

It is unclear precisely when the depression ended—estimates range from 1877 to 1879—but even after it ended, the U.S. continued to suffer from chronic deflationary pressures. For this reason, the roughly twenty-year period that ended in the mid-1890s is often described as a "long-wave depression." There is considerable debate about the causes and the extent of the suffering because the statistics at the time were distorted by deflation. The persistence of deflation itself, however, is not debated. Figure 10.1 shows the price index for all commodities from 1873 to 1895. Prices declined by nearly 50 percent over the twenty-two-year period.

Many Americans are familiar with the damaging effects of persistently high inflation, but few have experienced persistent deflation, which causes similar pain but in different ways. One effect of long periods of deflation is rising tension between borrowers and creditors because deflation increases the wealth of creditors but decreases the wealth of borrowers. The reason is that borrowers owe a fixed amount of debt even though declining prices cause their incomes to shrink. Creditors experience the opposite, as they receive fixed payments on loans, while the purchasing power of the payments increases due to broad-based declines in the price level. Persistent deflation in the U.S. from 1873 to the mid-1890s increased tension between borrowers and creditors. Borrowers (especially farmers) argued for an increase in the money supply to reverse the deflationary pressure, while creditors (especially Wall Street financiers) defended the status quo. The solution that was pushed by the "inflationists" was known as free silver, and it dominated politics for two decades.

Chapter 11

FREE SILVER AND THE PANIC OF 1893

"If they dare to come out in the open field and defend the gold standard as a good thing, we shall fight them to the uttermost, having behind us the produc-ing masses of the nation and the world . . . We shall answer their demands for a gold standard by saying to them, you shall not press down upon the brow of labor this crown of thorns. You shall not crucify mankind upon a cross of gold."[1]

—WILLIAM JENNINGS BRYAN (July 9, 1896)

The free silver movement traces its origins to the passage of the U.S. Coinage Act of 1873, which dramatically reduced the coinage of silver in the U.S. by stopping the minting of silver dollars. This seemingly innocuous legislation effectively moved the U.S. away from a bimetallic currency standard and toward a gold standard. The Coinage Act was soon followed by the Resumption Act of 1875, which estab-lished a timeline for returning the U.S. to full specie redemption for all legal-tender notes by 1879. This meant that greenbacks would be redeemable in gold or silver. It also called for the reduction of the number of greenbacks in circulation, which would reduce the money supply. In combination, these two acts created significant deflation-ary pressure in the United States.[2]

The End of the Line for Jay Gould

"There is never any difficulty deciding that a Gould movement is really on. The real difficulty is discovering when it is finished."[3]
—Unnamed stockbroker

On December 2, 1892, Jay Gould quietly passed away in the company of his family. He was only fifty-six years old, but he had suffered from tuberculosis for many years. Gould's death came as a surprise, as he was intensely private in his personal affairs. Gould's estate was estimated to be $100 million.

Jay Gould remains an enigma to this day. He was generally regarded as the personification of evil in the Gilded Age, but one of his more recent biographers, Maury Klein, casts Gould's life in a more favorable light. There is some legitimacy to this perspective, as his behavior was a bit more mixed in his later years. After being ousted from the Erie Railroad in 1872, Gould purchased a controlling interest in the Union Pacific. Initially, he appeared to be a reformed man. Over several years, he made improvements to the railroad, cleaned up the balance sheet, and increased earnings. But then the old Jay Gould reemerged, and he tainted his legacy by purchasing a competitor and blackmailing fellow Union Pacific board members to force them to buy the properties at inflated prices.[4]

After Gould left the Union Pacific, he assembled a new railroad network called the Missouri Pacific. He also controlled Western Union, which was the largest telegraph operator at the time. In 1885, Gould barely avoided bankruptcy when he was caught in a bullish position during a brief panic and recession. Spooked by the incident, Gould stopped speculating on Wall Street and began fading into the background.

Gould's waning influence in corporate boardrooms and the stock market made room for a new generation of corporate executives, financiers, and stock operators. The most notable rising star was J. Pierpont Morgan, who emerged as the new financial titan of Wall Street soon after Gould's passing.

Deflation tormented borrowers throughout the mid-1870s. In 1878, prices had declined by 31 percent over the prior five-year period. Farmers and debtors argued for a return of monetary silver to counterbalance deflationary pressures. The silver mining lobby supported their efforts. The first major win for the free silver movement was the passage of the Bland-Allison Act of 1878, which authorized the Treasury to purchase between $2 million and $4 million of silver each month. Over the next four years, wholesale prices increased by approximately 4 percent per year. But in 1883, deflationary forces returned. In 1890, the free silver movement scored a second victory with the passage of the Sherman Silver Purchase Act, which substantially increased purchases of silver to 4.5 million ounces per month.[5]

Prices stabilized for a few years after the passage of the Sherman Silver Purchase Act, but then a new problem emerged because silver had become much more plentiful than gold. During the ten years ending on December 31, 1895, the ratio of U.S. silver to gold production was approximately 30:1 (i.e., 30 ounces of silver were produced for every 1 ounce of gold). Foreign production also accelerated even though foreign demand for silver was declining because countries were abandoning the use of silver for monetary purposes. Despite the production imbalance, the Treasury continued to issue Treasury notes to purchase silver and allowed redemption for either gold or silver at the fixed ratio of 16:1. This would not have been problematic if market forces

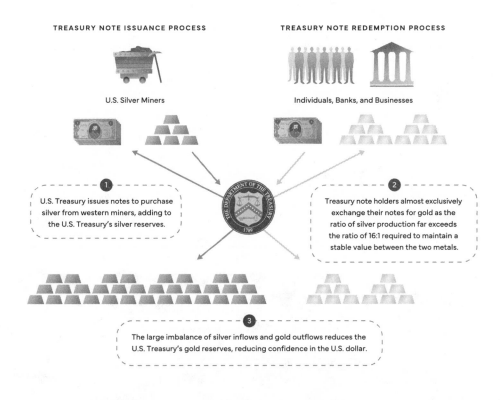

TREASURY NOTE ISSUANCE PROCESS

U.S. Silver Miners

TREASURY NOTE REDEMPTION PROCESS

Individuals, Banks, and Businesses

1. U.S. Treasury issues notes to purchase silver from western miners, adding to the U.S. Treasury's silver reserves.

2. Treasury note holders almost exclusively exchange their notes for gold as the ratio of silver production far exceeds the ratio of 16:1 required to maintain a stable value between the two metals.

3. The large imbalance of silver inflows and gold outflows reduces the U.S. Treasury's gold reserves, reducing confidence in the U.S. dollar.

Figure 11.1: Treasury Notes of 1890 Issuance/Redemption Imbalance

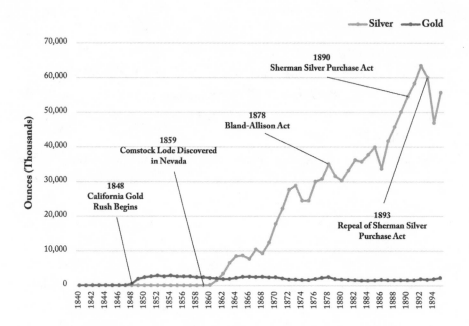

Figure 11.2: U.S. Gold and Silver Production (Thousands of Troy Ounces) (1840–1895)[6]

determined the exchange ratio between gold and silver; the amount of notes required to purchase an ounce of silver would simply adjust to reflect increased supply. But the U.S. maintained the fixed rate of exchange at 16:1. It did not take a genius to realize that it made more sense to redeem U.S. currency for gold (which had a more limited supply) as opposed to silver (which had a rapidly increasing supply). This skewed incentive led to a flood of gold withdrawals from the Treasury's reserves. This phenomenon is referred to as Gresham's law. According to the law, bad money drives good money out of circulation, as people have an incentive to hoard the money that holds its value (i.e., gold) and use the money that loses value (i.e., silver). Figure 11.1 shows the mechanics of this phenomenon. Figure 11.2 shows the sharp increase in silver production relative to gold production, which began in 1860 after the discovery of the Comstock Lode in Nevada.[7]

POINT OF INTEREST

What Is the Gold Standard?

The most fundamental purpose of money is to serve as a store of value, medium of exchange, and unit of account. Without money, people would be forced to barter, and trade would slow to a crawl. For thousands of years humans avoided bartering by using a variety of physical materials as money. Examples include seashells, beads, silver, and gold. The fact that so many civilizations settled on gold as the preferred medium is not a coincidence. Relative to other substances, gold has several attractive attributes, such as:

- **Chemical Stability**—Gold is a highly stable element that is immune to corrosion under normal conditions. Therefore, gold is unlikely to transform into something less valuable over time.
- **Malleability**—Gold is highly malleable, meaning that one can easily shape it into different forms, such as coins.
- **Scarcity**—The biggest threat to the value of a currency is overproduction or unexpected discoveries. Gold's natural scarcity is what makes it truly exceptional. It is plentiful enough to facilitate trade but sufficiently scarce to make it difficult to expand the supply rapidly. The perfect balance of scarcity and availability makes it a reliable store of value.

The Gold Standard

The unique attributes of gold explain why many civilizations used it as money. But there is one attribute that limits its usefulness in physical form: Gold is heavy, making it cumbersome to carry in large quantities. Many civilizations addressed this by using paper notes exchangeable for gold rather than trading with physical gold. In such systems, issuers of notes held gold reserves and allowed noteholders to redeem them for gold at a fixed rate. When people refer to the "gold standard," they are describing this system.

The U.S. employed a bimetallic currency standard throughout most of the 1800s, and then shifted to a gold standard at the turn of the twentieth century. Bimetallism ended after the currency crisis in the 1890s, as overproduction of silver caused holders of U.S. dollars to lose faith in its value.

The Future of Gold

In 1971, the U.S. delinked its currency from gold, and the U.S. dollar became a fiat currency—meaning that the currency is not backed by an underlying commodity. Fiat currencies provide greater monetary policy flexibility, but they also have risks. The primary risk is that the U.S. will fail to exercise discipline in managing the money supply, which could cause people to lose faith in the value of the U.S. dollar. It seems unlikely that this will happen soon, but it is conceivable that the risk will rise in the more distant future.

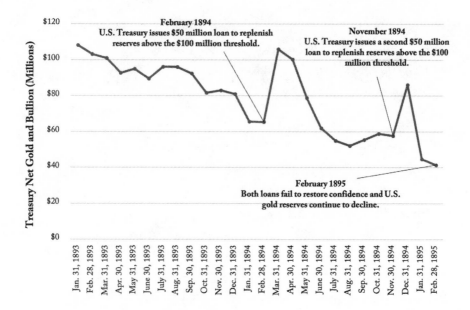

Figure 11.3: U.S. Treasury Intra-Month Minimum Gold Balance (January 31, 1893–February 28, 1895)[8]

The bimetallic currency standard was unsustainable, but the free silver movement remained firmly committed because of the weight of deflationary pressure.[9] Financiers and corporate leaders, on the other hand, preferred a stable currency with low inflation, as it made raising capital in foreign markets easier and it preserved the real value of their loan portfolios.[10]

By 1893, the U.S. was in a precarious position. Consistent with Gresham's law, silver poured into the Treasury, while Treasury note redemptions drained the Treasury's gold reserves. The problem was made worse by the fact that most developed nations at the time were firmly committed to the gold standard. Fearful of the U.S.'s lack of discipline, foreigners increasingly demanded payment for goods and services in gold, which placed even more pressure on the nation's reserves. Despite two concerted efforts to shore up the Treasury's gold supply in 1893 and 1894, the run on U.S. gold reserves intensified. Figure 11.3 shows the intra-month minimum Treasury holdings of gold by month from January 1, 1893, to February 28, 1895. Despite a total of $100 million in new debt issuance by the Treasury, the run on gold persisted, and U.S. reserves bottomed at $41.3 million on February 28, 1895.

THE PANIC OF 1893

During the Hard Times of the 1840s, leaders of European financial institutions regularly mocked Wall Street bankers. The most vicious insults emanated from the Houses of Barings and Rothschild. Capturing this sentiment, the following quote appeared in the London *Times* when the U.S. desperately sought a loan from England in 1842, "The people of the United States may be fully persuaded that there is a certain class of securities to which no abundance of money, however great, can give value, and that in this class their own securities stand pre-eminent."[11] To everybody's surprise—including most preeminent financiers in the U.S.—this sentiment would be turned on its head by the end of the nineteenth century.

In perhaps the greatest twist of all, the near failure of Barings Bank itself in 1890 set the stage for the Panic of 1893. The problems at Barings stemmed from its overexposure to risk in South America. Looking to diversify its holdings outside of Europe and the U.S., Barings invested heavily in Argentina during the late 1880s. A series of catastrophic events in 1890, which included a massive failure of the Argentinian wheat crop and an attempted coup, created a gaping hole in Barings's balance sheet. By November 1890, Barings was technically insolvent. It was only a quick bailout orchestrated by the Bank of England that allowed it to remain in operation.

The rescue of Barings spared the world from what could have been a much deeper crisis, but there were still ripple effects. In the U.S., it sparked a large outflow of foreign capital because the British needed to shore up their own financial system. These outflows consisted primarily of gold, and between June 30, 1890, and June 30, 1892, U.S. gold reserves declined by nearly 40 percent. Despite the outflows, U.S. securities markets were largely unaffected. It was not until February 1893 that signs of panic appeared. The immediate trigger was the bankruptcy of the Philadelphia and Reading Railroad, which entered receivership in February 1893. The next domino was the National Cordage Trust, which unexpectedly declared bankruptcy in May 1893. Although less impactful on the overall economy, the suddenness of the failure (which was largely attributable to a lack of transparency into the Trust's finances) took a toll on investor confidence. Losses in securities markets intensified and outflows of gold accelerated.[12]

Amid the panic on Wall Street, President Grover Cleveland took action to stop the flight of gold from the Treasury. A stopgap measure requiring banks to purchase government bonds provided some short-term relief, but Cleveland knew that a durable solution required a halt to silver purchases under the Sherman Silver Purchase Act. In retrospect, the only silver lining, so to speak, of the Panic of 1893 is that it finally provided Cleveland with the leverage that he needed to persuade Congress to repeal the Sherman Silver Purchase Act, but this would not occur until October 1893. Unfortunately, by the time it was repealed, the crisis of confidence in the U.S. had advanced too far, and the nation entered the dreaded, self-reinforcing cycle in which credit

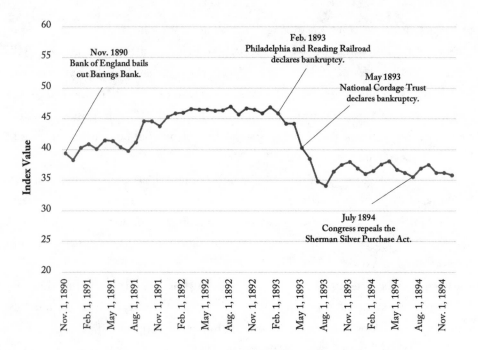

Figure 11.4: Cowles and Standard and Poor's Index of All U.S. Common Stock Prices
(November 1, 1890–December 1, 1894)[13]

contraction causes businesses and bank failures, which leads to more credit contraction, and so on. Securities prices declined sharply throughout this period, as illustrated in Figure 11.4.[14]

The repeal of the Sherman Silver Purchase Act occurred approximately one year after the stock market bottomed, but it failed to spark a meaningful rally. Further, the impact beyond Wall Street was worsening. In addition to a wave of bank and business failures throughout 1894, millions of Americans lost their jobs. The most pressing issue, however, continued to be the flight of gold from the Treasury. By February 8, 1895, the U.S. faced an impending catastrophe when gold reserves dipped to $44.7 million. At this point, the process was self-reinforcing: fear that the vaults would soon be empty caused redemptions to accelerate. Without immediate intervention, the U.S. would be forced to suspend gold redemptions, which would dramatically amplify loss of confidence in the U.S. dollar.

J. PIERPONT MORGAN LENDS HIS NAME

J. Pierpont Morgan established himself as a leader on Wall Street well before the Panic of 1893. His role in organizing a syndicate to support the stock market in the wake of William Vanderbilt's death in 1885 marked his rise as Wall Street's de facto leader. However, his actions in February 1895 solidified this role in the eyes of politicians and the public. As the nation's gold reserves evaporated, President Grover Cleveland found himself in an untenable position because he lacked the political capital and personal credibility that was needed to stop the run on gold. Populist support for free silver remained a threat, and many investors (especially foreign investors) had lost confidence in the United States. Not only did investors lack faith in the Cleveland administration, but they also feared the potential policies of the next administration. If the populists made significant gains in Congress, the free silver movement could regain momentum.

POINT OF INTEREST

The Confidence Game

"When you expect things to happen—strangely enough—they do happen."
—J. Pierpont Morgan

Market panics always seem unprecedented in the moment even though they are quite common. Over the past two centuries, the U.S. experienced dozens of panics of varying degrees of intensity and for various reasons. The damage that they caused depended on the severity of the underlying conditions and the speed and strength of the response.

When market panics hit, the media often focuses on the technical components of the response when, in fact, the most important factor is often restoring confidence in the system itself. In the twenty-first century, rescues orchestrated by the Federal Reserve and federal government are the primary tactics used to restore confidence. However, the most intense panics may also require support from private citizens. One such moment occurred in the fall of 2008 when Warren Buffett announced a $5 billion investment in Goldman Sachs, signaling his faith in the U.S. financial system.[15]

In 1895, the burden of confidence primarily rested on the private sector because the U.S. lacked a central bank. This explains why the contributions of J. Pierpont Morgan were so important. In contrast to Gilded Age stock operators, such as Jay Gould, Morgan possessed a unique ability to inspire confidence when markets were vulnerable to collapse. This enabled the country to avoid catastrophic depressions in the aftermath of the Panic of 1893—and a more severe panic that would arrive in 1907.

The run on gold was ultimately a crisis of confidence. The Treasury had already stopped purchasing silver after the repeal of the Sherman Silver Purchase Act, but it was too late to stop the run. Fortunately, confidence was an asset that Morgan possessed in abundance, and he correctly concluded that he could lend it to the federal government by signaling his faith in the integrity of U.S. gold reserves. After a series of meetings in February 1895, Morgan convinced President Cleveland to authorize an elegant solution. The first step was to leverage Morgan's domestic and foreign contacts to accumulate 3.5 million ounces of gold (approximately $62 million). The U.S. Treasury would then purchase the gold in exchange for a bond that was payable in gold. This would restore the Treasury's gold reserves above the $100 million statutory limit, but, more importantly, it would signal to the market that J. Pierpont Morgan *believed* in the integrity of U.S. gold reserves. Finally, Morgan promised that the new inflow of gold would remain in the government coffers. It is questionable whether Morgan had the ability to honor such a guarantee, but it had a strongly positive impact on market sentiment, regardless.[16]

The bond issue was precisely what the market needed, much to the chagrin of free silver advocates. The nation's gold reserves were restored to a level above $100 million, and Morgan's stamp of approval restored confidence in the dollar. From that point forward, the country's ability to honor its commitment to the gold standard was affirmed, and gold outflows waned. Morgan's reputation as the bulwark of Wall Street was firmly established, which would prove to be essential when the nation faced its next crisis in 1907. Gold reserves ebbed and flowed over the next year due to perceptions that the free silver movement could regain momentum. But President William McKinley's defeat of William Jennings Bryan in the election of 1896 effectively ended the free silver debate forever.[17]

LESSONS FROM THE GILDED AGE

The Gilded Age was a fascinating era of American history, and it is unfortunate that rampant corruption masked the underlying progress. By the time the U.S. entered the twentieth century it was armed with a strong culture of innovation, expansive transportation and manufacturing infrastructure, and relatively deep securities markets. These competitive advantages drove America's transition from an emerging market into an emerging empire by the middle of the 1900s. However, several formidable obstacles stood in the way of America's transformation, such as:

- **Growing Cost of Unregulated Markets**—Cheating the market was the preferred method of wealth accumulation for almost all Gilded Age speculators. As U.S. securities markets became more critical to the health of the nation's economy, the lack of regulation became increasingly problematic. J. Pierpont Morgan had little tolerance for the shenanigans of stock operators, which kept these problems reasonably contained for a few decades. But the costs of unregulated markets would intensify after Morgan passed away in 1913.

- **Flaws of the National Banking Regime**—The national banking system was becoming increasingly untenable by the end of the Gilded Age. In comparison to the wildcat banking days following the dissolution of the Second Bank of the United States in the 1830s, the system was a vast improvement. At the turn of the twentieth century, however, the flaws that remained had become intolerable. The severity of the danger would be revealed in 1907, which would prompt the third and final introduction of a central banking system in the United States.

- **Increased Efficiency in Securities Markets**—In the twenty-first century, most discussions regarding the efficiency of securities markets rest on the implicit assumption that market efficiency only recently emerged as a headwind for U.S. investors. However, the truth is that markets became highly efficient much earlier. By the late 1800s, it was already difficult for most investors to outperform a randomly assembled portfolio of U.S. equity securities. The first convincing evidence to this effect emerged in the 1920s.

This explains, at least in part, why Gilded Age speculators rarely bothered with security selection. Instead, they embraced the dark arts of market manipulation, insider trading, and pool operations. Jay Gould, Jim Fisk, and Daniel Drew distinguished themselves by the scale and daringness of their schemes, but countless men employed similar tactics on a smaller scale. This is an important principle because it explains why securities regulations remain so critical today. It will always be more lucrative to cheat rather than beat the system, and sophisticated market participants will always find new methods to circumvent laws and safeguards designed to prevent such abuses.

Part 3

Growing Pains of an Emerging Empire

1896–1929

"If we look forward to a period not far distant, we shall perceive that the productions of our country will infinitely exceed the demands which Great Britain and her connections can possibly have of them. And as we shall then be greatly advanced in population, our wants will be proportionately increased."[1]

—ALEXANDER HAMILTON (1775)

S oon after J. Pierpont Morgan restored confidence in the U.S. dollar, the American economy began to rebound, but the strength of the recovery was initially weakened by the nagging threat of free silver. Believing that political events would determine free silver's fate, investors anxiously awaited the results of the 1896 presidential election, which pitted William McKinley, a staunch advocate of the gold standard, against William Jennings Bryan, the nation's champion of free silver.[2] McKinley defeated Bryan decisively, gaining 271 electoral votes to Bryan's 176 votes. His victory weakened free silver, but the decisive blow was delivered by an unexpected expansion of the global gold supply. This was driven by several major discoveries in Alaska, South Africa, and Colorado, coupled with increased mining yields from improvements in the extraction process. The subsequent expansion of U.S. gold reserves increased the money supply, reversed deflationary pressures, and rendered the free silver movement obsolete. The passage of the Gold Standard Act of 1900 marked the official end of bimetallism in the United States.[3]

Part 3 recounts a series of events that enabled the U.S. to shed the last vestiges of its colonial past and emerge as the leading industrial and financial power of the twentieth century. By 1929, the U.S. would become the world's largest creditor, leading industrial power, and emerging rival to Great Britain as the dominant financial power. But in October 1929, a major stock market crash and subsequent implosion of the global economy threatened to derail America's progress.

Chapter 12 recounts an extraordinary ten-year period of economic growth that began in 1896. Frank Vanderlip, a leading American financier, referred to this period as the "American Commercial Invasion." For the first time in its history, the U.S. unleashed the full power of its economic potential by combining its rich natural resources, expansive transportation network, innovative mass manufacturing capabilities, and maturing financial system. By 1906, the U.S. had replaced Britain and Continental Europe as the world's workshop.

Chapter 13 recounts the end of the American Commercial Invasion, which coincided with the near implosion of the financial system during the Panic of 1907. The panic revealed fatal weaknesses of the national banking system, which could no longer support the U.S. economy. Despite continued resistance, a small majority of congressmen managed to pass the Federal Reserve Act of 1913, thus creating a U.S. central bank for the third time.

Chapter 14 recounts the unexpected onset of World War I in the summer of 1914. Rigid alliances among the great powers of Europe allowed what seemed like an inconsequential assassination in the streets of Sarajevo to escalate into one of the deadliest wars in human history. The U.S. unintentionally profited by remaining on the sidelines until April 1917. The arrival of U.S. troops in Europe tipped the scales in favor of the Allies but also helped spread a new, deadly strain of the H1N1 influenza virus. In 1919, the U.S. returned to a peacetime economy and the Great Influenza pandemic ran its course; however, Americans soon experienced a painful burst of inflation that was eerily similar to what Americans would experience nearly one hundred years later in the wake of the COVID-19 pandemic.

Chapter 15 concludes part 3 by recounting the robust economic recovery that followed the short but severe economic depression in 1920–1921. By the end of the 1920s, the recovery had devolved into a speculative mania, which was fueled by America's new addiction to credit-based speculation in the stock market. The Great Crash arrived in October 1929, and it was followed by the worst depression in U.S. history.

Chapter 12

THE AMERICAN
COMMERCIAL INVASION

*"It is as certain as anything in the future that industrial securities will
become the principal medium of speculation in this country."*[1]

—CHARLES DOW (MARCH 1900)

In 1880, Charles Dow arrived in New York City to pursue a career in journalism.
Prior to his arrival, Dow worked for several regional newspapers. After spending a
few years in New York City, Dow developed a passion for financial news and quickly
established a strong reputation as a financial reporter. After two years on the beat, Dow
decided to strike out on his own. He teamed up with two colleagues, Edward Jones and
Charles Bergstresser, and they launched a new company called Dow Jones & Company. In November 1883, the company released its first publication called the *Customer's
Afternoon Letter*, which quickly became a "must read" for both amateur and professional
investors. Building on their success, in 1889, Dow Jones & Company launched the *Wall
Street Journal*, which remains the premier financial newspaper in America today.[2]

Dow was an accomplished entrepreneur, but his commitment to reporting the
truth is what distinguished him most from his peers. The motto for the *Wall Street
Journal* was "The Truth in Its Proper Use."[3] Unlike many Gilded Age reporters, Dow
rejected bribes from stock operators in exchange for writing stories favorable to their
schemes, and he abstained from profiting from his access to insider information. Dow
demanded the same integrity from companies that he covered. His ethical standards
not only improved information access for his contemporaries, but they also inspired
federal regulations that would later arrive during the depths of the Great Depression.

The Original Dow Jones Industrials

In the 1880s, Charles Dow experimented with various techniques to predict market returns. His first step was to create a single return stream for a group of securities, which he called "indexes." After experimenting with multiple indexes for more than a decade, he settled on an index consisting of "industrials" due to his belief in the transformative impact of the American Commercial Invasion. In 1896, Dow published the Dow Jones Industrial Index for the first time. The index tracked twelve company stocks spanning multiple industrial sectors. The original Dow Jones Industrials are listed below. All but one, General Electric, has since been absorbed by a larger entity or disappeared entirely.

Original Dow Jones Industrials[4]

1. **American Cotton Oil**—Currently part of Unilever.
2. **American Sugar**—Currently part of Domino Foods.
3. **American Tobacco**—Broken up in 1911 under the Sherman Antitrust Act.
4. **Chicago Gas**—Now part of Integrys Energy.
5. **Distilling & Cattle Feeding**—Business units sold to various companies.
6. **General Electric**—Remains an independent company but was removed from the index in 2018.
7. **Laclede Gas**—Primary subsidiary of Laclede Group.
8. **National Lead**—Currently owned by Valhi.
9. **North American**—Dissolved in 1938.
10. **Tennessee Coal & Iron**—Acquired by U.S. Steel as part of a deal to end the Panic of 1907.
11. **U.S. Leather**—Dissolved in 1911.
12. **United States Rubber**—Currently part of The Michelin Group.

The Dow Jones Industrial Average remains an important gauge of stock market performance today, but it is no longer limited to traditional industrials. Recognizing the continual evolution of the U.S. economy, the index now includes software (e.g., Microsoft), health insurance (e.g., United Healthcare), financial services (e.g., Goldman Sachs), and energy (e.g., Chevron).

Dow's other notable contribution to financial history was the establishment of the Dow Jones Industrial Index in 1896. He constructed the index using only the returns of industrial company stocks because he believed that these companies represented the future of America. His foresight proved to be correct, but even he did not anticipate the magnitude of the growth of U.S. industrials that began that same year.[5]

AMERICA'S INDUSTRIAL ARSENAL

"For four years, I had seen at close range the growth of a favorable trade balance, which had assumed a total in that brief period greater than had been the net trade balance from the founding of the Government up to that time. That was a phenomenon which had had few parallels in our economic history, and the desire to study it from the European view led me to visit nearly all countries in Europe."[6]

—**FRANK VANDERLIP,** vice president, National City Bank (1902)

Similar to Charles Dow, Frank Vanderlip began his career in journalism. In the 1880s, he served as a financial reporter and editor in Chicago. While taking a course in political economy at the University of Chicago, Vanderlip met Lyman J. Gage, who moved to Washington in 1897 to become secretary of the Treasury. Gage recruited Vanderlip to join the Treasury, and after only six weeks, Gage promoted him to the position of assistant Treasury secretary. Following a successful five-year stint at the Treasury, Vanderlip joined National City Bank as a vice president in 1902. At the time, the U.S. was experiencing an explosive growth spurt that had unexpectedly catapulted U.S. industry ahead of global competitors as if they were standing still. National City executives sought to understand the causes and sustainability of this advancement, and they sent Vanderlip to tour Europe on a fact-finding mission.[7]

Vanderlip was stunned by what he observed. He marveled at the widespread use of American manufactured products, which ranged from inexpensive textiles to heavy industrial equipment, such as locomotive engines. He developed a deeper appreciation for the expansiveness and efficiency of American railroads, which transported much larger loads for a fraction of the cost. Finally, he was surprised to discover the primitive conditions of financial systems in Continental Europe. Frequent panics and crashes in the U.S. had hidden the incremental progress that Americans made in the aftermath of each crisis.

Vanderlip wrote a short pamphlet describing his experiences, which he titled, "The American 'Commercial Invasion' of Europe." His observations provide a unique

perspective on how America's unique competitive advantages simultaneously matured
in the 1890s. Specifically, Vanderlip attributed America's success to its vast trove of
natural resources, expansive transportation network, advanced manufacturing capabilities, and comparatively mature financial system. The remainder of this chapter
explains the role of each of these competitive advantages and the dramatic impact of
their convergence.[8]

Natural Resources

Since America's inception, settlers unearthed vast troves of natural resources scattered
across the countryside. Successful extraction—especially during the late 1800s—was a
major contributor to America's cost advantage in industrial production. Cheap energy
in the form of coal and petroleum enabled manufacturers to reduce operating costs
and transportation costs. The discovery of rich and easily accessible iron ore deposits,
especially in the Great Lakes region, provided cheap input for steel producers. Major
discoveries of gold and silver also fueled economic expansion, but in ways that Americans may not have fully appreciated at the time. One benefit was the expansion of the
nation's money supply. Finally, agricultural production (especially wheat and cotton)
continued to add value as exports, albeit to a lesser degree over time. The following
series of figures provides a snapshot of the dramatic increase in U.S. natural resource
production during the late nineteenth century and early twentieth century.

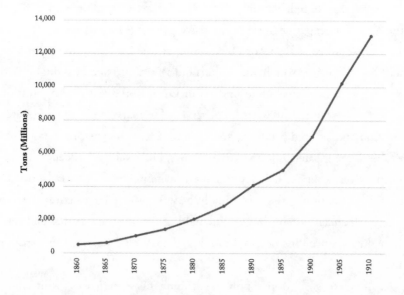

Figure 12.1: Coal Production in the United States (1860–1910)[9]

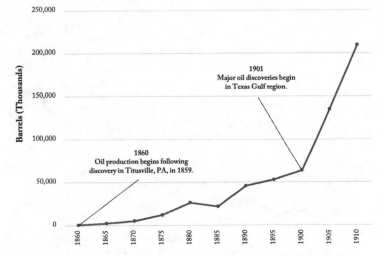

Figure 12.2: Crude Oil Production in the United States (1860–1910)[10]

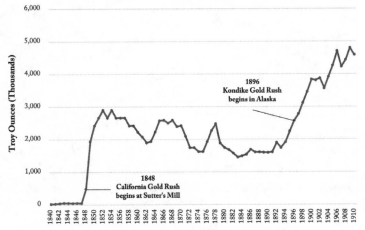

Figure 12.3: U.S. Gold Production (1840-1910)[11]

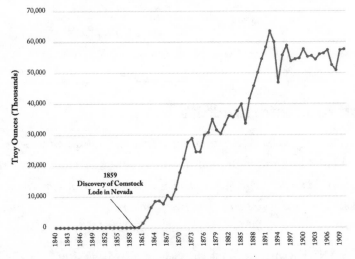

Figure 12.4: U.S. Silver Production (1840-1910)[12]

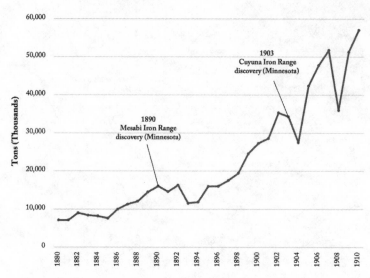

Figure 12.5: Manufacturing Raw Materials, Iron Ore (1880–1910)[13]

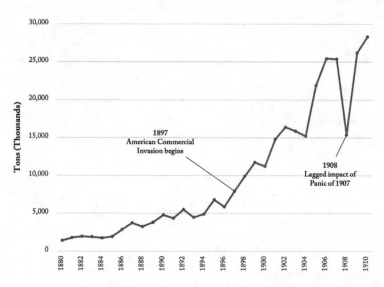

Figure 12.6: Manufacturing Raw Materials, Steel (1880–1910)[14]

Transportation Infrastructure

"One of the important factors in the strength of our industrial position is the unquestioned superiority in our transportation system. If one has, fresh in mind, the picture of our luxurious trains, mammoth engines, and more important still, our standard 50-ton freight cars, it makes the Europeans seem like amateurs in the science of transportation when we see their toy cars, small locomotives, and generally slow-going administration."[15]

—FRANK VANDERLIP, vice president, National City Bank (1902)

The endless scheming of stock operators and corporate owners during the Gilded Age had an unexpected silver lining—it enabled the U.S. to construct a vast railroad network that facilitated the inexpensive movement of raw materials and manufactured products to domestic and foreign markets. Moreover, by the turn of the twentieth century, a new generation of railroad owners had replaced the likes of Jay Gould, Collis Huntington, and Daniel Drew. The next generation was led by men such as Edward Harriman and James Hill, who were considerably more competent and ethical. The quality and efficiency of America's railroads dramatically improved, which added a new level of scale, efficiency, and reliability to match its expansiveness. In his book *The Tycoons*, Charles Morris observed this unexpected outcome by stating:

> The fact that railroads had so irrationally spread themselves over the empty plains, in stark defiance of every tenet of conventional economics and common sense, was a major factor in the explosive rate of American growth.[16]

Frank Vanderlip was stunned by the superior quality and efficiency of U.S. railroads in comparison to those in Europe. He noted that costs of freight averaged between 1.6 cents per ton per mile in France to 2.4 cents per mile in Great Britain. The average in America was only 0.75 cents per ton per mile. U.S. railroads were also constructed optimally for mass manufacturing. The efficiency and scale of U.S. railroad networks dramatically reduced prices of everything from commodities to heavy industrial equipment, which created a formidable competitive advantage for the entire American economy.[17]

Manufacturing Innovation and Advancement

"Heretofore our sales had been made up almost wholly of foodstuffs and raw materials. Europe was the workshop. But that has changed, and we find, year after year, an astonishing increase in our exports of manufactured articles . . . The increase in our exports of manufactured articles can, in the main, be traced to advances made in the manufacture of iron and steel, and to the display of inventive talent in the making of machinery."[18]

—FRANK VANDERLIP, vice president, National City Bank (1902)

The American System of Manufactures, which favored the use of specialized machinery to produce interchangeable parts, was perfectly suited for mass production. American precision manufacturing capabilities began advancing in the 1850s, but Europe's failure to keep pace enabled the U.S. to extend its lead over the subsequent decades. The

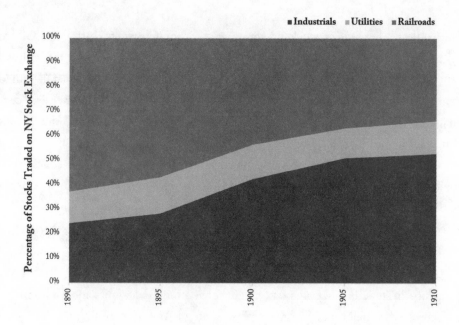

Figure 12.7: Percentage of Securities Traded on the NYSE (1890-1910)[19]

lead was then extended further still because of America's unique experience managing large industrial organizations and their philosophical commitment to mass production strategies. In contrast, European industrialists continued manufacturing products at relatively small scales and with greater customization. For the American strategy to succeed, however, industrialists were forced to construct large facilities designed for maximum efficiency. The obsessive focus on cost reductions, maximum capacity utilization, and continual technological improvement enabled U.S. manufacturers to strengthen their competitive advantage with each passing year.[20]

Evidence of U.S. advancements in manufacturing were also evident in securities markets. In 1890, industrial companies constituted approximately 25 percent of common stocks on the New York Stock Exchange; only twenty years later, industrials constituted approximately 50 percent (Figure 12.7).

Financial Infrastructure

"The banking methods of Continental Europe are cumbersome and time-consuming, and the people generally have learned but the first lessons in the uses of credit machinery. That forms a handicap upon industry that is just as real as that caused by their persistence in using out-of-date machines and methods of manufacture which we have long ago abandoned as slow-going and expensive."[21]

—**FRANK VANDERLIP,** vice president, National City Bank (1902)

POINT OF INTEREST

From Debtor to Creditor

During the nation's first 110 years, businesses relied heavily on foreign capital to fund businesses, government projects, and federal and state debt. The American Commercial Invasion tipped the scales in the other direction. In 1902, the U.S. had accumulated nearly $2.5 billion in trade surpluses. This money was used initially to buy back securities held by Europeans. Vanderlip recalled touring a bank vault in Germany that had several empty shelves. His host explained that the shelves once were filled with U.S. securities that had since been repurchased by Americans.

By the end of the American Commercial Invasion, Americans began investing meaningfully in foreign securities. This trend would accelerate in the coming decades.

The backwardness of European financial systems was among the more shocking observations of Frank Vanderlip. In fairness, during the Gilded Age, the U.S. financial system was hardly flawless, and Americans suffered frequent panics, crashes, and depressions as a result. However, to America's credit, they learned from their errors and made incremental improvements after each crisis subsided. By the turn of the twentieth century, the cumulative impact of these improvements was the creation of a financial system that was more advanced in comparison to most systems in Continental Europe.[22] Several practices in Continental Europe were so backward as to be comical. For example, transactions between two banking customers in Vienna required individuals who held accounts at the same bank to withdraw funds from one account, count it, and then allow the bank to re-deposit the cash in the other account. Even more absurd was a practice employed by the Bank of France to hand collect loan payments due from depositors, rather than simply credit each borrower's corresponding deposit account for monthly payments.[23]

The American financial system remained flawed at the turn of the twentieth century, but it had advanced far more quickly than most European systems. Some even argued that the U.S. had achieved par with England, which at the time issued the world's reserve currency and was the world's undisputed financial center.

Convergence of America's Competitive Advantages

America's dominance in industrial manufacturing at the turn of the twentieth century was so formidable because it was supported by multiple competitive advantages. Leadership in any one area would make a nation the envy of its competitors, but the combination of all advantages was a recipe for the emergence of a new empire. But before Americans could entertain such ambition, a nagging problem remained.

RUINOUS COMPETITION, CONSOLIDATION, AND STANDARDIZATION

During the 1800s, foreign investment in the U.S. frequently devolved into periods of indiscriminate investment in U.S. companies. This often resulted in the building of excess capacity, which then fueled vicious price wars. This problem was especially acute in the transportation and industrial sectors, which operated with high fixed costs funded by substantial amounts of debt. When entering periods of excess capacity, companies cut prices to levels barely exceeding operating costs just to avoid bankruptcy. These price wars sparked waves of bankruptcies that rippled through the financial system. Lacking a central bank and strong regulatory guardrails, financial panics often devolved into self-reinforcing economic contractions that ended in painful depressions.

J. Pierpont Morgan famously coined the phrase "ruinous competition" to describe this phenomenon. In the early years, industrialists attempted to prevent price wars by establishing "pooling agreements," which were effectively pacts to allocate market share among groups of competitors to avoid price competition. In the railroad industry, competing lines assigned territories and then agreed to refrain from price competition. These arrangements made sense in theory, but they repeatedly failed when one or more pool members cheated to gain market share and quick profits. In addition, pooling agreements were eventually outlawed with the passage of the Interstate Commerce Act of 1887 and the Sherman Antitrust Act of 1890.

Frustrated by the ineffectiveness of pooling agreements, Morgan concluded that industry consolidation was the only viable long-term solution. In the 1890s, he led aggressive consolidation in the railroad industry, and executives in other industries followed his lead. In the early phases, trusts were the preferred vehicle for company consolidation rather than outright acquisitions. The reason was that the trust structure allowed companies to circumvent state laws, which prohibited one corporation from owning shares in another corporation. Under a trust structure, individual companies deposited their company shares into a trust in exchange for trust certificates and a share of the trust's profits. A small number of trustees exercised control over production, distribution, and pricing for the underlying companies. This had the same effect of purchasing full ownership in other companies, but because trusts were not legally recognized as a corporation, state laws were not violated. Many of the more familiar business combinations of the Gilded Age, most notably Standard Oil, were organized in this manner.[24]

The second type of business consolidation involved the outright purchase (or rollup) of multiple companies under a single holding company. The "holding company" model was the preferred strategy during the "merger mania" in the late 1890s. Like the trust movement that preceded it, the holding company model was a legal rather than strategic innovation. In 1888, New Jersey became the first state to permit the formation of holding companies, which could then purchase controlling interests in other companies. Other states soon followed New Jersey's lead, rendering the trust model obsolete. Thus, the massive consolidation of commercial enterprises into holding companies in the late 1890s was largely a continuation of the trust strategy. The pace of consolidation, however, accelerated substantially at the turn of the twentieth century.[25]

MERGER MANIA AND THE MYTH OF THE AMERICAN MONOPOLY

When people recall the formation of U.S. industrial conglomerates at the turn of the twentieth century, they often assume that the primary objective was to monopolize markets for specific products, raise prices, and then fleece customers. The truth was usually less nefarious. Instead, most consolidations were defensive strategies that were intended to ensure a firm's survival rather than generate unfair profits.[26] As revealed in part 2, the most profitable schemes during the Gilded Age were usually less visible to the public. Abusing monopolistic power was neither the most profitable nor the most subtle tactic. The primary motive for industry consolidation was usually the creation of scale efficiencies, securing access to raw materials, reducing costs, and squeezing out excess capacity from the system.[27] Even the most notorious trustbuster of all, President Theodore Roosevelt, acknowledged this distinction. Despite his general hostility toward big business, Roosevelt made the following statement in a public speech:

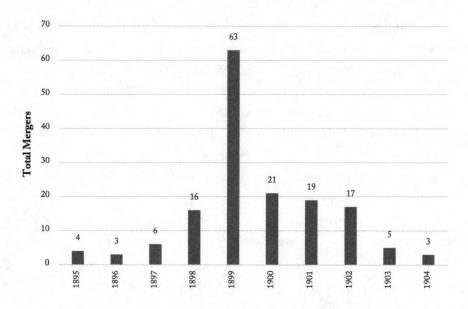

Figure 12.8: Total Mergers of Manufacturing Companies in the United States (1895–1904)[28]

It is unfortunate that our present laws should forbid all combinations instead of sharply discriminating between those combinations which do good and those combinations which do evil . . . The antitrust laws should not prohibit combinations that do no injustice to the public, still less those the existence of which is on the whole of benefit to the public.[29]

Although the motives driving industry consolidation are often mischaracterized, the sheer scale of consolidation at the turn of the twentieth century was not. The only time in which America experienced a comparable pace of mergers occurred in the 1980s. Figure 12.8 provides a snapshot of merger activity in the manufacturing industry alone from 1895 to 1904.

Industry consolidation radically transformed the U.S. economy at the turn of the twentieth century. No longer impeded by ruinous price wars, industrial companies enjoyed strong revenue growth, margin expansion, and powerful operational scale advantages. Individuals benefitted in the form of wealth accumulation, while companies accessed a new source of internally generated capital to self-fund future expansion. With this final phase of evolution completed, the U.S. had all the necessary pieces to execute its commercial invasion.

IMPACT OF THE AMERICAN COMMERCIAL INVASION

It must have been humbling to witness the American Commercial Invasion from the British Isles. The timing was particularly bad because the British were already suffocating from the rising costs of maintaining a global empire. The combined impact of mounting imperial costs and a deteriorating competitive advantage in manufacturing would prove too much to bear. The pound sterling survived as the world's dominant reserve currency for a few more decades, but the American Commercial Invasion marked the beginning of Britain's economic decline. The U.S. experience, however, was precisely the opposite. The world's insatiable appetite for American products dramatically increased the wealth of the nation and its citizens. The following series of figures captures several of these effects.

Industry consolidation and convergence of America's competitive advantages drives substantial productivity gains relative to global competitors (as illustrated by a comparison to Britain in Figure 12.9).

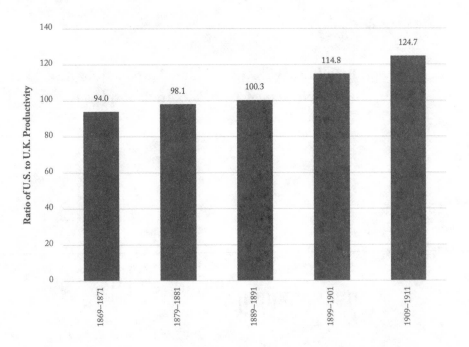

Figure 12.9: Ratio of U.S. to British Total Economic Productivity (1869–1911)[30]

Productivity enhancements, combined with operational and technological innovation, strengthen the competitiveness of U.S. manufacturing companies, altering the composition of U.S. exports.

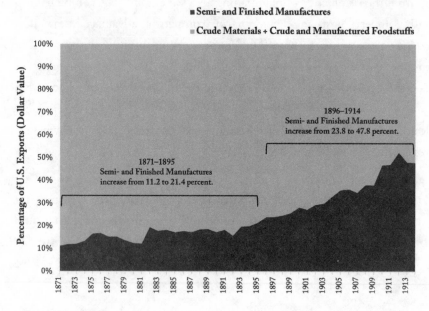

Figure 12.10: Composition of United States Exports to the Rest of World (1871–1914)[31]

Higher profitability of U.S. manufactured products drives a sharp and sustained increase in U.S. trade surpluses.

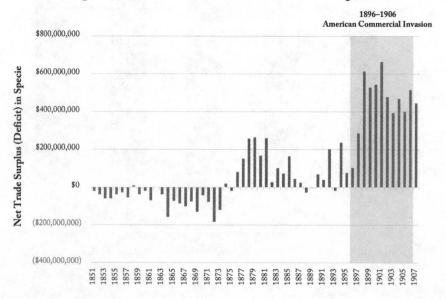

Figure 12.11: United States Net Trade Surplus (Deficit) in Specie (1851–1907)[32]

Expanding profit margins drive substantial gains in U.S. stocks.

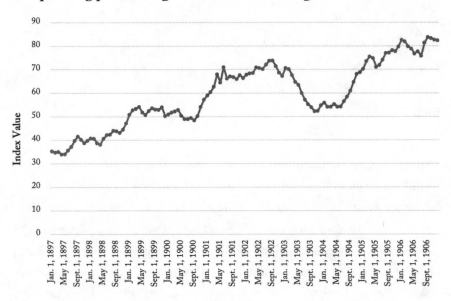

Figure 12.12: Total Return of Standard & Poor's Cowles Commission Index of
All Common Stocks (January 1, 1897–December 31, 1906)[33]

Large trade surpluses enable U.S. commercial enterprises and individual citizens to rapidly accumulate wealth.

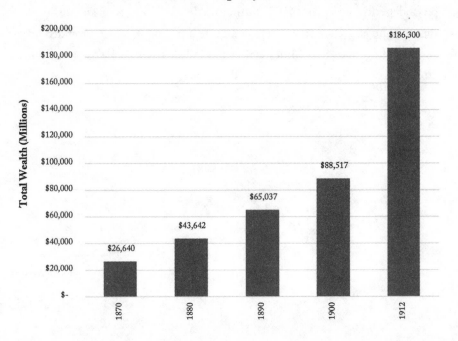

Figure 12.13: Estimated Value of Total U.S. Wealth in 1929 Prices (Millions) (1870–1912)[34]

THE HEIR TO THE BRITISH EMPIRE

"With such a combination [of competitive advantages] the country is bound to make the very greatest progress. It will go on and on, and will be greater and still greater. America is especially fortunate in that she has no great military burden. Militarism is the nightmare and the ruin of every European finance minister." [35]

—SERGEI WITTE, Russian foreign minister (1902)

The American Commercial Invasion ranks among the more significant inflection points in U.S. financial history. In the span of ten years, the country shed its agricultural roots forever and transformed into the world's leading industrial manufacturer. The impact on American life cannot be overstated. Incomes and savings rates rose sharply, and many Americans could afford both necessities and luxuries that were previously unobtainable. Dynamics in the business world also shifted, as corporations no longer depended on foreign capital for expansion and improvement. Instead, companies financed growth with free cash flow from operating activities. Securities markets blossomed, as trading volume increased, and the diversity of publicly listed companies broadened. Finally, as more Americans accumulated excess savings, a new group of investors caught the attention of Wall Street.

Russia's finance minister, Sergei Witte, met with Vanderlip during his tour of Europe and perfectly explained what America looked like from an outsider's perspective. But the above statement revealed quite a bit more. Witte provided an eerie premonition of Europe's fate. Militarism would indeed become the bane of Continental Europe and lead to the fall of the British Empire.

Chapter 13

THE LAST PRIVATE LENDER
OF LAST RESORT

"There are two rules: First: That these loans should only be made at a high
rate of interest . . . Secondly. That at this rate these advances should be
made on all good banking securities, and as largely as the public ask for
them. The reason is simple. The object is to stay the alarm, and nothing
therefore should be done to cause alarm. But the way to cause alarm
is to refuse someone who has good security to offer."[1]

—WALTER BAGEHOT (1873)

In 1873, Walter Bagehot formulated a principle that has guided central bank policy for 150 years. The principle is that central banks should lend freely to solvent banks during a crisis, but at a high rate of interest. This lender-of-last-resort principle ensures that solvent banks receive adequate liquidity, while the high cost of capital deters them from engaging in unsound practices. Bagehot was likely unaware that Alexander Hamilton employed the same principle nearly one hundred years earlier. Regardless of who invented the principle, the U.S. refused to embrace it until the passage of the Federal Reserve Act of 1913. Without a central bank to serve in this capacity, many banking panics spiraled out of control and triggered deep depressions. During such events, government and financial leaders scrambled to create solutions using improvised tools. For example, on multiple occasions in the late 1800s, the U.S. Treasury injected deposits in New York City banks, and the New York Clearing House (NYCH) issued a pseudo currency, known as "clearinghouse certificates," to increase bank liquidity.

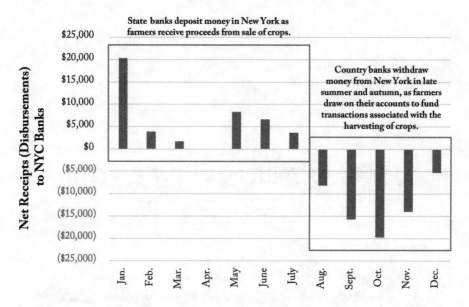

Figure 13.1: Average Receipts and Disbursements of Cash from New York Banks (1905-1908)[2]

Sometimes improvised solutions worked and sometimes they failed. After each failure, bankers learned from their mistakes and made incremental improvements. Despite the frequent crises, many politicians remained stubbornly resistant to the concept of a central bank. Even with incremental improvements in the private sector, the absence of a central bank became more costly as the U.S. economy grew during the American Commercial Invasion. Demand for reform was amplified by the frustrating predictability of financial crises. Since the establishment of the national banking system in 1864, bank panics almost always occurred in the fall months for reasons that were both understandable and predictable. The cause was the agricultural financing cycle. Each year, during September and October, funds flowed out of New York City banks because farmers withdrew capital from country banks to pay for the transport of crops to market. Country banks, in turn, withdrew funds from Central Reserve City National Banks located in New York City. After receiving payment for their crops in the winter, the process reversed. Figure 13.1 shows the net receipts and disbursements from New York City banks by month from 1905 to 1908.

The agricultural financing cycle created a chronic shortage of cash in New York City in September and October, which made banks especially vulnerable to panics and bank runs. This problem was referred to as "currency inelasticity," because banks were poorly equipped to adjust their liquidity in response to seasonal demands for cash and unexpected shocks.[3]

The inelasticity of the U.S. currency and the absence of a lender of last resort made major financial crises inevitable. If a crisis were to occur, it would likely happen in September or October, and this is precisely what happened in 1907. The remainder of this chapter recounts the events that culminated in the Panic of 1907. America's near miss with catastrophe inspired the passage of the Federal Reserve Act of 1913, which resurrected a central bank for the third time in the nation's history and gave it the power to serve as a lender of last resort.

A NEW FINANCIAL INSTITUTION GROWS IN THE SHADOWS

In July 1884, Frederick Eldridge, a former classmate of J. Pierpont Morgan, founded the Knickerbocker Trust Company with the goal of providing a suite of financial and investment products to serve a burgeoning new class of individual investors. Eldridge used the trust company structure, as opposed to a national bank, due to the relative ease of obtaining a charter and the comparatively light regulatory oversight in the state of New York. Located on a corner facing the Waldorf Astoria—a hotel and residence catering to New York's financial elite—the Knickerbocker became one of the largest trust companies in New York City by the turn of the twentieth century.

The growth of trust companies began several decades before the Panic of 1907.

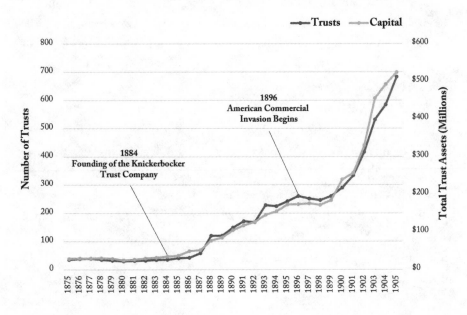

Figure 13.2: Number of U.S. Trust Companies and Total Trust Assets (1875–1905)[4]

Throughout the 1880s and 1890s, hundreds of trusts were launched across the country, accumulating assets at a breathtaking pace. Figure 13.2 shows the growth of trust companies and trust company assets for the thirty-year period ending December 31, 1905.[5]

The catalyst for trust company growth was the rapid accumulation of wealth by American citizens and businesses during the American Commercial Invasion. As their accounts grew, customers demanded more traditional banking services. Trust companies obliged by offering more traditional commercial banking services, such as short-term commercial loans, call loans on stock exchanges, and even securities underwriting. These services satisfied customers' demands and bolstered trust company profitability. This, in turn, enabled trusts to offer higher interest rates on deposits in comparison to national and state banks. Higher rates entailed greater risk, but clients paid little heed, and deposits flooded indiscriminately into trust company vaults. By 1906, total trust company deposits were nearly equivalent to the deposits held by the entire national banking system.[6]

POINT OF INTEREST

The Danger of Shadow Banking

A "shadow bank" is a financial institution that offers bank-like services but without the same regulatory constraints and protections. The existence of a massive shadow banking system during the GFC in the early 2000s amplified the panic and made the crisis especially difficult to stop (see chapter 28). The Federal Reserve was well equipped to resolve the failure of traditional banks, but non-members, such as investment banks, money market funds, and insurance companies, lacked protection.

Trust companies presented a similar challenge in the early 1900s. They had accumulated assets that were roughly equivalent to those held by national banks, but they were not subjected to national bank regulations. Instead, they were regulated at the state level, and many states allowed trust companies to take considerably more risk than national banks.

Trust company executives took full advantage of lighter regulations, which enabled them to enjoy exceptional growth and rising profits at the turn of the twentieth century. As is always the case, however, trust companies eventually paid a price for the risks that enabled them to achieve this growth.

Deposit growth and expansion into traditional commercial banking services was dangerous for trust companies because they were not designed to function in this capacity. For most of the nineteenth century, trust companies provided much more mundane services, such as the sale of insurance products and various estate planning services. These services were much less risky than providing loans. Adding commercial banking services on the margins may have posed little risk initially, but by the early 1900s, trust companies were virtually indistinguishable from national banks, yet they lacked the same safeguards. The most concerning gaps were:

- **Lower Reserve Requirements**—National banks were required to maintain reserves equivalent to 25 percent of the bank's capital. New York trust companies were only required to hold capital reserves of 15 percent—and only one-third was required to be held in cash. This provided a thin cushion to weather a financial crisis.[7]

- **Less Restrictive Investment Guidelines**—Trust companies were less restricted with respect to the type of assets they could hold for investment. Many states allowed trust companies to purchase equity securities and real estate, both of which were prohibited at national banks. This allowed trusts to take greater risk and hold fewer liquid assets.[8]

- **Restricted Access to the New York Clearinghouse (NYCH)**—Unlike commercial banks, trust companies did not engage heavily in activities that required clearing services, such as check processing. This did not pose a problem directly, but because it eliminated the need for trusts to join the NYCH, it created a major problem indirectly. The primary function of the NYCH was to facilitate the settlement of debits and credits among banks as part of the normal check clearing process, but it also offered an important safeguard during financial panics by allowing banks to settle debts using *clearinghouse certificates* rather than cash. The mechanics were a bit complex, but the use of clearinghouse certificates enabled member banks to conserve cash during a financial crisis or bank run by settling debts with other members of the NYCH with clearinghouse certificates rather than cash. In effect, the NYCH served as a private lender of last resort.[9]

The rapid growth of trust companies created a dangerous situation. It was only a matter of time before trust company stability would be tested in a financial crisis.

A BUTTERFLY TAKES FLIGHT IN SAN FRANCISCO

An important principle of chaos theory is that small changes in complex systems can spark a chain reaction that produces unpredictable outcomes far from the site of origin. The oft-used metaphor is that of a butterfly flapping its wings on one side of the world at just the right place and time to eventually produce a hurricane on the other side of the world. Although less subtle than the flutter of a butterfly's wings, America experienced a similar event on April 18, 1906, when residents of San Francisco, California, were jolted awake by a violent tremor. The earthquake lasted for nearly a minute and registered an estimated 8.3 on the Richter scale. Within a matter of days, most of San Francisco was reduced to rubble from the quake itself or to ashes from the fires that swept through the city in the days that followed. Estimated damages ranged from $350 million to $500 million, or roughly 1.5 percent of GDP at the time. In today's dollars, this would equate to roughly $300 billion—a painful but tolerable loss.[10]

Financial markets initially held up reasonably well. There was an initial sell-off, but losses were concentrated in sectors most affected, such as railroads and insurance companies. Beneath the surface, however, the earthquake had a dangerous but much less visible impact on the flow of money throughout the nation. These effects slowly but steadily made their way to New York City.

THE UNANTICIPATED CONSEQUENCES OF A SHRINKING MONEY SUPPLY

More than sixteen months passed before the snowball that formed in San Francisco on April 18 slammed into New York City. In the meantime, cracks in the financial system appeared in unexpected places. The first signs of distress did not even appear in America. London took the initial hit, as nearly half of San Francisco's fire insurance policies were issued by British insurance companies. To satisfy claims, British insurers liquidated assets and sent several large shipments of gold to America. Normally, this would have provided much-needed relief to the U.S. financial system, but only if the gold remained in New York–based banks and trusts. The problem was that New York banks were simultaneously experiencing even larger withdrawals of cash to fund reconstruction in San Francisco.[11]

From April 1906 to October 1907, tight monetary conditions tormented America. On several occasions, New York banks required intervention by the Treasury in the form of emergency deposits. One such example occurred on March 26, 1907, when Secretary of the Treasury George Cortelyou deposited $15 million in New York City banks. Figure 13.3 shows the increasing pressure on the money supply by tracking the interior flow of money in and out of New York City banks from 1905 to 1907. In addition to capturing the magnitude of the outflows, it is interesting to contrast the spring months of 1905 with those of 1906 and 1907. What were typically periods of strong inflows, due to the dynamics of the agricultural financing cycle, transformed into periods of outflows in 1906 and 1907. This was most acute in April and May of 1906, as New York banks experienced a net loss of approximately $54 million versus a net gain of $17.7 million during the same period in 1905 (Figure 13.4).[12]

POINT OF INTEREST

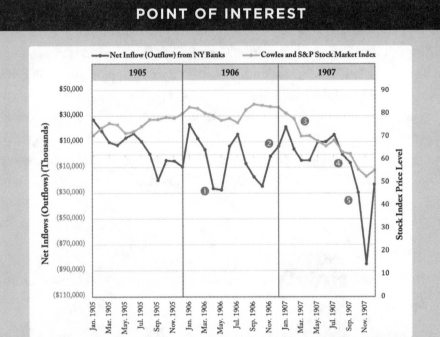

Figure 13.3: Panic of 1907 from the Perspective of New York City Banks and the Stock Market (1905–1907)[13]

Key Events

1. San Francisco earthquake triggers $54 million in cash outflows from New York City banks in April and May 1906.
2. For the entire year of 1906, New York City banks experience net outflows of $36.3 million versus net inflows of $62.7 million in 1905.
3. Equity market declines intensify as investors liquidate securities to raise cash. New York City banks experience net withdrawals (rather than seasonal inflows) in March and April of 1907.

(continued)

4. England bans the use of finance bills in London, forcing massive out-flows of gold from the United States. Gold reserves decline by 10 percent between May and August of 1907, placing further downward pressure on the money supply.
5. The Panic of 1907 begins after Otto Heinze's failed corner of United Copper. Trust companies and banks associated with Heinze suffer bank runs, which quickly spread in New York City.

Despite continual pressure on the New York City money supply, the stock market fared relatively well until the early months of 1907 but then steadily deteriorated through the spring and summer. Unlike prior bear markets, this decline was a slow bleed, which is why it was dubbed the "silent crash." The losses added up, however, and by October 1, 1907, the stock market had declined by approximately 30 percent since the beginning of the year.[14]

By October 1907, the U.S. financial system was fragile. Money was extraordinarily tight due to the combination of capital withdrawals to fund reconstruction in San Francisco and seasonal outflows associated with the agricultural financing cycle. Finally, the bear market in stocks weighed on investor sentiment. It would not take

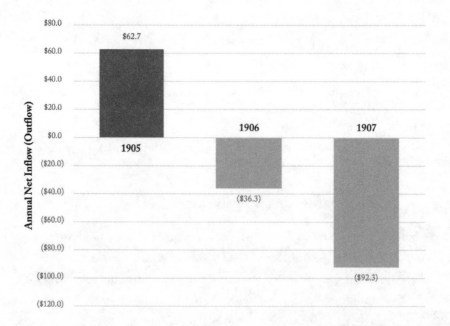

Figure 13.4: Annual Net Cash Inflows/(Outflows) from New York City Banks (Millions)
(January 1, 1905–December 31, 1907)

much to push the financial system into a full-blown panic. In fact, many historians argue that the Panic of 1907 was bound to happen even without another unanticipated shock to the system. Regardless of whether it was inevitable, by the third week of October, the foolish behavior of a Wall Street novice wreaked more than enough havoc to send financial markets into a tailspin.[15]

OTTO HEINZE LIGHTS THE FUSE

"In the history of every great catastrophe, you'll find some masterly bit of stupidity set fire to the oil-soaked rags."[16]

—EDWIN LEFEVRE (1908)

Otto Heinze followed his brother, F. Augustus Heinze, to Wall Street in early 1907. The move was prompted by the relocation of the headquarters of United Copper, a company founded by Augustus. After making a fortune in the copper mines of Montana, Augustus sought to test his mettle in the financial markets of New York. Seeking a Wall Street veteran for guidance, he formed a close relationship with Charles Morse, an ill-reputed stock operator who controlled several New York financial institutions. Leveraging Morse's connections, Augustus quickly purchased large ownership stakes in several banks and trust companies. His most notable purchase was the Mercantile National Bank, for which he also served as president. Although Otto Heinze lacked the notoriety of his brother Augustus, he participated in many of his brother's mining ventures and harbored similar ambitions in the financial markets. Soon after arriving on Wall Street, Otto launched a brokerage firm located directly across the hall from the United Copper headquarters and began to experiment as a stock operator.[17]

Within a year of their arrival on Wall Street, the Heinze brothers found themselves in a difficult situation. In October 1907, United Copper stock had plummeted, which placed Augustus under extreme financial pressure. He had pledged the stock as collateral for multiple loans that he used to purchase shares in several financial institutions. The significant drop in the stock price made his creditors uneasy. To support the falling price, Augustus organized a bull pool and began purchasing large amounts of shares on margin. But Heinze's efforts failed, and by the beginning of October 1907, the stock hovered around $50/share, a roughly 30 percent decline since the beginning of the year.[18]

Having assisted his brother with the failed bull pool, Otto devised a new plan to recoup their losses. After taking inventory of the family's ownership position, Otto hypothesized that most United Copper shares were under their control, which provided them with an opportunity to corner the stock. If successful, their profits could erase their losses from the unsuccessful bull pool. Otto shopped the idea to a few Wall Street veterans, but they all warned him that a successful corner required the purchase of far more stock than Otto estimated. One warning came from none other than Charles Barney, the CEO of the Knickerbocker Trust Company, which ultimately failed due to Otto's foolishness. After refusing to provide a loan, Barney warned Otto that his caper required purchases of up to $3 million in United Copper stock. This was roughly three times the amount Otto had budgeted.[19]

As one may recall from chapter 9, a market corner is a daring gambit that requires meticulous planning and a lot of experience. Like "shooting the moon" in a game of hearts, attempting a corner was a foolish act for a Wall Street amateur. But Otto Heinze was oblivious to his amateur status, and on October 14, he began aggressively purchasing shares of United Copper to corner the stock. After only a single day of trading, he then convinced himself that the corner was complete, and he initiated phase two. On October 15, Otto attempted to "squeeze" short sellers by calling in all securities on loan through multiple brokerage firms. However, to his horror, there were plenty of shares in circulation, and the stock price did not rise as Heinze had anticipated. The corner had failed, and the price of United Copper shares began to plummet.[20]

Heinze's failed corner was catastrophic. Not only had he borrowed heavily to establish the corner, but he had also purchased several large blocks of stock completely on his word. On Wednesday, October 16, the brokerage firm of Gross & Kleeberg ceased operations, citing the refusal of Otto Heinze & Company to pay for 6,000 shares of United Copper that they had purchased on the firm's behalf. After hearing the news, several brokers concluded that Otto was unlikely to honor payments to them as well, and they immediately dumped shares of United Copper on the market to raise cash. The flood of selling caused the stock to crater from a high of $60 per share on Monday, October 14, to $10 per share by the end of the week. On Thursday, October 17, having defaulted on its debt to several brokerage firms, Otto Heinze & Company was suspended from the New York Stock Exchange. On the very same day, the State Savings Bank of Butte, Montana, announced it was closing. Although only indirectly related to the failed United Copper corner, the bank happened to be owned by Augustus Heinze. The relationship alone prompted fear that Heinze's entire financial empire

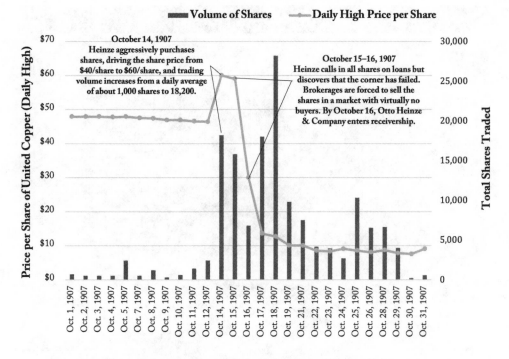

━━ Volume of Shares   **━━━ Daily High Price per Share**

October 14, 1907
Heinze aggressively purchases shares, driving the share price from $40/share to $60/share, and trading volume increases from a daily average of about 1,000 shares to 18,200.

October 15–16, 1907
Heinze calls in all shares on loans but discovers that the corner has failed. Brokerages are forced to sell the shares in a market with virtually no buyers. By October 16, Otto Heinze & Company enters receivership.

Figure 13.5: United Copper Daily High Price and Trading Volume
(October 1, 1907–October 31, 1907)[21]

could collapse—and that was all depositors needed to start queuing at the teller windows. The Panic of 1907 had begun.[22]

NEW YORK CITY ENTERS THE END GAME

An interesting fact about the Panic of 1907 is that, unlike prior financial panics in the U.S., inflated asset values were not a meaningful contributor. It is true that the ten-year bull market in stocks rewarded investors with double-digit returns, but these returns were supported by similarly impressive earnings and productivity growth stemming from the American Commercial Invasion. In fact, the price-to-earnings ratio of stocks in October 1907 was only 12.81—a valuation that would be considered attractive by today's standards. Instead, the problem in 1907 was primarily a function of tight monetary conditions in New York. If money had been plentiful, the failed corner of United Copper would, at most, have been a footnote in U.S. financial history.[23]

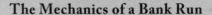

The Mechanics of a Bank Run

The Run on the 19th Ward Bank

The business model of a bank is to invest its capital, which is primarily provided by depositors, and earn a spread between the return on its investments (primarily loans) and the cost of capital (i.e., operating costs and interest paid to depositors).[24] The most dangerous situation for a bank is when a large percentage of depositors withdraw their cash simultaneously, as no bank is capable of liquidating its entire investment and loan portfolio at a moment's notice. When this happens, it is referred to as a bank run. The main defense against a bank run prior to the Federal Reserve Act of 1913 was for a bank to manage public perception of its solvency. If depositors ever suspected that a bank was at risk of insolvency, they would immediately withdraw their cash before the vaults were emptied.

Bank runs are fickle in that the only thing required to trigger one is the *perception* that a bank may be insolvent—or even just short on cash. A simple rumor, regardless of its validity, can trigger a bank run. Once a run starts, it is extraordinarily difficult to stop, as each depositor has a rational incentive to withdraw their money as fast as possible. If a bank is truly insolvent (i.e., the value of its assets is less than the value of its liabilities), withdrawal requests at the end of the queue may not be honored—at least not in full.

Few Americans today appreciate the terror of uncontrolled bank runs—although Silicon Valley Bank depositors, who suffered a run in March 2023, are a notable exception. In general, however, Americans' lack of experience with bank runs is a luxury they owe to the reforms inspired by the suffering of Americans who lost their life savings in the Great Depression. Recollections of bank runs from the 1800s and early 1900s provide a glimpse of how frightening they were to behold. Unlike today, the only way to withdraw money from a bank was to show up at the teller window; and the mere sight of a line forming at a bank could trigger a run. In fact, there are stories of bank runs occurring after people mistook lines forming at neighboring stores as an early symptom of a run.

When bankers and government officials encountered bank runs in the early 1900s, the first challenge was determining whether a bank was insolvent or simply short of cash to satisfy temporarily elevated demand for withdrawals. If the bank was merely short on cash (or even just slightly insolvent), it made sense to extend the required credit to weather the crisis. If the bank was insolvent (meaning its liabilities exceeded a reasonable estimate of the market value of its assets), the best approach was to place the bank in receivership and craft an organized liquidation plan. As if making this determination was not challenging enough, these decisions often needed to be made within extraordinarily tight time frames. Once bank runs start, every minute counts. Wasted time not only can make the difference between success and failure of the bank experiencing a run, but delays can also allow the panic to spread.

Bank runs began almost immediately after the failures of Otto Heinze & Company, Gross & Kleeberg, and the State Savings Bank of Butte. The runs initially targeted banks and trusts associated with the Heinze brothers. Sensing the risk posed by the mere association with the Heinze family, National Mercantile Bank assembled an emergency board meeting on the night of October 16 and announced the forced resignation of Augustus Heinze the next morning. Unfortunately, the announcement was too late, too little, or perhaps just ignored. Queues began forming at the National Mercantile Bank that very same day, and they did not stop there. Within a few days, queues were forming at any bank or trust company suspected of having any association whatsoever with Augustus Heinze and his partner Charles Morse. Whether these institutions were truly experiencing financial distress was irrelevant.[25]

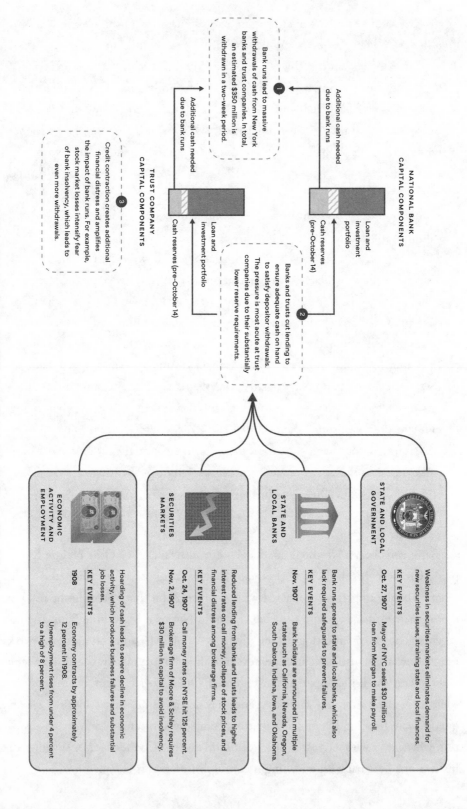

NATIONAL BANK CAPITAL COMPONENTS

Cash reserves (pre–October 14)

Loan and investment portfolio

1 Bank runs lead to massive withdrawals of cash from New York banks and trust companies. In total, an estimated $350 million is withdrawn in a two-week period.

Additional cash needed due to bank runs

TRUST COMPANY CAPITAL COMPONENTS

Cash reserves (pre–October 14)

Loan and investment portfolio

Additional cash needed due to bank runs

2 Banks and trusts cut lending to ensure adequate cash on hand to satisfy depositor withdrawals. The pressure is most acute at trust companies due to their substantially lower reserve requirements.

3 Credit contraction creates additional financial distress and amplifies the impact of bank runs. For example, stock market losses intensify fear of bank insolvency, which leads to even more withdrawals.

STATE AND LOCAL GOVERNMENT

KEY EVENTS

Oct. 27, 1907   Mayor of NYC seeks $30 million loan from Morgan to make payroll.

Weakness in securities markets eliminates demand for new securities issues, straining state and local finances.

STATE AND LOCAL BANKS

KEY EVENTS

Nov. 1907   Bank holidays are announced in multiple states such as California, Nevada, Oregon, South Dakota, Indiana, Iowa, and Oklahoma.

Bank runs spread to state and local banks, which also lack required safeguards to prevent failures.

SECURITIES MARKETS

KEY EVENTS

Oct. 24, 1907   Call money rates on NYSE hit 125 percent.

Nov. 2, 1907   Brokerage firm of Moore & Schley requires $30 million in capital to avoid insolvency.

Reduced lending from banks and trusts leads to higher interest rates on call money, collapse of stock prices, and financial distress among brokerage firms.

ECONOMIC ACTIVITY AND EMPLOYMENT

KEY EVENTS

1908   Economy contracts by approximately 12 percent in 1908. Unemployment rises from under 4 percent to a high of 8 percent.

Hoarding of cash leads to severe decline in economic activity, which produces business failures and substantial job losses.

Figure 13.6: The Panic of 1907 First- and Second-Order Effects of Bank Runs[26]

Once bank runs reach a critical mass, they spread like wildfire; and if they are not extinguished quickly, a deep depression is virtually guaranteed to follow. Bank runs accompanied the depressions that began in 1819, 1837, 1857, 1893, and 1929. The link between bank runs and depressions derives from the role that banks play in the transformation of money into credit. Although admittedly simplified, one way to visualize this is to first think of the total net worth of the United States (including checking accounts, savings accounts, real estate, stocks, bonds, etc.). On December 31, 2019, these holdings amounted to roughly $130 trillion. Although this wealth is valued in U.S. dollars, it is not the same as money. On the contrary, as of December 31, 2019, the U.S. monetary base (which includes currency in circulation and Reserve balances) was only roughly $4 trillion.[27] This means that the majority of U.S. wealth was in the form of credit. This is the inevitable and intentional product of a fractional reserve banking system.[28]

Now imagine that every person and institution tried to convert their wealth to cash at the same time. If that were to happen, the total wealth of the nation would no longer be $130 trillion. Instead, with only $4 trillion of actual money, investors would be forced to lower the price at which they are willing to sell assets to attract the limited amount of cash available to buy them. As *deflation* of asset values intensifies, it becomes self-reinforcing. The sale of assets at progressively lower prices increases fear, which encourages more selling at even lower prices. The reason that bank runs are especially dangerous is because when depositors drain enough cash from the banking system, it sparks a chain reaction of forced asset liquidations, which kickstarts a self-reinforcing cycle of asset price deflation. Once the deflationary process bottoms out—and if the nation survives the civil unrest that often accompanies such catastrophes—it takes years to rebuild institutions and public confidence before economic activity and asset values return to previous levels.[29] The bank runs that began in October 1907 started this process, and bankers were rightly fearful of the consequences. To illustrate specifically how bank runs impact an economy, Figure 13.6 shows actual first- and second-order effects associated with the bank runs of October 1907.

THE PLACE TO STOP THE TROUBLE

When the Panic of 1907 began, J. Pierpont Morgan was in Richmond, Virginia, attending an annual conference held by the Episcopal Church. For several days, colleagues urged him to return to New York, but he was concerned that his unplanned departure from the conference would only intensify fear in the market. On Saturday, October 19, Morgan's colleagues convinced him that the severity of the situation left him no choice, and he returned on Sunday morning. Entire books have been written about the events that transpired from the day Morgan returned to New York to the day the panic finally subsided on November 4. Throughout each day and most nights, Morgan hastily assembled meetings involving leaders of New York's largest national banks, trusts, corporations, and civic institutions. Attendees desperately crafted improvised plans to halt the flight of depositors, while simultaneously fighting second-order consequences in securities markets and within state and local governments. On several occasions, large-scale rescues were executed with only minutes to spare. If not for Morgan's extraordinary leadership, it is almost certain that the battle would have been lost.[30]

POINT OF INTEREST

Morgan's Lost Art . . . of False Imprisonment

"But for the powerful influence of Mr. J. P. Morgan it is probable that no united action whatever would have been taken. It is certainly an element of weakness in our central money market that influential credit institutions should have to be dragooned into doing what is after all in their own interest as well as the general advantage."[31]

—O. M. W. Sprague (1910)

The Panic of 1907 did not affect the entire U.S. banking system equally. In fact, the national banks held up reasonably well, and their willingness to extend loans to troubled institutions played a critical role in ending it. Trust companies, on the other hand, were in bad shape. After the Knickerbocker Trust failed on October 22, the Trust Company of America appeared to be the next domino to fall. But unlike the Knickerbocker, the Trust Company of America was sufficiently solvent to be worth saving.

Trust companies were more vulnerable because of the structural weaknesses highlighted on page 151. In addition, trust company executives were unaccustomed to collaborating with competitors during financial crises. Thus, the stronger trust companies were initially resistant to assisting weaker ones despite the danger that they would all suffer the same fate if they failed to collaborate. The resistance of trust company executives peaked on the evening of Saturday, November 2. After Morgan demanded that trust company executives create another $25 million rescue package, he instructed them to remain in the building until they had raised the funds. Morgan then exited the room and locked the doors behind him. The trust company executives eventually relented to Morgan's demands. At four thirty a.m. on Sunday, November 3, they committed the final $25 million, and Morgan released them from captivity.[32]

The scale and speed of the rescues are evident in Figure 13.7 on page 164, which provides an accounting of the major capital injections that occurred between October 22 and November 4. Most of these actions were arranged in a matter of hours, and Morgan was at the center of nearly all of them. When the crisis ended, Morgan had personally facilitated the injection of approximately $200 million of capital to aid a variety of organizations experiencing severe financial distress. To translate this into modern times, measured as a percentage of GDP, Morgan's accomplishment would be roughly equivalent to a private citizen arranging roughly $200 billion in relief packages from competing companies in just two weeks. The rescues proved just enough to prevent financial markets from spiraling into a deep depression.

POINT OF INTEREST

Wall Street Crowns Its Queen

"I saw this situation developing three years ago, and I am on record as predicting it. I said the rich were approaching the brink, and that a 'panic' was inevitable."[33]

—Hetty Green

The most distinguishing feature of a master investor is their ability to sense the movement of monetary currents that shape economic expansions and contractions. In his book *The Ascent of Money*, Niall Ferguson uses a game of Monopoly to explain how fluctuations in the money supply affect asset values. Early in the game, when money is plentiful, players spend liberally to purchase land and construct rental properties. Late in the game, when money is scarce, players are forced to sell properties at distressed prices to pay the rent.[34]

(continued)

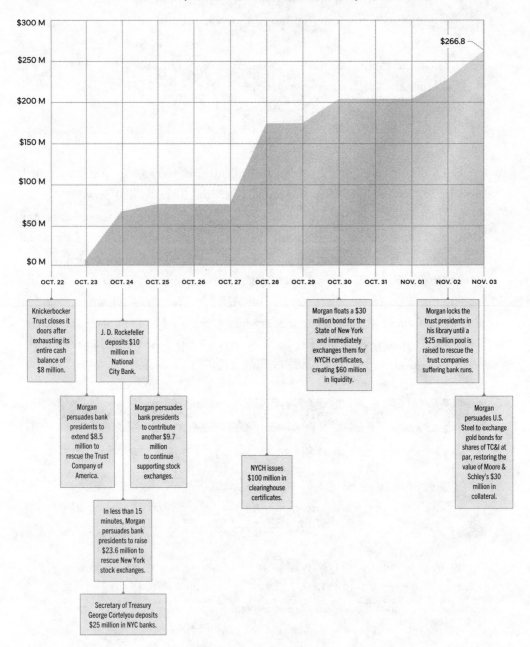

CUMULATIVE CAPITAL RAISES AND CREDIT EXPANSION
(October 22, 1907–November 3, 1907)

$300 M

$250 M — $266.8

$200 M

$150 M

$100 M

$50 M

$0 M

OCT. 22   OCT. 23   OCT. 24   OCT. 25   OCT. 26   OCT. 27   OCT. 28   OCT. 29   OCT. 30   OCT. 31   NOV. 01   NOV. 02   NOV. 03

Knickerbocker Trust closes it doors after exhausting its entire cash balance of $8 million.

J. D. Rockefeller deposits $10 million in National City Bank.

Morgan floats a $30 million bond for the State of New York and immediately exchanges them for NYCH certificates, creating $60 million in liquidity.

Morgan locks the trust presidents in his library until a $25 million pool is raised to rescue the trust companies suffering bank runs.

Morgan persuades bank presidents to extend $8.5 million to rescue the Trust Company of America.

Morgan persuades bank presidents to contribute another $9.7 million to continue supporting stock exchanges.

NYCH issues $100 million in clearinghouse certificates.

Morgan persuades U.S. Steel to exchange gold bonds for shares of TC&I at par, restoring the value of Moore & Schley's $30 million in collateral.

In less than 15 minutes, Morgan persuades bank presidents to raise $23.6 million to rescue New York stock exchanges.

Secretary of Treasury George Cortelyou deposits $25 million in NYC banks.

Figure 13.7: Panic of 1907: Timeline of Key Events[35]

Real-world economies are much more complex than a game of Monopoly, but the fundamental dynamics are surprisingly similar. The rare investor who can anticipate shifts in monetary currents has an extraordinary advantage over those who remain oblivious. By the end of 1906, Hetty Green sensed that the monetary tide was receding, and she began raising cash aggressively to prepare for a crisis. Few others appreciated what was happening. At the same time, Hetty feared that trust companies were especially vulnerable to a panic. When one of her friends asked for her opinion on the financial condition of the Knickerbocker Trust in the spring of 1907, Hetty responded, "If you have any money in that place get it out the first thing tomorrow," and then sarcastically added, "The men in that bank are too good-looking. You mark my words." J. Pierpont Morgan reached the same conclusion six months later, but only after frantically examining the books after a run on the Knickerbocker was well underway.[36]

When the Panic of 1907 began, Hetty Green was one of the only Americans with plentiful cash. Morgan is rightly credited for facilitating a rescue of the financial system by raising more than $200 million in private capital in less than three weeks, but unlike Hetty Green, he was caught by surprise. It was only after intense lobbying by several of his partners that he finally grasped the gravity of the situation on October 19.[37]

Recognizing her acumen as a leading financier, Hetty Green was the only woman invited to attend a critical meeting at the Morgan Library during the height of the panic. If the times were different, perhaps she would have led this meeting.[38]

The Panic of 1907 ended after the acquisition of Tennessee Coal & Iron (TC&I) by U.S. Steel. The TC&I acquisition was designed to halt the collapse of Moore & Schley, a major Wall Street brokerage firm. Moore & Schley's troubles stemmed from $30 million worth of outstanding loans, which were collateralized by shares of TC&I stock. As the price of TC&I shares declined in conjunction with the broader sell-off on Wall Street, creditors became concerned about Moore & Schley's solvency. After examining the books, Morgan's team concluded that shoring up the firm's balance sheet required another $30 million, but New York City banks and trusts no longer had enough lending capacity to provide the capital. It was at this point that Lewis Cass Ledyard, a friend of Morgan, suggested a creative solution. He proposed having U.S. Steel, which had a total of $76 million of free cash on its balance sheet, to acquire TC&I. The acquisition would resolve Moore & Schley's problems by restoring the value of its collateral. The challenge was convincing U.S. Steel's board of directors that the deal also served the interests of shareholders. Several directors were initially opposed, but after two days of intense debate, the board of U.S. Steel approved a roughly $35 million acquisition of TC&I in a non-cash exchange of gold bonds for stock at par value. Having obtained the approval of the board, the last remaining obstacle was to secure the blessing of the president of the United States, as board members feared that antitrust concerns could prevent the deal from closing. On the morning of November 4, several Morgan partners virtually forced their way into the room where President Theodore Roosevelt was eating breakfast and convinced him to voice his approval for the deal. Seeing no other option to end the panic, Roosevelt granted his approval despite his concerns about U.S. Steel's growing market share.[39]

U.S. Steel announced the acquisition of TC&I late in the morning of November 4, and from that point forward, the panic subsided and credit conditions improved. Although the acquisition of TC&I was essential, it left a blemish on Morgan's legacy. Critics accused him of self-dealing because he served as a board member for U.S. Steel and major holder of the company's stock. Despite this criticism, Morgan's reputation was generally enhanced by his leadership during the Panic of 1907. Considering the sheer scale of the rescue efforts, it is hard to imagine that anybody today could accomplish anything close to what Morgan did. In fact, his leadership was so impressive that fear of his mortality was cited by several politicians as a reason to back the Federal Reserve Act of 1913.

POST-PANIC REFORM

The economic damage from the Panic of 1907 was severe but fell far short of a worst-case scenario. Nevertheless, the event was disturbing enough to prompt one of the most important reforms in U.S. financial history. More than all panics that preceded it, the Panic of 1907 revealed the danger of currency inelasticity and the absence of a lender of last resort. The bank runs and ad hoc rescues made these weaknesses glaringly obvious, and the U.S. financial system had grown much too large to continue operating in this manner. Had the Federal Reserve existed in 1907, it could have extended emergency loans using a bank's assets as collateral or simply purchased the assets directly from distressed banks and trusts. Either method would have immediately provided distressed institutions with the cash that they needed to satisfy depositor withdrawals. Taking this one step further, if depositors knew that the Federal Reserve had this capability, there would be no reason to fear that banks and trust companies would run out of money, and it is likely that they never would have lined up at the teller windows in the first place. Without the support of a Federal Reserve–like institution, however, the only option was for bankers to hastily assemble pools of capital using whatever money was available in the system.[40]

Even though most financial leaders and many politicians were well aware of the need for a central bank, political opposition in certain quarters remained strong. At the root of the opposition was fear that a central bank would place too much power in the hands of the federal government and New York's financial elite. This was not the first time that this fear surfaced in the United States. The very same fear drove Thomas Jefferson's vehement opposition to the establishment of Alexander Hamilton's First Bank of the United States in 1791, and it was also behind President Andrew Jackson's decision to veto the renewal of the charter of the Second Bank in 1832. Even after teetering on the brink of financial ruin in 1907, many Americans still believed that the risk of federal overreach outweighed the benefits of reestablishing a central banking system. The Panic of 1907 convinced just enough politicians that the pros outweighed the cons, and politicians began drafting legislation to reintroduce a U.S. central bank for the third and final time.

THE FEDERAL RESERVE ACT OF 1913

POINT OF INTEREST

The Ghosts of Jekyll Island

In November 1910, six men boarded a private rail car at a train station in New Jersey. The men referred to each other only by first name to shield their true identities. The group included renowned Wall Street financiers (Paul Warburg, Henry Davison, and Frank Vanderlip), an assistant secretary of the U.S. Treasury (A. Piatt Andrew Jr.), and a U.S. Senator and his personal secretary (Senator Nelson Aldrich and Arthur Shelton). Their destination was the exclusive Jekyll Island Club located on an island off the coast of Georgia. Upon arriving, the men began hammering out a plan to reestablish a central banking system and stop the recurrent financial panics once and for all.[41]

Fearful of political opposition, the men never confirmed that the meeting even took place until the 1930s—although rumors of the meeting surfaced as

(continued)

early as 1916. Over the course of a week, the "First Name Club" engaged in intense daily sessions from morning to evening to hammer out the details of the plan. By the end of their stay, the fundamental framework of the Federal Reserve Act was on paper, and the men departed as quietly as they had arrived.

Nelson Aldrich delivered the Jekyll Island plan to the National Monetary Commission in 1911, but he did not reveal its source. The plan was later dubbed "The Aldrich Plan," and it became the model for the Federal Reserve Act of 1913. Because the Aldrich Plan was conceived in secret, contentious debate arose over the ensuing decades with respect to who deserved credit for the creation of the Federal Reserve System. Paul Warburg was especially critical of Senator Carter Glass's claim that he had drafted the act. In a book published in the 1930s, Warburg revealed the close similarity between the version produced by the ghosts of Jekyll Island and the final Federal Reserve Act.[42]

The truth of who contributed what to the Federal Reserve Act will never be known with certainty. Regardless of its origins, after its passage, the U.S. financial system would never be the same. Financial executives would no longer be left to their own devices to escape financial panics that inevitably occur in a fractional reserve banking system.

The sheer intensity of political opposition to the concept of a central bank prevented an immediate reintroduction of legislation. Instead, there were several interim steps. The first was the passage of the Aldrich-Vreeland Act, which was signed into law on May 30, 1908. The mechanics were a bit complex, but the act essentially provided the existing national banking system with greater flexibility to expand the money supply in emergency situations by loosening restrictions on the type of securities that were acceptable as collateral for the issuance of banknotes. The act also mandated the creation of the National Monetary Commission, which was a group tasked with evaluating various banking systems used throughout the world and recommending changes to the U.S. financial system. Over the next four years, the findings and recommendations of the National Monetary Commission were revealed in more than fifty reports. The most important report, referred to as the Aldrich Plan, included a reintroduction of a central banking system.[43]

A second mandate of the National Monetary Commission was to investigate the possible existence of a "money trust" in the United States. This reflected a growing fear among politicians that a loosely knit cabal of leading financiers held monopolistic power over both the financial system and corporate America. From May 1912 to February 1913, Congress convened a series of public hearings, known as the Pujo hearings, to determine whether a money trust existed. The hearings did not reveal conclusive evidence either way, but there were more than enough embarrassing testimonies from Wall Street bankers to intensify the public's distrust of Wall Street and increase political opposition to legislation that could potentially increase its power. Many politicians believed that the reestablishment of a central bank would do just that. In fact, opposition to a central bank was so intense that both the Democratic candidate (Woodrow Wilson) and Republican candidate (William Howard Taft) voiced their opposition in the run-up to the election of 1912. After Woodrow Wilson won the presidency in 1912 and Democrats took control of the House and Senate, many feared that the Aldrich Plan was dead.[44]

POINT OF INTEREST

The Atlas of Twentieth-Century America

"The first thing in [credit] is character . . . before money or anything else. Money cannot buy it . . . Because a man I do not trust could not get money from me on all the bonds in Christendom."[45]

—J. Pierpont Morgan

In Greek mythology, the gods of Mount Olympus battled the Titans of Mount Othrys to decide who would rule the universe. The Olympians defeated the Titans and imprisoned many of them in a dungeon known as Tartarus. To deter future rebellions, Zeus reserved the harshest sentence for Atlas, the leader of the Titan rebellion. As punishment for his crime, Atlas was condemned to hold the heavens upon his shoulders for eternity.

One cannot recount the history of the late Gilded Age and early twentieth century without honoring the contributions of J. Pierpont Morgan. Often compared by contemporaries to Atlas, Morgan led the country on its path to economic prosperity and rescued it from several potentially catastrophic financial crises. Although surely motivated by wealth creation, his top priority was living up to his principles of honor and duty to the country. Despite suffering from chronic overwork and ailing health, whenever the financial system neared the brink of collapse, Morgan worked tirelessly to orchestrate a rescue.

(continued)

Morgan also served as the nation's last private lender of last resort. The disappearance of the Second Bank of the United States in the 1830s rendered the country ill-equipped to stop financial crises. When panics struck, Americans depended on hastily assembled private capital pools to prevent downward spirals into depressions. Sometimes these efforts worked and other times they failed. During Morgan's unofficial reign over Wall Street, efforts never fell short. The gold loan in 1895, which restored confidence in the U.S. dollar, was the first such episode, but Morgan's commanding presence during the Panic of 1907 secured his legacy.

Finally, Morgan's greatest contribution to the U.S. was reestablishing moral leadership in corporate boardrooms and securities markets. Prior to his arrival, Gilded Age corruption had taken a toll on the country. The patience of foreign and domestic investors for the schemes orchestrated by men like Jay Gould, Collis Huntington, and Daniel Drew was running thin. In contrast, Morgan never wavered in his commitment to honesty, order, and fair dealing.[46]

J. Pierpont Morgan passed away on March 31, 1913, in Rome, Italy, during his annual vacation in Europe. As if he sensed that the opportunity was approaching to remove the American financial system from atop his shoulders, the Federal Reserve Act of 1913 was signed into law less than one year after his death. America would never again depend so heavily on the leadership of a single individual, as a third and final iteration of a central bank would thereafter serve as the backbone of the U.S. financial system.

Fortunately, President Wilson proved far more pragmatic than his populist colleagues, and after consulting with Congressman Carter Glass and key members of the financial community, he was persuaded that the country desperately needed a central bank. The trick was crafting legislation that was palatable to the opposition. After months of negotiations and compromises, Carter Glass and Robert Owen introduced the Federal Reserve Act of 1913, which gained narrow approval in both the House and Senate. The act included most elements of the Aldrich Plan, with the primary differences being modest adjustments to the structure of the system and some careful word choices. The most notable example of clever semantics was the avoidance of the term "central bank." Instead, the system was described as a public/private entity that mimicked the city reserve bank structures and clearinghouse associations that were already in place under the national banking regime. Another tactic to temper opposition was the creation of regional "Federal Reserve Banks" rather than a single central bank.

This eased fear of federal overreach and provided each reserve bank with flexibility to respond to local market conditions. On December 23, 1913, the Federal Reserve Act was signed into law, and the U.S. prepared to reinstate the financial institution that was deemed so essential by Alexander Hamilton more than one hundred years earlier. But before the system could be implemented, yet another panic would strike U.S. financial markets.

Chapter 14

WAR AND PESTILENCE

"All past experience, it is true, had proved that a foreign war was apt to enrich neutral countries which were large producers of necessaries of life and war supplies . . . But in no previous war had a neutral state been confronted with what appeared to be the financial insolvency of the entire outside world."[1]

—ALEXANDER DANA NOYES, financial editor, *New York Times*

The U.S. narrowly avoided a catastrophic financial crisis in October 1907, but a severe economic contraction was unavoidable. Over the next year, the nation experienced a sharp but relatively short recession. Economic growth resumed by late 1908, and the U.S. began generating substantial trade surpluses once again. Securities markets continued to mature, as the number of listings on securities exchanges multiplied and trading volume increased. Market integrity, on the other hand, improved only modestly. The example set by Charles Dow forced corporations to increase financial transparency, but market manipulation remained largely unchecked. Outside of Wall Street, the broader economy generally improved during the seven-year period following the Panic of 1907, but the U.S. entered a moderate recession in 1913. The stock market ended the year with a decline of nearly 15 percent, and the economy continued contracting modestly in 1914. The primary cause was tight fiscal policy, which was largely a byproduct of the nation's first federal income tax. Despite the setback, sentiment in the U.S. was reasonably optimistic. Few Americans envisioned the series of events that were about to unfold in Europe.

A TRAGIC WRONG TURN IN THE BALKANS

On June 28, 1914, Archduke Franz Ferdinand, heir to the throne of the Austro-Hungarian Empire, arrived in Sarajevo to inspect imperial forces stationed in the city. Sarajevo was the capital of Bosnia-Herzegovina, a province that the Austro-Hungarian Empire had formally annexed in 1908. At the time of the archduke's visit, tensions in the city were high. Serbia opposed annexation, and a large population of ethnic Serbs residing in Bosnia-Herzegovina were sympathetic to this position. Emboldened by Serbia's aggressive territorial expansion following the 1903 coup led by Dragutin Dimitrijević, Serbian nationalists sought to provoke a conflict with Austria-Hungary. After learning of the archduke's planned visit, a terrorist group known as the Black Hand settled on his assassination as a means of accomplishing this objective.[2]

Immediately after arriving in Sarajevo, the archduke and his wife, Sophie, traveled by motorcade to the Sarajevo Town Hall for a brief reception. Along the route, five members of the Black Hand prepared to ambush the motorcade using crudely constructed bombs. The first two assassins lost their nerve and stood idly as the motorcade passed, but the third assassin, Nedeljko Čabrinović, tossed his bomb toward the archduke's vehicle. Čabrinović's aim was slightly off, and the bomb bounced off the hood and exploded beneath the next car in the motorcade. The archduke's driver and remaining members of the motorcade sped away and arrived at the town hall within a few minutes. Barely containing his anger, the archduke delivered a brief speech before discovering that several members of the motorcade suffered injuries in the attack. Further outraged, he demanded to visit the wounded at the hospital. Meanwhile, several members of the Black Hand repositioned themselves on the streets, hoping for another opportunity to attack the motorcade. Armed with only a pistol, a nineteen-year-old co-conspirator named Gavrilo Princip awaited on a side street near the Latin Bridge.[3]

Despite misgivings among members of the archduke's security team, the motorcade departed from the town hall less than one hour after the initial attempt on the archduke's life. To reduce the motorcade's vulnerability to a second attack, the security team planned to travel to the hospital along the Appel Quay, which ran along the river on the outskirts of the city. Although less direct, the route circumvented the crowded city center. In the rush to depart, the head of security neglected to notify the lead driver of the new plan, and he mistakenly led the motorcade on a direct route to the hospital by turning right onto a side street near the Latin Bridge. After being alerted to his error, the driver stopped the motorcade and began to reverse course. In a horrible stroke of misfortune, the archduke's vehicle stalled within feet of Gavrilo Princip's improvised position. Seizing the opportunity, Princip fired his pistol into the vehicle, striking both the archduke and the duchess. The motorcade raced to the hospital, but the Archduke Ferdinand and Duchess Sophie were both pronounced dead soon after their arrival.[4]

EVERYBODY BLUFFS AND NOBODY FOLDS

"If there is to-day high probability of a war involving the great Powers of Europe, we are not left in ignorance of the chief cause. No vital interest of Germany, Russia, France, England, or Italy is directly threatened. Yet they are all on the verge of war. Why? Not because they approve or disapprove of Austria's high-handed attack on Servia [sic].[5] It might indeed be a localized war but for one thing. This is the Alliances, offensive and defensive, into which the leading European Powers are grouped. These treaties have been held up to us for years as the brilliant conception of statesmen to safeguard peace. But at this moment they reveal themselves as the fatal cause of war."[6]

—*THE COMMERCIAL & FINANCIAL CHRONICLE* (August 1, 1914)

Few imagined that the death of the archduke and duchess of Austria-Hungary would set in motion a series of events that would plunge the entire European continent into one of the most destructive wars in human history. Numerous books and research papers have examined the rationale underlying the tragic decisions made by European leaders. It is beyond the scope of this book to examine these in detail, but suffice it to say that the root of these miscalculations was the existence of inflexible defense pacts that forced countries to mobilize their military forces (in some cases preemptively) to support their allies despite having little incentive to engage in combat. Time pressure also impaired decisions. The clock began ticking when Austria-Hungary demanded a long list of concessions from Serbia as punishment for the archduke's assassination. The Austro-Hungarians granted Serbia only forty-eight hours to comply. Surprisingly, Serbia agreed to most of the demands, but Austria-Hungary accepted nothing less than full compliance, and they responded by declaring war on Serbia on July 28, 1914.

The irony of World War I is that the alliances that drove the great European powers to war were designed specifically to *prevent* it. In fact, Europeans downplayed the risk of escalation specifically because their defense pacts had worked as intended for several decades prior to World War I. Unfortunately, the strategy failed in the summer of 1914, and the major powers of Europe found themselves careening toward an unwanted war to honor their alliances. By the first week of August 1914, all the major powers of Europe had issued declarations of war. On one side were the Allied Powers of France, Russia, and Great Britain, and on the opposing side were the Central Powers of Germany, Austria-Hungary, and a reluctant Italy. Few politicians realized that a war of this scale was possible, and even fewer imagined the magnitude of human suffering and economic devastation that would accompany it. Instead, as is often the case, the public greeted the initial war declarations with ad hoc celebrations to display national pride, giving little thought to the potential carnage that was to come. British Secretary of State for Foreign Affairs Sir Edward Grey was among the few who foresaw the potential devastation, which he memorialized with the following statement made in July 1914.[7]

> The possible consequences of the present situation were terrible. If as many as four great Powers of Europe—let us say Austria, France, Russia and Germany—were engaged in war, it seemed to me that it must involve the expenditure of so vast a sum of money and such an interference with trade, that a war would be accompanied or followed by a complete collapse of European credit and industry. In these days, in great industrial states, this would mean a state of things worse than that of 1848, and, irrespective of who were victors in the war, many things would be completely swept away.[8]

The escalation of European hostilities played out like a dystopian poker game. Multiple players holding weak hands wagered their nations' health, welfare, and economic future on the false hope that their adversaries would cave to their bluffs. Instead, each bluff was called, and the players reluctantly played the game out to its horrific conclusion. Meanwhile, sitting on the opposite side of the Atlantic, the only remaining Western power remained ignorant to the strength of its own hand—or even that it was dealt into the game. Soon after the war began, the U.S. adopted a shrewd policy of neutrality, which allowed Americans to inadvertently benefit from Europe's unforced error.

AN UNEXPECTED PANIC

"While the standing armies of Europe were a constant reminder of possible war, and the frequent diplomatic tension between the Great Powers cast repeated war shadows over the financial markets, the American public, at least, was entirely unprepared for a world conflagration."[9]

—HENRY GEORGE STEBBINS NOBLE,
president of the New York Stock Exchange (1915)

The commencement of World War I initially caught the U.S. off guard, as most Americans were too preoccupied with domestic affairs to pay much attention to European geopolitics. Even those who were concerned with escalating tensions believed that cooler heads would prevail. Most Americans could not fathom that the European powers would willingly enter a war with such devastating consequences. It was not until Austria-Hungary officially declared war on Serbia on July 28, 1914, that signs of panic appeared in U.S. financial markets.

In the immediate aftermath of the war declarations, the primary concern in the U.S. was the flight of foreign capital, as many Americans feared that European investors would liquidate their investments and ship the proceeds (largely in the form of gold) across the Atlantic to fund war expenses. The potential consequences were dire, as foreign investors held $7 billion worth of U.S. securities. This fear seemed to be validated during the three-day period beginning on July 27, 1914, as $28.6 million worth of gold was withdrawn from the United States. This was a small fraction of the nearly $1 billion of gold reserves, but bankers knew that a trickle of outflows could quickly accelerate into a flood. After all, this was precisely what had happened during the bank runs in October 1907. The second concern centered on how the war would affect trade with Europe. If trade collapsed, the U.S. economy could spiral into a deep depression.[10]

POINT OF INTEREST

Echoes of July 1914: The COVID-19 Crisis

On March 11, 2020, the World Health Organization (WHO) officially declared the onset of the COVID-19 pandemic. The number of reported cases had increased exponentially over the prior several months, and the world was completely unprepared for the consequences.

The Federal Reserve and the U.S. federal government responded immediately and aggressively to prevent a rapid descent of the economy into a depression. The international community responded in a similar fashion. Unlike 1914, the U.S. was well-trained to deal with the financial effects of a "sudden stop" economic crisis, but that does not mean that collateral damage was completely avoided.

In the spring of 2021, Americans began to spend the large portion of the fiscal stimulus that had remained in savings during the long period of quarantine. The result was a burst of inflation that persisted despite the Fed's initial assessment that it would be "transitory." As of the publication of this book, the Federal Reserve continued to fight inflationary pressures.

AMERICA FLEXES ITS CURRENCY

The timing of World War I was somewhat fortuitous in the sense that memories of the Panic of 1907 were relatively fresh. These memories preconditioned government and Wall Street leaders to respond aggressively to the first signs of panic. They did not have to wait long—a full-blown panic erupted on Wall Street on July 30, 1914. The Dow Jones Industrial Average declined by several percentage points on a huge spike in volume to nearly 1.3 million shares. Concerned that July 31 would be a bloodbath, prominent bankers, leaders of the New York Stock Exchange, and government leaders convened to discuss the potential closure of the Exchange. Initially, the decision was unanimous to remain open, as a market closure would reverse the precedent established by J. Pierpont Morgan during the Panic of 1907. However, by the morning of July 31, it was clear that closure was the only option. All major foreign exchanges had shuttered their doors, leaving U.S. exchanges as the only remaining source of liquidity for the entire world. In the hours prior to the scheduled opening, traders received a flood of sale orders and virtually no offsetting buy orders. Just minutes before trading was set to begin, the New York Stock Exchange announced it would close its doors indefinitely. It did not fully reopen until December 15, 1914, making it the longest closure by far in its 230-year history.[11]

POINT OF INTEREST

The Eternal Folly of the Spotless Mind

"For practical purposes, the financial memory should be assumed to last, at a maximum, no more than twenty years. This is normally the time it takes for the recollection of one disaster to be erased and for some variant on previous dementia to come forward to capture the financial mind."[12]

—John Kenneth Galbraith

A thorough review of 230 years of U.S. financial history reveals many patterns that are imperceptible over the course of a single person's lifetime. One such pattern is the slow, steady, and predictable erosion of society's collective memory

(continued)

of past financial traumas. Had people recalled these traumas, they would have avoided making the same catastrophic errors. John Kenneth Galbraith's twenty-year rule is by no means precise, but it provides a reasonable estimate of the amount of time that typically transpires before the memory of a prior financial trauma loses its potency.

Americans' reaction to the COVID-19 pandemic in the early 2020s is an excellent example of this phenomenon. Preconditioned by the memory of the Global Financial Crisis that occurred a decade earlier, the nation's leaders enacted massive monetary and fiscal stimulus programs in a matter of weeks and with little objection from the public. This was a remarkable accomplishment given the amount of political divisiveness at the time. On the other hand, the collective memory of the dot-com bubble had just breached the twenty-year mark. As a result, Americans once again engaged in unconstrained speculation in the newest tech stocks and financial innovations, such as cryptocurrencies and non-fungible tokens (NFTs).

Because financial memories tend to quickly fade, when venturing a guess as to how society will react to a financial crisis, it can be helpful to take inventory of the collective memory from which the reaction will likely draw. The more familiar a crisis is in the context of the recent past, the more predictable the response.

The closure of the New York Stock Exchange prevented a catastrophic crash, but the banking system remained in a precarious position. The Federal Reserve Act had passed in December 1913, but the system would not be operational until November 1914. Fortunately, the U.S. had a backup. The Aldrich-Vreeland Act of 1908 remained on the books, and it provided a powerful mechanism to support the banking system in a crisis. The act allowed the Treasury to expand the type of securities that national banks could use as collateral to issue banknotes. Under normal circumstances, only bonds of the federal government were eligible for rediscounting.[13] The Aldrich-Vreeland Act expanded eligibility to include securities, such as municipal bonds and various forms of commercial paper. Secretary of the Treasury William McAdoo invoked the Aldrich-Vreeland Act on July 31, 1914, and publicly announced that the Treasury was prepared to authorize the issuance of $500 million in "emergency currency" to counterbalance potential liquidity pressure on the banking system. Over the next several months, banks tapped this liquidity, and currency issued under the Aldrich-Vreeland Act peaked at $364 million in November 1914 (Figure 14.1).[14]

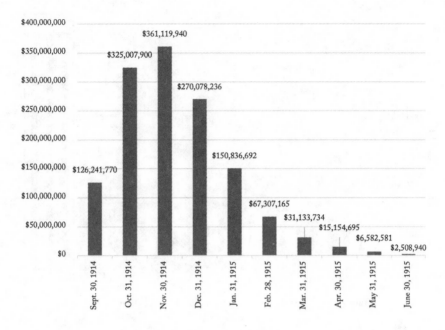

Figure 14.1: Emergency Currency Issued Under
the Aldrich-Vreeland Act (September 1914–June 1915)[15]

Decisive action by public and private sector leadership stopped the financial panic of 1914 before it spiraled out of control. The closure of the New York Stock Exchange stopped the decline of stock prices and flight of gold from the U.S., while the use of emergency currency authorized under the Aldrich-Vreeland Act prevented a run on the banking system. But after the panic on Wall Street was contained, Americans remained terrified that global trade would collapse and trigger a depression.

THE SPOILS OF NEUTRALITY

The fear that World War I would negatively impact the U.S. economy proved to be unfounded. Instead, after adopting a policy of neutrality, the U.S. experienced its largest increase of exports in its history. As one of the few developed nations that remained safely removed from European battlefields, demand for American exports skyrocketed. During the two decades preceding the war, U.S. trade surpluses averaged approximately $450 million per year. By 1916, demand for U.S. exports drove the trade surplus to more than $3 billion per year. Figure 14.2 shows the spike in the U.S. trade surplus beginning in 1915.

Satisfying the surge of demand from European countries was not easy. As demand outstripped supply, inflationary pressures built up, and before long the government

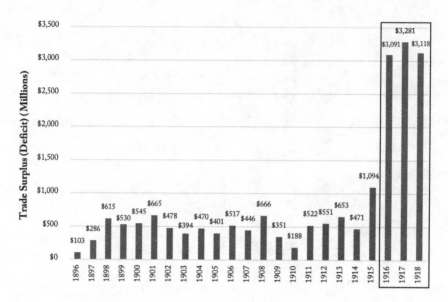

Figure 14.2: U.S. Trade Surpluses by Year (Millions) (1896-1918)[16]

was forced to recruit many of the nation's corporate leaders to bring order to chaotic supply chains. The financial sector was an especially attractive recruiting ground because the closure of the New York Stock Exchange had left many financial executives with plenty of spare time. The House of Morgan played an especially important role by working with the Wilson administration to set up what became known as the Export Department. Conceived by Morgan partner Harry Davison, the House of Morgan functioned as a centralized purchasing agency on behalf of the British government. Centralization helped to moderate inflationary pressures at least to a degree, while also bolstering output by streamlining the purchasing and production process. Under the leadership of Edward Stettinius, the Export Department facilitated the sale of more than $3 billion in war supplies to the Allied powers over the course of the war. Stettinius proved so effective that U.S. intelligence feared that the Central powers were plotting his assassination. To ensure his protection, Stettinius and his family resided on a navy ship anchored in the New York harbor for the entirety of the war.[17]

At the outset of World War I, it appeared that the U.S. would remain committed to its policy of neutrality, but American sympathies soon drifted toward the Allies. This shift began a few months after the start of the war when corporate leaders convinced the Wilson administration to allow "back door" lending to the Allied powers. Under the arrangement, Wilson allowed companies to extend trade credit for the purchase of goods even though direct lending to belligerents was prohibited. The value of trade credit balances increased over time and were heavily skewed toward the Allied powers in large part due to the effectiveness of the British Navy's blockade of the European continent. Even if Americans desired equal trade among the Allied and Central powers, they were unable to penetrate the blockade. As the war dragged on, the Allied powers were much more heavily indebted to the U.S. than were the Central powers. All else being equal, this increased American sympathy for the Allies, as a victory by the Central powers could compromise the Allies' ability to make good on their trade credits. A shared cultural heritage also shaped American sympathy for the Allies. There were pockets of support for the Central powers among immigrants from continental Europe (especially in the Midwest), but most Americans related more to the Allied cause. This position intensified dramatically when Germany made a fateful gamble in the winter of 1917.[18]

THE KAISER'S GAMBIT

By 1917, German military leaders feared that their opportunity for victory was slipping away. The British naval blockade had taken a toll on the morale of the military and German citizenry. Military leaders were especially frustrated that the U.S. had neutralized Germany's U-boat operations, which would have otherwise provided Germany with a formidable advantage at sea. The limits on U-boat attacks began when President Wilson issued a stern warning to the Germans after U-boats sunk the RMS *Lusitania* on May 7, 1915, and the SS *Arabic* on August 15, 1915, killing a total of 130 Americans. The Germans responded by changing their rules of engagement so that, prior to firing torpedoes on ships with Americans onboard, U-boats were required to issue a warning and allow passengers and crew to abandon ship. For seventeen months, Germany operated under these "prize rules." Then, on December 16, 1916, Admiral Henning von Holtzendorff drafted a memorandum recommending that Germany resume unrestricted submarine warfare. The thesis was that German U-boats would be so disruptive to British supply lines that it would force the British to surrender within six months.[19] Holtzendorff acknowledged that his strategy was risky and would likely prompt the U.S. to join the war on the side of the Allies, but he argued that the British would surrender before the U.S. could effectively mobilize. Kaiser Wilhelm II accepted the proposal despite the risks, and Germany resumed unrestricted submarine warfare on February 1, 1917.[20]

The subsequent German U-boat offensive ravaged British supply lines.[21] Figure 14.3 shows the sharp increase in shipping losses after the resumption of unrestricted submarine warfare. Within five months, German U-boats sunk nearly 40 percent more ships than they had in all of 1916. Only after the British adopted the convoy system in the summer of 1917 were they able to reduce the destruction to a survivable level.[22]

Americans were outraged by the U-boat offensive, as many American ships and

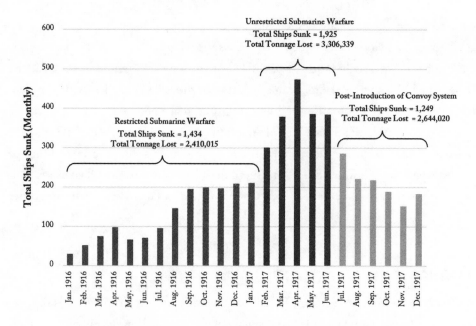

Figure 14.3: Shipping Losses in the Vicinity of British Territory (1916–1917)[23]

crew were among the casualties. Yet these acts of aggression alone did not convince President Wilson to join the war. It took a more brazen act of aggression to convince Wilson that neutrality was no longer an option. In March 1917, British intelligence intercepted a communication indicating that Germany was seeking an alliance with Mexico to take up arms against the United States. Germany planned to offer Mexico assistance in regaining lost territory in Texas, Arizona, and New Mexico if the U.S. entered the war on the side of the Allied powers.[24] Outraged by the audacity of the plot, political and public support shifted decisively in favor of war.[25] On April 2, 1917, President Wilson delivered a speech asking Congress to pass a war resolution. Two days later, the resolution passed, and on April 6, the U.S. declared war on Germany.

The subsequent speed and scale of America's mobilization exceeded Germany's projections. The nation rapidly transformed from a seemingly docile state of neutrality to a single-minded state of total war against the German nation. Prominent leaders of American corporations and financial institutions were recruited to lead critical war departments. The secretary of the Treasury, William McAdoo, spearheaded aggressive drives to sell war bonds to Americans to fund war expenses. A military draft was enacted, and several million Americans joined the armed forces and support services. From across the Atlantic, Germans shuddered at the speed, scale, and intensity of the American war effort. They had underestimated the American will and strength of its war machine, which was aided by the nation's formidable mass production capabilities.

The entry of the U.S. into World War I provided the Allies with the edge they needed to defeat the Central powers. Not only were the additional weapons and troops critical, but the psychological impact was also important. Having endured horrific trench warfare for three years, the arrival of fresh U.S. troops provided much-needed relief to Allied troops and also demoralized the German troops. In the summer of 1918, the Allies launched what became known as the Hundred Days Offensive, which delivered a decisive blow to the German army. Simultaneously losing ground on the battlefields and dealing with uprisings on the home front, the Germans surrendered on November 11, 1918.

POINT OF INTEREST

The World's Deadliest Assassin Awakens in Haskell County

Demonstration at the Red Cross Emergency Ambulance Station in Washington, D.C., during the Influenza Pandemic of 1918

On March 4, 1918, Private Albert Gitchell reported to the infirmary at Fort Riley, a major military training facility located outside of Topeka, Kansas. Gitchell suffered from a sore throat, headache, and fever. The illness resembled a cold or flu but with much more severe symptoms. Within a few days, nearly one hundred more soldiers reported to the infirmary with similar complaints. Unbeknownst to medical personnel at the time, Fort Riley was ground zero for a novel H1N1 variant of the influenza virus. Soon after the first reports at Fort Riley, military bases

(continued)

throughout the country reported similar outbreaks, and within a matter of weeks, the Great Influenza pandemic began ravaging the planet.[26]

Conditions in 1918 could not have been worse for the emergence of a pandemic. For starters, the H1N1 variant was highly contagious and deadly—but not quite deadly enough to kill too many hosts before spreading. Second, the U.S. was training several million troops in preparation for the war in Europe. Military barracks were packed with recruits, creating ideal breeding grounds for the virus. Third, the new H1N1 variant happened to be deadliest for victims aged fifteen to thirty-four—almost precisely the demographic of most inhabitants of military encampments.[27] Fourth, upon completing their training, troops were quickly transported overseas where they immediately sheltered with Allied troops in close quarters. Finally, in perhaps the worst twist, members of the media in most major countries were forbidden from even acknowledging the existence of the virus, much less the severity of the danger. This is because the pandemic coincided with one of the most draconian censorship operations in world history. One week after declaring war on Germany, the Wilson administration formed the Committee on Public Information (CPI) under the direction of George Creel. The CPI forbade the media from writing about anything that could jeopardize the war effort by weakening public morale. This included the spread of a deadly new strain of influenza. In fairness, the U.S. was not the only country suppressing information about the pandemic. In fact, because Spain was one of the few countries that lacked censorship policies, people erroneously concluded that the virus originated there. This is why the Great Influenza is often referred to as the "Spanish Flu."[28]

The Great Influenza ranks among the top two deadliest global events since the founding of the United States—second only to World War II. During the four years of trench warfare on the European continent, an estimated twenty million people lost their lives. In just nine months, the Great Influenza claimed at least fifty million more—with some estimates running as high as one hundred million. There is also evidence that the pandemic may have impacted the outcome of World War I. The second wave of the pandemic, which was by far the deadliest, coincided with the Meuse-Argonne offensive in the fall of 1918. Already suffering from dwindling supplies and hunger, the misery of influenza crushed German morale. In his best-selling book *The Great Influenza*, John Barry cited a statement by General Erich Ludendorff, who identified influenza as a contributing factor in the failure of Germany's final offensive:

Ludendorff himself blamed influenza for the loss of initiative and the ultimate failure of the offensive: 'It was a grievous business having to listen every morning to the chiefs of staffs' recital of the number of influenza cases, and their complaints about the weakness of their troops.' Influenza may have crippled his attack, stripped his forces of fighting men.[29]

It is conceivable that the Great Influenza expedited the surrender of the German army in World War I. In addition, it is undoubtedly true that the pandemic significantly impacted the postwar economy in the United States. Although disentangling the effects of World War I from those of the pandemic is difficult, the 1920s likely would have turned out quite differently had the pandemic never occurred.

THE FINANCIAL EFFECTS OF WORLD WAR I

It is common knowledge that World War I permanently reshaped the economies of Europe, but the way in which it changed the U.S. economy is often less appreciated. Prior to the war, the U.S. had largely shed its 140-year status as a net debtor to the world, but few people expected that, by 1919, it would become the world's largest creditor. After the signing of the Treaty of Versailles, New York City had, at a minimum, matched London as a global financial center, and the U.S. dollar was threatening to replace the pound sterling as the world's dominant reserve currency. The effects of World War I were not limited to its new role in the international community. It also prompted important changes within the nation's borders. Two of the more notable changes were the expansion of the "investor class" and the accumulation of massive gold reserves.[30]

Expansion of the Investor Class

"Just consider the 3,000,000 who bought the last issue of Liberty bonds. It shows we must devote more and more of our time to the small investor. That is going to come to this country. It has been a long time coming, but I venture to predict that we will sell government bonds before the war is over to 8,000,000 to 20,000,000 people."[31]

—CHARLES E. MERRILL, founder of Merrill Lynch

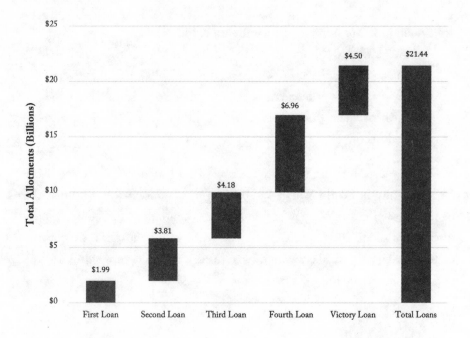

Figure 14.4: Final Allotments of Liberty and Victory Bonds (1917–1919)[32]

After declaring war on Germany, the U.S. was forced to raise substantial amounts of capital to fund the manufacture of armaments and compensate a military force that peaked at nearly four million Americans. Thanks to the precedent set by Alexander Hamilton, the credit of the U.S. was impeccable. Unlike prior wars, however, few foreign investors were capable of providing capital, as most were already deeply indebted to the United States. The only viable source was the nation's own citizens. This forced the federal government to rely heavily on the domestic issuance of bonds (referred to as Liberty and Victory bonds). Under the leadership of Treasury Secretary William McAdoo, Liberty bond drives spanned the nation throughout 1917 and 1918. The effort combined an interesting mix of patriotic appeal and public shaming for nonparticipation. The bond drives raised a total of $21.4 billion, which provided most of the required funding for the war. Figure 14.4 tracks the amount of capital raised during each Liberty and Victory bond issue, as well as the cumulative amount raised as of April 1919.[33]

After the war ended, the war bond drives had a lasting impact on U.S. securities markets. This was largely attributable to the sheer number of Americans who purchased the bonds. According to a survey of thirteen thousand urban wage workers in 1918 and 1919, nearly 68 percent of respondents owned Liberty bonds. Most of these individuals had no prior experience owning a piece of paper that produced a steady stream of income. After making the initial leap into government bonds, many members of this new class of investors were open to exploring other types of securities, such as corporate stocks and bonds. The bond drives had dramatically expanded the "investor class" in the United States. By the mid-1920s, these investors were engaging in increasingly risky forms of speculation, adding momentum to a bubble that would begin forming in the mid-1920s.[34]

The Dark Side of Gold

When World War I began, Americans initially feared that Europeans would withdraw gold from the country. Instead, it flowed in the opposite direction. This was a natural byproduct of large U.S. trade surpluses with European countries, as foreigners bought U.S. exports in far greater quantities than America imported European goods. Gold inflows were generally desirable, but too much of a good thing can sometimes be bad. One unwanted side effect was inflation. The reason is that each ounce of gold that was added to U.S. bank reserves increased lending capacity several-fold. But this was not the only inflation driver. Others included the Federal Reserve's monetization of debt; wage inflation driven by extremely low unemployment, which bottomed at 1.4 percent; and a general scarcity of products and raw materials as businesses adjusted their supply chains. During World War I the U.S. experienced sustained, double-digit inflation for the first time since the Civil War. This was a new experience for many Americans. Figure 14.5 shows the annual rate of inflation for the fifty-year period ending December 31, 1920, and Figure 14.6 shows the accumulation of gold in the U.S. banking system.[35]

After World War I ended, the accumulation of gold in the U.S. created a much bigger problem in Europe. The gold standard limited the ability of European central banks to adjust their monetary policies in response to changing economic conditions. The reason is because outflows of gold would force central banks to reduce the money supply to ensure that they retained adequate reserves to redeem their currency in gold at a fixed rate. But retaining gold required raising interest rates, which threatened to derail reconstruction efforts. By the mid-1920s, this placed the Federal Reserve in a difficult position. On one hand, the Federal Reserve leadership sought to support U.S. efforts to assist European countries with reconstruction by keeping U.S. interest rates low and preventing further gold flows from Europe into the United States. The problem, however, is that this policy forced the Fed to keep rates too low for too long. By the mid-1920s access to inexpensive capital in the U.S. began fueling speculation throughout the country.

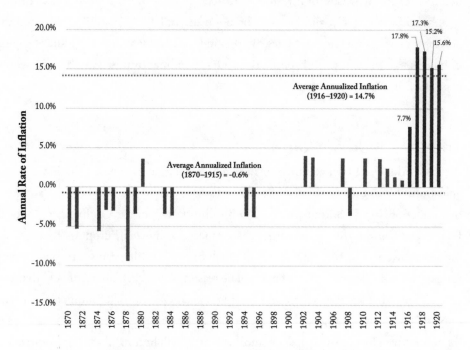

Figure 14.5: U.S. Annual Rate of Inflation (1870–1920)[36]

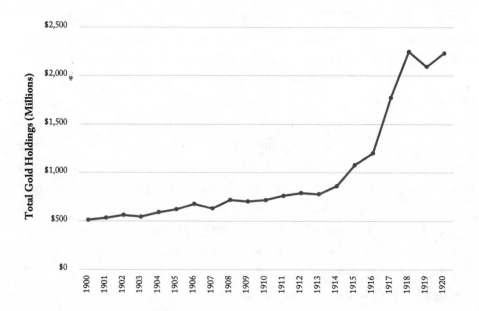

Figure 14.6: Total Gold in U.S. Treasury, National Banks, and Federal Reserve Banks (1900–1920)[37]

THE FEDERAL RESERVE STRUGGLES TO GAIN A FOOTHOLD

After the announcement of the Armistice on November 11, 1918, most Americans feared that a deep depression was imminent. This fear was understandable, given that the U.S. experienced a sharp decline in exports and government spending immediately after the ceasefire. During the first few months in 1919, the country appeared to be entering a recession.

The post-war recession was short-lived, however, and the economy began accelerating in March 1919. A sharp rise in consumer spending was at the root of the recovery. Having survived a horrific war and pandemic, Americans were excited to spend on luxuries that were previously discouraged or forbidden. Cheap credit also played a role, as the Federal Reserve maintained a highly accommodative monetary policy for too long.[38] In addition to concerns regarding European reconstruction, the Fed was hesitant to raise rates for several reasons. First, the U.S. Treasury was concerned about servicing a floating rate portion of the war debt issued over the prior two years, and higher rates would have increased the cost. Second, both the Treasury and Federal Reserve were concerned about the impact of higher rates on the health of the banking system, as many banks had loaded their balance sheets with Liberty and Victory bonds to fulfill their patriotic duty. Therefore, despite growing concern about inflation and speculation, the Federal Reserve was reluctant to raise rediscount rates.[39]

POINT OF INTEREST

A One-Hundred-Year Event: The Inflation of 1919 and COVID-19

The post–World War I/Great Influenza inflation that lasted from 1919 to 1920 had much in common with the post–COVID-19 inflation that began in March 2021. In addition, both events prompted the Federal Reserve to raise interest rates more aggressively than investors initially anticipated.

The post–World War I/Great Influenza inflation officially began in March 1919 and lasted for approximately two years. The key drivers were (1) massive fiscal stimulus in the form of increased war-related spending, (2) highly accommodative monetary policy to support the financial system, (3) spending of excess savings following the end of the Great Influenza and World War I, and (4) supply chain shocks resulting from the rapid conversion of a wartime economy back to a peacetime economy.

(continued)

The factors driving the post–COVID-19 inflation included (1) massive fiscal stimulus to prevent a sharp economic contraction and rise in unemployment, (2) monetary stimulus in the form of asset purchases by the Federal Reserve, (3) large accumulations of excess savings and subsequent release of the savings after COVID-19 subsided, and (4) severe supply chain disruptions as the world shifted from a pandemic-oriented economy back to normalcy.

Many investors, economists, government policymakers, and even the leadership of the Federal Reserve were caught off guard by the intensity and persistence of inflation after the worst economic effects of COVID-19 subsided in the spring of 2021. Yet the event was nearly identical to the one the nation experienced nearly one hundred years earlier. The lessons from the post–World War I/Great Influenza inflation provide yet another example of how revisiting the experiences of our predecessors allows one to envision future events with greater clarity.

In this respect, the recovery in 1919 resembled the recovery that the U.S. experienced during the second half of 2021 after the COVID-19 pandemic subsided. An important difference, however, was that the consumer spending binge did not last as long in 1919 as it did in the 2020s. The brief recovery in 1919 was followed by a short but severe decline in economic activity that began in January 1921. The most significant catalyst was aggressive (albeit delayed) tightening of monetary policy by the Federal Reserve.[40] In contrast to the standards employed today, the Federal Reserve banks offered little warning. Faced with inflation approaching 20 percent and gold reserves falling close to statutory minimums, the Federal Reserve raised rediscount rates from 4.75 percent to 6 percent in January 1920, and then followed with a second increase to 7 percent in June 1920.[41] The Federal Reserve was caught off guard by the suddenness and severity of the reversal of prices. By June 1921, wholesale prices collapsed by a jaw-dropping 56 percent.[42] This caused substantial collateral damage, including the collapse of stock prices (Figure 14.7).[43]

The Federal Reserve quickly reversed its monetary policies as the economy declined. In May 1921, the Federal Reserve Bank of New York took the lead by cutting its rediscount rate to 6.50 percent. By December 1921, a series of additional cuts reduced the rediscount rate to 4.50 percent. In early 1922, the economy regained its footing, and the short but severe depression of 1920–1921 came to an end. The remainder of the decade, which is now referred to as the Roaring Twenties, was a period of extraordinary prosperity, but it concluded with one of the most intense periods of speculation in U.S. history.[44]

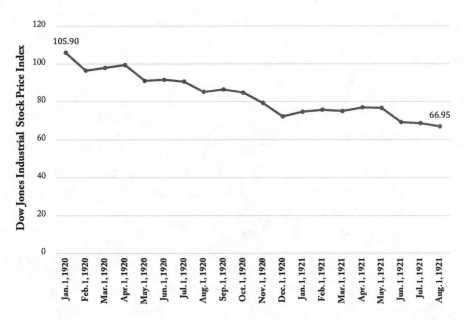

Figure 14.7: Dow-Jones Industrial Stock Price Index (January 1, 1920–August 1, 1921)[45]

Chapter 15

A HOLLOW ROAR
ON WALL STREET

*"This is truly a new era in which formerly well–established standards
of value for securities no longer retain their old significance . . . The type
of support by investors creates almost ideal opportunities for speculators,
and so the new conditions have destroyed the old standards."*[1]

—COLONEL LEONARD P. AYRES,
vice president of Cleveland Trust Company (August 16, 1929)

Americans entered the 1920s in an unsettled state. As if it were not enough to
have suffered through a war and pandemic that claimed the lives of at least
seventy million people worldwide, they also suffered a depression from 1920 to 1921.
As the economy recovered in 1922, Americans slowly regained their optimism. The
subsequent economic expansion lasted for the remainder of the decade and was inter-
rupted only by a couple of mild recessions.

The "Roaring Twenties" is often categorized as a decade of excess, but this applied
primarily to the final few years. There is debate as to the precise moment when the bull
market began, but most historians converge around 1924. This is when a new class
of investors took interest in the stock market, and Wall Street created several financial
innovations to cater to them. But increased stock market participation was not the
only story. Many forces combined to transform enthusiasm that was initially justified
into mass delusion. The inevitable crash and depression that followed were the worst
in all of U.S. history.

BUY IT FORWARD

Americans today routinely purchase goods and services on installment plans or with other forms of credit, such as a credit card. Buying on credit occurred as early as the mid-1800s, but it was generally frowned upon as it was viewed as an act of desperation. This perception changed at the turn of the twentieth century. It was likely prompted by the introduction of several new consumer products, such as the automobile, radio, and multiple household appliances. These products offered enormous productivity and lifestyle benefits, but the high price points made cash purchases unrealistic for most Americans. Convinced that such items were necessities—which was a perception that was amplified by messaging crafted by a rapidly expanding advertising industry—Americans no longer feared the stigma formerly associated with credit-based purchases. During the decade preceding World War I, credit-based purchases became more common. Frugality briefly returned during the war years, but after it ended, the consumer spending binge resumed. Immediately after the war, General Motors added momentum to the trend when the company launched the first credit-based purchase program for new automobiles. Competing automobile companies quickly adopted similar tactics, and before long companies offered credit-based purchases for a wide variety of consumer products, such as radios, washing machines, vacuum cleaners, furniture, and other household appliances. Figure 15.1 illustrates the proliferation of consumer credit by showing sales of radios, which were typically purchased with a relatively modest down payment of 25 percent.[2]

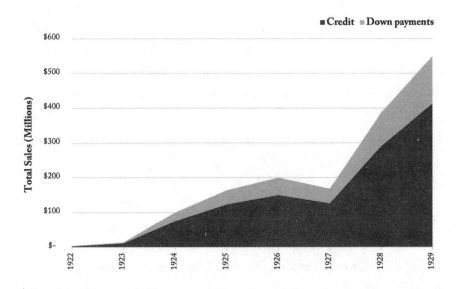

Figure 15.1: Total Radio Sales in the United States (1922-1929)[3]

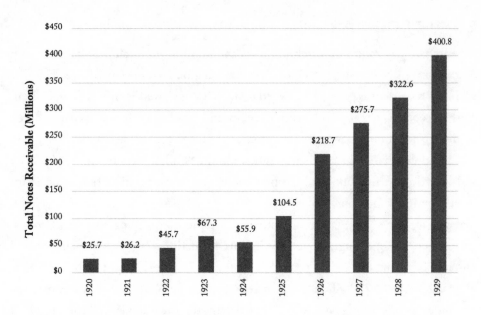

Figure 15.2: General Motors Corporation Acceptance of Total Notes Receivable (Millions) (1920-1929)[4]

Liberal use of credit allowed Americans to improve their living standards, but it also created risks. The biggest one was that it pulled demand forward from future years, creating distorted perceptions of future economic growth. Companies reported record revenue and profits, but much of it came from purchases that would have occurred in future years if not for the use of consumer credit. Investors mistakenly concluded that future sales growth would build on an artificially inflated baseline. The second problem was the steady deterioration of credit standards. As memories of the depression of 1920–1921 faded, lenders grew confident that the good times would continue indefinitely, and they applied less scrutiny to borrowers. Many companies systematically underestimated the probability of consumer defaults. One example of just how exposed companies were to consumer credit is visible in Figure 15.2, which shows a more than fifteen-fold increase in consumer loans on the General Motors balance sheet during the 1920s.

Americans were living beyond their means in the 1920s, yet most were oblivious to the risk. Historian Robert Sobel articulated the tradeoff that Americans unknowingly made by stating:

All of these purchases took massive amounts of credit and involved the mortgaging of tomorrow for today. The American consumer was willing to make this deal, and he traded a decade of unemployment and hunger for a decade of tinsel, much like the man who sold his soul to the devil.[5]

STOCKS CAPTIVATE MAIN STREET

The World War I Liberty and Victory bond drives introduced millions of Americans to the concept of investing. Initially, most Americans restricted their purchases to ultrasafe government bonds, but by the mid-1920s, many had developed an appetite for common stocks. An important catalyst was the 1924 publication of a book by Edgar L. Smith, *Common Stocks as Long Term Investments*. The book presented statistical analyses of common stock and bond returns over several holding periods ranging from the late 1800s to 1923. The results painted a favorable picture of common stock returns relative to bond returns. The superior performance of stocks during periods marked by elevated levels of inflation and a depreciating dollar were especially enticing because the U.S. had just experienced such an event during and after World War I. Smith's book was well received by academics and the public, and it added momentum to the growing interest in stocks as an investment.[6] Figure 15.3 below shows the scale of the shift from bonds to stocks that occurred between 1909 and 1929 by showing the change in individual U.S. savings invested in common and preferred stocks versus U.S. government securities.[7]

In the 1920s, Americans were accustomed to using credit to purchase a wide variety of consumer products, and they applied the same philosophy to stock purchases. In fact, many Americans believed that credit-based stock purchases were *less risky* than credit-based consumer purchases. They reasoned that securities were assets that always

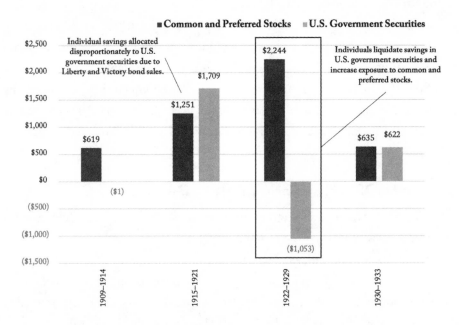

Figure 15.3: Annual Individual U.S. Savings by Major Components (Millions)
(Economic Period Averages 1909–1933)[8]

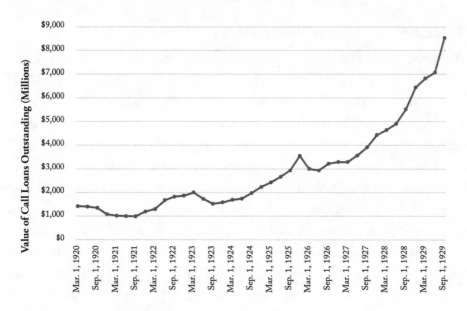

Figure 15.4: Total Value of Call Loans Outstanding (Millions) (March 1, 1920–September 1, 1929)[9]

appreciated in value. Of course, this is only correct in a rising market, but people did not think that way in the Roaring Twenties and purchasing stock on margin became standard practice. In fact, buying on margin was so common that people who bought securities with 50 percent down were classified as "investors." Only individuals who bought securities with less than 10 percent down qualified as "speculators." Illustrating the popularity of margin-based stock purchases, Figure 15.4 shows the rapid growth of call loans outstanding during the 1920s.[10] The use of margin debt was so ubiquitous in the 1920s that the availability and price of call loans was among the most important metrics monitored by the financial press. Illustrating its importance, the financial section of the *New York Times* almost always led with a one-sentence headline describing the direction of the stock market and price of call loans. Everybody was acutely aware that a threat to the call loan market also threatened the great bull market in stocks.[11]

THE END OF THE GENTLEMEN BANKER'S CODE

During World War I, there was a tectonic shift beneath the foundation of Wall Street, but most Americans were unaware of its significance. During the era of J. Pierpont Morgan, investment banking was dominated by a handful of privately owned firms. Major firms included the Houses of Morgan, Kuhn Loeb, Goldman Sachs, and a handful of others. These firms adhered to the unwritten Gentlemen Banker's Code. The code consisted of only a few rules, but they were rarely violated. The first was that bankers did not solicit business from clients, as it was considered unseemly. Instead, the goal was to establish long-term relationships grounded in trust and exceptional service. When clients required financial services, bankers assisted, but it was always reactive rather than proactive. The second rule was that once a client was under the umbrella of a major banking house, competing houses were forbidden from approaching that client without the approval of the existing banker. This rule led naturally to the dominance of specific houses in various industries and geographic locations. For example, the Houses of Morgan and Kuhn Loeb dominated railroads and large industrials. The third rule was that speculation on Wall Street was considered a vice, as it was viewed as a threat to the investment banking profession and the U.S. economy generally.[12]

The Gentlemen Banker's Code worked well from the perspective of corporate leaders and bankers, but it did not sit well with the public. Concentration of power and overlap among corporate and banking directorships sparked fear that America was under the control of a "money trust." This issue came to a head during the Pujo hearings in 1912–1913, which featured several contentious exchanges between congressional leaders and the most prominent bankers of the day, including J. Pierpont Morgan himself. The final report from the Pujo hearings fell short of confirming the existence of a money trust, but it implied that informal practices produced roughly the same outcome, nonetheless.[13]

The money trust investigation created a public relations nightmare for the banking industry, and it emboldened entrepreneurs who wished to compete with the major houses. Guilty of conspiracy in the court of public opinion, major investment banking houses were reluctant to suppress competition from upstarts. Even so, emerging competitors lacked existing relationships with corporate executives, making it difficult to compete under the terms of the Gentlemen Banker's Code. Instead, the only viable strategy was to adopt aggressive sales tactics and poach clients from the established houses. Early evidence of this strategy appeared in 1916 when Charles E. Mitchell accepted a position as president of National City Company, a small investment banking affiliate of National City Bank. Over the next thirteen years, Mitchell transformed a small, four-person office into the largest investment banking house in the nation. Fundamental to Mitchell's growth strategy was the abandonment of the Gentlemen Banker's Code. As one business executive stated, "Instead of waiting for investors to come, he [Mitchell] took young men and women, gave them a course of training on the sale of securities, and sent them out to find investors. Such methods, pursued with such vigor and on such a scale, were revolutionary." Following Mitchell's lead, the financial services industry rapidly transformed from a service- to a sales-oriented culture. And with clients no longer captive to the leading Wall Street houses, the industry was inundated with upstarts employing aggressive sales tactics and offering an array of new products.[14]

This cultural shift was especially ill-timed, as it coincided with the transition of the U.S. from the world's largest debtor to its largest creditor. The enormous costs of World War I and reconstruction forced European countries to spend much of their wealth on U.S. goods. Once their wealth was thoroughly depleted, Americans issued credit in its place. This created an interesting challenge for American bankers. Whereas in the past they had relied on a steady supply of foreign capital to fund business expansion, the only remaining source of capital was in the hands of their fellow Americans. Beginning in the early 1920s, the newly initiated wolves of Wall Street began preying on their own.

INVESTMENT COMPANIES CATER TO A "NEW CROP OF SPECULATORS"

"The most notable piece of speculative architecture of the late 20s, and the one by which, more than any other device, the public demand for common stocks were satisfied, was the investment trust or company."[15]

—JOHN KENNETH GALBRAITH

By the mid-1920s, Americans were participating in the stock market in record numbers. Due to their limited experience and lack of discipline, Wall Street veterans often referred to them as a "new crop of speculators." Despite their interest in stocks, they held back on their speculative impulses to a degree due to fear of selecting the wrong securities. Even in the early 1920s, Americans understood that regardless of whether stocks tend to rise in aggregate, any individual stock could decline for any number of reasons. They knew the best defense was to diversify their portfolio by purchasing multiple securities so that the failure of any single security would be tolerable.[16] The problem, however, was that many investors lacked the means to buy enough stocks to diversify adequately.

Wall Street responded by creating a new investment product, referred to as the *investment company*.[17] Investment companies purchased a pool of securities and then sold shares in the company to investors. In effect, a share in the investment company provided the shareholder with exposure to a diversified portfolio with the purchase of a single security. It is debatable when the very first investment company appeared in the U.S., although they were quite popular in Britain by the late 1800s. The earliest reference appears to be the New York Stock Trust, which was launched in 1889. The investment company that triggered rapid expansion of the industry in the 1920s, however, was the Massachusetts Investors Trust (MIT), which was officially incepted

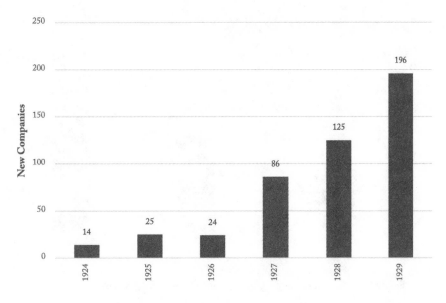

Figure 15.5: New Investment Funds by Year (1924–1929)[18]

on July 15, 1924.[19] Within a few years of its founding, several dozen additional investment companies were established, and by the end of the decade, hundreds more would follow. Figure 15.5 shows the rapid increase in the number of new investment companies founded between 1924 and 1929. Figure 15.6 shows the increase in assets held by these funds in the final years of the Roaring Twenties.[20]

Investment companies were primarily structured as either closed-ended or open-ended funds.[21] Under a closed-ended structure, the investment portfolio was fixed and shares traded in the open market. Depending on supply and demand, shares could trade at either a premium or discount to the market value of the securities held in the portfolio. Under an open-ended structure, the size of the portfolio was flexible, so if new investors entered the fund, additional shares were issued, and the investor's cash was used to purchase securities in proportions that matched those in the existing portfolio. If investors sold their shares, assets were liquidated, and the shares were retired. This "self-liquidating" feature enabled open-ended funds to trade close to the net asset value (NAV) of the underlying portfolio of securities, which was determined daily.

In the 1920s, closed-ended funds dominated the market. The main reason was that, in a bull market, closed-ended funds substantially outperformed open-ended funds. But strong relative performance disguised several risks. The first was that the fixed size of the fund allowed closed-ended fund shares to trade at either a premium or discount to the fund's NAV. In a bull market, closed-ended funds tended to trade at substantial premiums to the NAV, and in a bear market, shares tended to trade at a significant discount. This magnified gains when markets were rising, but it also

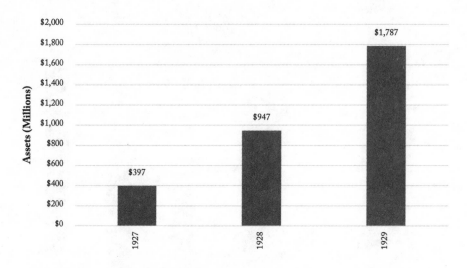

Figure 15.6: New Investment Company Funds by Assets (Millions) (1927–1929)[22]

magnified losses when they fell. The second problem was the use of leverage, which closed-ended fund managers employed liberally to create portfolios that exceeded the amount of invested capital. Once again, this worked well when returns were strong but had the opposite effect in bear markets. Investors in closed-ended funds could be completely wiped out well before the portfolio of securities itself hit zero. The combination of premiums/discounts to NAVs and leverage had a devastating impact on investors who bought these securities in 1929. A $1.00 investment in the average closed-ended investment company in July 1929 was worth only $0.02 in June 1932—a staggering loss of 98 percent.[23]

Closed-ended funds were much riskier than open-ended funds, but both types suffered from a universal set of flaws that affected virtually all investment companies. After factoring in these flaws, the diversification benefits paled in comparison to the costs and risks. A few of the more noteworthy flaws are described in the following box.

POINT OF INTEREST

The Price of Diversification[24]

- **Sales and Underwriting Fees**—Investment companies charged many fees, but the most significant were sales and underwriting fees. The amount varied, but on average they were much larger than those charged today. According to a 1939 SEC study, the average sales load for a closed-ended fund was 5.8 percent. When underwriting spreads were added, the estimate rose to 7–8 percent. In other words, when investors purchased $100 of investment company shares, they gained exposure to only $92 to $93 worth of securities.

- **Investment Management Fees**—Both closed- and open-ended investment companies charged annual investment management fees to compensate them for the "expertise" that they employed to identify the most attractive securities. The average investment management fee for closed-ended funds was not compiled during this time, but open-ended funds averaged 1.00 percent per year. Given the instinct of closed-ended fund managers to charge fees for any activity that involved a hint of effort, it is a reasonable assumption that closed-ended fees were comparable.
- **Dumping of Undigested Securities**—Many investment companies were sponsored by financial institutions that also underwrote stocks and bonds. When sales failed to meet expectations, investment company portfolios served as a convenient dumping ground, and shares were sold to them at prices above market value. This practice intensified in October 1929 when insiders found themselves in financial distress. In its 1939 report, the SEC identified at least $76 million of such transactions in 1929 alone but hypothesized that many more transactions likely remained undetected.
- **Accounting Abuses**—Investment companies were almost completely unregulated in the 1920s, which provided them with plenty of latitude on how they reported the value of assets, liabilities, and returns to investors. Many companies took advantage of this flexibility to paint a more favorable picture of their results and hide fees.

SHADOW BANKS EXTEND THE PARTY

"It was accepted as evidence that, despite the fundamental firmness in the money situation, funds are available in large supply any time that the rates go unusually high. Yesterday the inflow of money from out of town, from corporations and from foreign sources was so great that after renewing at 8%, the call loan-rate sank to 7%."[25]

—NEW YORK TIMES (October 4, 1928)

As the bull market raged in 1928 and 1929, demand for call loans frequently outstripped supply.[26] Banks initially satisfied demand by expanding loan capacity in the

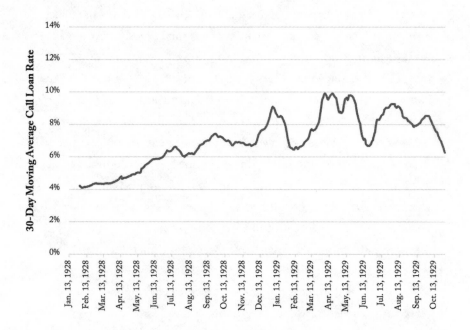

Figure 15.7: Interest Rate on Call Loans—30-Day Moving Average
(January 30, 1928–October 31, 1929)[27]

mid-1920s, but they could only go so far before breaching their risk management thresholds. As supply failed to keep pace with demand, lenders began charging higher interest rates. Figure 15.7 illustrates this by showing the thirty-day moving average call loan rate from January 1928 through October 1929.

A fundamental rule of economics is that when demand for a product exceeds supply, the price rises and attracts new market entrants. Sure enough, as the price of call loans rose on Wall Street, new lenders appeared. Beginning in 1928, most of the additional capital came from lenders operating outside the Federal Reserve system (i.e., shadow banks). These included corporations, investment funds, and even wealthy individuals who had spare cash in their brokerage accounts. The thesis was that call loans offered an attractive return with little risk. From a return perspective, the average interest rate on call loans was approximately 6.1 percent for the entirety of 1928 and 7.6 percent for the entirety of 1929. From a risk perspective, lenders were attracted by the short-term nature of the loan (i.e., callable in one day), as well as the fact that the loans were collateralized by securities that seemed to never decline in value. Figure 15.8 shows the dramatic rise in call loans issued by banks and other sources beginning in 1920. As the graph indicates, shadow banks became the dominant funding source for Wall Street speculation by the spring of 1928, and there seemed to be no limit to how much capital they were willing to provide.[28]

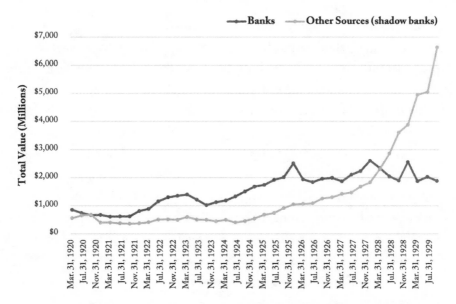

Figure 15.8: Total Value of Call Loans by Source (Millions) (March 31, 1920–September 30, 1929)[29]

Table 15.1: Selected Sample of Companies Providing Call Loans in 1929

COMPANY	MILLIONS
Electric Bond and Share	$157.58
Bethlehem Steel	$157.45
Standard Oil (NJ)	$97.82
Tri-Continental	$62.15
Chrysler	$60.15
Cities Service	$41.90
Anaconda Copper	$32.50
American & Foreign Power	$30.32
General Motors	$25.00

The growth of shadow banking created many problems. First, it enabled specula-tion to persist despite efforts by the Federal Reserve to contain it. Repeated warnings by the Federal Reserve were reasonably effective in curtailing lending by member banks, but they had no impact on shadow banks. Second, corporations earned sub-stantial income from call loans, which padded their earnings. This added to the perception that valuations of U.S. companies were reasonable on a price/earnings basis. But earnings from call loans were fueled by an unsustainable stock market bubble. Once the bubble popped, companies would not only take a hit from a decline in revenue from their core businesses, but they would also take a hit from the loss of income from call loans. Finally, the most absurd impact of call loans was in the portfolios of investment companies. By 1929, many investment companies began using investors' capital to issue call loans to investors rather than to purchase stocks. This is a particularly ludicrous example of circular economics. Many investment companies literally issued loans to investors, who then immediately turned around and invested the proceeds in the same investment fund that issued the loan. Noting the absurdity, John Kenneth Galbraith wrote: "People who speculated in the stock of investment trusts were in effect investing in companies which provided the funds to finance their own speculation."[30]

The explosion of call loans issued by shadow banks was probably the most potent driver of the stock market bubble that ultimately ended the Roaring Twenties. Had it not been for the abundance of call loans, the market would not have the required capital to rise as far as it did in 1928 to 1929. That said, the Federal Reserve also had an important role to play.

THE CREDITOR'S DILEMMA

"I really have a feeling in my own mind that the prosperity of our country is so wrapped up in general world prosperity that, aside from any declaration of purpose in the [Federal Reserve] Act, the best that we can do for our people is to try in any way that we can to maintain these markets on which our prosperity so largely depends . . . I earnestly believe that the greatest service that the Federal Reserve System is capable of performing today in this matter, is to hasten so far as it has the power wisely and without undue hazard, this question of monetary reform in the countries that have suffered from the war."[31]

—**BENJAMIN STRONG,** governor of the Federal Reserve Bank of New York (1926)

It is impossible for asset bubbles to form without a continuous supply of fresh capital. This is why monetary policy is usually a contributing factor. Recall for a moment the asset bubbles described earlier in this book. The real estate bubbles that triggered the Panics of 1819 and 1837 would not have risen nearly as high had state banks throughout the country constrained their lending practices. In the late 1920s, shadow banks were certainly guilty of fueling the speculative fever, but the Federal

Reserve was not an innocent bystander. A bloated money supply lay at the base of the bull market.

In fairness, hindsight is 20/20, and the Federal Reserve was in a tough spot. Suffering from intense bipartisan criticism for having allegedly caused the depression of 1920–1921, the Federal Reserve Board and Federal Reserve Bank regional governors wished to avoid repeating their prior mistake. All else being equal, this created a bias toward keeping rates lower for longer rather than raising them prematurely. In addition, the Federal Reserve was under pressure from both U.S. politicians and European central bankers to keep rates low. If the Federal Reserve were to raise rates, investors would seek higher returns in the U.S., and gold would flow out of Europe. This, in turn, would threaten post–World War I reconstruction efforts by forcing European central banks to raise interest rates to stem the flow. This was the conundrum to which Ben Strong referred in the opening quote.

The Federal Reserve's commitment to European reconstruction was first tested by the British in 1925. After World War I, the British Empire had largely forfeited its reserve currency status to the U.S., but they were eager to get it back. Many political conservatives and leaders of the Bank of England believed that reinstating the gold standard was critical. The British had suspended convertibility to gold during World War I. Despite having reservations, Winston Churchill (chancellor of the Exchequer at the time) caved to pressure to reinstate convertibility, and in April 1925 he announced the return of the pound sterling to the prewar fixed rate of $4.86 per pound. The problem, however, was that the British pound sterling was substantially overvalued at this exchange rate. This made British goods more expensive, which, in turn, caused British exports to plummet. The resulting trade deficit increased gold shipments from Britain to the U.S., which created problems for both the British and the Americans. In Britain, it sparked a painful recession, and in the U.S., it fueled unwanted expansion of the money supply.[32]

By the spring of 1927, inflation and speculation were making the Federal Reserve leadership uneasy. The heads of major European central banks were worried that the Fed would respond by raising interest rates. To preempt this scenario, leaders of the British, German, and French central banks traveled to the U.S. and encouraged leaders of the Federal Reserve to continue supporting European reconstruction by maintaining an easy monetary policy. But not only did the Federal Reserve leadership agree not to raise interest rates, *they cut them*. Shortly after the meeting, the New York Federal Reserve Bank reduced the rediscount rate from 4 percent to 3.5 percent. The reduction was approved with broad consensus, but one dissenter, Adolph C. Miller, presciently described the decision as "the greatest and boldest operation

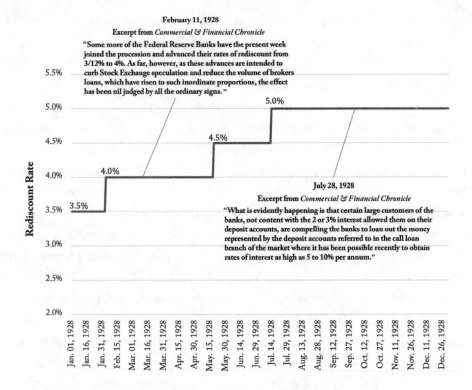

Figure 15.9: Federal Reserve Bank of New York Rediscount Rates
(January 1, 1928–December 31, 1928)[33]

ever undertaken by the Federal Reserve System, and . . . [it] resulted in one of the most costly errors committed by it or any other banking system in the last seventy-five years!"[34]

Clear signs of excessive speculation in the stock market were evident by the spring of 1928, and the Federal Reserve leadership became increasingly alarmed. The Federal Reserve regional banks responded by raising rediscount rates three times and issuing a series of verbal warnings to member banks to restrain the issuance of call loans, but these actions had little impact. Figure 15.9 shows the rediscount rate of the Federal Reserve Bank of New York in 1928, along with selected quotes from *The Commercial & Financial Chronicle* documenting the failure of the Fed's actions to reduce the supply of call loans and the stock market speculation that it fueled.

In fairness, the Federal Reserve Board was acutely aware of the dangerous speculation in the stock market and that call loans were the primary culprit. They made several attempts to curb speculation using the tools that they had, but by the end of 1928, it was clear that stronger action was required.

A BARBARIAN HOLDS THE GATE

"So far as this institution is concerned we feel that we have an obligation, which is paramount to any Federal Reserve warning, or anything else . . . While we are averse to resorting to rediscounting, for the purpose of making money in the call market, we certainly would not stand by and see a situation arise where money became impossible to secure at any price."[35]

—CHARLES E. MITCHELL, chairman, National City Bank (March 26, 1929)

In January 1929, many Federal Reserve leaders felt that speculation on Wall Street had become too dangerous, but a rift emerged between the Federal Reserve Board (situated in Washington) and the Federal Reserve Regional Bank of New York. The New York leadership wanted to increase rediscount rates, and they made their first proposal for a rate increase in February 1929. But the Federal Reserve Board vetoed the proposal out of fear that the negative impact on the broader economy would be too severe. It is also believed that President Herbert Hoover pressured the board to adopt this position. The Federal Reserve Board preferred to use "moral suasion" to temper the public's appetite for stocks and encourage member banks to voluntarily reduce call loans.[36]

In February 1929, the Federal Reserve Board issued a public statement warning commercial banks to refrain from using the Federal Reserve's rediscount facilities to borrow funds for use in speculation. In other words, they were warned not to borrow federal funds at 5 percent and loan them in the call loan market for 10 percent—which was a highly profitable activity. The problem, however, was that the banks were no longer the primary suppliers of call loans. Shadow banks had replaced them, so the statement had little impact.[37]

In March 1929, the bull market almost ended after word leaked of a secret Federal Reserve Board meeting in Washington, DC. Investors assumed that the meetings were prompted by Wall Street speculation, and they began to panic. On March 25, it appeared that the bubble was finally ready to pop. The immediate trigger was a sudden shortage of call loans, which caused rates to spike to 14 percent on March 25. On March 26, call loan rates hit 20 percent, and the stock market opened to a wave of selling. The market averages were on their way to a nearly 10 percent decline, and many believed that the Great Bull Market had finally ended. Instead, the audacity of Charles E. Mitchell, chairman of National City Corporation, bought speculators another seven months. Observing the tremendous selling pressure and contraction of the call loan market, Mitchell announced that National City would provide $25 million of additional call loans, using the Federal Reserve's rediscount facilities if necessary. He then chastised the Federal Reserve by saying, "For the Federal Reserve Board to deny investors the means of recognizing economies which are now proved, skill which is now learned, and inventions that which are almost unbelievable seems to justify doubt whether it is adequately interpreting the times."[38]

Mitchell would later pay a steep price for his brazen act of defiance, but, at the time, it was just what the market needed. Mitchell's statement sparked an immediate rally, and by the market close, prices had returned to only slightly below the prior day's close. Mitchell's pledge to provide an additional $25 million in call loans was relatively small, but the insinuation that there was "organized support" from the banking community was powerful. Mitchell's words restored investor confidence and allowed the stock market to resume its meteoric rise.

THE FALL OF 1929

"Men have been swindled by other men on many occasions. The autumn of 1929 was, perhaps, the first occasion when men succeeded on a large scale in swindling themselves."[39]

—JOHN KENNETH GALBRAITH

The month of October is always precarious on Wall Street due to the lingering fears associated with the agricultural financing cycle. In October 1929, fear was once again palpable. The Federal Reserve Board finally granted approval to the Federal Reserve Bank of New York to raise the rediscount rate to 6 percent, and soon thereafter, the U.S. economy decelerated. There were no immediate signs of doom on Wall Street— just subtle whiffs of fear that strengthened with each passing day. Hints of trouble first appeared in September when the stock market suffered several sharp declines followed by weak rallies that added up to a 9.9 percent total decline for the month. By the end of September, demand for call loans softened, signaling that the appetite for speculation was waning. Figure 15.10 shows the steady decline of the stock market during the months of September and October 1929, along with the decline in the average daily rate on call loans.[40]

Hyman Minsky's financial instability hypothesis asserts that speculative bubbles (defined as "Ponzi markets") form when enough people value an asset based primarily (if not entirely) on the belief that they can soon sell it to another buyer for an even higher price. Nobody knows the precise moment when the U.S. stock market entered the Ponzi phase, but it clearly crossed the threshold at some point in 1928. The problem with speculative bubbles is that they can never inflate forever. It inevitably reaches

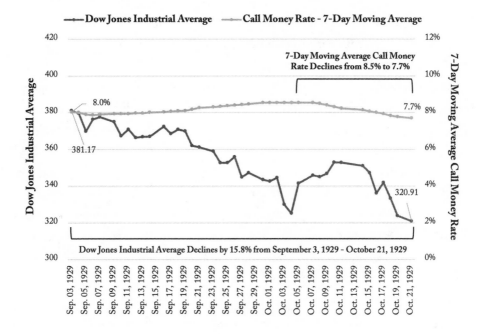

Figure 15.10: Dow Jones Industrial Average and Daily Average Call Money Rate
(September 3, 1929–October 21, 1929)[41]

a point at which the supply of fresh capital runs dry. Just like a Ponzi scheme collapses once a con artist runs out of new victims, a Ponzi market collapses when speculators run out of money. When the market turns, investors initially fear they will be unable to sell their securities at a higher price, and then, seemingly out of the blue, they become petrified they will be unable to find a buyer at any price. Perusing the financial section of the *New York Times* in September and October 1929, one can sense this fear building. Whereas price declines in prior months were almost welcomed as new buying opportunities, investors reacted to sharp declines in September and October of 1929 with increasing trepidation.[42]

The knockout punches arrived during the final days of October 1929. The week began with a sharp sell-off on Monday, October 21, and was followed by a weak rally that left the market flat at the close on Tuesday, October 22. On Wednesday, October 23, selling pressure returned, prompting a 6.3 percent decline in the Dow Jones Industrial Average. The decline triggered massive margin calls at the end of the day. Spooked by the margin calls, distressed investors finally capitulated, and the stock market collapsed on the morning of Black Thursday, October 24, 1929. The decline temporarily stalled when the leading bankers of Wall Street announced the formation of a "Bankers' Pool," which immediately purchased $125 million in securities to signal confidence in the market. When the market closed on Black Thursday, losses from earlier in the day were almost completely erased. Hope that further "organized support" was forthcoming helped stabilize prices on Friday, October 25, and Saturday, October 26.[43]

At some point between the market close on Saturday, October 26, and the opening bell on Monday, October 28, a critical mass of investors concluded that more organized support was not coming. Black Monday and Black Tuesday were catastrophic. In retrospect, the conclusion that organized support would never materialize was hardly unfounded. What person or entity was both willing and able to provide it? The Federal Reserve had discouraged speculation on Wall Street for nearly two years. It was not irrational to think that they would view the collapse of the speculative bubble as tolerable—some board members may have even welcomed it. Investment companies, which many presumed could provide a reliable floor for stock prices, had leveraged their portfolios recklessly, while encouraging clients to leverage themselves even more recklessly by buying shares with call loans. Investment companies were in no position to support prices, and in fact would soon become forced sellers themselves. European investors were, of course, not an option given that they were already deeply indebted to the United States. Finally, the heroic return of the bankers who stopped the Panic of 1907 was all but a pipe dream in 1929. The Gentlemen Banker's Code died with J. Pierpont Morgan in 1913, and the discipline among the leading houses of Wall Street evaporated after his passing. In many cases, the great financial houses and their senior partners were just as exposed to the crash as their clients. For all these reasons, investors were entirely justified in their fear that organized support would not arrive. Unlike virtually every other calculation they had made over the prior two years, they got this one right.

When the market opened on Black Monday, October 28, 1929, it was a full-blown panic. In just two days, the Dow Jones Industrial Average declined by another jaw-dropping 23.0 percent on volume of nearly thirty million shares (Figure 15.11). After the market rout on Black Tuesday, the total decline since the beginning of September was just shy of 40 percent.

During the first two weeks of November, the market suffered an additional decline of approximately 10 percent, bringing cumulative losses to nearly 50 percent for the final four months of 1929. The market slowly recovered in December, but the rally soon fizzled. Over the first several months of 1930, the stock market experienced multiple weak recoveries followed by declines to even greater depths. Simultaneously, economic activity collapsed, and before long, waves of bank failures and bank runs spread. This toxic combination plunged the U.S. into the deepest economic depression in the nation's history.

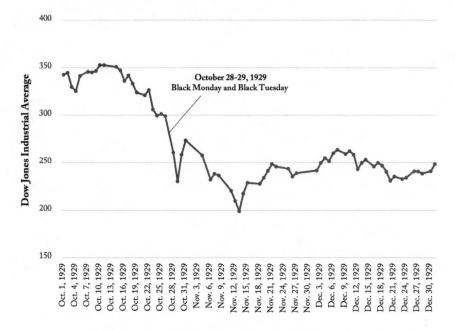

Figure 15.11: Dow Jones Industrial Average Daily Closing Price
(October 1, 1929–December 31, 1929)[44]

Seven years would pass before the market returned to the high achieved in 1929 in terms of real value.[45] But when investors returned to the market, the rules of the game had fundamentally changed. The stock operators who had ruled the markets since the time of Alexander Hamilton were no longer in command. Perhaps recognizing that the 140-year run of unconstrained speculation was over, famed stock operator William C. Durant stated, "We may as well tell the truth and put the blame where it belongs. It's up to Washington now. We have stepped aside. Eventually, we will take control again."[46]

A sustained recovery finally gathered momentum in the mid-1930s, but the days of unregulated securities markets were gone. Before the next era could begin, however, the U.S. would have to navigate its way out of the deepest depression in its history. Americans would emerge stronger, but the destabilizing forces of the Great Depression would break much of the world. The chapters covering the next fifteen years are the most extensive of this book but are also the most important. Several of the forces that shaped the Great Depression and World War II era will be hauntingly familiar to those living in the present.

Part 4

The Great Depression and Global Destabilization

1930–1945

"The world was a miserable, wretched place to be in the 1930s. It was a time when death lurked around every street corner—death which could be as slow as starvation or as quick as a whistling machine gun bullet . . . everyone and everything—including the immediate future—was in doubt. The average citizen was being whittled shorter and shorter with every skimpy meal."[1]

—BILLIE JEAN PARKER MOON

I nvestors often pay little attention to financial events that occurred prior to the Great Depression, which is unfortunate because many of these events remain just as relevant today. The oversight is understandable, however, because the United States that existed before the Depression seems so different than the one that emerged after the Depression and World War II. **Part 4** recounts the financial events that reshaped the United States between 1930 and 1945. For fifteen years, the nation's survival required Americans to leverage every strength that they had built over the prior 140 years.

Chapter 16 recounts the Great Depression, which remains the most traumatic economic event in U.S. history. The Depression officially began in August 1929 and technically ended in March 1933, but the economy did not achieve escape velocity until the end of the 1930s. Americans suffered from a devastating loss of wealth, chronic unemployment, and frequent spasms of civil unrest. This led many Americans to question the sustainability of the capitalist system.

Chapter 17 reviews the Stock Exchange Practices hearings that were held by the U.S. Senate in 1932 and 1933. The issue was the proliferation of fraud, market manipulation, and insider trading prior to and immediately after the Great Crash in October 1929. The lead counsel, Ferdinand Pecora, uncovered extensive corruption that allowed stock operators and insiders to profit at the public's expense. The revelations provided just enough momentum to pass a series of critical securities regulations that would serve as the backbone of the U.S. financial system and securities markets.

Chapter 18 reviews five groundbreaking regulations passed between 1933 and 1940. The Banking Act of 1933 (Glass-Steagall) strengthened the powers of the Federal Reserve, established federal deposit insurance, and forced the separation of investment and commercial banking at large financial institutions. The Securities Act of 1933 and Securities Exchange Act of 1934 created transparency in the securities underwriting business and established federal oversight of securities exchanges. The days of legal market manipulation and insider trading ended after these two regulations passed. Finally, the Investment Company and Investment Advisers Acts of 1940 created the regulatory foundation for the asset management and investment advisory professions.

Chapter 19 recounts the rise of the Nazi Party in Germany and militarism in Japan. The brutal ideologies of the Axis Powers were fueled by the misery of the Great Depression. The chapter is among the most important in the book because it reveals that the true costs of depressions are more accurately measured in terms of losses of life rather than wealth. The chapter concludes with the surprise attack by the Japanese Navy on the U.S. Pacific Fleet based in Pearl Harbor, which instantly converted the American people into the most powerful and motivated military force on the planet.

Chapter 20 recounts the mobilization of America's industry, financial system, and people in World War II. It explains how America's unique competitive advantages enabled the country to lead the Allied Powers and emerge victorious from an unprecedented two-front war spanning the entire globe. After defeating the Nazis on May 7, 1945, and the Empire of Japan on August 15, 1945, the British Empire faded, and the U.S. took its place as the leader of the Western World.

Chapter 16

THE LAST
GREAT DEPRESSION

*"The singular feature of the Great Crash of 1929 was that the worst
continued to worsen. What looked one day like the end proved on the next
day to have been only the beginning. Nothing could have been more inge-
niously designed to maximize the suffering, and also to ensure that
as few as possible escaped the common misfortune."*[1]

—JOHN KENNETH GALBRAITH

The statement by John Kenneth Galbraith is correct in the sense that the decline
of the U.S. economy was unrelenting after the Great Crash, but it also reinforces
the common misperception that the stock market crash was the primary cause. The
truth is that the crash triggered the decline, but the policies enacted in the aftermath
bear much more responsibility for the depth and duration of the Great Depression.

Few Americans today can relate to the misery of the 1930s. By March 1933, the
U.S. had suffered an 18.8 percent cumulative decline in real GDP. Unemployment
peaked at approximately 25 percent and did not return to pre-Depression levels until
the 1940s. (Figure 16.1). The Global Financial Crisis (GFC) in 2008–2009 was caused
by similar factors, but the actions by the Federal Reserve and federal government produced a dramatically different outcome. When the GFC ended in March 2009, the
U.S. had suffered a 4.3 percent cumulative decline in real GDP and peak unemployment of 10 percent. The different policy responses explain the sharp differences in
outcomes and reveal the paradox of deflationary depressions. In the wake of financial
crises, human instinct is to assign blame bluntly, dole out punishment liberally, and

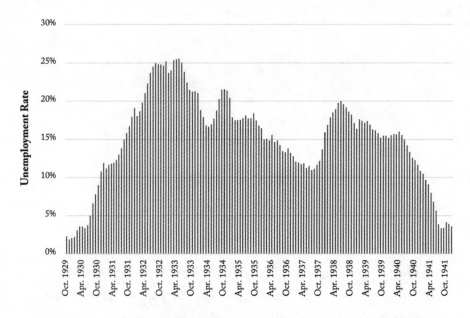

Figure 16.1: U.S. Rate of Unemployment (October 1929–December 1941)[2]

end all behavior that contributed to the crisis immediately. The Great Depression demonstrates that, while these solutions may seem sensible instinctively, they prove disastrous in the real world.[3]

INFLATIONARY AND DEFLATIONARY DEPRESSIONS

The Great Depression followed several years of debt-fueled speculation. When speculative manias like this end, economic depressions often follow. In *Principles for Navigating Big Debt Cycles*, Ray Dalio defines two types of depressions. The first is an *inflationary* depression, which is best known for the terrifying phenomenon of hyperinflation. The inflationary depression in Germany under the Weimar Republic in the early 1920s is an oft-cited example. By the end of this catastrophic event, Germany experienced hyperinflation of 322 percent per month.[4] The root cause of the Weimar hyperinflation was the fact that Germany had an unsustainable debt that was denominated in a foreign currency. This is the hallmark of inflationary depressions, and it is what makes them so difficult to manage. Adjusting the domestic currency (i.e., printing money) is an effective tactic to counteract *deflationary* depressions, but this tool is unavailable to nations suffering from *inflationary* depressions. The U.S. is fortunate to have never experienced an inflationary depression, and it is unlikely that it will experience one as long as it can continue issuing debt in its own currency.[5]

The second type of depression is a *deflationary* depression. These have occurred several times in the United States. The most severe ones occurred in the 1820s (chapter 3), 1840s (chapter 4) and the Great Depression in the 1930s. Deflationary depressions occur when the debts of a nation are denominated primarily in its own currency. Countries experiencing deflationary depressions are fortunate in that they have greater flexibility in crafting policy responses. The challenge is to understand which specific policies are needed and to assemble an optimal combination. If well executed, countries can navigate relatively smooth exits from deflationary depressions by spreading out the impact of the damage over multiple years.[6]

The Great Depression was unnecessarily catastrophic because policymakers employed tactics that intensified the depression rather than reversing it. These responses were understandable, however, because the most effective responses to deflationary depressions are counterintuitive. We now understand this at a deeper level, but it is only with the benefit of hindsight. The remainder of this chapter explains the most critical errors that led to the Great Depression.

THE DANGER OF AUSTERITY

One way to think about the behaviors that cause a depression is to consider the relationship between a spendthrift child and a financially responsible parent. If the parent discovers that their child has been racking up unsustainable credit card debt, their instinct is to cancel the credit card and force the child to use their savings to pay off their debts. Such strategies are often referred to as "austerity," and in situations in which the child is the only irresponsible actor, it is a sound approach. The child is taught to behave responsibility, and society is better off because there is one less fiscally irresponsible person in the world.

The problem is that this strategy only works when irresponsible behavior is reasonably contained. It does not work when a large portion of the population engages in the same behavior. If every parent in the country were to simultaneously enact austerity measures, it would destabilize the entire financial system, rendering it vulnerable to collapse. For example, if the "child" represents the American consumer, aggregate spending sharply declines, which places stress on businesses, which then forces layoffs, which leads to further declines in spending, and so on. This self-reinforcing process causes the entire economy to descend into a depression. If the "child" represents a bank, the stakes are even more dire. Austerity causes many banks to fail, which leads to a contraction of credit available to businesses and individuals, which leads to declines in spending and investment, which metastasizes into the same type of self-reinforcing process that applies to consumers.

The worst depressions occur when austerity measures are applied bluntly to individuals and the banking system simultaneously, and this is precisely what happened in the early 1930s.

Fiscal Policy Errors

"Liquidate labor, liquidate stocks, liquidate the farmers, liquidate real estate. It will purge the rottenness out of the system. High costs of living and high living will come down. People will work harder, live a more moral life. Values will be adjusted, and enterprising people will pick up from less competent people."[7]

—ANDREW W. MELLON, U.S. secretary of the Treasury

Fiscal policy refers to the use of government spending to either stimulate or dampen economic activity. During depressions, the government can reduce taxes and/or increase spending to fill the void left by declines in spending by individuals and businesses. After the Great Crash, Americans suffered massive losses of wealth. The natural reaction was to reduce their spending and rebuild their savings. Again, this is a logical and responsible reaction, but if everybody behaves this way simultaneously, it causes a sharp, self-reinforcing economic contraction. The federal government can short-circuit the process by either increasing spending or reducing taxes. This approach can lead to massive government deficits, which must be paid back over time, but creating a practical repayment plan is less costly in the long run than allowing a self-reinforcing deflationary spiral to run its course.

The opening quote from Treasury Secretary Andrew Mellon captures the essence of the Hoover administration's approach. Austerity measures placed intense pressure on individuals and businesses to reduce spending and investment. Examples included the refusal to extend emergency credit to distressed businesses, reductions in government spending, and even income tax increases that were intended to balance the federal budget. In fairness, Hoover created a few government programs to stimulate the economy, but for the most part, his strategy entailed austerity, coupled with verbal attempts to restore confidence in the business community. By the time Hoover began implementing more aggressive measures, such as the launch of the Reconstruction Financing Corporation (RFC) in January 1932, the Depression had deepened to a point that required much more aggressive intervention.[8] Further, by the end of 1932, Hoover's credibility had deteriorated to such a degree that he was unable to inspire confidence regardless of the sensibility of his strategies.[9]

POINT OF INTEREST

The Paralyzing but Legitimate Fear of Moral Hazard

Moral hazard refers to the weakening of incentives of people to behave responsibly. Opponents of stimulative fiscal policies during a depression often justify their position by citing their desire to reduce moral hazard. It is difficult to counter this argument because they raise a legitimate point. If financially irresponsible individuals and businesses are not held accountable for irresponsible behavior, they have no incentive to behave responsibly in the future.

Moral hazard must be considered when creating stimulative fiscal and monetary policies to combat a depression. Ignoring these risks incentivizes bad actors to repeat their behavior without fear of consequence, which allows instability to build up in the system. On the other hand, preventing moral hazard at all costs can cause depressions that are so extreme that the system fails.

The Hoover administration prioritized the reduction of moral hazard at the expense of system stability in the early 1930s, and the U.S. experienced a dangerous breakdown of society. These policies were reversed in the mid-1930s, but it took nearly a decade before the U.S. economy reached escape velocity. The economy did not fully recover until the outbreak of World War II forced the federal government to increase spending sharply.

Monetary Policy Errors

"The only change made by the board during the year [1931] in its regulations applicable to member banks was in its regulation G governing the rediscount by Federal reserve banks of notes secured by adjusted service certificates issued under the provisions of the World War adjusted compensation act."[10]

—ANNUAL REPORT OF THE FEDERAL RESERVE BOARD FOR THE YEAR 1931

The above quote describing changes to Federal Reserve policies in 1931 is revealing not because of what was said, but rather because of what was unsaid. In 1931, a total of 4,305 bank suspensions had occured over the prior three years, which was nearly equal to the total suspensions from 1921 to 1928. In fairness, the Federal Reserve Board eased credit conditions quickly after the Great Crash, but they did not act aggressively

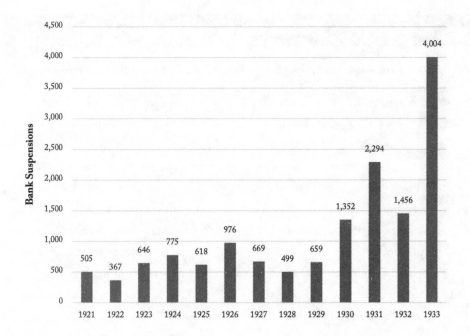

Figure 16.2: Total Bank Suspensions by Year (1921–1933)[11]

enough to stop the spread of bank failures. Each bank closure created a contraction of credit and painful losses to depositors, which intensified the deflationary spiral.[12]

By the end of 1933, more than nine thousand state, Federal Reserve member, non–Federal Reserve member, and private banks had been suspended, and most had not reopened (Figure 16.2). This left a gaping hole in credit markets. Consumers and businesses were unable to obtain loans, forcing them to cut spending and magnify the deflationary spiral. The failure to contain the banking crisis is regarded as the worst mistake in the Federal Reserve's history. In a tribute to famed economist Milton Friedman, former Chairman of the Federal Reserve Board Ben Bernanke lamented the Fed's role in causing the Great Depression, stating: "Let me end my talk by abusing slightly my status as an official representative of the Federal Reserve. I would like to say to Milton [Friedman] and Anna [Schwartz]: Regarding the Great Depression. You're right, we did it. We're very sorry. But thanks to you, we won't do it again."[13]

A Dark Comedy of Errors

Figure 16.3 tracks several key milestones during the Great Depression, as well as several of the more impactful fiscal and policy errors made by the Hoover administration and the Federal Reserve. Along the bottom of the chart are several key metrics that reveal the economic consequences. As the graphic illustrates, fiscal policies shaped by

KEY MILESTONES AND POLICY ERRORS OF THE GREAT DEPRESSION
(January 1, 1930–March 31, 1933)

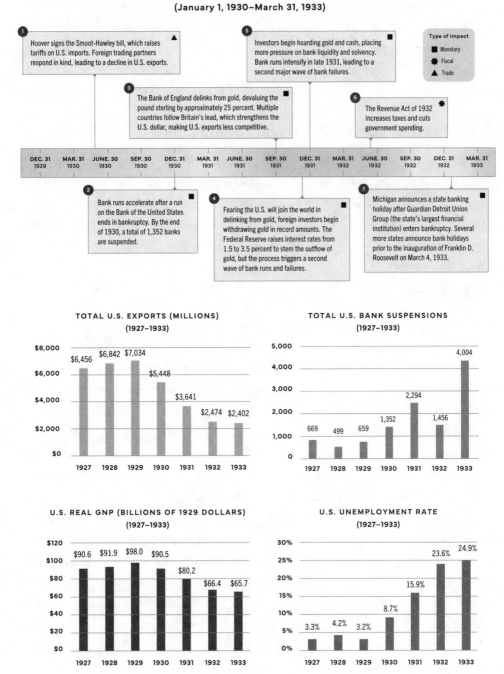

Figure 16.3: Key Milestones and Policy Errors of the Great Depression[14]

austerity and the Federal Reserve's neglect of the banking system were almost precisely counter to what was needed to reverse the self-reinforcing deflationary spiral. The graphic also references destructive trade policies, which caused significant harm to the U.S. and its global trading partners. The damage caused by trade policies is reviewed in greater depth in chapter 21.

Roosevelt Reverses the Deflationary Spiral

"While leaving the gold standard, printing money, and providing guarantees [of the financial system] were by far the most impactful policy moves that Roosevelt made, they were just the first of an avalanche of policies that were unrolled during his first six months in office. The shock and awe of all those big announcements of spending, coming week after week, built confidence among investors and the public, which was critical to putting the economy on a good footing."[15]

—RAY DALIO

The foundation of Franklin Delano Roosevelt's presidential campaign was providing a "New Deal" for Americans. Given the dire condition of the country, it is unsurprising that his message resonated with the American people even though Roosevelt rarely explained what exactly the New Deal meant. It is unclear whether Roosevelt's ambiguity was intentional or simply reflected a genuine absence of a specific plan— he was reported to have a penchant for procrastination. Regardless of motive, by refusing to make specific campaign promises, Roosevelt entered office with plenty of flexibility to design and implement creative solutions.[16]

After winning the presidency in a decisive electoral victory, and backed by a Democratic majority in both houses of Congress, Roosevelt entered office with a powerful mandate. During his first one hundred days, he introduced a tidal wave of new economic policies. His top priority was restoring faith in the banking system, which was on the verge of a complete collapse. On March 5, 1933, which was the day after his inauguration, Roosevelt signed an executive order closing all U.S. banks for four days. On March 9, Roosevelt signed the Emergency Banking Act of 1933, which retroactively legalized the banking holiday and extended it for an additional four days. The act also authorized the use of additional financial tools, such as authorizing the Federal Reserve to issue emergency currency backed by a much broader array of assets.[17] On March 12, Roosevelt delivered one of his signature "fireside chats" to the nation and explained his administration's plan to begin reopening banks on March 13. He also explained how a rigorous testing process would gauge bank solvency, ensuring that banks would only reopen when it was safe to do so. On the morning of March 13, the Roosevelt administration watched nervously as the strongest banks in the nation reopened. To their relief, not only did the banks open without suffering additional bank runs, but customers also lined up to redeposit cash that they had previously hoarded. The success of the national bank holiday and steady stream of successful bank reopenings marked the bottom of the Great Depression.

POINT OF INTEREST

The Flimsy Moral High Ground of the Monday Morning Quarterback

The Hoover administration and Federal Reserve made many costly errors that caused the Great Depression to worsen unnecessarily, but it is easy to criticize their behavior with the benefit of hindsight. It has taken nearly a century to understand the governing dynamics of deflationary depressions and the policies required to end them. Many discoveries were possible only because researchers had the luxury of observing the consequences of Hoover's failed policies. It is unfair, therefore, to assume that policymakers in the 1930s should have known better.

By applying lessons from the Great Depression over the last ninety years, U.S. fiscal and monetary authorities have avoided a repetition of this catastrophe. It is also important to acknowledge that many former members of the Hoover administration, such as Arthur Ballantine and Ogden Mills, graciously volunteered their time to assist the Roosevelt administration despite being excoriated in the press for "having caused the crisis." Raymond Moley, a close advisor to President Roosevelt, would later credit their patriotism, stating "except for the expertness, the information, and the plans of the lower level of the Hoover administration, the crisis could never have been surmounted." These were acts of patriotism, not treachery or incompetence.[18]

From a purely factual perspective, the Hoover administration's policies caused the depression to worsen, and it is important to understand why. But this can be accomplished without maligning the character of people who made mistakes—often despite their positive intentions.

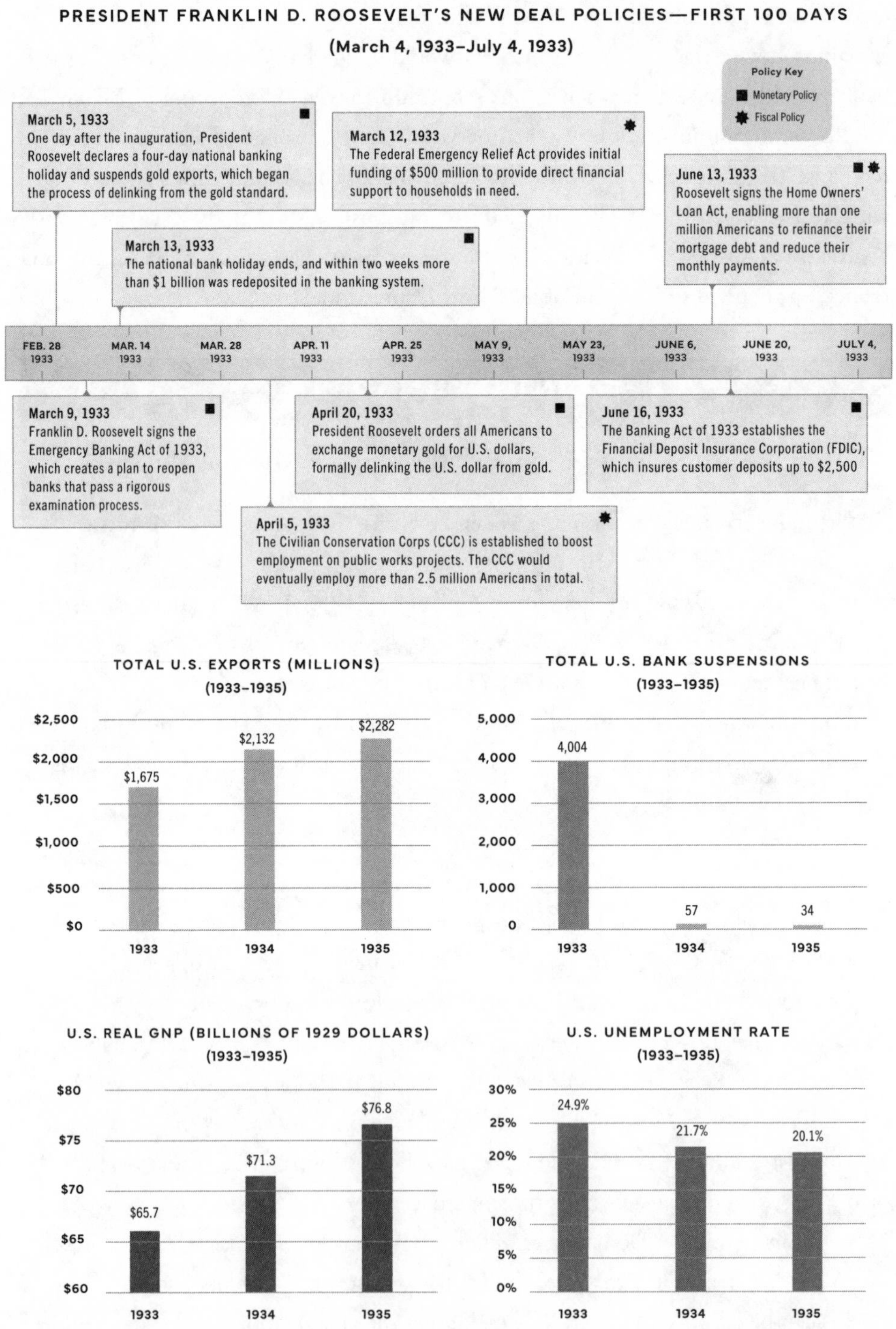

PRESIDENT FRANKLIN D. ROOSEVELT'S NEW DEAL POLICIES—FIRST 100 DAYS

(March 4, 1933–July 4, 1933)

Policy Key

■ Monetary Policy
✱ Fiscal Policy

March 5, 1933 ■
One day after the inauguration, President Roosevelt declares a four-day national banking holiday and suspends gold exports, which began the process of delinking from the gold standard.

March 12, 1933 ✱
The Federal Emergency Relief Act provides initial funding of $500 million to provide direct financial support to households in need.

June 13, 1933 ■ ✱
Roosevelt signs the Home Owners' Loan Act, enabling more than one million Americans to refinance their mortgage debt and reduce their monthly payments.

March 13, 1933 ■
The national bank holiday ends, and within two weeks more than $1 billion was redeposited in the banking system.

| FEB. 28 1933 | MAR. 14 1933 | MAR. 28 1933 | APR. 11 1933 | APR. 25 1933 | MAY 9, 1933 | MAY 23, 1933 | JUNE 6, 1933 | JUNE 20, 1933 | JULY 4, 1933 |

March 9, 1933 ■
Franklin D. Roosevelt signs the Emergency Banking Act of 1933, which creates a plan to reopen banks that pass a rigorous examination process.

April 20, 1933 ■
President Roosevelt orders all Americans to exchange monetary gold for U.S. dollars, formally delinking the U.S. dollar from gold.

June 16, 1933 ■
The Banking Act of 1933 establishes the Financial Deposit Insurance Corporation (FDIC), which insures customer deposits up to $2,500

April 5, 1933 ✱
The Civilian Conservation Corps (CCC) is established to boost employment on public works projects. The CCC would eventually employ more than 2.5 million Americans in total.

TOTAL U.S. EXPORTS (MILLIONS)
(1933–1935)

	1933	1934	1935
	$1,675	$2,132	$2,282

TOTAL U.S. BANK SUSPENSIONS
(1933–1935)

	1933	1934	1935
	4,004	57	34

U.S. REAL GNP (BILLIONS OF 1929 DOLLARS)
(1933–1935)

	1933	1934	1935
	$65.7	$71.3	$76.8

U.S. UNEMPLOYMENT RATE
(1933–1935)

	1933	1934	1935
	24.9%	21.7%	20.1%

Figure 16.4: President Franklin D. Roosevelt's New Deal Policies[19]

During the remainder of Roosevelt's first one hundred days, he experimented with many additional programs to stimulate the economy. These policies were often mirror images of those employed by Hoover. Roosevelt also made mistakes, but in the end, his administration's actions enabled the U.S. to begin a long recovery. A timeline of Roosevelt's first one hundred days is provided in Figure 16.4. Over the next several years, the economy slowly reversed course, but the severe damage caused by the Great Depression stubbornly lingered for the remainder of the decade. It was only the uptick in war spending in 1939 that allowed the U.S. to end the Great Depression for good.

THE WEIGHT OF GOLD

"If gold is at last deposed from its despotic control over us and reduced to the position of constitutional monarch, a new chapter of history will have opened. Man will have made another step forward in the attainment of self government."[20]

—JOHN MAYNARD KEYNES

The refusal of the U.S. to delink from gold was another impediment to its efforts to exit the Great Depression. The gold standard prevented the Federal Reserve from printing currency in sufficient quantities to counteract deflationary pressures. The reason that the Federal Reserve was constrained was because it was legally required to maintain gold reserves that equated to at least 40 percent of the total issuance of Federal Reserve notes. For most of the Depression, gold reserves were comfortably above this floor, but excess gold reserves (referred to as "free gold") were not sufficient to back the printing of enough currency to counter deflationary forces and stabilize the banking system.

The only thing preventing the U.S. from printing more dollars was fear that it would cause the world to lose faith in the U.S. financial system and the U.S. dollar. To be fair, this was not an insignificant concern. England's departure from the gold standard during World War I contributed to its decline as a global financial center and accelerated the pound sterling's replacement as the world's reserve currency. But the circumstances in the 1930s were quite different. By the end of 1932, most major countries had already delinked from gold, so the U.S. would hardly be alone. Soon after these countries delinked, their economies began recovering, as devalued currencies made exports more competitive and gave central banks more flexibility to print currency to reverse deflationary pressures.[21] Their departures from the gold standard also deepened the depression in the U.S., as their depreciated currencies made U.S.

exports less competitive. Finally, fearing that the U.S. would delink from gold eventually, foreign investors rushed to convert dollars to gold and ship the proceeds back home. From 1930 to 1932, the U.S. lost more than $600 million dollars' worth of gold, which placed more downward pressure on the U.S. money supply.[22]

The gold standard was a big problem for Roosevelt. Despite having repeatedly emphasized his commitment to the gold standard during his campaign, in March 1933, he began the process of delinking the U.S. dollar. On March 5, he placed restrictions on gold transactions and gold exports as part of the executive order declaring a national bank holiday. On May 12, Roosevelt signed a farm bill, which granted him the authority to embargo gold exports and adjust the gold content of the U.S. dollar. For all practical purposes, these actions delinked the U.S. dollar from gold. Over the subsequent year, additional actions included the forced conversion of monetary gold into U.S. dollars, outlawing the hoarding of monetary gold, adding further restrictions on gold exports, and passage of the Gold Reserve Act of 1934, which officially ended the use of gold as money. The delinking of the U.S. dollar from gold provided the country with greater flexibility to reverse the self-reinforcing deflationary spiral. Further, because the U.S. was not alone in its decision to delink from gold, it did not threaten the nation's status as the world's leading financial center and issuer of a major reserve currency. It was yet another irony of history that the discovery of gold at Sutter's Mill lifted the U.S. out of its second Great Depression in the 1840s, while the abandonment of gold in 1933 ended its final Great Depression in the 1930s.[23]

THE LEGACY OF THE GREAT DEPRESSION

The Great Depression was a seminal event in U.S. history. Many Americans who lived through it developed a visceral aversion to debt, speculation in the stock market, and, in more extreme cases, use of the banking system. Lingering fear of financial panics also dampened stock market valuations for nearly twenty years. But the most enduring impact of the Depression was its effects on monetary and fiscal policy. To this day, U.S. policies express a bias toward minimizing the likelihood of repeating a Great Depression–level event. For example, lessons from the Great Depression clearly shaped the response of the Federal Reserve and politicians to the GFC in 2008 and COVID-19 panic in 2020.

The second philosophical shift stemming from the Great Depression involved banking reform. The failure to stop several waves of bank failures in the early 1930s significantly deepened the Depression. Congress passed several important banking reforms to protect the financial industry from future systemic crises. The Banking Act of 1933 (often referred to as the Glass-Steagall Act) separated commercial and investment banking activities and established federal deposit insurance under the Federal Deposit Insurance Corporation (FDIC). The substance and impact of this regulation are explained in greater detail in chapter 18.

The final impact of the Great Depression involved behavior on Wall Street. The stock market crash was less important than monetary and fiscal policy errors as a cause of the Great Depression, but it fueled significant outrage in America, nonetheless. As is typical in the aftermath of any financial crisis, Congress scheduled hearings to diagnose the causes and expose misbehavior. The Stock Exchange Practices hearings inspired several regulations that permanently reshaped Wall Street. The history, details, and impact of these regulations are the subject of chapters 17 and 18.

There is no question that the U.S. avoided considerable economic pain over the last ninety years by applying many lessons from the Great Depression. However, as the nation progresses through the twenty-first century, the blind application of these lessons may create imbalances that are not fully appreciated. In other words, America's bias toward depression avoidance may set the stage for a crisis that is unlike those experienced since the Great Depression. For example, now that the U.S. dollar is no longer tied to gold, monetary and fiscal policymakers are less sensitive to the potential long-term consequences of running unsustainable budget deficits. The consequences of this practice may not be felt in the near term, but it cannot continue forever. Perhaps the next major financial crisis will arrive after foreign countries abandon the U.S. dollar as a reserve currency, just as the world abandoned the pound sterling in the mid-1900s. As of the publication of this book, this seemed unlikely to occur in the near term, but every reserve currency that preceded the U.S. dollar eventually forfeited its status. Is the U.S. dollar any different? Those who study history know that principles that seem permanent prove to be temporary with the passage of enough time. This suggests that the replacement of the U.S. dollar as the world's reserve currency is a matter of "when," not "if."

Chapter 17

THE SHAMING OF THE STREET

*"There is no way of constructing a rascality index, but if one could
be made, the highs of the Drew–Fisk–Gould era would be
overshadowed by the peaks of the 1920s."*[1]

—ROBERT SOBEL

The stock market crash in October 1929 was severe, but its overall contribution to the Great Depression is overstated. Its impact on securities market regulation, however, was monumental. Outraged at the profiteering by Wall Street insiders, Congress finally outlawed many of the more egregious abuses. If not for the trauma of the Depression, intense lobbying by Wall Street may have prevented meaningful reform, just like it had in prior decades. In fact, it initially appeared that reform efforts would fizzle because the Hoover administration expressed a strong bias toward self-regulation. But even Hoover lost his patience when Wall Street leaders repeatedly disregarded the few demands he placed on them. Frustrated by the lack of progress, in February 1932, Hoover asked the Senate to open an investigation into securities exchange practices. Under the leadership of Senator Peter Norbeck, the Senate Committee on Banking and Currency commenced hearings on April 11, 1932.[2]

The first two weeks of hearings fell flat, and it appeared that Wall Street might escape unscathed. Senator Norbeck and his staff had limited experience in financial matters, which made it difficult for them to uncover the depths of abuse on Wall Street. Witnesses exploited their weakness by dodging questions and distracting committee members. But on April 26, 1932, the tone suddenly changed when Representative Fiorello La Guardia was called as a witness. La Guardia shared receipts proving that a publicist, A. Newton Plummer, had collected nearly $286,000 from stock operators, which he then used to pay journalists and editors to run stories favorable to their schemes. In addition to capturing the public's attention, exposure to the numerous schemes provided multiple targets for future investigations. Over the next two months, the committee exposed several insider trading and market manipulation schemes orchestrated by well-known stock operators of the time. Unfortunately, the subsequent witness testimonies were less explosive than the Plummer revelation. The committee adjourned in June 1932 having failed to strike a fatal blow, but it had established enough momentum to continue the hearings after the November presidential election.[3]

Senate hearings resumed in January 1933, but during the recess Senator Norbeck replaced William Gray with Ferdinand Pecora, a little-known district attorney from New York. Pecora almost instantly breathed new life into the hearings. His meticulous gathering of evidence, combined with skilled questioning and a flare for theatrics, enabled the committee to finally expose the depth of abuse by America's financial institutions. Pecora's skewering of Charles Mitchell remains one of the more devastating congressional testimonies on record. Historian Joel Seligman recounts Mitchell's shocking fall, stating, "On February 21, the seemingly indomitable Mitchell strode into the Banking Committee's hearing room flanked by a retinue of senior associates. Ten days later, Pecora would spy Mitchell walking to Union Station alone, carrying his own grip, a discomfited and beaten man."[4]

POINT OF INTEREST

The Birth of a Salesman

Senator Couzens: Mr. Mitchell, which are you, a better salesman, or a better financier?

Mr. Mitchell: I will say this, Senator Couzens: I have rarely seen an executive who had to do with the public and the management of a great corporation who was not inherently, by personality or otherwise, in the class that might be called a good salesman.

Senator Couzens: That is what I understand; and from my observations of you here, and on numerous occasions, I should judge you to be a better salesman than a financier—and that is no disparagement on your financial ability at all.[5]

In the wake of major financial crises, the American public tends to focus blame primarily on unscrupulous individuals, when, in truth, the primary causes are

(continued)

systemic weaknesses. In such cases, assigning individual accountability is roughly akin to blaming an impending war on the soldier who happened to fire the first shot. But every so often, situations arise in which a single individual bears disproportionate responsibility for causing a crisis and creating structural instabilities that persist long after they pass away. John Law achieved this feat when he single-handedly fueled the Mississippi Bubble, which ruined the French economy for the entire eighteenth century. In October 1929, Charles E. Mitchell, chairman of National City Bank and Corporation, joined John Law in this exclusive club.

Mitchell's stained legacy often focuses on his blatant abuse of national banking laws, which inspired the separation of commercial and investment banking activities under the Glass-Steagall Act. These misdeeds were shameful, but they were not enough to earn him a place beside John Law. To appreciate the significance of Mitchell's misdeeds, it may be helpful to contrast him with the financial titan who preceded him, J. Pierpont Morgan. First, Mitchell's success derived from the use of aggressive sales tactics. Often referred to as the best bond salesman in history, Mitchell would sell anything to the public. Salesmanship, rather than client service, was the spirit of his philosophy. In contrast, Morgan never deviated from the spirit of the Gentlemen Banker's Code. Despite its flaws, the core of this philosophy was solving clients' problems reactively and maintaining their trust indefinitely. Mitchell behaved in ways that J. Pierpont Morgan would have never considered because of the harm it could cause to clients. For example, Mitchell happily engaged in speculation and pool operations using his personal funds and those of his clients. Morgan religiously avoided such activities as he considered them to be little more than gambling. Mitchell exhibited little care for the quality of securities underwritten by National City Corporation, nor did he express remorse when commercial banking clients were duped into purchasing questionable securities. In contrast, Morgan felt a paternal obligation to foster the success of companies that he underwrote both before and after securities offerings. Finally, Mitchell expressed little regret for the countless lives that he and his employees ruined. Morgan could be defensive and irritable when exposed to public scrutiny, but he never hesitated to sacrifice his time and wealth for the greater good.

Morgan was the last of a generation of investment bankers who embraced principles that extended beyond self-interest. Many failed to uphold these principles, but the Gentlemen Banker's Code at least provided a target at which to aim. What earned Charles Mitchell a ticket into the club of the worst financial villains was the role he played in killing this code. Mitchell broke no existing laws—although many argued that he should have been convicted of tax evasion—but the damage he caused was immeasurable because he poisoned the ethos of his profession. This rendered the letter of the law as the primary constraint on behavior, but a profession bound only by the letter of the law soon loses touch with the spirit.

The spirit of Charles Mitchell persists today. Many financial and investment professionals divorce their conscience from the outcomes that they create because they believe that it is their clients' responsibility to own them. Lawmakers have proposed countless regulations to right these wrongs, but there is no regulation on earth that can replace a rudderless conscience.

The legacy of Charles Mitchell aside, the securities and banking regulations passed during the Roosevelt administration significantly strengthened investor protections. If not for the revelations at the Stock Exchange Practices hearings of 1932–1933, many of these regulations likely would have floundered. In recognition of Pecora's leadership, the Securities Exchange Practices Hearings of 1932–1933 are now referred to as the Pecora hearings. The remainder of this chapter details several of the more noteworthy revelations.

THE GRAND INQUISITOR

"After five short years, we may now need to be reminded what Wall Street was like before Uncle Sam stationed a policeman at its corner, lest, in time to come, some attempt be made to abolish that post."[6]

—FERDINAND PECORA

Ferdinand Pecora was born in Sicily and, at the age of four, he immigrated with his parents to Manhattan. Pecora excelled in school, graduating as valedictorian of his high school class. His college studies were sidetracked, however, after his father suffered a workplace injury, which forced Pecora to take a job as a junior clerk at a small law office to support his family. Undeterred by the setback, Pecora enrolled part time at the New York Law School. He graduated with a law degree in 1906 and passed the bar in 1911. In 1918, Pecora was appointed district attorney of New York, where he developed an exceptional reputation as a tough but honest prosecutor.[7]

Pecora accepted Senator Norbeck's invitation to replace William Gray as the new lead counsel for the Stock Exchange Practices hearing even though his knowledge of Wall Street was limited. His prosecutorial experience dealt primarily with the uglier financial schemes in New York, having successfully prosecuted nearly one hundred bucket shops.[8] What Pecora lacked in direct experience he made up for with his tireless work habits and sharp intellect. Pecora had limited time to prepare for witness testimonies, but he had an uncanny knack for sifting through troves of company documents and finding obscure but undeniable evidence of legal and ethical violations. As a digital monument to Pecora's efforts, many of the greatest abuses committed during the Roaring Twenties are accessible online in the nearly ten thousand pages of witness testimony and supporting artifacts. To fully appreciate the groundbreaking laws enacted after the Pecora Hearings, it is helpful to first understand the behaviors that these laws targeted.[9]

Abuse #1: Back Door Investment Banking

The National Banking Acts of the 1860s prohibited national banks from offering investment banking services. The most important consequence was that national banks could not underwrite securities. There were two reasons for this restriction. First, securities underwriting was much riskier than offering commercial loans to businesses and individuals. Prohibiting these activities at national banks reduced the risk to depositors. Second, the restriction mitigated conflicts of interest that emerged when banks offered both commercial and investment banking services. The most concerning conflict occurred when investment bankers pressured commercial banking clients to purchase securities that their firm was underwriting.

For nearly fifty years, national banks abided by these rules. Then, in 1911, National City Bank executives discovered a loophole. Rather than offering investment banking services directly, they offered them through a separate company, called a "securities affiliate." On paper, National City Corporation (the securities affiliate of National City Bank) was a legally distinct entity, but in practically every other way National City Bank and National City Corporation were one and the same. The two entities had the same shareholders, nearly the same name, and eventually they shared the same chairperson, Charles E. Mitchell. The companies even shared the same stock certificates. Shares of National City Bank were printed on the front, and shares of National City Corporation were printed on the back.

It was common knowledge that securities affiliates violated the spirit of national banking laws, but few realized that they also violated the letter of the law. Pecora revealed this when he presented a memorandum prepared on November 6, 1911, by Solicitor General Frederick Lehmann, which concluded that National City Corporation was "in usurpation of Federal authority and in violation of Federal law." Lehmann also explicitly warned the attorney general of the dangers inherent in merging commercial and investment banking businesses. For reasons that remain unexplained, the attorney general chose not to enforce the violation. The lack of enforcement emboldened competitors, and they soon established securities affiliates to compete with National City. Before long, many of the major national banks had combined commercial and investment banking services under a single corporation despite the existence of a law that prohibited it.[10]

Once commercial and investment banking services were combined, abuses soon followed. The most damaging abuse was the one that Solicitor General Lehmann had most feared—the dumping of low-quality securities on commercial banking clients. Pecora revealed this in his interrogation of Hugh Baker, president of National City Corporation. Baker reluctantly confessed that National City not only engaged in such practices, but that it was the "usual thing."

Baker's casual responses to Pecora's questions made the practice seem benign, but it inflicted serious harm on clients. A few days later, a former client of National City Bank, Edgar Brown, described the harm in vivid detail. Brown was encouraged by his client representative at National City Bank to enlist the services of Mr. Fred Rummel, a representative of National City Corporation. Given the similarity of the company names (i.e., National City Bank and National City Corporation), Mr. Brown assumed that the service was part of his commercial banking relationship with National City. Within a period of two years, Mr. Rummel's advice caused Mr. Brown to lose his entire life savings of $100,000, which were previously invested conservatively in U.S. government bonds. Mr. Rummel recommended an assortment of high-risk investments, including foreign bonds, speculative stocks, and even stock in National City Bank itself. Rummel also convinced Brown to leverage his portfolio by using 60 percent margin debt. A decline of greater than 40 percent would completely wipe out Mr. Brown's portfolio—and this is precisely what happened. In fact, Mr. Rummel's advice was so terrible that most of Mr. Brown's losses occurred even before the October 1929 crash.[11]

Hugh Baker's testimony, coupled with the testimonies of clients who fell victim to National City's practices, further inflamed public outrage. The separation of commercial and investment banking interests seemed like a long shot at the start of the Pecora hearings, but political pressure tipped in favor of it soon thereafter.

Abuse #2: Misuse of Federal Reserve Lending Privileges

The bull market in the late 1920s was fueled by an enormous increase in the use of call loans to purchase stock on margin. By 1929, the danger of this practice was a top concern among leaders at the Federal Reserve. The national banks generally heeded warnings from the Federal Reserve to limit these loans, which is why call loans issued by national banks plateaued by 1927. The shadow banking system, on the other hand, showed no such constraint. By the late 1920s, shadow banks met the increased demand and became the primary supplier of call loans (see page 203).

Banking executives may have avoided blame for the Great Crash if not for Charles E. Mitchell's defiance of the Fed. By the end of March 1929, the supply of call loans was shrinking, stock prices were declining, and it appeared that the bubble was ready to deflate. Then, on March 26, Mitchell announced that National City Bank would rescue investors from the liquidity crunch by providing $25 million in fresh call loans.[12]

Not only had Mitchell derailed the Federal Reserve's efforts to tame the stock market, he admitted that, if necessary, he was willing to use the rediscounting facilities at the Federal Reserve Bank of New York. This was an action that the Federal Reserve Board had specifically discouraged, and Mitchell was a director at the Federal Reserve Bank of New York when he issued this statement. Politicians were outraged by his behavior. Senator Carter Glass, who was already busy crafting legislation to rein in Wall Street, demanded Mitchell's immediate resignation. Nevertheless, immediately following Mitchell's statement, the sell-off on Wall Street ended, and the stock market bubble continued to inflate. If not for Mitchell's actions, it is conceivable that the bubble would have ended in the spring of 1929, and the fallout from the crash would have been less severe.[13]

Abuse #3: Inadequate Securities Disclosures

Disclosures regarding risks associated with newly issued securities were sparse during the 1920s. Even the most resourceful investors had little information on the securities they purchased. Prior to federal securities laws, underwriters commonly used misleading statements, material omissions, and outright lies. Pecora's meticulous research shined a spotlight on the severity of these abuses and the damage that resulted from them. One of the more dramatic moments occurred when Pecora revealed the existence of several internal memorandums circulating at National City that questioned the stability of the Peruvian government and stated that there was a low probability that the government could service debt payments on bonds that National City was preparing to issue. The content of these memorandums conflicted with statements made to prospective investors. When confronted by Pecora, even National City's president, Hugh Baker, conceded that an investor would have been unlikely to buy the bonds if they had seen the internal memorandum. This admission is captured in the following excerpt:

Mr. Pecora: Do you think that the public here would have subscribed at 91 ½ for these bonds if they had been given the information that was given to your Company by its overseas manager and Vice-President, that "there are two factors that will long retard the economic importance of Peru"?

Mr. Baker: I doubt if they would.

Mr. Pecora: And do you think that the public would have subscribed to these bonds at 91 ½ if they had been told in the circular that Mr. Durrell in July 1927 advised the company that "Peru's political situation is equally uncertain. I have no great faith in any material betterment of Peru's economic condition in the near future"?

Mr. Baker: I doubt if they would.[14]

—EXCERPT FROM THE TESTIMONY OF HUGH BAKER, president of National City Corporation

Mr. Baker deserves some credit for his candor. Other witnesses brazenly countered Pecora's revelations with ludicrous denials and rationalizations. Charles Mitchell was notorious for employing this tactic. One memorable exchange occurred when Mitchell attempted to excuse the use of newly raised equity capital from National City shareholders to remove $25 million of worthless bonds in Cuban sugar farms from the company's balance sheet. Mr. Mitchell explained the transaction as a "conversion of a short-term asset to long-term asset." In other words, he insinuated that investors were better off losing 5 percent per year over twenty years than the full 100 percent in a single year. This was technically correct, but neither scenario was attractive. Nonsensical rationalizations such as these probably kept Mitchell out of prison, but they did not absolve him of guilt in the public eye. His twisted rationalizations were arguably more infuriating than his abuses, as they allowed the public to witness the same insincerity that he used to swindle them.[15]

Abuse #4: Self-Dealing and Conflicted Transactions

The stories of self-dealing and conflicted transactions during the Roaring Twenties could fill several books. These practices were often legal, and it was difficult to find Wall Street insiders who did not partake. That said, some were more prolific than others, and the chairman of Chase National Bank, Albert Wiggin, was among the worst.

In the late 1920s, Wiggin was in a privileged position. As the chairman of Chase National, he effectively controlled five securities affiliates and served as a director on more than fifty corporate boards. These positions provided access to troves of insider information, and he used it unsparingly to enrich himself and his family. One of Wiggin's more egregious schemes involved trading in the stock of his own bank during the fall of 1929. As if this were not bad enough, a large percentage of his profits were generated between September 19, 1929, and December 11, 1929, which is when Chase National Bank stock was plummeting along with the rest of the market. This meant that Wiggin had sold the stock of his own company short during the October 1929 crash. Pecora revealed this shameful act by sharing incontrovertible evidence that Wiggin shorted more than 40,000 shares of Chase National stock and realized a profit of more than $4 million. Wiggin claimed that he did not intend to profit from these transactions but rather that he only intended to boost liquidity in the stock. Pecora countered by presenting the financial results of two trading accounts for Chase National stock. The first used corporate funds and the second used Wiggin's personal funds. Wiggin claimed that both were used only to stabilize the price of Chase National stock, yet his personal account generated a $10.4 million profit, while the corporate account barely broke even (Table 17.1).

Table 17.1: Results of Trading Accounts of Chase National and Albert Wiggin[16]

	CHASE NATIONAL TRADING ACCOUNT	ALBERT WIGGIN TRADING ACCOUNT
Purchases	$429,949,210	Not Disclosed
Sales	$430,772,795	Not Disclosed
Total Profit	$159,000	$10,425,000

Albert Wiggin's abuses were among the more egregious ones, but they were hardly unique. Executives, board members, and corporate insiders routinely leveraged privileged information at the expense of ordinary Americans. The public was not entirely naïve to these practices, but the Pecora hearings revealed that the scale was more extensive than most feared.

Abuse #5: Market Manipulation

POINT OF INTEREST

Return of the Stock Pool: The Meme Stock Mania of 2021

In the spring of 2021, Americans witnessed what many believed to be a unique event when members of a Reddit online chat group aggressively bought shares in small cap stocks, such as GameStop, American Airlines, and AMC Theaters.[17] The objective was to force short sellers to cover their positions at a substantial loss. The use of social media to form "bull pools" was a novel approach, but the fundamental technique was hardly new.

Many Americans applauded the crowdsourced stock pools presumably because the highest-profile victims were hedge fund managers. Lost in the conversation was the fate of millions of individual investors who lost fortunes in the crossfire. The widespread damage caused by pool operations throughout the Gilded Age and Roaring Twenties serves as a healthy reminder of the damage caused by such behavior if it is left unchecked.

If there is a law of securities markets that is comparable to the law of gravity, it is that skillful market manipulation has and always will provide the quickest and surest path to wealth creation. In effect, it enables investors to profit from knowing the future, rather than guessing it. Gilded Age stock operators were well aware of this law, which explains why they pioneered the various tactics covered in chapter 9.

Market manipulation was so ubiquitous during the Roaring Twenties that rumors of the latest pool operations frequently appeared in newspapers. The average investor often welcomed these "tips," as they believed that they could profit alongside the stock operators. This worked well while the market marched steadily upward, as individual investors were happy to ignore massive wealth creation by a handful of insiders if they shared in the spoils. But when markets declined by nearly 90 percent in the early 1930s, the average investor lost everything, while many stock operators retained much of their wealth. The symbiotic relationship was severed, and the public began viewing market manipulation to be yet another example of Wall Street corruption.

POINT OF INTEREST

Guilt by Dissociation

Arthur Cutten was one of the more prolific market manipulators in the Roaring Twenties, but he was one of Pecora's more evasive witnesses. Rather than rationalizing his behavior like many witnesses, Mr. Cutten sought to completely dissociate himself by claiming ignorance or forgetfulness in response to nearly all Pecora's questions. Pecora must have seethed as Cutten's

(continued)

statements of "I don't know" piled up. Ironically, although Cutten's obtuse responses protected him from inadvertently admitting to illegal acts, the sheer absurdity of his forgetfulness was unpersuasive to the public. Cutten's repeated claims that he could remember nothing convinced the public that he was guilty of everything.

In the end, karma had a say in the fate of Arthur Cutten. Even before his testimony, his fortune had dwindled. He had lost much of his wealth during the Great Depression, and his finances were further drained by a series of criminal and tax evasion investigations. Arthur Cutten passed away on June 24, 1936, at the age of sixty-six. Once worth as much as $100 million, Mr. Cutten's estate had shrunk to $350,000 by the time of his death.[18]

The final report from the Pecora hearings identified at least 105 stocks that were manipulated by pool operators in 1929 alone. Arthur W. Cutten was among the more prolific stock operators. On November 9, 1933, Pecora called Cutten to the stand to testify about his involvement in a pool operation targeting Sinclair Consolidated Oil Company. Cutten denied direct knowledge of almost every element of the operation, but the absurdity of his denials convinced the public that he was guilty on all charges.[19]

Abuse #6: Insider Trading and Preferred Lists

Market manipulation during the 1920s was far more damaging than insider trading. Nevertheless, profiteering by Wall Street insiders was sufficiently revolting to persuade the public that it was time to outlaw it. What seemed to tilt public sentiment in this direction was not the unfair profits of any single insider, but rather it was the use of privileged access by Wall Street financiers to reward (and presumably influence) politicians and high-powered corporate executives. Pecora used the House of Morgan as the poster child of this practice.

Testimony by Morgan executives, such as Jack Morgan, Thomas Lamont, and George Whitney, revealed that Morgan companies were prolific users of preferred lists. Evidence included documentation that implicated numerous politicians, corporate executives, wealthy individuals, and financiers. Throughout the 1920s, individuals on preferred lists received pre-IPO shares with no minimum required holding period. It seemed obvious to everybody but the Morgan executives that these riskless profit opportunities would, at a minimum, secure goodwill from influential people. Table 17.2 shows a small sample of notable individuals who appeared on Morgan preferred lists, along with the profits they realized on just one issuance (many received several issuances). The list includes a former president of the United States, U.S. secretary of the Treasury, a sitting Senator, and numerous directors of major U.S. corporations.[20]

Table 17.2: Notable Members of J.P. Morgan and Co. Preferred Lists[21]

NAME	ROLE	COMPANY	SHARES	ISSUE PRICE	MARKET VALUE	GAIN ON ISSUANCE
Charles Francis Adams	Ex-Secretary of the Navy	Alleghany	1,000	$20.00	$33.00	$13,000
Newton Baker	Former Secretary of War	Alleghany	2,000	$20.00	$33.00	$26,000
Calvin Coolidge	Former President of the United States	Standard Brands	3,000	$32.00	$36.63	$13,875
Charles Hayden	Director of 70 Large U.S. Companies	Johns Manville	1,000	$57.50	$79.00	$21,500
H.E. Manville	Chairman and Director, Johns Manville Corporation	Alleghany	1,000	$20.00	$33.00	$13,000
John J. Raskob	Director, General Motors	Johns Manville	1,000	$57.50	$79.00	$21,500
Alfred Sloan, Jr.	President, General Motors Corporation	Alleghany	10,000	$20.00	$33.00	$130,000
Myron Taylor	Chairman of the Finance Committee, U.S. Steel	Standard Brands	10,000	$32.00	$36.63	$46,250
Richard Whitney	President, New York Stock Exchange	Alleghany	1,000	$20.00	$33.00	$13,000
William H. Woodin	United States Secretary of the Treasury	Alleghany	1,000	$20.00	$33.00	$13,000
Owen Young	Chairman of the Board, General Electric	Alleghany	5,000	$20.00	$33.00	$65,000
William Gibbs McAdoo	Former U.S. Secretary of the Treasury and U.S. Senator	Alleghany	500	$20.00	$33.00	$6,500

The publication of Morgan's preferred lists was arguably more theater than substance. While it is conceivable that preferred lists were used to establish quid pro quo–type relationships with influential corporate executives and politicians, many were simply private banking clients. Nevertheless, the existence of these lists constituted another example of how insiders were able to profit in ways unavailable to the average American.

Abuse #7: Pyramiding of Holding Companies

The "pyramiding" of holding companies was the final major abuse revealed in the Pecora hearings. These complex corporate structures enabled a small group of investors to control massive utilities conglomerates. Under a typical pyramid structure, investors bought nonvoting shares in multiple holding companies, while a small group of investors owned a controlling position in the company at the top of the pyramid. In some cases, large conglomerates spanning multiple states were controlled by investors who had contributed less than 1 percent of the capital. In one of the more extreme cases, the Standard Gas and Electric Company had a total capitalization of $1.2 billion but was controlled by investors who contributed only $23,100 of capital (roughly 0.0019 percent of the firm's total capitalization).[22]

In 1932, three holding companies produced 46 percent of the electricity in the entire country, and four holding companies controlled 56 percent of the total mileage of the nation's natural gas transportation system. The most infamous corporate pyramids were run by Samuel Insull, the Van Sweringen Brothers, and Ivar "the Match King" Krueger. The complexity, lack of transparency, and concentration of control enabled them to engage in a variety of abuses, several of which were reminiscent of nineteenth-century railroad schemes. One such practice involved the return of the "construction and finance company" scheme. In a slightly modified form, the top level of a public utility overcharged operating companies for services—some of which were never performed. The operating companies passed these charges to their customers via regulated rates, which effectively forced the public to subsidize the scheme.[23]

Ferdinand Pecora spent a considerable amount of time unraveling the corruption of holding company pyramids, but the sheer complexity necessitated further investigation. Several years later, the Federal Trade Commission issued a scathing report, which inspired the passage of the Public Utility Holding Company Act of 1935. The act empowered the SEC to regulate public utilities; granted the SEC broad powers to alter the holding company structure; and forced the divestiture of several business units. In addition, buried within the act was a little-noticed provision that commissioned an SEC study to further investigate the practices of public utility holding companies and investment companies. Although not the primary intent, the final report revealed staggering abuses by investment companies before and after the Great Crash. These revelations inspired the creation of the Investment Company Act of 1940, which continues to serve as a powerful protection for investors to this day.

Chapter 18

RESTORING CONFIDENCE
IN AMERICA

"States, like individuals, who observe their engagements, are respected and trusted: while the reverse is the fate of those, who pursue an opposite conduct."[1]

—ALEXANDER HAMILTON

The worst effect of the Great Depression was the shattering of Americans' faith in the financial system itself. The banking holiday was an important step toward restoring confidence in the nation's banks, but faith in the financial system as a whole remained tenuous. Widespread distrust of financiers made it difficult and expensive for companies to raise capital. Securities exchanges were viewed as little more than upscale bucket shops that were rigged in favor of wealthy insiders and well-connected stock operators. Finally, investors had little faith in the integrity of the emerging investment company and investment advisor profession.

Federal reforms enacted between 1933 and 1940 helped restore confidence in the financial system in its entirety. The sheer scale of these reforms begs the question: would it have been possible if not for the Great Depression? Most evidence suggests that the answer is "no." Many similar regulations were attempted in prior years, but Wall Street lobbyists successfully killed them. The intensity of Americans' desperation during the Depression, coupled with disgust with Wall Street in the wake of the Pecora hearings, generated just enough support to overcome opposition from Wall Street lobbyists. Historian Joel Seligman brilliantly articulated this phenomenon by stating, "To reverse a popular saying of the day, the period of the first hundred days of the Roosevelt administration was that rare time when money talked and nobody listened."[2]

In retrospect, the irony of the financial profession's opposition to market reforms is that they stood to benefit just as much (if not more) than the public. Restoring public confidence in the financial system enabled the U.S. to stabilize its banking system, lower the cost of capital for businesses, and ultimately resuscitate a depressed economy. This, in turn, increased demand for financial services.

Chapter 18 details several of the most important reforms that emerged during the Great Depression. The first was the Banking Act of 1933 (Glass-Steagall), which restored confidence in the integrity of the U.S. banking system. Next, the Securities Act of 1933 created uniform disclosure requirements for securities underwriters. The Securities Act was followed by the Securities Exchange Act of 1934, which established the Securities and Exchange Commission (SEC) and forced U.S. securities exchanges to submit to federal regulation for the first time. Next, in 1935, the Public Utility Holding Company Act forced much-needed reform of the utilities industry, which was controlled by a small cadre of individuals who had contributed a shockingly small percentage of capital to their respective companies. The act also sparked a ground-breaking investigation into the practices of investment companies and investment advisors, which culminated in the final two regulations of the era. The Investment Company Act of 1940 sought to end egregious abuses of investors by investment companies (the precursor of the modern-day mutual fund), while the Investment Advisers Act of 1940 sought to bolster the public's trust in investment professionals in whose hands Americans entrusted their financial well-being. Contrary to the fears of the financial lobby, these reforms enhanced the nation's reputation for market integrity, thereby strengthening, rather than weakening, America's role as the new financial center of the world.

BANKING REFORM

Rebuilding confidence in the banking system was President Roosevelt's most urgent priority upon taking office. Whether Americans like it or not—and often they do not—ensuring that a nation's banks are stable and well-capitalized is critical to economic prosperity. Roosevelt's nationwide bank holiday reestablished a solid foundation of confidence in the U.S. banking system, but it did not resolve several remaining vulnerabilities that, if left unaddressed, could cause similar crises in the future. The Banking Act of 1933, hereto referred to as Glass-Steagall, addressed several remaining vulnerabilities.

The Banking Act of 1933 (Glass-Steagall)

The Glass-Steagall Act was the first major piece of banking reform since the Federal Reserve Act of 1913. Senator Carter Glass, a Democrat from Virginia, is credited for his leadership in crafting the legislation and orchestrating its approval by Congress. It may seem odd that Senator Glass would champion this cause. Aside from his support of the Federal Reserve Act and the Glass-Steagall Act, Senator Glass was a staunch proponent of states' rights and opposed almost every effort to expand federal authority. Glass was also outspoken in his opposition to most elements of the New Deal, including the Works Progress Administration (WPA), the abandonment of the gold standard, and even the candidacy of Franklin Roosevelt in all three Democratic primaries. Expressing his vehement opposition to the New Deal, Senator Glass once stated, "I've no objection to communist Russia; we're so far beyond Russia that I am amused that Russia is willing to recognize us." Glass was also unapologetically supportive of discrimination against African Americans. He took pride in his successful efforts to undermine African American voting rights in the state of Virginia, which left a permanent stain on his legacy.[3]

To understand why Senator Glass championed the Glass-Steagall Act, it is important to recall the Jeffersonian political philosophy that shaped his beliefs. While it is true that President Thomas Jefferson opposed most efforts to increase federal power, he was equally, if not more, hostile toward "the money changers" of Wall Street. One may recall from chapter 1 that it was Thomas Jefferson who led the savage attacks on Alexander Hamilton's financial programs. In this respect, Glass's support of the Glass-Steagall Act was consistent with the Jeffersonian philosophy. Glass simply viewed the expansion of federal power as a lesser evil than the expansion of Wall Street's power.

The purpose of the Glass-Steagall Act was to mitigate many of the systemic weaknesses that contributed to the collapse of the U.S. banking system during the Great Depression. The four most impactful components included:[4]

- **New Federal Reserve Powers to Restrain Speculation**—The inability of Federal Reserve regional banks and the Board of Governors to restrict the use of call loans made speculation much more dangerous in the 1920s. The Federal Reserve Board relied heavily on moral suasion to discourage member banks from expanding the supply of call loans in March 1929, but their efforts were obstructed by Charles Mitchell's public defiance. The Glass-Steagall Act empowered the Federal Reserve to conduct regular examinations of member banks and to suspend a bank's access to the Federal Reserve's credit facilities if unsound practices were discovered. The act specifically referenced the monitoring and restriction of bank credit used to support "speculative carrying of or trading in securities, real estate, or commodities." The act also restricted member banks from acting as agents to facilitate the offering of call loans by non-banking entities. The intent of this provision was to constrain lending by shadow banks, which provided most of the call loans to speculators in the late 1920s. Had the Federal Reserve possessed these powers in 1929, they could have prevented both member banks and shadow banks from recklessly lending to speculators.[5]

- **Separation of Commercial and Investment Banking Activities**—The signature provision of Glass-Steagall was the forced separation of commercial and investment banking activities. Under the act, bank holding companies that had both securities affiliates and commercial banking services were forced to separate the two businesses within one year. The objective was to eliminate the conflicts of interest that were revealed so vividly in the testimony of Hugh Baker, president of National City Corporation, and Edgar Brown, the client who lost $100,000 at the hands of one of Mr. Baker's employees. This was one of the more controversial provisions of the act. Many argued that separation was unnecessary, while others argued it was essential. Seventy-five years later, the debate was reignited when many contended that the failure of the U.S. to reinstate this provision in the wake of the GFC constituted a dereliction of duty by Congress. Regardless of which side is correct—and there are legitimate points on both sides—this provision dramatically reshaped Wall Street in the 1930s by forcing many of the largest financial institutions to separate two of their largest business units.

- **Expansion of Branch Banking**—In contrast to the GFC, most bank failures during the Great Depression involved small banks. Larger financial institutions, particularly national banks, fared reasonably well. Senator Glass believed that supporting larger banks would stabilize the system, but the prohibition against branch banking limited their ability to grow. Glass-Steagall significantly reduced these restrictions, thereby allowing branch banking to expand.[6]

- **Federal Deposit Insurance**—The establishment of federal deposit insurance and the formation of the Federal Deposit Insurance Corporation (FDIC) was arguably the most valuable component of the Glass-Steagall Act. Since 1933, FDIC insurance has served as a powerful deterrent against bank runs by removing the incentive for depositors to withdraw funds during a financial panic. As several banking panics covered in this book reveal, bank runs occur because depositors have a rational motive to withdraw their funds when they suspect that a bank may be insolvent. But if depositors are insured against losses, the incentive to withdraw funds disappears—at least for the balance covered by the insurance. To this day, FDIC insurance serves as a critical source of stability for the U.S. banking system. It may seem surprising, therefore, that deposit insurance was a late addition to the Glass-Steagall Act and was vehemently opposed by both President Roosevelt and Senator Glass. Both men feared that deposit insurance would encourage reckless lending by small banks, which constituted most of the failures during the Great Depression. They also feared that deposit insurance was bound to fail, as seven states had attempted it over the prior thirty years, and each attempt had failed.[7] Nevertheless, Representative Henry B. Steagall's insistence on including the provision prevailed, and President Roosevelt permitted its inclusion in the final bill.

President Roosevelt signed the Glass-Steagall Act into law on June 16, 1933, and the clock began ticking for the breakup of several of the largest financial institutions in the United States.[8] By June 16, 1934, iconic financial houses such as J.P. Morgan, Chase National, and National City split their commercial and investment banking businesses into two separate entities. The Federal Reserve embraced new powers to regulate the U.S. banking system and constrain debt-fueled speculation on Wall Street. Finally, the FDIC began functioning as an invaluable deterrent of bank runs, while simultaneously accelerating the expansion of membership in the Federal Reserve System. Perhaps the greatest testament to the success of Glass-Steagall is the fact that, to this day, the U.S. has never suffered bank runs or economic depressions that are even remotely comparable to those that plagued the nation during the early 1930s.

POINT OF INTEREST

Too Big to Fail or Too Small to Survive?

During the aftermath of the 2008–2009 GFC, many politicians justifiably demanded that the nation's largest financial institutions embrace reform. Some insisted on breaking up the big banks and/or reinstating the separation of commercial and investment banking interests, which was repealed by the Gramm-Leach-Bliley Act in 1999. A common catchphrase during the GFC was that no bank should be "too big to fail," as this created untenable moral hazards. The argument was that if bank executives know they are too big to fail, they will no longer fear adverse consequences of their decisions. This would allow large financial institutions to enjoy the potential rewards of risky behavior without worrying about the consequences.

(continued)

The "too big to fail" argument has merits, but the irony is that the U.S. faced precisely the opposite problem during the Great Depression. Most Depression-era bank failures involved smaller institutions, especially those operating in rural areas with agricultural economies. From 1930–1933, banks with less than $500,000 in assets constituted 83 percent of U.S. bank failures. This was not just an artifact of the Depression. Figure 18.1 shows the distribution of bank failures from 1921–1935 by asset size. Small banks suffered suspensions at a much higher rate than large institutions.[9] In light of this trend, the primary concern among politicians and regulators after the Depression was not whether large banks were too big to fail—it was whether small banks were fit for survival. This is why President Roosevelt and Senator Glass initially opposed deposit insurance. They feared that it would reinforce the same reckless behavior that led the U.S. banking system to the brink of ruin during the Depression. It also explains why Representative Henry B. Steagall insisted on adding deposit insurance to the Glass-Steagall Act. Steagall hailed from Alabama, which was a state that relied heavily on a network of small rural banks. His constituency believed—correctly as it turns out—that the viability of Alabama's banking system depended on the availability of deposit insurance.[10]

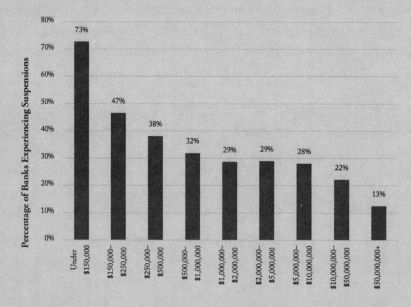

Figure 18.1: Percentage of Banks Suspended by Size of Loan and Investment Portfolio as of June 30 of Fiscal Year (1921–1935)[11]

The differing views on moral hazard risks in the banking system during the GFC and Great Depression reveal a persistent flaw in the way societies react to financial crises. The human instinct to simplify problems and isolate a distinct group to blame often leads to incomplete solutions that address only the latest manifestation of a problem rather than the underlying root cause. The existence of moral hazard is just as likely to occur in small banks as it is in large institutions, which makes it important to design solutions that address the risks in both. Solutions that only address banks that are "too big to fail" may neglect weaknesses that cause the next crisis.

SECURITIES REFORM

The second major area of financial reform under the Roosevelt administration targeted securities markets. The Pecora hearings revealed that the two areas most prone to abuse were the issuance of new securities and trading on securities exchanges. The Securities Act of 1933 targeted the former, and the Securities Exchange Act of 1934 targeted the latter. There was also a lesser-known third piece of securities legislation called the Public Utility Holding Company Act of 1935, which addressed the problem of holding company pyramiding and prompted an SEC investigation of the practices of investment companies. The subsequent report inspired the creation of the Investment Company Act and the Investment Advisers Act, both of 1940.

The securities regulations passed during the Roosevelt administration reshaped Wall Street forever. The SEC steadily stamped out the worst abuses of Wall Street stock operators, company insiders, and unethical investment bankers. The days when stock operators and insiders could brazenly manipulate markets and trade on inside information officially ended in 1934. Wall Street would need to search elsewhere for new profit opportunities or risk criminal penalties for indulging in the Gilded Age dark arts.

The Securities Act of 1933

"Publicity is justly commended as a remedy for social and industrial diseases. Sunlight is said to be the best of disinfectants; electric light the most efficient policeman."[12]

—PRESIDENT FRANKLIN DELANO ROOSEVELT

The Securities Act of 1933 was the first U.S. federal law regulating the underwriting of securities. Prior to its passage, securities underwriting was regulated by individual states under laws collectively known as "blue sky" laws. Companies easily evaded these laws by issuing securities across state lines to avoid the law of any individual state. Even securities issued within a single state often circumvented blue sky laws because of various exemptions or because underwriters flew under the radar, knowing that enforcement was lax. This left the nation with a complex patchwork of well-intended state laws that were utterly ineffective.[13]

The Securities Act of 1933 addressed this deficiency by establishing federal laws that superseded state laws. The Securities Act of 1933 had broad public support, especially for the concept of disclosure. The core thesis was that if underwriters fully disclosed potential risks, rewards, and fees, investors would have sufficient information to make prudent decisions. More contentious issues were the degree of liability that issuers would incur for inadequate disclosure, as well as whether the federal government would pass judgment on the quality of securities (referred to as "merit reviews").

In the final Securities Act, merit reviews were abandoned and the scope of liability was narrowed, but the disclosure requirements remained largely intact. The act was signed into law on May 27, 1933, and securities underwriters were henceforth required to provide a detailed prospectus that included information such as the company's capital structure, history of financial performance, fees associated with the flotation, and other qualitative and quantitative information that enabled investors to understand the prospects and risks of the investment. Underwriters were required to submit prospectuses to the Federal Trade Commission (FTC), which then had twenty days to review the material. If there were deficiencies, the FTC could bar the sale of the securities. Finally, the act authorized the FTC to establish uniform accounting standards for financial reporting. This provision was not considered particularly important at the time, but many people would later describe it as the most impactful provision in the long run, as it led to the development of universal accounting standards.[14]

The Securities Act of 1933 was relatively modest in scope initially, but it nevertheless constituted an essential first step in the history of federal securities regulation. After its passage, unscrupulous sellers of questionable securities risked severe penalties for failing to disclose the true risks and potential rewards of securities. Future regulations would build on this solid foundation. President Roosevelt acknowledged the importance of the Securities Act in the larger regulatory framework, stating:

> This is but one step in our broad purpose of protecting investors and depositors. It should be followed by legislation relating to the better supervision of the sale and purchase of all property dealt in on [sic] Exchanges, and by legislation to correct the unethical and unsafe practices on the part of officers and directors of banks and other corporations.[15]

The Securities Exchange Act of 1934

The Securities Exchange Act of 1934 was arguably the most important piece of securities legislation in U.S. history. It included a broad array of provisions to regulate securities transactions on exchanges and in over-the-counter markets. The act also created the SEC to enforce U.S. securities laws. The most notable provisions are as follows:

- **Establishment of the Securities and Exchange Commission (SEC)**—Section 4 of the act established the SEC, which consisted of five commissioners. Each commissioner received a five-year term, and a maximum of three commissioners could be associated with a single political party. The commissioners were authorized to hire staff and compensate them in a manner consistent with their objectives.[16]

- **Registration of Securities Exchanges**—Section 6 required all U.S. securities exchanges to register with the SEC and adhere to all terms of the act. Upon registering with the SEC, securities exchanges agreed to provide extensive information regarding their governance and operations, as well as provide amendments in a timely manner. Examples of required documentation included articles of incorporation, bylaws, membership lists, and "other information as the Commission may by rules and regulations require as being necessary or appropriate in the public interest or for the protection of investors."[17]

- **Additional Powers Granted to the Federal Reserve to Regulate Margin Requirements**—During the drafting of the act, there was debate as to whether the SEC or Federal Reserve should be granted additional authority to regulate the use of margin debt on securities exchanges. Under Section 7, authority was granted to the Federal Reserve rather than the SEC. The act included specific requirements with respect to the maximum allowable margin on securities, and the Federal Reserve was given latitude to adjust these requirements as market conditions evolved.[18]

- **Banning of Various Market Manipulation Techniques**—Section 9 outlawed market manipulation, which had plagued U.S. securities markets for generations. It banned many of the Gilded Age dark arts, such as wash sales, pool operations, publication of false information, and publication of impending major market activity. The act also left the door open for additional regulations to restrict manipulative practices. Section 10 outlawed any "manipulative or deceptive device or contrivance in contravention of such rules and regulations as the Commission may prescribe as necessary or appropriate in the public interest or for the protection of investors." Enforcement of these laws took time, but Section 9 and Section 10 were death blows to the stock operators of old.[19]

- **Registration Requirements for Securities**—Section 12 and Section 13 established registration requirements for securities traded on national securities exchanges. The initial list of required documentation was extensive, and it expanded over time. The act also included a catch-all phrase allowing the SEC to request additional financial documents that were not listed in the original legislation. A phrase that received little notice at the time proved to be vital in future years. Section 13(a)(3) stated that "the Commission may prescribe, in regard to reports made pursuant to this title, the form or forms in which the required information shall be set forth, the items or detail to be shown in the balance sheet and the earning statement, and the methods followed in the preparation of the reports." In other words, the SEC was authorized to demand the submission of financial data according to specific "accounting standards." This would prove to be a critically important power as accounting standards evolved in the United States.[20]

- **Penalties for Noncompliance**—While members of Congress drafted the Securities Exchange Act, Roosevelt repeatedly demanded the creation of a bill that had "teeth in it." It took many years before violators of the Securities Exchange Act suffered meaningful financial and criminal penalties, but the authority to establish such penalties was explicitly established in the act. After Roosevelt signed the act, many of the most lucrative practices employed by stock operators since the establishment of the Buttonwood Agreement in 1792 could land them in prison.[21]

POINT OF INTEREST

A Momentary Lapse of Scheming

"Everybody says that what business needs is confidence. I agree. Confidence that if business does the right thing it will be protected and given a chance to live, make profits, and grow, helping itself and the country . . . We at the SEC do not regard ourselves as coroners sitting on the corpse of financial enterprise. On the contrary, we think of ourselves as the means of bringing new life into the body of the security business . . . If we of the SEC do our job well and if we are helped by those we want to help, the New Deal in finance will be found to be a better deal for all."[22]

—**Joseph P. Kennedy, chairman of the SEC**

On June 6, 1934, President Roosevelt signed the Securities Exchange Act. Many members of the financial community feared that Roosevelt would nominate James Landis to serve as the first SEC chairman. Landis had previously served as the head of the FTC's securities division and was instrumental in drafting both pieces of securities legislation. If Roosevelt were to appoint Landis, the financial community feared an aggressive enforcement campaign would follow.[23] It came as a shock, therefore, when newspapers reported Roosevelt's intention to nominate Joseph Kennedy.[24] New Dealers believed that Roosevelt was recklessly placing the proverbial fox in the hen house, while Wall Streeters believed their luck was too good to be true.

Skeptics and supporters agreed that Kennedy understood Wall Street abuses, but only because he committed many of them himself. Kennedy made a fortune participating in pool operations throughout the 1920s. He then added to his wealth by selling his stock portfolio and adding short positions prior to the crash.[25] Ferdinand Pecora, another nominee to the SEC, was outraged by Kennedy's appointment. Pecora was especially troubled by Kennedy's participation in one of the higher-profile stock pools that he had exposed.[26]

Despite widespread opposition, Roosevelt refused to withdraw Kennedy's name. Roosevelt believed that a conciliatory approach to Wall Street was essential in the run-up to the 1934 midterm elections, as opposition to the New Deal was growing. He also believed that Kennedy was genuinely committed to personal reform, which was an opinion supported by Kennedy's outspoken support of the New Deal and repeated statements in private that his greatest ambition was to be "a credit to his family."[27]

Despite what seemed like long odds, Kennedy lived up to Roosevelt's expectations. Immediately upon taking the chairmanship, he wasted no time gaining the trust and respect of his fellow commissioners. Despite initial misgivings, each man—even Ferdinand Pecora—credited Kennedy for his leadership. Kennedy struck a delicate balance of effective outreach to his Wall Street contacts to reinforce Roosevelt's conciliatory message, while simultaneously making it clear that the SEC would not tolerate failures by firms to police their own people. Kennedy's financial savvy also came in handy, and he was able to secure an initial budget for the SEC that far exceeded James Landis's own assessment of their needs. At Kennedy's urging, Congress raised the original $300,000 appropriation to $2.3 million. Kennedy also had a knack for attracting talent. By the end of his tenure, the SEC's staff of nearly seven hundred employees had a strong

(continued)

reputation for competence and integrity. Kennedy's greatest accomplishment, however, was ending the "capital strike" on Wall Street by using a skillful combination of outreach and occasional public shaming. In March 1935, companies abandoned their silent protest of securities legislation by refusing to issue securities to the public. On March 7, 1935, Swift and Company registered a $43 million bond issue, which was soon followed by a $45 million issue of Pacific Gas and Electric. By the end of 1935, public listings totaled $2.7 billion versus only $641 million in 1934.[28]

By the end of Joe Kennedy's fourteen-month term as SEC chairman, his balanced approach had revived U.S. securities markets, improved market integrity, and established a strong reputation for the SEC. Had he ended his career at the SEC, he may very well have sealed his legacy as a reformer. Instead, he accepted an appointment as the U.S. ambassador to Great Britain and summarily ruined his legacy. Prior to joining the SEC, Kennedy was rumored to harbor antisemitic leanings. The depths of these prejudices would later surface in letters sent to family members and in documents seized from the Nazi regime. The documents revealed that, at best, Kennedy was a Nazi appeaser. Making matters worse, Kennedy was an outspoken defeatist who mocked what he perceived to be the futility of British resistance during the Battle of Britain.

There are countless stories throughout history of people who seek redemption, and many live their final years in peace knowing that their contributions late in life have outweighed the suffering caused in their earlier years. Joe Kennedy's failure to complete such a journey makes him a tragic figure. His interactions with the Nazi government and defeatist attitude in the presence of a desperate ally overshadowed his accomplishments as the nation's first SEC chairman. Sadly, when people recall his public service today, they likely view it as a brief flirtation with redemption that preceded the most shameful acts of his life.

The Public Utility Holding Company Act of 1935

The Public Utility Holding Company Act of 1935 is rarely discussed today, which is understandable because the purpose of the act was almost exclusively to address abuses committed by large holding companies that dominated the public utilities industry in a bygone era. Few investors noticed Section 30, which directed the SEC to conduct further study of practices employed by public utility holding companies and investment companies. After a four-year investigation, the SEC published the results of its investigation in a series of reports released in 1939 and 1940 under the general title of *Investment Company and Investment Trusts*. The reports revealed many disturbing abuses by investment companies and investment trusts during the 1920s and 1930s. It also included a preliminary evaluation of practices by investment counselors (later referred to as investment advisors). The results of the study inspired the creation of the Investment Company Act and the Investment Advisers Act, both of 1940.

The Investment Company and Investment Advisers Acts of 1940

"So similar were M.I.T.'s bylaws to the Investment Company Act of 1940, which laid the ground rules for the funds, that the M.I.T. had to change only a few commas."[29]

—STATEMENT OF THE MASSACHUSETTS INVESTORS TRUST

The SEC's report on investment company abuses initially seemed to be perfectly timed, as Congress was already working on bills to regulate investment companies. Senator Robert F. Wagner introduced the first bill on March 14, 1940, but it immediately encountered stiff opposition. The first obstacle was waning enthusiasm for the New Deal, as the economy was improving and several major banking and securities reforms had already addressed the worst abuses on Wall Street. The second hurdle was the growing threat of Nazi aggression in Europe, which now demanded most of the attention of politicians. The final hurdle was predictable opposition from the investment company industry. For all of these reasons, few politicians believed that Wagner's bill would pass before the end of the year. In fact, only three days after introducing the bill, even Senator Wagner and Congressman Clarence Frederick Lea signaled that they were uncommitted to passage of the bill in its present form.[30] Yet despite the long odds, the Wagner Bill refused to die and soon evolved into two separate bills—one covering investment companies and the other covering investment advisors. Then, on August 23, 1940, both bills were unexpectedly signed into law as the Investment Company Act of 1940 and Investment Advisers Act of 1940.

Given the initial opposition, journalists were shocked that these laws made it through Congress at all, much less so quickly. It was later revealed that investment companies themselves pressured Congress to pass them. But why would an industry encourage regulation of itself? The answer is that it was in their financial interest. To understand why, it is important to briefly recount the evolution of investment companies over the sixteen years that preceded the passage of these laws.

EVOLUTION OF THE INVESTMENT COMPANY

In March 1924, Edward G. Leffler founded a new type of company modeled after British investment trusts that started in the late 1800s. The objective of the company, which he named the Massachusetts Investors Trust (MIT), was to provide investors with an opportunity to own a diversified portfolio of securities by buying shares in a single company. The MIT issued common stock representing ownership in an under-lying portfolio of securities and allowed the daily issuance and redemption of shares. Over the next year, the State Street Corporation and Parker, Putnam, and Nightingale, Inc. launched similar companies. These three products are now regarded as the first open-ended investment companies in the United States.[31]

The MIT and other open-ended investment companies grew steadily during the Roaring Twenties but not nearly as fast as closed-ended investment companies, which operated with a different set of rules. Under a closed-ended structure, investors pur-chased a finite issuance of shares in the investment company, and those shares could be traded for either a discount or premium to the value of the underlying portfolio of secu-rities. Closed-ended investment companies also added leverage to portfolios by issuing debt and preferred shares. During the late 1920s, this structure produced extraordinary returns, as investors benefitted from (a) the price appreciation of the securities in the underlying portfolio, (b) leverage applied to the portfolio, and (c) the premium that buyers were willing to pay for the shares. In contrast, investors in open-ended companies benefitted only from the price appreciation of securities in the portfolio.

Closed-ended investment companies outperformed open-ended funds in the 1920s, but they significantly underperformed after the crash. The use of leverage and the shift of market premiums to market discounts had the opposite effect in the early 1930s. The extreme losses of closed-ended investment companies effectively killed their business model. In contrast, as the stock market recovered in the mid-1930s, investors reentered open-ended investment companies.

In 1935, investment companies were enjoying strong inflows when their business model was suddenly threatened by the Revenue Act of 1935. Under the new law, income that investment companies received from securities in their portfolios was no longer fully exempt from corporate taxes; 10 percent of income was taxed at the investment company level, and 100 percent was taxed at the individual investor level. In prior years, income from the portfolio was fully passed through to investors, who were then responsible for paying tax on the income that they received. This law pre-sented a significant deterrent to growth, so representatives from many of the leading open-ended investment companies lobbied the Roosevelt administration to change the rule. Under the Revenue Act of 1936, a full exemption for dividend distributions was reinstated—but only for open-ended companies. Closed-ended companies continued to suffer from double taxation, which further weakened their business model.[32]

Open-ended investment companies were in an enviable position by the late 1930s due to their superior performance relative to closed-ended investment companies during the Great Depression and favorable tax treatment. In addition, after the Securities Act and Securities Exchange Act outlawed market manipulation and insider trading, financial firms were searching for new revenue streams. Investment companies were a compelling solution because they provided recurring revenue, healthy fees, and attractive scale economies.

Open-ended investment companies had only one remaining obstacle to growth. Many investors were skittish about investing in investment companies because they were not regulated by the SEC. Investment company executives observed the rapid growth in the issuance of new securities following the passage of the Securities Act of 1933 and Securities Exchange Act of 1934, and they concluded that growth was driven by investors' belief that federal oversight reduced their risk. Investment company executives believed that federal regulations would produce similar results for investment companies. Moreover, the draft bill circulating in Congress required few changes to their current practices. The bill targeted the more egregious abuses that were committed mostly by closed-ended investment companies during the 1920s, and these companies had largely disappeared after the crash. With a few tweaks, the bill would have a minimal impact on open-ended investment companies that survived the Depression.[33]

From the perspective of closed-ended investment companies, the Investment Company Act of 1940 was initially viewed differently. The draft bills targeted practices that remained in place such as the use of leverage and issuance of different classes of stock. However, there was one critical change to the law that closed-ended investment companies still desperately desired—relief from double taxation. This made them willing to compromise on other issues to eliminate double taxation once and for all. Therefore, in an unlikely alliance of convenience, open-ended and closed-ended companies joined forces and pushed for the passage of the Investment Company and Investment Advisers Acts of 1940.

Broad-based industry support explains why the Investment Company and Investment Advisers acts of 1940 sailed through Congress despite what the media believed to be the slimmest of odds. Both acts were signed into law on August 22, 1940. Two years later, the Revenue Act of 1942 eliminated double taxation on closed-ended funds. This helped closed-ended funds to a degree, but the legacy of their performance during the Great Depression was something that investors never forgot. Open-ended investment companies continued to gain market share at a faster pace, and they remain the dominant type of investment fund in the market to this day.

A NEW DEAL FOR AMERICA

The regulatory environment established under the New Deal permanently transformed the U.S. banking system and securities markets. Glass-Steagall granted the Federal Reserve new powers to constrain speculation on Wall Street while simultaneously introducing new safeguards such as federal deposit insurance. The Securities Act and Securities Exchange Act provided powerful defenses against Wall Street's worst abuses. The birth of the SEC ended the reign of stock operators, who had dominated U.S. securities markets since the mid-1800s. Finally, the Investment Company Act of 1940 and the Investment Advisers Act of 1940 created a regulatory framework to limit abuses by investment companies and investment advisors for the first time.

Soon after the passage of the Investment Company Act of 1940, investors returned to U.S. securities markets, and most of their money was funneled into investment companies. Tragically, in the midst of this transition, investors missed out on what could have been the greatest financial innovation in the entire history of the United States. Buried deep in the SEC's *Investment Trust and Investment Companies* study was incontrovertible evidence that most investment companies (both open- and closed-ended) consistently failed to beat the return of a broad index of comparable securities. In other words, even in the 1920s and 1930s, the value proposition of an investment company was almost entirely limited to its ability to provide inexpensive diversification. Active management detracted value in most cases. In fairness, the country had bigger problems demanding its attention. France was under Nazi occupation and Great Britain was barely able to defend its homeland from the relentless bombing by the German *Luftwaffe*. Many Americans feared that the U.S. would be drawn into the conflict. By September 1940, Roosevelt's attention was focused squarely on the immediate threat of Nazi Germany and looming threat of Imperial Japan. The era of transformational reform on Wall Street was over.

Chapter 19

THE WORLD DESCENDS
INTO DARKNESS

*"Today we know that World War II began not in 1939 or 1941 but
in the 1920s and 1930s when those who should have known better
persuaded themselves that they were not their brother's keeper."*[1]

—**HUBERT HUMPHREY,** former vice president of the United States

Americans suffered tremendously during the Great Depression but emerged with
the fabric of society still intact. Many countries were less fortunate. Germany
turned toward fascism, and Japan embraced a genocidal form of colonialism. Chapter
19 may seem out of place in a financial history book, but it is quite relevant. Understanding the magnitude of destruction and human suffering caused by World War II
is important because the war probably would not have happened if not for the Great
Depression. It is not a coincidence that the worst war in modern history immediately
followed the worst global depression in modern history. The failure of world leaders
to treat the Depression with prudent and peaceful economic policies provided fuel
for the twisted ideologies of the Nazi Party and Japanese militarists. The passage of
time always renders policymakers vulnerable to losing sight of the connection between
depressions and wars. In fact, some people cavalierly invite the collapse of financial systems without considering the consequences, but the death and destruction of World
War II are horrors that should not be taken lightly.

THE RISE OF NAZI GERMANY

It is a chilling reality that Hitler persuaded tens of millions of Germans to participate in, applaud, or at least tolerate his depraved acts of aggression, cruelty, and genocide. What disturbs historians most about the Holocaust is their knowledge that there are few events in history that fail to repeat. In fact, similar atrocities have already occurred multiple times, and the total number of atrocities committed since the end of World War II already exceed those committed during the war.[2] Nevertheless, despite it seeming like a lost cause, prevention efforts are always worthwhile. It is important, therefore, to understand the factors that led to the rise of the Nazi Party, which oversaw a particularly horrific program of systematic genocide. Some factors were political, others economic, and some were solely attributable to Hitler's toxic personality. The pages that follow explain many of these factors by recounting the events in Germany leading up to World War II.

An Imaginary "Stab-in-the-Back"

"War is never cheap, but let me remind you that it's a million times cheaper to win than to lose."[3]

—HENRY MORGENTHAU, U.S. secretary of the Treasury (January 4, 1942)

On August 8, 1918, the Allied powers routed German troops in Amiens, France. The victory marked the beginning of the Hundred Days Offensive, which broke the stalemate of trench warfare and thoroughly demoralized German troops. As the Allies advanced, General Erich Ludendorff and Field Marshal Paul von Hindenburg reluctantly conceded that surrender was their only option. Unwilling to face the humiliation themselves, they turned over the process to the civilian government under the leadership of the Social Democratic Party. This was also a calculated maneuver, as it enabled the military and conservative politicians to shift blame for what they suspected would be brutal terms of a peace treaty. These fears turned out to be well founded. Outraged by the horrors of trench warfare and Germany's perceived instigation of hostilities, the Allies showed no mercy at the Paris Peace Conference. The Treaty of Versailles confiscated Germany's foreign capital holdings; forced Germany to cede approximately 10 percent of its territory; demanded a humiliating disarmament of the German military; and created a framework for crushing reparation payments to cover the cost of both personal and government property destruction. John Maynard Keynes, who was one of the more renowned economists at the time, departed early from the Paris Peace Conference after failing to convince world lead-ers of the dangers. Keynes correctly predicted that the treaty would ruin the German economy, which would then create precisely the type of instability on the European Continent that the Allies sought to avoid.[4]

After the signing of the Treaty of Versailles, extreme German nationalists sought to save face by crafting a conspiracy theory that blamed the civilian government, rather than the military, for the German defeat. The myth asserted that Germany was on the cusp of victory when civilian political leaders surreptitiously signed the Armistice out of cowardice and the pursuit of personal gain. Before long, hatred of the so-called "November criminals" intensified when the myth merged with preexisting racial and political prejudices. Soon it was not just that the civilian government had sold out their countrymen, but it was also the Jewish money changers and communists. The constant repetition of the "stab-in-the-back" conspiracy theory by extremists, military leaders, and sympathetic members of the media transformed an easily provable lie into an incontrovertible truth in the minds of many Germans. Once the lie was entrenched, most Germans ceased viewing World War I as a military defeat and, instead, viewed it as a racially tinged betrayal by enemies of the state.[5]

Adolf Hitler was a little-known corporal in the German army when he learned of Germany's surrender on November 11, 1918. He was only twenty-four at the time, but his virulent beliefs in German nationalism and the genetic superiority of the Aryan race were already fundamental to his worldview. Germany's humiliating defeat struck a devastating blow to the heart of his being. In *Mein Kampf*, Hitler recalled the psychological trauma of the German surrender, "I could stand it no lon-ger. Everything went black again before my eyes; I tottered and groped my way back to the ward, threw myself on my bunk, and dug my burning head into my blanket and pillow . . . So it had all been in vain . . . Did all this happen only so that a gang of wretched criminals could lay hands on the Fatherland?" Hitler's rabid belief in the superiority of the Germanic people and the Aryan race could not coexist with the reality of an unconditional surrender. This forced him to make a choice that all people must make when presented with evidence that contradicts the validity of their belief system: (a) accept new beliefs that better reflect the facts, or (b) fabricate a new reality that better reflects their disproven beliefs. Hitler chose the latter and embraced the stab-in-the-back conspiracy theory. Vengeance against the November criminals became the rallying cry of the Nazi Party, enabling Germans to convert the shame of defeat into a thirst for vengeance. The subsequent rage would be turned on political and racial enemies, many of whom were already too marginalized to resist (or even flee) the horrors to come.[6]

An Inflationary Depression

Broad acceptance of the stab-in-the-back conspiracy theory and Hitler's mesmerizing demagoguery were a dangerous combination. However, the Nazi Party almost certainly would have remained a fringe movement if not for the dysfunctional economy in Germany after World War I. The first catastrophe struck in the early 1920s soon after reparation payments mandated under the Treaty of Versailles were established under the London Ultimatum. After months of contentious negotiations, the Allies fixed German reparation debt at 132 billion gold marks (or approximately 330 percent of German GDP). To put this in perspective, this would be like the U.S. losing a war in 2023 and being forced to pay more than $80 trillion to compensate the victors. Servicing such a crushing debt was impossible. The Allies soon adjusted the repayment schedule, but even modified payments amounted to roughly 10 percent of German GDP, and the Allied powers reserved the right to increase payments if the German economy improved. The Germans objected to the proposal, but they had little negotiating power. On May 5, 1921, the Allies gave the Germans six days to accept the terms or face a military invasion. The Germans reluctantly signed the agreement.[7]

The sheer size of the reparation debt payments created a balance of payments crisis in Germany, as foreigners lost faith in the value of the German currency. This prompted a self-reinforcing run on the mark as Germans converted worthless marks as quickly as possible into real assets and hard currency. This resulted in a persistent shortage of marks, forcing the German central bank to print more and more currency. By the summer of 1922, Germany was suffering from one of the worst hyperinflationary episodes in history. Between July 1922 and November 1923, prices rose by a cumulative 387,000,000,000 percent. The German economy plunged into a deep depression, and the government defaulted on reparation payments. In January 1923, France and Belgium responded by occupying the Ruhr Valley (Germany's industrial heartland) and seized German coal and steel to compensate them for missed reparation payments. Recognizing that the situation was unsustainable, the Allies eventually intervened to relieve pressure on Germany. In August 1924, under the Dawes Plan, reparation payments were reduced from 10 percent of GDP to a more palatable 1 percent of GDP. In exchange, Germany agreed to cap the money supply, cease debt monetization, and eliminate fiscal deficits. This stabilized the German currency, but it was not without cost. The elimination of the fiscal deficit alone forced the government to lay off 25 percent of its workers and cut the salaries of the remaining workers by 30 percent. The additional economic stress reignited German resentment toward the Allies and the mythical November criminals.[8]

During these tumultuous years, Hitler consolidated various nationalist groups under the Nazi banner. Outrage at the Weimar hyperinflation attracted many followers, but Hitler sensed that his movement was losing momentum when the German government began negotiating the Dawes Plan. Passive resistance among Ruhr Valley laborers, which was supported by the Social Democratic leadership, seemed to unite Germans behind the Weimar Republic and weakened sympathy for nationalist causes. Hitler's supporters were similarly concerned, and they pressured him to foment a revolution before their political movement fizzled out.[9]

Hitler reluctantly conceded to the demands of his followers even though he feared that a revolution was premature. On the night of November 8, 1923, in what became known as the Beer Hall Putsch, Hitler enacted a hastily crafted plan to declare a national revolution. His objective was to gain the support of enough army and police to execute a bloodless coup. Supported by the S.A., a Nazi paramilitary unit, the Putsch began in Munich at the Bürgerbräukeller beer hall when Hitler held three political leaders of Bavaria hostage at gunpoint and forced them to declare allegiance to the revolution. Through a bit of trickery, Hitler also secured the backing of General Erich Ludendorff, who was still regarded as a hero of World War I. The coup initially appeared to be working, but by the morning of November 9, support from the army and police forces fizzled out. Lacking the manpower and desire to foment a bloody civil war, Hitler, General Ludendorff, and the S.A. made a last-ditch effort to gain sympathy from the army and police by marching to the War Ministry. They hoped that the mere sight of the mob would inspire them to join the cause. As they approached the police line, shots were fired, and sixteen Nazis and three police officers fell dead. General Ludendorff was immediately arrested, and Hitler fled the scene. The Beer Hall Putsch had failed. Hitler and ten co-conspirators were later found, detained, and tried for treason. Hitler received a five-year prison sentence but was eligible for parole in six months.[10]

The Great Depression Breathes New Life into the Nazi Party

"The month of September 1930 marked a turning point . . . [business leaders] might not like the party's demagoguery and its vulgarity, but on the other hand it was arousing the old feelings of German patriotism and nationalism which had been so muted during the first ten years of the Republic."[11]

—WILLIAM SHIRER, *The Rise and Fall of the Third Reich*

Hitler spent a little less than nine months in prison before gaining release on parole. During that time, he wrote much of *Mein Kampf,* which provided a disturbingly detailed game plan for German domination of the European continent. He also learned several valuable lessons from the failed Putsch, the most important of which was that a coup could not succeed without support from key institutions, especially the armed forces. Hitler vowed never to repeat this mistake.

In 1924, Hitler resumed leadership of the Nazi Party, but he encountered a less receptive audience. As a rule, extremist movements lose momentum when the population of disenchanted people shrinks. The renegotiation of reparation payments and stamping out of hyperinflation sparked an economic recovery in Germany. By 1927, economic output had risen above 1913 levels, and by 1928, unemployment dipped to 8.4 percent. Waning appeal for Nazi extremism was evident at the ballot box. In 1928, the Nazi Party won only 12 of a total of 491 seats in the Reichstag. However, Germany's prosperity was more fragile than it appeared. The nation's savings were wiped out by hyperinflation in 1923, and German economic expansion relied heavily on foreign loans. Hitler remained confident that foreign lending would dry up one day, and when it did, the good times would end. In the meantime, he worked tirelessly to prepare the Nazi Party to seize the opportunity when it arrived.[12]

The Great Depression was the event that Hitler longed for. Global trade collapsed, German exports fell sharply, and foreigners withdrew capital. This caused the economy to spiral into a depression, and the German people fell into poverty once again. Between 1929 and 1932, German output declined by 50 percent, and millions of Germans were suddenly unemployed. Bitterness spread throughout Germany to the benefit of the Nazi Party. In 1930, the Nazis received 6.9 million votes and gained 107 seats in the Reichstag, which was nearly ten times their representation only two years earlier.[13]

The 1930 elections legitimized the Nazis as a major political party, but Hitler knew that the eventual takeover of the government still required military support. He immediately began courting military leaders through direct outreach and offering unsolicited praise in speeches. Simultaneously he used propaganda to brainwash the rank and file. Hitler also garnered support from the business community, which provided desperately needed financial assistance. Despite their distaste for Hitler's demagoguery, many business leaders contributed to the Nazi Party simply because they wished to benefit from what they believed would be a bigger role for the Nazis in the government. Hitler's efforts paid off across the board. Within a few years, the business community and military were aiding rather than impeding his rise.

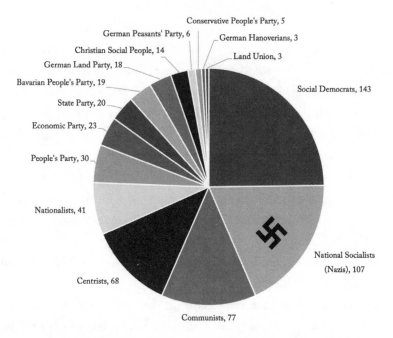

Figure 19.1: Reichstag Seats Awarded after September 1930 Election[14]

A Constitutional Putsch

The United States effectively functions under a two-party political system, with the Republican and Democratic parties dominating most elections. Critics correctly identify flaws of the system, such as the tendency to suppress less popular but potentially valuable perspectives, greater susceptibility to influence from special interest groups, and more limited choices of political candidates. But the same critics often ignore several offsetting benefits, the most important of which is stability of the system itself. In the early 1930s, Germany's political system was the opposite of America's two-party system. The Reichstag seated representatives from fifteen different parties, none of which was close to a majority (Figure 19.1).

Fragmented political parties made it nearly impossible to create a governing majority, which was necessary to appoint a chancellor and cabinet members. This produced constant dysfunction in the Reichstag, which forced the president—who was elected separately by popular vote—to repeatedly use emergency powers to govern. This was accomplished by invoking Article 48 of the German Constitution, which gave much broader executive powers to the president to deal with national emergencies. Article 48 was only intended to be used sparingly to address true crises, but leaders used it habitually throughout the 1920s and 1930s because political dysfunction made it impossible to govern otherwise. This created a dangerous precedent, which Hitler exploited.[15]

Hitler's intent was always to seize absolute power, but an important lesson from the Beer Hall Putsch was that gaining the support of powerful institutions must come first. This is why he never wavered from his strategy to acquire power through constitutional means and then seize absolute power once he was firmly entrenched. The gains in the 1930 Reichstag elections provided Hitler with the platform that he needed to put his plan into action. Over the next two years, Hitler and his close advisors, such as Joseph Goebbels and Hermann Göring, leveraged their political influence to maneuver their way into higher echelons of power. The ultimate objective was to find a way for Hitler to gain appointment as chancellor of the Reich, which would give him the authority to convert constitutional power into absolute power. There were two paths to the chancellorship. First, he could form a coalition government in the Reichstag and gain appointment by majority vote. Alternatively, President Paul von Hindenburg could appoint him by emergency decree.[16]

Hitler's chances of gaining the chancellorship through either of these scenarios seemed unlikely in 1930. President Hindenburg detested Hitler, referring to him privately as the "little corporal." His chances in the Reichstag seemed equally unlikely. The Nazis had the second largest representation (controlling 18.6 percent of the seats in 1930), but assembling a coalition to elect Hitler by majority vote was virtually impossible. Over the next two years, with the assistance of duplicitous aides to President Hindenburg, such as General Kurt von Schleicher, Hitler conspired to create chaos in the Reichstag until President Hindenburg viewed Hitler's appointment as chancellor to be a risk worth taking. The sheer number of schemes and conspiracies that occurred between 1930 and 1933 are too extensive to cover in this book. General Kurt von Schleicher, who served as chancellor for only fifty-seven days before being forced to resign, described the level of scheming when he stated, "I stayed in power only fifty-seven days, and on each and every one of them I was betrayed [fifty-seven] times."[17] Germany cycled through three chancellors and dissolved the Reichstag three times. Exhausted by the instability and under pressure from the growing popularity of the Nazis, Hindenburg reluctantly appointed Hitler as the chancellor by decree on January 30, 1933. Hitler had gained the power he craved while operating roughly within the bounds of German law.

The Weimar Republic Goes Down in Flames

"The only one who really knows about the Reichstag is I, because I set fire to it!"[18]

—HERMANN GÖERING (April 20, 1942)

Hindenburg and his conservative advisors appointed Adolf Hitler to the chancellorship with the naïve belief that he could be controlled. This seemed feasible at first, as the Nazis held only three positions in the eleven-person cabinet, and Hindenburg would not even allow Hitler in his presence without Vice Chancellor Franz von Papen by his side. Hitler would not be so easily deterred, however, and he immediately crafted a plan to counter efforts to contain him. The first step was to force new elections in the Reichstag so that he could establish a Nazi majority and repopulate the eleven-person cabinet with Nazi Party members. This was easily accomplished when he simply informed Hindenburg that he could not form a governing majority in the Reichstag (despite making no attempt) and was thus forced to dissolve the Reichstag and hold new elections. Once new elections were declared, Hitler used state institutions and the S.A. to unleash an intense propaganda campaign, political violence, and voter intimidation. Hitler hoped to tilt the election in favor of the Nazis and provoke a communist revolt, which he could then use as an excuse to convince President Hindenburg to restrict civil rights under an emergency decree. To Hitler's surprise, his efforts failed to incite a communist revolt. Something more dramatic was needed.[19]

On February 27, 1933, the Reichstag caught fire. German police arrested a communist party member named Marinus van der Lubbe at the scene, and he was eventually executed for the crime. Evidence presented at the Nuremberg trials, however, strongly suggests that the Nazis were the true culprits. In an affidavit, General Franz Halder claimed that he witnessed Hermann Göring boasting about having set the Reichstag on fire.[20] Moreover, physical evidence revealed that large amounts of gasoline were used as an accelerant, yet Lubbe was armed only with rags. Finally, there is evidence that Nazi infiltrators pretending to be communists encouraged Lubbe to attempt arson to provide cover for the real arsonists.[21]

Irrespective of who started the fire, there is no question that it provided the Nazis with the emergency they needed to deal another devastating blow to the Weimar Republic. Hitler convinced President Hindenburg that Germany was on the brink of a communist revolution, making it essential to issue an emergency decree restricting civil rights and authorizing the arrest of thousands of political opponents. When the Reichstag elections took place on March 5, 1933, opposition parties were weakened, and anti-Nazi voters were thoroughly intimidated. Yet even with this advantage, the Nazis only secured 44.5 percent of the Reichstag seats, which was short of a majority.[22]

Hitler remained undeterred because he knew the elections gave him enough political cover to pull off his final power grab. Two weeks after the elections, he introduced the Enabling Act (officially entitled a "Law to Remedy the Distress of People and the Reich") to the Reichstag. The act placed all legislative power in the hands of Hitler for a period of four years. Hitler positioned the act as a necessity to contain political violence, never mind the fact that the violence was instigated by the Nazis themselves. In his speech before the Reichstag, Hitler backed his argument with barely concealed threats against anybody who opposed it, and he reinforced his message by stationing members of the S.A. throughout the Reichstag just in case politicians failed to read between the lines. Most politicians understood the threat, and on March 23, 1933, the Enabling Act passed by a vote of 441 to 94. The Reichstag was relieved of its responsibilities for four years, but in reality they had relinquished them indefinitely. The Weimar Republic had fallen, and Hitler had become dictator of the Third Reich.[23]

Ethnic Cleansing and *Lebensraum*

The Enabling Act ended phase one of Hitler's grand plan. There were a few more tasks required to consolidate power, such as eliminating the position of president after Hindenburg passed away and murdering dozens of political enemies during the "Night of the Long Knives," but Hitler largely had the power he needed under the Enabling Act. Phase two of his plan commenced almost immediately thereafter.

Thousands of pages have been written on the nature of Hitler's ambitions, but in truth, he was a simple, ignorant sociopath, and his plan for Germany reflected this. Hitler's objective was to create *lebensraum* ("living space") for the Germanic people of Aryan ancestry. Ironically, Hitler was Austrian by birth, but he attached at an early age to German nationalism and the myth that German people of Aryan descent were superior to all other races. He was especially hostile toward the Jewish and Slavic races. Consistent with nationalist rhetoric at the time, Hitler believed that Germans were robbed of their destiny by a chronic shortage of land and natural resources. To fulfill Germany's destiny, Hitler's plan was to (a) destroy France, which was a check on German territorial expansion; (b) conquer eastern Europe and eventually Russia to secure lebensraum; and then (c) integrate annexed territory into a greater German nation, dubbed the Third Reich. Once additional living space was secured, Hitler intended to enslave non-Aryans for as long as they could survive as free labor and remove the rest via deportation or extermination. Germany would then repopulate the new territories with Aryans. Hitler's plan was clearly laid out in *Mein Kampf*, but world leaders either ignored it or believed that his ideas were too far-fetched to be taken literally. Over the next twelve years, Germans and citizens of conquered nations who possessed an insufficient amount of Aryan blood discovered that Hitler meant every word.[24]

Ethnic cleansing commenced slowly but escalated steadily within Germany's borders, as Jews and political enemies were gradually stripped of their rights, imprisoned, or murdered.[25] Citizens who resisted suffered a similar fate or were persuaded to remain silent after witnessing their friends suffer such fates. Terror rose to new heights during *Kristallnacht*, when the Nazis encouraged paramilitaries and citizens to punish the Jewish population to avenge the murder of a German diplomat in Paris. On November 9, 1938, mobs destroyed nearly three hundred synagogues and seven thousand Jewish businesses. Nearly thirty thousand Jews were arrested and sent to concentration camps, and hundreds were murdered. To all but those in the deepest state of denial, it was clear that the Nazi terror had no bounds.[26]

POINT OF INTEREST

The Inhumanity of Nazi Germany

"We are told that the American soldier does not know what he is fighting for. Now at least, he will know what he is fighting against."[27]
—**General Dwight D. Eisenhower (April 12, 1945)**

The Nazi goal of securing *lebensraum* for a racially purified nation had primacy over all other human rights. There were few (if any) crimes that the Nazi party found intolerable in pursuit of this objective. Theft, murder, and torture were rationalized because Nazis believed that their enemies were lesser forms of human beings who were unworthy of the rights afforded to Aryans. This perspective gave the Nazis license to behave in ways that were incomprehensible to the Allied powers. The murder of hundreds of Jews on *Kristallnacht* was viewed as a legitimate means to punish the entire Jewish race for the death of a single German diplomat by a Jewish assassin. Theft of property, trial without jury, and eventually mass extermination of millions of Jews, Slavs, and political enemies were just the means to achieve the Nazi prime directives of increased living space, racial purity, and vengeance.

Ironically, Hitler professed his loyalty to his Aryan followers, but his respect for their rights was conditioned on total loyalty to him. Aided by his propagandist-in-chief, Joseph Goebbels, Hitler felt no obligation to be truthful with the public. He lied repeatedly without remorse to support his twisted narrative. Those who dared to speak up against him met a fate that was no different than the fate of the races that they had once deemed to be inferior.

The Price of Appeasement

"Each one hopes that if he feeds the crocodile enough, the crocodile will eat him last. All of them hope that the storm will pass before their turn comes to be devoured."[28]

—**WINSTON CHURCHILL** (January 20, 1942)

Hitler's plan to expand the Third Reich beyond Germany's existing borders created a new challenge, as he suspected that it would provoke a military conflict eventually. The entirety of eastern Europe and Russia would not just roll over and allow their territory to be occupied and their non-Aryan populations to be systematically slaughtered. Hitler feared that countries would eventually resist, but he hoped to use deception to gain as many concessions as possible before the military conflict began. His primary tactic was to exploit his adversaries' fear of repeating the horrific trench warfare of World War I. Hitler believed that the mere hint of this possibility would enable him to extract enormous concessions.[29]

By 1936, the German military had strengthened, but it was no match for the combined forces of France, Great Britain, and several eastern European nations. Nevertheless, Hitler believed that his military was powerful enough to deter countries from responding militarily to the initial phases of German territorial expansion and violations of terms of the Treaty of Versailles. Hitler's first act of aggression occurred on March 7, 1936, when he ordered the German army to reoccupy the Rhineland, which was German territory that was demilitarized under the Treaty of Versailles. As Hitler predicted, France ignored this flagrant violation of the treaty even though French forces could have easily decimated German troops. General Alfred Jodl later testified to this fact at the Nuremberg trials, stating, "I can only say that, considering the situation we were in, the French covering army alone could have blown us to pieces."[30]

For the next three years, Hitler claimed additional territory and demanded economic concessions from the international community. Examples included the annexation of Austria, Sudentenland, Slovakia, and the territory of Memel in Lithuania. His demands were met each time without firing a single bullet. This emboldened Hitler to demand more, despite promising that each would be his last. By 1939, Hitler had significantly expanded German borders; bolstered the German military with hundreds of thousands of additional troops; and fortified German defenses on the western and eastern fronts.

The cost of appeasement was not just measurable in lost territory, natural resources, and population. In fact, one could argue the biggest cost was the strengthening of Hitler's grip over his own people. Each time Hitler scrapped a provision of the Treaty of

Versailles or acquired new territory, he claimed, quite accurately, that he had improved the condition of Germany without resorting to violence—at least against Nazi Party supporters. Responding to American criticism of Nazi aggression, Hitler boasted of his "peaceful" conquests. In a speech before the Reichstag on April 28, 1939, Hitler stated, "I have brought back to the Reich provinces stolen from us in 1919; I have led back to their native country millions of Germans who were torn away from us and were in abject misery; I have reunited the territories that have been German throughout a thousand years of history; and, Mr. Roosevelt, I have endeavored to attain all this without bloodshed and without bringing to my people and so to others, the misery of war."[31]

After World War II ended, the Allies discovered that appeasement policies had disrupted several assassination plots by convincing German military leaders that they lacked the popular support necessary to remove Hitler from power. One particularly tragic example was the abandonment of an advanced plot organized by General Hans Oster to assassinate Hitler in 1938. The co-conspirators abandoned the plot at the last minute after British Prime Minister Neville Chamberlain conceded to the terms of the Munich Agreement, which enabled Hitler to annex the Sudetenland from Czechoslovakia without resorting to war. The co-conspirators believed that public support was critical to their success, and an unwanted war with Czechoslovakia would have provided the support they needed. Deprived of this element of their plan, they abandoned the plot. Recalling this episode after World War II, one co-conspirator, Hans Gisevius, lamented that "Chamberlain saved Hitler."[32]

In retrospect, appeasement policies almost certainly allowed Hitler to survive at a time when he was highly vulnerable. If not for appeasement, Hitler may have died by a self-inflicted gunshot wound after suffering an overwhelming defeat in battle or in a coup long before World War II began.

Blitzkrieg, Dunkirk, and the Battle of Britain

On March 15, 1939, Hitler violated the terms of the Munich Agreement and invaded the remaining territory of Czechoslovakia. Great Britain and France belatedly recognized the nature of Hitler's deceitful game, and they issued an ultimatum that they would declare war on Germany if Hitler invaded Poland, which appeared to be his next target. The threat had little effect. Over the next several months, Hitler pressured Poland to make impossible territorial concessions or face invasion. Unbeknown to the Allied powers, Hitler also reduced the risk of a German attack on Poland by negotiating a secret nonaggression pact with Russia (referred to as the Molotov-Ribbentrop Pact). This pact effectively divided Polish territory between Russia and Germany in the event of a German invasion. Hitler never intended to honor the pact, but it eliminated the possibility of a conflict with Russia for the time being.[33]

No longer threatened by a Russian military response, Germany invaded Poland on September 1, 1939. The new German technique of *blitzkrieg* was lethal. Relentless bombings by the *Luftwaffe*, followed by fast-moving armored columns and tireless infantry overwhelmed Polish forces despite their valiant resistance using inferior weaponry. Within approximately two weeks, western Poland was in Nazi hands. A few weeks later, eastern Poland was overrun by Russian troops in accordance with the Molotov-Ribbentrop Pact.

On September 3, 1939, England and France declared war on Germany and began mobilizing their forces. Hitler never admitted it publicly, but he was surprised by the declaration of war—especially the British declaration. Emboldened by his previous deceptions, Hitler believed that the two allies would continue cowering from war. Hitler was also frightened by their combined military power, as the size of their forces and equipment far exceeded that of the Nazis even after five years of German rearmament. Despite his bluster, Hitler had little desire to fight a war with Britain and France.[34]

Hitler's sense that the French and British wanted to avoid war was correct, but he failed to understand that they were no longer naïve to his insatiable desire to expand German territory. This led them to conclude that war was a matter of "when" rather than "if," and the longer they waited, the more painful it would be. Despite their belated start, France and Britain were also confident in their ability to defeat the Nazis. They soon discovered, however, that what Germany lacked in manpower and armaments, they made up for with tactical innovation. First, the *blitzkrieg* technique combined overwhelming air power with fast-moving armored columns, artillery, and infantry to destroy enemy lines and demoralize enemy troops. France and Britain failed to comprehend the effectiveness of this tactic against technically superior forces. Second, the Germans had the advantage of ignoring international norms. For example, they were willing to invade neutral countries, such as Belgium and the Netherlands, to circumvent the fortified Maginot Line that protected France's eastern border. Finally, the Germans had developed new battlefield capabilities that were unknown to the Allies. The most devastating was their ability to send armored divisions through the dense Ardennes Forest, which France and Britain believed to be impenetrable.[35]

On May 10, 1940, the German army invaded western Europe, ending a nine-month quiet period known as the "Phony War." The attack began with an invasion of the Netherlands and Belgium. Employing *blitzkrieg* techniques, the Nazis defeated Dutch and Belgian forces within a week. Meanwhile, a thin line of French defenses was quickly overwhelmed by a surprise assault of armor and infantry through the Ardennes Forest.[36] The two-pronged assault left French forces disoriented in the northwest and rendered the heavily fortified Maginot Line irrelevant. By May 24, the German military had surrounded 400,000 British and French troops on the beaches of Dunkirk, France. Then, in perhaps the only meaningful error of an otherwise perfect invasion, Hitler ordered the German frontline to pause its advance for several days and allow infantry to catch up to armored divisions. The British government took advantage of the pause and rallied every civilian and government ship available to evacuate the stranded soldiers. In what became known as the Miracle of Dunkirk, the British evacuated nearly 340,000 British and French soldiers, which was an astonishing feat considering that initial estimates were that only 45,000 could be rescued. By June 3, the last shots were fired at Dunkirk, and the German military turned to Paris. France fell within two weeks, placing western Europe firmly in Hitler's hands.[37]

In the summer of 1940, Great Britain was the only western European power standing in the way of total German domination of Europe. But with a large portion of their equipment and munitions abandoned on the Dunkirk beaches, Britain was nearly devoid of land defenses. Prime Minister Churchill reportedly confided to a friend that there were fewer than twenty tanks in Britain after the defeat at Dunkirk. The freedom of the British people now depended solely on British naval and air power. From July to October 1940, the German *Luftwaffe* tested British resolve by terrorizing the British Isles with relentless air raids. At the same time, the German Army and Navy prepared for an amphibious assault, dubbed Operation Sea Lion. The British barely survived the *Luftwaffe*'s relentless attacks during a terrifying four-month period, known as the Battle of Britain, but the Royal Air Force's resistance was enough to deprive Hitler of air superiority. The Nazis subsequently abandoned Operation Sea Lion. Britain remained free from Nazi occupation for the time being, but it was unlikely to last without assistance from the United States.[38]

THE RISE OF IMPERIAL JAPAN

American recollections of World War II often focus on the war in Europe, yet it was the Japanese attack on Pearl Harbor that started the war, and the detonation of a second atomic bomb at Nagasaki that ended it. The disproportionate focus on Europe is unfortunate because the rise of Imperial Japan reinforces many important lessons related to the rise of Nazi Germany, the most important of which is the danger of deep depressions.

Japan Emerges from Isolation

Japan was isolated from the world and almost entirely self-sufficient from the early 1600s until the mid-1850s. During this period, Japan employed a feudal system of government under the rule of the Tokugawa Shogunate. Isolationism abruptly ended on July 8, 1853, when Commodore Matthew Perry of the U.S. Navy arrived in Tokyo Bay and demanded that Japan open its ports to U.S. ships and begin trading with the United States. Commodore Perry's small fleet was hardly sufficient to force compliance, but the Japanese realized that the pressure campaign would only intensify from not only the United States, but also Britain, Russia, and other Western nations. Acknowledging the futility of resisting a technologically superior enemy, Japan opened its ports. Over the next fifteen years, Japan signed multiple trade agreements with the U.S. and other Western nations. This benefited the U.S., as Japan offered a new, untapped market for exports, which would help the U.S. accelerate its transition to an industrial economy.[39]

The opening of the Japanese economy marked the end of the Tokugawa Shogunate. In 1868, power shifted back to the emperor, which marked the beginning of an era known as the Meiji Restoration. The Japanese initially resisted engagement with the West, but once the door opened, they embraced many Western practices, such as the formation of a parliamentary government and transition to an industrial economy. Over the next several decades, the Japanese economy thrived, thereby increasing the nation's wealth and allowing it to strengthen its military. Figure 19.2 shows the rise in total exports from Japan between 1885 and 1930, which was critical to its prosperity. By the end of the 1800s, Japan was the most advanced Asian economy.[40]

As the economy expanded, Japanese leaders grew frustrated by its lack of a colonial empire. This deficiency was especially painful for Japan because it had an acute scarcity of natural resources, such as oil, coal, and iron. At the same time, rapid population growth outstripped the supply of land. This forced many Japanese citizens, a large percentage of whom still relied on farming for survival, into poverty and even starvation. As these issues intensified in the late 1800s, military leaders concluded that territorial expansion was critical to Japan's prosperity.[41]

In 1895, Japan secured its first major territorial gain when Japanese forces defeated Chinese forces in the first Sino-Japanese War. The victory enabled Japan to establish control over the Korean Peninsula, Liaodung Peninsula, and Formosa (present-day Taiwan). In 1905, Japan achieved a shocking victory over Russian forces in the Russo-Japanese War. The Treaty of Portsmouth forced a Russian withdrawal from Manchuria and allowed Japan's Kwantung Army to control the South Manchuria Railway, which was a critical transportation route connecting Manchuria's vast reserves of coal and iron to end markets.

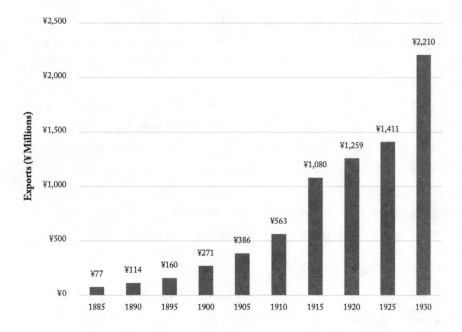

Figure 19.2: Total Japanese Exports (¥ Millions) (1885–1930)[42]

Japan's reputation as an emerging world power was further reinforced during World War I. Japan aided the Allied Powers by seizing German territory in China and defending Allied ships from German U-boats in the Mediterranean. Japan was honored to be the only Asian nation invited to the Paris Peace Conference in 1919, but they departed deeply resentful of their treatment by the Allies. Bitterness stemmed from the refusal of the Allied powers to approve a racial equality provision in the Treaty of Versailles, which would have provided Japanese citizens with immigration rights equal to those granted to citizens of Western nations. Despite a majority vote among the Allied powers, President Woodrow Wilson overturned it, and the Japanese viewed this as a racist slight.[43]

Japan entered the 1920s with simmering resentment at the racist policies of Western nations. Simultaneously, Japan's growing military strength, accelerating industrial output, and rapid population growth strained its resources. Japanese leaders concluded that expansion of a colonial empire was essential, yet Western powers continued to obstruct their ambitions. By the end of the 1920s, military officers, particularly those in the lower ranks, were angered by Western hypocrisy and the perceived treachery of Japanese politicians and business leaders who caved to Western demands. They believed it was unfair that Western nations, such as Britain, France, and the Netherlands, maintained colonial holdings throughout Southeast Asia, but the Japanese were forbidden. The Japanese were further angered by Western efforts to restrict the power of the Japanese armed forces. Military officers were especially outraged by the London Naval Treaty signed by the civilian government in 1930. The treaty limited the size of the Japanese naval fleet, ensuring its permanent inferiority to the combined American and British fleets.[44]

Resentment of the West was amplified by the fact that many enlisted troops and young officers were peasants, whose families suffered the most from anti-colonial policies. Their direct exposure to poverty reinforced the perception that Japanese civilian and political leaders profited at the expense of the masses and deprived Japan of its rightful place as the leader of a new Asian Empire. Tension was barely suppressed during the prosperous years in the 1920s, but it quickly became unmanageable when the Japanese economy collapsed during the Great Depression.[45]

The Great Depression and a False Flag in Manchuria

Rapid industrialization during the Meiji Restoration enabled the Japanese economy to thrive throughout the early 1900s. The October 1929 stock market crash and trade policies that followed threatened to undo all of Japan's achievement. Exports, which consisted primarily of industrial products and luxury items, such as silk, were particularly vulnerable to a global depression. Figure 19.3 demonstrates the impact by showing the collapse of U.S. silk imports, most of which were sourced from Japan. By 1934, U.S. silk imports had declined by more than 80 percent relative to the average for the five-year period ending in 1930.

The collapse of Japanese exports was not limited to luxury items. Price declines of agricultural products also devastated Japanese farmers, many of whom lived at a subsistence level even before the Depression. The collapse in demand for Japanese exports was also made much worse in June 1930 by the passage of the Smoot-Hawley tariffs, which virtually eliminated the market for Japanese manufactured products in the United States. In combination, these events decimated the Japanese economy. Suffering was especially pronounced among members of the lower classes, and many joined the military to escape poverty and starvation. This, in turn, increased pressure on military leaders to improve the situation in the only way they knew how: expanding Japan's colonial empire.[46]

The U.S. military operates under a strict chain of command that must be followed unless orders clearly violate international law or the Constitution. In the 1930s, the Japanese military operated under a similar philosophy, but with the glaring exception of *gekokujō*. The word *gekokujō* roughly translates to "the low overcomes the high." Under *gekokujō*, insurrection by low-level military officers could be excused (or even

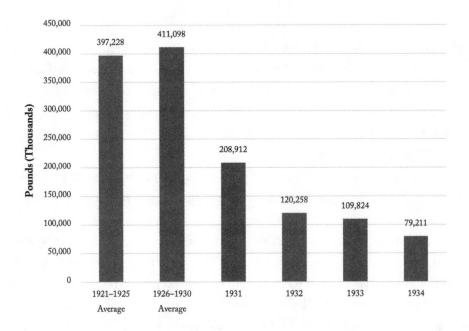

Figure 19.3: Total U.S. Silk Imports (Pounds) (1921–1934)[47]

encouraged) if the goal was the betterment of the Japanese nation. Judgment as to what constituted "betterment" was, of course, subjective, so insurrectionists who claimed to act under *gekokujō* did so at their own risk. But these risks were usually modest, as soldiers rarely received harsh punishment. This created a dangerous precedent in Japan, as it inspired entire military units to act independently with little fear of consequence if they claimed that they were acting in the interest of the Japanese people. Moreover, when officers employed *gekokujō*, they often appealed to the public for support, and populism was a powerful weapon in the 1930s.[48]

In 1931, Japan's economy was in shambles, and it appeared that their position as a leading Asian power was in jeopardy. Military leaders responded by pursuing colonization opportunities in continental Asia. Territories in Manchuria were an especially attractive target, as it was rich in natural resources and offered a captive population to sell Japanese industrial products. Capturing Manchuria would alleviate Japan's dependence on foreign nations for industrial raw materials, while simultaneously dampening the impact of U.S. tariffs. In 1931, Japan had a significant presence in Manchuria, but it was limited to a narrow, 124-meter corridor lining each side of the South Manchuria Railway Zone.[49]

The Kwantung Army was a unit of the Imperial Japanese Army (IJA) charged with maintaining security of the South Manchuria Railway Zone. The leaders of the Kwantung Army, Colonel Seishirō Itagaki and Lieutenant Colonel Kanji Ishiwara, understood how Manchuria could help alleviate Japan's economic woes. Operating under the principle of *gekokujō*, in September 1931, Itagaki and Ishiwara orchestrated a plot to incite a conflict with Chinese forces stationed along the railway. This, in turn, could be used to justify a Japanese invasion of Manchuria. The operation, which was dubbed the Mukden Incident, was poorly concealed. Japanese troops simply detonated dynamite close to the railway tracks and then blamed a Chinese military unit stationed nearby. The Kwantung Army then attacked the Chinese garrison with artillery, and Chinese forces retreated.[50]

Despite the obviousness of the ploy, the Kwantung Army used it as justification to invade Manchuria. Being far more advanced than the Chinese military, the Kwantung Army easily overwhelmed Chinese resistance. Within six months, Japan controlled a large percentage of Manchurian territory, and they proceeded to set up a Japanese puppet state, which they named Manchukuo. The new territory provided Japan with greater access to natural resources and a captive market for exports, but there was also a significant cost. In 1932, the League of Nations issued a report, known as the Lytton Report, concluding that the Japanese military had intentionally orchestrated a false flag attack on the South Manchuria Railway, and the League refused to recognize Manchukuo as a state.[51] Japan withdrew from the League of Nations in protest, placing further strain on relations with Western nations.[52]

Government by Assassination and the Rise of Militarism

The Manchurian Incident and Japan's subsequent withdrawal from the League of Nations marked an inflection point. The U.S. Ambassador to Japan, Joseph Grew, later commented, "Nobody could miss the political significance of Japan's decision to quit the League of Nations. It marked a clear break with the Western powers and prepared the way for Japan's later adherence to the Axis."[53]

The break with Western powers widened in the years following the Manchurian Incident. It also produced internal discord. Disgusted by the perceived corruption of government officials, coupled with empathy for Japanese citizens suffering from poverty, many young military officers began assassinating politicians who expressed insufficient support for the military. Hugh Byas later coined the term "government by assassination" to describe this tumultuous period. Throughout the mid-1930s, assassinations of Japanese cabinet members occurred with increasing regularity, and public sympathy for the assassins ensured that they received light penalties. As cabinet members became more fearful of displeasing the military, government policy was increasingly shaped by military priorities. Although the emperor remained the official authority in Japan, by the late 1930s, military leaders were effectively dictating Japanese domestic and foreign policy.[54]

The Second Sino-Japanese War

After the end of the Boxer Rebellion in 1901, the Chinese government permitted foreign countries to station troops in the vicinity of Beijing for security purposes. On July 7, 1937, Chinese and Japanese troops stationed at the Marco Polo Bridge exchanged fire in an apparent misunderstanding. Despite several truces, an unknown third party repeatedly reignited the conflict by firing on Japanese troops. Whether it was Chinese soldiers or expansionist Japanese troops orchestrating a false flag operation remains unknown. Regardless of the cause, and despite genuine efforts to resolve the incident peacefully, the crisis escalated. Anti-Japanese rhetoric from Chiang Kai-shek, leader of the Chinese Nationalists, further angered Japanese military leaders, and Japan responded by sending reinforcements to teach him a lesson.[55]

The Japanese military response quickly escalated to a full-scale invasion of China, thus beginning the Second Sino-Japanese War. Japan's goal was to defeat the Chinese decisively and force them to a negotiated settlement within three months. Initially, Japanese military superiority was overwhelming. As more Chinese cities fell, Japanese troops suffered a complete breakdown in discipline and committed horrific atrocities. The most egregious incident occurred in Nanking, where up to 300,000 Chinese men, women, and children were systematically murdered, tortured, and raped. The atrocities were so barbaric that even Nazi observers condemned the Japanese Army, describing it as a "bestial machinery." Stories included captured civilians being used as live dummies for bayonet practice and timed contests in which Japanese troops competed to see who could behead the most prisoners.[56]

The brutality of the Japanese military hardened Chinese resistance. Although Japan gained control over several coastal regions, guerrilla resistance persisted throughout the mainland. Months of battle morphed into years, costing the Japanese hundreds of thousands of lives. The negative attention from Western nations, especially the U.S., was even more costly. Horrified by Japanese atrocities, Americans began viewing the Japanese Empire as no different than the Nazi regime.

The Horror of Unconstrained Barbarity

"It may be pointless to try to establish which World War II Axis aggressor, Germany or Japan, was the more brutal to the peoples it victimised. The Germans killed six million Jews and 20 million Russians; the Japanese slaughtered as many as 30 million Filipinos, Malays, Vietnamese, Cambodians, Indonesians and Burmese, at least 23 million of them ethnic Chinese . . . Both conquerors enslaved millions and exploited them as forced labourers— and, in the case of the Japanese, as prostitutes for front-line troops."[57]

—Chalmers Johnson

Nazi atrocities were so horrific that it is hard to imagine another country could have matched them. But the Japanese military committed atrocities at a scale and with a level of cruelty that matched, if not exceeded, that of the Nazis. Japanese POWs and civilians were routinely subjected to torture, rape, starvation, medical experimentation, and murder.

In contrast to Nazi Germany, many atrocities were not specifically ordered by higher-ups, but there was virtually no accountability for lower-level officers and soldiers who committed them. The ultimate verdict on the character of a leader is based on the outcomes of their command. The Japanese sin of permissiveness created outcomes that were no different than those produced by the explicit policies of the Nazis. Willful ignorance does not excuse tacit approval made possible by a lack of accountability.

The Empire of Japan Goes South

In the spring of 1940, mounting Japanese casualties and the rising financial costs of war weighed on Japan. Military leaders quietly planned to accept modest territorial gains and pull back if the war was not won within a year. But the plan suddenly changed when Japan witnessed the unexpected fall of western Europe in May 1940. With the Netherlands and France under Nazi control, their former colonies in China and Southeast Asia were open for the taking. Not only did this harden Japan's resolve in its war against China, but it also inspired them to expand farther into Southeast Asia and the Dutch East Indies. The slogan among Japanese militarists became "don't miss the bus," and they set out to seize former Dutch, French, and British colonies in the South Pacific Islands and Southeast Asia. The most attractive assets were oil fields in the Dutch East Indies and reserves of tin, coal, and rubber scattered throughout the South Pacific.[58]

In July 1940, the Japanese cabinet unanimously approved the total mobilization of the Japanese nation to lead the creation of a greater Asian empire. Fearing that Japan was merely a clone of the Nazis, the U.S. responded by freezing all Japanese assets and tightening trade restrictions. Roosevelt had also sent a signal earlier in the year that military confrontation with Japan was not out of the question when he relocated the Pacific Fleet from southern California to Pearl Harbor on the island of Oahu, Hawaii.[59]

Japanese militarists were undeterred by the American response. In August 1940, Japan began its move into Southeast Asia by signing an agreement with Vichy France to take control of Vietnam. Next, in September 1940, Japan signed the Tripartite Pact, solidifying its relationship with Nazi Germany and Fascist Italy. The Japanese movement into Vietnam was the final straw for the United States. Roosevelt responded by tightening trade restrictions even further and banning oil exports to Japan. At the time, the U.S. provided 80 percent of Japanese fuel oil. When the Dutch East Indies and Britain joined the embargo, 88 percent of Japanese oil imports disappeared, and Japanese military leaders estimated they would run out of fuel oil in three years. Once supplies ran out, the Japanese Empire would collapse. Militarists knew that ending the oil embargo was critical to their survival. The preferred option was a negotiated settlement with the U.S., but if negotiations failed, war was their only alternative. The clock was ticking, and Japan would not wait for its oil reserves to run dry before acting.[60]

Admiral Yamamoto's Gamble

"A military man can scarcely pride himself on having 'smitten a sleeping enemy'; it is more a matter of shame, simply for the one smitten. I would rather you made your appraisal after seeing what the enemy does, since it is certain that, angered and outraged, he will soon launch a determined counterattack."[61]

—ADMIRAL ISOROKU YAMAMOTO (January 9, 1942)

Admiral Isoroku Yamamoto was one of the few Japanese military officers who disapproved of Japan's expansionist policies. He opposed the invasion of Manchuria in 1931, the invasion of China in 1937, and the plan to attack the U.S. in response to the oil embargo. Yamamoto's perspective was informed by experiences that most of his comrades lacked. From 1919 to 1921, he resided in the U.S. as a student at Harvard University, and he later returned as a naval attaché in the mid-1920s. Yamamoto marveled at America's wealth of natural resources, large-scale industrial capabilities, and relentless spirit of innovation. Most importantly, having immersed himself in the American culture, he was skeptical of the Japanese belief that Americans would cower in response to an attack.[62]

Despite Yamamoto's reservations, he knew his opinion was unpopular in Japan. He accepted that eventual war with the U.S. was likely, so rather than wasting his time trying to persuade his comrades to stand down, he focused on crafting a military strategy that had the best chance of success. Core to Yamamoto's strategy was his fundamental belief that Japan could not defeat the U.S. in a protracted war. The U.S. had too many competitive advantages in terms of natural resources, industrial capacity, and technological sophistication. Moreover, the country's natural defenses were insurmountable, as it was separated from Europe and Asia by vast oceans and bordered by friendly nations to the north and south. Instead, Yamamoto concluded that the only chance of victory would be to deliver a devastating blow at the outset of a war and hope that the U.S. would sue for peace. Yamamoto doubted that even this strategy was likely to succeed, but at least it would have a chance.[63]

In 1941, the Japanese military began planning their expansion into Southeast Asia, accepting the risk that it would trigger a military confrontation with the United States. The consensus among militarists was that the Japanese should focus their offensive operations in Southeast Asia, create solid defensive positions, and then wait for the Americans to counterattack. Yamamoto argued against this strategy because it neglected to account for the fact that America's significant competitive advantages would only strengthen while Japan waited for the Americans to attack. Delaying a war would effectively guarantee Japan's defeat. He argued that the more attractive option was to hit the U.S. where it hurt the most by launching a surprise attack on the Pacific Fleet stationed at Pearl Harbor. If successful, the attack would incapacitate America's aircraft carriers and battleships, thereby eliminating the risk of an immediate counterattack. As the U.S. rebuilt its fleet, Japan could seize critical oil reserves in the Dutch East Indies and fortify their defensive positions. The attack would also maximize the element of surprise. Just like the French never expected armored divisions to emerge from the Ardennes Forest, Yamamoto believed that an attack on Pearl Harbor was beyond the bounds of American imagination.[64]

Yamamoto's plan, which was code-named Operation Z, was conceptually brilliant, but execution was initially deemed to be beyond the navy's capabilities. Several technical hurdles, such as refueling ships in rough seas and launching torpedoes in a shallow harbor, had to be overcome. The attack also required the utmost secrecy; if the U.S. detected a Japanese fleet enroute to Pearl Harbor, they would retaliate and end Japan's expansion into Southeast Asia before it even began. Over the next ten months, Yama-moto overcame each technical challenge by designing new weaponry and rigorously training naval crews to refuel at sea. By November 1941, he was confident that he had surmounted the technical obstacles, but even then, he estimated that the probability of victory was 50/50, at best.[65]

While Yamamoto was preparing Operation Z, the government of Japan engaged in what proved to be a futile effort to negotiate a peaceful settlement. Throughout 1941, negotiations suffered from countless miscommunications, misperceptions, and clumsy translations on both sides. There is even credible evidence that a Russian intelligence operation dubbed Operation Snow successfully shaped U.S. policy to increase the chance of diplomatic failure.[66] The American asset used for this operation was Harry Dexter White, who would express similar sympathies for Russia when architecting a new international monetary system at Bretton Woods in July 1944 (see chapter 21). Even after factoring in the potential influence of Russian intelligence, it is likely that the U.S. and Japan would have arrived at the same place. A peaceful solution was perhaps possible if there was more time, but Japan was on the clock, as each passing day brought them closer to running out of fuel oil reserves. On November 26, 1941, Japan reached its internal deadline, and six aircraft carriers accompanied by eighteen warships departed from Hitokappu Bay enroute to the Hawaiian Islands.[67]

The Japanese fleet experienced few complications during its eleven-day journey. Seas were calm, making refueling easier than anticipated, and the fleet remained undetected. U.S. military leaders were alarmed by intelligence reports revealing that Japanese embassy employees suddenly began destroying documents on November 26, but nobody anticipated an attack on Pearl Harbor.[68]

On the morning of December 7, 1941, the Japanese fleet arrived at its launch site for Operation Z, which was approximately two hundred miles north of the island of Oahu. The first planes took off at 6:10 a.m. and headed south. At approximately eight a.m., a Japanese bomber radioed, "Tora, tora, tora," signaling the commence-ment of the first wave of attacks. Americans were completely unaware of the attack until the first bombs began exploding. The bombers targeted the airfields first, destroying or incapacitating virtually every aircraft on the island within minutes. With America's air defenses neutralized, the bombers swarmed over the defenseless warships moored at Pearl Harbor. For two hours, Japanese bombers attacked at will, flooding Pearl Harbor with torpedoes and penetrating ship decks with armor-pierc-ing bombs. After two attack waves, the last planes departed around ten a.m., having devastated the Pacific Fleet. The assault destroyed three battleships and inflicted heavy damage on an additional eighteen warships. Damage to U.S. aircraft was even worse, with 188 of 402 aircraft completely destroyed and another 159 damaged. The human cost was also severe, with the U.S. suffering 2,403 soldiers killed and another 1,173 wounded. The only positive (but not insignificant) news was that the Pacific Fleet's three aircraft carriers were spared, as they were performing maneuvers at sea during the attack. Had they been present, the U.S. Pacific Fleet would have been totally incapacitated.[69]

The Japanese military and citizenry were ecstatic when they heard the news of their victory at Pearl Harbor, but Admiral Yamamoto fell into a deep depression. Unlike his comrades, he knew that Pearl Harbor was a monumental failure. First, from a purely tactical perspective, the attack failed to sink America's aircraft carriers, which were by far the most critical assets of the Pacific Fleet. More importantly, even if Japan had sunk the aircraft carriers, it was America's reaction that revealed the futility of Yamamoto's gamble. Rather than cowering in fear and suing for peace, Pearl Harbor galvanized the nation. In a single day, Americans abandoned their isolationist leanings and unified behind the single goal of destroying their newest enemy: the Empire of Japan. Unlike his comrades, Yamamoto knew that the attack on Pearl Harbor was a psychological operation. Its success depended on its ability to demoralize the American people. When he witnessed the opposite reaction, he knew what his fellow citizens would only come to appreciate after suffering millions of deaths from grueling combat, urban firestorms, starvation, and two nuclear explosions. On December 7, 1941, Japan had won a memorable surprise attack against an unarmed opponent, but the war was already lost.[70]

Chapter 20

THE U.S. ARSENAL
OF DEMOCRACY

*"America is like a giant boiler . . . once the fire is lighted under it,
there is no limit to the power it can generate."*[1]

—SIR WINSTON CHURCHILL, British prime minister

In the spring of 1942, the U.S. military was surviving but not yet winning the war. Two of the nation's four aircraft carriers were incapacitated in the Battle of the Coral Sea, rendering the Pacific Fleet outmatched by the Japanese fleet of six carriers. In the European Theater, Hitler had opened a second front by declaring war on the U.S. only four days after the attack on Pearl Harbor. Meanwhile, the Nazis had advanced deep into Russian territory, and it appeared that the country would soon fall into Nazi hands.

It almost certainly did not seem so at the time, but 1942 was the high watermark of the Axis power's advances. The Nazi invasion of Russia and Japanese conquests in the South Pacific were like rogue waves. Such waves are lethal to anybody standing close to the shoreline, but the initial terror quickly subsides once the wave disperses and recedes back into the sea. The war machine of the United States was more like a tsunami. Supported by a massive seismic movement of the ocean floor itself, 99.99 percent of a tsunami's energy remains hidden beneath the surface and is only revealed when the wave crashes on the beach and refuses to stop.

The Nazi and Japanese advances were like rogue waves because they lacked the power to sustain their conquests. In contrast, the U.S. was like a tsunami, drawing its power from a rich bounty of raw materials, seemingly limitless industrial production capacity, and deadly technological innovation. In the summer of 1942, a flood of American war materiel began making its way to the front lines, overwhelming the under-resourced and overextended German and Japanese forces. Many unconscionable atrocities lay ahead, but each new day from the summer of 1942 onward brought the world closer to the end of the Nazi and Japanese reigns of terror.

AWAKENING THE SLEEPING GIANT

It is tempting to assume that the U.S. victory in an unprecedented, two-front global war was written in the stars, but the truth is that the U.S. was woefully unprepared for war when Hitler invaded western Europe. Over the prior twenty years, the U.S. had neglected its military, allowing it to plummet from the fourth largest force in the world in 1918 to the eighteenth largest in 1939—trailing even the Netherlands. There were many explanations for this decline, including pervasive isolationist leanings, budgetary constraints stemming from the Great Depression, and a general desire to punish the defense industry for alleged war profiteering during World War I. The last issue was especially problematic, as the Neutrality Acts passed in 1935 and 1936 effectively banned the sale of war materiel to belligerent nations. This forced a substantial reduction in defense-related manufacturing capacity and complicated Roosevelt's effort to aid the British.[2]

In May 1940, the Netherlands, Belgium, and France were overrun in a matter of weeks, and the Roosevelt administration accepted the disturbing reality that not only was the U.S. unprepared to assist Great Britain, but America itself was vulnerable to invasion. In an eye-opening meeting, Army Chief of Staff General George C. Marshall warned Roosevelt that "if five German divisions landed anywhere on the coast, they could go anywhere they wished . . . If you don't do something, and do it right away, I don't know what's going to happen to the country." Upon hearing this grave warning, Roosevelt knew that Americans needed to prepare for total war at a scale that far exceeded even the most extreme estimates.[3]

On May 23, 1940, as Nazi tanks encircled British forces at Dunkirk, President Roosevelt called Bernard Baruch, who was one of his most trusted outside advisors. Baruch headed the War Industries Board in 1917 and had brought order to the production process after two of his predecessors had struggled to convert the U.S. industrial infrastructure into an efficient producer of war materiel. Roosevelt asked Baruch to return to his post, but in a heroic act of self-awareness, he declined, confessing that the assignment was beyond his capabilities. When Roosevelt asked who Baruch would recommend as his top three alternatives, Baruch repeated a single name three times— Bill Knudsen.[4]

The National Defense Advisory Commission (NDAC)

"I'm not a soldier, and I'm not a sailor. I am just a plain manufacturer. But I know if we get into war, the winning of it will be purely a question of material and production. If we know how to get out twice as much material as everyone else—know how to get it, how to get our hands on it, and use it—we are going to come out on top—and win."[5]

—BILL KNUDSEN, chairman of the National Defense Advisory Commission

Bill Knudsen immigrated to the U.S. from Denmark in February 1900 at the age of twenty-one. Despite having to learn a new language and having no benefit of a personal network, Knudsen's career blossomed due to his uncanny ability to disassemble manufactured products and design efficient assembly lines to mass-produce them. After designing most of the assembly lines for the Ford Motor Company, Alfred Sloan hired Knudsen to turn around the failing Chevrolet division at General Motors. Within two years, Knudsen transformed Chevrolet from GM's most unprofitable division into one of the company's most profitable brands. He followed this success by reengineering the entire manufacturing process at GM. His greatest innovation was adding flexibility to mass production. Whereas Ford produced only one automobile model, Bill Knudsen's system produced customized vehicles that suited different client preferences without compromising operational economies of scale. Knudsen's flexible manufacturing system sparked yet another game-changing innovation in America. It would also prove essential when American manufacturers were forced to quickly convert production from consumer goods to military equipment, armaments, and ammunition. In 1936, Bill Knudsen became president of GM, but it was a position he soon abandoned.[6]

On May 28, 1940, President Roosevelt called Bill Knudsen and asked if he could come to Washington, DC, to help the military with production issues. On the very next day, Knudsen flew to New York and asked Alfred Sloan for a leave of absence from GM. Sloan begrudgingly granted the leave despite voicing strong disapproval and warning Knudsen that the Roosevelt administration and media would ultimately ruin him. On May 30, Knudsen arrived at the White House and, after a brief meeting with Roosevelt, he was ushered into a conference room filled with many of the nation's leading corporate executives, government leaders, and financiers. Roosevelt briefly introduced Bill Knudsen and explained the group's mandate, which was to work with the military and private sector in an advisory capacity to convert the U.S. from a peacetime, consumer-oriented economy to a total war economy—and to do it in record time. The group was dubbed the National Defense Advisory Commission (NDAC).[7]

NDAC's mandate was daunting. Not only did they need to convince American industrialists to produce war materiel at an unprecedented scale, but they also needed to guide the military in determining what was required in the first place. The eighteen-page plan provided to NDAC for an emergency mobilization was shockingly naïve with regard to the speed and complexity of converting the U.S. industrial infrastructure to a total war footing. Adding to the challenge was the fact that NDAC had no formal authority, which meant that convincing private industry to cooperate depended entirely on trust and the power of persuasion. Finally, everything needed to be accomplished at a time when two-thirds of Americans held strong isolationist leanings. This meant that the Roosevelt administration would face stiff congressional opposition to increased military spending and had limited political capital to protect industrialists from accusations of war profiteering.[8]

Americans were fortunate to have Bill Knudsen leading the NDAC. His skill and knowledge far surpassed that of his peers, while his selflessness enabled him to focus solely on the task at hand despite a constant barrage of unfair attacks by the media and politicians. Knudsen's colleagues quickly recognized his talents and selflessness, and they soon deferred to Knudsen as NDAC's leader. Like many of the "one-dollar men" in Washington, DC, at the time, Knudsen demanded no payment for his services. When explaining to his family why he was willing to place himself in such an unenviable position, he simply responded, "This country has been good to me, and I want to pay it back."[9]

An American Tsunami Takes Shape

"There was a race between the Kaiser draftsmen and the field people as to whether we could build it first or the engineers and architects could draw it first."[10]

—CLAY BEDFORD (recalling the construction of a shipyard foundation in three weeks, which was five months ahead of schedule)

POINT OF INTEREST

The Capitalist's Challenge in War: Balancing Profit and Patriotism

"Mr. President, do you want statistics or do you want guns?"[11]

—Bill Knudsen

One of the greatest challenges for Bill Knudsen was balancing the profit require-ments of corporations with production demands of the military. On one hand, the profit incentive is what had inspired American economic advancement and innovation since the nation's founding in 1788; on the other hand, profiting from war was often condemned by the public. Balancing these conflicting perspectives was challenging for Roosevelt, given the anti-corporate lean of many New Dealers.

Knudsen convinced Roosevelt to provide sufficient profit incentives so that corporations could justify shifting production from consumer to military prod-ucts. Important changes included:

- **Civilian Production Allowance**—It seemed counterintuitive to Roosevelt, but Knudsen knew that forcing companies to shift exclusively to the produc-tion of war materiel would be catastrophic because it would require plants to temporarily shut down, and engineers and workers would seek employment elsewhere. By the time the new plant was ready, there would be no workers to staff the assembly lines. The solution was to allow companies to continue producing consumer goods throughout the run-up to the war.

- **Accelerated Depreciation**—Accelerated depreciation was a tactic that could help improve cash flow for companies by granting them larger tax deductions on the purchase of new equipment and plants. This was par-ticularly valuable in 1940 because corporate taxes were high to help fund the military buildup and New Deal programs. The debate with President Roosevelt over accelerated depreciation prompted the above quote from Bill Knudsen. Roosevelt responded wisely by choosing guns over statistics.

- **Capital Expense (Capex) Advances**—Shifting to wartime production required substantial capital investment in new equipment and facilities. Companies faced the risk that the investments would be in vain if a war never materialized. To alleviate this risk, Knudsen established a policy allowing the government to fund capex, thereby minimizing the financial risk of retooling and building new facilities.

NDAC made rapid progress during its first year, but much of it was invisible to politicians, the media, and the public. This was unsurprising to Knudsen. He had specifically told President Roosevelt that it would take approximately eighteen months for American industry to retool and add the required capacity to meet unprecedented production goals. The bigger challenge was convincing companies to shift from the production of consumer products to war materiel. Knudsen skillfully overcame this

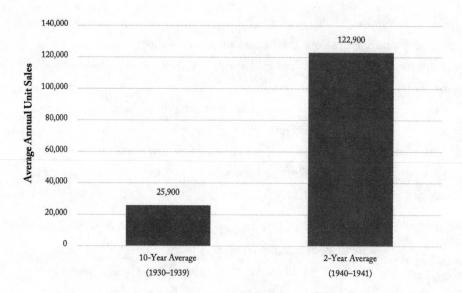

Figure 20.1: Annual U.S. Machine Tool Sales (1930-1941)[12]

problem by convincing Roosevelt to preserve the profit incentive of U.S. companies and change laws that threatened to eliminate it.[13]

Bill Knudsen knew better than anybody that mass production was not a function of speed, but rather it was a function of proper sequencing of activities and the quality of the output. Accomplishing these two objectives required substantial retooling and the construction of new facilities. Knudsen spent his first six months persuading company executives to retool and build massive new plants. Figure 20.1 shows the sharp increase in machine tool production in 1940 and 1941 versus the average of the prior ten years.[14]

Knudsen's encyclopedic knowledge of the unique capabilities of hundreds of companies scattered across the nation was also invaluable. His credibility also enabled him to secure many essential commitments to produce war materiel based only on a handshake.[15]

On December 29, 1940, President Roosevelt delivered one of his famous fireside chats to inform Americans of the effort underway to support U.S. allies and bolster its own defenses by partnering with private industry. He described the U.S. as the "Arsenal of Democracy," which was a term coined by Knudsen himself. Hitler scoffed at Roosevelt's production targets, believing them to be so outrageous that they must have been propaganda. The American media and public were also skeptical. Few believed that America was on track to produce an unimaginable 50,000 planes, 130,000 engines, 380 Navy ships, 9,200 tanks, 17,000 heavy guns, and equipment to outfit 1.4 million troops. Tragically, even fewer Americans appreciated that output at this scale was achievable only by retooling first. The failure to appreciate the long ramp-up time led to skepticism of Knudsen's methods among several members of the Roosevelt administration. Critics were especially irritated by Knudsen's approach to labor, which was a repeated thorn in his side. Numerous strikes disrupted production with serious consequences for the British supply effort. Knudsen estimated that more than 3,500 strikes in 1941 cost 23 million man-days of labor, which was "enough to build 124 Fletcher-class destroyers."[16]

Pressure from organized labor waned after Japan attacked the U.S. on December 7, 1941, but animosity toward Knudsen remained. Opposition to Knudsen boiled over when Leon Henderson, head of the Supply Priorities and Allocation Board (SPAB), responded to the attack on Pearl Harbor by ordering the shutdown of all civilian production in the auto industry to increase capacity for war production. As Knudsen had warned, this resulted in layoffs of nearly half a million workers. But rather than blaming Henderson, Knudsen was targeted as the culprit. Critics claimed that he should have converted the auto industry gradually over the prior eighteen months. In an unfortunate lapse of judgment, President Roosevelt caved to pressure from within his administration to replace Knudsen. On January 16, 1942, he announced the formation of the War Production Board to replace NDAC and appointed Donald Nelson to lead it. Knudsen was devastated and was especially hurt by Roosevelt's neglect in delivering the news himself. Nevertheless, his primary

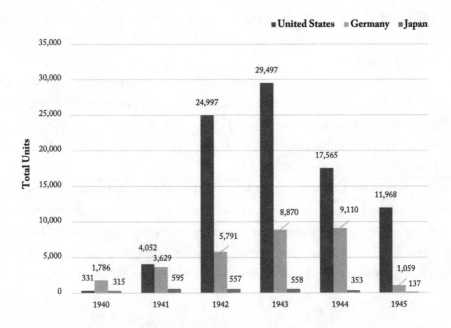

Figure 20.2: Annual Production of Tanks and Self-Propelled Artillery (1940-1945)[17]

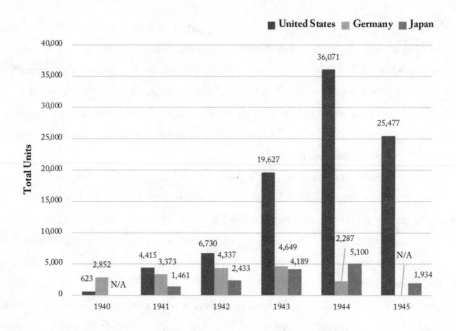

Figure 20.3: Annual Production of Light, Medium, and Long-Range Bombers (1940–1945)[18]

interest was always helping the U.S. and its allies prepare for war, and he continued to offer his help in any way he could. Fortunately, Knudsen had many supporters who knew that his talents were irreplaceable. They lobbied Roosevelt to commission Knudsen as a three-star general so he could continue assisting the military. To this day, Bill Knudsen is the only American civilian to receive an appointment as a three-star general, and his contributions to the war production effort were just as valuable in his new position.[19]

Roughly eighteen months after Bill Knudsen's first meeting with Roosevelt, the massive retooling effort began to bear fruit. American production increased exponentially, exactly as Knudsen had predicted. Figures 20.2, 20.3, and 20.4 show selected metrics of war production output of the U.S. juxtaposed against the production of Nazi Germany and Japan.

The contributions of American industry during World War II were extraordinary. The personal sacrifice of American and Allied troops ultimately won the war, but they could not have succeeded without the arsenal of democracy behind them. The sheer volume of war materiel begs an important question, "How did America pay for it?" The answer reveals yet another of America's unique competitive advantages.

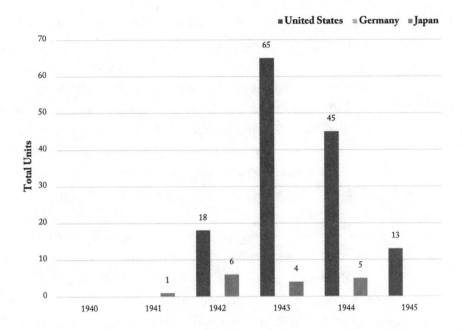

Figure 20.4: Annual Production of Aircraft Carriers (1940–1945)[20]

American Financial Weapons of War

"Exigencies are to be expected to occur, in the affairs of nations, in which there will be a necessity for borrowing. That loans in times of public danger, especially from foreign war, are found an indispensable resource, even to the wealthiest of them . . . it is essential that the credit of a nation should be well established."[21]

—ALEXANDER HAMILTON, *First Report on the Public Credit*

Alexander Hamilton did not know when the U.S. would replace Great Britain as the world's leading industrial power, nor did he know when a totalitarian alliance would present an existential threat to American democracy. But he knew that the former was possible, and the latter was inevitable. This is why establishing sound credit for the nation was his top priority in 1790. Hamilton's wisdom and the countless innovations introduced by his successors armed the country with a deep trove of financial resources to fund the arsenal of democracy. One hundred and fifty years after the founding of the country, the U.S. drew upon its accumulated wealth and sterling credit to protect democracy at home and restore it abroad. The following were the main financial weapons employed by the U.S.

- **The Allied Bank of the United States**—U.S. industrial production during World War II yielded enough war materiel for America to win a two-front war while simultaneously producing a large percentage of war materiel for America's allies. However, a problem was that our allies quickly ran out of money to pay for it. By December 1940, Great Britain, which was the largest purchaser of American war materiel, was nearly insolvent. Secretary of the Treasury Henry Morgenthau calculated that Britain would exhaust its gold reserves within six months and would then have to resort to purchasing war materiel on credit. This was a big problem because selling armaments to belligerents on credit was forbidden under U.S. Neutrality Acts.

  The solution was simple but elegant. Beginning in December 1940, all British orders were officially purchased by the U.S. military. After taking stock of what it needed, the remainder was "lent" or "leased" to the British. In this way, the U.S. provided Britain with essential equipment without technically violating the Neutrality Acts. In March 1941, the legality of this arrangement was codified into U.S. law by an act of Congress, and for the next four years American allies "borrowed" more than $50 billion in war materiel.[22]

- **Tax Increases**—Prior to World War II, federal taxes were rising to pay for several New Deal programs. The commencement of World War II prompted even greater hikes. Figure 20.5 shows the total federal tax receipts collected from 1940 to 1945 as well as the steep progression of the highest marginal income tax rate from 1933 to 1945. The sharp rise in federal tax receipts during the war years mirrored the dramatic increase in corporate and individual incomes due to war-related production.[23]

- **Deficit Spending and Debt Monetization**—The U.S. raised substantial amounts of capital via tax increases, but it was far from sufficient to fund the war. This forced the U.S. to run massive budget deficits, which were funded by the sale of Treasury and war bonds (Figure 20.6). The sheer volume of bond sales created upward pressure on interest rates. To keep rates low, the Federal Reserve purchased a large portion by printing money. The fancy term for this is "debt monetization." This, of course, increases the money supply, which drives higher inflation. Debt monetization during the war years, coupled with chronic supply disruptions that accompanied a shift from a peacetime economy to a total war economy, drove higher rates of inflation during World War II. From 1941 to 1945, inflation averaged more than 5 percent per year.

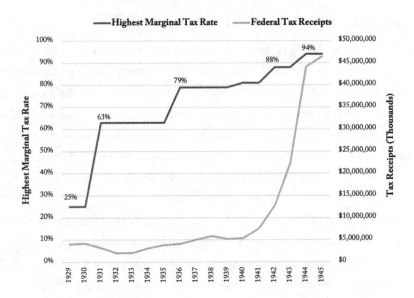

Figure 20.5: Federal Tax Receipts and Highest Marginal Tax Rate (1929–1945)[24]

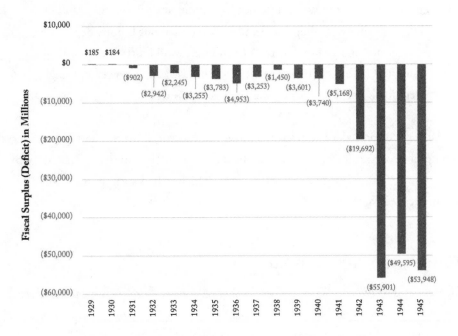

Figure 20.6: Fiscal Deficits (1929–1945)[25]

As Alexander Hamilton had warned Congress in 1790, it was impossible to win a war without financing it first. The financial power of the United States, which strengthened over 150 years, enabled the country to fund the enormous costs of total war both for itself and its allies without starving its own people.

The New World Liberates the Old

On May 10, 1940—the very same day that Germany launched its attack on western Europe—Winston Churchill was named prime minister of Great Britain. Within only three weeks, the British Expeditionary Force was driven off the European continent, abandoning almost all its equipment on the beaches of Dunkirk. On June 4, 1940, after the miraculous rescue of more than 300,000 British forces, Prime Minister Winston Churchill sought to resuscitate a demoralized nation by delivering his most famous speech. Churchill's speech concluded with the following words:

> We shall go to the end, we shall fight in France, we shall fight on the seas and oceans, we shall fight with growing confidence and growing strength in the air, we shall defend our Island, whatever the cost may be, we shall fight on the beaches, we shall fight on the landing grounds, we shall fight in the fields and in the streets, we shall fight in the hills; we shall never surrender, and even if, which I do not for a moment believe, this Island or a large part of it were subjugated and starving, then our Empire beyond the seas, armed and guarded by the British Fleet, would carry on the struggle, until, in God's good time, the New World, with all its power and might, steps forth to the rescue and the liberation of the old.

Aided by unprecedented industrial power, vast financial wealth, bottomless reserves of natural resources, innovation that enabled the seemingly impossible, selfless sacrifice by its youth, and empathy for a nation from which it had sprung, the United States of America led the New World toward the liberation of the old in the spring of 1945.

Turning the Tables in Europe

"Surrender is forbidden; Sixth Army will hold their position to the last man and the last round and by their heroic endurance will make an unforgettable contribution towards the establishment of a defensive front and the salvation of the Western World."[26]

—ADOLPH HITLER (rejecting General Paulus's request to surrender at Stalingrad)

Hitler's lack of self-awareness ultimately led to his demise. Throughout the 1930s, he correctly identified and exploited the Allied powers' big fear, which was reliving the horrors of trench warfare in World War I. Appeasement policies enabled Germany to claim territory and resources without applying military force. Emboldened by his early successes, Hitler concluded that the Western powers would always cower to Nazi aggression. It never crossed his mind that, once World War II was deemed inevitable, the Allies' fear would transform into iron resolve. In fact, it was bitter resentment for having been duped, coupled with the horror of Hitler's atrocities, that intensified the Allies' resolve to accept nothing less than total victory.

Hitler's big fear, on the other hand, became an ever-growing liability. As he revealed in *Mein Kampf,* his most traumatic life experience was suffering the humiliating surrender to the Allied powers on November 11, 1918. He preferred to die rather than allow himself to relive this trauma, and he expected the same commitment from his military. Hitler's aversion to surrender compelled him to sacrifice entire armies rather than authorize sensible, tactical retreats. The best example was Hitler's refusal to allow a strategic retreat from an unwinnable battle in Stalingrad, which ended in the almost complete annihilation of Germany's Sixth Army. Out of nearly 250,000 soldiers in the besieged unit, only five thousand returned to Germany alive. From that moment forward, Russian forces steadily pushed the hobbled Nazi troops back to Berlin. In December 1944, Hitler ordered a similarly reckless offensive to retake the Port of Antwerp. The attack initially caught the Americans off guard, but mostly because they could not fathom why the Nazis would behave so foolishly. After the bloody two-week Battle of the Bulge, the Americans decimated what was left of Germany's western army.[27]

It is probably true that once the U.S. joined the Allies, the Third Reich's chances of survival were slim regardless of Hitler's decisions—but the odds were not zero. Hitler's reckless refusal to permit tactical retreats reduced those chances substantially, if not eliminated them entirely. Hitler never surrendered to Allied Forces, but he spent his final days reliving the humiliation that precedes surrender. He then spared the world of his continued existence by firing a bullet into his head on April 30, 1945.

The Turning of the Tide in the Pacific

The Japanese code of Bushido expresses the core values of the samurai, which was a warrior class that defended feudal lords for 250 years during the Tokugawa shogunate. Among the most important tenets of Bushido was the refusal to surrender. This principle was embedded in the Kanji, which all Japanese troops were forced to commit to memory. The principle stated that "duty is heavier than a mountain; death is lighter than a feather." Hitler tried instilling a similar ethos in the minds of Nazis, but most abandoned it when they encountered a real-life choice between death and surrender. This was not the case for the Japanese. Almost all troops (and even many civilians) fought to their last bullet and then died in suicidal assaults using whatever weapons

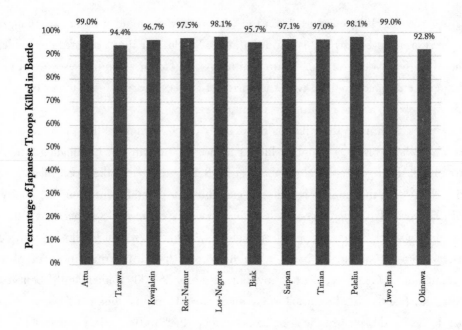

Figure 20.7: Death Rates of Japanese Troops on Eleven Island Battles (1941–1945)[28]

remained in their possession. The Japanese armed forces may have been less intimidating than the Nazis in terms of their resources and quality of weaponry, but the ferocity of their attacks made them a much more terrifying enemy to behold. After the Battle of Midway, momentum in the war shifted decidedly in favor of the United States, and U.S. Marines began clearing the South Pacific of Japanese troops island by island. But this gruesome task required the killing of almost every Japanese soldier defending the islands. It also resulted in painful American casualties. Figure 20.7 shows Japanese casualty rates on eleven islands liberated by the U.S. during World War II. Of the 200,000 Japanese troops defending these islands, roughly 190,000 perished in battle.[29]

The Japanese military's refusal to surrender heavily influenced the most controversial decision of the United States. Americans made significant gains after taking islands such as Guadalcanal, Iwo Jima, and Okinawa, but the Japanese were not even close to surrendering. This meant that an invasion of the Japanese mainland was necessary. Based on the U.S. experience in Okinawa, even the most optimistic projections of American casualties from a full-scale invasion were horrifying. There was also no guarantee that it would force a surrender. In fact, later evidence emerged that the Japanese were training citizens of all ages to resist American advances using whatever weapons they could get their hands on. The alternative to an invasion was to use a new weapon that the U.S. had developed in secret. Hidden in a blur of unprecedented production volumes of conventional weaponry was the development of a new weapon by leading American scientists in a top-secret undertaking called the Manhattan Project. On July 16, 1945, the project was completed, and the U.S. detonated the world's first atomic bomb in Alamogordo, New Mexico. Calculating that the use of the atomic bomb was the better of two horrific options, President Harry S. Truman approved its use against the empire of Japan.[30]

On August 6, 1945, the U.S. dropped the first atomic bomb on Hiroshima, instantly killing at least 66,000 civilians and soldiers. Surprisingly, the Japanese refused to surrender—in fact, military leaders refused to even meet to discuss the possibility of surrender. On August 9, 1945, the U.S. dropped a second atomic bomb on the city of Nagasaki, instantly killing at least another 39,000 Japanese.[31] Even after the second atomic bomb, military leaders were evenly divided on whether to surrender. Emperor Hirohito was called to break the deadlock and wisely concluded that surrendering was a better option than suffering the complete annihilation of the Japanese nation. On August 15, 1945, Emperor Hirohito addressed the nation directly for the first time ever to announce the surrender.[32] A formal agreement was signed by the Japanese on September 2, 1945, officially ending the worst war in human history. Over the span of four years, 100 million people perished and much of Europe and Asia lay in ruins. The post–World War II era would begin with massive reconstruction efforts under the leadership of the United States, which was now the sole occupant of the commanding heights formerly held by the British Empire.[33]

LESSONS FROM THE GREAT DEPRESSION AND WORLD WAR II

The Great Depression and World War II shaped the world as we know it today. The U.S. emerged as the world's largest economy and was supported by the world's most formidable military. The U.S. dollar replaced the British pound sterling as the world's dominant reserve currency. Finally, for the first time in history, U.S. securities exchanges were subjected to federal regulation, which enabled U.S. securities markets to establish a level of integrity to match its depth and breath. Although there is not enough room to summarize all the lessons from the Great Depression and World War II, listed below are a few that are especially relevant today.

- **Recognizing the Life-and-Death Stakes of Deep Depressions**—Many Americans understand the severity of the Great Depression at an intellectual level but underestimate the true scope of the consequences. In the case of the Great Depression, the costliest consequence was not the decline in the U.S. stock market, the 25 percent rate of unemployment, or even the estimated twenty thousand additional suicides that occurred from 1930 to 1933. The costliest consequence was World War II. If not for the Great Depression, it is probable that the Nazi Party would have drifted into obscurity, while the desperate need for Japan to expand its colonial empire would never have materialized. In other words, there is an argument that the total lives lost as a result of the Great Depression are measurable in the tens of millions rather than the tens of thousands. It is important to never lose sight of the fact that the loss of human life, rather than asset price declines, is the most meaningful metric to gauge the costs of depressions. Sadly, these costs are often underestimated at the outset of a depression and forgotten in the aftermath.

- **The Necessity of Counterintuitive Solutions during a Systemic Financial Crisis**—The biggest challenge for policymakers during a major depression is that many of the more effective solutions are opposed by the public because they seem counterintuitive. Deep depressions usually occur after periods of irresponsible credit expansion and speculation; therefore, the natural reaction is to punish individuals guilty of the most egregious behaviors by enacting austerity measures. The problem with austerity is that it only works if irresponsible behavior is relatively contained. If the behavior is systemic, austerity only makes the problem worse. It seems counterintuitive, but the most effective solutions are considered irresponsible under normal circumstances. Tactics such as debt monetization, recapitalization of banks, and deficit spending enable countries suffering from a depression to spread out the cost rather than suffer a sudden and self-reinforcing economic collapse.[34]

- **Balancing the Motivating Force of Capitalism and Stabilizing Force of Wealth Equality**—The U.S. has a strong tradition of capitalism—much stronger than those of many developed nations. This tradition has proven essential to the nation's success. There would have been no transcontinental railroads if not for the enterprising (and often shady) entrepreneurial ventures launched during the Gilded Age. There would have been no American Commercial Invasion if not for the extraordinary innovations of entrepreneurs such as Thomas Blanchard, John Hall, and Thomas Edison. American inventions may never have reached end markets if not for the support of financiers such as J. Pierpont Morgan, Jacob Schiff, and Otto Kahn. Finally, it is almost certain that the U.S. would not have been capable of ridding the world of the tyranny of Nazi Germany and Imperial Japan without the arsenal of democracy. This capability only existed because of 150 years of innovation and economic expansion. At the same time, the U.S. has experienced several periods of social instability, which were amplified by wealth disparity.

Managing the tension between these opposing forces is among the great challenges for Americans in the twenty-first century. Continued prosperity requires Americans to maintain their unique drive for innovation and progress without allowing widening wealth gaps to destabilize society. There is no foolproof prescription to address this challenge, but perhaps a good place to start is to acknowledge that the tension exists. Those who argue for extreme forms of capitalism and socialism embrace belief systems that are equally likely to fail. Author Ray Dalio offers a useful analogy in his book *Principles for Dealing with the Changing World Order*. Dalio explains that capitalism is the best solution for "growing the pie," while wealth equalization policies are essential corrective mechanisms for "sharing the pie" and stabilizing the system. America's ability to balance these seemingly opposing philosophies will shape its future prosperity or decline.[35]

- **Replacement of Market Manipulation and Insider Trading with Securities Analysis**—The securities markets that existed in the U.S. prior to the Great Depression do not resemble the markets that have existed since. Prior to the Securities Exchange Act of 1934, stock operators ruled Wall Street by engaging in market manipulation and insider trading. Serious investors rarely bothered with diligent securities analysis, as it was much more difficult and slow going. The passage of the Securities Exchange Act of 1934 changed Wall Street forever. Stock operators could incur hefty fines or even jail time for employing tactics that made them fortunes in the past. When markets returned to normal after the end of World War II, a new investment professional emerged on Wall Street: the financial analyst. However, it would not take long before the lackluster track record of these analysts proved why the stock operators of the past shunned securities analysis in the first place. Even in the mid-1900s, it was extraordinarily difficult to discover something that the market had not already incorporated into the price of a security, yet many decades would pass before investors would begin wakening to this reality.

After Japan officially surrendered on September 2, 1945, most of the world celebrated a much-welcomed peace. The unspeakable horrors of the worst war in human history had finally come to an end. But there was much more work to do, as cities throughout Europe, Russia, and Asia lay in ruins. By default, the U.S. took center stage in the rebuilding effort, as it had become the world's largest creditor and one of the few countries with an infrastructure that remained intact. The next era ushered in another period of extraordinary wealth creation, an increasing portion of which would accumulate in institutional rather than individual accounts.

Part 5

The Wealth of the American Empire

1946–1982

"You should fully understand the special position that the United States now occupies in the world, geographically, financially, militarily, and scientifically, and the implications involved. The development of a sense of responsibility for world order and security, the development of a sense of overwhelming importance of this country's acts, and failures to act, in relation to world order and security—these, in my opinion, are great musts for your generation."[1]

—GENERAL GEORGE C. MARSHALL

Americans celebrated when World War II ended on September 2, 1945, but policymakers shuddered at the daunting task of reconstruction. Most major cities in Europe, China, Japan, and southeast Asia were in ruins, and their occupants struggled to survive in a state of virtual anarchy. Starvation, looting, rape, and murder were daily occurrences long after the Axis powers surrendered. At the same time, Britain, Japan, France, and the Netherlands lacked the financial and military wherewithal to maintain their colonial empires. As their stabilizing presence evaporated, bloody civil wars erupted throughout Asia, Africa, and the Middle East.

Americans old enough to recall life in the 1950s often describe it with nostalgia. This sentiment reflects the nation's exceptional wealth, military strength, and vastly superior economic production relative to global competitors. Beneath the surface, however, new threats were growing. The most notable was the Soviet Union. Despite suffering extensive damage to its industrial infrastructure and a horrific loss of 10 percent of its population, the Soviets exited World War II with control over vast territory in Eastern Europe. Joseph Stalin, the nation's autocratic leader, soon abandoned his alliance with the U.S., viewing it as an obstacle to his aspirations to expand Soviet territory and convert the world to a communist system of government. The philosophical conflict between these two superpowers was dubbed the Cold War. It officially began on March 5, 1946, with the delivery of Winston Churchill's famous "Iron Curtain" speech. Shortly thereafter, the fate of hundreds of millions of civilians depended on the outcomes of proxy wars fought between the U.S. and the Soviet Union—and, to a more limited extent, China.

Part 5 recounts the creation of the Post–World War II financial system under the leadership of the United States. The chapters are written from a distinctly American viewpoint, but also acknowledge that the experiences of the remaining world were quite different. The chapters also recount several important trends in financial markets that continue to shape investor behavior today. Finally, it concludes by recounting the Great Inflation, which tested American resilience and altered the Federal Reserve's perspective on the importance of price stability.

Chapter 21 explains the fundamental dynamics of the new financial world order established under the Bretton Woods Agreement. The agreement restored international trade, reestablished the international gold standard, and set new rules for cross-border capital flows.

Chapter 22 shifts back to the U.S. financial system and explains how institutional investors replaced stock operators as the dominant force on Wall Street. It also describes the origin of the greatest financial innovation of the twentieth century, the index fund. It then concludes by explaining why most investment professionals denied its merits.

Chapter 23 concludes part 5 by recounting the Great Inflation of 1965 to 1982, which is one of the few events in U.S. financial history that is truly unprecedented. Neither before nor since has the U.S. experienced an inflationary event of this magnitude and duration. The Great Inflation ended when Federal Reserve Chairman Paul Volcker enacted draconian monetary policies to reset Americans' inflation expectations and reestablish price stability. The subsequent recession and rise in unemployment were painful, but when the Great Inflation ended, the U.S. was prepared to commence a new era of economic prosperity.

Chapter 21

THE FOUNDATION OF
THE NEW WORLD ORDER

*"[T]he kid who owns the ball is usually the captain and decides
when and where the game will be played and who will be on the
team . . . Since the U.S. now owns some twenty-two billions of the
world's reported twenty-eight billions of gold, we think Uncle Sam
is going to be the captain of the team or there will be no game."*[1]

—NEW YORK WORLD-TELEGRAM (APRIL 1943)

B y the end of 1943, an Allied victory over the Axis powers appeared inevitable, and Allied leaders began architecting a framework for a new world order. The top priority was establishing new rules to govern international trade and cross-border capital flows. There was urgency assigned to this task because policymakers believed that the dysfunctional trade policies of the 1930s—collectively known as "beggar-thy-neighbor" policies—had caused the war.[2] The tragedy of these policies is that the leaders of each individual country genuinely believed that trade barriers would benefit their people. By increasing the price of imports and reducing the price of exports, they hoped to stimulate a recovery of their domestic economies. This, in turn, would create a favorable trade balance, lower unemployment, and end the Depression.

Beggar-thy-neighbor policies only seemed logical, however, because policymakers failed to foresee that trading partners would retaliate by erecting trade barriers of their own. This tit-for-tat retaliation caused all nations to suffer by producing a broad-based collapse of international trade (Figure 21.1). This, in turn, weakened the benefits of comparative advantage, thereby amplifying the effects of the Depression

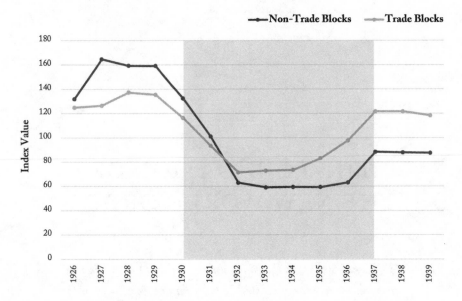

Figure 21.1: International Trade Index (1926–1939)[3]

rather than mitigating them.[4] Beggar-thy-neighbor trade policies were a classic example of a concept known as the prisoner's dilemma. By independently pursuing their own self-interest, all nations suffered.

POINT OF INTEREST

The Prisoner's Dilemma and Beggar-Thy-Neighbor Trade Policies

Game theory is a theoretical framework used to evaluate the likelihood of potential outcomes when rational decision-makers base their decisions on the expected behavior of other participants. The *Prisoner's Dilemma* is a well-known scenario in game theory. The fundamental principles are revealed in the following example.

Prisoner's Dilemma Example[5]

Police arrest two business partners who are suspected of fraud. Upon arriving at the police station, the suspects are placed in separate rooms, thereby preventing them from communicating. The police know that both suspects are guilty, but they lack evidence to prove it. But the police do have sufficient evidence to convict the suspects on a lesser charge of tax evasion. The lead detective decides that the best course of action is to seek confessions for the fraud scheme by offering each suspect a reduced sentence if they confess. The police sweeten the deal by offering full immunity if only one suspect confesses. The potential outcomes in this scenario are:

1. **Both confess:** Both prisoners receive three-year sentences.
2. **Neither confesses:** Both prisoners receive six-month sentences.
3. **One confesses:** The prisoner who confesses receives immunity, while the prisoner who remains silent receives a <u>five-year sentence</u>.

The "dilemma" stems from the fact that each prisoner has a rational incentive to minimize their sentence by confessing because it eliminates the possibility of receiving a five-year prison sentence if their partner confesses and they remain silent. The most likely outcome, therefore, is that both suspects confess and receive three-year prison sentences, which is worse than the six-month sentences that they would have received if they had both remained silent. In other words, the two prisoners forfeit the possibility of receiving a six-month sentence because they are unable to coordinate their decisions.

Beggar-thy-neighbor trade policies were considerably more complex than this example, but the fundamental principles were identical. The optimal choice for all nations was to coordinate trade policies and maximize trade benefits for every nation. Instead, nations pursued their own self-interests, and everybody suffered a worse outcome as a result.

The decline in global economic output was not the only negative consequence of beggar-thy-neighbor policies. Reduced trade also lowered barriers to armed conflict. All else being equal, economic interdependence lessens the probability of war because the financial costs of trade disruptions are too high.[6] Combined with a deep global depression that destabilized governments, reduced economic interdependence made armed conflicts more likely in the 1930s.

THE BRETTON WOODS AGREEMENT

In July 1944, representatives from forty-four nations convened at the Mount Washington Resort in Bretton Woods, New Hampshire, to create a new international financial system. The primary goals were to restore international trade and prevent the recurrence of beggar-thy-neighbor trade conflicts. Other goals included the creation of institutions to manage postwar reconstruction and alleviate periodic balance-of-payments crises.

The American delegation shared the fundamental goals of other attendees, but they also used their leverage to advance American interests. Among these interests included the dismantling of the closed trading bloc of the British Empire and replacing the pound sterling with the U.S. dollar as the world's reserve currency. Despite vehement objections from Britain's prickly economic ambassador, John Maynard Keynes, U.S. preferences ruled the day. America's lead negotiator, Harry Dexter White, ensured that U.S. priorities were incorporated into the draft Bretton Woods Agreement, thus setting the stage for the U.S. to replace Great Britain as the world's financial center.[7]

On December 27, 1944, twenty-eight nations ratified the agreement, and the Bretton Woods System officially became the foundation of the new financial world order. At the end of 1945, Bretton Woods took effect, and two new international institutions, the International Monetary Fund (IMF) and World Bank, were introduced to the world. The IMF was charged with managing balance-of-payments shocks among its members, and the World Bank was charged with funding post–World War II reconstruction. The full implementation of the system of fixed exchange rates did not take effect until 1958. At that point, the U.S. dollar was firmly established as the world's new reserve currency and was exchangeable for gold at a fixed rate of $35 per ounce. All parties to the Bretton Woods Agreement then pegged their currencies to the U.S. dollar, thereby reestablishing the international gold standard.[8]

POINT OF INTEREST

Sunset on the British Pound Sterling

"In another year's time we shall have forfeited the claim we had staked out in the New World and, in exchange, this country will be mortgaged to America."[9]

—John Maynard Keynes

A popular saying from the late 1700s to the mid-1900s was that Britain was the "empire on which the sun never sets." This saying captured the fact that British Commonwealth nations and colonies spanned every longitudinal meridian across North America, Southeast Asia, Africa, South America, the Middle East, and the South Pacific. The Bretton Woods Agreement rendered this saying obsolete and marked the decline of the British Empire and demotion of the pound sterling as the world's reserve currency.

The loss of reserve currency status was painful for the British. Reserve currencies provide empires with a powerful competitive advantage because they compel foreign central banks to accumulate the reserve currency to facilitate international trade and reduce exchange rate risk. For example, if a country requires British pounds to settle international transactions, and the central bank holds plenty of pounds, it reduces the exchange rate risk inherent in purchasing pounds in the open market. Holding sufficient reserves is especially important when countries suffer balance-of-payments disruptions (e.g., they import more than they export).

The dominant reserve currency in world trade does not change frequently. Over the past five hundred years, there have been only three: the Dutch guilder, the British pound sterling, and the U.S. dollar. The guilder rose to prominence in the late 1500s after the Dutch freed themselves from Spanish rule. The Dutch then dominated international trade for nearly two centuries. In 1784, the Dutch lost this privilege after the British prevailed in the Fourth Anglo-Dutch War. Dutch finances, which were already strained by the burden of maintaining a colonial empire, collapsed in the aftermath. This, in turn, compromised their ability to control overseas trade, and the pound sterling replaced the Dutch guilder.[10]

For the next 120 years, the British dominated world trade, and the pound sterling was the world's reserve currency. It was only at the turn of the twentieth century that the U.S. emerged as a potential heir. Bolstered by enormous trade surpluses from the American Commercial Invasion, the U.S. became a formidable economic rival to Britain in the early 1900s. But it was the devastating costs of World War II that sealed the pound sterling's fate. Britain was nearly bankrupted by the war, rendering it unable to maintain its global empire, much less dictate the terms of the Bretton Woods Agreement. Thus, in 1945, the pound sterling faded, and the dollar remains the world's dominant reserve currency to this day.[11]

The Bretton Woods Agreement helped resurrect global trade and accelerate reconstruction of war-ravaged nations, but the system was not flawless. In fact, the fixed exchange rate system was fatally flawed at the outset. This deficiency would be exposed in 1971, forcing the U.S. to abandon the gold standard and convert the U.S. dollar to a fiat currency. The IMF and World Bank, however, have stood the test of time and remain important institutions to this day.

THE COLD WAR AND DECOLONIZATION

The Soviet Union was the only major power to reject the Bretton Woods Agreement. This was especially disappointing to its architect, Harry Dexter White, who was suspiciously sympathetic to the Soviets. After White's death, U.S. intelligence revealed the source of White's biases when it declassified evidence that White may have engaged in espionage on behalf of the Soviet Union for many years.[12]

The fissure between the Soviet Union and United States extended beyond monetary issues. Tensions included fundamental differences in governing philosophies (e.g., autocratic versus democratic), divergent economic philosophies (e.g., communism versus capitalism), and conflicting territorial aspirations in Germany and Eastern Europe. The Soviet Union and Western powers also disagreed on the treatment of the Axis powers after the War. The Soviet perspective was shaped by their devastating loss of life and wealth in World War II. They believed that weakening the former Axis powers was the best deterrent. The U.S. position was shaped by a desire to avoid repeating the mistakes of the Treaty of Versailles. They believed that rebuilding cities and rehabilitating governments were the best defense. The contrast between the two philosophies was captured in the following exchange between Joseph Stalin and Winston Churchill while discussing Soviet demands for extreme German reparations.

> **Churchill**: If you want a horse to pull your wagon, you have to give him some hay.

> **Stalin**: Feeding the horse could be dangerous. It might just turn around and kick you.[13]

The clash between Soviet and U.S. philosophies was the most important driver of geopolitical events from 1946 until the Soviet Union collapsed in 1991. Cold War conflicts destabilized dozens of nations, as the U.S. and Soviet Union used various groups as proxies in a larger battle to expand their spheres of influence. Cold War–related conflicts and civil wars prompted by the disintegration of European colonial empires produced horrific atrocities over several decades. In *The Cold War: A World History*, Odd Arne Westad provides a bone-chilling inventory of such atrocities. In China alone, fifty-seven million deaths occurred between 1920 and 1980—and this does not count twenty to thirty million additional deaths from World War II. Intense fear of international communism also metastasized into the costliest proxy war for the United States: the Vietnam War.[14]

Many conflicts that trace their roots to the Cold War continue to this day. Examples include Afghanistan, Israel and Palestine, and North Korea. But these threats were not yet apparent to Americans. Instead, most Americans entered the postwar era with an abundance of wealth and optimism. Over the next several decades, U.S. policymakers, financiers, and business leaders erected powerful financial institutions to channel their newly acquired wealth.

POINT OF INTEREST

Marshaling the Wealth of the U.S. Empire

In April 1948, the U.S. launched the Marshall Plan, which provided European countries with massive aid for reconstruction. The Marshall Plan is recognized as one of America's most altruistic acts, but it was also a strategic necessity. After the Nazi surrender, Germany no longer presented a military threat to the West, but the Soviet Union was a hostile rival with clear ambitions to expand its borders. U.S. leaders viewed the spread of the Soviet Union's communist philosophy in western Europe to be an existential threat to the new world order. The best way to deter the Soviets was to rebuild western European nations under capitalist economic systems and democratic governments.

In March 1948, Congress passed the Marshall Plan (officially called the Economic Cooperation Act of 1948). Total aid provided to western Europe under the act amounted to approximately $13 billion. This aid was critical in rebuilding European economies and cementing the alliance of many western European countries against the Soviet threat.[15]

The Marshall Plan did not cover reconstruction in Japan, but the U.S. would later provide more than $2 billion for Japanese reconstruction. The strategic importance of a Japanese alliance increased dramatically after Mao Zedong's communist forces emerged victorious from the Chinese Civil War that ended in October 1949. Defeated nationalist forces, which were supported by the U.S., were exiled to the island of Taiwan, which substantially reduced the U.S. sphere of influence in Asia. The strategic importance of an alliance with Japan was further elevated after the North Korean invasion of South Korea, which triggered the Korean War.

Chapter 22

INSTITUTIONS
TAKE THE STREET

*"If the types of speculators and manipulators of the fifties differed from
those of the twenties, the manner of institutional support in the two was
still more dissimilar . . . During the fifties their places had been taken
by the often-faceless managers of mutual funds, trusts, pension funds,
insurance portfolios, and foundations . . . The men who controlled these
vast resources were the new key men of Wall Street."[1]*

—ROBERT SOBEL, financial historian

After the Great Crash, U.S. securities markets entered a period of hibernation that lasted until the late 1940s. When activity returned to pre-Depression levels, the structure of securities markets was forever changed. The nation's largest financial institutions had separated their commercial and investment banking businesses, and the outlawing of the Gilded Age dark arts disarmed stock operators. The void was quickly filled, however, by a new group consisting of institutions rather than individuals.

By the mid-1980s, institutional investors had fundamentally reshaped securities markets. It was also during this era that the investment profession attached to the misguided belief that investment professionals trained in the art of securities analysis were sufficiently skilled to beat ruthless market efficiency. The founding father of the financial analyst profession himself, Ben Graham, would later challenge this belief, but his warnings were largely ignored. Too many investment professionals had staked their careers on denying this reality. To this day, most members of the investment profession reject the "inconvenient truth" of market efficiency, and the final section of this chapter explains why.

THE SERVANTS BECOME THE MASTERS

Prior to the mid-1930s, stock operators and their brokers dominated U.S. securities markets. Many staffers supported their conquests. Runners delivered buy and sell tickets to traders on exchange floors; typists transmitted and received orders by telegraph; and statisticians collected what little data companies offered in public disclosures. Many of these positions were rendered obsolete by new technologies; but statisticians were a notable exception.[2]

Prior to the late 1930s, statisticians were rarely seen. They usually sat in back offices sifting through piles of financial documents to supply their employers with routine financial data such as bond ratings and earnings. Brokers had little respect for statisticians because insider information was much more valuable, and it was only obtainable from personal networks or more nefarious means. One former statistician expressed the lowliness of his status when he lamented that they had "a professional rating and financial reward of third-class library clerks."[3]

Federal securities legislation completely altered the playing field. The Securities Act of 1933 required publicly traded companies to provide extensive disclosures to the public, while the Securities Exchange Act of 1934 outlawed market manipulation and insider trading. By 1935, financial information was plentiful, and analyzing it was the only legal way to gain an edge. Skilled financial analysis was suddenly in high demand, and statisticians were the only suppliers. In the 1997 publication *From Practice to Profession*, the Association for Investment Management and Research (AIMR) captured the impact of federal securities regulations, stating, "The infant profession of financial analysis obviously prospered by it [securities regulations] too. Indeed, if the profession can be said to have had a 'founding legislation,' then this clearly was it."[4]

A New Profession on the Street

"All the conditions were right. The age of disclosure had dawned. Theory was developing to comprehend information. The postwar boom was about to turn into the longest sustained period of economic growth in American history. Capital was being mobilized on a scale up to then unknown in peacetime. Yet a favorable environment alone did not determine the subsequent steady evolution of the profession."[5]

—FROM PRACTICE TO PROFESSION

The CFA® designation is often regarded as the gold standard of investment professional certifications. Before receiving a CFA® charter, candidates must complete thirty-six months of relevant experience and pass three rigorous examinations covering topics such as economics, accounting, financial statement analysis, corporate finance, portfolio management, and ethical principles. As of March 2023, there were more than 190,000 CFA® charterholders worldwide, far surpassing even the most optimistic forecasts of the program's founders. The rapid growth of the profession makes sense, however, when one understands the corresponding evolution of U.S. securities markets.[6]

The Wind of Change Hits the Streets of Chicago

In 1925, a group of Chicago-based statisticians formed a club that convened regularly over lunch to discuss general business conditions. Membership in the club, which was dubbed the Investment Analysts Club, grew rapidly during the Great Bull Market, and discussions shifted from business conditions to the evaluation of individual stocks. In 1929, membership was a highly coveted honor, but it quickly collapsed during the Great Depression. Statisticians were considered nonessential employees, and club dues were unaffordable for those who lost their jobs.[7]

The New Deal programs ended the Great Depression in 1933, and demand for statisticians rebounded. However, it faltered again during the deep recession of 1937–1938 and then remained stagnant during World War II.[8] After the war ended, market activity gradually returned to pre-Depression levels, and club membership recovered. At the same time, similar societies thrived in Boston, New York, and Philadelphia. In 1947, leaders of the four societies joined forces to form the Financial Analysts Federation (FAF). The goal was to coordinate membership expansion and leverage the benefits of information sharing. From that day forward, demand for the services of financial analysts enjoyed uninterrupted growth. In addition to 1930s securities regulations, the profession benefited from several additional tailwinds:[9]

- **Postwar Capital Requirements**—After World War II, the U.S. served as both the factory and financier for much of the world. U.S. companies issued a flood of new securities to fund expansion projects. These securities were accompanied by extensive disclosures that required analysis by qualified professionals.

- **Dawning of the Information Age**—On February 15, 1946, the U.S. War Department publicly announced the invention of a groundbreaking machine that was originally intended to improve the analysis of ballistics data during World War II. The invention of the Electronic Numerical Integrator and Computer (ENIAC) marked the dawn of the Information Age. In accordance with Moore's Law, computing power advanced exponentially with each passing year. This, in turn, increased demand for financial analysts, who collected and analyzed increasingly large volumes of financial data.[10]

- **Research-Driven Competitive Differentiation**—By the late 1940s, memories of the Great Depression had faded. Americans reentered securities markets, which created demand for new investment products. As the field became more crowded, institutions differentiated their products by showcasing the depth of their research capabilities. The quality and number of financial analysts on staff became one of the more effective means of differentiation.

POINT OF INTEREST

The Dean of Wall Street

"I have learned whatever I know about economics in the same way I learned about finance—by reading, meditation, and practical experience."[11]

—Ben Graham

Benjamin Graham was born in London on May 9, 1894. His family immigrated to the U.S. in 1895 after Ben's father, Isaac Graham, was asked to lead a new outpost of the family business in New York City. The Grahams lived comfortably during their first eight years in America, but then suffered a devastating setback when Isaac died of pancreatic cancer in 1903. Without the support of the family business, the Grahams struggled financially for the remainder of Ben's childhood.[12]

Ben excelled academically, which earned him a full scholarship at Columbia University. His Wall Street career began soon after graduation in 1914. After working his way up to a statistician position, Graham noticed that brokers ignored information that could be used to identify mispriced securities. In his memoirs, he proudly recalled discovering detailed financial reports that gas pipeline companies submitted to the Interstate Commerce Commission (ICC). After reviewing the reports, he discovered that the Northern Pipeline Company traded for $65 per share, paid an annual dividend of $6 per share, and had $95 per share worth of net cash and high-quality bonds on its balance sheet. Graham purchased the stock, collected a hefty dividend, and then forced the company to distribute its excess cash.

Graham documented his financial analysis techniques in classic books such as *Security Analysis* and *The Intelligent Investor*. To this day, his teachings inspire

(continued)

legendary investors such as Warren Buffett. Yet Graham later realized that investment opportunities that were abundant in the 1930s and 1940s were anomalies. As more financial analysts embraced Graham's techniques, markets returned to a high state of efficiency. Acknowledging this shift, Graham later confessed, "I have little confidence even in the ability of analysts, let alone untrained investors, to select common stocks that will give better than average results."[13]

Ben Graham passed away on September 21, 1976. He dedicated much of his life to developing the financial analyst profession, but his greatest contributions were his impeccable ethical standards. From the moment he entered Wall Street, he employed investment strategies that relied solely on intellectual prowess rather than market manipulation and insider trading. His behavior inspired countless members of the burgeoning financial analyst profession, and nearly fifty years after his passing, his ethical principles and analytical techniques continue to serve as the cornerstone of the CFA Institute's Body of Knowledge.

The Quest for Professional Status

Financial analysts had the wind at their back during the postwar years. As the profession grew, leaders of the FAF explored the creation of a certification program. The thought was that it would provide credibility on par with other professions such as

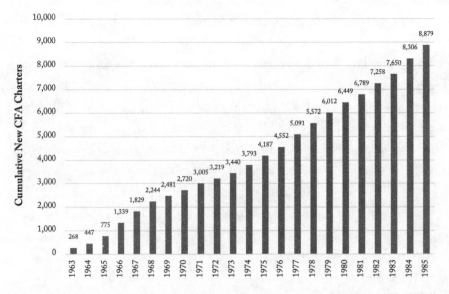

Figure 22.1: Cumulative Number of New CFA® Charters Awarded by Year (1963–1985)[14]

accounting, law, and even medicine. Ben Graham first proposed a certification program in 1942, but more than two decades passed before it came to fruition. The challenge was building consensus among local societies, many of which held markedly different opinions on issues such as experience requirements, educational curriculum, and ethical standards. The FAF finally agreed upon a certification framework, and the first CFA examinations were administered in 1963. A total of 268 charters were awarded in the first year, and the number of new charter awards increased rapidly with each passing year (Figure 22.1).

POINT OF INTEREST

Impact of the CFA Institute on the Financial Analyst Profession

"For the free market to operate successfully henceforth and for its fruits to achieve the greatest social good, the notion of 'privileged' access to information would have to give way to the doctrine of disclosure."[15]

—*From Practice to Profession*

For more than eighty years, CFA* charterholders and their predecessors have incrementally improved the ethical standards of investment professionals, transparency of corporations, and investment performance reporting standards. Many protections that investors take for granted trace their roots to the efforts of CFA* charterholders. Examples include a slew of SEC policies, investment performance reporting standards, and even the establishment of the Financial Accounting Standards Board (FASB). The CFA Institute also provided venues for the distribution of groundbreaking research, including works by Nobel Laureates such as Harry Markowitz, Eugene Fama, Merton Miller, and William Sharpe. If not for the collective efforts of this group, U.S. securities markets would almost certainly be less transparent and suffer from weaker integrity. At the same time, the CFA Institute's commitment to continuous improvement ensures that emerging flaws are identified and addressed.[16]

As of March 2023, there were more than 190,000 CFA* charterholders representing more than 150 countries. The program's impressive track record continues to enhance the credibility of new charterholders. That said, this track record is ever evolving, and the ability of CFA* charterholders to continually prove their merit will determine whether its reputation is sustained.[17]

The postwar period was a time of massive change in the financial analyst profession. As institutional investors replaced stock operators, hiring financial analysts became a necessity for brokerage firms, mutual fund companies, and a variety of institutional investment plans such as pension funds and endowments. The former statisticians would soon occupy the corner offices in many of the nation's largest financial institutions, thereby securing their position as the new masters of Wall Street.

Merrill Lynch Revives the U.S. Stock Market

"When Charles Merrill and Winthrop Smith entered Wall Street, Americans were wary of stock buyers. At most 15% of households were in the market. Today almost half of the adult population has money socked away in equities—either directly or through a 401(k) retirement program. The financial world has changed, in large part because of these far-sighted co-leaders."[18]

—WINTHROP SMITH JR., author of *Catching Lightning in a Bottle*

Prior to the 1950s, most Americans viewed the stock market as little more than a gambling venue. They suspended this belief temporarily during the mania of the late 1920s, but then re-embraced it after many lost their life savings in the Great Depression. During World War II, Americans began investing in securities cautiously, but primarily limited their purchases to war bonds. After the war, fear of the stock market gradually waned as memories of the Great Depression faded and federal securities regulations shielded investors from Wall Street's worst abuses. By the late 1940s, the average investor was ready to reconsider the merits of stocks, and an emerging financial powerhouse welcomed them back.[19]

The Origins of Merrill Lynch

Charles E. Merrill founded Merrill Lynch on January 6, 1914, after leaving his former employer, Eastman Dillon & Company. A few months after founding the firm, Merrill asked his close friend and former colleague, Edward Lynch, to join the venture. This unlikely duo created a surprisingly effective partnership. Merrill was the innovator and visionary, while Lynch's skepticism kept Merrill grounded in reality.[20]

Prior to the Great Depression, Merrill Lynch only offered investment banking services. It was one of many upstarts that entered the industry after Wall Street shed the constraints of the Gentlemen Banker's Code. New firms battled for clients by proactively pitching their services to corporate executives. Charles E. Mitchell, president of National City Corporation, trained his sales force to use aggressive marketing tactics and make exaggerated claims. Merrill also marketed aggressively, but unlike Mitchell, he never wavered from his belief that honesty and integrity were an investment banker's most valuable assets.[21]

Merrill Lynch's values fueled the firm's success for fifteen years. Its most lucrative underwriting clients were chain stores, which proliferated during the early 1900s. Many companies underwritten by Merrill Lynch are recognizable today. Examples include Safeway, Walgreens, and JCPenney. In March 1928, the firm was in a strong financial position, but Merrill sensed danger on the horizon. He feared that lax monetary policies had driven stock prices to dangerously high levels, and he encouraged clients and employees to trim their exposure. Despite his warnings, the stock market continued to rise for the remainder of 1928 and most of 1929, prompting relentless ridicule by Merrill's friends, colleagues, and journalists. The criticism was so unbearable that Merrill questioned his own sanity. It took several consultations with a psychiatrist before he was convinced that he was not losing his mind. Despite the unpopularity of his beliefs, Merrill persuaded the partnership to substantially reduce the firm's exposure to stocks well in advance of the Great Crash in October 1929.[22]

The Great Crash vindicated Merrill. The firm's conservative balance sheet enabled it to weather the Great Depression better than almost all competitors. Nevertheless, Merrill grew disenchanted with securities markets, and throughout the 1930s, he shifted his attention to the management of his chain store holdings. Most of his time was dedicated to the management of Safeway, which he considered the crown jewel. He also jettisoned Merrill Lynch's brokerage business via a sale to E. A. Pierce and Company. Merrill's sabbatical from Wall Street was another example of his impeccable timing. Brokerage firms and investment banks struggled during the 1930s, but Safeway thrived. Americans still needed to buy groceries, and Safeway's low prices were attractive during hard times. By the end of the 1930s, Safeway was thriving under Merrill's leadership, and he had little desire to return to Wall Street.[23]

The Rehabilitation of the American Stockbroker

In 1940, the U.S. economy shed the last vestiges of the Depression, as World War II fueled massive demand for industrial products. However, E. A. Pierce, the acquirer of Merrill's former brokerage business, struggled to compete as an independent entity. Realizing that the firm's survival was at stake, Winthrop Smith, one of the firm's managing partners, approached Charles Merrill with a proposal to recombine Merrill

Lynch and E. A. Pierce into a single firm with the goal of opening U.S. securities markets to the average American. Merrill initially dismissed the proposal, but after hours of discussion, Smith persuaded him to join.[24]

While Merrill and Smith plotted the future of the newly merged company, they were alarmed by the results of a New York Stock Exchange survey, which revealed that the American public had a disturbing level of mistrust in the brokerage industry. Merrill commissioned his own survey to pressure test the findings, but the results were identical. The surveys convinced Merrill that restoring trust in the brokerage profession was not only critical to the future of Merrill Lynch, but it was also essential for the entire industry.[25]

As executives brainstormed strategies, a rising star by the name of Ted Braun crafted a radical proposal. The chief complaint in the Merrill survey was the common practice of "churning" portfolios to generate commissions, which was a broker's primary source of compensation.[26] To neutralize the incentive to churn, Braun proposed switching from commission-based compensation to a salary and bonus-based system. Merrill initially rejected the proposal, but Braun refused to back down, and Merrill eventually conceded.[27]

POINT OF INTEREST

The Long-Term Rewards of Honesty versus the Destructive Fear of Obsolescence

"The customer may not always be right, but he has rights.
And upon our recognition of his rights and our desire
to satisfy them rests our chance to succeed."[28]

—Charles Merrill

When faced with moral dilemmas, characters in old cartoons consulted with an imaginary devil on one shoulder and an angel on the other. The devil encouraged acts that were wrong but self-serving, while the angel encouraged them to do what was right but seemed self-destructive. In the long term, the angel's advice always proved to be both right and rewarding, while the devil's advice provided short-term relief at the expense of long-term self-destruction.

Investment professionals are constantly presented with this dilemma. Serving clients honestly—which is in every investment professional's long-term interest—often requires accepting truths that seem self-defeating in the moment. This is because the truth forces them to recognize their limitations, alter their behavior, and adapt to a new reality. Those who respond well to these existential dilemmas place themselves in an unexpectedly powerful position because an investment professional's greatest asset has always been and always will be their willingness to communicate the truth. Over many years, adherence to this principle ebbs and flows. During periods in which collective fear of obsolescence dominates, the few who buck the trend and communicate honestly with their clients are rewarded beyond their wildest expectations.

Merrill Lynch's commitment to honesty, integrity, and transparency rehabilitated the reputation of Wall Street in the decades following World War II. The firm, its employees, its customers, and Americans in general benefitted from their bold decision. Sadly, their commitment eventually weakened, as it almost always does as companies age. After the firm's adherence to its core values eroded in the early 2000s under the leadership of Stanley O'Neal, Merrill Lynch nearly disappeared forever beneath the wreckage of the Global Financial Crisis.

Merrill Lynch survived as a subsidiary of Bank of America, but its reputation is not what it was in the 1950s and 1960s. History demonstrates that it is never too late to regain the trust of Americans, but doing so requires them to open-mindedly explore what customers need and humbly accept the limits of what they can provide. It is unclear if Merrill Lynch will resurrect the principles of Charles E. Merrill and Winthrop Smith, but if they do, their employees and customers will once again enjoy benefits that they never anticipated were possible.

On April 3, 1940, the leadership of Merrill Lynch assembled its senior management at the Waldorf Astoria in New York City to unveil its strategy to regain America's trust and welcome Main Street back to Wall Street. Merrill leveraged many of the lessons he had learned in the grocery business, which were unexpectedly transferable to the brokerage industry. For example, the strategy relied heavily on innovative advertising techniques and relentless public outreach. Finally, Merrill crafted a code of ethics that served as the moral compass for multiple generations of Merrill Lynch employees. The code, which was dubbed the Ten Commandments, was constantly reinforced to ensure that the behavior of Merrill Lynch employees aligned with the spirit of the firm.[29]

The Ten Commandments of Merrill Lynch[30]

1. **Supremacy of Client Interests**—Our customer's interest MUST come first. Upon our ability to satisfy him rests our chance to succeed.

2. **Acceptance of Ethical Obligations**—Our business deals with people and their money. This creates financial and ethical responsibilities which we accept completely.

3. **Modesty and Impartiality**—Eliminating all expensive frills which do not make a direct contribution to the fundamental requirements of our customers, we offer simple offices, competent manpower and efficient, impartial service.

4. **Full Disclosure of Potential Conflicts of Interest and Biases**—When our relationship with a customer is other than that of a commission broker, the fact will be made known before the transaction. When supplying printed reports concerning a security in which the firm is not acting as principal, we intend to indicate the extent of the aggregate direct and indirect owner-ship, as for the date of the report by the firm and its general partners. The purpose of such disclosure is to help the customer estimate the possibility and extent of bias on the part of the firm in its presentation of facts related to a particular security.

5. **Incentive Alignment with Customers**—Salaries of our Registered Rep-resentatives are related primarily to the success in satisfying the service requirements of customers—thus eliminating conditions which indirectly create pressures to increase the trading of customers.

6. **Equal Treatment of Customers**—Our managers and partners are available for consultations with all customers, large or small. And, upon request, we will assist our customers in working out the investment, speculative, and hedging problems. However, we will not foist gratuitous advice upon our customers and all reports issued by our Research Department will be limited to facts—impartially presented.

7. **Respect for Operational Constraints**—During periods of extraordinary activity, no new accounts will be opened on any day when the volume of trading at any time indicates that the facilities of the firm may be overtaxed.

8. **Conservative Financial Management**—Our working capital position

> will at all times exceed the requirements of the law, the New York Stock Exchange and other exchanges, and our financial statements will be issued in a form designed for maximum clarity and understanding.
>
> 9. **Respect for the Law**—We heartily support the laws and other controls designed to protect the investor by preventing manipulation and fraud.

Many senior managers entered the Waldorf Astoria fearful about Merrill Lynch's future, but they all left inspired by a new sense of mission. Members of the media were also impressed. The *Chicago Daily News* called the Ten Commandments "the most refreshing document that has come to LaSalle St. in years." Many other newspapers lavished similar praise. The strategy was a hit, but whether Merrill Lynch could execute remained an open question.[31]

MAIN STREET FOLLOWS THE THUNDERING HERD BACK TO WALL STREET

The first few years under the new strategy were difficult. The firm's profitability depended on aggressive cost reductions and rapid client acquisition—two goals that do not usually coexist. Nevertheless, Merrill Lynch persisted, and just as the tide turned in World War II, so did Merrill Lynch's fortunes. Sadly, Charles Merrill suffered a severe heart attack in 1944, leaving him unable to lead the firm on a day-to-day basis. Merrill Lynch was supported, however, by a large pool of talented executives, the most impressive of whom was Winthrop "Win" Smith. Over the next decade, Smith and Merrill resurrected the spirit of the old Merrill-Lynch partnership and rehabilitated the brokerage industry. The three elements that proved most impactful included:[32]

- **Educational Advertising**—Under the leadership of Lewis Engel, Merrill Lynch abandoned the common practice of using boring tombstone ads in newspapers. Instead, Merrill Lynch sought to educate the public on the discipline of investing. The hope was that free education would, in turn, cement Merrill Lynch's reputation as the most trusted brokerage firm in America. The firm's educational campaigns used a variety of mediums, such as newspaper ads, television ads, conference seminars, state fair exhibits, information stands in Grand Central Station, and many others.

- **Paid Employee Education and Training**—Consistent application of the Ten Commandments was the cornerstone of Merrill Lynch's brand. Reinforcement required intense training and repetition. In 1945, Merrill Lynch hired Dr. Birl "Doc" Schultz to formalize training for new employees. Not only did the program ensure that new employees adhered to the firm's core values, but it also attracted many highly qualified World War II veterans. After abandoning his plans to attend business school, one veteran (and future Merrill Lynch president) commented, "My Lord, I'm getting paid for learning what I would have had to borrow money to do." The Merrill Lynch training program became the gold standard for the investment industry, and it helped the firm attract the most qualified entry-level employees.

- **Operational Innovation**—The decision to eliminate commission-based compensation reduced portfolio churning, but it also reduced revenue. Merrill Lynch offset this by implementing innovative cost reduction programs. Often these programs were made possible by the firm's proactive investment in new technologies. For example, Merrill Lynch was the first investment firm to use IBM mainframes to automate back-office functions. Over subsequent decades, Merrill Lynch continued to excel in operational efficiency and was a reliable early adopter of the latest information technologies.

The strategy employed by Charles Merrill and Win Smith enabled the firm to reinvent itself and prosper. It also proved that brokers who traded in truth had a formidable competitive advantage. Finally, the firm's values helped restore America's faith in the capitalist system at a time when the Soviet Union's central planning model was creating doubts. The series of charts on the pages that follow provides a snapshot of the impact of Merrill Lynch's strategy on U.S. securities markets after World War II.

THE INSTITUTIONAL MISSING LINKS

Merrill Lynch helped rehabilitate the brokerage industry and strengthen its influence in U.S. securities markets, but it was not the only institutional investor to emerge from the wreckage of the Great Depression. In the 1970s, Merrill Lynch discovered they had overlooked the rise of two other types of institutional investors. The first group consisted of institutional investment plans, which amassed large portfolios as corporations and not-for-profit institutions rapidly accumulated wealth. The second consisted of mutual fund companies, which rebounded after the passage of the Investment Company Act of 1940.

Renewed faith in U.S. securities markets helps facilitate a flood of new securities issues by U.S. companies.

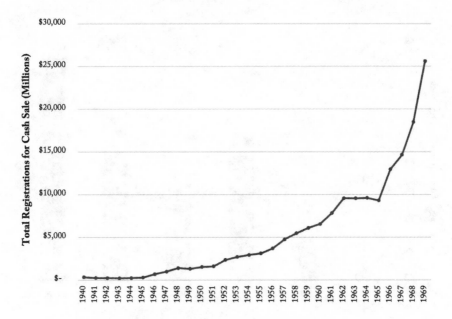

Figure 22.2: Three-Year Rolling Average New Registrations under the Securities Act of 1933 (Millions) (1940–1969)[33]

Increased investment in growth and innovation helps fuel a multi-decade bull market in U.S. stocks.

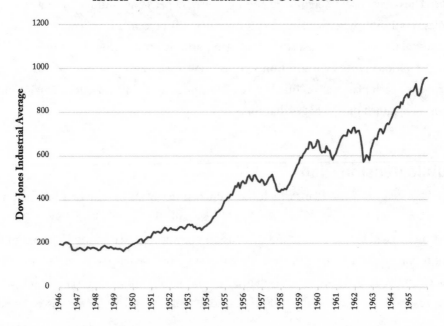

Figure 22.3: Dow Jones Industrial Average Price (Monthly)[34]

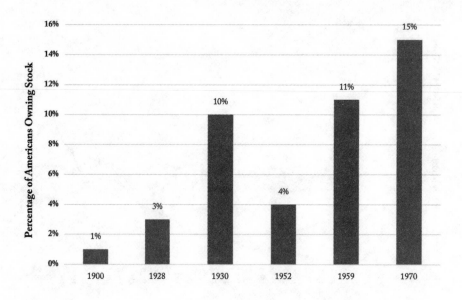

Broader stock ownership enables more Americans to share in the rewards.

Figure 22.4: Percentage of U.S. Population with Ownership in Stocks (Selected Years)[35]

The Emergence of Institutional Investment Plans

After World War II ended, institutional investment plans accumulated assets at a rapid pace. The largest plans were public pensions, private pensions, and life insurance companies. By 1985, these plans held approximately 20 percent of the entire U.S. stock market.[36] Figure 22.5 shows institutional plan portfolio growth from 1945 to 1985.[37]

The various types of institutional plans grew at similar rates, but the origin and purpose of each plan was unique. A brief description of the history of the major plan types is explained on the pages that follow.

Public Pension Plans

The U.S. Navy Pension Plan, which was launched in 1800, was the first funded pension plan in the U.S., but it exhausted its funds soon after the Panic of 1837.[39] Nearly a century passed before funded public pension plans reappeared in the U.S. in significant numbers. When they reemerged, most plans employed a pay-as-you-go funding model. In the 2020s, trustees consider pay-as-you-go schemes to be reckless, but they seemed less risky in the early 1900s because it took many years for plans to accrue

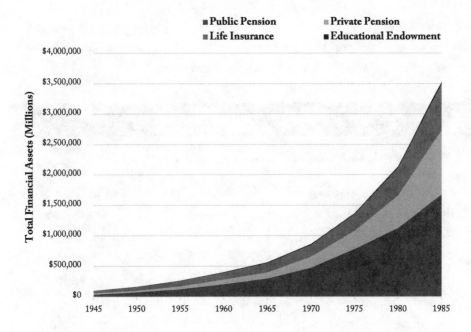

Figure 22.5: Total Market Value of U.S Institutional Investment
Plan Assets (Millions) (October 1, 1945–July 1, 1985)[38]

substantial liabilities. Therefore, paying distributions with current tax revenue initially
had little impact on public finances. New York City launched the first pay-as-you-go
plan in 1857, and many major U.S. cities soon followed. Most early plans covered
police officers, firemen, and teachers.[40]

By the 1920s, actuarial science had improved, annual distributions were no longer immaterial, and governments began abandoning the pay-as-you-go model and
adopting funded models. Public pension plans were funded via regular contributions
from both employers and employees. By the late 1930s, assets and liabilities of state
and local pension plans were growing rapidly. The initial catalyst was the passage of
the 1935 Social Security Act, which provided a safety net for many Americans but
excluded state and local employees due to concerns of potential constitutional violations. State and local governments responded by establishing separate plans for public
employees. Over the next fifteen years, more than half of the large state and local plans
in existence today were established.[41]

The investment strategies of early public pension plans were unlike those employed
today. Most invested only in government bonds and, in some cases, high quality corporate bonds. Investments in common stocks were rare. Public pensions only began
branching out into stocks after World War II ended, largely because new federal

regulations appeared to make them less risky. Even so, allocations to stocks were usually capped at 35 percent. It was not until the 1980s that public pension plans began allocating heavily to equity securities and alternative assets.[42]

POINT OF INTEREST

The Stubborn Challenge of Governance

Since the U.S. Navy established the first funded pension plan in 1800, institutional plans have constantly struggled with governance. The crux of the issue is that most plans are governed by committees of volunteer trustees, rather than full-time investment professionals. Trustees usually serve for a limited time (typically four years or less), and many lack experience managing multi-asset class portfolios. Trustees are also forced to make decisions with limited time to prepare, as meetings are typically held quarterly and run for only a matter of hours. The combination of time constraints, limited trustee tenure, and variable levels of investment experience create a second problem, which is that trustees must place enormous trust in the advice provided by staff and service providers. Many of these individuals are prone to prioritize their own self-interest, and it is difficult for trustees to detect when this is occurring.

The structurally flawed governance of institutional investment plans, combined with poor alignment of incentives among trustees and service providers, produces enormous waste. Examples include excess complexity of investment portfolios, overuse of actively managed funds, excessive hiring and firing of fund managers, and the adoption of misleading benchmarks. These problems have only worsened over time. Repairing flawed governance practices remains the greatest challenge for institutional investment plans in the 2020s.

Private Pension Plans

In 1875, the American Express Company offered the first private pension plan in the United States.[43] Over the next several decades, a handful of companies emulated American Express, but private pensions were not widespread until after World War I began in 1914. Key drivers included an informal IRS policy that allowed companies to deduct employer contributions from taxable income, as well as a sharp increase in corporate profitability stemming from the sale of goods and services to the Allied powers in World War I. Finally, pension plans made it easier for employers to gracefully replace older workers with younger workers by enforcing mandatory retirement. This was especially important in industries with significant physical labor requirements, such as railroads, public utilities, and manufacturing companies.[44]

Private pensions grew steadily in the 1920s, but then the Great Depression forced many corporations to cut benefits (or eliminate them entirely). After the start of World War II, private pensions became popular again for a few reasons. First, the federal government introduced wage caps to contain inflation during the war. Pension benefits, which were not subjected to wage caps, were used to increase compensation to employees without violating wage caps. Second, tax rates for individuals and corporations were extremely high during and immediately after the war. Using pension benefits rather than wage increases effectively functioned as tax-free compensation. Third, U.S. corporations were extremely profitable due to massive war-related spending. Flush with cash, corporations and labor unions had ample cash to fund pension liabilities.[45]

In the 1950s and 1960s, private pension plan growth continued but at a slower pace. Ironically, the event that ultimately led to the decline of private pensions was a regulation that was intended to save them. On September 2, 1974, President Gerald Ford signed the Employee Retirement Income Security Act (ERISA) to strengthen protections against employer abuses of pension beneficiaries. The unintended consequence was a significant increase in plan administration costs. Employers responded by switching to defined contribution plans, thereby transferring retirement funding risk to employees.[46]

Educational Endowments

Educational endowments managed a small sliver of total institutional plan assets. But it is not the amount of assets that makes this group interesting, rather it is the impact of the investment strategies that they began employing in the late 1980s. Despite their limited size, investment professionals often view university endowments as especially innovative. This aura is largely attributable to the performance of a single institution: the Yale University Endowment. Under the leadership of Chief Investment Officer David Swensen, the Yale University Endowment embraced an unorthodox strategy that generated exceptional returns for nearly forty years.

Over the past several decades, institutional investment plans—and, more recently, investment consultants and OCIOs who advise them—sought to replicate Yale's performance, but they overlooked the true source of Yale's competitive advantage. The most costly error was their mistaken belief that mere access to "alternative asset classes" would automatically produce Yale-like returns. This issue is discussed in greater depth in chapter 25.

Life Insurance Companies

Life insurance companies lost their status as the largest institutional investors in the U.S. in the late 1950s, but they remain the oldest. In 1752, Benjamin Franklin founded the Philadelphia Contributionship, which insured the homes of Philadelphians. Insurance companies grew at a modest pace over the next century but were mostly limited to fire and marine policies. It was not until the late 1800s that these companies established a meaningful presence in America, and longer still before they became a major force in securities markets.[47]

At the turn of the twentieth century, life insurance policies were the dominant policy in the U.S., but property and disability insurance were steadily catching up. The industry landscape then shifted dramatically in the 1940s. The first catalyst was the passage of the McCarran-Ferguson Act, which shifted regulation from the federal to state level. The second was the gradual allowance of multi-line insurance products by state insurance commissions.[48] By the end of the 1950s virtually all states permitted multi-line insurance, which allowed companies to diversify underwriting risks more effectively and increase in size.

The growth of insurance portfolios during the early 1900s primarily involved assets held in the general account. In the 1970s, insurance companies began offering an array of new insurance products, such as whole life, universal life, and variable annuities, which required the investment of policyholders' assets separate from the insurance company's general account. The sale of these products fueled an uptick in growth of insurance assets in the post–Great Inflation Era.

Mutual Funds Rise from the Ashes

Investment companies—heretofore referred to as mutual funds—were a welcome financial innovation in the 1920s.[49] By purchasing shares in a fund, investors gained exposure to a diversified portfolio of securities with a single purchase. Unfortunately, in most cases, diversification benefits were more than offset by careless speculation, reckless use of leverage, and exorbitant fees. In a disturbing warning issued only six months prior to the Great Crash of 1929, Paul C. Cabot, founder of the State Street Investment Corporation, described the practices of fund managers, stating, "Some months ago, in testifying before a committee of the New York Stock Exchange, I was asked to state briefly what were, in my opinion, the present abuses in the investment trust movement. My reply was: (1) dishonesty; (2) inattention and instability; and (3) greed."[50]

Mutual funds were given a second chance in the post-World War II era. In his book recounting the history of the mutual fund industry, Matthew Fink, former president of the Investment Company Institute (ICI), concluded that "by 1940 the entire foundation for mutual fund success had been put in place. All that was needed was a period of prosperity and rising stock prices."[51] The industry did not have to wait very long for this tailwind to arrive, as one of the longest bull markets in U.S. history commenced soon after World War II ended. The rally accelerated in the 1950s and lasted well into the 1960s. Stock prices also benefited from the brokerage industry's aggressive marketing efforts, especially those of Merrill Lynch. Upward momentum in stocks made mutual funds more attractive, as most funds were tilted heavily toward stocks rather than bonds. These tailwinds fueled massive growth in mutual fund assets. Over a twenty-year period, assets grew at an annualized rate of 18 percent per year. Figure 22.6 and Figure 22.7 show the growth of mutual fund assets under management (AUM) and total mutual funds from 1945 to 1965.

AN INCONVENIENT TRUTH

"The people who came to Wall Street in the 1960s had always been—and expected to be— winners . . . The trouble with winner's games is that they tend to self destruct because they attract too much attention and too many players—all of whom want to win. That's why gold rushes always finish ugly."[52]

—CHARLES ELLIS, founder of Greenwich Associates (July 1975)

Large inflows of capital into mutual funds continued unabated for decades. Under pressure to differentiate their products, funds offered a wide variety of strategies covering different asset classes and sub-asset classes. To their credit, many fund managers simultaneously improved governance practices, fund transparency, and overall fee levels. The problem, however, is that these improvements disguised the existence of a fundamental flaw at the heart of the business model itself. The flaw was the claim that professional management of an investment portfolio added value beyond what investors could obtain by simply investing blindly in the entire market.[55] Strong evidence that market indexes outperformed most professionally managed portfolios surfaced even before the first mutual fund was created in the U.S. in

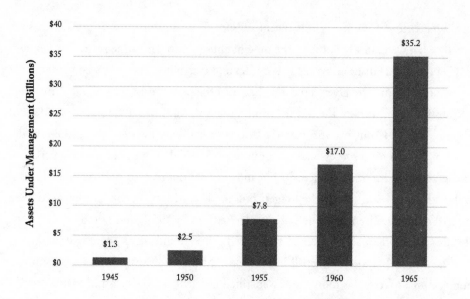

Figure 22.6: Total Mutual Fund Assets Under Management (Billions) (1945–1965)[53]

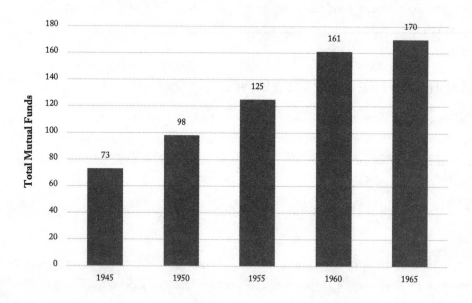

Figure 22.7: Number of U.S. Mutual Funds (1945–1965)[54]

1924. Countless academic papers, government studies, and actual experience have since reaffirmed this truth. For all but the most skilled investors, active management is a waste of money and time, yet most investment professionals refuse to accept this harsh reality.

THE WISDOM OF THE CROWD
AND FOLLY OF THE GAMBLER

"My basic point here is that neither the Financial Analysts as a whole nor the investment funds as a whole can expect to 'beat the market,' because in a significant sense they (or you) are the market."[56]

—BENJAMIN GRAHAM, "The Future of Financial Analysis" (1963)

The stubborn refusal of investors to accept that professional management is highly unlikely to add value is perplexing. Perhaps it stems from a general lack of understanding as to why active management, in aggregate, is doomed to fail. The primary reason—but certainly not the only one—is explained by a mathematical concept known as the "wisdom of crowds." The concept was introduced by Francis Galton in 1907 to explain the results of a contest in which people were asked to guess the weight of an ox. Galton analyzed 787 guesses and noted that the average guess of 1,198 pounds differed from the actual weight by only nine pounds. Galton also observed that 90 percent of individuals failed to come closer than the average guess. In other words, only 10 percent of individuals outperformed.[57]

Galton's observation was not an anomaly. Many people witness the wisdom of crowds when participating in a common contest at charitable events. For a small fee, contestants are asked to guess the number of jelly beans in a jar. The participant who comes closest to the actual number wins a prize. An interesting thing about this game is that even the most thoughtful participants are unlikely to beat the average guess of all participants once enough contestants enter the contest. Assuming every participant has access to the same information (i.e., no cheating), the total guesses above the actual amount tend to cancel out the total guesses below the actual amount, and the average guess comes remarkably close to the actual number of jelly beans. Figure 22.8 shows the results from one of these contests, which was held at Riverdale High School in Portland, Oregon, in March 2023. The average guess was 1,180, which was close to the actual number of 1,283. Out of the seventy-one guesses, only three beat the average guess. Anders Nielsen came closest with a guess of 1,296.

Figure 22.8 may look familiar because it illustrates the same principle that was explained in chapter 9, which is that it becomes increasingly difficult to create a better-than-average estimate of an uncertain value as the number of estimates increases. This rule applies to the jelly bean guessing contest, forecasting GDP growth, creating asset class return assumptions, and countless other economic uncertainties. Estimating securities prices is admittedly more complex than a jelly bean–guessing contest, but

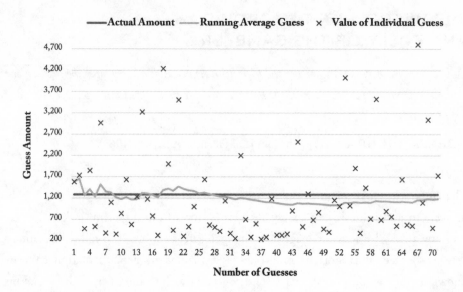

Figure 22.8: Average Participant Guess by Number of Participants[58]

the same rule applies. As the number of market participants increases, it becomes more difficult to estimate a fair price that is superior to the average.

The Gilded Age stock operators intuitively understood the wisdom of crowds, which is why they resorted to insider trading and market manipulation. Market efficiency was already formidable in the late 1800s. Immediately after the passage of the Securities Act of 1933 and Securities Exchange Act of 1934, these techniques were no longer permitted. An unanticipated side effect was that it created a temporary state of higher market inefficiency because companies were forced to release troves of financial information, but there were few market participants who knew how to analyze it. Ben Graham was among the few, and it enabled him to outperform market averages for many years. But within a few decades, the number of trained financial analysts increased, and the market returned to a high level of efficiency. Graham inadvertently accelerated this process by publishing several books and papers explaining his techniques, thereby weakening his competitive advantage.

By 1963, Graham concluded that beating market averages was no longer viable for most financial analysts. That did not mean that he had lost faith in the value of the profession; he just knew with mathematical certainty that beating the market averages was no longer a worthy endeavor for most analysts. Despite his indisputable logic, Ben Graham's message was largely ignored. By the 1960s, there were simply too many investment firms and investment professionals that had staked their businesses and livelihoods on the premise that beating the market was broadly achievable.

More than a decade passed before several courageous innovators embraced Ben

Graham's warning by creating funds that replicated indexes. These included people like Rex Sinquefield, Eugene Fama, and William Sharpe. In 1975, Jack Bogle commercialized the concept for the mass market when his firm, the Vanguard Group, introduced its first indexed mutual fund on December 31, 1975. The sole objective was to replicate the performance of the U.S. equity market and charge investors the lowest possible fee. The combination of fee savings and avoidance of non-value-added security selection enabled the Vanguard fund to persistently beat most actively managed funds for nearly fifty years.[59]

Despite the indisputable logic and incontrovertible evidence to support it, the deep-seated belief that financial analysts can beat market averages persists to this day. Making matters worse, overconfidence has spread to new markets such as hedge funds, venture capital, and private equity. The only difference is that the purported skill of fund manager selection replaced the purported skill of security selection. The failure of the investment profession to accept the mathematical impossibility of their purported value proposition impedes their ability to add real value to the investors whom they serve. The profession must come to terms with this reality to restore its credibility.

POINT OF INTEREST

The Irresistible Allure of the Wall Street Casino

"The dopamine rush we get from long shots is why we play the lotto, invest in IPOs, keep too much money in too few stocks, and invest with active portfolio managers instead of index funds."[60]

—Jason Zweig, financial journalist

By 1963, Ben Graham concluded that most financial analysts could not outperform market indexes. If he were alive today, he would consider it a veritable fool's errand—just like his protégé, Warren Buffett. The reason that their prospects have only worsened is because the number of market participants has increased exponentially. The CFA® program alone has churned out 244,285 new charterholders since Ben Graham issued his warning in May 1963. But even this number massively underestimates the number of "market participants" who regularly estimate the fair value of stocks, bonds, and many other types of securities. Hedge fund analysts, mutual fund analysts, pension fund staff, and skilled amateur investors

(continued)

all play the game. There are literally millions of participants in securities markets on any given day, making it extremely difficult to beat market indices.

Most people stubbornly deny this reality despite the preponderance of evidence. Mass denial is likely due to a durable flaw of human nature—the same one that explains why casino floors never lack gamblers even though each gambler is explicitly told that the odds are stacked against them. Investors gamble with active management because they convince themselves that the rules do not apply to them. This belief is amplified by the axiom expressed by J. Pierpont Morgan, who stated that "nothing so undermines your financial judgment as the sight of your neighbor getting rich." Just like a gambler cannot resist adding more of their hard-earned money to a slot machine after seeing the adjacent machine spewing out chips, the active management gambler cannot stomach watching peers benefit from market-beating performance. Probabilities do not matter. Active management gamblers roll the dice in the hope that magical thinking will render them immune from the laws of mathematics.

Chapter 23

INFLATED EXPECTATIONS

"The stamping of paper is an operation so much easier than the laying of taxes, that a government, in the practice of paper emissions, would rarely fail in any such emergency to indulge itself too far . . . If it should not even be carried so far as to be rendered an absolute bubble, it would at least be likely to be extended to a degree, which would occasion an inflated and artificial state of things incompatible with the regular and prosperous course of the political economy."[1]

—ALEXANDER HAMILTON

The U.S. exited the 1940s as the wealthiest nation in the world, and it extended its lead in the 1950s. Under the Eisenhower administration, the U.S. enjoyed rapid economic growth, modest unemployment, low inflation, and the unique privilege of holding the world's new reserve currency. The stock market responded with tremendous gains and experienced only a few temporary pullbacks. Figure 23.1 captures several of these trends.

Eisenhower's second term was coming to an end in the fall of 1959, and Americans were anxious about whether prosperity would continue. Confidence was soon restored with the election of John F. Kennedy, who became the youngest president in U.S. history. The restoration of confidence was especially important in the business community. After taking office, President Kennedy's policies were more pragmatic than many executives feared. That is not to say that Kennedy's presidency was without setbacks. The most significant were the aborted U.S. invasion of Cuba and a terrifying nuclear standoff with the Soviet Union during the Cuban Missile Crisis. From an economic perspective, however, his leadership was viewed positively.

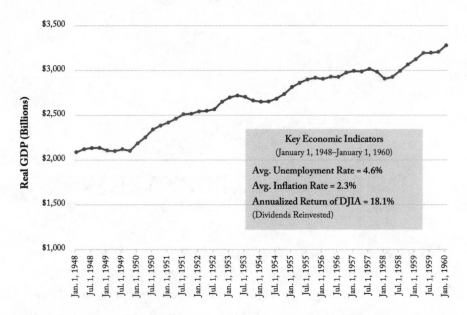

Figure 23.1: U.S. Real Gross Domestic Product (2012 Dollars) (January 1, 1948–January 1, 1960)[2]

President Kennedy's presidency was tragically cut short on Friday, November 22, 1963, after he suffered a fatal gunshot wound at the hands of Lee Harvey Oswald during a campaign stop in Dallas, Texas. Within hours, Lyndon Baines Johnson took the oath of office aboard Air Force One. Johnson's unexpected ascendency to the presidency marked a fateful shift in U.S. economic, domestic, and foreign policy. Despite positive intent, Johnson's ambitious policies were tainted by fundamentally flawed theses and woefully inadequate execution. Many of his programs produced outcomes that were precisely the opposite of what he intended. Johnson's blunders drained the nation's wealth, needlessly sacrificed the lives of its youth, and ultimately contributed heavily to the onset of the Great Inflation.

In 1963, the famed monetarist Milton Friedman stated that "inflation is always and everywhere a monetary phenomenon in the sense that it is and can be produced only by a more rapid increase in the quantity of money than in output."[3] This explanation is simple and logical, but policymakers failed to take heed in the 1960s and 1970s. Flawed monetary policies—which were significantly amplified by intense political pressure from members of both the Democratic and Republican parties—ignited the Great Inflation in the late 1960s.

Chapter 23 details the underlying causes of the Great Inflation and explains why draconian monetary policies were needed to end it. It begins by recounting the subtle onset, which was triggered by President Johnson's Great Society programs and escalation of the war in Vietnam. It then details how fundamental miscalculations and flawed philosophies of the Federal Reserve allowed inflation to persist. The chapter concludes by detailing the painful monetary policies introduced by Fed Chairman Paul Volcker in October 1979, which finally brought the Great Inflation to an end in 1982. After inflation was tamed, the U.S. enjoyed a new era of prosperity, which lasted until the turn of the twenty-first century.

GREATLY INFLATED EXPECTATIONS

"Let this session of Congress be known as the session which did more for civil rights than the last hundred sessions combined; as the session which enacted the most far-reaching tax cut of our time; as the session which declared all-out war on human poverty and unemployment in these United States; as the session which finally recognized the health needs of all our older citizens; as the session which reformed our tangled transportation and transit policies; as the session which achieved the most effective, efficient foreign aid program ever; and as the session which helped to build more homes, more schools, more libraries, and more hospitals than any single session of Congress in the history of our Republic . . . All this and more can and must be done. It can be done by this summer, and it can be done without any increase in spending."[4]

—PRESIDENT LYNDON B. JOHNSON

On November 3, 1964, President Lyndon Baines Johnson won his first elected presidential term in a landslide victory over Republican candidate Barry Goldwater. Democrats simultaneously won large majorities in both the House and Senate, clearing the path for an ambitious legislative agenda. Reform priorities included civil rights, voting rights, expansion of entitlement programs, and strengthening of labor unions. At the root of these reforms was Johnson's grand ambition to eliminate poverty in America. In his State of the Union speech on January 8, 1964, Johnson confidently proclaimed that all these reforms were achievable in record time and without compromising the federal budget. Perhaps emboldened by America's victory in World War II, successful execution of postwar reconstruction, and economic growth that was the envy of the world, Johnson discounted the possibility of failure.

THE WAR ON POVERTY

Civil rights reform and the war on poverty topped Johnson's legislative agenda. Civil rights legislation is beyond the scope of this book, but it is worth noting that Johnson's accomplishments were commendable. The Civil Rights Act of 1964 prohibited discrimination in schools and public institutions, while the Voting Act of 1965 enfranchised millions of African American voters victimized by "Jim Crow" laws. Johnson's War on Poverty, however, was far less successful.

The seeds of Johnson's War on Poverty were planted by the Kennedy administration. Poverty concerns were rising in the early 1960s for a few reasons. First, American perceptions of poverty changed due to the nation's newly acquired wealth. Poverty levels that were once viewed as an unfortunate part of life became intolerable for a wealthy empire. Second, reductions in the poverty rate that Americans enjoyed during the 1950s had stalled in the 1960s. The Kennedy administration sensed that further poverty reduction was a priority for Americans, and he experimented with several federal programs to reduce it. These programs consisted mostly of small-scale pilots, many of which proved ineffective.[5]

In comparison to Kennedy, President Johnson was much more enthusiastic about the potential social and political benefits of addressing poverty at the federal level. First, he believed that poverty reduction would enhance progress on civil rights, as African Americans disproportionately suffered from lower incomes, higher unemployment, and lower standards of living. Second, Johnson correctly sensed that Americans were less tolerant of poverty even though poverty rates had declined substantially during the 1950s. Finally, Johnson saw the political benefits, as anti-poverty programs appeared to have broad appeal with voters.[6]

Johnson's aides initially proposed modest anti-poverty initiatives that consisted primarily of pilot projects to test various academic theories. But Johnson demanded much bolder action. In a review of recorded conversations recovered from the Johnson archives, the historian Guian A. McKee observed that "[Johnson's advisors'] initial proposal had called for a limited series of demonstration projects to perfect the community action concept and determine whether it represented an effective solution . . . Lyndon Johnson, however, had little interest in pilot projects. He wanted action, and he wanted to make bold strides in attacking a social evil . . . this meant that an academic concept that had barely been tested in a real-world setting would suddenly form the core of a major federal social policy endeavor." The tapes revealed that rather than moving cautiously, Johnson pushed his administration to roll out experimental programs on a national scale.[7]

Only three months after settling on poverty reduction as the cornerstone of his second presidential term, Johnson introduced the Economic Opportunity Act (EOA) of 1964 to Congress. The EOA created multiple federal programs, such as the Job Corps, the Neighborhood Youth Corp (NYC), and the Volunteers in Service to America (VISTA) program. The funding requirements were modest, but the EOA created momentum for further legislation that was far more costly. Most importantly, on July 30, 1965, Johnson signed the Social Security Amendments of 1965, which created Medicare and Medicaid to provide health insurance coverage for the elderly, disabled, and poor.[8]

The aggregate impact of the War on Poverty was and continues to be a topic of intense disagreement. Opining on the overall effectiveness of every program is beyond the scope of this book; however, it is important to acknowledge two effects. The first relates to the sheer size of the long-term financial liabilities created by the War on Poverty. Over the past sixty years, the liabilities have grown substantially and now pose a significant threat to the long-term financial health of the United States. This is not a judgment of the benefits; it is simply an acknowledgement of the costs. Funding these liabilities presents a daunting challenge for all Americans. The second is that the chaotic implementation of the War on Poverty severely impaired Johnson's presidency. The Community Action Program (CAP) in particular, which was the most controversial element of the EOA, contributed significantly to Johnson's inability to pursue a second presidential term.

POINT OF INTEREST

Einstein's Special Theory of Financial Relativity

"A calm and modest life brings more happiness than the pursuit of success combined with constant restlessness."

—Albert Einstein

Most people judge their wealth relative to the wealth of others rather than precisely defining their unique needs. This is unfortunate because once people ignore their relative standing, they often find that their needs are more modest than they thought. Instead, many people needlessly sacrifice their happiness in the pursuit of riches that offer no incremental benefit.

In the U.S., studies reveal that the relationship, in aggregate, between income and reported levels of happiness disappears once annual earnings exceed around $100,000 per year. Yet many people with incomes far above this threshold consider themselves poor, while others are perfectly content earning less.[9]

The relativism of wealth perceptions creates an interesting paradox. On one hand, the incentive to accumulate wealth fuels human progress. Proponents of capitalism oppose programs to equalize wealth because they correctly point out that it deprives entrepreneurs and innovators of incentives that perpetuate human progress. The achievements of these individuals are critical to a nation's

(continued)

overall competitiveness and long-term economic well-being. The absence of such incentives explains why socialist countries such as the Soviet Union failed to keep pace with the U.S. during the Cold War. On the other hand, when wealth disparity becomes too pronounced, resentment and desperation build among the "have nots." This can destabilize governments and lead to the decline of civilizations.

In *Principles for Dealing with the Changing World Order*, Ray Dalio credits capitalism for increasing the aggregate wealth of a society, but he also acknowledges the important role of policies to correct excessive wealth disparity. Financial history confirms that nations that allow wealth to become too concentrated risk revolution, but nations that distribute wealth evenly suffer from economic stagnation. The fate of the U.S. will depend on the ability of policymakers to strike a balance between these two extremes.[10]

COMMUNITY ACTION AND REACTION

"This is not what I set up poverty [for]. I set up poverty for people to just work like hell and get paid so they'd have something to eat . . . All this theoretical stuff, a bunch of goddamn social workers going out and shoveling money through a bunch of half-baked organizations . . . I put in the interview the other day . . . and the boys made me take it out. I said, 'I think it's a waste, and I think it's graft, and I think it's mismanagement, and I think it's political.'"[11]

—PRESIDENT LYNDON B. JOHNSON

POINT OF INTEREST

A Perfect Storm of Paper

"When you traced the arc of the Johnson presidency, you could see that Johnson translated everything into legislation, a new aide, Joseph Califano, noticed. At one point, Califano's young son swallowed a bottle of aspirin and was sent to the hospital to have his stomach pumped. When Johnson learned of the accident, he promised legislation to make medicine bottles child-resistant."[12]

—Amity Shlaes, author of *Great Society*

Lyndon Johnson's ability to shepherd legislation through Congress was legendary during his reign as Speaker of the House. This skill morphed into a virtual superpower when he entered the White House with a dominant majority in both houses of the Congress. Ironically, the ease with which Johnson passed legislation led to his undoing. In the 2000s, U.S. presidents struggle to pass a single piece of significant legislation, but Johnson's problem was passing too much legislation. Although a law to save children from drug overdoses is not the best example of unneeded legislation, the overarching point is that Johnson's instinctive response to societal problems was to fix them with new laws. Such laws often had undesirable side effects, and the sheer volume made it difficult to implement anything effectively.

Pushing legislation through Congress was President Johnson's greatest strength, but it also proved to be a fatal weakness. The blizzard of reform legislation that swept through the Capitol during Johnson's presidency all but guaranteed chaotic implementation. Moreover, many of the legislative initiatives were so poorly constructed that even perfect implementation was bound to fail.

In the case of the EOA, the problem was that it was based almost entirely on unproven academic theories. The Community Action Program (CAP), which was part of the EOA, was the poster child of a program that seemed sensible in theory but was disastrous in practice. The CAP provided federal funding to community groups in cities and localities throughout the country. The goal was to allow local leaders to decide the best use of the funds. This seemed reasonable on the surface, but the problem with CAP stemmed from language buried deep in the law that mandated "maximum feasible participation" of program design and implementation. These seemingly benign words produced several unwanted side effects, including:[13]

- **Federal Funding of Civil Unrest**—The intent of CAP was to empower local community activists to provide training and opportunities to underprivileged citizens. The "maximum feasible participation" language, however, allowed funds to be funneled to radical groups, which then used it to support their causes rather than the poor. In many cases, groups incited violent conflicts with local political leaders. All else being equal, the CAP intensified civil unrest that was already on the rise in the 1960s due to opposition to the Vietnam War and civil rights abuses.

- **Perverse Incentives and Unintended Consequences**—A combination of perverse incentives and misdirected leadership by groups with ulterior motives caused

CAP to produce outcomes that often hurt the very people it was intended to help. One of the worst outcomes was the systematic razing of African American neighborhoods and replacement of single-family homes with community housing, often referred to as "projects." In one of the worst examples, local leaders in St. Louis replaced an entire neighborhood of single-family homes with large apartment buildings and then encouraged behavior that was detrimental to the well-being of the residents. The most egregious example was the employment of hall monitors to catch families with fathers living on the premises. In effect, intact families with limited financial means were either evicted or encouraged to separate.

- **Absence of Jobs**—President Johnson idolized President Franklin Roosevelt, often referencing the New Deal as the inspiration for the Great Society. However, unlike many New Deal programs, such as the Tennessee Valley Authority and Works Progress Administration, Johnson's programs did not create jobs directly. Many of Johnson's programs provided training for jobs that simply did not exist. All else being equal, this amplified discontent rather than mitigating it.

In fairness, Johnson's anti-poverty programs were not universally ineffective, but at a minimum, they were a political disaster. The costs were then significantly amplified by Johnson's disastrous escalation of the Vietnam War, which placed further strain on the federal budget and produced a frightening spasm of civil unrest.

THE WAR IN VIETNAM

"Men and women, old and young, regardless of creeds, political parties or nationalities, all Vietnamese must stand up and fight the French colonists to save the Fatherland. Those who have rifles will use their rifles. Those who have swords will use their swords. Those who have no swords will use spades, hoes, or sticks . . . We must sacrifice even our last drop of blood to safeguard our country."[14]

—HO CHI MINH (December 19, 1946)

The Vietnam War is the most controversial war in U.S. history. Despite an enormous mobilization of personnel and capital, America failed to achieve its objectives—or even agree on what the objectives were. Retrospective analysis reveals countless failures that ultimately forced the U.S. to withdraw from Vietnam. Fatal errors included faulty assessments of North Vietnamese objectives, capabilities, resilience, and the nature of the actual threat to U.S. interests. These errors were amplified by the refusal of several administrations to admit their mistakes to the American people. The costs of the Vietnam War were substantial. The U.S. spent $138.9 billion (approximately $1 trillion in 2023 dollars); suffered 58,220 fatalities; and suffered a loss of faith in the integrity of U.S. government leaders. Many of these wounds have not fully healed.[15]

The section that follows focuses primarily on the financial costs of the war, which explain much of the political pressure that politicians placed on the Federal Reserve to maintain an accommodative monetary policy. This, in turn, contributed to the Great Inflation. But it also seeks to honor the countless Americans and Vietnamese who lost their lives in a war that neither side desired. Not only did American soldiers return to the U.S. scarred from the horrors of war, but many also suffered abuse from the very Americans whom they sought to protect. The war itself was a tragic error, but most American soldiers served honorably and deserved more respect and gratitude than they received. On the flip side, several million Vietnamese lost their lives in a war that most viewed as a fight for independence rather than a movement to spread international communism. Their motives and sacrifice are also deserving of honor.

The U.S. and the Republic of Vietnam now maintain friendly relations. Given the atrocities and horrors suffered by both sides, their reconciliation is a credit to both nations. Many wars persist for multiple generations because the thirst for vengeance persists long after the fog of war dissipates. The ability of the Vietnamese and Americans to avoid this fate is both rare and commendable.

A Misapplication of the Domino Theory

The conclusion of World War II marked the beginning rather than the end of wars for much of the world. The withdrawal of European countries from their former colonies triggered many conflicts. Battles to fill the power vacuum resulted in tens of millions of deaths in countries such as Korea, China, Indonesia, Pakistan, and Vietnam. Many conflicts eventually morphed into proxy wars between Western democratic groups led by the U.S., and communist groups led by the Soviet Union and China. Involvement among the major powers was usually restricted to financial support and the provision of armaments, but some proxy wars escalated into full-scale wars. Such was the case for the United States in Vietnam.

POINT OF INTEREST

Origin of the Domino Theory

*"Finally, you have broader considerations that might follow what you
would call 'the falling domino principle.' You have a row of dominoes set
up, you knock over the first one, and what will happen to the last one is the
certainty that it will go over very quickly. So, you could have a beginning
of a disintegration that would have the most profound influences."*[16]

—President Dwight D. Eisenhower (April 7, 1954)

U.S. involvement in Vietnam slowly escalated after the French abandoned their
former colony in 1954. The belief was that if Vietnam fell under communist
control, other nations in southeast Asia, such as Laos, Burma, and Malaysia,
would fall like a row of dominos. The domino theory was not far-fetched during
Eisenhower's presidency. At the time, the Soviet Union operated an international
organization known as the Cominform that sought to destabilize governments
and spread communism throughout the world. Sending a clear message that
the U.S. would resist such efforts made sense. The problem was that the risk
of a domino-like spread of communism diminished over time, and the theory
was misapplied to Vietnam. The primary goal of Vietnamese nationalists was to
achieve independence from foreign rule. They had little interest in contributing
to an international communism movement. Further, in 1956, the Soviet Union
dissolved the Cominform as part of its de-Stalinization efforts. This significantly
reduced the threat of international communism even if the North Vietnamese
desired to take part.[17]

By the 1960s, the domino theory provided weak justification for escalation
in Vietnam, but it continued to be used irrespective of its merits. Instead, the
primary motive for escalation became a failure to acknowledge mistakes and
admit that Americans were dying based on a flawed theory.

U.S. involvement in Vietnam began imperceptibly in 1947. After World War
II ended, France attempted to reoccupy its former colonies of Vietnam, Cambo-
dia, and Laos. Vietnamese nationalists, who had sought independence for decades,
immediately resisted the French. Under the spiritual leadership of Ho Chi Minh and
military leadership of Vo Nguyen Giap, the Viet Minh used guerilla warfare tactics to
demoralize French occupying forces.[18] The U.S. reluctantly expressed public support

for the French reoccupation, but it was largely because U.S. leaders feared that with-holding support would push the French toward an alliance with the Soviet Union. By the early 1950s, the Viet Minh were inflicting heavy damage on French occupation forces, and President Dwight D. Eisenhower expanded support by providing finan-cial aid and armaments to French forces.[19]

In 1954, while negotiating with the French on a withdrawal, the Viet Minh scored a decisive victory over French forces after a four-month siege of Dien Bien Phu. The unexpected victory convinced the French that their continued presence was futile, and they withdrew from Vietnam. For the remainder of the 1950s, there were several attempts to resolve the ongoing civil war by dividing the nation into a communist regime in the north and a democratic regime in the south, but both sides violated terms of the agreement, and the civil war only intensified. The U.S. supported the Southern regime despite serious concerns with corruption and incompetence of its prime minister, Ngo Dinh Diem. When President Kennedy took office in 1960, he increased support for the South Vietnamese by substantially increasing financial assis-tance and shipments of armaments. Kennedy also dramatically increased the number of "military advisors" who trained South Vietnamese troops and secretly accompanied them on combat missions. By the time Kennedy was assassinated in November 1963, the Vietnam War looked like more than a proxy war.[20]

The End of the Proxy War

We will never know whether President Kennedy would have ended or prolonged the Vietnam conflict. Prior to his assassination, he privately conceded that the war was unwin-nable but also confessed that withdrawal may not be politically feasible. Initially, President Lyndon Johnson's opinions mirrored those of his predecessor. Following the advice of military and civilian advisors, Johnson ultimately chose to escalate, but many activities were done in secret to minimize the impact on public opinion in an election year.

POINT OF INTEREST

A Timeless Miscalculation:
Underestimating Local Contempt of Foreign Rule

"Without gas or without you? Without you."[21]
—Volodymyr Zelensky, president of Ukraine

(continued)

On February 24, 2022, Russia launched a full-scale invasion of Ukraine. The invasion represented a significant escalation of Russian President Vladmir Putin's overarching plan to reclaim lost territory of the former Soviet Union. Immediately following the invasion, the consensus in the U.S. military and intelligence community was that the Russian military would quickly overrun Ukrainian resistance, install a puppet regime, and then turn its eyes toward further conquests in eastern Europe. As is often the case in warfare, however, the results became much less predictable once the bullets and artillery shells began to fly.

As of the writing of this book, the outcome of the Russo-Ukrainian war remained uncertain. At a minimum, however, it was clear that the Russian military substantially underestimated the strength of its adversary and overestimated the effectiveness of its own military. Perhaps more importantly, Russia also severely underestimated the will of the Ukrainian people. Many (if not most) Ukrainians would rather perish on the battlefield than live under the oppression of Russian rule.

Russia's miscalculation is an error that has occurred repeatedly throughout history. For thousands of years, invading armies have made the same mistake. Notable examples include the Roman invasion of Great Britain, the English invasion of Scotland, the Nazi invasion of Russia, the U.S. war in Vietnam, and the Russian invasion of Afghanistan. Sadly, both the U.S. and Russia recently repeated their errors despite having supposedly learned their lessons. After the 9/11 attacks in 2001, the U.S. spent twenty years in Afghanistan attempting to install a system of government that its people rejected. In 2023, Russia finds itself trapped in a Ukrainian quagmire.

It is a mystery why invading nations repeatedly attach to the false hope that local populations will welcome foreign rule rather than despise its presence. In the case of the U.S., denial often stems from a genuine belief in the merits of its system of governance and personal freedoms. This causes Americans to mistakenly conclude that foreign populations will abandon their history, education, traditions, values, and religion to embrace those of a foreigner. The truth, however, is that the merits of a foreign civilization often matter little to local populations. What matters is their freedom to choose their own destiny. Many local populations would rather die fighting for independence than submit to foreign rule, yet invaders repeatedly underestimate this timeless truth.

The Vietnam War took a fateful turn when the North Vietnamese fired torpedoes on the U.S. Navy on August 2, 1964. The torpedoes missed, but U.S. military leaders recommended an aggressive response. Johnson initially showed restraint but vowed to retaliate in response to any future North Vietnamese attack. On August 4, 1964, the U.S. Navy erroneously reported a second attack by the North Vietnamese, and Johnson responded by authorizing the first bombing missions in North Vietnam. He also sent pre-drafted legislation to Congress to authorize further escalation if needed. The Gulf of Tonkin resolution sailed through Congress and was signed into law on August 10, 1964. The legislation did not specify the catalysts and limits of further escalation.[22]

Armed with the Gulf of Tonkin Resolution, the Johnson administration steadily increased U.S. involvement in Vietnam. In 1965, the military commenced a relentless bombing campaign, dubbed Operation Rolling Thunder, which was intended to weaken the North Vietnamese will to resist. Next, Johnson made the fateful decision to send the first American ground troops to Vietnam. On March 8, 1965, approximately 3,500 U.S. Marines arrived on the beaches of Danang. The war in Vietnam was no longer a proxy war.[23]

The American Tsunami Stalls

"Once you put that first soldier ashore, you never know how many others are going to follow them."[24]

—GENERAL MAXWELL D. TAYLOR, U.S. ambassador to the Republic of Vietnam

POINT OF INTEREST

Winning Bodies but Losing Souls

"Secretary [Robert] McNamara decided that he would draw up some kind of a chart to determine whether we were winning or not. And he was putting things in like numbers of weapons recovered, numbers of Viet Cong killed—very statistical. And he asked Edward Lansdale, who was then in the Pentagon as head of Special Operations, to come down and look at this. And so Lansdale did and he said, 'There's something missing.' McNamara said, 'What?' And Lansdale said, 'The feelings of the Vietnamese people.'"[25]

—Rufus Phillips

(continued)

In 1960, Robert McNamara resigned as president of the Ford Motor Company and joined the Kennedy administration as secretary of defense. Known for using data collection to measure performance at Ford, McNamara applied a similar approach to measure progress in the Vietnam War.

The metric that McNamara favored most was body count because he believed that the North Vietnamese would surrender if the U.S. could achieve much higher kill ratios. McNamara failed to comprehend that the cost of American fatalities was far higher than the cost of Vietnamese fatalities for several reasons. First, reliance on "kill ratios" as a proxy for victories in battle created incentives for U.S. soldiers to artificially inflate high body counts. Not only did this create false optimism, but it encouraged soldiers to be less discerning about who they killed. As the war progressed, civilians constituted a larger percentage of Vietnamese fatalities, which the Viet Cong used to persuade neutral civilians to join their cause. Second, because the North Vietnamese viewed the war as a fight for independence, their military force was not limited to young men. As casualties mounted, women and children joined the military. Finally, and most importantly, kill ratios were irrelevant to the American public. The cost of a single American life in terms of American public opinion far exceeded the cost of a Vietnamese life in terms of Vietnamese public opinion. The loss of tens of thousands of Americans triggered massive protests, civil disobedience, and violence in the U.S., but the loss of an estimated one million Vietnamese lives only strengthened their resolve.[26]

North Vietnamese resistance intensified during Johnson's first elected term. In the south, the Viet Cong tormented U.S. troops with guerilla warfare tactics that they had perfected during their campaign against the French. The U.S. responded by sending more combat troops, ratcheting up the bombing campaign, and reluctantly supporting South Vietnamese politicians despite their ineffectiveness and corruption. The rise in U.S. troop levels led to sharp increases in American casualties. In 1964, the U.S. suffered 216 killed in action; only four years later, 16,889 Americans were killed. The nature of the casualties also changed. In the early years, casualties consisted primarily of military advisors who were highly trained career soldiers who had volunteered to fight in Vietnam. In the late 1960s, a growing portion of American troops were draftees who had less training and less desire to complete tours.[27]

On January 31, 1968, the Viet Cong launched a massive offensive in South Vietnam. The attacks, which were dubbed the Tet Offensive, were intended to end the war by seizing major cities, including the South Vietnamese capital of Saigon. The Tet Offensive failed to end the war, but it had a devastating impact on U.S. public opinion. President Johnson reacted by scolding the media for portraying the battles as setbacks. In a recorded conversation with one reporter, President Johnson described the Tet Offensive as a "major dramatic victory" for U.S. forces. Johnson based his assessment on the fact that the U.S. suffered four hundred killed, while the North Vietnamese suffered approximately twenty thousand killed. Johnson failed to see that his rationale revealed the most fundamental flaw of U.S. strategy in Vietnam.[28]

The core of the war plan conceived by Robert McNamara was to inflict asymmetrical casualties on the North Vietnamese so that they would eventually run out of replacements. The U.S. achieved this objective: at the conclusion of the Vietnam War, the U.S. suffered 58,220 fatalities, while the North Vietnamese suffered an estimated one million fatalities. The problem, however, was that this was the wrong metric to gauge progress in the war. The Vietnamese were fighting to rid their country of foreign rule, and each loss of life only strengthened their resolve. The opposite was true for the United States. Each American casualty strengthened public opposition to the war. By 1968, American cities were erupting with massive protests, civil disobedience, and violence. In other words, the cost of an American life in terms of public opinion far exceeded the cost of a Vietnamese life. This multiplier effect never found its way into McNamara's scorecards.[29]

The Tet Offensive marked the end of the Johnson administration. The combination of failures with the War on Poverty and Vietnam War were insurmountable. On March 31, 1968, Johnson announced that he would not seek a second term in the White House. Only five days later, the Reverend Martin Luther King Jr. was assassinated, and riots erupted again in U.S. cities. Later that year, Hubert H. Humphrey won the Democratic nomination at a chaotic Democratic National Convention in Chicago. Outside of the convention, violence erupted among police, National Guard troops, and various protest groups, creating a public relations nightmare for the entire Democratic Party.[30]

On November 5, 1968, President Richard Nixon narrowly defeated Hubert Humphrey, in part due to his pledge to bring the Vietnam War to an honorable conclusion.[31] The fate of Johnson's Great Society and Vietnam War were now in Nixon's hands. Nixon would soon discover that it was much more difficult to solve these problems than he had anticipated. After initially escalating the war to strengthen the U.S. negotiating position, Nixon adopted a policy of "Vietnamization" to gradually turn military activities over to South Vietnamese forces. Privately, Nixon confided that this would almost certainly lead to the fall of South Vietnam, but it provided the U.S. with a viable exit. Over the next four years, the U.S. scaled down its presence in Vietnam, but an additional twenty thousand Americans lost their lives before the final combat troops exited in March 1973. Two years later, Saigon fell to the North Vietnamese, and the war of independence in Vietnam ended.

The emotional scars from the Vietnam War involve far more than the financial costs, and covering them in detail is beyond the scope of this book. From a purely financial perspective, one of the more enduring legacies of the Vietnam War was the deterioration of Americans' faith in the government and the Federal Reserve. Political interference in monetary policy—which was, in part, due to a desire to support the funding of the war—contributed to the Federal Reserve's loss of credibility regarding its ability to maintain price stability. This led to the longest period of elevated inflation in U.S. history.[32]

THE PHANTOM MENACE

"'Maximum' or 'full' employment, after all, had become the nation's major economic goal—not stability of the price level . . . Fear of immediate unemployment—rather than fear of current or eventual inflation—thus came to dominate economic policymaking. At any time within that period, it [the Federal Reserve] could have restricted the money supply and created sufficient strains in financial and industrial markets to terminate inflation with little delay. It did not do so because the Federal Reserve was itself caught up in the philosophic and political currents that were transforming American life and culture."[33]

—ARTHUR BURNS, chairman of the Federal Reserve Board

By the late 1960s, the fabric of American society appeared to be disintegrating. Racial tensions, perceptions of wealth inequality, and the war in Vietnam led to violent confrontations in city streets and on college campuses. The Nixon administration yielded to public opposition to the Vietnam War and gradually brought troops home, but another insidious menace had quietly taken root in America. By 1970, Americans were suffering from persistently high rates of inflation. For the five years ending December 31, 1970, inflation averaged 4.3 percent per year versus only 1.3 percent per year for the five years ending December 31, 1965. The Federal Reserve had failed to quell the expansion of the U.S. money supply, which allowed elevated inflation expectations to become entrenched. The scourge of inflation lasted until the early 1980s. Economists would later refer to this seventeen-year period as the Great Inflation. Never before nor since has the U.S. suffered a persistently high rate of inflation for such an extended time. Figure 23.2 shows the annual change of

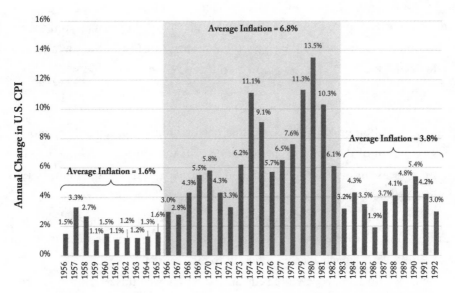

Figure 23.2: Annual Change in the CPI by Year (January 1, 1956–December 31, 1992)[34]

the U.S. consumer price index (CPI) during the Great Inflation in comparison to the ten years prior and ten years after this event.

POINT OF INTEREST

The Swelling of the Community Chest

The board game Monopoly is a surprisingly effective tool to explain several economic concepts, including inflation. For example, imagine a game of Monopoly in which four players are prepared to purchase the final unowned property, and each player has only $100 in cash. Additionally, each player is only willing to spend 50 percent of their remaining cash on the property. All else being equal, each player would bid a maximum of $50 for the property.

Now imagine a second scenario in which the bank "prints" an additional $4,000 and distributes it equally to the four players. If each player is still willing to spend 50 percent of their cash at auction, they would now budget up to $500 for the property. This is because the supply of property is the same, but the supply of money has risen.

The inner workings of a nation's economy are considerably more complex than this example, but the fundamental rule is the same. If the money supply increases at a rate that exceeds the increase in goods and services available

(continued)

for sale, people are willing to spend more per item. People may think they have more wealth because they have more money, but in fact their wealth has remained static because it costs more to purchase goods and services.

In 1963, Milton Friedman declared that persistent inflation can only be produced by an expansion of the money supply that exceeds the growth in economic output. This makes sense intuitively—when economic participants have more money without a commensurate change in resources available to purchase, they are willing to pay more for the limited resources available. This is precisely what happened during the Great Inflation. The Federal Reserve failed to contain the growth of the money supply for seventeen years, which allowed inflation to take root.[35]

The bigger question is why the Federal Reserve allowed this to happen. Several of the more important factors are explained on the pages that follow.[36]

Factor #1: Structural Imbalance of the Federal Reserve Mandate

The Federal Reserve currently has an explicit mandate to balance the competing objectives of maximizing employment and maintaining price stability. This dual mandate was established with the Federal Reserve Reform Act of 1977 in response to the Great Inflation. During the 1960s and early 1970s, however, the Federal Reserve mandate was focused squarely on maximizing employment. There are multiple explanations for this bias. First, the Federal Reserve leadership interpreted the language in Section 2 of the Employment Act of 1946 as a mandate for the federal government to pursue maximum employment by law.[37] This interpretation was strengthened during the Kennedy administration, and a specific target of 4 percent unemployment was generally assumed to constitute full employment.[38] This target was later determined to be far too low. Second, the American public (and the politicians elected by them) had a visceral fear of unemployment due to lingering scars from the 1930s. In contrast, few Americans recalled the painful inflation that occurred during and after the World Wars, in part because it did not last nearly as long. Finally, there was a general belief that the Federal Reserve and federal government were obligated to synchronize fiscal and monetary policy. This belief had weakened after the Treasury–Federal Reserve Accord of 1951, but it then returned in the 1960s. In fact, the Kennedy administration formed a committee, known as the Quadriad, which conducted regular meetings to coordinate fiscal and monetary policy. Members included leaders of the Fed, Treasury, and Council of Economic Advisors. This framework made the Federal Reserve leadership hesitant to tighten monetary conditions when the president and Congress enacted expansionary fiscal policies regardless of whether they threatened price stability. Former Federal Reserve Chairman Arthur Burns described this mentality when recalling the mistakes during the 1970s, stating, "Every time the government moved to enlarge the flow of benefits to the population at large, or to this or that group, the assumption was implicit that monetary policy would somehow accommodate the action."[39]

Factor #2: Vulnerability to Political Pressure

The nation's financial founding father, Alexander Hamilton, believed that a central bank must operate independently of political interference. In his proposal to establish the First Bank of the United States, Hamilton cautioned that "the stamping of paper is an operation so much easier than the laying of taxes, that a government, in the practice of paper emissions, would rarely fail in any such emergency to indulge itself too far."[40] Despite Hamilton's warning, the Federal Reserve has never achieved complete immunity to political influence, but pressure was especially intense during the Great Inflation. For example, when Chairman William McChesney Martin Jr. informed President Johnson that rate increases or spending reductions were necessary during a meeting at Johnson's ranch, the president reportedly pinned Martin against a wall and shouted, "Martin, my boys are dying in Vietnam and you won't print the money I need."[41] President Richard Nixon succeeded Johnson in 1970, and appointed Arthur Burns as the new chairman of the Federal Reserve. Despite a dramatically different set of priorities, President Nixon proved just as willing to bully the Federal Reserve. Describing his relationship with Arthur Burns, Nixon ominously stated, "I respect his independence. However, I hope that, independently, he will conclude that my views are the ones he should follow."[42]

William McChesney Martin Jr. and Arthur Burns clearly failed to resist pressure from Presidents Lyndon Johnson and Richard Nixon, but this was not entirely their fault. Federal Reserve independence was not nearly as strong at the time, and both Martin and Burns justifiably feared that both the executive and legislative branches would weaken their independence further if they challenged them.

Factor #3: Flawed Interpretation of the Phillips Curve

During the Great Inflation, many leaders at the Federal Reserve believed that there was a stable trade-off between inflation and unemployment—a relationship known as the Phillips Curve. The belief was that by allowing inflation to rise, the country would always enjoy an offsetting benefit of reduced unemployment. Unfortunately, this is not how the Phillips Curve works in the real world. Milton Friedman pointed this out in 1968 when he argued that increases in inflation would no longer produce lasting reductions in unemployment once unemployment reached its natural rate. Increases in accommodative policies beyond that point could temporarily reduce unemployment, but it would not last. Instead, people's expectations of future inflation would increase, and unemployment would then rise back to its natural rate—which was higher than the 4 percent target assumed at the time. The Federal Reserve would then loosen monetary policy again to bring unemployment back to the 4 percent level, which would increase the rate of inflation. This process repeated over and over, and each time the rate of inflation rose higher and higher. The leadership of the Federal Reserve failed to understand this vicious cycle.[43]

Factor #4: Absence of Inflation Target

In a scene from the Showtime television series *Homeland*, a group of senior CIA officials asked an undercover agent if the U.S. strategy in the Middle East was working. The agent responded, "Tell me what the strategy is. I will tell you if it is working." The Federal Reserve suffered from a similar problem during the Great Inflation. Prior to the appointment of William McChesney Martin Jr., the Federal Reserve had an informal target of matching monetary growth to output growth. This objective—which would have proven quite useful during the Great Inflation years—disappeared after Martin took the helm. In the years that followed, the Federal Reserve failed to replace it with a new framework. This prevented the Fed from establishing discrete inflation goals; and without them, it was much more difficult to resist political and public pressure to contain inflation. Economist Allan Meltzer lamented the lack of inflation targets, stating, "Since there was no generally accepted framework relating unemployment, inflation, budget deficits, balance of payments, and Federal Reserve actions, there was no agreement about a long-term strategy."[44]

Impact of the Great Inflation

An unbalanced Federal Reserve mandate, relentless political pressure, and flawed monetary theory was a toxic combination. In 1968, inflation exceeded 4 percent for the first time since 1951, and it remained well above this level until 1983.[45] The Great Inflation years caused tremendous suffering. In the 1960s, the economist Arthur

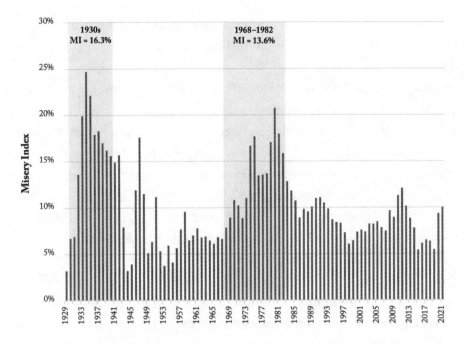

Figure 23.3: Misery Index of the United States (1929–2021)[46]

Okun constructed the Economic Discomfort Index to capture the combined effect of inflation and unemployment. The index is now commonly referred to as the "Misery Index," and it is calculated by adding the unemployment rate and inflation rate. Figure 23.3 shows the Misery Index from 1929 to 2020.

It is noteworthy that the average misery index during the 1930s was comparable to the misery index during the peak years of the Great Inflation. This is an important insight because some Americans today continue to fear unemployment more than they fear inflation. Even worse, politicians tend to fear high unemployment more than high inflation because it is easier to blame them for unemployment. In contrast, high inflation is easier to blame on exogenous factors and can take many years before the full effect is felt. The Great Inflation revealed the danger of prioritizing maximum employment at the expense of price stability. A few of the more notable consequences are covered in greater detail on the pages that follow.

The Fall of Bretton Woods

The fixed exchange rate system established under Bretton Woods was fatally flawed from the start. Even if the Great Inflation never happened, the system was destined to fail, but the Great Inflation expedited the process. The flaw of Bretton Woods was identified by Robert Triffin in 1960 and was subsequently called the "Triffin Paradox." The paradox was that an international fixed exchange rate system pegged to the U.S. dollar (which was, in turn, convertible to gold) could only function if the U.S. ran continuous balance-of-payments deficits. In other words, the integrity of the system depended on the U.S. shipping more dollars abroad than it received from foreign countries. If the U.S. ran a surplus, central banks of other countries would be unable to accumulate the dollars they needed for use in trade. On the other hand, if the U.S. continuously ran balance-of-payments deficits, the amount of dollars held by foreign central banks would eventually exceed the amount of gold for which the dollars could be exchanged. Once foreign central banks figured this out, they would convert their dollars into gold before the U.S. could devalue the dollar. This made a run on U.S. gold reserves inevitable under Bretton Woods.

Throughout the 1950s, U.S. monetary gold reserves slowly declined at an annualized rate of 2.2 percent. Immediately after the Bretton Woods fixed exchange rate system went active in 1958, outflows accelerated to 5.4 percent per year. Large U.S. deficits in the 1960s added to this pressure. Figure 23.4 shows the monthly balance of U.S. monetary gold reserves from 1947 through 1970. By 1968, U.S. gold reserves hovered just above the statutory minimum of $10 billion. The U.S. protected its gold reserves as best it could by implementing stop-gap solutions in coordination with

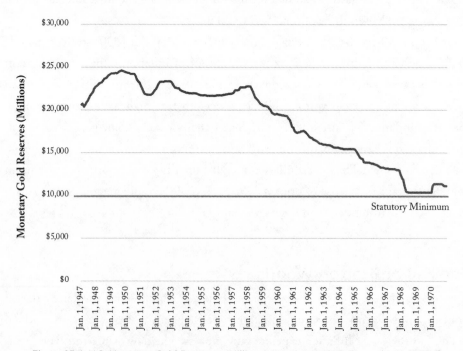

Figure 23.4: U.S. Monetary Gold Reserves (Millions) (January 1, 1947–December 1, 1970)[47]

other major central banks, but these failed to resolve a problem that was structural in nature.

In 1971, the U.S. reached the breaking point. Persistent fiscal and balance of payments deficits created a glut of U.S. dollars that substantially exceeded the nation's gold reserves. European central bankers correctly questioned whether the U.S. could honor its commitment to exchange dollars for gold at $35 per ounce. Suspecting that devaluation was inevitable, they began redeeming U.S. dollars for gold in large amounts in the spring and summer of 1971. The outflows forced the U.S. to concede that the system was no longer tenable, and on August 15, 1971, President Nixon announced that the U.S. would no longer allow foreign-held dollars to be converted into gold. This marked the end of the fixed currency exchange rate system established under Bretton Woods. An attempt was made to create a modified system of fixed exchange rates under the Smithsonian Agreement, but it only lasted for fifteen months. The U.S. dollar had become a fiat currency, and countries would have to choose whether to continue pegging their currency to the U.S. dollar or allow exchange rates to float. Most chose the latter, and floating exchange rates and fiat currencies became the norm for most developed nations.[48]

POINT OF INTEREST

Money by Fiat

For most of U.S. history the dollar derived its value from the ability of holders to redeem it for gold and silver at a fixed price. Only during times of financial distress did the U.S. alter the conversion rate or temporarily suspend it entirely. One may recall from chapter 18 that temporarily delinking the U.S. dollar from gold proved essential in helping the U.S. to exit the Great Depression. In 1934, the U.S. reestablished the conversion rate for gold at $35 per ounce, and then Bretton Woods established the international gold standard by fixing rates of exchange with the U.S. dollar.

In contrast to currencies backed by precious metals, fiat currencies derive their value from the scarcity of the currency itself. Fiat currencies are not convertible to an underlying commodity at a fixed rate. When the U.S. exited Bretton Woods, the U.S. dollar converted to a fiat currency. Many developed nations followed, thus beginning a new era dominated by fiat currencies and floating exchange rates.

(continued)

The benefit of a fiat currency is that it provides central banks with currency elasticity, which history has repeatedly demonstrated to be invaluable during a financial crisis. The danger is that it eliminates a constraint on reckless expansion of the money supply. No longer bound by the obligation to convert currency to a scarce commodity at a fixed price, nations can expand the money supply more easily, which can produce high rates of inflation. Countries issuing a reserve currency are especially vulnerable to this abuse.

A half century has transpired since the era of fiat currencies began on August 15, 1971. Over the years, Americans have experienced both the pros and cons of fiat-based currency systems, and the final verdict on the system's sustainability remains unclear. That said, the large accumulation of debt in the U.S., which is enabled by the nation's use of a fiat currency and status as the world's reserve currency, is beginning to cast doubt about the long-term viability of this experiment.

SECURITIES MARKETS AND VALUATIONS

The Great Inflation was a dreadful time for U.S. investors. As inflation rose, bond investors demanded greater compensation in the form of higher interest rates. Not

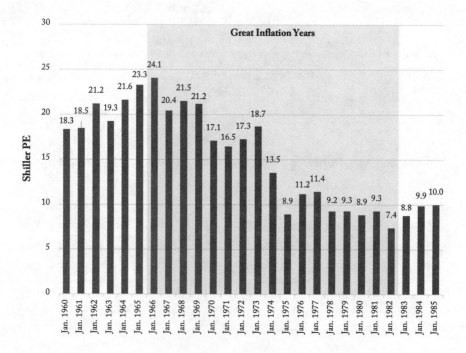

Figure 23.5: The Shiller P/E Ratio (1960–1985)[49]

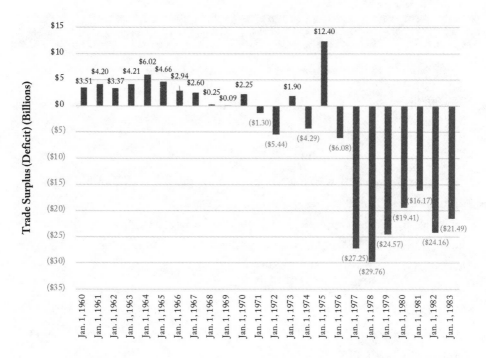

Figure 23.6: The U.S. Balance of Trade on Goods and Services (Billions) (1960–1983)[50]

only did this lead to price declines for existing bondholders, but it also affected stock valuations. This is because higher interest rates were used to discount future earnings, which reduced the value of expected earnings streams. Figure 23.5 shows the decline of the average annual Shiller price-to-earnings ratio (Shiller PE) of the S&P 500 Index from 1960 to 1985. By the mid-1970s, stock investors suffered from both lower valuations and reduced pricing power due to inflation. Investors who invested in the S&P 500 on January 1, 1966, realized an annualized nominal return of roughly 6.8 percent on December 31, 1982. On the surface, this return seems modest but certainly not problematic. But when returns are adjusted for inflation, investors realized an average annualized real return of only 0.01 percent. In other words, for seventeen years, an investor in U.S. stocks earned almost nothing after adjusting for inflation.

DETERIORATION OF U.S. COMPETITIVENESS

There is little question that U.S. competitiveness declined during the Great Inflation. Figure 23.6 shows the U.S. trade balance for the twenty years ending January 1, 1983. The 1960s were the last decade in which the U.S. recorded a positive trade balance. Beginning in the 1970s, chronic trade deficits became the norm.

POINT OF INTEREST

The Japanese Commercial Invasion

"Success is not final, failure is not fatal:
it is the courage to continue that counts."[51]

—Japanese Proverb

The Japanese economy was in total ruin after World War II. Moreover, U.S. aid under the Marshall Plan was directed toward western Europe, placing a greater burden on the Japanese to self-fund their reconstruction. The fate of Japan, however, took a fortunate turn in 1949 when Chinese communist forces under Mao Zedong defeated nationalist forces. Mao immediately made overtures to the Soviet Union, substantially increasing the communist sphere of influence in Asia. Faced with a more formidable communist threat, the U.S. viewed Japan as a critical ally to check the expansion of communism in Asia and began investing in Japanese reconstruction.

Throughout the 1950s, the Japanese economy improved steadily. Heavily reliant on exports once again, Japan initially focused on its traditional strength in textiles. In 1953, the Japanese government shifted the focus to heavy industrial products, choosing the automobile sector as a priority. The former textile manufacturer Toyota led this movement, and within a few decades Japanese auto companies became a formidable rival to U.S. companies.

Like the American Commercial Invasion at the turn of the twentieth century, Japanese manufacturers benefited from a convergence of multiple competitive advantages, including a weak currency, cheap labor, and strong tariff protection. This made Japanese automobiles considerably more price competitive in the United States. Second, during the 1960s and 1970s, labor unions were much weaker in Japan than they were in the United States. This enabled Japanese companies to adapt more rapidly to evolving consumer demands. Third, Japanese management proved to be innovative in their manufacturing techniques. For example, Toyota allowed any employee to shut down the production line if they identified a problem. Finally, the Japanese also got a little lucky. They made a fortuitous decision to produce smaller, more fuel-efficient vehicles, which paid off during the 1970s oil embargoes.

U.S. auto manufacturers operated under an entirely different set of conditions. The U.S. dollar was strong relative to the yen and tariffs were low. Labor

unions demanded higher wages and enforced rigid procedures that stifled innovation. Finally, U.S. vehicles were larger and less fuel efficient, making them less
attractive during the 1970s.

By the end of the 1970s, Japan had become a formidable threat to U.S.
automobile manufacturers and was rapidly gaining market share in electronics.
But the Japanese miracle would not last. The nation's success attracted a deluge
of capital that was recklessly invested in stocks and real estate. This created a
speculative bubble that burst in the late 1980s, and Japan has yet to fully recover.

The extent to which U.S. competitiveness deteriorated as a direct result of the
Great Inflation is difficult to quantify because many other factors coincided with it.
For example, the U.S. experienced a decline in productivity growth during the 1970s,
but the effects were concentrated in energy-sensitive industries. This suggests that
the oil embargoes—independent of their effect on inflation—also played an important role. Second, many foreign countries were naturally becoming more competitive
because the destruction from World War II was no longer an impediment. Increased
competitiveness of West Germany and Japan were especially intense.[52]

For these reasons, it is difficult to precisely quantify the impact of inflation on U.S.
competitiveness. At a minimum, however, it amplified the effects of other factors.
Increased uncertainty and volatility of future inflation expectations also undoubtedly
weighed on business confidence and depressed investment. Finally, inflation negatively
impacted labor relations when wages failed to keep pace with the rising costs of living.

DEFLATION OF THE AMERICAN DREAM

*"I think it's inevitable that there will be a lower standard of living than what everybody
had always anticipated, constant growth . . . I think there's going to have to be a
reorientation of what people value in their own lives. I believe that there has to be a more
equitable sharing of what we have."*[53]

—PRESIDENT JIMMY CARTER

During the Great Inflation, Americans suffered three recessions (1973–1975, 1980, and
1981–1982). Workers received higher paychecks but suffered significant losses of real
income; home loans and commercial loans were often unaffordable; and stock returns
were abysmal. Like victims of a chronic, undiagnosed disease, Americans felt a weight of

hopelessness that was made worse by the fact that nobody could put their finger on the cause. Politicians often made the situation worse by refusing to question the merits of their economic assumptions, and instead blamed inflation on exogenous events such as oil embargoes and the Vietnam War. Yet when these shocks subsided, inflation remained.[54]

POINT OF INTEREST

The Weight of Despair

"Learned helplessness is the giving-up reaction, the quitting response that follows from the belief that whatever you do doesn't matter."[55]

—Martin E. P. Seligman

In May 1967, Professors Martin E. P. Seligman and Steven F. Maier of the University of Pennsylvania published a groundbreaking research study entitled "Failure to Escape Traumatic Shock." The study subjected dogs to painful electric shocks in two controlled experiments. In Group A, the subjects were unharnessed, which allowed them to escape the shock. In Group B, the dogs were harnessed, which prevented escape.

When dogs from both groups were subsequently unharnessed and exposed to electric shocks, the subjects from Group A took evasive action, but the subjects from Group B passively endured the pain. This is because the subjects from Group B believed that they were powerless to escape, so they made no attempt to do so. Professors Seligman and Maier referred to this phenomenon as "learned helplessness."[56]

The timing of this discovery was eerie, as the American people were, at the same time, internalizing the belief that they were helpless to escape the pain of high inflation. Throughout the 1970s, Americans accepted that unaffordable mortgages, chronic shortages of gasoline, and perpetual declines in stocks were phenomena beyond their control. This took a toll on their faith in their future. According to an August 1979 Gallup poll, a record 84 percent of Americans believed the nation was on the wrong track.[57]

This was the true cost of the Great Inflation, and because it persisted for so long, ending it required more than a shift in monetary policy—it required the reestablishment of the belief that a solution was even possible. This was the challenge handed to Paul Volcker when he replaced G. William Miller as the new chairman of the Federal Reserve Board on August 6, 1979.

We now know that many of the explanations for the Great Inflation offered by economists and politicians were incorrect. The primary cause was persistent, overly accommodative monetary policy. It was only when Chairman Paul Volcker began his relentless campaign to shrink the money supply that the Federal Reserve reestablished its credibility and ended the Great Inflation. But Volcker's campaign was not without cost. The nation suffered an excruciating recession from 1981 to 1982, and unemployment peaked at 10.8 percent in 1982. This was the price Americans paid for more than a decade of monetary profligacy. It is not something that U.S. central bankers will easily forget nor willingly repeat.

PAUL VOLCKER AND THE DAWN OF THE MODERN ERA

"Inflation is as violent as a mugger, as frightening as an armed robber, and as deadly as a hitman."[58]

—RONALD REAGAN, president of the United States

Four U.S. presidents and three Federal Reserve chairmen failed to tame inflation. The time had come to consider alternatives. On January 31, 1978, Arthur Burns completed his term as Fed chair. President Jimmy Carter appointed G. William Miller as Burns's replacement, but after eighteen months, Miller left to become the new secretary of the Treasury. The move was considered a promotion, but many at the Fed were relieved, as Miller had limited experience with monetary issues and his leadership was viewed negatively by many Fed leaders. On July 25, 1979, Carter nominated Paul Volcker, the former chairman of the New York Federal Reserve Bank, to replace Miller. Carter's motivations for this nomination are unclear. Volcker was not secretive about his plans for monetary policy, which Carter likely suspected would harm his reelection prospects. Volcker's memoirs revealed that he was convinced he had ruined his nomination prospects after he gave a blunt answer in his interview with Carter. When discussing whether he would tighten monetary policy, Volcker responded, "I would have tighter policy than that fellow" while pointing to William Miller, who was also attending the interview. On the other hand, Volcker's appointment may have simply resulted from Carter's rush to appoint a new Fed chair, which caused him to underestimate Volcker's commitment to his hawkish policy. That said, after Volcker's appointment, Carter knew Volcker's plans would hurt his presidency. Several aides expressed concerns with Volcker's program and reported to Volcker that President Carter concurred with their opinions. Nevertheless, Carter never asked to meet with Volcker to express his concerns directly, which was a measure of restraint that did not go unnoticed. In his memoirs, Volcker noted, "It was significant to me that the president did not ask to see me directly. My reading of the situation was that while the president would strongly prefer that we not move in the way we proposed, with all its uncertainties, he was not going to insist on that judgment in an unfamiliar field over the opinion of his newly appointed Federal Reserve chairman."[59]

President Carter made many mistakes during his presidency, but he deserves credit for respecting the Federal Reserve's independence. For the program to work, lack of political opposition was essential, and Carter's restraint likely sacrificed his reelection. Carter's successor, President Ronald Reagan, deserves equal credit for allowing Volcker to finish the job, but Carter's self-sacrifice is less frequently mentioned.

MONETARISM SAVES THE DECADE

"Inflation is always and everywhere a monetary phenomenon, in the sense that it is and can be produced only by a more rapid increase in the quantity of money than in output."[60]

—MILTON FRIEDMAN, economist

On August 6, 1979, Paul Volcker took office as the new chairman of the Federal Reserve Board. He immediately began preparing to implement a monetary policy that differed dramatically from those of his predecessors. Volcker's thinking drew from the monetarist theory of economics, which was founded by famed University of Chicago Professor Milton Friedman. Monetarism rested on the belief that persistently high rates of inflation were always a function of the money supply expanding at a rate that exceeded the underlying growth of the economy. Monetarists acknowledged that temporary supply shocks could cause sudden bursts of inflation, but persistent inflation was explainable only by excessive expansion of the money supply. Prior to the emergence of monetarism, the theories of John Maynard Keynes dominated economic theory and government policies. The core of the Keynesian philosophy was the belief that government spending was the most important tool for managing demand and unemployment. Economists' attachment to the Keynesian philosophy was understandable, as the fiscal stimulus associated with the New Deal and World War II did, in fact, help the U.S. exit the Great Depression and end the sluggish recovery that defined the 1930s.[61]

Paul Volcker was not a staunch monetarist, but he acknowledged that the stagflation of the 1970s was consistent with monetarist predictions. Since the 1960s, Milton Friedman had argued that the flawed policies of the Federal Reserve would inevitably produce the type of stagflation that Americans experienced in the 1970s. Volcker was ready to try something new, and the monetarist school of thought seemed compelling.

POINT OF INTEREST

The Hidden Danger of High Inflation Expectations

"Shortly after October 6, 1979, [US Federal Reserve Chair Paul Volcker] met with some chief executives of medium-sized firms . . . One CEO announced that he had recently signed a three-year labor contract with annual wage increases of 13 percent—and was happy with the result. Only bitter experience would purge inflationary expectations and behavior."[62]

—Robert J. Samuelson

The cost of extinguishing inflation in 1979 was much higher than it would have been in the mid-1960s because higher inflation expectations had become woven into the fabric of the U.S. economy. Examples included automatic CPI adjustments in labor union contracts, automatic price increases by companies, and the day-to-day planning by the average American.

Higher inflation expectations first became evident in Gallup poll results in 1968, yet only 8 percent of respondents considered rising prices to be their top concern. Beginning in 1973, however, inflation regularly polled as the top concern by more than 50 percent of respondents to Gallup polls.[63]

The Federal Reserve was unable to precisely quantify how Americans' elevated concerns about inflation translated into long-term inflation expectations, but they knew that it was well-entrenched in the American psyche. The Federal Reserve had lost credibility, and reestablishing it required a much more intense effort than had been attempted previously.

The Subtle Anguish of an Upside-Down Depression

Stagflation occurs when an economy suffers from both high inflation and high unemployment. The term is commonly used to describe the U.S. experience during the Great Inflation; however, a more apt term is an "upside-down depression." Americans felt as if they were in a depression, but the cause was excessive inflation rather than deflation. Psychologically, it is much easier for policymakers to end a depression than it is to end an upside-down depression because the solution is to use massive monetary and fiscal stimulus, which provides Americans immediate relief. In contrast, ending an upside-down depression requires the withdrawal of monetary and fiscal stimulus, neither of which is welcomed by the public nor the politicians whom they elect. This explains why the biggest challenge during the late stages of the Great Inflation was convincing the American people to accept significant short-term pain before they could enjoy the long-term benefits. Volcker knew that painful monetary tightening would produce unattractive side effects such as job losses, reduced access to loans, and sharp asset price declines. Even worse, he knew that the pain would last a long time because the Fed had lost credibility with the American public by prematurely abandoning previous efforts to tame inflation.[64]

These thoughts tormented Volcker as he began building consensus among members of the Federal Open Market Committee (FOMC) to launch a new strategy to tame inflation. After two months of deliberation, the Fed had a plan. At the core of the program was a commitment among the leadership of the FOMC to continue tightening until inflation was extinguished for good. Once the process began, there would be no turning back.

POINT OF INTEREST

The Volcker Plan: A Penance of Pain

"The reality was that only a recession, "shock treatment" or something similar could cure double-digit inflation, precisely because Americans had come to believe that inflation was indestructible. The assumption could be dislodged only by actual experience that disproved it."[65]

—Robert J. Samuelson, economist

Americans had become accustomed to elevated rates of inflation for more than ten years when Paul Volcker took the helm at the Federal Reserve. Volcker's predecessors made several attempts to tame inflation, but each premature retreat only reinforced the public's belief that the Fed lacked the will to follow through. Volcker knew that extinguishing inflation required much greater fortitude and a high tolerance for pain among politicians and the American public. The Volcker plan consisted of the following components, the most important of which was the refusal to surrender:

- **Targeting Bank Reserves Rather Than Interest Rates**—The Fed's traditional approach to inflation reduction is to increase the federal funds rate. Higher rates then filter through the economy and indirectly reduce the money supply (measured in terms of bank reserves) and economic activity. At the later stages of the Great Inflation, however, there were several problems with this approach. First, the Fed was fighting elevated inflation *expectations*, but it was very difficult to quantify those expectations. The money supply, at least initially, was easier to quantify. Second, Volcker suspected that lowering inflation expectations would require raising the federal funds rate to unprecedented heights. He feared that political blowback would force them to abandon the program before rates were high enough. Repositioning the federal funds rate as a *consequence* of monetary policy rather than a distinct target created the impression that interest rates were beyond the Fed's control. Finally, Volcker believed that the simple act of changing the methodology signaled the seriousness of the Fed. Even if the new strategy was no more effective technically, he thought the signal value alone could boost the Fed's credibility.

- **Strong and Unified Messaging**—Volcker believed that taming inflation expectations was as much about regaining credibility as it was about reducing the money supply. The sooner Americans *believed* that the Fed meant what it said, the sooner the Fed could loosen monetary policy. Volcker believed that maintaining a unified message among the Fed's leadership would strengthen their credibility and ultimately reduce the pain that they were forced to inflict on Americans.[66]

- **Refusal to Surrender**—Volcker knew that he had only one chance. The worst thing that he could possibly do was to start a new program and then backtrack before inflation expectations were tamed. This would only reinforce the American public's lack of faith in the Fed. Once the tightening began, the Fed could not quit until the job was done.

- **Political Support**—Gaining outspoken political support for Volcker's plan was not a prerequisite but avoiding opposition was essential. After taking office in January 1981, President Ronald Reagan never wavered in his support for Volcker's plan. It is surprising, therefore, that Paul Volcker never felt a close relationship with Reagan. Nevertheless, he deeply appreciated Reagan's deference to the Fed on monetary matters. Volcker later reflected on Reagan's perspective, stating, "I had the sense that, unlike some of his predecessors, he [Reagan] had a strong visceral aversion to inflation and an instinct that, whatever some of his advisers might have thought, it wasn't a good idea to tamper with the independence of the Federal Reserve."[67]

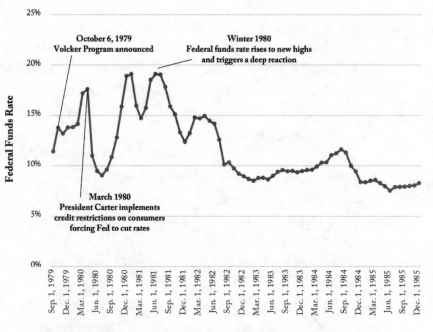

Figure 23.7: The Federal Funds Rate (September 1, 1979–December 1, 1985)[68]

Arthur Burns Fires the First Shot

On September 30, 1979, Paul Volcker attended an IMF conference in Belgrade, the former capital of Serbia. At the event, Arthur Burns delivered his famous "Anguish of Central Banking" speech, in which he detailed all the Federal Reserve's errors that allowed inflation to take root in America. Burns's speech extinguished whatever remaining doubts Volcker had about the Fed's imminent plans, and he returned to the U.S. with stronger resolve.[69]

On October 6, 1979, the FOMC voted to implement the plan. Volcker then held a press conference, which was unprecedented at the time, to present the program to the American people. Over the next two years, monetary policy tightening inflicted severe pain on the American people. By the winter of 1980, the federal funds rate peaked at approximately 20 percent, and the U.S. plunged into a painful recession that lasted from July 1981 to November 1982. The unemployment rate began climbing almost immediately after Volcker's program began and peaked at 10.8 percent in December 1982. The following series of charts captures some of the effects of the 1981–1982 recession.[70]

A Light at the End of the Tunnel

In July 1982, the monetary tightening cycle finally seemed to be having its desired effect. But the sheer duration of the recession took a toll on the U.S. economy and

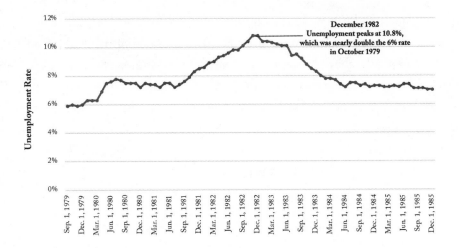

Figure 23.8: Unemployment Rate (September 1, 1979–December 1, 1985)[71]

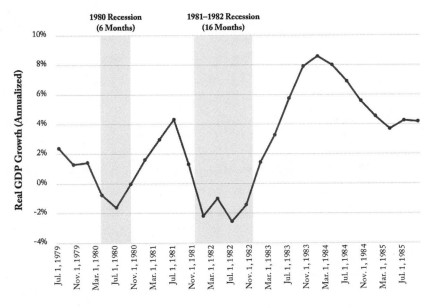

Figure 23.9: Real GDP Growth (July 1, 1979–November 1, 1985)[72]

the economies of many foreign nations. In the U.S., a high-profile failure of the Penn Square National Bank of Oklahoma caused significant stress in the financial system. In foreign markets, a strengthening of the U.S. dollar caused balance-of-payments crises in several emerging market countries. In August 1982, Mexico defaulted on its foreign debt, becoming the highest-profile victim of the Volcker program.[73]

The Federal Reserve loosened monetary policy over the next several quarters and were relieved to see that they had reestablished the credibility that their predecessors had lost. American businesses began hiring, and by the fall of 1985, unemployment settled at an average level of 7.0 percent. For the remainder of the decade, inflation remained modestly above levels that preceded the Great Inflation but well within range of the Fed's tolerance. The era of the Great Inflation and post–World War II period was over, and America was positioned to embark on a new period of growth. In many ways, the modern era that followed resembled all that preceded it. Most events were repetitions of the past, but a handful were unique. Part Six begins in 1983 and recounts America's final journey to the present.

Part 6

The American Empire Strikes Back

1983–2023

"The pioneer spirit is still vigorous within this nation. Science offers a largely unexplored hinterland for the pioneer who has the tools for his task. The rewards of such exploration both for the Nation and the individual are great. Scientific progress is one essential key to our security as a nation, to our better health, to more jobs, to a higher standard of living, and to our cultural progress."[1]

—DR. VANNEVAR BUSH, director of the
Office of Scientific Research and Development (1945)

The Great Inflation ended in 1982, and optimism was rekindled in America. Soon thereafter, the Cold War ended, as the inefficiencies of central planning in the Soviet Union failed to keep pace with market-based economies. **Part 6** recounts the most recent forty years of U.S. financial history. It begins with the birth of Silicon Valley, which firmly established America's position as the world's innovation engine in the Information Age. It also reveals several challenging side effects of technological advancement from the perspectives of different groups of Americans. In securities markets, new investment principles and investment vehicles drove increasing portfolio complexity, while proponents of active management rejected research that questioned their collective results. Finally, **part 6** recounts a series of manias, panics, and financial crises that plagued Americans during the first twenty-three years of the twenty-first century, which added to an unsettled feeling that had been quietly growing for several decades. The book concludes with a recap of the COVID-19 pandemic and the persistent inflation that tormented Americans in the aftermath. As this manuscript was completed, the Federal Reserve continued its battle to reestablish price stability.

Chapter 24 recounts the evolution of the world's leading high-tech ecosystem in Silicon Valley. The story begins with a new generation of entrepreneurs who launched a slew of technology companies, most of which were funded by a new form of investment called venture capital. The rapid evolution of technology reshaped the U.S. economy, securities markets, and the investment management profession.

Chapter 25 explores the growing complexity of investment strategies, as new asset classes emerged and active management thrived. Many investors drew inspiration from the success of the Yale University endowment, mistakenly concluding that asset allocation and skillful active manager selection was sufficient to replicate Yale's results.

Chapter 26 explores several undesirable side effects accompanying America's transition from a mass-producing industrial economy into a technology/services-oriented economy. Examples include the displacement of low-skilled workers and expansion of the wealth gap.

Chapter 27 recounts the rise and fall of the dot-com bubble. The chapter demonstrates how individual segments of the financial system succumbed to a common delusion and fueled the first of several asset bubbles in the twenty-first century. The chapter also explains how the response to the dot-com bubble planted the seeds of the Global Financial Crisis (GFC).

Chapter 28 recounts the GFC, which was the most dangerous financial crisis since the early 1930s. The chapter explains how the U.S. applied the lessons of financial history to avoid the onset of a fourth Great Depression-level event.

Chapter 29 addresses the growing economic resentment and frustration that festered in the U.S. during the decade that followed the GFC. It also explains several headwinds that threaten to dislodge the U.S. as the world's dominant economic power. These include the growing U.S. debt burden, rising competitive threat of China, and diminishing advances in productivity.

Chapter 30 recounts the COVID-19 pandemic and the ongoing fallout. The long-term consequences of this event were uncertain as this book went to print. But as always, history provides some guidance on what the future may hold.

Chapter 31 concludes the book by reflecting on several of the more important lessons from the study of more than two centuries of U.S. history. It then concludes by forecasting how these lessons may shape the coming decades.

Chapter 24

THE SECOND AMERICAN COMMERCIAL INVASION

"You can't really understand what is going on now unless
you understand what came before."[1]

—STEVE JOBS, cofounder of Apple Computer

M ost historical accounts of the 1970s focus on the Vietnam War, civil rights conflicts, and chronic inflation. All were critically important, but they masked the exciting technological progress percolating below the radar. By the 1980s, high-tech companies in the Santa Clara Valley were developing a slew of exciting high-tech products. This fueled a Second American Commercial Invasion, which firmly established the U.S. as the undisputed leader of the Information Age.

Many people instinctively attribute America's extraordinary advancements to the sheer genius of people like William Shockley, Robert Noyce, David Packard, Gordon Moore, Steve Jobs, and Bill Gates. Contemporaries of Alexander Hamilton showered him with similar praise, but he corrected them by asserting that his achievements were simply the product of obsessive "labor and thought." The magic of Silicon Valley is explainable in similar terms. For more than three decades, engineers and technology enthusiasts spent endless hours experimenting with cutting-edge technology. Each new generation added another layer of innovation atop the groundbreaking innovations of their predecessors. They also drew support from tight-knit economic ecosystems that combined exceptional academic research, targeted government funding, creative venture capitalists, and fearless entrepreneurs. At the center of the most successful ecosystem was Stanford University, which eventually surpassed Harvard and MIT as the world's leading producer of high-tech innovation.[2]

The Second American Commercial Invasion positioned the U.S. as the high-tech engine of the world. Similar to the First American Commercial Invasion at the turn of the twentieth century, it was rooted in timeless American strengths of hard work, personal sacrifice, resilience in the face of failure, freedom of expression, financial innovation, and symbiotic government support. It all began during the dark years of World War II when the Allied Powers desperately sought a new solution to defend cities from relentless attacks by the Nazi's *Luftwaffe*.

COLLATERAL CREATIONS OF WAR

It is disheartening to acknowledge, yet undeniably true, that many of the world's great commercial innovations are byproducts of war.[3] The modern computer is a recent example. During World War II, the Allied powers—especially Great Britain—suffered horrific attacks by the Nazi's *Luftwaffe*. Allied anti-aircraft guns were dreadfully inaccurate, but efforts to improve their aim were stymied by the daunting number of calculations needed to estimate trajectories of ordinance. The Allies employed scores of mathematicians—commonly referred to as "computers"—to create ballistics tables, but the sheer number of variables was overwhelming. This rendered tables incomplete and riddled with errors, and military leaders desperately sought a more effective solution.[4]

In 1943, two physics professors, John Mauchly and J. Presper Eckert, received funding to create a digital machine to automate ballistics calculations. The project was called the Electronic Numerical Integrator and Computer (ENIAC), and development began immediately at the University of Pennsylvania's Moore School of Electrical Engineering. The ENIAC suffered many delays, and World War II ended before it was completed. But when it performed its first calculations on December 10, 1945, the Information Age had officially begun. On February 15, 1946, the *New York Times* introduced the ENIAC to the world by running the understated headline, "Electronic Computer Flashes Answers, May Speed Engineering."[5]

The ENIAC was a groundbreaking advancement, but the timing was suboptimal, as U.S. defense funding plummeted soon after the war ended. Fortunately, the pause was short lived. In 1949, the Soviet Union announced that it had acquired nuclear weapons, making the Soviet campaign to expand international communism much more frightening. The federal government responded by investing heavily once again in advanced missile technology. Soon thereafter, a new high-tech ecosystem began forming in the Santa Clara Valley, and it would quickly become a destination of choice for the most advanced electronics research in the world.

The Foundation of the Silicon Valley Ecosystem

"All of the energetic scientists were forming around Stanford. The reason for that, in my opinion—although some will differ—is because of Fred Terman."[6]

—**ARTHUR ROCK,** venture capitalist

POINT OF INTEREST

Leland Stanford's Thoroughbreds

"You have to think of it like a horse race . . . That's how the high-tech game worked. The horse was the technology. The race was the market. The entrepreneur was the jockey. And the fourth and last ingredient was the owner and trainer—the high-tech investor."[7]

—**David Morgenthaler, venture capitalist**

Leland Stanford made a fortune in the late 1800s as one of the four, shall we say, horsemen of the Central Pacific Railroad. As revealed in chapter 7, the Central Pacific's profits often derived from unscrupulous business practices.

History is teeming with individuals who live their entire lives without expressing remorse for their vices, but others achieve redemption. Leland and Jane Stanford are among the latter. After losing their only child to typhoid fever in 1884, they decided to build a university to memorialize his life. Funding for the Stanford Endowment included an 8,180-acre tract of land in Palo Alto, which Leland Stanford previously used to raise thoroughbred racehorses. Little did he know that it would become the premier incubator for the high-tech racehorses of the twentieth and twenty-first centuries.

Stanford's rise as a preeminent high-tech research ecosystem began long after Jane and Leland Stanford's passing, but Fred Terman happily took the reins. If the high-tech game is analogous to horse racing, then Stanford continues to lead the field by producing the fastest horses, most skilled jockeys, and most capable trainers. The market is largely outside of a race participant's control—although Silicon Valley entrepreneurs have been known to create markets

(continued)

that were previously unknown to exist. Examples include the Apple iPhone and the Tesla series of electric vehicles.

People who question the durability of Silicon Valley's competitive edge likely underestimate the power of an integrated high-tech ecosystem. There are few places on earth capable of repeatedly producing groundbreaking, high-tech innovations, and Silicon Valley is the best of the best. At its center sits Stanford University, which continues to serve as a wellspring of renewable, entrepreneurial energy. This natural resource is uniquely American, and it is unlikely to be depleted in the foreseeable future.

In 1925, Fred Terman returned to his hometown of Palo Alto after accepting a professorship in Stanford University's Engineering Department. Believing that electronics research was vitally important to the nation's future, he developed Stanford's first electronics course. Over the subsequent fifteen years, Terman became a highly acclaimed professor and prolific writer in the electronics field. But those who recall his classes remember him less for his lectures and more for his constant encouragement to launch new business ventures. It was Fred Terman who pushed William Hewlett and David Packard to launch Hewlett-Packard in their garage in 1939.[8]

In 1942, Terman's academic career was put on hold when Vannevar Bush asked him to relocate to Harvard University and lead a military effort to develop new radar-jamming technologies. For the next three years, Terman supervised hundreds of research scientists who created several invaluable inventions for the military. One of the group's most important inventions was the aluminum strip that Allied aircraft dropped over enemy territory to disrupt Nazi radar defenses. This technique saved the lives of thousands of Allied airmen.[9]

Immediately after the war, Terman returned to Stanford as dean of the Engineering Department and immediately resumed his quest to elevate the university's reputation. He believed that the postwar years offered a once-in-a-lifetime opportunity for Stanford to become the West Coast equivalent of Harvard University or MIT. He also realized that World War II placed Stanford in a unique position in the field of electronics. Prior to the war, the Santa Clara Valley was an agricultural community known mostly for its fruit orchards. But after Japan attacked Pearl Harbor on December 7, 1941, it became an important production site for advanced electronics used in aircraft and missiles. The U.S. military tested many of its newest models over the vast, unpopulated deserts of the American southwest, and Stanford's proximity to the testing grounds was an important competitive advantage. From 1941 to 1945,

Santa Clara Valley businesses thrived, and a handful of small electronics startups were established. The most notable was Hewlett-Packard (HP), which was founded by two Stanford alums, William Hewlett and David Packard.[10]

Terman believed that Stanford had most of the necessary components to raise its profile, but a nagging problem was that most of the brightest students headed east after graduation. Keeping Stanford graduates in the surrounding community was critical to his vision. He learned this lesson during his time at Harvard, having observed how the presence of large companies in the Boston area was critical to their success. Terman sought to create a similar ecosystem for Stanford, but it required establishing a strong business community in the Palo Alto area. He believed that the first step was to persuade American companies to set up operations near Stanford to slow the flight of graduates. Terman began by creating a curriculum that was sensitive to the needs of industry, as he believed that this would convince companies that Stanford offered the most attractive job candidates. Terman constantly reworked the curriculum to ensure that students acquired knowledge and skills that aligned with practical needs of businesses. At the same time, he encouraged graduates to launch entrepreneurial ventures in the local area.[11]

Terman knew it would take years for his strategy to yield meaningful results, but he persisted. Then in 1951, he seized an opportunity to accelerate his plan. At the time, Stanford was still recovering financially from the decline in defense spending in the late 1940s. The administration hired financial consultants to find ways to strengthen the school's financial position. The consultants advised them to generate rental income by developing residential housing on the school's vast land holdings. Terman was one of the few people who objected. Instead, he proposed the construction of an industrial park that would cater to local entrepreneurs and research divisions of large companies. He believed that the Class A office space and close proximity to Stanford's campus would be highly attractive to technology businesses. If successful, the Stanford Industrial Park (later renamed the Stanford Research Park) would become the cornerstone of Palo Alto's high-tech ecosystem.[12]

Construction on the Stanford Research Park began in 1951. Varian Associates, one of Silicon Valley's first high-tech companies, became the first occupant in 1953. In the decades that followed, scores of entrepreneurs and leading high-tech companies flocked to the park to gain privileged access to Stanford research, faculty, and students. The Palo Alto business community soon became the most desirable destination for premier engineering talent. Companies that currently or once resided in the park include names such as Fairchild Semiconductor, Google, Hewlett-Packard, Lockheed Martin, PARC, Facebook, Tesla, and many others.[13]

The completion of the Stanford Research Park came just in time for the next high-tech revolution in America. A research scientist and Nobel Laureate, William Shockley, was frustrated with his work developing transistors at Bell Laboratories. Shockley was looking for a change of scene, and Fred Terman convinced him to set up shop in the Santa Clara Valley.

Less is Moore

"We [the traitorous eight] don't like him [William Shockley] and he doesn't like us, but we like each other."[14]

—EUGENE KLEINER, cofounder of Kleiner Perkins Caufield & Byers

In 1955, Fred Terman was appointed provost of Stanford University. During the same year, he persuaded William Shockley to relocate to California to launch his new venture, a semiconductor laboratory within Beckman Instruments. The Shockley Semiconductor Laboratory produced silicon-based transistors which were more durable and less expensive than the germanium-based transistors invented at Bell Labs.[15] Silicon-based transistors soon replaced the more cumbersome and expensive vacuum tubes that were used in the first mainframe computers.[16]

Shockley was initially successful, but his horrendous managerial skills drove a particularly talented group of engineers out of the company. Nicknamed the "traitorous eight," the group joined forces in October 1957 to start a new semiconductor venture known as Fairchild Semiconductor.[17] Sherman Fairchild, the owner of Fairchild Camera and Instrument, provided the initial funding. The Fairchild Semiconductor launch was impeccably timed. During the same month, the Soviet Union launched Sputnik, which became the world's first satellite to reach orbit. Sputnik's success not only embarrassed Americans, but it also revealed an existential threat. Since the nation's founding, Americans were shielded from foreign attack by vast oceans to the east and west and friendly nations to the north and south. But if the Soviet Union could launch a satellite into space, it would not be long before it could send nuclear weapons across the Pacific Ocean.

Federal funding for missile and space-related R&D increased astronomically after the Sputnik launch. Advanced electronics and digital computing were critical components, making demand for Silicon-based semiconductors accelerate virtually overnight. Then, in 1959, Fairchild Semiconductor introduced an innovation that radically transformed the electronics industry forever. Jean Hoerni, a member of the traitorous eight, invented

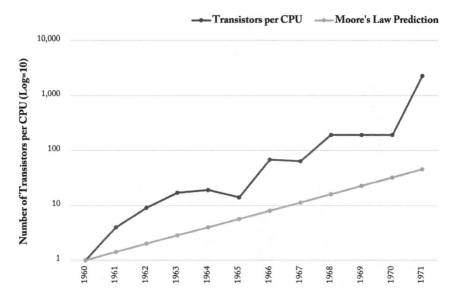

Figure 24.1: Transistors (Number per CPU) (1960-1971)[18]

the "planar process," which enabled engineers to link multiple transistors on a single silicon chip.[19] Prior to this invention, each chip could only accommodate a single transistor.
Dubbed the "integrated circuit," the potential commercial applications were extraordinary and the economics were even more impressive. With each passing year, Fairchild
Semiconductor packed more and more transistors on each chip, thereby increasing the
power of each unit, while simultaneously reducing the price. In 1965, having observed
this trend for several years, Gordon Moore predicted that the power of the silicon chip
would double roughly every two years. Moore's Law proved remarkably accurate, albeit
a bit conservative initially. Figure 24.1 uses data from Fairchild Semiconductor and Intel
Corporation to show the average number of transistors on silicon chips produced from
1960 to 1971. The dark line shows actual transistor counts, while the light line shows the
count predicted by Moore's Law.[20]

The only hurdle that prevented integrated circuits from entering the mass market was the fact that they were prohibitively expensive. Fortunately, price was not an
impediment for the newly formed National Aeronautics and Space Administration
(NASA). Launching satellites into orbit—and eventually sending astronauts to the
moon—required computers that packed as much power as possible in the smallest
amount of space. The demand for integrated circuits from NASA and other branches
of the military provided Fairchild with a critical bridge to the commercial market.
Within a few years, economies of scale dramatically reduced the price per unit, making integrated circuits affordable in the commercial market (Figure 24.2). In 1962,
100 percent of the integrated circuits produced in the U.S. were purchased under

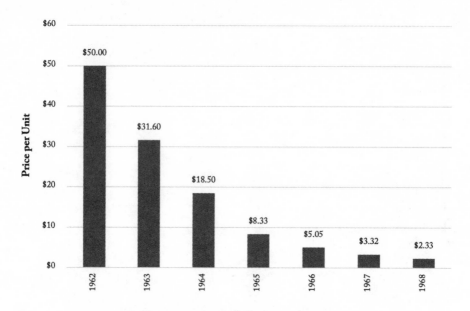

Figure 24.2: Average Uncorrected Price of Integrated Circuits (1962–1968)[21]

government contracts, but by 1968, government purchases made up only 37 percent of the total.[22]

Throughout the 1960s, demand for semiconductors grew at an astonishing rate, and many new semiconductor firms formed to supply the market. Over the fourteen-year period, production increased at a compound annual rate of 33 percent per year. Figure 24.3 shows the production of semiconductors and integrated circuits in the U.S. from 1957 to 1971, as well as the dates in which new semiconductor firms were established.

Fairchild Semiconductor thrived, but the founders grew frustrated by their small share of their profits. The original investment gave Sherman Fairchild the option to buy out the founders at a preestablished price of $3 million, and he exercised the option in 1959. From that point forward, Fairchild Semiconductor operated as a business unit within Fairchild Camera and Instrument, and the profits from the semiconductor division were used to fund several unsuccessful ventures elsewhere in the company. Disappointed with Fairchild's management, many of the founders left to start new semiconductor companies. The most notable departures were Robert Noyce and Gordon Moore, who founded Intel Corporation in 1968.[23]

By the start of the 1970s, Fred Terman's work at Stanford, combined with explosive demand for semiconductors, had reshaped the landscape of the Santa Clara Valley. But this was not enough to establish the valley as the nation's new high-tech hub. Boston's 128 corridor still held the lead, and Texas Instruments was a formidable competitor in the south. One key component of the high-tech ecosystem was still missing: capital

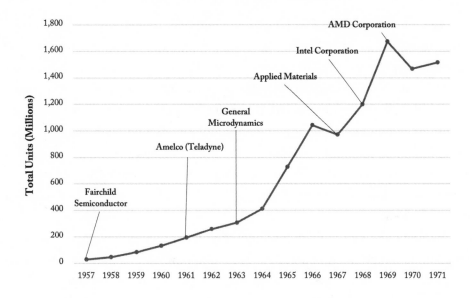

Figure 24.3: Total U.S. Production of Semiconductors and Integrated Circuits (1957–1971)[24]

remained in short supply, and the venture capital industry had yet to establish a significant presence on the West Coast.

CREATIVE CAPITAL

"As president of the Federal Reserve Bank of Boston, I became seriously concerned with the increasing degree to which the liquid wealth of the nation is tending to concentrate in fiduciary hands . . . We cannot float indefinitely on the enterprise and vision of preceding generations. To be confident that we are in an expanding instead of a static or frozen economy, we must have a reasonably high birth rate of new undertakings."[25]

—RALPH FLANDERS, president, Federal Reserve Bank of Boston (1946)

Boston's 128 corridor was the nation's leading source of engineering research and talent during and after World War II. Companies relied heavily on the deep resources of Harvard University and MIT, which in turn attracted government funding for research and development. The darling of the Boston tech community was Digital Equipment Corporation, which was established in 1957 by two former MIT researchers, Ken Olsen and Harlan Anderson. Digital Equipment was the leading producer of minicomputers, which were much smaller and less expensive than mainframes, making them more affordable for small- and medium-sized companies.

Digital Equipment's commercialization of the minicomputer was an important milestone in the history of computing, but what was more interesting was the company's funding source. Digital Equipment was the first blockbuster investment for Georges Doriot's venture capital firm, American Research and Development Corporation (ARD). Founded in 1946, ARD was the first professionally managed venture capital firm in the United States.[26] The founders included several prominent local leaders in academia, finance, and industry, including Karl Compton, president of MIT; Ralph Flanders, president of the Federal Reserve Bank of Boston; Merrill Griswold, head of Massachusetts Investors Trust; and Donald K. David, dean of the Harvard Business School.[27]

ARD's founders believed that the dominance of large companies in America weakened the nation's competitiveness. Making the problem worse was the fact that small companies had limited access to capital. Banks were still recovering from the Great Crash of 1929, and funding new ventures in unproven markets was considered much too risky. Insurance companies and pension plans were equally risk-averse, rarely venturing beyond high-quality bonds and stocks. These factors made it difficult for small companies to obtain financing. Most entrepreneurs relied on wealthy individuals, and this pool of capital was small and difficult to access.[28]

Georges Doriot and his cofounders aspired to fill this void by creating a private investment company that specialized in providing "venture capital" to small, high-growth companies. In December 1946, ARD raised $3.5 million in initial capital and began investing in a variety of small companies across many industries.

ARD struggled through its first decade. The portfolio generated a modest return but not at a level that justified the increased risk, illiquidity, and uncertainty regarding the viability of the new investment model. By the mid-1950s, investors were frustrated with the lackluster returns, and Doriot was growing weary of his constant battles with the SEC to gain exceptions to rules that were not intended for the firm's unique investment strategy. Many feared that ARD's investment model was attractive in theory but simply not practical.[29]

Perceptions changed after ARD's $70,000 investment in Digital Equipment provided a monster return. On August 19, 1966, Digital Equipment went public, valuing ARD's holdings at $38.5 million. ARD's original investment in 1957 had produced a compound annualized return of approximately 100 percent per year. This single investment legitimized the venture capital model, but at the same time, it revealed the most critical difference between venture investing and investing in more traditional publicly traded companies. Because so many of the companies in a venture capital portfolio either provide mediocre returns or fail outright, success depends almost entirely on generating outsized returns from one or two blockbuster investments. Funds that fail to find a blockbuster investment are almost certainly doomed to produce lackluster returns.[30]

POINT OF INTEREST

Hunting the Future Whales of Wall Street

"While some vessels on their voyages have made but poor returns, even bringing, in numerous cases, positive and at times damaging loss to their owners, others have done extraordinarily well and brought in fortunes to those investing in them."[31]

—Alexander Starbuck, author of
History of the American Whale Fishery (1878)

The most fundamental challenge of venture investing is that most portfolio companies produce subpar returns. The success of a venture fund, therefore, depends on the ability of fund managers to find one or two blockbusters that make up for the shortfall. The problem is that few markets offer such opportunities, and even fewer entrepreneurs can execute successfully. This dynamic creates heavily skewed return distributions that are unattractive to most investors. This is why most investors avoided direct investments in early-stage ventures prior to the introduction of venture capital funds.

Venture capital seemed like a novel concept when ARD was established in 1946, but investments with similar attributes had existed for much longer. In *VC: An American History*, Tom Nicholas draws an interesting parallel between modern venture investments and investments in American whaling expeditions in the early nineteenth century. Like venture investments, whaling investments were illiquid, subject to long holding periods, and produced returns that were heavily skewed by one or two blockbuster investments. Finally, the most skilled and well-connected whaling agents (a rough equivalent of a premier venture firm) repeatedly constructed portfolios of voyages that produced the best outcomes.[32] Figure 24.4 shows the heavy skew of whaling and venture capital return distributions. Figure 24.5 demonstrates return persistence by showing the profitability of the top whaling agents and the average internal rate of return (IRR) for the top venture capital firms.[33] The data for the whaling industry is based on 1,566 voyages for the top twenty-nine agents between 1830 and 1887. Venture capital IRRs are based on returns for all venture funds with vintage years spanning from 1981

(continued)

to 2006. An important caveat is that whaling data *only* includes profitability of the top twenty-nine agents. If all agents were included, the distribution would likely resemble more closely those produced by venture firms.[34]

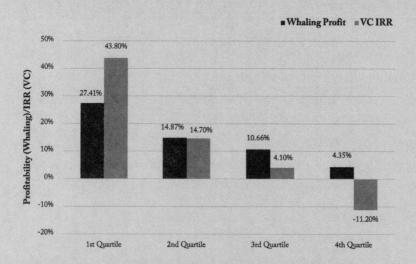

Figure 24.4: Distribution of Returns in Whaling and Venture Capital

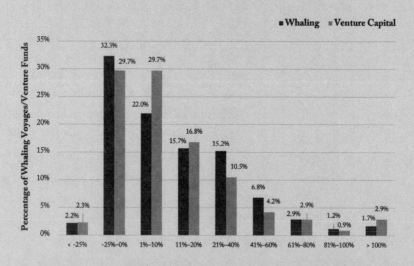

Figure 24.5: Distribution of Profitability (Whaling) and IRR (VC) by Quartile[35]

The scarcity of blockbuster investments and the tendency of the best whaling agents to repeatedly produce the best outcomes is similar to the experience of venture capitalists. Successful whaling investors were rewarded with extraordinary wealth, but imprudent ones produced disappointing results. Similar rules apply to venture investors: Most venture firms fail to generate attractive returns, and those that do are very difficult to access. Sadly, most limited partners suffer from overconfidence in their ability to identify the best firms, and fail to acknowledge that even if they do, they are unlikely to gain access.

Venture Capital Heads West

Over its twenty-one-year history, ARD funded many successful ventures and inspired the formation of several new venture capital firms. But ARD itself did not last. Its fatal flaw was that it was structured as an investment company, which was subject to SEC regulation. This placed significant constraints on portfolio construction and the firm's ability to compensate investment professionals. As a result, ARD missed out on several attractive opportunities and suffered a chronic loss of top talent. Doriot despised the SEC for meddling in ARD's affairs, but the truth is that his problems were circumstantial rather than personal. Running the firm as an investment company was suboptimal from the start. After twenty years of battling the SEC (and later the IRS), ARD merged with Textron Corporation in 1972. Despite expressing public support, Doriot knew that ARD could not thrive as a corporate subsidiary. In 1976, Doriot's instincts were proven correct when Textron dissolved the ARD board of directors, and the former venture firm became a business unit within Textron.[36]

Despite ARD's disappearance, the merits of venture investing were proven, and it became the preferred funding model for early-stage companies. Throughout the 1960s and 1970s, aspiring venture capitalists—many of whom were former Doriot students or employees—launched new venture firms. But the next generation operated without the flaws that tormented Doriot. By structuring their firms as limited liability partnerships, they avoided SEC regulation and enjoyed much more flexibility in compensating employees.

The second generation of venture capitalists had a deeper appreciation for the fact that the success of each fund hinged on their ability to find one or two investments that produced outsized gains. The high-tech industry was the most attractive source of such opportunities, as new companies could quickly dominate large markets and then defend their position with strong patent protection. Venture firms gravitated toward this industry sector, and Silicon Valley was considered the optimal hunting ground. By 1970, the valley had established its reputation as the new high-tech capital of America. In 1972, two of the most prestigious venture firms, Sequoia Capital and Kleiner Perkins Caufield & Byers (Kleiner Perkins), opened offices on Sand Hill Road, which sat between the Stanford University Campus and Silicon

Valley. Many firms soon joined them, and Sand Hill Road became the destination of choice for venture capitalists.

The Dry '70s

"The most common exit strategy was that we lost all our money."[37]

—JACK MELCHOR, venture capitalist

On September 2, 1974, President Gerald Ford signed the Employee Retirement Income Security Act (ERISA). The objective was to strengthen protections for employees covered by private pension plans. As is often the case, however, the new regulation produced several unexpected side effects. The biggest one for venture capital firms was language that defined the fiduciary responsibilities of plan trustees.

The problematic language derived from the interpretation of the Prudent Man Rule, which guided trustees to discharge their duties "by diversifying the investments of the plan so as to minimize the risk of large losses." Most trustees interpreted this language as an implicit ban on venture investments, which constructed portfolios with several companies that would likely produce large losses. ERISA plan trustees responded by limiting investments to traditional fund managers that invested in publicly traded stocks and high-quality bonds. Non-ERISA plans, such as public pensions, foundations, and endowments, adopted similar practices out of an abundance of caution. This starved venture funds of institutional capital.[39]

The impact of ERISA on the nascent technology industry was painful. Desperate to reestablish relationships with institutional plan trustees, the National Venture Capital Association (NVCA) lobbied the Department of Labor (DoL) to exercise greater flexibility in its interpretation of the Prudent Man Rule. In 1979, the DoL obliged, and the venture industry was once again able to raise sufficient capital to fund the next wave of high-tech innovation. Four years later, David Swensen arrived at the Yale University Endowment as the new chief investment officer. Almost immediately, he and Dean Takahashi saw an extraordinary opportunity for investors willing to stray beyond traditional investments in stocks and bonds—and venture capital was especially compelling. The relationships that Swensen and Takahashi developed in the 1980s helped drive exceptional returns of the Yale University Endowment. But those who failed to enter this asset class early were not afforded this privilege.

As the 1970s commenced, almost all the pieces were in place for an economic renaissance in Silicon Valley. The field of computing was advancing rapidly, Stanford University was producing a constant flow of cutting-edge research, and venture capital firms provided a new source of funding for aspiring entrepreneurs. The only remaining obstacle was the U.S. economy, which unfortunately took a turn for the worse. The Fed had failed to contain inflation in the late 1960s, which allowed stagflation to persist throughout the 1970s. Making matters worse, spending on the space race dropped off in the mid-1970s, as the U.S. achieved its mission to land on the moon.

The venture capital industry was hit especially hard in the 1970s. Rising interest rates compressed equity valuations, which reduced venture capital returns and made new fund investments less attractive to limited partners. Venture firms also struggled to attract talent, as higher capital gains tax rates reduced the value of stock options in portfolio companies and carried interest. But the biggest problem was an unexpected side effect of the Employee Retirement Income Security Act (ERISA), which was signed into law on September 2, 1974. The act required trustees of ERISA plans to abide by the Prudent Man Rule when selecting investments. Fearful of violating the rule, most trustees restricted investments to traditional stocks and bonds. Trustees who oversaw non-ERISA plans adopted similar practices. Venture funding—which was already struggling due to mixed results for several second-generation funds—all but evaporated after the passage of ERISA.[40]

Despite the capital drought, innovation never ceased in Silicon Valley. Capital would eventually return at the end of the 1970s. In the meantime, an unlikely ragtag group of technology enthusiasts set the groundwork for the next phase of innovation.

The Mother of All Demos

On December 8, 1968, Douglas Engelbart, the founder of the Augmentation Research Center at the Stanford Research Institute (SRI), gave a presentation that was later dubbed the "Mother of All Demos." The presentation demonstrated how office workers would interact with computers in the future. The two thousand audience members gasped in wonderment as Engelbart revealed an array of never-before-seen technological innovations. Many inventions would not be commercialized for years—even decades. Examples included the computer mouse, a graphical user interface, word processor, collaborative editing, the internet, and even video conferencing. Few in the audience knew these technologies were even possible, much less already in existence. In fact, the presentation was so far ahead of its time that most attendees concluded that such systems had no commercial application. The Augmentation Research Center was dissolved soon after the demonstration, and many years transpired before Engelbart's technologies resurfaced.[41]

POINT OF INTEREST

Silicon Valley Goes Small Time

The rapid expansion of the computer market was a natural consequence of Moore's Law. The exponential increase in the number of transistors on silicon chips enabled computer manufacturers to create progressively smaller products without sacrificing power or price competitiveness. The first major transition occurred in the late 1950s when Digital Equipment commercialized the minicomputer. This broadened the market to include companies that could not afford mainframes. The next transition was the creation of the personal computer in the mid-1970s. Mainframes and minicomputers were far too expensive and unwieldy for American households, but personal computers were a viable option once the price was right.

The potential profits from sales of an affordable personal computer were mind-boggling. Yet most leading computer manufacturers, such as HP and Digital Equipment, remained skeptical. By the late 1970s, a new generation of entrepreneurs saw the potential, but these individuals differed from their predecessors. Many considered personal computing to be a hobby rather than an occupation. Therefore, the great companies that emerged in the 1970s and 1980s were not inspired by government scientists or academic researchers. The most notable examples were Apple Computer (founded by Steve Jobs and Steve Wozniak) and Microsoft Corporation (founded by Bill Gates).

Further, as computers became more powerful, software applications that performed essential business functions, personal tasks, and entertainment constituted an entirely new market. Software applications included operating systems, business applications, and computer games.

A Xerox Copy of Engelbart's Vision

The research team that created the technology in Engelbart's demonstration disbanded shortly after the presentation. Several joined the Palo Alto Research Center (PARC), which was established by the Xerox Corporation in 1970. At the time, Xerox was awash in cash, having virtually monopolized the copying machine market. Executives established PARC to explore the commercial viability of various computer technologies, hoping that one could replicate the profitability of the copier market. Soon after PARC was established, several researchers sought to re-create Engelbart's personal computer. They completed their mission in 1973, and PARC introduced the Alto computer. It included most of the features of a modern computer, such as a mouse, keyboard, graphical user interface, and even email. The only problem was the high production costs and Xerox Corporation's lofty margin requirements. With a build cost of approximately $12,000, Xerox could only meet its margin targets by charging a retail sales price of approximately $36,000 per unit. This severely limited the market size, and Xerox refused to invest much in marketing the Alto. Sales were lackluster, and Xerox failed to profit meaningfully from the innovation. The functionality of the Alto, however, did not go unnoticed. Inspired by the proof of concept, many hobbyists sought to replicate the design in their garages.[42]

Homebrewing Personal Computers (PCs)

The Stanford Augmentation Research Center and the Xerox Corporation failed to create a mass market for PCs, but efforts continued at the grassroots level. Hobbyists throughout the country formed loosely knit groups and experimented with new computing technologies. Initially, progress was stymied by the lack of low-cost components, but this changed virtually overnight when a little-known company called MITS announced the release of the Altair 8800. To the layperson, the Altair looked useless: it had no screen, mouse, or even a keyboard. But through the eyes of a do-it-yourselfer, the Altair had all the essentials. First, it had enormous flexibility to add accessories and memory. Second, it was surprisingly powerful because MITS had negotiated a sharply discounted price to purchase the new Intel 8080 processor. Finally, and most importantly, the Altair cost only around $500, which was a steep discount to minicomputers.[43]

After the release of the Altair, participation in computing communities exploded throughout the country. The most notable group was the Homebrew Computer Club in Silicon Valley. The club's first meeting was held in Gordon French's garage on March 5, 1975, but it attracted only thirty-two attendees.[44] The second meeting drew a larger audience, forcing the group to meet in a bigger house and eventually move again to the Stanford Linear Accelerator Center (SLAC). The most notable members of the club were two former phone phreaks, Steve Wozniak and Steve Jobs.[45]

After experimenting with the Altair, Homebrewers discovered that the device was not only optimal for testing different technologies, but it also could be resold at a profit after adding software and accessories. Throughout the mid-1970s, small computer manufacturers sprouted up in garages across Silicon Valley and in cities across the country. Most were relatively small, generating less than $25 million in revenue. But two former Homebrewers, Steve Wozniak and Steve Jobs, distanced themselves from the pack soon after launching Apple Computer on April 1, 1976.[46]

Apple's early computer models differed little from those of other small startups. What made Apple different was Steve Wozniak's and Steve Jobs's ability to assemble the critical elements of a successful high-tech company. First, Wozniak and Jobs were talented entrepreneurs who possessed complementary skills. Wozniak was the technical genius, while Jobs was a mesmerizing and relentless technology evangelist. Second, the company secured funding from Don Valentine, one of the founders of the up-and-coming venture capital firm Sequoia Capital. Third, Steve Jobs persuaded famed marketing guru Regis McKenna to represent Apple, which gave the firm an enormous advantage relative to competitors who lacked sophisticated marketing strategies.

Using the horse race analogy, Apple's technology was the horse; Wozniak and Jobs were skilled jockeys; and Sequoia Capital's Don Valentine was an exceptional trainer. In addition, the combination of Steve Jobs's evangelism and Regis McKenna's marketing genius accelerated the development of the consumer market. Sales of personal computers grew rapidly in the late 1970s. By 1979, only two impediments remained in the way of a second American commercial invasion. The first was a weak economy that was hobbled by persistent inflation. Paul Volcker would soon eliminate this obstacle. The second was the scarcity of venture capital, which the Department of Labor (DoL) would soon resolve by announcing a new rule to relieve trustees' anxiety regarding the Prudent Man Rule.

THE DEPARTMENT OF LABOR MAKES IT RAIN

"Although securities issued by a small or new company may be a riskier investment than securities issued by a blue chip company, such an investment may be entirely proper under ERISA's prudence rule."[47]

—IAN LANOFF, administrator of pension and welfare programs, U.S. Department of Labor (June 21, 1979)

The drought of venture capital funding in the mid-1970s was devastating for the fledgling profession. For the three years ending December 31, 1977, new commitments declined by 56 percent relative to the prior three-year period. The National Venture Capital Association (NVCA) lobbied hard to convince the DoL to introduce a more flexible interpretation of ERISA's Prudent Man Rule. Recalling the intensity of the NVCA's efforts, Ian Lanoff, former administrator of pension and welfare programs, stated, "It was the only time I was summoned to the White House in my five-year tenure."[48]

On June 21, 1979, the DoL issued new guidance that provided trustees with the flexibility they needed to invest in venture capital funds without fear of violating ERISA. Commitments to venture firms skyrocketed in the subsequent years, giving high-tech entrepreneurs the funding they needed to meet demand for the personal computer (PC) revolution (Figure 24.6).[49]

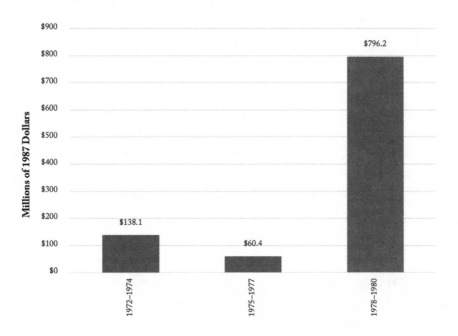

Figure 24.6: New Commitments to VC Firms (1972–1980)[50]

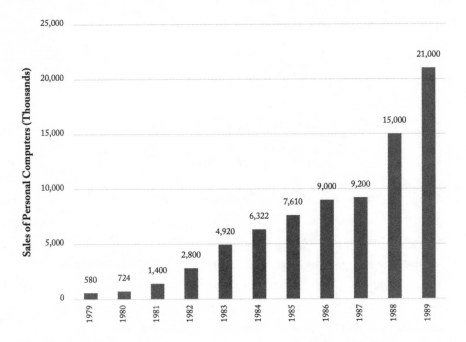

Figure 24.7: Annual Sales of Personal Computers (Thousands) (January 1, 1979–December 31, 1989)[51]

THE INFORMATION AGE GOES MAINSTREAM

By 1982, inflation was declining, venture firms were flush with cash, and sales of PCs were increasing rapidly. For the ten-year period ending on December 31, 1989, PC sales increased at a rate of 43 percent per year (Figure 24.7).

Selling hardware soon proved to be just the tip of the iceberg. Enormous demand for operating systems and software soon followed. The first opportunity came when established tech companies, such as IBM, were under intense pressure to accelerate the launch of their own PCs. Creating a proprietary operating system took time; therefore, licensing an existing operating system was more viable. IBM took a risk with a new start-up company called Microsoft that was founded by William H. Gates III and Paul Allen. Microsoft licensed the MS-DOS operating system to IBM in 1980, thereby accelerating the introduction of IBM PCs to market. Another wave of innovation involved software. The enormous success of VisiCalc (a spreadsheet application) in 1979 demonstrated that PCs were not just a novelty. Throughout the 1980s, a slew of "killer applications" were launched and quickly achieved rapid sales growth and breathtaking profit margins. Examples included Lotus 1-2-3 (spreadsheets), WordPerfect (word processing), PowerPoint (slide presentations), AutoCad (architectural design), and PageMaker (desktop publishing). In the span of less than twenty years, the personal computing industry transformed from a

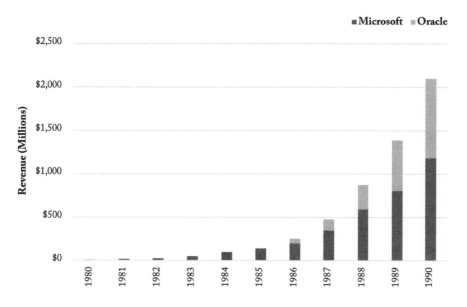

Figure 24.8: Total Annual Sales of Microsoft Corporation and Oracle Systems (FY 1980-1990)[52]

hobby of fringe technologists into the fastest-growing industry in America. Figure 24.8 provides a snapshot of the enormous growth in software during the 1980s by tracking the revenue of Microsoft Corporation and Oracle Systems, which achieved combined revenue growth of 75.6 percent per year over the ten-year period ending on June 30, 1990.[53]

THE BULL MARKET RETURNS

The bull market returned to Wall Street soon after the recession ended in the fall of 1982. The success of America's computer industry played an important role in improving investor sentiment—although it was less impactful than the wave of leveraged buyouts (LBOs). Nevertheless, buoyant markets ensured robust demand for multiple tech IPOs, many of which remain household names today. Figure 24.9 shows the strength of the bull market by showing the closing price of the S&P 500 during the 1980s, as well as the dates of several notable tech IPOs.

The stock market was not the only place to generate exceptional investment returns in the 1980s. In fact, it was difficult for investors to lose money regardless of their skill. Bonds, stocks, and real estate generated strong returns that dwarfed those achieved in the 1970s. Figure 24.10 shows the ten-year annualized return for investment grade corporate bonds, 10-Year US treasury bonds, and real estate.[54]

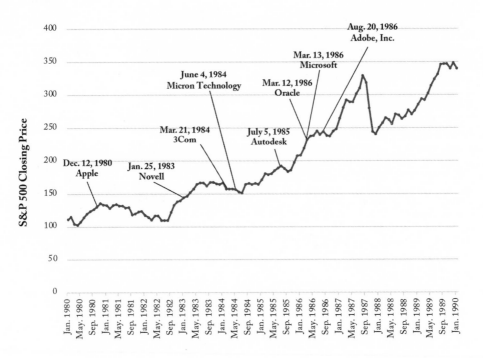

Figure 24.9: S&P 500 Index Closing Price (Monthly) (January 1, 1980–January 1, 1990)[55]

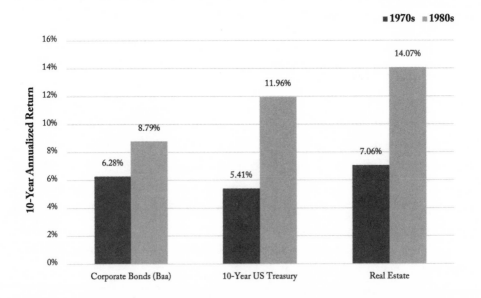

Figure 24.10: Annualized Returns for U.S. Treasuries, Corporate Bonds, and Real Estate (January 1, 1970–December 31, 1989)[56]

POINT OF INTEREST

The Cost of Blind Mean Reversion

Many asset management and investment advisory firms create proprietary capital market assumptions, which shape the asset allocation of their clients' portfolios. Often they base future return assumptions on the expectation that valuations will "mean revert" to some type of long-term average. There is some merit to this belief, but it is problematic when it fails to incorporate the direction of interest rates. For example, if a firm projects that interest rates will remain low for twenty years, but at the same time assumes that equity valuations will mean revert to average valuation levels of the last one hundred years, they are ignoring the tight relationship between interest rates and valuations.

Blind mean reversion assumptions in the 2010s were costly for institutional investors because they caused many to direct money away from public equities and into more expensive asset classes such as hedge funds and private equity. In many cases, the superior expected returns in these asset classes were simply the result of a lack of historical data which prevented advisory firms from using mean reversion on these "alternative" asset classes. This, in turn, artificially inflated the expected returns of alternative asset classes relative to public equities. Even worse, in many cases, return expectations in alternative asset classes did not account for higher fees and the critical necessity of manager selection skill. This contributed to over-investment in asset classes that were unlikely to reward investors for the corresponding risks and fees.

Stock market returns during the 1980s mirrored those of the first American Commercial Invasion at the turn of the twentieth century. For the ten-year period ending December 31, 1989, the S&P 500 generated a real return of 11.2 percent per year, which was close to the 12.4 percent real return for the ten-year period ending December 31, 1906.[57] But there was one important difference. Returns during the 1980s were closely tied to the broad-based decline in interest rates that followed Paul Volcker's successful battle with inflation.

The reason for the tight relationship between interest rates and the returns produced by other asset classes is simple and logical. In the postwar era, investors valued assets based on the return premium that they expected relative to the safest investment— U.S. Treasury securities. Therefore, when the yield on Treasurys declined, investors accepted a correspondingly lower yield on riskier asset classes. All else being equal, this

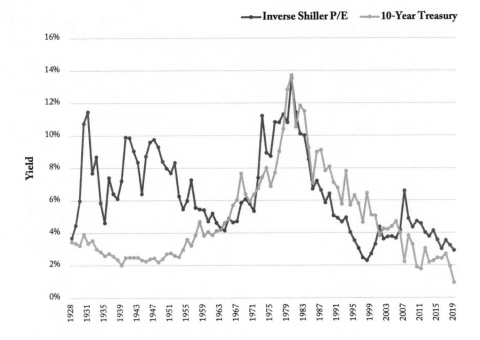

Figure 24.11: 10-Year Shiller Earnings Yield vs. 10-Year Treasury Yield
(January 1, 1928–December 31, 2019)[58]

increased the price that investors were willing to pay for different types of investments. Illustrating the relationship between interest rates and stock market returns, Figure 24.11 shows the ten-year average trailing earnings yield of the S&P 500 and the yield on the 10-year Treasury. As the 10-year Treasury yield declined, investors accepted lower earnings yields from stocks. A regression analysis reveals that approximately 68 percent of the change in stock valuations between 1960 and 1990 was attributable to the change in interest rates.

A NEW STREET HAZARD

Advancements in computing technologies provided many benefits on Wall Street. Brokerages, asset management firms, and stock exchanges embraced these advancements to speed up the process of trading and strengthen risk management. The benefits far outweighed the costs, but computers also introduced new risks. The terrifying crash on October 19, 1987, revealed one such risk. When the market closed, the Dow Jones Industrial Average (DJIA) had lost 22.6 percent in a single day, far exceeding the prior record of 12.8 percent that had occurred on October 28, 1929.

The crash of 1987 involved the convergence of multiple extreme circumstances. First, pessimism was rising on Wall Street in October for the simple reason that the stock market had experienced a strong bull market for five years and many investors anticipated a correction. Concerns were especially pronounced at the start of September, as stocks had returned approximately 40 percent over the prior eight months. Second, during the week prior to the crash, the House Ways and Means Committee introduced legislation that threatened to end the spree of LBOs, which had propped-up stock prices. Third, the U.S. recorded an unfavorable trade balance on October 14. This raised fear that depreciation of the dollar was needed to close the gap, which, in turn, could reignite inflation and force the Fed to raise interest rates. Fourth, as markets declined during the week prior to the crash, the use of portfolio insurance accelerated. A common form involved the sale of futures. The sudden spike in futures sales depressed futures prices, and arbitrageurs responded by purchasing futures and selling the underlying assets. This significantly added to selling pressure on Wall Street. Fifth, Wall Street experienced what is known as a "triple witching" day on October 16. This meant that several different forms of derivative contracts expired simultaneously, which tends to amplify market volatility.[59]

The sixth and final contributor to the crash was unique from a historical perspective. The culprit was the automation of security sales based on stop-loss orders, which automatically triggered sales when prices breached specific limits. As the panic intensified, it triggered automatic selling as stocks hit progressively low prices. Technology also proved troublesome due to the sheer volume of sales, which exceeded levels that systems were designed to handle. Describing the widespread technical failures, economist Barrie Wigmore stated, "At the worst point, limit orders were backed up more than an hour. Computers as well as printers gave out, software malfunctioned, and computer memory capacity was exceeded. Execution reports were often delayed for hours, and some were even lost."[60]

The crash of 1987 remains the single largest one-day decline in U.S. stock market history. Wall Street has not come close to repeating this event, but it has suffered several more flash crashes. Much like rogue waves, these events are infrequent and unpredictable, but given the uncertain behavior of markets, market participants, and technology, flash crashes will likely remain a market feature in the future.

POINT OF INTEREST

Flash Crashes: The Rogue Waves of Wall Street

Rogue waves are large, highly destructive waves that seem to materialize out of nowhere. These waves are caused by the rare and unpredictable interaction

(continued)

of multiple waves that occasionally combine in just the right way to form a much bigger wave. Flash crashes are the Wall Street equivalent of rogue waves. They occur when multiple market forces combine to produce a sharp and unexpected crash. Once the panic subsides, the market recovers in a relatively short amount of time (often within days).

The crash of 1987 was the worst flash crash in U.S. history, but it was not the first. The term was coined to describe a sudden 5.7 percent decline in the market on May 28, 1962. But unlike all prior crashes, the activity of computers amplified the crash of 1987. The sheer magnitude of the crash prompted many reforms, such as the use of market circuit breakers, but technologies will always be unpredictable when confronted with unforeseen circumstances. It is not surprising, therefore, that the U.S. has experienced several additional flash crashes. One of the more dramatic ones occurred on May 6, 2010, when the stock market declined by nearly 10 percent in a matter of minutes, and then recovered most of its losses by the end of the day.[61]

Flash crashes will likely remain a feature of securities markets. It is possible that we will never again witness a single-day decline of 22.6 percent, but as the famed stock operator Jesse Livermore once warned, "Whatever happens in the stock market today has happened before and will happen again."[62]

Chapter 25

MANUFACTURING
PORTFOLIO COMPLEXITY

"The members of the establishment in any field have too much to lose in institutional stature, their carefully developed reputations as experts, the value of their many years of past work, and their earning power—all dependent on the status quo. So they defend against the new. Usually they are proven right—so they win. But not always."[1]

—CHARLES D. ELLIS, former investment committee chairman,
Yale University Endowment

The shift in ERISA's interpretation of the Prudent Man Rule enabled venture capital (VC) firms to attract billions of dollars of capital from institutional investors in the 1980s. Those who invested early in the leading funds enjoyed outstanding returns. The less restrictive interpretation also opened the door for institutional investors to experiment with other new fund types, such as private equity and hedge funds. The 1980s provided ideal market conditions for the former, while the 1990s provided excellent conditions for the latter. Finally, in 1990, Harry Markowitz received the Nobel Prize for his pioneering work on modern portfolio theory (MPT). The theory encouraged portfolio diversification but placed less emphasis on the associated costs. Prior to the 1980s, most institutional investment plans invested primarily in publicly traded stocks and bonds. By the turn of the twenty-first century, investment consultants were aggressively pushing plans into more exotic "alternative assets" under the implicit argument that greater diversification would produce better returns.

Chapter 25 recounts the origins of two particularly important alternative asset classes and explains why institutional investment plans "diversified" their portfolios into these sectors with little regard for costs and whether they were properly equipped to succeed.[2]

THE GOLDEN ERA OF THE LEVERAGED BUYOUT

The steady decline of interest rates in the 1980s fueled the rise of a new form of private equity fund known as the buyout fund (also referred to as LBO funds).[3] Similar to VC funds, buyout funds were structured as limited liability partnerships; these funds also charged management fees and carried interest on the fund's profits.[4] Kohlberg Kravis Roberts (KKR) is often regarded as the first buyout fund. In truth, the firm of Thomas H. Lee Partners predated KKR by two years, but the KKR founders had a longer history of leading buyouts.[5]

Jerome Kohlberg, Henry Kravis, and George Roberts formed KKR in 1976 after Bear Stearns Chairman Cy Lewis repeatedly rejected proposals to form a buyout practice. Prior to their departure, they had led multiple LBOs, but their returns were relatively unimpressive. Lackluster performance was largely attributable to challenging economic conditions. The modus operandi of an LBO is to purchase a company using mostly debt, improve its operations, and shed non-value-added business units. Then, over the course of several years, management pays down debt aggressively, improves profitability, and eventually sells the company at a higher valuation. Prior to the 1980s, it was difficult to make money from LBOs because the cost of debt was high and equity valuations were declining. After Paul Volcker tamed inflation in the early 1980s, these headwinds transformed into tailwinds.[6]

Highly favorable market conditions enabled buyout firms to purchase companies at attractive prices, pay down debt aggressively by eliminating extraneous costs and selling non-value-added business units, and then selling the company within a few years at a valuation multiple that was substantially higher than the one applied to the purchase price. Figure 25.1 shows the basic mechanics of how this worked. Actual transactions were admittedly more complex, but it captures the fundamental mechanics. The annual return of 66 percent for the sample fund may seem exceptional today, but such returns were not uncommon in the 1980s.

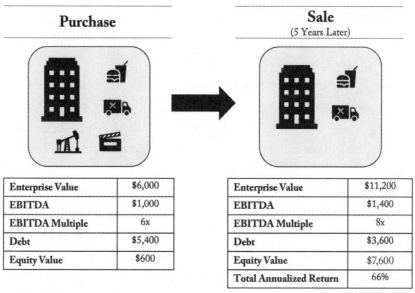

Enterprise Value	$6,000
EBITDA	$1,000
EBITDA Multiple	6x
Debt	$5,400
Equity Value	$600

Enterprise Value	$11,200
EBITDA	$1,400
EBITDA Multiple	8x
Debt	$3,600
Equity Value	$7,600
Total Annualized Return	66%

Return Drivers

✓ Sales of non-strategic businesses reduce debt by $800 million (but reduce EBITDA by $100 million).
✓ Excess cash flow is used to reduce debt to $3,600 million in year 5.
✓ Revenue growth and cost reductions increase EBITDA to $1,400 million in year 5.

Figure 25.1: Hypothetical LBO Transaction

POINT OF INTEREST

A Beautiful Day in the Neighborhood for a Leveraged Buyout

The 1980s provided optimal conditions for LBOs. Several of the more noteworthy tailwinds included:

- **Relative Attractiveness of Debt Financing**—In the early 1980s, the cost of debt was high by historical standards but reasonable relative to the risk of LBO transactions. Moreover, as inflation declined, the cost of debt correspondingly declined. There was also a significant tax advantage associated with the use of debt rather than equity, as interest was tax deductible, while dividends were not.[7]

- **Junk Bond Boom**—LBOs were typically funded with a rough combination of equity (~10 percent), senior bank loans (~60 percent), and junk bonds (~30 percent).[8] In the early 1980s, insurance companies were the primary buyers of junk bonds, and it often took several months to absorb new issues,

(continued)

which limited the volume of LBOs. In the mid-1980s, this changed when an especially prolific middleman, Michael Milken, created an expansive network of junk bond buyers. Milken's junk bond team at Drexel Burnham Lambert single-handedly could raise billions of dollars within days to fund LBOs. Drexel's infamous "highly confident letter" was often enough to convince targets of friendly or hostile takeovers that funding was secured.[9]

- **Rising Equity Valuations**—Price-to-earnings (P/E) ratios of U.S. companies were extremely low in the 1970s because of the tight correlation between earnings yields and interest rates. But as inflation subsided in the 1980s, interest rates declined, which allowed P/E ratios to climb. This created a perfect environment for LBOs—especially ones that were purchased in the early 1980s when P/E ratios were low. Not only could buyout funds profit by paying down debt and improving performance, but they could also command higher valuations when they exited their investments.

- **Overdiversification of Corporations**—In the 1960s and 1970s large corporations diversified their revenue streams by acquiring multiple businesses. As companies became more complex, many business units became uncompetitive due to inefficiencies and inattention. In addition, business unit values were often improperly reflected in the stock price of the larger corporate entity. In such cases, the business unit could be sold off for a multiple that was higher than the one assigned to the larger business. Buyout firms used this to their advantage by selling nonstrategic business units immediately and using the proceeds to accelerate debt repayment.[10]

The Barbarians Storm the Gates

"Investment discipline is the phrase that's got to come back and be talked about. In the beginning, the innovators of this idea, of whom I was one, had a great deal of discipline . . . What has happened is imitators by the hundreds have gotten into this business and as imitators flocked in, discipline has eroded, and as a result, breakups that didn't make sense have occurred."[11]

TED FORSTMANN, founder of Forstmann Little

J. Pierpont Morgan observed that few people have the mental fortitude to watch their neighbor get rich and then resist the temptation to copy them even after the opportunity is long gone. The upper echelons of Wall Street often succumb to the same vice. Outsized returns generated by buyout funds in the mid-1980s attracted a stampede of investors—especially institutional investment plans. In 1978, KKR was thrilled to raise $30 million in its first fund for institutional plans. Less than ten years later, it raised $5.6 billion (mostly from institutional investors) in only four months. By the late 1980s, buyout funds had far more capital than they could deploy at an attractive rate of return. Wall Street's latest watering hole had become overcrowded. The prospects for LBOs took a major hit in 1987 in the wake of the October flash crash. Fund-raising fell precipitously by the early 1990s, and the LBO craze went dormant for more than a decade.[12]

POINT OF INTEREST

How Much Greed Is Good?

"Any Neanderthal can go in there and whack away and cut costs, show me a guy that can spend money."[13]

—Ross Johnson, CEO of RJR Nabisco

In 1987, Oliver Stone directed the classic movie *Wall Street* starring Michael Douglas as the ruthless corporate raider Gordon Gekko. The character was reportedly modeled after several iconic figures of the time, such as Carl Icahn and Ivan Boesky. In the movie, Gekko delivers a speech to a management group and explains why "greed, for lack of a better word, is good."[14] He then explains how corporate takeovers force management to become more disciplined with shareholders' money. Gekko's toxic personality made him a poor spokesperson for capitalist principles, but his statement contained some truth. The desire to generate wealth is a key factor that explains the competitiveness of market-based economic systems, including that of the United States. But taken too far, greed eventually becomes toxic.

The LBO boom of the 1980s undoubtedly had merit—especially during the early years. The competitiveness of many U.S. corporations had deteriorated, and LBOs forced management to become more disciplined, focused, efficient, and ultimately more competitive. RJR Nabisco was the poster child of corporate excess and waste in the 1980s. The opening quote from Ross Johnson, former CEO of RJR Nabisco, encapsulates his sense of entitlement to such excesses, and his attitude invited the hostile takeover by KKR.

(continued)

By the end of the 1980s, the buyout craze had gone too far. Corporate excesses were replaced by excesses of buyout fund managers, junk bond promoters, and investment bank M&A departments. The opportunity for exceptional returns had largely evaporated, and returns in the 1990s paled in comparison to those generated in the 1980s. As the tide receded, the typical detritus of fraud and abuse surfaced. Many of the decade's iconic characters, such as Michael Milken, Ivan Boesky, and Martin Siegel, forfeited much of their wealth and served time in prison. Like many before them, they became intoxicated by greed. Dissatisfied with legitimate profits from the LBO boom, they resurrected several Gilded Age dark arts such as insider trading, self-dealing, and market manipulation.

The excesses of the 1980s were relatively extreme but certainly not unique. Unconstrained greed returned in the late 1990s, mid-2000s, and early-2020s. Each mania seemed unlike the one that preceded it, but beneath the surface, there was little difference. At the root lay some combination of greed, envy, impatience, and self-delusion.

Return of the Stock Operators

"We may as well tell the truth and put the blame where it belongs. It's up to Washington now. We have stepped aside . . . Eventually, we will take control again."[15]

—WILLIAM C. DURANT (October 1929)

POINT OF INTEREST

A Quantum Leap to the Gilded Age

"The first thing I heard when I got in the business—not from my mentor—was, 'Bulls make money, bears make money, and pigs get slaughtered. I'm here to tell you I was a pig. And I strongly believe the only way to make long-term returns in our business that are superior is by being a pig."[16]

—Stanley Druckenmiller, cofounder of the Quantum Fund

The stock pool was a formidable weapon wielded by stock operators prior to the 1930s. It enabled them to control the rise and fall of a stock, and it is much easier to profit when the future is known. In the late twentieth century, currency markets presented an opportunity to resurrect this lost art. Unlike stock exchanges, there were no rules preventing large investors, such as hedge funds, from pooling their resources to shape the future.

In 1979, the first opportunity emerged when the European Union (EU) created the exchange rate mechanism (ERM) to keep exchange rates of EU members in a narrow band. Keeping currencies within specified ranges often required central bank intervention. When a currency appreciated too far, a nation's central bank sold its currency, and when it depreciated too far, it purchased its currency using its foreign exchange reserves.

In 1992, the British pound sterling had depreciated too far relative to the German mark. The Bank of England purchased pounds to prop up its value, but George Soros and Stanley Druckenmiller, cofounders of the Quantum Fund, calculated that the Bank of England's foreign exchange reserves were insufficient to defend the pound. This would ultimately force the Bank of England to abandon the ERM, which would cause a sharp depreciation of the pound.

Shorting the pound promised massive profits, but the challenge was creating sufficient selling pressure. No single hedge fund had enough capital, but a coordinated effort would likely work. Soros and Druckenmiller shared the plan with several hedge fund managers, such as Bruce Kovner and Paul Tudor Jones, and they agreed to launch a coordinated bear pool. In September, the group shorted the pound aggressively, and as predicted, the Bank of England abandoned the ERM. After covering their positions, the Quantum Fund made a $1.5 billion profit, while Bruce Kovner's and Paul Tudor Jones's funds made $300 million and $250 million, respectively.[17]

Wall Street was awed by the profits but even more excited to discover a legal application of the stock pool. The breaking of the Bank of England also triggered rapid growth of hedge fund assets under management (AuM). In 1990, total AuM was less than $10 billion. In 2000, it exceeded $250 billion.

Alfred W. Jones is often credited for having invented the hedge fund in 1949, but this overlooks the fact that Ben Graham ran a hedge fund more than twenty years earlier. His protégé, Warren Buffett, revealed this to financial journalist Kristin Aguilera in 2012. Graham's fund, which was called the Benjamin Graham Joint Account, combined a portfolio of long and short positions, seeking to make money on both market advances and declines. In the wake of the Great Crash of 1929, Graham suffered devastating losses, and he liquidated the fund in 1936. Thirteen years later, Jones resurrected the model and was mistakenly given credit for having invented it.[18]

For the next forty years, hedge funds grew at a glacial pace. It was only in the 1990s that they began attracting significant attention after George Soros's Quantum Fund emerged victorious from his epic battle with the Bank of England in 1992. Two years later, interest in hedge funds was further bolstered by the adoption of the American Law Institute's Restatement of the Law (3d) of Trusts, which embraced the diversification principals of modern portfolio theory (MPT).[19]

By the late 1990s, the hedge fund industry was well positioned for growth. The return of the stock pool enabled global macro funds, such as the Quantum Fund, to attract billions of assets. But much like the experience of private equity, investors rushed into the asset class with too little regard for the costs and prospects of the strategies. Thousands of hedge funds were launched, offering a wide variety of strategies such as long/short equity, merger arbitrage, fixed income arbitrage, and many others. Like private equity funds, hedge funds charged hefty fees of 1–2 percent per year plus carried interest of 15–20 percent.

The growth of the hedge fund industry also benefited from a development that fueled increased investment in all alternative asset classes. By the turn of the twenty-first century, the Yale University Endowment had generated eye-popping returns, and many investors blindly replicated their allocation strategy.

An Uncommon Approach to Investment Excellence

"I liked the competitive aspects of Wall Street, but—and I'm not making a value judgment here—it wasn't the right place for me because the end result is that people are trying to make lots of money for themselves. That just doesn't suit me."[20]

—DAVID SWENSEN, late CIO of the Yale Investments Office

The 1980s were a decade remembered mostly for its excesses, which makes it especially refreshing that it also marked the emergence of one of the nation's most skilled, ethical, and successful institutional investors. The Yale University Endowment began its extraordinary run in 1985 after extracting one of its alums from Wall Street.

Founded in 1701, Yale University is one of the oldest universities in the nation, and it continues to rank among its best. Yale's academic philosophy is particularly sensitive to the preservation of its independence—especially from unwanted influence from state and federal politicians. This perspective is understandable given its history. On several occasions over the last three centuries, politicians threatened to withhold funds if Yale refused to compromise values that it held dear. In *Pioneering Portfolio Management*, David Swensen recounts many of these conflicts. The importance of intellectual independence made the leadership of Yale especially sensitive to the strength of its endowment. The more they could rely on stable, annual distributions from the portfolio, the less they needed to worry about outside pressure that could threaten their core values.[21]

Swensen and Takahashi Chart a New Course

David Swensen received a PhD in economics from Yale University in 1979 and then moved to New York to begin a career on Wall Street. After only six years, he developed an exceptional reputation working the fixed income trading desks at Salomon Brothers and Lehman Brothers. In fact, he is credited with having invented the currency swap to manage currency exposure of IBM and the World Bank. But Swensen's Wall Street career was short-lived. In 1985, his former dissertation advisors, William Brainard and James Tobin, presented David with an unsolicited offer to lead Yale's investment operations. Swensen initially hesitated, fearing that he lacked the necessary experience, but his love of Yale, deep sense of mission, and natural talent for teaching persuaded him to accept the offer.[22]

After returning to Yale, David asked his friend and fellow alum Dean Takahashi to join him as his second-in-command.[23] In close consultation with leading academics in portfolio management theory, Swensen and Takahashi crafted a new investment strategy. At the time, the portfolio consisted mostly of publicly traded stocks, bonds, and cash, which was consistent with the strategies employed by most institutional investment plans at the time. But Swensen and Takahashi concluded that the allocation was suboptimal for Yale's long-term objectives. Over the next several years, they implemented a new strategy that included a heavy equity bias, diversification into illiquid asset classes, and highly selective use of active managers. Their rationale is laid out in detail in *Pioneering Portfolio Management* and the Yale Endowment Reports that Swensen began issuing in 1990. For those seeking to emulate Yale's strategy, reading these reports is a non-negotiable prerequisite. The documents explain Yale's investing requirements, capabilities, constraints, and most importantly, its exceptional culture. Understanding these distinctions reveals why Swensen asserted that few institutional investors should seek to replicate the Yale Model.

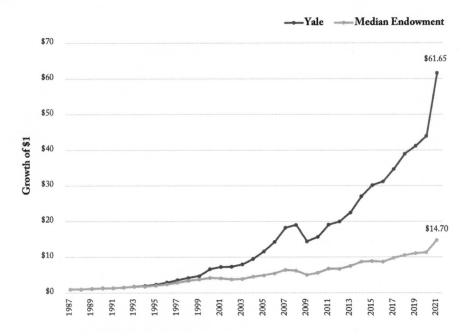

Figure 25.2: Growth of $1 Invested in the Yale University Endowment and Median University Endowment (July 1, 1987–June 30, 2021)[24]

Unconventional Success

The Yale University Endowment thrived under Swensen's and Takahashi's leadership. Figure 25.2 shows a dollar invested in the Yale University Endowment relative to the median endowment from July 1, 1987, to June 30, 2021.[25] The endowment is now approximately four times larger than it would have been had it generated a return equivalent to the median university endowment.

It was only a matter of time before the institutional investing community noticed Yale's performance. In 1997, Professor Josh Lerner published a Harvard Business School case study profiling the Yale Investments Office. Three years later, David Swensen published *Pioneering Portfolio Management*, which outlined the Yale investment philosophy in detail. Soon after its publication, institutional investors rushed to reengineer the "Yale Model," but as is almost always the case, most followers failed to produce comparable results. The reason is that they copied Yale's strategy only at a superficial level, mistakenly concluding that mere access to alternative asset classes, such as venture capital, buyout funds, and hedge funds, was all that was required. Few appreciated that the key to Yale's success was the courage, discipline, open-mindedness, and integrity that was hardwired into the minds of all the investment professionals who touched the Yale portfolio.

Pioneering People Management

"In 2000, when David first wrote the book [Pioneering Portfolio Management*], many wondered if it was a mistake to publish the playbook for the Yale Model. Why give away all of Yale's intellectual property? But as I continue to learn, I realize that the real secret ingredient was not just David's conceptual framework for the endowment portfolios, but vitally, his extraordinary investment in people. The Yale Model needs highly intelligent, committed, and selfless team players to excel. David's investment in people—that is the secret sauce!"*[26]

—DEAN TAKAHASHI, former senior director, Yale Investments Office

The Yale Investments Office staff and alumni understand the secret to their success in a way that few others appreciate. The root was Swensen's ability to find great people and mold them into exceptional investors. This talent was not limited to Yale's investment professionals. Every person who invested or received a dollar from the Yale University Endowment impacted performance in some way. A few notable examples include:

- **Endowment Beneficiaries**—Members of the Yale Investments Office share a passion for investing, but serving the beneficiaries is held in much higher regard. It is easy for investment professionals to lose sight of this responsibility, but David Swensen and his staff never have. Commitment to the mission is evident in every speech, annual report, and informal communication.

- **Yale Alumni and Academics**—Yale University produced (and still produces) many of the world's leading academics and industry leaders. In the early years, economists such as William Brainard and James Tobin were instrumental in assisting with portfolio construction and spending policy. More recently, professors and alumni have helped Yale establish contacts with leading investors, as well as navigate new market challenges. For example, over the past three years, several Yale alumni specializing in public health helped the Yale Investments Office understand potential scenarios during and after the COVID-19 pandemic.

- **Investment Staff Members**—The Yale Investments Office is populated by an extraordinary staff of investment professionals. But what is interesting is that many of the most successful alums had little investment background prior to joining the office. The 2020 Annual Endowment Report profiles fourteen Yale Investments Office alumni—nine of whom are women—who now serve as successful CIOs. Undergraduate majors include philosophy, biology, math, anthropology, and history. Although their interests varied, they shared an unwavering commitment to Yale's mission and genuine passion for investing. If there is one universal sentiment expressed by Swensen's proteges, it is that his greatest talent was teaching and mentoring. Illustrating Swensen's ability to mold great investors, in 2022, Dean Takahashi reviewed the performance of eight ten-year track records of CIOs with Yale pedigrees. All eight produced returns that rank in the top decile relative to other endowments. The odds of this occurring randomly are 1 in 100 million.[27]

- **Investment Committee Members**—One of the greatest threats to the long-term success of an institutional investment plan is the structural instability of its governance. All perpetual funds are supervised by temporary stewards, and with each changing of the guard there is risk that the strategy and culture will suffer. The patience, discipline, and guidance of Yale's Investment Committee members—many of whom were coached by Swensen—is an invaluable competitive advantage. Few institutional investors are capable of replicating this, and those that do often lose it eventually. Yale's ability to neutralize this risk is a rare feat in and of itself.

- **Investment Fund Managers**—Yale published its 2021 Endowment Report after David Swensen passed away. It includes many personal attestations to David's positive influence. Comments from investment managers were especially noteworthy. Most staff members of institutional investment plans view investment managers as mere service providers who are hired and fired based on their ability to meet relatively short-term performance benchmarks. In contrast, Yale seeks long-term partnerships. This philosophy benefits Yale in several ways. First, close relationships with managers often lead to introductions to emerging managers, which enables Yale to consistently "arrive early" to the most attractive opportunities. Second, Yale often adjusts allocations to managers based on the strength of the opportunity set. This has proven valuable to both investment managers and Yale. On many occasions, Yale has served as a reliable supplier of capital in distressed markets when many investors are withdrawing capital rather than adding it. This benefits the investment manager, as it enables them to take advantage of attractive opportunities that tend to accompany major market dislocations. It benefits Yale because they profit from the opportunity.

Re-Creating the Yale Model Is Not Impossible . . .
But It's Pretty Close

"You either have the passive strategy that wins the majority of the time, or you have this very active strategy that beats the market . . . For almost all institutions and individuals, the simple approach is best."[28]

—DAVID SWENSEN, late CIO of the Yale Investments Office

David Swensen passed away on May 5, 2021, after suffering a long battle with cancer. He left behind an exceptional legacy. In 1987, distributions from the endowment funded only 11 percent of Yale's operating budget. In 2021, they funded more than 34 percent. Swensen's positive impact on Yale will last for generations, and his proteges are having a similar impact on institutions such as Princeton, Bowdoin, and Wesleyan.

The only regretful but unintended impact of Yale's strategy is that many institutional plans have failed in their attempts to replicate it. A trustee's most important fiduciary responsibility is to only pursue investment strategies that are achievable. Therefore, before attempting to replicate the Yale Model, trustees have a fiduciary obligation to ask themselves honestly whether they have, or can realistically create, an investment ecosystem with all the attributes described on the previous pages. Most trustees who ponder this question honestly will conclude that they cannot. Admitting this is not shameful, it is simply an acknowledgement of a statistical reality. The law of investing dictates that the number of market-beating organizations will always be small. Most trustees, therefore, are better off limiting their exposure to traditional asset classes and relying mostly on low-cost index funds. Trustees to which this truth applies have a fiduciary duty to respect this law.

POINT OF INTEREST

The Law of Late Arrival

"The trouble with winner's games is that they tend to self-destruct because they attract too much attention and too many players—all of whom want to win. That's why gold rushes always finish ugly."[29]

—Charles Ellis, former chairman of the Yale University Endowment

Human beings exhibit a strong herd instinct. This is hardwired into our brains because it was critical to our survival for hundreds of thousands of years. When

(continued)

tribes of human beings identified an attractive resource, neighboring tribes benefited by following their lead. For most of history, the human population was sufficiently small to allow followers to benefit as much as early arrivers.

Unfortunately, this instinct does not work in the investment profession. In fact, the result is precisely the opposite because when followers flock to a new investment, the price increases and quickly exceeds its intrinsic value. Nevertheless, humans repeatedly engage in this self-destructive behavior. Examples from history include canal securities in the 1820s, real estate in the 1830s, railroads in the late 1800s, almost anything traded on Wall Street in the late 1920s, consumer electronics in the 1960s, internet stocks in the 1990s, and now cryptocurrency in the 2020s.

If there is a single law of investing that most humans fail to appreciate, it is that late arrival to an investment is nearly a guarantee of failure. Further, the number of early arrivals will always be small. This is why most investors are better off investing in broad market indices. Attempting and failing to establish oneself as a member of what will always be an exclusive group is risky, costly, and usually produces bad outcomes. To this day, most investment professionals dismiss this risk. The Yale University is a notable exception to the rule, and few should seek to emulate them.

Out of the Frying Pan and into the Fire

"Consultants express conventional views and make safe recommendations . . . Clients end up with bloated, fee-driven investment management businesses instead of nimble, return-oriented entrepreneurial firms."[30]

—DAVID SWENSEN, late CIO of the Yale University Endowment

Over the last fifty years, institutional investment plans have accumulated massive portfolios. As of 2021, total assets held by public and private pensions alone exceeded $40 trillion.[31] To this day, investment committees provide fiduciary oversight over most institutional investment plans.[32] Most committees are populated by volunteers, many of whom have limited investment experience and significant time constraints.[33] This forces trustees to rely heavily on the advice of investment consultants to shape investment strategy and day-to-day investment decisions.

The investment consulting profession traces its roots to the early 1960s. At the time, most trustees relied on services of bank asset management departments and insurance companies to manage their portfolios.[34] One of the frustrations of trustees was that they had very little information to gauge whether performance and fees were competitive. In the early 1960s, the brokerage firm A.G. Becker leveraged new computing technologies to create performance reports to provide this information. The firm soon discovered that performance reporting was also a great tool to promote its more lucrative brokerage services. They began offering reports free of charge to trustees in exchange for directing all the plan's brokerage needs to A.G. Becker.[35]

The performance reports were well-received, and A.G. Becker responded by forming a new business unit. By the early 1970s, A.G. Becker had one thousand client relationships. Several brokerage firms took note and launched performance-reporting practices of their own. Brokerage firms were especially attracted to performance reporting because they were under enormous pressure to secure new revenue streams and retain clients. The May 1975 decision by the SEC to abolish fixed-rate commissions on trades caused brokerage firms to lower commission rates or add services to remain competitive. Merrill Lynch was especially enamored with performance reporting, as it also provided an opportunity to enter the institutional investment plan market, which it had neglected in the 1960s. A group of Merrill Lynch brokers began offering performance reports and consulting in exchange for directed brokerage services.[36]

In the early 1980s, investment consultants ran into a big problem. Over the prior decade, they had migrated clients' portfolios away from insurance companies and banks and replaced them with best-of-breed asset managers. At the same time, many brokerage firms had moved aggressively into the mutual fund business. The problem was that consultants' performance reports often revealed that the brokerage firms' funds underperformed. This created internal tension as the performance reports suggested that trustees should terminate the brokerage firms' funds and/or remove them from consideration in searches. In his memoirs, Richard Ennis recalled being summoned into the office of the senior leadership of A.G. Becker after a large brokerage client terminated its relationship because the manager research team provided inadequate coverage of its funds. Unable to resolve this conflict, Richard Ennis launched an independent firm, EnnisKnupp, which was free of this conflict of interest.[37]

Merrill Lynch's performance reporting consultants encountered the same problem. Performance reports often revealed that Merrill Lynch's funds underperformed those of competitors. This led to internal discord, and Merrill Lynch decided to exit the performance reporting business altogether in the mid-1980s. After shuttering its institutional performance reporting practice, a group of performance reporting consultants launched their own firms. Several of these companies remain the largest investment consulting firms in the country.

The Seeds of Complexity

In the early years, investment consulting firms focused primarily on performance reporting, but they soon expanded their businesses by offering new services such as manager search, asset allocation optimization, fiduciary audits, and other investment products. Slowly but steadily their value proposition morphed from providing independent and objective performance assessments to offering services that were intended to help trustees outperform their peers and broad indexes. Convincing clients that they were better than their competitors required beefing up research teams. This was costly, and consultants raised their fees accordingly. In addition, to prove to clients that their fees were well spent, consultants added complexity to portfolios by making greater use of active management and alternative asset classes. Consultants often justified the added complexity by using Harry Markowitz's Mean Variance Optimization (MVO) models to show that adding more to the portfolio always (or at least almost always) increased risk-adjusted returns.

POINT OF INTEREST

The Conflicted Conscience of the Unconflicted Consultant

"Consultants' agency interests . . . are economically focused on keeping the largest number of accounts for as many years as possible. These agency interests are not well aligned with the long-term principal interests of the client institution."[38]

—**Charles D. Ellis, former chair of the Yale University Endowment**

Investment consultants originally intended to help trustees evaluate the performance of their portfolios, but many soon morphed into businesses that performed no better than the bank and insurance company asset management departments from which they had freed trustees.

Investment consultants often claim that their business models are "conflict free," but they suffer from a deep-seated conflict at the heart of the business model itself. Most investment consulting firms base their value proposition on their implied claim that they can generate superior returns relative to competitors. The problem is that even back-of-the-envelope math reveals that it is statistically impossible for the investment consulting industry, in aggregate, to outperform broad benchmarks and peer averages. In 2022, the top thirty investment consulting firms advised on $18.0 trillion in assets. There is simply not enough market inefficiency for these firms to exploit.

Nevertheless, the quest for outperformance compels many consultants to encourage the creation of portfolios that are overly diversified, supported by unnecessary staff, and overly invested in alternative asset classes and active managers. The inevitable outcome is subpar performance and higher fees. Consulting firms rarely admit this truth to themselves (much less their clients) due to fear of obsolescence. Eventually, this flaw will be revealed, and those who move early and adapt to a new reality will be rewarded.

The Nondiscretionary Cloak of Invisibility

An irony of the investment consulting profession is that firms were created to provide objective assessments of performance, yet their nondiscretionary status shields them from having to apply the same standards to themselves. The most egregious example is the case of active manager selection. Many investment consultants routinely recommend the use of active managers, yet there is no independent entity that reports whether, in aggregate, their firm's recommendations add value or not. Few firms voluntarily provide this information because (a) they never thought to do the analysis; (b) they refuse to do the analysis because they fear what it *may* reveal; or (c) they have done the analysis but refuse to share it because of what it *does* reveal.[39] None of these explanations are acceptable from the client's perspective. The cloak of invisibility of the nondiscretionary investment consulting profession protects them from providing the very transparency that prompted the formation of the profession to begin with.

Chapter 26

SOWING THE SEEDS
OF DISCONTENT

"When there is no middle class, and the poor greatly exceed in number,
troubles arise and the state soon comes to an end."

—ARISTOTLE

The long economic recovery that began in 1982 probably did not feel different than prior recoveries, but the passage of four decades has demonstrated otherwise. Most prior economic recoveries were accompanied by federal budget surpluses, trade surpluses, broad-based real wage gains, and strong stock returns. The rebound that began in 1982 produced strong stock returns but lagged on the other metrics. Federal budget and trade deficits grew substantially, and the gap between the highest-earning and lowest-earning Americans widened. There are many factors that explain the difference in this recovery. Among the more powerful drivers was the shift of the U.S. from a mass-production industrial economy to a technology and services-driven economy. This shift gained traction in the 1970s, gathered momentum in the 1980s, and then accelerated even further in the 2010s.

Many Americans now see a future that seems dimmer, but it is difficult to explain precisely why. They are perplexed by the fact that the U.S. is one of the wealthiest nations, yet many Americans feel they cannot afford the necessities. This chapter explains several economic factors that may explain this malaise. Several emerged in the 1980s and have slowly intensified ever since. It begins by outlining several key metrics of the post–Great Inflation recovery that differed from past recoveries. It then presents several theories that may help explain why.

THE FEDERAL BUDGET DEFICIT

"If now the most classical, hardline president in fifty years [Ronald Reagan] accepts indefinite deferral of a balanced budget, who will any longer be inhibited by fear of deficits?"[1]

—HERB STEIN, economist

POINT OF INTEREST

Art Laffer's Curveball

"If a tax cut increases government revenues, you haven't cut taxes enough."[2]

—Milton Friedman

President Ronald Reagan announced a bold economic plan after taking office in 1980. The fiscal component included a combination of tax and spending cuts. The original plan was conceptually sound, but the final legislation deviated from its core principles. Proposed spending cuts were watered down to gain support from various constituencies in Congress, but tax cuts were left relatively intact. Reagan was ultimately persuaded by a fringe group of economists who claimed that aggressive tax cuts would "pay for themselves." At the core of the thesis was a U-shaped curve that Art Laffer hastily sketched on the back of a napkin. The curve shows total tax receipts on the y-axis and the tax rate on the x-axis. Laffer used the curve to argue that a reduction in tax rates would increase tax revenue. He assumed that the U.S. was positioned on the right side of the curve.

Art Laffer's Drawing

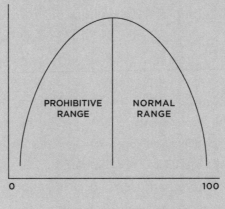

PROHIBITIVE RANGE   NORMAL RANGE

0   100

Replication of Laffer's Curve[3]

(continued)

In fairness, there is a kernel of truth to the Laffer Curve. Tax rate increases beyond a certain threshold will prompt the tax base to find ways to avoid paying them, and economic growth will slow as people have less incentive to work. But the crudely conceived "Laffer Curve" was little more than a thought experiment. Laffer made no attempt to quantify the tradeoff, and he just assumed that the U.S. was on the right side of the curve in 1980. Nevertheless, supply-side economists embraced the visual and implicitly argued that the U.S. was located on the right of the curve, which would ensure that tax cuts increased revenue.

For the eight years ending December 31, 1988, Americans enjoyed real GDP growth of 3.1 percent per year. Unemployment had settled at 5.3 percent, and inflation was running at approximately 4 percent per year. Republican Party members often describe the Reagan years as a golden era, and some of it is merited. But the Reagan administration also reinforced a disturbing habit that began in the 1960s. For most of its history, the U.S. reserved the use of public debt primarily to address emergencies. Initially, emergencies consisted only of war but were later expanded to include extreme economic shocks, such as the Great Depression. The principle of issuing public debt only to address emergencies was specifically cited by Alexander Hamilton in his *First Report on the Public Credit*. But Hamilton also believed in paying down the debt when the emergency subsided, stating, "The creation of debt should always be accompanied with a means of extinguishment."[4]

Adherence to Hamiltonian principles enabled the U.S. to finance its responses to multiple existential threats for more than 150 years. The most notable examples were the American Civil War and the two World Wars. Beginning in the 1960s, however, Hamiltonian principles began to erode. During the Johnson, Nixon, Ford, and Carter presidencies, the U.S. relaxed fiscal restraint during times of peace. Discipline has not yet returned. Figure 26.1 shows the U.S. federal budget deficit as a percentage of GDP from 1791 to 2022.[5]

Figure 26.1 begs the question as to why the U.S. continued running budget deficits after the conclusion of World War II. One reason is that once the U.S. dollar became the world's dominant reserve currency, Americans had the means to do it. Surplus countries, such as Saudi Arabia and China, were more than willing to fund U.S. deficits by purchasing U.S. Treasuries as a store of value for their savings. A second reason is because the U.S. massively expanded its entitlement programs, which soon exceeded the nation's ability to fund them. Figure 26.2 shows the growth in U.S. spending on the social safety net, which includes healthcare (Medicare and Medicaid), social

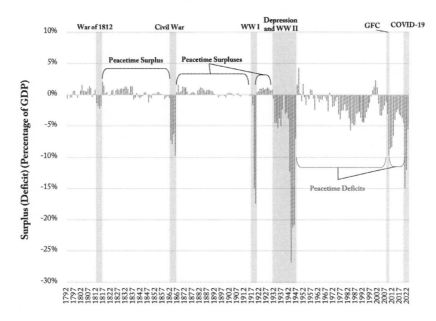

Figure 26.1: U.S. Federal Budget Deficits as a Percentage of GDP (1792–2022)[6]

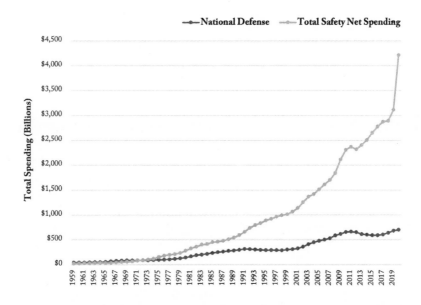

Figure 26.2: U.S. Spending on National Defense and Social Safety Net Programs (1959–2020)[7]

security, unemployment insurance, and various anti-poverty initiatives. Contrary to conventional wisdom, these programs vastly exceed the spending on national defense, which has steadily declined as a percentage of GDP. Figure 26.3 shows total federal tax receipts from 1959 to 2020 as a percentage of GDP. The surprising observation is that total tax receipts as a percentage of GDP have changed little since 1959.

Figure 26.3: U.S. Total Tax Receipts as Percentage of GDP (1959–2021)[8]

The prior series of figures paints a picture of an empire that has lived beyond its means for more than half a century. Both political parties tend to blame their opponents, but the truth is that neither Democrats nor Republicans have embraced thrift.

LABOR PRODUCTIVITY AND WORKER DISPLACEMENT

"Put simply, a large share of the changes in the U.S. wage structure during the last four decades are accounted for by the relative wage declines of workers that specialized in routine tasks at industries that experienced labor share declines."[9]

—DARON ACEMOGLU, economist, Massachusetts Institute of Technology

The technological revolution in the U.S. during the 1980s fueled exceptional stock market returns, but it did not affect real economic growth as much as people often assume. Figures 26.4 shows the total annualized real GDP growth in the 1970s and 1980s. Growth was admittedly stronger in the 1980s relative to the 1970s, but not by much.

The more interesting observation is the source of economic growth in the 1980s. To explain this, it is necessary to first define the term. Economic growth constitutes the increase in total economic output (i.e., goods and services) that a society produces.[10] There are a few ways to increase output. First, a country can increase the size of its

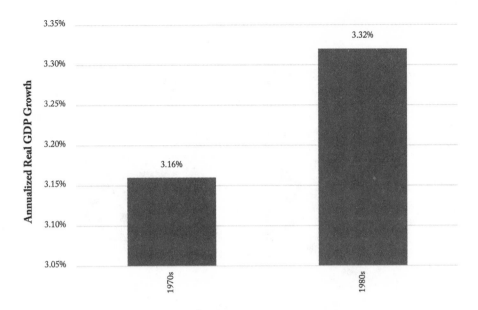

Figure 26.4: 10-Year Annualized Real GDP Growth (1970 vs. 1980s)[11]

labor force. This can be accomplished through organic population growth, immigration, and expansion of labor force participation. Second, it can come from increases in the number of hours worked by the labor force. Finally, it can come from increases in labor productivity. Increased productivity, in turn, is a function of three factors: educational advancement, increases in the capital stock, and technological advancement.

The most important economic growth driver is productivity because population growth has slowed substantially in the U.S., and the labor force participation rate and hours worked have flattened. Productivity growth, however, is still additive to growth because it enables workers to produce more output per unit of work. One of the more surprising statistics related to U.S. technological advancement is that total productivity growth over the past several decades was much weaker than it had been during the fifty-year period ending in 1970. For the forty-four-year period ending in 2014, total productivity advanced at an annual rate of 1.62 percent versus an annual rate of 2.82 percent for the fifty years ending in 1970. Productivity growth was especially slow in more recent years. During the 2010s, productivity growth advanced at a rate of only 1.1 percent per year. Many Americans assume that technological advancements are destined to translate into massive productivity gains, but for almost the entirety of the information age, the opposite was true. Figure 26.5 shows annualized labor productivity growth during the 1970s and 1980s.[12]

These statistics do not mean that technology does not improve productivity. It just indicates that the impact of recent advancements is less powerful than people

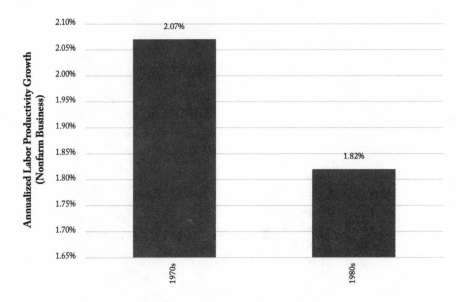

Figure 26.5: Annualized Labor Productivity Growth (1970s vs. 1980s)[13]

often assume. There are a few explanations for this overestimation. First, many people underestimate the impact of technological advances that drove productivity gains from the late 1800s until 1970. Inventions such as electricity, combustion engines, household appliances, and electric power tools had a much more substantial impact on the workforce than the invention of computing technologies. There are few Americans alive today who recall the exhausting and time-consuming work required to perform routine tasks that never cross our minds today. Comparatively, the work reduction achievable from information technology is simply less substantial and broad-based. The second reason is that productivity gains from technology are offset to a degree by the simultaneous displacement of workers performing routine tasks. In other words, recent technological advancements enhance the productivity of *highly skilled* workers, but it decreases the productivity of less-skilled workers. It some cases, it eliminates their employability all together. According to a June 2021 study by the National Bureau of Economic Research, between 50 and 70 percent of the changes in U.S. wage structure from 1980 to 2016 are explainable by the replacement of workers performing routine tasks.[14]

Decline of Manufacturing

American manufacturing workers were among the more notable victims of worker displacement due to technological advancement. The reason is because routine manufacturing tasks were especially easy to automate. Moreover, tasks that were not subject

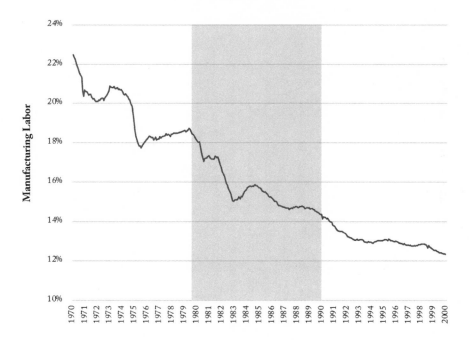

Figure 26.6: U.S. Manufacturing Labor Force as Percentage of Total Labor Force (1970-2000)[15]

to automation could be outsourced to countries with lower labor costs. The loss of manufacturing jobs began in the early 1970s, flattened in the late 1970s, and then resumed in the 1980s. The U.S. shed a total of 1.4 million manufacturing jobs in the 1980s despite adding a total of 17.9 million jobs to the labor force. This reduced the share of manufacturing jobs in the labor force from 18.1 percent to 14.1 percent (Figure 26.6).

The transition away from mass-production manufacturing was not solely a function of automation. Other causes included the erosion of the U.S. productivity advantage relative to Europe and Japan and the strength of the U.S. dollar in the mid-1980s, which made imports more attractive to Americans. Finally, reduced power of U.S. labor unions during the 1970s and 1980s made it easier for companies to move manufacturing operations offshore and take advantage of cheaper labor. The following series of graphics provide evidence of these causal factors. Figure 26.7 shows union membership as a percentage of all manufacturing jobs, and Figure 26.8 shows the increase in the U.S. dollar index.

In combination, slower productivity growth, worker displacements, and the shift away from manufacturing have increased fear and uncertainty among large segments of the American population. This is a difficult problem to solve because regressing to prior phases of economic evolution would harm the overall competitiveness of the U.S., while blind economic progress threatens to disenfranchise large pockets of the population.

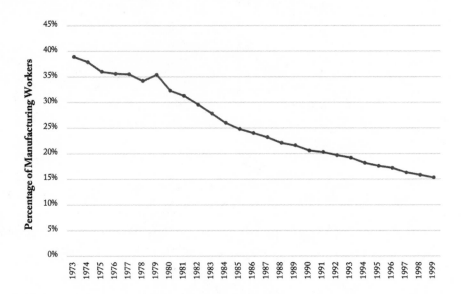

Figure 26.7: Percentage of U.S. Manufacturing Labor Force with Union Membership (1973–1999)[16]

Figure 26.8: U.S. Dollar Index (January 1, 1980–December 1, 1989)[17]

The U.S. Trade Deficit

In the 1980s, the U.S. began running persistent trade deficits. Figure 26.9 shows the history of the U.S. trade balance in the post–World War II era. The implications of persistent trade deficits are a common source of confusion. On the surface, chronic trade deficits are alarming, but the phenomenon is more nuanced. Before discussing these nuances, it is important to explain two different ways of calculating trade deficits.

- **Trade Balance–Based Calculation**—The most common calculation of a trade deficit is to simply subtract a nation's imports from its exports. If imports exceed exports, the country has a trade deficit; if exports exceed imports, a country has a trade surplus. Countries that run trade deficits make up the shortfall by running capital account surpluses. This can be accomplished by issuing public debt, selling investment securities, or attracting foreign direct investment (FDI).

Trade Surplus (Deficit) = Exports – Imports

- **Savings/Investment–Based Calculation**—A second calculation of a trade deficit evaluates a nation's savings versus investment. Countries that save less than is required to fund domestic investment run a trade deficit. Countries that save more than is required to fund domestic investment run a trade surplus.

Trade Surplus (Deficit) = Savings – Investment

The second calculation is more insightful for the U.S. because there is evidence that the trade deficit is heavily influenced by differences in foreign savings rates. It is further amplified by the attractiveness of U.S. government securities due to the

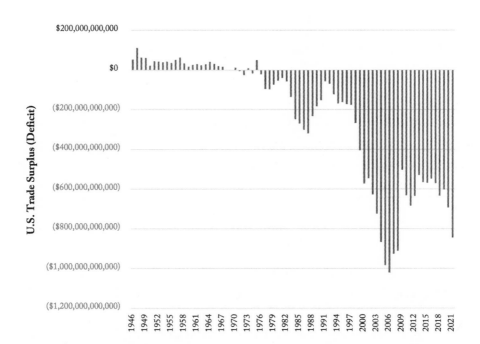

Figure 26.9: U.S. Trade Surplus (Deficit) in 2021 Dollars (1946-2021)[18]

U.S. dollar's status as the dominant reserve currency and the perceived safety of U.S. debt securities. Finally, America's well-regulated securities markets and strong track record of innovation make U.S. securities especially attractive to foreign investors. All of these factors suggest that America's trade deficit may be heavily influenced by the "glut of savings" abroad, combined with the attractiveness of U.S. investment opportunities.[19]

To the extent that this thesis is true, the trade deficit is not necessarily a sign of deteriorating U.S. competitiveness. In fact, it may be an indicator of strength. On the other hand, it is a problem if the deficit mostly reflects inadequate savings (especially by the federal government), weakening innovation, and eroding competitiveness. Determining the extent to which these different factors impact the trade deficit remains a subject of contentious debate, and it is one that is discussed in greater depth in chapter 29, particularly as it relates to the rise of China.

Creative Destruction and Compression of the Corporate Life Cycle

"Situations emerge in the process of creative destruction in which many firms may have to perish that nevertheless would be able to live on vigorously and usefully if they could weather a particular storm."[20]

—JOSEPH A. SCHUMPETER

The U.S. has a well-established track record of allowing market forces to reward companies that innovate to meet evolving market demands and punish those that fail. This does not mean that the U.S. is or has ever been a purely market-based economy. Markets are constantly distorted by regulations, political influence, and uncompetitive behavior by companies. Compared to other nations, however, the U.S. tends to have a greater respect for market forces. Joseph Schumpeter famously coined the phrase "creative destruction" to describe the continual process of destruction and renewal in capitalist economies.[21] This process forces companies to continuously improve or descend into obsolescence. The financial history of the United States clearly reveals the many benefits of creative destruction. The downside, however, is that the demise of companies and entire industries can cause significant pain because it forces workers to develop new skills.

In 1990, Ichak Adizes published research that described the phases of corporate

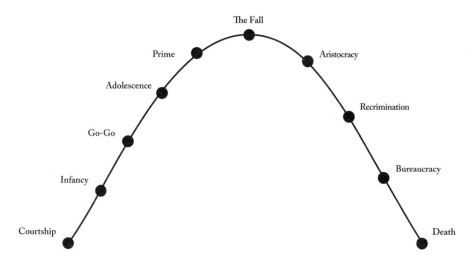

Figure 26.10: Phases of the Corporate Life Cycle[22]

growth and decline (Figure 26.10). On the front end of the cycle, Adizes identified five phases through which companies must pass before achieving peak performance. For most of U.S. history, companies spent many years (even decades) working through each phase of the corporate life cycle. During the 1980s, however, high-tech companies began racing through the life cycle in record time. This is because massive markets for high-tech products emerged so quickly that it forced companies to skip along the path from birth to prime in the span of years—or even months in some cases. Moreover, the death of a company, which can be a painfully drawn-out process, occurred almost instantaneously in many cases.[23]

The compression of the corporate life cycle persists today, and it is not restricted to high-tech companies. Many industries must keep pace with evolving technology to maintain a competitive edge. Success requires continuous upgrades with little room for error or delay. Failure to evolve accelerates a company's demise. All else being equal, this may add to the unsettled feeling among members of the U.S. labor force.

THE SHRINKING OF MIDDLE CLASS AMERICA

America accumulated immense wealth over the past fifty-five years, but it was not evenly distributed. The bottom quintile remained roughly unchanged, while the top quintile substantially increased its income share. Almost all the gains came from the middle three quintiles, which declined from 52.3 percent in 1967 to 44.5 percent in 2021. Figure 26.11 reveals this phenomenon by showing the percentage of income received by the middle 60 percent of earners in the U.S. from 1967 to 2021.

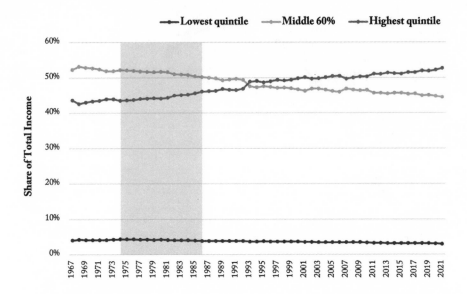

Figure 26.11: Share of Total U.S. Income by Quintiles (January 1, 1967–December 31, 2021)[24]

Erosion of the middle class is especially painful in the U.S. because Americans have historically expressed a strong aversion to socialist policies. In fairness, there is strong justification for this philosophy. Respect for capitalist principles has served as one of the nation's greatest competitive advantages for more than two hundred years. The danger, however, is that once certain thresholds of wealth disparity are breached, there is risk that the "have nots" will seek to reallocate resources by force if necessary. The conflict between socialism and capitalism has existed for thousands of years, and history demonstrates that both philosophies are unstable in their purest forms. For the U.S. to maintain its competitive advantage it must balance its deep respect for property ownership, entrepreneurship, and the corrective power of market forces with sensible policies that temper its vulnerability to rebellion when wealth disparity breaches critical thresholds. This is among the greatest challenges for the U.S. in the twenty-first century, and it is discussed in greater depth in chapter 29.

An Unsettled Feeling Takes Root in America

Paul Volcker's successful battle with inflation helped Americans firmly establish their position as the world's innovation engine at the dawn of the Information Age. At the same time, many Americans felt more insecure. Gains in the stock market were offset by increasing job insecurity. Faith in the durability of one's skills eroded as technology replaced jobs that Americans once believed were permanent. Retirement security felt less achievable as companies closed pension plans and adopted employee-funded retirement plans. Finally, the middle-class lifestyle was becoming less common among Americans. As the 1990s commenced, however, these feelings were temporarily suppressed as Americans embraced the mass delusion that the internet offered a path to effortless riches.

Chapter 27

THE ANCIENT WONDERS
OF THE PRESENT

*"There can be few fields of human endeavor in which history counts for
so little as the world of finance. Past experience to the extent that is part
of memory at all, is dismissed as the primitive refuge of those who do not
have the insight to appreciate the incredible wonders of the present."*[1]

—JOHN KENNETH GALBRAITH

On November 9, 1989, the world was stunned when the government of East Germany announced that they would allow its citizens to cross the wall that separated East and West Germany for nearly thirty years. A few days later, the Berlin Wall fell, thus marking the beginning of the end of the Soviet Union. Two years later, the Soviet Union had completely dissolved, thus ending the Cold War. The disintegration of the Soviet Union elevated the role of the U.S. as a global leader, accelerated the creation of the European Union, and reshaped the economic strategy of China.

The Cold War also inspired technological advancements that radically changed the world. The most important was a new networking technology called ARPANET. The technology was originally designed to ensure government continuity in the event of a nuclear attack. In the early 1990s, ARPANET was adapted to the private sector, at which point it was referred to as the internet. The seemingly endless commercial applications of the internet fueled rampant speculation in Silicon Valley and on Wall Street.

Chapter 27 begins by recounting the collapse of the Soviet Union and the end of the Cold War. It then explains the irrational exuberance that accompanied the transition of the internet from a military experiment to a mainstream technology. Indiscriminate investment in internet-related businesses then fueled the dot-com bubble at the dawn of the twentieth century. The bubble eventually burst, and the U.S. suffered a sharp but relatively brief recession. The experience was traumatic for those caught in the mania, but it paled in comparison to a much more severe financial crisis that would arrive less than ten years later.

THE COLLAPSE OF THE SOVIET UNION

"In the U.S. small children play with computers. Here, we don't even have computers in every office of the Defense Ministry. And for reasons you well know, we cannot make computers widely available in our society."[2]

—GENERAL NIKOLAI OGARKOV, chief of the Soviet General Staff

In the 1950s and 1960s, Soviet military and technological advancements rivaled those of the U.S., but the advantage shifted decisively in America's favor in the 1970s and 1980s. America's most powerful competitive advantage was its market-based economy, which fueled technological advancements that far outpaced those of its rival. In contrast, the Soviet Union suffered from economic stagnation, several unforced policy errors, and some bad luck. The Soviet Union's biggest weakness was its stubborn adherence to central planning. Chronic inefficiencies and the absence of innovation resulted in food shortages, a scarcity of consumer goods, and technological stagnation. The Soviets' most costly policy error was the invasion of Afghanistan in 1979. Military leaders expected an easy victory within a few months, but after making little progress, they withdrew in total defeat after ten years. Finally, bad luck came in the form of a collapse in oil prices in the mid-1980s, which starved the nation of foreign currency which was desperately needed to purchase imports. The Soviet central bank responded by printing money freely, which stoked inflation. When the Soviet Union began to crumble in the 1980s, Americans were shocked to discover that they had grossly overestimated the strength of the Soviet military and economy.

Gorbachev's Hail Mary

"The aging Politburo simply refused to experiment with the economy in any meaningful sense. Even limited reforms such as those in Eastern Europe, not to mention China, were off the table."[3]

—MIKHAIL GORBACHEV, former general secretary of the CPSU

On March 11, 1985, the Communist Party of the Soviet Union (CPSU) realized that the status quo was unsustainable, and they elected the youthful Mikhail Gorbachev as the general secretary to lead reform efforts. Unlike his predecessors, Gorbachev believed that migrating to a market-based economy and increasing government transparency were critical to the nation's survival. For five years, Gorbachev worked tirelessly to achieve these goals. His most notable programs were *perestroika*, which involved market reforms, and *glasnost*, which increased government transparency. In retrospect, these programs may have succeeded had they been launched a decade or so earlier, but by the late 1980s, citizens of the fifteen Soviet republics were uneasy. Then, the lifting of media censorship under *glasnost* revealed how far the Soviet Union had fallen behind the West, and citizens would not wait long to catch up.[4]

By 1988, the sense of unity binding the fifteen Soviet republics began to disintegrate. A key component of Gorbachev's reforms was allowing each republic to choose its own government. No longer fearful of Soviet interference, citizens embraced their independence and rejected the status quo. Poland moved first by electing a non-communist government in August 1989, but the most dramatic moment came on November 9, 1989, when the East German government approved a policy allowing travel between East and West Germany. Border crossings required a permit, but thousands of East German citizens ignored this requirement and crossed the Berlin Wall later that night. Within a week, East and West German citizens were dismantling the wall with sledgehammers. Guards who would have shot them for even approaching the wall a few months earlier watched in awe or joined in the demolition.[5]

Declarations of independence spread rapidly after the fall of the Berlin Wall. Even Russia, the largest of the Soviet republics, charted its own path after Boris Yeltsin was elected chairman of the Supreme Soviet of the Russian SFSR and announced that Russian law superseded Soviet law. By the end of 1990 the complete disintegration of the Soviet Union appeared inevitable. The end arrived in August when Mikhail Gorbachev traveled to Crimea for vacation and was placed under house arrest while members of the conservative wing of the CPSU staged a coup. But the coup attracted little support and fizzled within a matter of days. On December 8, 1991, leaders of Russia, Belarus, and Ukraine secretly signed a document with a provision that stated, "The USSR as a subject of international law and a geopolitical reality no longer exists." The Soviet Union was no more, and the U.S. was the world's only remaining superpower.[6]

The End of the Cold War

The Cold War lasted forty-five years. It was less deadly than a direct military confrontation, but it was still costly. Americans suffered 58,220 lives fighting a proxy war in Vietnam and spent hundreds of billions of dollars on Cold War–related defenses and other proxy wars. Nations caught in the crossfire endured even more pain. The Vietnamese suffered more than one million fatalities in the war with the U.S., and Afghanis suffered between 850,000 and two million fatalities in a war with the Soviet Union. Henry Morgenthau Jr. brilliantly stated that "war is never cheap, but it is a million times cheaper to win than to lose." The U.S. emerged victorious but paid a heavy price in terms of lives lost and dollars spent. The Soviet Union lost, and the former Soviet republics continue to suffer much more severe consequences to this day.[7]

The end of the Cold War marked the beginning of a new era in the U.S., and with it came new financial challenges. The first major financial crisis arrived at the turn of the century with the collapse of the dot-com bubble. The subsequent recession was magnified by a devastating terrorist attack on the nation's centers of finance and government on September 11, 2001. The economy recovered, but Americans immediately fueled a new bubble that would cause far more damage. But to fully appreciate the causes of the GFC of 2008–2009, it is important to understand the bubble that preceded it.

POINT OF INTEREST

Cold War Remnants

Several decades passed before the consequences of the Cold War became fully apparent—and some have only recently materialized. The campaign by President Vladmir Putin to reabsorb Ukraine in 2022 is one example. From a financial perspective, several of the more notable consequences included:

- **German Reunification and the Formation of the EU**—On September 12, 1990, East and West Germany reunited after the signing of the Two Plus Four Agreement in Moscow. Latent fear over a reunified Germany, coupled with fallout from a disintegrating Soviet Union, increased momentum to strengthen political cooperation in Europe. On February 7, 1992, the European Union (EU) was officially established with the signing of the Maastricht Treaty. Seven years later, the EU launched the euro as its official currency.
- **American Technological Leadership**—The Cold War arms and space races supercharged R&D efforts in the United States. The Soviet acquisition of

(continued)

nuclear weapons in 1949 triggered massive funding of computer technologies, which accelerated the advancement of semiconductors, mainframes, and minicomputers. The launch of Sputnik in 1957 subsidized integrated circuits at a time when they were prohibitively expensive in commercial markets. Over the next several decades, America's technological leadership advanced even further, creating many more advantages.

- **The Rise of China**—The failure of Soviet central planning did not go unnoticed in China. On September 9, 1976, Mao Zedong passed away, and Deng Xiaoping emerged as China's new leader. Xiaoping immediately implemented a series of reforms intended to migrate China steadily toward a market-based economy but without abandoning the one-party communist system of government. The verdict on this approach remains uncertain, but current signs are that China may soon rival the U.S. both economically and militarily in the twenty-first century.

- **Rise of the Internet**—Fearful of a nuclear holocaust in the 1960s, the Department of Defense (DoD) researched ways to maintain government continuity in a worst-case scenario. A key priority was ensuring redundancy of computer networks. A DoD unit known as the Advanced Research and Projects Agency (ARPA) developed technology to standardize communications among disparate computing devices. The hardware and software were referred to as ARPANET. In the 1990s, academic institutions and private corporations created a public version of the ARPANET, which was renamed the internet. The exponential increase in digital connectivity quickly reshaped economies and societies.

THE RISE OF THE INTERNET

"Speculation does not depend entirely on the capacity for self-delusion . . . It is another feature of the speculative mood that, as time passes, the tendency to look beyond the simple fact of increasing values to the reasons on which it depends greatly diminishes."[8]

—JOHN KENNETH GALBRAITH

In 1962, Joseph Licklider joined the Advanced Research Project Agency (ARPA) at the Department of Defense (DoD) as the director of the Information Processing Techniques Office (IPTO). Shortly thereafter, he distributed a memo addressed to

"Members and Affiliates of the Intergalactic Computer Network," which proposed the creation of a network of computers that could share information using a common language. Licklider departed before making his vision a reality, but his replacement, Robert Taylor, aggressively pushed the project forward. In 1967, Taylor secured $1 million in funding to create the ARPANET, which would allow military computers to communicate. On October 29, 1969, ARPANET went live, and the first message was sent from a node at UCLA to a node at the Stanford Research Institute.[9]

ARPANET steadily added nodes at military and academic institutions during the 1970s and early 1980s. In 1985, having observed the success of the ARPANET, researchers at the National Science Foundation (NSF) issued a research grant to study the use of the technology to allow shared access to high-end supercomputing resources scattered throughout the country. In 1986, NSFNET went live, allowing computer networking technology to spread outside of military networks.

In 1991, Tim Berners-Lee, a researcher at the European Organization for Nuclear Research (CERN), developed a software application called the World Wide Web. The application created primitive web pages that made it easier to access information on NSFNET. Intrigued by Berners-Lee's creation, two employees at the National Center for Supercomputing Applications (NCSA) at the University of Illinois, Urbana-Champaign, developed a free software application called Mosaic that students could use as a "browser" to find and download information on NSFNET. In 1993, more than one million users were using the Mosaic browser, thus marking the beginning of the Internet Age.

The internet was a monumental innovation that had undeniable commercial applications, but it was unclear which companies would profit, how they would profit, and whether it was sustainable. This created a land grab mentality. Hordes of entrepreneurs armed with hastily written business plans and billions of dollars of venture capital raced to develop the next big idea. Inspired by the instant riches of the first internet IPO in 1994, the U.S. was primed for an asset bubble.

The Navigators of the Netscape

"You literally had insatiable demand. It wouldn't have mattered where they priced the offering, it was going to go to some outrageous price."[10]

—ROGER MCNAMEE, Integral Capital Partners (August 10, 1995)

In 1991, Marc Andreesen was working part time at the National Center of Supercomputing Applications (NCSA), while studying computer science as an undergraduate at the University of Illinois at Urbana-Champaign. After using Tim Berners-Lee's World Wide Web, Andreesen and a colleague, Eric Bina, joined forces to write the Mosaic software, which was a primitive web browser. The first version of Mosaic was offered for free to users in April 1993. After graduating in December 1993, Andreesen moved to Silicon Valley where he met Jim Clark, who had recently left Silicon Graphics. Clark believed that the Mosaic software had huge commercial applications. In April 1994, Clark provided seed funding, and the two partnered to launch Netscape Communications.[11]

Netscape quickly captured the attention of John Doerr, a partner at Kleiner Perkins. In September 1994, Kleiner Perkins invested $5 million for a 25 percent stake in the company. Three months later, Netscape released the first version of its browser, Netscape Navigator, and it was an instant hit. On August 9, 1995, Netscape went public, valuing the company at nearly $3 billion. The IPO was priced at $28 per share, traded as high as $74.75, and closed at $58.25 on the first day. In the span of only fifteen months, Andreesen and Clark had transformed a business plan into a multibillion-dollar company.[12]

Netscape struggled after its IPO, as several startups launched competitive browsers. Its most formidable rival was Microsoft, which launched its Explorer browser only a week after Netscape's IPO. The browser was bundled with Microsoft's operating system, giving it a powerful competitive advantage. Netscape sued Microsoft for antitrust violations, but the browser wars ended before the suit was resolved. In 1998, AOL acquired Netscape, and the browser disappeared entirely by the early 2000s.[13] Nevertheless, Netscape's short-lived success proved that internet companies could achieve multibillion-dollar valuations in a matter of months and without proof of profitability. This resurrected animal spirits in the United States. VC firms soon raised enormous amounts of capital, and many chased half-baked business plans that they would have tossed in the garbage only a few years earlier.[14]

The Delusion of the Crowd

"[Stock market] bubbles do not grow out of thin air. They have a solid basis in reality, but reality as distorted by misconception."[15]

—GEORGE SOROS, founder of the Quantum Fund

In retrospect, the absurdity of asset bubbles always seems obvious, but few people realize it in real time. One way to understand the dot-com delusion is to explain how and why the same flawed thinking was widely accepted by venture capitalists, entrepreneurs, investment bankers, sell-side analysts, members of the media, and individual investors. Almost everybody was blinded by the seemingly limitless upside. Profits were of little concern, and investors crafted new metrics to rationalize valuations once they became detached from reality. By the end of the frenzy, most investors hoped only for an early rise in price, which is the hallmark of an asset bubble. The remainder of this chapter explains how each participant in the dot-com supply chain contributed to the rise and fall of the bubble.

POINT OF INTEREST

Six Phases of an Asset Bubble

Americans have experienced multiple asset bubbles over the past 230 years, and they will experience many more in the future. Asset bubbles occur repeatedly because they tap into multiple deeply entrenched human instincts, including greed, envy, and herd behavior. Although every bubble seems unique, they tend to progress through several distinct phases.

1. **Emergence of a New Innovation with Mass Market Appeal**—Asset bubbles often form around a promising innovation that has the potential to radically transform society. Examples include railroads, consumer electronics, e-commerce, and blockchain technology. The mass market appeal is what makes them so frustratingly difficult to detect in real time. Bubbles only happen when a large number of people believe they are not happening, and the contagious excitement around groundbreaking new technologies makes them especially prone to irrational enthusiasm.

2. **Boasts from Early Investors Fuel the Mania**—Early investors often enjoy gargantuan returns, but many delude themselves into believing that their fortuitous early arrival is evidence of previously undiscovered genius. Emboldened by adulation in the media, they encourage new investors to join the stampede. This attracts new investors, which drives prices higher, increases their wealth, and reinforces their self-confidence.

3. **Late Adopters Inflate the Bubble**—Envious of the riches acquired by market gurus, latecomers join the frenzy. The flood of new capital inflates prices beyond even the most optimistic metrics of fundamental value. Battle-tested investment principles are discarded and replaced with new ones to

(continued)

rationalize the insanity. Dot-com companies no longer need to generate profits, they just need to acquire users.

4. **The Money Supply Contracts**—If a central bank exists, the mania eventually reaches a point at which inflated asset values and tight labor markets begin stoking inflation. Central banks react by tightening monetary policy, thereby reducing the money available to drive prices up further.

5. **Panic and Crash**—As the pool of new capital dries up, sellers begin to outnumber buyers. Before long, investors conclude that the innovation may not be as valuable as they thought. The pain of falling asset prices soon morphs into terror that total losses are possible, and the bubble bursts. In the aftermath, investors discover that many companies and newly established market gurus were at best wildly optimistic and at worst clueless grifters or outright frauds.

6. **Forget and Repeat**—Chastened investors pledge to never make the same mistake again. But John Kenneth Galbraith once warned that "for practical purposes, the financial memory should be assumed to last, at a maximum, no more than twenty years." Sure enough, within a decade or two, most investors fail to keep their promise.

Venture Capitalists

"What risk? If the company doesn't work out, we'll sell it for $150 million. If the company kind of works out, we'll sell it for $500 million, and if it really works, it'll be worth between $2 billion and $10 billion. Tell me how that's risk."[16]

—**GEOFFREY YANG**, cofounder, Redpoint Ventures

The Netscape IPO triggered a massive allocation of capital to VC funds. Well-established firms, such as Sequoia Capital and Kleiner Perkins, raised the largest funds in their history, but they did not come close to satisfying demand. The remaining capital was absorbed by newly formed VC firms, most of which lacked the experience, access, and judgment to succeed. Figures 27.1 and 27.2 show total new commitments to venture capital by year from 1990 to 2010.

The VC industry that existed in the late 1990s would be unrecognizable to Georges Doriot. ARD's primary objective was to provide capital to small businesses to enable them to compete with larger firms. Many VCs that popped up in the late 1990s aspired only to build companies that met the minimum qualifications of an IPO or high-priced acquisition in a market that had become completely untethered from reality. The fate of the company after the IPO was of little concern.

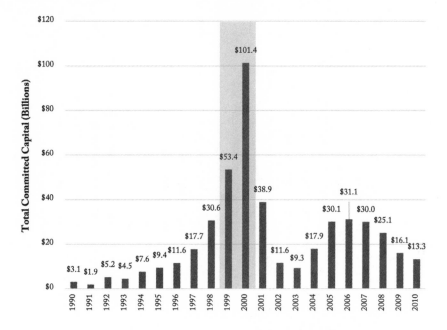

Figure 27.1: Total Committed Capital at U.S. VC Funds (1990–2010)[17]

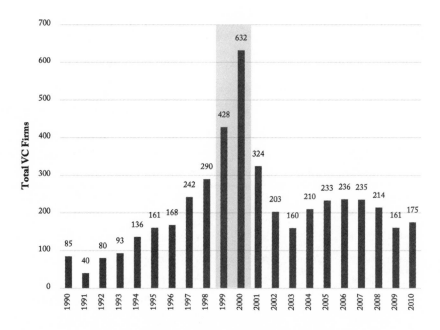

Figure 27.2: Total U.S. Venture Capital Firms (1990–2010)[18]

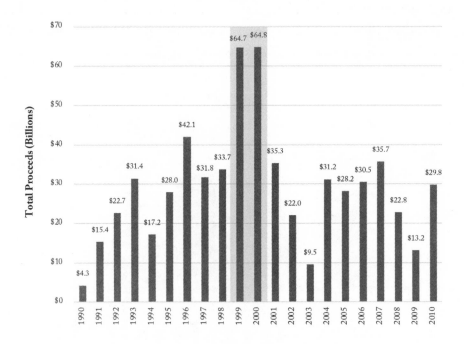

Figure 27.3: Total IPO Proceeds (Billions) (1990–2010)[19]

Investment Bankers

"Right now, it is hang on to the rocket ship and giggle all the way to the moon."[20]

—**MARK G. SHAFIR,** investment banker

In 1916, Charles Mitchell established salesmanship as a core competency of the investment banker. Over the next eighty years, many investment bankers honed this skill to sell corporate executives on a wide variety of transactions. Sometimes these transactions added value and other times they did not, but they always generated attractive fees. In the early 1990s, investment banking revenues were stagnant due to the end of the LBO boom. After witnessing the Netscape IPO, however, even inexperienced associates sensed that the dot-com mania was a gold mine. Investment bankers immediately descended on Sand Hill Road to secure access to the latest hot IPOs. A few years would pass before many venture-backed startups reached the point at which there was at least some possibility of generating a profit, but once they did, investment bankers were ready to sell the shares to the public—charging a mere 6 percent to 7 percent of proceeds for the privilege. Figure 27.3 shows the total proceeds of tech IPOs from 1990 to 2010.

Sell-Side Analysts

"Jack Grubman is the king of conflicted analysts. A strong case can be made that he used his picks to generate investment banking business for his firm and abused investor trust in his picks. He personifies the blurring of lines between investment banking and objective analysis."[21]

—JACOB H. ZAMANSKY, securities attorney

Brokerage firms employ sell-side analysts to evaluate companies and issue reports for use by the firm's brokers. These brokers, in turn, provide the reports as a value-added service to their brokerage clients. Internal policies and SEC regulations prohibit a firm's investment banking division from securing new business or boosting the price of securities by manipulating the content of sell-side analyst reports. The virtual separation of investment banking and sell-side analysts is often described as a Chinese Wall.

Investment bankers had the wind at their backs at the turn of the twenty-first century, but competition for new deals was intense, and bankers grasped for advantages to boost their business development prospects. Before long, some began piercing the Chinese Wall and leveraging the firm's sell-side analyst relationships to differentiate their investment banking services. A mere hint that investment bankers could persuade sell side analysts to initiate coverage and/or issue a favorable rating of a client's securities could be enough to win a new deal. The depth of the corruption varied by institution, but among the more prominent offenders were Jack Grubman (Salomon Smith Barney) and Henry Blodget (Merrill Lynch).

To be fair, these practices were not nearly as pervasive and egregious as they were in the late 1920s. Nevertheless, in April 2003, the SEC reached a record settlement with ten leading financial institutions. The firms admitted no wrongdoing, but agreeing to pay a $1.4 billion fine was a hefty act of contrition for a group of people with a clear conscience. It is impossible to know the extent to which conflicted analyst recommendations inflated a market that had plenty of assistance from other quarters, but it certainly did not serve as a corrective mechanism.[22]

POINT OF INTEREST

The Price of Assigning Blame Bluntly

The dot-com bubble was created by the shared misperception regarding the economic potential of the internet. While it is true that some individuals acted

(continued)

more irresponsibly than others, few understood how their actions combined with those of others to create a much larger systemic risk. One way to understand asset bubbles is to think of them like a manufacturing supply chain. Each component of the assembly line contributes to the production process, but individual actors often lack insight into the disastrous financial risks that pop out at the end. Millions of individuals contribute to the mass delusion, but most remain oblivious to the danger that they create together.

When asset bubbles collapse, people instinctively search for people to punish for having caused the crisis. While it is true that some individuals should be punished for particularly egregious behavior, systemic flaws and the collective behavior of millions of individuals are almost always the more important factors. After the dot-com collapse, sell-side analysts took the brunt of the blame, and several of them deserved to be held accountable. But the danger of isolating a few bad actors is that policymakers overlook other systemic risks that are less visible. These risks then become the seeds of future crises.

In the case of the dot-com bubble, there was less accountability for venture capital firms, investment bankers, overly enthusiastic members of the media, and individual investors. Moreover, other contributors, such as institutional investment plan trustees, were hardly even noticed. Overlooking the role of trustees was especially costly because they continue to engage in the same behaviors today. Allocations by trustees to alternative investments, such as venture capital, private equity, and hedge funds, far exceed levels that can be deployed responsibly. In recent years this has led to malinvestment in areas such as cryptocurrencies, cryptocurrency exchanges, and digital healthcare companies. Unfortunately, such behavior is likely to continue so long as trustees remain unaccountable.

Mutual Fund Managers

"This correction spells a once-in-a-lifetime opportunity . . . We're still in the bottom of the first inning."[23]

—ALBERTO VILAR, portfolio manager of the Amerindo Technology Fund (May 25, 2000)

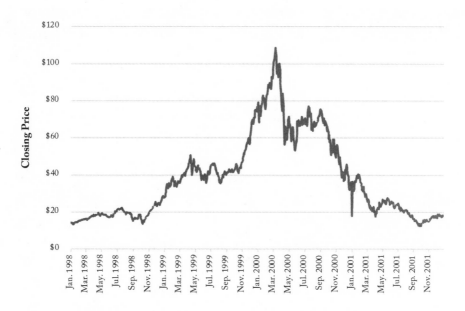

Figure 27.4: Closing Price of the Munder NetNet Fund (MNNAX)
(January 1, 1998–December 31, 2001)[24]

Portfolio managers of mutual funds often behave like a surfer who catches a monstrous wave, rides it to shore, and then boasts to spectators that they could have accomplished the same feat in a calm sea. Any portfolio manager with even a slight tilt toward technology stocks at the turn of the twenty-first century was bound to outperform broad market averages for a couple of years. But few predicted the intensity of the speculative fever, and even fewer exited their positions before the crash obliterated their gains. Making matters worse, once the tech wave began to crest, asset management companies began hawking an assortment of tech-focused funds, while simultaneously adding tech stocks to existing funds to attract more assets. At the end of 1999, there were fifty-six different tech-focused mutual funds. By the end of 2000, it had swollen to 123 funds.[25]

Tech-focused mutual funds ultimately suffered losses that matched or exceeded their gains. Figure 27.4 shows the rise and fall of the Munder NetNet Fund, which was launched in 1996. After a meteoric rise in 1999 and 2000, the Munder NetNet Fund returned to where it started. This outcome may not seem catastrophic to the untrained eye, but it was for many investors. Most entered the NetNet Fund in late 1999 and 2000, meaning that they experienced little of the upside but suffered a lot of the downside. Few investors in the NetNet Fund broke even, which mirrored the experience of most investors who entered tech funds during the dot-com mania.[26]

POINT OF INTEREST

The Perennial Peril of Chasing Performance

Many investors are unaware that returns reported by mutual funds do not accurately reflect the returns received by investors. This is because mutual funds report time-weighted returns which do not incorporate the impact of cash flows in and out of the fund. This is a fair method of reporting returns from the perspective of mutual fund managers because they cannot control investors' cash flows. The problem, however, is that from the investor's perspective, the timing of cash flows matters quite a bit. Consider a scenario in which a mutual fund generates a 35 percent return in Year 1 and a 7 percent return in Year 2. The mutual fund would report a time-weighted annualized return of 20.2 percent for the two-year period, but an investor's money-weighted return often differs substantially depending on when they invested in the fund. The table below shows a simple example of how two investors in the same fund have different money-weighted returns.

Table 27.1: Money-Weighted Returns of Two Sample Investors

	YEAR 1 INVESTMENT	YEAR 2 INVESTMENT	MONEY WEIGHTED RETURN	ENDING VALUE (YEAR 2)
Investor A	$50,000	$10,000	19.2%	$82,925
Investor B	$10,000	$50,000	11.2%	$67,945

Investor A and Investor B both experience money-weighted returns that are below the time-weighted return reported by the fund because they added to their investment after the fund's exceptional return in Year 1. Unfortunately, this scenario is not only possible, it is the norm. Just like investors tend to buy stocks at the peak and sell at the low, they tend to add money after a fund experiences a strong year and take money out after a bad year.

Each year, Morningstar publishes a report called *Mind the Gap*, which compares thousands of time-weighted and money-weighted returns of mutual funds. The document consistently reports that money-weighted returns lag time-weighted returns by a substantial amount. In the 2022 report, money-weighted returns lagged time-weighted returns by 170 basis points per year over the past ten years. The implications of this observation are dire. Not only are active managers unlikely to outperform inexpensive index funds, but investors are also likely to cause additional damage by poorly timing their cash flows into and out of funds.[27]

The Media

"You have to throw out all of the matrices and formulas and texts that existed before the Web. You have to throw them away because they can't make money for you anymore, and that is all that matters. We don't use price-to-earnings multiples anymore . . . If we talk about price-to-book, we have already gone astray. If we use any of what Graham and Dodd teach us, we wouldn't have a dime under management."[28]

—**JIM CRAMER,** host of *Mad Money* (February 29, 2000)

American media companies have a simple business model: they generate revenue by selling advertising space and subscriptions. The more attention they get, the more revenue. Over the past two hundred years, mediums through which the media has delivered news, opinions, and analyses have evolved, but the fundamental revenue model has changed little. One drawback of this model is that it creates a structural bias toward sensationalism. Sometimes, this benefits Americans by raising awareness to important issues that would otherwise be ignored. The downside, however, is that it often creates distorted perceptions of reality. In financial markets, sensationalism tends to amplify irrational behavior. That does not mean that there are no journalists who offer contrarian opinions. It just means that their voices tend to be drowned out by those who engage in sensationalism.

The behavior of the financial media during the dot-com bubble was consistent with this pattern, although the effects were likely more pronounced than they were in years past. The introduction of specialized programming, such as CNBC, and the launch of financial websites, made it especially difficult to ignore the hype.[29]

POINT OF INTEREST

The Subtle Signs of Insanity

Subtle signs of irrational exuberance often appear in the media just as an asset bubble enters the most intense phase. These signs are often overlooked because

(continued)

most people have already bought into the hype. One red flag is the introduction of new metrics to track whatever is driving the bubble. These often appear with little fanfare and are rarely noticed even after the bubble bursts. A few examples from history include:

- **Call Loan Metrics (March 1928)**—The Roaring Twenties entered the bubble phase in 1928. It was fueled by heavy use of margin debt funded by call loans. By October 1929, the use of call loans rose by nearly threefold relative to 1927, and most of it was provided by shadow banks and nonfinancial lenders. In March 1928, the *New York Times* recognized the critical role of call loans and began supplementing its financial market updates with a subtitle that summarized both overall market performance and the cost of call loans.

- **Nasdaq Composite Index (February 2000)**—On February 25, 2000, the business section of the *New York Times* listed four broad indicators of financial market activity. These included the Dow Jones Industrial Index, the Thirty-Year Treasury Yield, the euro, and the U.S. dollar. On February 26, 2000, the tech-heavy Nasdaq Composite Index was quietly added to the list. The closing price of the Nasdaq Composite on the prior day was 4,590.50. Only fourteen days later, the Nasdaq Composite peaked at 5,132.52 and then began its precipitous decline. Another fifteen years passed before the Nasdaq returned to its high in March 2000.[30]

- **Cryptocurrency Index (February 2021)**—On February 2, 2021, CNBC displayed links to eight broad-market indices at the top of its home page. These included U.S. stocks, European stocks, Asian stocks, bond markets, oil, gold, and foreign exchange. On February 3, 2021, CNBC quietly added a "Crypto" link. Bitcoin traded around $35,000 at the time. Six days later, *Business Insider* reported that CNBC's *Mad Money* host, Jim Cramer, stated that "every treasurer should be going to boards of directors and saying: should we put a small portion of our cash in Bitcoin?"[31] Michael Saylor, former CEO of MicroStrategy, took it one step further by instructing his treasurer to invest all the cash sitting on its balance sheet in Bitcoin. Also, just to squeeze out the last drop of insanity, he borrowed funds to add to MicroStrategy's Bitcoin position. The price of Bitcoin peaked around $69,000 in October 2021 and has steadily declined as this book went to print.

The American Public

"There is nothing so strong as the determination of vast numbers of public opinion . . . They do not want to sit outside and have their neighbors guess right and they guessed wrong. So, they go along, and the combined power of millions of people in doing that is infinitely stronger than anything that a combination of bankers can do."[32]

—**OTTO KAHN,** partner of Kuhn Loeb

The tech stock mania was encouraged by venture capitalists, investment bankers, sell-side analysts, mutual fund managers, and members of the media. But it would be a mistake to absolve individual investors of accountability. Human beings have many vices that impair financial decision-making. Topping the list are greed, envy, and the herd instinct. When people observe a neighbor rapidly acquiring wealth, they often succumb to all three vices simultaneously and blindly copy whatever it is that their neighbor is doing. By 1999, Americans had watched their neighbors amass enormous profits in a matter of days with each new tech IPO, and few could resist joining the frenzy.

Tech company shares entered the public markets at absurd valuations, only to increase by an average of nearly 60 percent on the first day of trading. The heavy lifting prior to tech IPOs was primarily the work of the previously mentioned perpetrators,

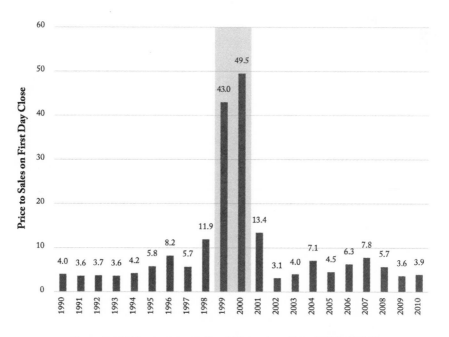

Figure 27.5: Price to Sales Ratio of Technology IPOs (1990-2010)[33]

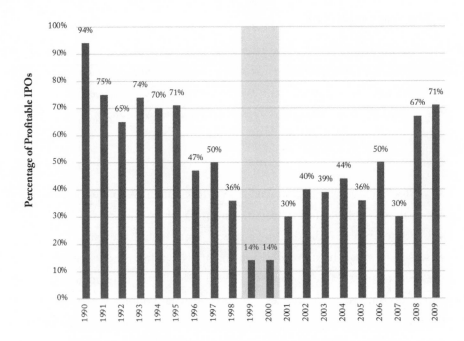

Figure 27.6: Percentage of Technology IPOs Reporting Positive Earnings
over Trailing 12 Months (1990–2009)[34]

but individual investors willingly followed and took the bubble to even greater heights.
Figure 27.5 and 27.6 shows the senselessness of the mania by revealing the absurdity of
the valuations of tech IPOs. Many should have known better. Many did know better
but participated anyway.

POINT OF INTEREST

The Risk of Excessive Regulation

*"The history of capitalism has been one of striking the right balance
between profit-driven market forces and the array of regulations and
laws necessary to harness these forces for the common good."*[35]

—Hank Paulson, former secretary of the Treasury

The understandable and appropriate response to a crisis is to identify and eliminate the problems that contributed to it. If reforms are thoughtfully constructed
and appropriately targeted, they strengthen the system to the benefit of all. The
securities laws of the 1930s are excellent examples. On the other hand, if regulations are poorly designed and excessively applied, the costs will exceed the

benefits. Many of the poorly conceived regulatory reforms passed during Lyndon Johnson's presidency fall squarely in this category.

History demonstrates that there are risks to underregulation and overregulation. In the financial industry, risks of underregulation are typically more visible to the public, especially in the immediate aftermath of a crisis. The risks of overregulation are often less obvious but can be very costly. One cost is the suppression of the type of innovation that has driven U.S. economic advancement for more than 230 years. The process of creative destruction works best when market forces hold individuals and businesses accountable when they fail to add value. If they are shielded from consequences, the incentive to innovate declines and society suffers from economic stagnation.

The vibrancy of the U.S. economy depends in large part on the willingness of its people to risk failure and then have the strength to recover. Regulations that strengthen the system are clearly beneficial, but when they go too far, they risk impairing a powerful competitive advantage on which America's future prosperity depends. Irresponsible financial institutions and financial professionals must be punished for the system to thrive, but individuals who provided them with the funds must also bear responsibility.

GREENSPAN PUTS A STOP TO IRRATIONAL EXUBERANCE

"How little, it will perhaps be agreed, was either original or otherwise remarkable about this history. Prices driven up by the expectation that they would go up, the expectations realized by the resulting purchases. Then the inevitable reversal of these expectations because of some seemingly damaging event or development or perhaps merely because the supply of intellectually vulnerable buyers was exhausted."[36]

—JOHN KENNETH GALBRAITH

Things that are too good to be true always reveal their true colors eventually. Every bubble that has happened in the past or will happen in the future ends the same way. In modern times, the collapse is typically triggered by the tightening of monetary policy. The mandate of the Federal Reserve is to balance its two competing objectives of price stability and maximum unemployment. The challenge is that data revealing the status of both is lagged, making it uncertain when a change in policy is necessary.

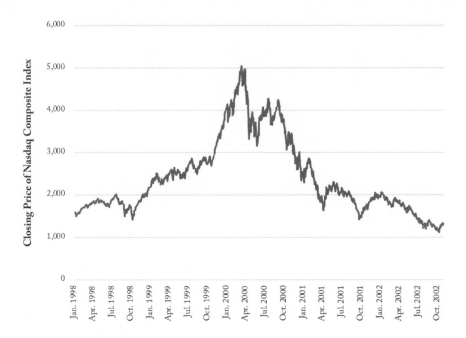

Figure 27.7: Daily Closing Price of the Nasdaq Composite Index (January 1, 1998–October 31, 2002)[37]

Making matters even worse, it can take anywhere from six to twenty-four months before adjustments are observed in the economy. These uncertainties make it difficult for Federal Reserve leaders to know exactly when adjustments are needed, how much they need to adjust, and when the adjustments have produced the desired effect.

In 1999, the Fed began tightening monetary policy, as speculation had reduced unemployment to levels at which inflation was becoming a threat. The Fed initiated a series of six, twenty-five-basis-point hikes on June 30, 1999, and then concluded the cycle with a fifty-basis-point hike on May 16, 2000. Over the next year, the tech bubble collapsed. Figure 27.7 shows the closing price of the tech-laden Nasdaq Composite Index from January 1, 1998, to October 31, 2002. The Nasdaq bottomed out at 1,114.11 on October 9, 2022.

The dot-com crash ruined many tech investors and triggered a recession. Relative to past recessions, however, the recession that began in March 2001 was relatively mild. Real GDP contracted by only 0.3 percent, unemployment peaked at 5.5 percent, and the contraction lasted for only eight months. The damage was less severe than many people feared because speculation was limited to a relatively small segment of the economy. This is also one of the reasons that it faded quickly from Americans' collective memory and lowered their resistance to the next bubble which appeared less than ten years later. In retrospect, the dot-com crash was merely an opening act to the main event of the twenty-first century.

Chapter 28

THE GREAT SHADOW
BANK RUN

*"The investing public is fascinated and captured by the great
financial mind. That fascination derives, in turn, from the scale of
the financial operations and the feeling that, with so much money
involved, the mental resources behind them cannot be less."*[1]

—JOHN KENNETH GALBRAITH

Americans have experienced many asset bubbles since 1790. Most ended in painful but tolerable recessions, but a few triggered deep depressions. One way to explain the potential destructiveness of bubbles is to separate them into two distinct types. Type One bubbles are primarily limited to a specific asset type. Distinct segments of the stock market are often (but not always) involved in Type One bubbles. The dot-com bubble in 2000 and cryptocurrency bubble in the 2020s are examples of Type One bubbles. Type Two bubbles can be thought of as credit bubbles in the sense that they involve large-scale participation of institutional lenders and financial institutions. These organizations both *facilitate* and *participate* in the speculation. Type Two bubbles are far more dangerous because when they implode, they destabilize the entire financial system. The bank runs that often accompany such events must be stopped promptly or deep depressions are all but certain to follow. The Global Financial Crisis (GFC) was a Type Two bubble—and a particularly dangerous one at that.[2]

There were many contributing factors to the GFC, but at the most fundamental level, it was a classic bank run. It caught nearly everybody by surprise because most people assumed that systemic bank runs were a thing of the past. After all, the Fed's powers were significantly strengthened in the 1930s to prevent systemic bank runs. But because these defenses worked for many decades, Americans became complacent. This allowed a massive shadow banking system to form beyond the reach of the Federal Reserve. By 2007, the shadow banking system was far larger than the commercial banking system. When the financial panic hit in 2008, the Federal Reserve stretched its powers as far as it could, but many financial institutions had ventured too far beyond the bounds of their authority.

This chapter outlines six problems that contributed to the GFC. The first problem was the speculative mania in the U.S. real estate market, which drove housing prices to unsustainable levels. The second was the massive expansion of the U.S. shadow banking system, which provided a continuous supply of capital to fuel the real estate bubble. The third was deterioration of mortgage lending standards, which enabled buyers with poor credit to purchase homes they could ill afford. This problem was especially acute in the subprime sector, which catered to the riskiest borrowers. The fourth problem was the compartmentalization of risk in the mortgage industry, which emboldened all participants in the mortgage securitization supply chain to take on reckless amounts of risk. Each participant discounted the risk because they believed that they could pass it on to the next participant in the supply chain. The fifth problem was the false sense of security provided by specialized insurance companies that insured mortgage-backed securities at levels that far exceeded their ability to pay. The sixth problem was the fragmented regulatory infrastructure in the United States. This proved especially problematic in the shadow banking system.[3]

In the summer of 2007, bank executives, government regulators, and central bankers began feeling the early symptoms of the crisis. Wholesale funding providers, such as money market funds and lenders in the tri-party repo market, abruptly withdrew funding from loan origination companies and investment banks. Over the next two years, a wave of bankruptcies swept the loan origination industry, and investment banks suddenly found their balance sheets laden with toxic mortgage-backed securities, collateralized debt obligations (CDOs), and other exotic derivatives that were unsellable at any price. Finally, insurance companies that had issued credit default swaps (CDSs) to protect investors from losses discovered that they lacked adequate reserves to satisfy mounting claims and margin calls. The combination of these factors allowed what initially appeared to be a significant but containable loss in the subprime mortgage sector to metastasize into the most intense global bank run in recorded history.

Fortunately, even the most severe financial panics can be stopped short of catastrophe if financial leaders, government regulators, central bankers, politicians, and the public set aside their differences and work quickly and collaboratively to stop the crisis before it spirals downward into a depression. The Dutch failed during the tulip mania in the 1630s; the French failed during the Mississippi bubble in 1720; and the United States failed after the Great Crash of 1929. But Americans and most of the developed world just barely succeeded in 2008 and 2009. Their success explains why the GFC was among the worst financial panics in U.S. history but only produced a relatively mild depression in comparison to the Great Depression of the 1930s. This outcome was possible because of the heroic efforts of people who worked around the clock for months on end to bring the financial system back from the edge of the abyss. Despite being vilified by politicians and the media, the selfless efforts of people like Hank Paulson, Tim Geithner, Ben Bernanke, George W. Bush, and Barack Obama spared the world from horrors that often lay at the bottom of major depressions.

PROBLEM #1: SPECULATION IN THE U.S. REAL ESTATE MARKET

"I define a speculative bubble as a situation in which news of price increases spurs investor enthusiasm, which spreads by psychological contagion from person to person, in the process amplifying stories that might justify the price increases and bringing in a larger and larger class of investors, who, despite doubts about the real value of an investment, are drawn to it partly through envy of others' successes and partly through a gambler's excitement."[4]

—ROBERT J. SHILLER, economist

At the core of every bubble lies a simple but widely accepted belief that is later revealed to be tragically flawed. In the 1920s, Americans believed that the stock market would always rise, so they saw little risk in using margin debt to leverage their positions. Few investors appreciated that it is this very belief that sits at the foundation of the most dangerous asset bubbles.

In 1992, the famed economist Hyman P. Minsky published a paper entitled "The Financial Instability Hypothesis," in which he explored the impact of debt on financial systems and asset bubbles. Minsky identified three distinct phases of debt-fueled asset bubbles, which he defined as hedge, speculative, and Ponzi. In the hedge phase, investors use debt conservatively, ensuring that their income is sufficient to cover interest and principal payments. In the speculative phase, investors are more

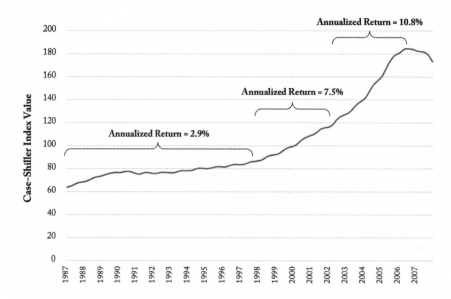

Figure 28.1: S&P Case-Shiller U.S. National Home Price Index (Monthly)
(January 1, 1987–December 1, 2007)[5]

aggressive. They still cover the interest on the debt, but they lack the required cash flow to pay down the principal, which forces them to renew the loans upon maturity. Finally, in the Ponzi phase, investors can neither cover interest nor principal payments. Their entire investment thesis rests on the hope that they can quickly sell their investments at higher prices, pay off the loan, and keep the profit. If they fail to find a buyer at a higher price, they face losses and/or financial ruin. Ponzi markets always collapse eventually because price gains can only be sustained when new investors enter the market. Eventually, the supply of new investors is exhausted and the bubble implodes.[6]

In the early 2000s, the U.S. real estate bubble moved quickly through the final two phases of the Minsky framework. Speculation was fueled by the simple but false belief that U.S. real estate prices had never declined on a national level. Many Americans projected this myth forward and dismissed the possibility of future declines. This belief was demonstrably untrue—real estate prices had declined on a national level on several occasions—but the myth provided Americans with the confidence they needed to drive real estate prices to absurd levels. Figure 28.1 shows the rising price of residential real estate using the S&P Case-Shiller Index from 1987 to 2007. The graph marks the rough transitions between the hedge, speculative, and Ponzi phases.

POINT OF INTEREST

The Lost Memories of American Real Estate Bubbles

"There is no national price bubble [in real estate].
Never has been; never will be."[7]

—David Lereah, chief economist,
National Association of Realtors (September 2004)

The above statement from David Lereah was clearly incorrect, and this is not only in retrospect. Chapters 3 and 4 detailed the real estate crashes that accompanied the depressions in the 1820s and 1840s. Moreover, even if his statement were true, the belief that it could never happen in the future would likely have made it a self-fulfilling prophecy.

During the early 2000s, members of the real estate profession and media reinforced the myth that real estate prices had never fallen on a national level. For the five-year period preceding Lereah's statement, housing prices increased at an unsustainable, annualized rate of 9.4 percent per year. Reassurances from market experts convinced Americans that there was little risk of loss.

The myth of ever-rising real estate prices encouraged all sorts of reckless behavior. Americans purchased homes with little, if any, money down. Lenders relaxed underwriting standards or ignored them entirely. Investment banks purchased mortgages aggressively and converted them into complex, securitized products that hid enormous risks. Specialized insurance companies such as AIG used overly optimistic underwriting standards to issue policies to protect investors from defaults. Finally, money market funds and tri-party repo counterparties provided funding for these activities, believing that their collateral was safe.

At the core of these errors was the simple but false narrative that the U.S. real estate market had never meaningfully declined on a national level. Americans soon discovered that real estate prices *had* declined previously on a national level and would do so again.

PROBLEM #2: THE RETURN OF SHADOW BANKING

Asset bubbles inflate to dangerous levels when speculation is fueled by massive amounts of debt financing. Bubbles are especially hazardous when shadow banks supply a large share of the loans because they lack access to the Federal Reserve's lender-of-last-resort facilities. This is precisely what happened in the early 2000s. First, government-sponsored entities (GSEs) purchased or guaranteed trillions of dollars of mortgages, a growing percentage of which involved subprime loans.[8] Second, investment banks relied heavily on overnight repos and the issuance of short-term, asset-backed commercial paper to fund their mortgage securitization businesses. These operations were often handled in off–balance sheet special investment vehicles (SIVs), which made the risks less apparent to regulators. Third, money market funds had assets under management of more than $3 trillion, yet they were highly vulnerable to a run because they lacked FDIC insurance and access to the Federal Reserve as a lender of last resort. Finally, specialized insurance companies underwrote credit default swaps that could force payouts that far exceeded their reserves.

POINT OF INTEREST

Fannie Mae and Freddie Mac Leveraged to the Hilt

Recollections of the GFC often focus disproportionately on the near collapse of America's largest investment banks, but the two GSEs Fannie Mae and Freddie Mac posed a much more significant systemic risk. Fannie Mae was established in 1938 to create a secondary market for mortgages. Mortgage originators sold mortgages to Fannie Mae, which enabled them to free up capacity to issue new mortgages. In 1970, Congress established Freddie Mac to further expand the market for secondary mortgages and introduce competitive pressure on Fannie Mae.[9]

The business model for the two GSEs was rather simple. The firms operated as quasi-private corporations but with support from the federal government. Most importantly, they had an implicit guarantee of their debt, which enabled them to issue debt at rates only slightly higher than U.S. Treasuries. This, in turn, enabled them to purchase mortgages from mortgage originators at higher prices, thus reducing the interest rates offered to borrowers.[10]

The problem with Fannie and Freddie is that their total mortgage exposure increased dramatically during the early 2000s, and it was almost entirely funded with debt rather than equity. By the end of 2007, Fannie and Freddie had total liabilities that were supported by shareholder equity of only 1.51 percent and 1.74 percent, respectively. The slightest increase in default rates would wipe out their equity and test the government's implicit guarantee of their debt.[11]

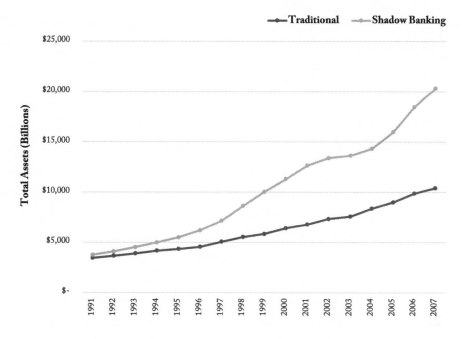

Figure 28.2: Total Assets of Commercial and Shadow Banks (Billions)
(January 1, 1991–December 31, 2007)[12]

By 2007, shadow banks had liabilities that were more than double that of the commercial banking system (Figure 28.2). In fact, the shadow banking system in 2007 was much larger than it was in the late 1920s. The total amount of call loans outstanding in September 1929 was an estimated 8 percent of GDP. In December 2007, the two most problematic sectors of the U.S. shadow banking system, the GSEs and asset-backed securities (ABS) issuers, had total liabilities exceeding $12 trillion, which was approximately 80 percent of GDP. The shadow banking system in the early 2000s resembled that of the trust companies in the early 1900s, and the subsequent bank runs resembled the ones that occurred during the Panic of 1907.

The most unbreakable rule of fractional reserve banking systems is that they will *always* suffer bank runs eventually in the absence of critical protections, such as having a lender of last resort, strong banking regulations, and deposit insurance. Shadow banking systems lack all three, which makes bank runs inevitable and much more dangerous. Americans discounted this possibility in the 2000s in part because it had been so long since they had suffered a systemic run on the banking system. The last major wave of bank runs had occurred in the 1930s, and most Americans assumed they were a thing of the past. The entire world of finance was complacent at the turn of the twenty-first century, which allowed a massive expansion of the shadow banking system to re-create conditions that existed before the Federal Reserve was established.

The system was ripe for a run, and the fragmented and outdated regulatory system was incapable of stopping it.

PROBLEM #3: DETERIORATION OF MORTGAGE UNDERWRITING STANDARDS

By 2004, U.S real estate prices were detached from reality, yet few Americans feared the possibility of price declines. Demand for new mortgage loans only accelerated, and commercial banks and private mortgage lenders relaxed standards to accommodate demand. Some lenders were motivated only by greed, but many simply suffered from the same delusion as borrowers. They too believed that housing prices would never decline meaningfully on a national level. Subprime mortgage loans, which were issued to the riskiest borrowers, were the biggest growth sector by 2004. Subprime lenders reasoned that even if the loans defaulted, the liability would be fully covered by the sale of the property. This assumption inspired the approval of loan applications that would have been instantly rejected only a few years earlier.

POINT OF INTEREST

Subprime's Deadliest Assassin: The NINJA Loan

Subprime borrowers were individuals who had one or more materially negative events that compromised their ability to obtain a traditional mortgage loan. Lending to subprime borrowers was risky but perhaps justifiable in certain cases. But before long, the most aggressive lenders even viewed the criteria for subprime lending to be too restrictive, and they began issuing loans using no standards whatsoever. As early as 2001, HCL Finance began offering loans to applicants who had "no income, no job," and "no assets." In March 2007, these loans were referred to as NINJA loans.[13]

The only thing more terrifying than the fact that these loans existed was the fact that they were sufficiently common to warrant a name. The only way borrowers could afford such a loan was if they flipped the property for a profit before their mortgage payments forced them into default. In some cases, borrowers could not even afford to make the first payment. NINJA loans were the most extreme form of reckless lending, but they were symbolic of the lax lending standards that prevailed during the early 2000s.

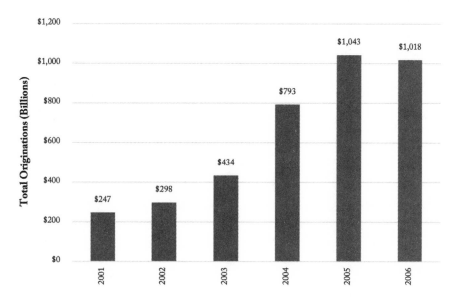

Figure 28.3: Total Subprime Mortgage Originations (Billions) (2001–2006)[14]

Subprime lending was made much worse by the backing of GSEs. This practice can be traced to March 10, 1994, when Fannie Mae launched "Impact 2000." The initiative was an ambitious effort to make homes more affordable to underserved populations. Many Impact 2000 initiatives focused on education and outreach, but Fannie Mae also relaxed underwriting standards. Initially, this only entailed lowering down payment requirements, but then on September 30, 1999, Fannie launched a pilot program to underwrite subprime mortgages. In a frighteningly accurate assessment of the risks, *New York Times* reporter Stephen A. Holmes wrote: "In moving, even tentatively, into this new area of lending, Fannie Mae is taking on significantly more risk, which may not pose any difficulties during flush economic times. But the government-subsidized corporation may run into trouble in an economic downturn, prompting a government rescue similar to that of the savings and loan industry in the 1980s." Holmes's warning was ignored, as times were good at the turn of the twenty-first century, and Fannie experienced no immediate repercussions. After weathering the brief recession in 2001 with acceptable losses, Fannie extended its foray into subprime mortgages, and Freddie Mac adopted similar practices. With the backing of the GSEs, private mortgage companies were free to lend aggressively to subprime borrowers. Figure 28.3 shows the growth of subprime mortgage originations from 2001 to 2006.[15]

The growing volume of subprime mortgages was not the only problem. By 2004, subprime borrowers had shifted into riskier products. Not only did this suggest that the GSEs were taking on additional underwriting risk, but it also suggested that borrowers

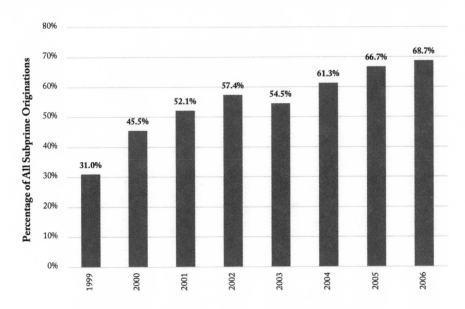

Figure 28.4: Percentage of Subprime Mortgage Originations
Using 2/28 ARM Methodology (1999–2006)[16]

were motivated by speculation rather than home ownership. Figure 28.4 shows the percentage of subprime mortgage originations using a 2/28 adjustable-rate methodology. This structure fixed the interest rate at a temporarily low level for two years, and then reset at a higher rate for the remaining twenty-eight years. All else being equal, such mortgages were preferred by speculators who purchased properties with the intent to flip them for a profit within a year or two. Consistent with Minsky's Ponzi phase, many borrowers lacked the cash flow to pay the interest and principal for an extended period.

PROBLEM #4: COMPARTMENTALIZATION OF RISK IN THE MORTGAGE MARKET

In the late 1970s, profit margins at savings and loans banks were under pressure as the gap closed between the interest rate paid to depositors and the interest collected on mortgage loans. Lew Ranieri, a trader at Salomon Brothers, devised a creative solution by pooling hundreds of mortgage loans and creating a bond-like security that could be sold to investors. Dubbed the "mortgage-backed security," this technique enabled savings and loans (as well as other mortgage loan originators) to increase loan origination volume by removing loans from their balance sheet and freeing up capital to issue new loans. The mortgage-backed security also benefited homeowners. The creation of a vibrant secondary market for mortgages allowed banks to increase their lending capacity, which then put downward pressure on interest rates. But there was a dark side to the securitization business. In prior years, most mortgages remained on banks' balance sheets, which created a natural incentive for loan officers to apply rigorous underwriting standards because the banks suffered the consequences of delinquencies. But as lenders increasingly originated mortgages with the intent to sell them in the secondary market, lending standards eroded. Further, specialized companies soon emerged that engaged only in mortgage origination, and their revenue models depended primarily on volume rather than quality of mortgage originations.[17]

The growth of the securitized mortgage market created a windfall for investment banks. The banks purchased mortgages, pooled them together into securities, and then sold the securities to investors such as investment managers, money market funds, and pension plans. Investment banks also discovered a substantial demand in international markets, as the glut of savings forced investors to find new opportunities to boost returns. As the market grew, investment banks created increasingly complex products to satisfy specific investor demands. For example, they created collateralized debt obligations (CDOs), which pooled different types of asset-backed securities (i.e., mortgages, auto loans, credit card debt, etc.) to offer greater diversification of cash flows. They also created different tranches of securities that varied the degree of investment risk from factors such as borrower defaults and prepayments. They even combined tranches of different CDOs to create synthetic CDOs, referred to as a "CDO-Squared."[18]

POINT OF INTEREST

Past Solutions Become Future Problems[19]

An enduring principle of financial history is that solutions to past crises often become the seeds of future ones. As an example, the Glass-Steagall Act of 1933 included a little-known provision known as Regulation Q. The provision capped interest rates paid to depositors by banks and thrifts to 6 percent per year. The objective was to limit competition for depositors and thereby stabilize the deposit bases of the banking system. Regulation Q was a nonissue for a long time because interest rates remained low for several decades.[20]

In the 1970s, high rates of inflation caused investors to demand interest rates that were higher than the Regulation Q cap of 6 percent. At the same time, brokerage firms were seeking new revenue streams, as the SEC abolished fixed commissions on stock trades in 1975. Several large brokerage and asset management firms, such as Merrill Lynch and Fidelity, launched money market funds

(continued)

that offered higher interest rates to investors but without the protection of the FDIC and Federal Reserve.[21]

Over the next thirty years, money market assets increased from $3.4 billion in the first quarter of 1977 to more than $3.1 trillion by the fourth quarter of 2007. Common securities found in money market fund portfolios were asset-backed commercial paper and repos. Thus, money market funds became a major source of credit for investment banks issuing mortgage-backed securities and securitized products in the years prior to the GFC. The problem with these loans is that they were short term. Asset-backed commercial paper maturities ranged from two weeks to nine months, while repos were often renewable daily. This was not a problem if money market assets were stable or growing, but if they contracted, a major funding source for investment banks could evaporate overnight.[22]

In the 1980s, commercial banks and thrifts lobbied Congress for legislation to restore their competitiveness with money market funds. One key piece of legislation was the Garn–St. Germain Act, which allowed commercial banks to issue interest-only and adjustable-rate mortgages. This helped banks manage their interest rate risk, but it also gave real estate borrowers access to riskier loans. During the years leading up to the GFC, these loans were issued recklessly by lenders and used inappropriately by speculators.[23]

Reliance on Wholesale Funding

One way to understand the mortgage industry in the early 2000s is to use the manufacturing supply chain analogy again. Loan originators created the raw materials in the form of mortgage loans. Issuers, such as the GSEs and investment banks, purchased the raw materials and converted them into mortgage-backed securities and structured products. Finally, investors purchased the final products. The originators and issuers required substantial amounts of capital to fund their inventory. The problem, however, was that many of them were not members of the Federal Reserve system and therefore could not rely on FDIC-insured deposits as a funding source. Instead, they relied heavily on short-term wholesale funding, which consisted primarily of asset-backed commercial paper and short-term tri-party repo contracts. Figure 28.5 shows the rapid growth in asset-backed commercial paper in 2005 to 2007.

Most people assumed that wholesale funding providers had little exposure to bank runs because they were collateralized by mortgages and mortgage-backed securities held in inventory. But this assumption was not much different than the assumption

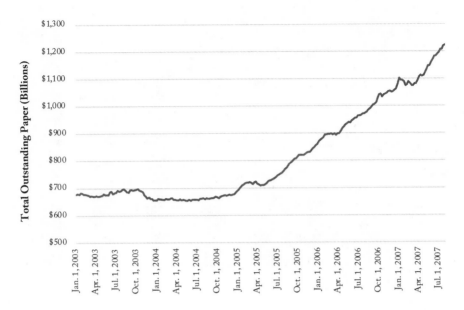

Figure 28.5: Total Outstanding Asset-Backed Commercial Paper (Billions)
(January 1, 2003–July 1, 2007)[24]

made by the shadow banks that provided call loans in 1929. As the mortgage securitization industry grew, the risks of a bank run–like event intensified, but few participants realized it because they only saw the risk in their segment of the supply chain. Loan originators were willing to relax their lending standards because most loans were sold off to issuers of securitized products. Issuers of securitized products discounted the risks embedded in their inventory because they planned to offload the risk to investors. Finally, investors discounted the risks of structured products because they trusted the issuers. But even if they did not trust the issuers, there were two additional participants in the supply chain that provided the assurance they needed.

PROBLEM #5: A FALSE SENSE OF SECURITY

The fundamental thesis of mortgage securitization is that the risk posed by any single loan can be substantially reduced by assembling a large, diversified portfolio of loans. If a borrower defaults, the impact on the portfolio is relatively immaterial. Securities issuers believed that they could provide added protection to investors by creating tranches of securities from a pool of loans. Those in the senior-most tranches received a lower return in exchange for greater protection from default and prepayment risk. The problem with these "structured products" was that it was too time consuming and complicated for investors to evaluate hundreds of individual loans in a pool, much less model out the impact of various economic scenarios on

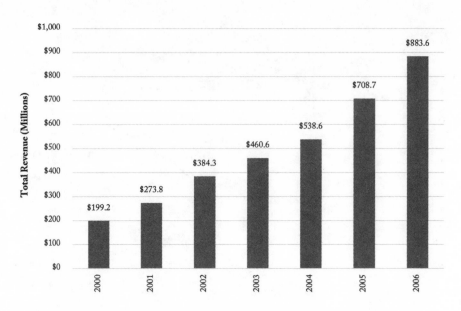

Figure 28.6: Total Structured Products Ratings Revenue—Moody's Investors Services (Millions) (2000-2006)[25]

default rates and prepayments. Issuers addressed the problem by soliciting ratings from the three major U.S. rating agencies: Moody's, Standard & Poor's, and Fitch. This seemed sensible because the rating agencies had decades of experience evaluating credit risk of corporate bonds. Few appreciated that the complexity of structured products required analytical skills that were well beyond the competency of ratings analysts—or any human being whatsoever in many cases. Nevertheless, the ratings agencies aggressively pursued contracts with structured product issuers. Figure 28.6 shows the total revenue of Moody's Investors Services from its structured product business unit. For the six-year period ending December 31, 2007, revenue increased at an annualized rate of 28 percent per year, while Moody's other business units increased at 19 percent per year.

The use of ratings agencies worked well for the senior-most tranches of securitized products, but issuers often struggled to sell the riskier mezzanine and equity tranches. If the agencies agreed to rate these tranches at all, they often received poor ratings. To alleviate investors' fears, issuers tapped specialized insurers such as MBIA, Ambac, and the financial products division of AIG to issue credit default swaps (CDS). Under a CDS contract, investors paid a premium to the insurer in exchange for the right to "swap" the security if it defaulted. In 2001, the total notional value of CDS was approximately $910 billion. By 2007, it had ballooned to $62.2 trillion. Figure 28.7 shows the net value of CDS from 2000 to 2007. The CDS industry itself constituted a massive risk that was ripe for a crisis.

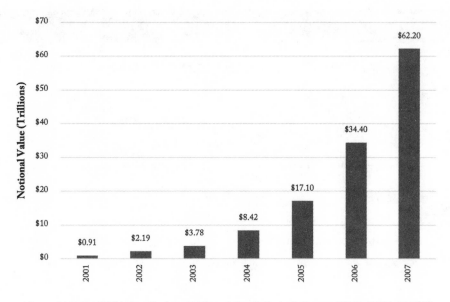

Figure 28.7: Total Mid-Year Notional Value of Credit Default Swaps (CDS) (2001–2007)[26]

PROBLEM #6: FRAGMENTED AND OUTDATED REGULATORY INFRASTRUCTURE

The financial regulatory infrastructure of the U.S. failed to evolve adequately to mitigate risks that had steadily accumulated in the financial system for decades. This deficiency was especially problematic in the shadow banking system. For example, money market funds and brokerage firms, which held trillions of dollars of assets, were primarily regulated by the SEC. But the SEC was primarily tasked with regulating securities issuance and trading. Evaluating the safety of the firms and systemic risks in the industry was beyond the SEC's mandate. Another example was regulation of GSEs. The Office of Federal Housing Enterprise Oversight (OFHEO) oversaw Fannie and Freddie, but regulation was comparatively weak relative to that of the Federal Reserve. Finally, the insurance giant AIG was the most dramatic example of a shadow bank operating outside the Federal Reserve's field of vision. To begin with, as an insurance company, AIG was regulated by state law. Making matters worse, CDSs fell in a regulatory gray area. This allowed AIG to issue nearly $500 billion of CDSs with very little oversight and without posting any collateral. When the value of these assets collapsed, a massive hole suddenly opened on AIG's balance sheet. The company ultimately required more than $180 billion of financial support to avoid what would have been a catastrophic bankruptcy.[27]

POINT OF INTEREST

The Twenty-First Century Associates

"The old political reality was that we always won, we took no prisoners . . . We used to, by virtue of our peculiarity, be able to write, or have written, rules that worked for us."[28]

—Daniel Mudd, former COO of Fannie Mae (2004)

In the late 1800s, Collis Huntington, Leland Stanford, Mark Hopkins, and Charles Crocker (i.e., the Associates) ensured favorable treatment of the Central Pacific and their corrupt construction and financing company by showering U.S. congressmen with bribes. Although records were conveniently lost, it is estimated that the Central Pacific budgeted $500,000 per year in political bribes, which is roughly equivalent to $15 million per year in 2023.[29]

Bribery was illegal for Fannie Mae and Freddie Mac but lobbying and making hefty contributions to political action committees (PACs) were not. Between 1999 and 2008, Fannie and Freddie spent a total of $164 million on lobbying fees, and its employees contributed another $15 million to PACs. This amounted to roughly $17.9 million per year, which is comparable to the Central Pacific's bribery budget. Not only did these contributions relieve Fannie and Freddie of aggressive regulation, but it also made it difficult for Hank Paulson to challenge the leadership of the companies during the GFC.[30]

THE DECK IS STACKED FOR A PERFECT PANIC

By 2007, the U.S. real estate market and the shadow banking system that supported it had become a gigantic house of cards. Figure 28.8 shows how borrowers, loan originators, structured product issuers, and investors had overextended themselves. It also illustrates how members of the media, GSEs, ratings agencies, and specialized insurers reinforced the false sense of security that existed on each level. At the foundation of the house of cards lay the false but widely accepted belief that housing prices would never decline meaningfully at the national level. The U.S. was primed for a financial panic and run on the fragile shadow banking system. The first cracks in the foundation appeared in July 2006 when real estate prices stopped rising.

Figure 28.8: The Twenty-First Century House of Cards

The House of Cards Comes Down

"Prospective subprime losses were clearly not large enough on their own to account for the magnitude of the crisis. Rather, the system's vulnerabilities, together with gaps in the government's crisis-response tool kit, were the principal explanations of why the crisis was so severe and had such devastating effects on the broader economy."[31]

—BEN BERNANKE, former chairman of the Federal Reserve

In 2001, the combined impact of the dot-com crash and the 9/11 terrorist attacks pushed the U.S. into a recession. The Federal Reserve responded by maintaining an accommodative monetary policy for several years. By early 2004, unemployment had returned to levels consistent with the presumed natural rate, and the Fed began a series of gradual interest rate increases. They moved cautiously because deflation was viewed as a greater threat to the economy at the time. They were also concerned with speculation in the real estate market, but it was not considered particularly severe because

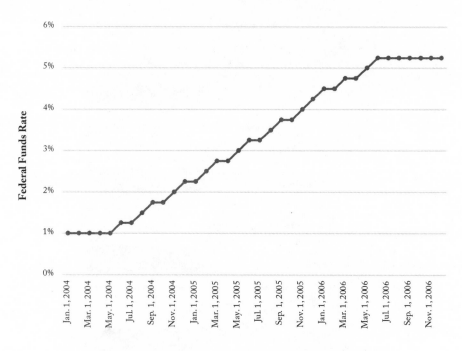

Figure 28.9: Federal Funds Rate (January 1, 2004–December 31, 2006)[32]

the risk appeared to primarily involve subprime mortgages in especially speculative markets, such as Florida and California. The Fed was also comforted by the fact that subprime mortgages were still, at the time, a reasonably small segment of the market. On June 30, 2004, the Fed began a series of seventeen consecutive twenty-five-basis-point increases to the federal funds rate (Figure 28.9). Immediately after the Fed made its final rate increase on June 29, 2006, phase one of the GFC began.[33]

Phase One: Subprime Borrowers Abandon Ship

On June 30, 2006, the S&P Case-Shiller Index hit 184.6, marking the top of the U.S. real estate bubble. Over the next year, prices declined modestly but then began falling rapidly in the summer of 2007 (Figure 28.10).

As prices declined, subprime borrowers entered delinquency in record numbers. In 2007, a sample of subprime loans reported delinquencies of 37.1 percent, which was a nearly fourfold increase from the 10.2 percent rate recorded in 2003. A disturbing number of borrowers failed to even make their first payment. Within a few months, many delinquencies transitioned into outright default, forcing lenders to foreclose and reclaim properties. Contrary to lenders' expectations, many properties had little equity, and those that did were soon underwater as real estate prices collapsed. Subprime lenders were completely unprepared to absorb the losses.[34]

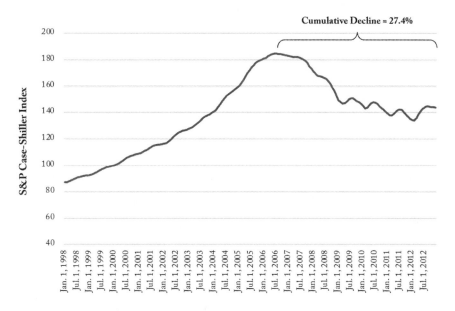

Figure 28.10: S&P Case-Shiller Index, (January 1, 1998–December 31, 2012)[35]

Phase Two: Bankruptcies Sweep the Subprime Mortgage Origination Industry

On February 7, 2007, New Century Financial announced that it would restate earnings for the prior three quarters. One month later, the company announced it would not be filing its 2006 annual report on time. These announcements triggered a series of margin calls from wholesale funding providers. Unable to obtain capital for new loans, New Century ceased processing loan applications in March 2007 and then filed for Chapter 11 bankruptcy on April 2, 2007.[36]

New Century was not the first subprime lender to fail, but it spooked investors because it was among the country's largest subprime lenders. Wholesale funding providers abruptly tightened collateral requirements and withdrew funding from subprime mortgage originators. Simultaneously, purchasers of whole loans, such as investment banks, demanded compensation for previously purchased loans that failed to meet contractual performance thresholds. The sudden withdrawal of wholesale funding and growing losses on subprime mortgages triggered a wave of bankruptcies. By the summer of 2007, the market for subprime loans had all but evaporated; home price declines began accelerating; and the biggest of all the dominos in the mortgage securitization supply chain began to shake.[37]

Phase Three: A Run on the Investment Banks

"When the music stops, in terms of liquidity, things will be complicated. But as long as the music is playing, you've got to get up and dance. We're still dancing."[38]

—**CHARLES PRINCE,** former CEO of Citigroup

On August 8, 2007, BNP Paribas suspended redemptions for three of its hedge funds. Each fund had substantial exposure to U.S. subprime mortgages, and portfolio managers could no longer value the portfolio because the market for many securities had completely evaporated. Several financial institutions, such as Bear Stearns, also reported losses from subprime exposure earlier in the year, but the failure of the BNP Paribas hedge funds is generally regarded as the first casualty in the GFC.[39]

Like a game of musical chairs, the room suddenly went silent on August 8. And when the music stopped, many of the nation's largest investment banks were caught holding massive inventories of subprime loans and structured products that awaited sale to investors. Much of the exposure was hidden because structured products were created by off–balance sheet special investment vehicles (SIVs). The SIVS were financed by asset-backed commercial paper and tri-party repos, which were constantly rolled over on a monthly (or even daily) basis. But after the announcement by BNP Paribas, demand for asset-backed commercial paper evaporated, and repo funding became scarcer and more expensive (Figure 28.11). In addition, with no buyers for any security that appeared even remotely affected by subprime defaults, the value of the assets in SIV inventories collapsed. This forced investment banks to backstop their SIVs with internal loans or bring SIV assets back on to their balance sheets, which resulted in a cascade of multibillion-dollar write-downs.

By September 2007, regulators and Federal Reserve leaders were alarmed by the rapid contraction of wholesale credit markets, but they did not yet fear a broader financial crisis. Despite recent growth, subprime still constituted a reasonably small share of the total mortgage market, and it seemed unlikely to trigger a major financial panic. But the problem was not the market size; it was that structured products were so complex that it was impossible to quantify their exposure to subprime. Rather than trying to gauge their risk, investors shunned any security that was even remotely associated with subprime. This was reminiscent of depositors fleeing any bank remotely associated with Augustus Heinze in October 1907. Comparing the reaction to an outbreak of mad cow disease, Hank Paulson stated, "Only a small portion of the available beef supply may be affected, but the infection is so deadly that consumers avoid all beef."[40]

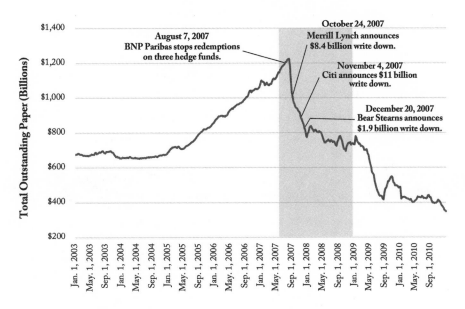

Figure 28.11: Total Outstanding Asset-Backed Commercial Paper
(January 1, 2003–December 31, 2010)[41]

The Federal Reserve leadership did not yet see the magnitude of the problem, but they initiated a series of precautionary interest rate cuts and reinforced their commitment to serve as a lender of last resort. On September 18, 2007, the Fed reduced the federal funds rate by fifty basis points. But the crisis continued to worsen, and the Fed passed a series of additional cuts that took the federal funds rate down by an additional 275 basis points over a seven-month period. The Fed's aggressive action failed to contain the panic, and the consequences of the run on shadow banks were becoming more dire.

Spring to Fall of 2008

On March 17, 2008, J.P. Morgan acquired Bear Stearns at a fire sale price. The demise of Bear Stearns can be traced to August 2007 when it announced the closure of two hedge funds with subprime exposure. Bear's financial performance deteriorated further in the fourth quarter of 2007, resulting in the company's first ever quarterly loss. Losses continued to mount in 2008, and by early March, wholesale funding providers lost confidence in the firm. On Thursday, March 13, Secretary of the Treasury Hank Paulson was informed that Bear Stearns was experiencing severe liquidity problems. In his memoirs, Paulson recalled, "Before Bob [Steel] finished, I knew Bear Stearns was dead . . . My years on Wall Street had taught me this brutal truth: when financial institutions die, they die fast." To avoid a catastrophic bankruptcy, the Federal Reserve invoked Section 13(3) of the Federal Reserve Act and approved an emergency loan to

J.P. Morgan, which was then used indirectly to give Bear Stearns an additional twenty-eight days of liquidity. It was clear, however, that Bear Stearns would be lucky to survive another week. After a weekend of frantic negotiations, J.P. Morgan announced the acquisition of Bear Stearns before the market opened on Monday, March 17. Shareholders were appalled by the purchase price of $2 per share, which was a fraction of the $171.51 per share that Bear had commanded fourteen months earlier.[42]

POINT OF INTEREST

Section 13(3) of the Federal Reserve Act

In 1932, Congress amended the Federal Reserve Act to expand its lender-of-last-resort powers. Known as Section 13(3), the provision authorized the Federal Reserve to provide emergency liquidity to both financial institutions and nonfinancial institutions that were not members of the Federal Reserve system. Prior to the GFC, these powers had not been used since the mid-1930s, and even then, they were used sparingly.

In December 2007, the Federal Reserve provided liquidity to a vast array of financial institutions by invoking Section 13(3). But even these expanded powers prevented the Fed from stopping the run on the shadow banking system in the Fall of 2008. Section 13(3) permitted emergency lending only if loans were backed by adequate collateral. Institutions unable to provide adequate collateral remained outside of the Fed's reach. In such cases, the Fed and other regulatory agencies sought alternative means to prevent systemically important financial institutions from failing. In September 2008, these alternatives finally reached their limits, and Lehman Brothers was forced to file for bankruptcy.

The run on Bear Stearns marked the beginning of the most perilous phase of the GFC. The Fed responded by cutting the federal funds rate by seventy-five basis points on the day after the Bear Stearns announcement, but it did little to help members of the shadow banking system. Instead, the Federal Reserve continued invoking emergency powers granted under Section 13(3) of the Federal Reserve Act. They also worked closely with other federal regulators and Wall Street executives to craft improvised solutions. The most notable tactics were:

- **Temporary Lending Facilities**—The Federal Reserve launched an unprecedented number of temporary lending facilities to provide liquidity to both members and nonmembers of the Federal Reserve system. Most facilities were authorized under Section 13(3). Temporary lending facilities helped ease credit conditions but eventually proved inadequate to stem the crisis completely. Table 28.1 shows a partial list of lending facilities launched between December 10, 2007, and October 7, 2008. In total, the Fed provided more than $1 trillion in liquidity under the programs. Before the crisis ended, the Fed would also use Section 13(3) to lend directly to several distressed corporations, such as AIG.

Table 28.1: Federal Reserve Temporary Lending Programs[43]

PROGRAM	ANNOUNCEMENT DATE	PEAK LOANS OUTSTANDING (BILLIONS)
Temporary Auction Facility (TAF)	December 10, 2007	$493
Term Securities Lending Facility (TSLF)	March 11, 2008	$236
Primary Dealer Credit Facility (PDCF)	March 17, 2008	$150
Asset-Backed Commercial Paper Money Market Mutual Fund Liquidity Facility (AMLF)	September 19, 2008	$152
Commercial Paper Funding Facility (CPFF)	October 7, 2008	$350

- **Acquisitions by Commercial Banks**—One way to prevent the bankruptcy of systemically important financial firms was to encourage Federal Reserve member banks to acquire them before they were rendered insolvent. From March 2008 through September 2008, leaders of the Federal Reserve, U.S. Treasury, FDIC, and Federal Reserve Regional Bank of New York worked closely with investment and commercial banking executives to orchestrate such acquisitions. Examples included Bank of America's acquisition of Merrill Lynch on September 15, 2008, and J.P. Morgan's acquisition of Washington Mutual on September 25, 2008.[44]

- **Government Takeover of GSEs**—By the summer of 2008, Fannie Mae and Freddie Mac seemed likely to be the next dominos to fall—and if one fell, the other would surely follow. The GSEs held or insured nearly $10 trillion of mortgage debt, and their failure would create a financial shock that would dwarf those created by any other Wall Street institution. On July 29, 2008, President George W. Bush signed legislation authorizing additional financial support to the GSEs and established a process for the federal government to take them over if their finances continued to deteriorate. Only one month later, a full takeover of the GSEs was necessary. On September 10, Hank Paulson informed the executive teams of Fannie and Freddie that they were being placed in conservatorship. The CEOs and several top executives were replaced with new leadership. The GSEs ultimately required $150 billion of additional support before the crisis ended, but once in conservatorship, they no longer presented a systemic threat to the financial system.[45]

Lights Out at Lehman Brothers

The credit crunch intensified after the acquisition of Bear Stearns. From March to September 2008, federal regulators and financial leaders scrambled to stop a cascade of runs on the shadow banking system. The Fed launched multiple temporary lending facilities while simultaneously encouraging the most vulnerable financial institutions to raise capital and shore up their balance sheets. These efforts were not enough, however, and it was clear to everybody that Lehman Brothers would be the next domino to fall.

On October 22, 1907, J. Pierpont Morgan and Ben Strong had just witnessed the failure of the Knickerbocker Trust, which had succumbed to bank runs that were spreading like wildfire through the streets of New York. Later that night, executives at the Trust Company of America pleaded for assistance. Morgan assembled several leading bankers to determine if the Trust should be rescued. When Morgan asked for Strong's verdict on the Trust's financials, he replied that it was solvent but lacked liquidity to stop the run. Morgan responded, "This is the place to stop the trouble, then." A group of bankers extended credit to the Trust Company of America, and it proved to be the turning point in the crisis.[46]

The GFC is often compared to the Great Depression, but it has more in common with the Panic of 1907. The bankruptcy of Lehman was reminiscent of the failure of the Knickerbocker Trust. In September 2008, Hank Paulson, Ben Bernanke, and Tim Geithner concluded that Lehman was insolvent and, therefore, ineligible for Section 13(3) loans from the Federal Reserve. The only option was to orchestrate an acquisition by a large commercial bank backed by the Federal Reserve or a foreign bank that had similar central bank support. Paulson led the effort to find a buyer, but there were few remaining options. Bank of America was the only U.S. bank capable of handling the acquisition, but it abandoned its due diligence after discovering the size of the hole on Lehman's balance sheet. On Friday, September 12, Lehman was almost out of cash. The only remaining acquirer was London-based Barclays, but executives refused to consider an acquisition without first removing tens of billions of dollars of toxic assets from Lehman's balance sheet. Over the weekend, Paulson assembled executives from many of Wall Street's largest financial institutions to create a private pool of capital to purchase Lehman's most toxic assets and pave the way for a Barclays acquisition. But these efforts were for naught. The UK's Financial Services Authority vetoed the deal on Sunday, September 14, leaving Lehman with no other options.[47]

On Monday, September 15, Lehman Brothers filed for bankruptcy. Founded in 1850, the firm had survived the Panics of 1857, 1873, 1884, 1893, 1907, and 1929, but the Panic of 2008 was too much. Nobody could predict the consequences of Lehman's failure, but everybody knew it would be bad. Lehman held more than $600 billion in assets and more than 900,000 derivatives contracts. Much like the failure of the Knickerbocker in 1907, Lehman's failure elevated the crisis to a new level. Less than two weeks later, Washington Mutual declared bankruptcy after suffering a relentless run by depositors and wholesale funding providers, and it appeared that Wachovia would soon follow.[48] Hank Paulson realized that the time had come for congressional intervention. The system could not withstand another Lehman or Washington Mutual bankruptcy, and existing powers of federal regulators had proved inadequate.[49]

POINT OF INTEREST

The Fall of Lehman Brothers: Intentional or Inevitable?

The bankruptcy of Lehman Brothers on September 15, 2008, is often regarded as the biggest mistake during the GFC. Criticism often hinges upon the assumption that federal regulators intentionally allowed Lehman to fail either because they underestimated the consequences, or they simply believed it was necessary to teach Wall Street a lesson. The truth, however, is that the leadership of the Fed, Treasury, and SEC did everything in their power to prevent a Lehman bankruptcy, but rescuing the firm using government funds would have violated their constitutional authority.

The problem with Lehman was that its insolvency was undeniable. The Federal Reserve had the power to lend to nonmember banks under Section 13(3), but only if the institution was fundamentally solvent. Therefore, the only option for Lehman was to find a larger bank to acquire them and guarantee their liabilities. Despite intense efforts to orchestrate an acquisition, Lehman failed to find a buyer and was forced to declare bankruptcy.[50]

It is impossible to penetrate the minds of Ben Bernanke, Hank Paulson, and Tim Geithner to know for sure, but most evidence suggests that the Lehman bankruptcy was an unfortunate consequence of the limits of federal

(continued)

regulatory powers rather than a conscious decision to punish the firm. Regulators simply lacked the tools to deal with Lehman. The failure of Lehman ultimately forced Congress to choose a depression or pass legislation to backstop the banking system. After witnessing the consequences of Lehman's bankruptcy, they chose the latter.

Phase Four: Hank Paulson Breaks the Glass

In early 2008, Treasury employees Phill Swagel and Neel Kashkari quietly crafted an emergency plan to be used if the crisis spiraled out of control. It called for hundreds of billions of dollars of federal appropriations to buy toxic assets from financial institutions and/or recapitalize them by purchasing equity. Realizing that Congress was unlikely to appropriate hundreds of billions of dollars to rescue Wall Street institutions unless no other options remained, Kashkari and Swagel called the plan the "Break the Glass Bank Recapitalization Plan," referring to the axes used to access fire extinguishers to stop fires before they spread.[51]

POINT OF INTEREST

The Unappreciated Sacrifice of the Financial Firefighter

"Our political tradition sets great store by the generalized symbol of evil. This is the wrongdoer whose wrongdoing will be taken by the public to be the secret propensity of the whole community or class. We search avidly for such people, not so much because we wish to see them exposed or punished as individuals, but because we cherish the resulting political discomfort of their friends."[52]

—John Kenneth Galbraith

Financial panics, frauds, and other forms of reckless behavior are painful but enduring features of every financial system. But what is more tragic is the tendency of Americans to demonize individuals who make enormous sacrifices to prevent financial crises from devolving into depressions. Many of America's most admirable financial leaders suffered this fate. Alexander Hamilton endured relentless attacks while crafting a financial system to resuscitate the nation's damaged credit in 1790. Hetty Green was labeled the "Witch of Wall Street" despite her selfless acts to support financiers and the entire city of New York when they were most vulnerable during the frequent panics of the late 1800s. J. Pierpont Morgan was excoriated by the media and congressmen only a few years after orchestrating an extraordinary rescue during the Panic of 1907.

Many financial firefighters during the GFC suffered similar fates. It is only by reading the memoirs of financial leaders such as Hank Paulson, Tim Geithner, and Ben Bernanke that it is possible to appreciate their noble intent and selfless sacrifice during the GFC. Nobody is perfect—and these individuals admitted many of their mistakes—but impugning their character is unfair. America's financial firefighters suffer from the sacrifices they make to extinguish the flames, while simultaneously bearing undeserved insults and character assassinations from those observing the infernos—usually from a safe distance. These heroes fight financial fires with full awareness of the reputational risks, which makes their sacrifices especially noble.

After the Lehman bankruptcy, Paulson knew that regulators' powers were insufficient to stop the run on the shadow banking system. The next two weeks only reinforced his fears. Credit markets contracted at a terrifying pace. The very next day, the $62 billion Primary Reserve money market fund broke the buck after investors discovered large holdings of Lehman commercial paper in the portfolio. This sparked a run on the $3.4 trillion money market fund industry. Money market funds ceased purchasing commercial paper and counterparties in the tri-party repo market pulled back, which deprived investment banks with access to short-term funding. The liquidity of Morgan Stanley and Goldman Sachs rapidly deteriorated, threatening the solvency of the nation's two largest investment banks. Outflows from money market funds even left corporations such as General Electric with no buyers for commercial paper. Many of the nation's largest corporations faced the real possibility of failing to make payroll. The U.S. was experiencing a full-blown bank run that was unlike anything since the early 1930s.[53]

The time had come to break the glass, but the plan required an enormous congressional appropriation. Paulson's team settled on $700 billion but privately conceded that even that amount could be insufficient. Passing a $700 billion piece of legislation in a matter of weeks was impossible under normal conditions, and it would still be difficult in dire circumstances. Many Americans blamed Wall Street for having caused the crisis, and many of their representatives in Congress relished the thought of watching these firms suffer for their transgressions. Such punishment was perhaps justified in some situations, but all Americans would suffer alongside them if the financial system imploded. The depressions in the 1820s, 1840s, and 1930s provided proof of this inevitability.

Over the next four weeks, Hank Paulson worked with Congress and members of the Bush administration to pass legislation to fund the "Break the Glass" plan. Dubbed the Emergency Economic Stabilization Act of 2008, the bill sought $700 billion to fund the Troubled Asset Relief Program (TARP), which would be used to recapitalize the financial system. In a stunning vote on September 29, the U.S. House of Representatives rejected TARP by a vote of 228 to 205. The S&P 500 index declined by 8.8 percent after the vote, giving members of Congress a glimpse into the abyss that the U.S. would plunge if they failed to reverse their decision.[54]

Facing a choice between rescuing a financial system they resented or inviting a fourth Great Depression–level event in the U.S., enough naysayers changed their votes, and the bill was passed on October 3, 2008. President Bush quickly signed the bill, and the Treasury Department immediately set to work on implementation. In the end, Paulson opted to use most TARP funds to purchase equity in financial institutions.

POINT OF INTEREST

Paulson Makes an Offer the Bankers Can't Refuse

"Look, we're making you an offer. If you don't take it and sometime later your regulator tells you that you are undercapitalized and you have to raise private-sector capital, but you are unable to do so, you may not like the terms if you have to come back to me."[55]

—Hank Paulson, secretary of the Treasury

Soon after the passage of TARP, Hank Paulson concluded that purchasing equity stakes in troubled financial institutions was the most effective use of TARP funds. Purchasing toxic assets was too complex and time consuming. Even more importantly, the math simply didn't work. Stabilizing banks required increasing the ratio of common equity to a bank's total liabilities. Basic math reveals that less money is required to increase the numerator (i.e., the value of a bank's equity) than to decrease the much larger denominator (i.e., the bank's total liabilities). The problem with purchasing equity in troubled financial institutions, however, was that it would reveal which institutions were the most troubled and potentially harm their businesses. Paulson believed that if TARP funds were initially invested in the most systemically important financial institutions regardless of whether they were in distress, the stigma would be eliminated.[56]

On Monday, October 13, 2008, Hank Paulson called the CEOs of nine of the most systemically important financial institutions in the country and requested them to be in Washington, DC, for a mandatory meeting on the very next day. At the meeting, Paulson, Geithner, and Bernanke presented the terms of a proposed $125 billion investment in preferred securities to recapitalize the nine financial institutions. Unable to force the CEOs to accept the money, Paulson made it clear that it was to their advantage to accept it voluntarily.

Most of the CEOs put up little resistance, as several were fully aware that they desperately needed the capital. Those who resisted were quickly persuaded to do the right thing. On October 14, the Treasury announced the launch of a $250 billion Capital Purchase Program (CPP) under TARP and revealed that $125 billion was invested in Bank of America, Bank of New York Mellon, Citigroup, Goldman Sachs, J.P. Morgan, Morgan Stanley, State Street, and Wells Fargo. The crisis was not yet over, but the firefighters were gaining the upper hand.[57]

Phase Five: Economic Fallout and Stress Tests

The passage of TARP was a key turning point, but the crisis was not over. Many more fires erupted over the next five months, and a few were barely contained. AIG appeared to be a bottomless money pit that ultimately required nearly $200 billion to prevent its demise. Wachovia barely avoided collapsing in a bank run, and Citigroup required an additional injection of TARP capital to fill the growing losses from its subprime holdings. Meanwhile, the lagged impact of financial panic was finally hitting Main Street. Real GDP in Q4 2008 declined at an annualized rate of 6.3 percent relative to the prior quarter. Unemployment was rising fast, increasing from 6.1 percent in September 2008 to 9.0 percent in April 2009. Finally, the U.S. stock market cratered, threatening consumer and business spending as Americans' wealth shrank. Figure 28.12 tracks the decline of the S&P 500 from the onset of the crisis in August 2007 to the market bottom in March 2009. Figure 28.13 shows the unemployment rate from January 2008 to December 2009. In retrospect, the six months ending March 31, 2009, were the worst of the GFC, but this was not clear in real time. Many feared that the economy would fall much further before reaching rock bottom.[58]

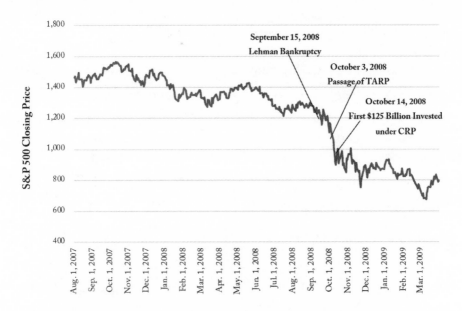

Figure 28.12: Closing Price of the S&P 500 Index (August 1, 2007–March 31, 2009)[59]

U.S. Banks Pass Their Stress Tests

"The key to any financial crash is the banking system. If banks can remain solvent and retain public confidence, then recovery may take place under their leadership. Every savior of the market in times of panic knew this, from Hamilton through U.S. Grant to J.P. Morgan."[60]

—ROBERT SOBEL, financial historian

Tim Geithner served as president of the Federal Reserve Bank of New York during most of the GFC. In November 2008, he joined President Obama's administration as the new secretary of the Treasury. When Geithner began his term at the Treasury, it seemed likely that the successes in the final months of 2008 would be insufficient. The U.S. economy was contracting, the stock market was cratering, and confidence in the banking system remained tenuous.[61]

In December 2008, Geithner hypothesized that the crisis could not end until confidence in the banking system was completely restored. He also believed that injecting capital and purchasing toxic assets would not suffice because potential future losses would remain hidden on banks' balance sheets. President Franklin D. Roosevelt faced a similar challenge when the national banking holiday began on March 6, 1933. He believed that confidence in the banking system would return only if the government restored faith in the solvency of the nation's banks rather than offering Band-Aid

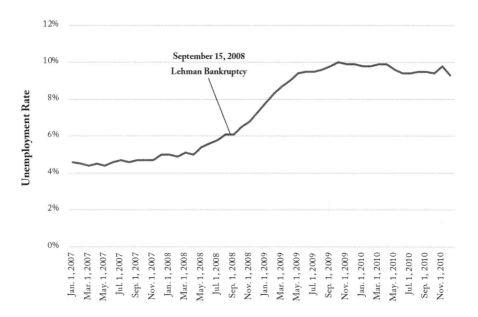

Figure 28.13: U.S. Unemployment Rate (January 1, 2007–November 31, 2010)[62]

solutions to cover up each new wound. Roosevelt created a tiered reopening plan, assuring the public that only solvent banks would reopen when the holiday was gradually lifted. The strategy worked, and it marked the beginning of the U.S. recovery from the Great Depression.[63]

Geithner proposed a similar stress test program that would reestablish confidence in the solvency of the nation's banks. Geithner's proposal was initially unpopular among several members of the Obama administration. Many feared that the public would view it as window dressing that merely allowed insolvent banks to survive. Nevertheless, President Obama signed off on the plan. Geithner announced the program in a hastily prepared press conference on February 10, 2009. The announcement did not go well, as the lack of details only increased uncertainty. Despite the setback, Geithner's plan was fundamentally sound. He believed—and the stress test would later confirm—that the banking system was stronger than the market assumed because ambiguous fear was depressing asset values far below their true value. By allowing an independent entity (i.e., the Federal Reserve) to complete rigorous stress tests on the most systemically important banks, investors would no longer default to their worst-case assumptions.[64]

The Federal Reserve began the stress tests on February 25, 2009. As part of the program, the FDIC provided an unlimited guarantee of deposits of banks subjected to the stress tests, and the federal government committed to filling any capital holes revealed by the tests. On May 7, 2009, the stress test results were announced, and the balance sheets of the banks appeared much stronger than the public feared. In total, the Fed estimated that the banks required an additional $75 billion in capital. Within one month, these shortfalls were mostly filled by $66 billion in fresh capital raises in private markets, leaving a gap of only $9 billion for the government. But the greatest valida-tion of the stress tests came from the private sector. In Bridgewater Associates's closely followed *Daily Observations*, the headline read, "We Agree!" Bridgewater estimated that the capital shortfall was $67 billion, which was nearly identical to the Fed's estimate.[65]

The stress tests marked the end of the bank run phase of the GFC. The U.S. had come dangerously close to a fourth Great Depression–level event. The outcome was a result of extraordinary actions of many individuals who to this day suffer from unfair criticism. Unfortunately, for the rest of America, more pain lay ahead. Over the next decade, the economy slowly recovered, but feelings of ambiguous fear and resentment increased more rapidly.

POINT OF INTEREST

Restoring Faith in the American Banking System

"Some of our bankers had shown themselves either incompetent or dishon-est in their handling of the people's funds . . . This was of course not true in the vast majority of our banks, but it was true in enough of them to shock the people for a time into a sense of insecurity and to put them into a frame of mind where they did not differentiate . . . It was the Govern-ment's job to straighten out this situation and do it as quickly as possible—and the job is being performed."[66]

—President Franklin Delano Roosevelt (March 12, 1933)

The U.S. likely would have failed without the financial reforms introduced by Alexander Hamilton in 1790. Nearly fifty years later, the nation descended into a depression from which it barely escaped after President Andrew Jackson vetoed the bill to renew the charter of the Second Bank of the United States. Finally, Americans descended into the worst depression in its history after allowing a wave of bank failures in the aftermath of the Great Crash of 1929.

Restoring faith in financial institutions—especially those led by executives who have acted irresponsibly—is an unenviable task, but it is essential to restor-ing prosperity in the wake of a financial crisis. Soon after taking the oath of office on March 4, 1933, President Franklin Roosevelt announced a national banking holiday by executive order. The U.S. Treasury Department and Federal Reserve used the holiday to examine the books of banks across the country. On March 13, 1933, the strongest banks began reopening with the full support of the Federal Reserve as a lender of last resort. The fact that banks could only reopen once the Treasury Department and Federal Reserve provided a stamp of approval restored confidence in the U.S. banking system.[67]

The stress tests performed by the Federal Reserve in 2009 had a similar objective and produced the same outcome. The stress tests concluded that the American banking system was fundamentally sound even in a worst-case scenario. Scars from the GFC would remain for years, but the crisis phase ended after stress test results were announced.

Chapter 29

A DECADE OF
DIMINISHING RETURNS

*"What this means is that they, like everyone else, are somewhat embarrassed by
the fact that what everyone feels to have been a technological revolution, a
drastic change in our productive lives, has been accompanied everywhere,
including Japan, by a slowing down of productivity growth, not by a step up.
You can see the computer age everywhere but in the productivity statistics."*[1]

—ROBERT SOLOW, economist

On March 17–18, 2009, the Federal Open Markets Committee (FOMC) convened its regularly scheduled meeting. Chairman Bernanke later remarked that "[the discussion] was the darkest I ever heard as a central banker, before or since." Credit markets continued to function poorly despite enormous fiscal and monetary policy stimulus. The crisis had also spread beyond financial markets, and the economy appeared to be careening off a cliff. March 2009 was later identified as the bottom of the panic phase of the GFC, but Americans suffered many more years of economic pain.[2]

In the decade that followed the GFC, economic anxiety, discontent, and resentment increased steadily in America. The figures presented on the pages that follow may help explain why. The first three reveal that real GDP, corporate profits, and stock prices returned to pre-crisis levels within three to five years, but this tended to favor wealthier Americans. In contrast, it took roughly ten years for unemployment and real estate prices to return to pre-crisis levels. This aspect of the recovery tended to disproportionately impact middle- and low-income Americans. To be clear, this does not suggest that the actions taken to prevent a financial collapse were ill-advised.

The misery of the Great Depression and horrors of World War II provide more than enough evidence to refute such arguments. That said, an unwanted side effect was the perception that government action favored the wealthy. This perception likely contributed to increased socioeconomic resentment and political polarization, although it is by no means the only causal factor.

Chapter 29 recounts the post-GFC recovery. It largely counters the common perception that the relative weakness and unfairness of the recovery were attributable to the nature of government and central bank intervention during and after the GFC. Instead, evidence suggests that these trends began long before the crisis hit in 2007. The observations in this chapter are important because economic stagnation in the U.S. appears likely to continue for several decades to come. The COVID-19 pandemic and post–COVID-19 inflation temporarily diverted Americans' attention, but once the crisis subsides, economic stagnation is likely to return. The ability of Americans to acknowledge, confront, and overcome this challenge constitutes yet another important test for the U.S. Empire.

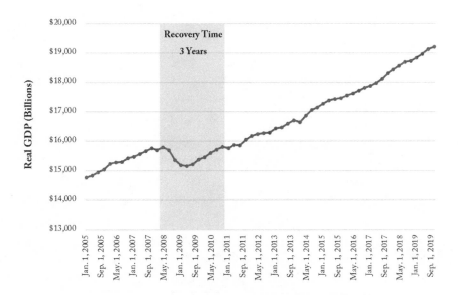

Figure 29.1: Rolling One-Year U.S. Real GDP (Quarterly) (January 1, 2005–October 1, 2019)[3]

The Secular Decline of Economic Growth

"The post–1972 growth is considered a disappointment precisely because the pace of growth during 1928–1972 was so rapid and so unprecedented."[4]

—ROBERT J. GORDON, economist

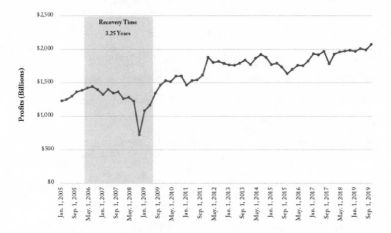

Figure 29.2: U.S. Corporate Profits After Tax (January 1, 2005–October 1, 2019)[5]

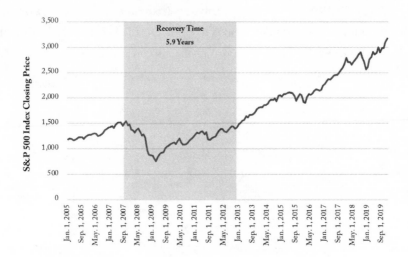

Figure 29.3: U.S. Stock Prices as Represented by the S&P 500 Index
(January 1, 2005–December 31, 2019)[6]

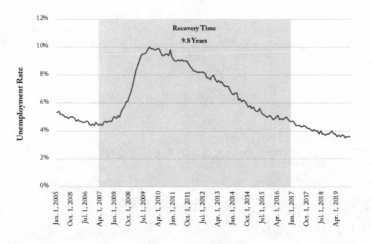

Figure 29.4: U.S. Unemployment Rate (January 1, 2005–December 31, 2019)[7]

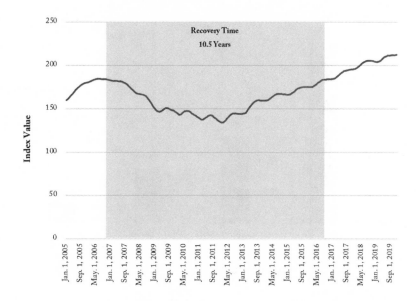

Figure 29.5: S&P Case-Shiller Index of Real Estate Values (January 1, 2005–December 31, 2019)[8]

$$Real\ GDP_{Annual} = Population \times \left(\frac{Labor\ Force}{Population}\right) \times \left(\frac{Employed\ Workers}{Labor\ Force}\right) \times \left(\frac{Hours\ Worked}{Year}\right) \times \left(\frac{Output}{Hours}\right)$$

| | **Labor Force Participation Rate** | **Natural Employment Rate** | **Total Hours Worked per Year** | **Productivity** |

Figure 29.6: Equation for Total Real Economic Output per Year

Real GDP measures the total economic output of a nation after adjusting for inflation. Mathematically, it is a function of the output produced by a combination of labor and capital (which can increase labor productivity). One way to think about the headwinds to future U.S. economic growth is to decompose real GDP by isolating the key drivers, which include: (a) total population, (b) total size of the labor force, (c) natural employment rate,[9] (d) total hours worked by the labor force, and (e) the total output per hour (Figure 29.6).[10]

The challenge for the U.S. in the coming decades is that at least three of the five factors—labor force participation, natural employment rate, and total hours worked per year—are expected to either decline or experience minimal levels of growth relative to history. Population is expected to grow but at a much lower rate relative to most of U.S. history. Finally, productivity is expected to increase, but also at a rate that is far less than the rate that the U.S. experienced for most of its history. Several of the more important factors explaining the depressed expectations of future growth are outlined on the pages that follow.[11]

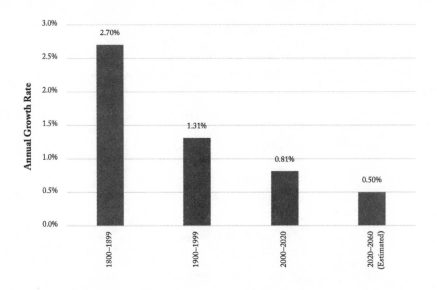

Figure 29.7: U.S. Population Growth by Time Period (1800–2060(e))[12]

Population Growth

Holding all other factors constant, population growth directly translates into economic growth. Population growth was a major contributor to the nation's economic expansion in the 1800s and was a moderate contributor in the 1900s. According to U.S. census data, the U.S. population increased by 2.7 percent per year in the 1800s and then slowed to 1.3 percent in the 1900s. Growth in the twenty-first century continued to slow, increasing by only 0.8 percent per year through 2020. The slowdown is expected to continue, with current estimates of approximately 0.5 percent annual growth from 2020 to 2060 (Figure 29.7).[13] Population growth is, therefore, expected to add little to economic growth in the coming decades.

Labor Force Participation

The labor force participation rate captures the portion of the population that is willing and able to work. Since 1948, the participation rate has ranged between 58 percent and 67 percent (Figure 29.8).[14] When all other factors are held constant, higher labor force participation translates into higher economic growth. In March 2000, the U.S. labor force participation rate peaked at 67.3 percent. Since then, it has steadily declined and now hovers around 62.3 percent. A significant portion of this decline is attributable to the aging of the U.S. population, which is a headwind that will intensify over the next decade due to upcoming baby boomer retirements. In fact, current estimates are that the labor force participation rate will contract by another two percentage points by

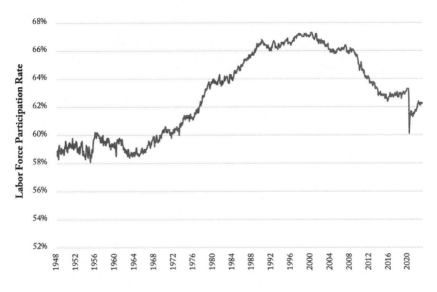

Figure 29.8: U.S. Labor Force Participation Rate (January 1, 1948–December 1, 2022)[15]

2031. Holding all other variables constant, labor force participation will, at best, have no effect on economic growth, but is more likely to detract from growth.[16]

Natural Rate of Employment

The natural *employment* rate is the opposite of the natural *unemployment* rate. In other words, it is the threshold at which the labor force is considered fully employed. Any remaining unemployed individuals are in normal transition for various reasons. If the natural *unemployment* rate is 5 percent, the natural *employment* rate is 95 percent. Estimates of the natural rate of employment have risen in recent years. According to estimates provided in the FOMC's quarterly *Summaries of Economic Projections*, the natural rate of employment has steadily increased from a range of 94.0 percent–94.8 percent in 2012 to a range of 95.8 percent–96.5 percent in 2022. It is not completely clear what is driving this trend. Theories include the greater mobility of workers, higher percentage of older and more experienced workers in the labor force, and the introduction of technology tools that speed up the matching of job candidates to vacancies.[17] There are two important caveats to this observation. First, the natural rate of employment is not static; while the current trend is positive, it is conceivable that it could reverse in the future. Second, even if improvement continues, there is a lower bound. The estimate in 2022 implies a natural rate of unemployment between 3.5 percent and 4.2 percent, which leaves little room for further improvement. Thus, the natural rate of employment may provide a slight tailwind to growth, but it is not guaranteed.[18]

Table 29.1: FOMC Estimates of Long-Run Natural Rate of Employment[19]

YEAR	IMPLIED NATURAL RATE OF EMPLOYMENT (PERCENTAGE)
2012	94.0–94.8
2013	94.0–94.8
2014	94.5–94.8
2015	94.8–95.0
2016	95.0–95.3
2017	95.2–95.5
2018	95.4–95.7
2019	95.6–96.0
2020	95.7–96.0
2021	95.7–96.2
2022	95.8–96.5

Hours Worked per Employee

The substantial reduction of the work schedule is one of the most dramatic changes to the U.S. work environment since the nation's founding. The first recorded data in 1830 reveals that the average hourly worker put in nearly seventy hours per week. In 2020, the average workweek was nearly cut in half to thirty-five hours per week. Figure 29.9 tracks the decline in the average hours worked by the U.S. labor force between 1830 and 2020. There are many caveats to this data, such as the inclusion of part-time employees in recent years, and the fact that several different methodologies were employed over the 190-year period, but the fundamental trend is undeniable. This does not mean that there are no benefits to reduced work schedules. For example, Americans have more time to spend with their families and enjoy the benefits of leisure. But the trade-off is that, all else being equal, it creates a headwind for economic growth. If the number of hours worked declines further, it will continue to be a headwind. On the flip side—although this observation will assuredly be unpopular—working more hours has the potential to bolster growth.

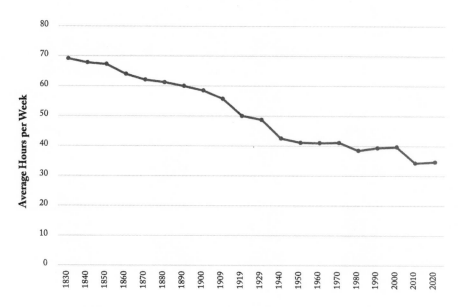

Figure 29.9: Average Work Week of the U.S. Labor Force (1830–2020)[20]

Productivity Growth

Productivity growth captures the increase in economic output per person. Productivity growth may come from educational advancement, capital accumulation, and techno-logical advancement. Productivity growth is the key to improving standards of living over time, but it is also subject to long cycles of elevated or depressed levels of growth. Further, when considering the entire history of human civilization, sustained peri-ods of productivity growth are a relatively recent and rare phenomenon. Prior to the industrial revolution in the nineteenth century, human beings experienced negligible productivity growth for nearly two thousand years.

The current challenge for the U.S. is that many Americans implicitly hope that future productivity growth rates will resemble those that Americans experienced in the mid-1900s. Those who cling to this belief often make the implicit assump-tion that rapid advancement in computing technology will revitalize productivity growth. The problem with this belief is that, while it is true that advancements in computing have driven and will continue to drive productivity gains, the gains are modest relative to those achieved in the mid-1900s (i.e., roughly 1920 to 1970). This is the most important insight from economist Robert J. Gordon's book *The Rise and Fall of American Growth*. Gordon explains how productivity gains from technological advances such as electricity, running water, the combustion engine, household appliances, electric machine tools, and air conditioning were far more dra-matic and broadly beneficial than those achieved from advancements in computing

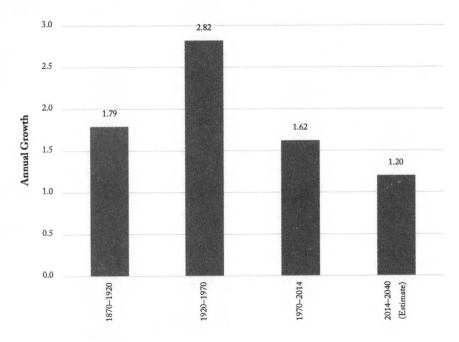

Figure 29.10: Average Annual Productivity Growth in the United States (1870–2040(e))[21]

technologies. Figure 29.10 shows the productivity gains during four eras of U.S. history, as well as Gordon's base case projection for productivity growth over the next eighteen years.[22] Absent a revolutionary innovation, Gordon projects that productivity will increase at a much slower pace than many Americans anticipate. All else being equal, this creates another significant headwind to growth.[23]

Threats to U.S. Competitiveness

The headwinds to U.S. economic growth are daunting and appear likely to intensify over the next several decades. Adding to America's economic challenges are several complications that threaten U.S. competitiveness, which could create even further downward pressure on growth. The remainder of this chapter highlights three of the more notable complications, which include the increasing U.S. debt burden, the rise of China as an economic rival, and the increasing income and wealth gap.

The Federal Debt Burden

Since the end of World War II, the U.S. has run annual fiscal budget deficits in almost every year. Expressed as a percentage of GDP, deficits have also steadily increased over time. Over the past fifteen years alone, debt has roughly doubled as a percentage of GDP.

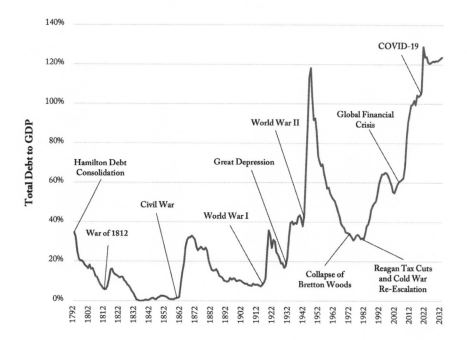

Figure 29.11: Total U.S. Debt as a Percentage of GDP (1792–2032(e))[24]

Figure 29.11 shows the total debt-to-GDP ratio from 1792 to the projected level as of 2032. The chart also denotes several events that prompted sharp increases in debt levels.

The U.S. debt-to-GDP ratio is now at an all-time high. An important caveat, however, is that most of the increase over the past fifteen years was the consequence of two severe and relatively rare events. The GFC, which was the worst financial crisis since the 1930s, caused the debt-to-GDP ratio to rise from 62 percent in 2007 to 100 percent in 2013. The COVID-19 pandemic, which was the worst global pandemic since of the Great Influenza in 1918, caused the debt-to-GDP ratio to increase from 106 percent in 2019 to 124 percent in 2022. The danger, however, is that these two crises have reduced the nation's capacity to address future crises. Making matters worse, budget deficits are expected to widen over the next several decades. The base case Congressional Budget Office (CBO) estimate projects that the debt-to-GDP ratio will remain flat over the next ten years, but projections beyond 2032 are daunting. Figure 29.12 summarizes the CBO's 2022 projection for the debt-to-GDP ratio for the debt held by the public through 2051.[25]

The biggest problem with this picture is not that the U.S. is destined to default on its debt—although that certainly is a possibility; the problem is that the current trajectory leaves little margin for error. In 2006, the CBO projected that the U.S. debt-to-GDP ratio in 2016 would be 28.1 percent, but the actual debt-to-GDP ratio as of December 31, 2016, was 105.3 percent. Most of the difference was attributable to the

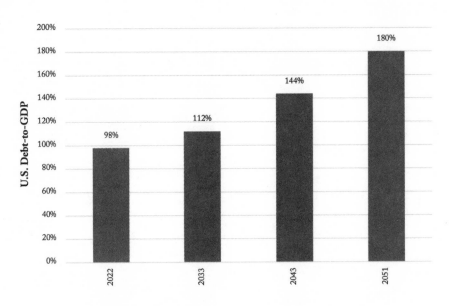

Figure 29.12: Estimated Total U.S. Debt to GDP (2022–2051)[26]

GFC and COVID-19, which were rare but not unprecedented events. The U.S. could experience another financial catastrophe in the next thirty years that will necessitate substantial emergency spending. The higher the debt level rises, the more difficult and expensive it will be to deal with such catastrophes. This is the risk that Hamilton feared when he asserted that "the creation of debt should always be accompanied with the means of extinguishment." The U.S. abandoned this principle after the conclusion of World War II and has yet to re-embrace it.[27]

The Rise of China

After the ratification of the Constitution in 1788, the U.S. gradually evolved from an agrarian economy into a global financial and technological empire. Along the way, the U.S. overcame multiple obstacles that threatened to derail its advancement. One recent scare was the rise of Japan in the 1970s and 1980s, but the threat turned out to be less significant than Americans feared. In recent decades, however, China has emerged as an economic rival, and this threat appears to be more formidable. Figure 29.13 shows the amount of time it has taken the U.S. and China to progress along their respective evolutionary paths. The most striking observation is the speed of China's economic advancement. The U.S. progression from an agricultural economy to a high-tech services economy took approximately 222 years (assuming a starting year of 1800). China accomplished most of its transformation in the span of less than fifty years.[28]

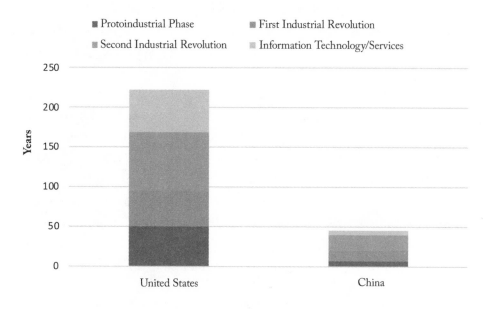

Figure 29.13: Total Years of U.S. and China Economic Evolution[29]

POINT OF INTEREST

The Reforms of Deng Xiaoping

"China's experiences (both good and bad, joyful and painful, successful and failed)
show that correct procedures of development, and proper industrial policies
and strategies of development based on a nation's own initial social–political
conditions matter . . . they matter not only for individuals'
welfare, but also for a nation's survival, dignity, and destiny."[30]

—Yi Wen, AVP, Federal Reserve Bank of St. Louis

In the fall of 1949, Mao Zedong's People's Liberation Army (PLA) was close to defeating Chiang Kai-Shek's Kuomintang (KMT) forces. Anticipating an imminent victory, Mao announced the formation of the People's Republic of China, which was to be governed under communist rule. By December 1949, KMT forces were surrounded in two besieged cities, and Chiang Kai-Shek fled to the island of Formosa, which would be renamed Taiwan.[31]

The end of the bloody civil war was initially welcomed, but Mao's leadership proved to be disastrous. The most damaging program was the "Great

(continued)

Leap Forward," which was intended to industrialize the economy and raise Chinese standards of living. The problem was that the centrally planned strategy allocated too many resources to industrial projects and too little toward agricultural production. The formation of large farming cooperatives simultaneously reduced accountability for individual farmers, which resulted in sharp declines in productivity. The combination of misallocation of resources and lower productivity resulted in the Great Chinese Famine of 1959–1961, which led to an estimated thirty million deaths from starvation.[32]

Mao died on September 9, 1976. After a few years of power politics, Deng Xiaoping emerged as China's new leader. Like Mao, Deng sought to revolutionize the Chinese economy, but he embraced a more practical approach that combined Chinese socialist ideology and capitalist-based market forces. Capturing the crux of Deng's philosophy was his famous statement that "it does not matter if the cat is black or white, as long as it catches mice."[33]

The U.S. and China have markedly different philosophies with respect to politics, human rights, and many other issues. Despite these differences, it is undeniable that Deng and his successors have achieved impressive economic results. Whether China will surpass the U.S. as the world's dominant economic power remains uncertain. Plenty of well-respected economists argue for and against this outcome, but there are few who dismiss the possibility.

Many Americans are perplexed as to how China's industrialization proceeded at such a fast pace. In 2016, Yi Wen, a research director at the Federal Reserve Bank of St. Louis, published a working paper that provided compelling answers. Wen attributed China's success to the proper sequencing of distinct stages of economic development. He also provided compelling evidence that improper sequencing explains why many nations fail in their quest to industrialize. Examples of such failures include Mao Zedong's industrialization attempts in the 1950s and 1960s, as well as numerous failures in eastern Europe, Latin America, and Africa. Wen identified the first phase, which he refers to as the protoindustrialization phase, as the most critical but often neglected phase. The next few pages explain each of the critical stages of industrialization and how China has navigated them successfully and rapidly.

Protoindustrialization (1978–1985)

Protoindustrial is the most critical but oft neglected stage of industrialization. Many nations neglect this stage in their rush to establish mass production capabilities. During the protoindustrialization stage, the goals (even if unstated) are to create the infrastructure and culture that are essential for a thriving industrialized nation. Key objectives include the establishment of food security, creation of entrepreneurial cultures, establishment of crucial supply chain networks, and encouragement of high savings rates to fuel domestic demand and investment. To be effective, these outcomes must occur at the grassroots level rather than from the top down. Many nations fail to make this transition because they succumb to the temptation to use foreign capital and leapfrog directly to the mass production stage. Those who fall into this trap often find that they lack the infrastructure to succeed. The U.S. was fortunate in that it passed through this stage in the early 1800s when neglecting it was not a realistic option. Mass production manufacturing simply did not exist at the time.[34]

China's entry into the protoindustrialization stage began with Deng Xiaoping's reforms in 1978. The first step was the creation of profit incentives for farmers by dissolving large collectives established during Mao's Great Leap Forward and replacing them with smaller farming units. Farmers were then allowed to keep excess revenue generated by production that exceeded government quotas. The second step was the encouragement of small business formation by promoting township and village firms (TVEs), which were funded and led by local leaders. TVEs expanded rapidly during the 1980s and 1990s, yielding countless economic benefits. One example was the fostering of entrepreneurship. In *The Making of an Economic Superpower*, Wen recounts the rise of the city of Yong Lian, which transformed from a poor farming village in 1978 into a major steel producer in the twenty-first century. The transformation began when farmers used profits from excess agricultural production to invest in fishponds. Profits from fishponds were then used to develop light manufacturing capabilities. Profits from light manufacturing eventually led to the development of major steel manufacturing facilities. These types of progressive grassroots industrialization efforts were common throughout China during the 1980s and 1990s.[35]

First Industrial Revolution (1985–1995)

By the mid-1980s, TVEs were transforming the Chinese economy. This provided a strong foundation for the nation's first industrial revolution. Like the U.S. economy in the mid-1800s, the first phase of industrialization focused on goods from light manufacturing. Examples included textiles, kitchenware, office furniture, bicycles, and many other relatively inexpensive items.[36] Demand came from domestic customers (who were accumulating savings from farming and TVEs), as well as international customers who were attracted by China's price competitiveness. By the mid-1990s, the number of TVEs had grown substantially. In 1995, TVEs employed nearly 130 million workers versus only 28 million in 1978. TVE output had also become a significant component of the Chinese economy. In 1995, TVEs generated nearly 30 percent of China's total economic output compared to only 14 percent in 1978.[37] The success of TVEs even surprised Deng. When asked by foreign leaders how China was advancing so quickly in the 1980s, he replied:

> The most unexpected consequence of our rural reform is the explosive growth of village firms, [and] the sudden emergence of so many businesses and varieties of professions and specialized regional products created by village firms. This was not designed by the government. It cannot be attributed to the central government . . . this is totally out of my expectations. It just happened, what a surprise.[38]

Second Industrial Revolution (1998–2018)

By the late 1990s, China had begun its transition to mass production. Using the U.S. as a benchmark, China's second industrial revolution resembled the American Commercial Invasion at the turn of the twentieth century. In the late 1990s, China's state-owned enterprises (SOEs) and private companies began mass producing heavy industrial products. Demand came from domestic and international markets, both of which benefitted from supply chains and customer relationships that were established during the first industrial revolution.

During its first industrial revolution, China generated modest trade surpluses, but by the early 2000s, mass production capabilities fueled massive trade surpluses. Again, China's experience was reminiscent of the U.S. experience during the American Commercial Invasion. Figure 29.14 shows China's trade surpluses from 1982 to 2021. In addition to increasing the wealth of its citizens, China's trade surpluses provided domestic funding for its economic advancement. This provided a solid foundation for the next phase of its economic evolution, which now threatens to compete directly with advanced economies such as the United States.[39]

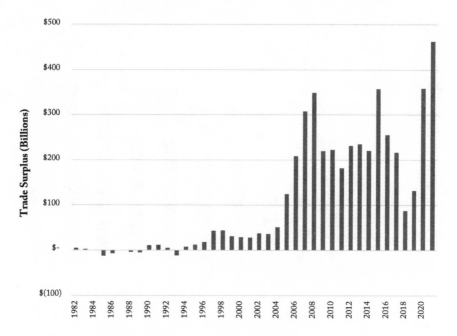

Figure 29.14: Trade Surplus of China (1982–2022)[40]

The Final Transition to a High-Tech Services Economy

China's growth has slowed considerably over the past decade, but its economic capabilities continue to evolve rapidly. China is now in the process of transitioning into a high-tech services economy. Evidence of this transition can be seen in Figure 29.15, which shows the rapid growth of software and services revenue in China. From 2010 to 2020, sales increased more than fivefold.

If China continues to evolve at its present pace, it may soon rival the U.S. for dominance in technological innovation. Those who dismiss this possibility often cite the many unattractive side effects of China's rapid industrialization as conclusive evidence that the nation is destined to fail. Examples include the impact of industry on the environment, violations of human rights, political corruption, financial fraud, and many other undesirable outcomes. But critics overlook that the U.S. experienced many of the same problems during its evolution from an agricultural economy to an economic superpower. Yi Wen explained this misconception, stating:

> China's rapid development compressed the typical 250–300 years of Western industrial achievements . . . into a mere 35 years. It must have also rapidly accumulated the typical 250–300 years' worth of major development problems and hurdles that the West encountered. These problems include but are not limited to rampant corruption,

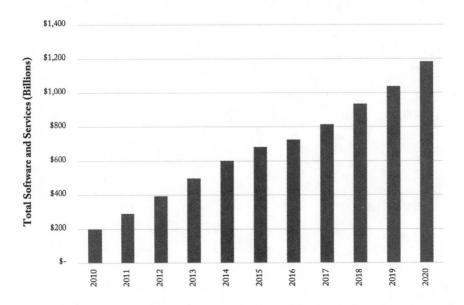

Figure 29.15: Total Software and Services Sales for Republic of China (Billions) (2010–2020)[41]

unprecedented pollution and environmental destruction, rapid break-down of traditional family values and an accelerated sexual liberation, rising divorce and suicide rates, wide-spread business fraud, markets-full of "lemons" and low-quality goods, pervasive asset bubbles, rising income inequality and class discrimination, frequent industrial accidents, organized crime, economic scandals, and unemployment.[42]

On the flipside, those who believe that China is destined to replace the U.S. as the dominant economic power may be too optimistic. China's challenges resemble those confronted by the U.S. in the 1800s and 1900s, but the U.S. prevailed over many of these challenges while other nations have failed. China has yet to prove that it will prevail. All things considered, the fate of China remains uncertain, but the fact that it has come this far is impressive. Only time will tell whether China will one day surpass the United States.

INCOME AND WEALTH INEQUALITY

American standards of living have improved exponentially over the past 235 years. When controlling for one's relative socioeconomic standing, few Americans would willingly trade places with individuals in comparable positions in the past. But human beings never have, and probably never will, gauge their quality of life in the context

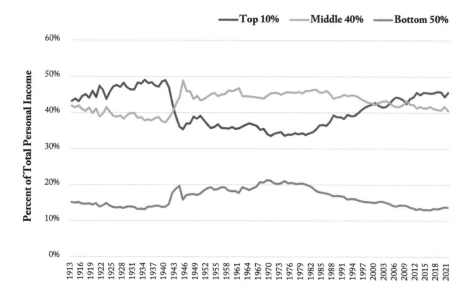

Figure 29.16: Percentage of Total U.S. Personal Income Percentile (1913–2021)[43]

of history. Instead, most compare themselves to what they observe in the present—whether it is their neighbors or people portrayed in the media. Wealth disparity is a tricky issue for Americans because it forces them to deal with two ideas that do not easily coexist. On one hand, Americans have always valued property ownership, entrepreneurship, and self-reliance. For more than two centuries, these values motivated Americans to work hard, innovate, and create better lives for themselves and their families. Collectively, these values also fueled impressive rates of real economic growth. Wealth and income inequality were both intentional and tolerable consequences of this value system. On the other hand, history has repeatedly proven that when wealth inequality breaches certain thresholds, civil unrest increases. If wealth and income inequality gaps become too extreme, the breakdown of civilization erases the benefits.

In 2015, the French economist Thomas Piketty assembled a database that reveals historical income and wealth data for the U.S. dating back to 1913. This data reveals that both income and wealth inequality have increased over the past several decades—although neither is at an all-time high. Figure 29.16 reveals that the top 10 percent of Americans substantially increased their share of income since the end of World War II but remain slightly below Roaring Twenties and Great Depression–era levels. Figure 29.17 shows a similar result for total wealth using the same percentiles. Although data is unavailable prior to 1913, it is also almost certain that income inequality was even more extreme.

Some economists argue that wealth inequality presents an immediate, existential

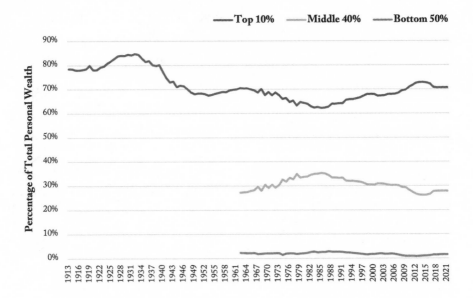

Figure 29.17: Percentage of Total U.S. Personal Wealth by Percentile (1913–2021)[44]

threat to the U.S., while others argue that the threat is overstated. The merits and flaws of each argument are beyond the scope of this book, but the mere fact that the issue invites debate demonstrates that it is worthy of further exploration. There is also evidence that increased wealth and income disparity have a negative impact on economic growth, as lower-income individuals are more likely to spend incremental increases in their income. Therefore, all else being equal, expansion of the wealth gap likely presents another obstacle to economic growth.

POINT OF INTEREST

Drivers of Income and Wealth Inequality

The steady expansion of U.S. income and wealth inequality over the past forty years is the byproduct of multiple forces. Isolating the relative importance of each force is difficult, and it is even more difficult to create solutions that reverse the trend. A few of the more notable causes of growing wealth and income inequality include:

- **Education**—On average, highly educated workers demand higher compensation. The income gap between those with higher educational achievement (e.g., college and advanced degrees) and those with lower achievement (e.g., high school or less) has widened over the past forty years. This effect is further amplified by the tendency of highly educated individuals to get married.[45]

- **Technology**—The Information Age has eliminated the need for workers performing routine tasks in both blue-collar and white-collar jobs. This has eliminated many administrative jobs.
- **Superstar Economics**—The replacement of workers performing routine tasks has had the opposite effect on individuals who excel at tasks that are not easily replaced by technology. By leveraging their impact, they can demand higher compensation.

Chapter 30

A 101-YEAR PANDEMIC

*"Two generations is an eternity in the minds of financial operators, and all
that was out of sight and out of mind in the world of the 1970s."*[1]

—PAUL VOLCKER, former chairman of the Federal Reserve Board

ackluster prospects of future economic growth, increasing global competition, stubborn deficits, and the widening of wealth gaps amplified economic anxiety in America during the 2010s. These concerns were temporarily put aside, however, when a new threat emerged at the end of the decade. On December 12, 2019, a cluster of patients were admitted to a hospital in the city of Wuhan, China. They were experiencing pneumonia-like symptoms that were unresponsive to standard treatment protocols. These patients are now believed to be the first victims of a novel coronavirus known as COVID-19.

POINT OF INTEREST

A Natural Cause or Laboratory Experiment Gone Awry?

There are two leading theories regarding the origin of the COVID-19 virus. The first theory is that it originated in another animal species, such as a bat, and then adapted to humans. The second theory is that it was created artificially in a laboratory and released accidentally. Existing evidence is inconclusive, but it appears moderately biased toward the theory that the virus had a natural origin.

The alternative theory that COVID-19 was genetically engineered in a lab is considered moderately less likely, but it is certainly a plausible explanation.

By the time this book is published, the scientific community may have converged on a definitive explanation. Regardless of its origin, however, few scientists debate that the rapid spread of the virus among human beings began in Wuhan, China, at some point between mid-October and mid-November of 2019.[2]

On December 31, 2019, the World Health Organization (WHO) discovered a media report issued by the Wuhan Municipal Health Commission warning citizens of the presence of severe "viral pneumonia." The very next day, Chinese authorities closed the Huanan Seafood Market, which they suspected to be the source of the pathogen causing the pneumonia outbreak. On January 3, 2020, Chinese authorities reported forty more cases of pneumonia to the WHO. Two days later, they shared the genetic sequence of the virus suspected to have caused the outbreak. On January 10, 2020, the WHO reported the outbreak of a novel coronavirus (later confirmed to be COVID-19), and three days later the first cases of COVID-19 were detected in Thailand.[3]

Over the next year, the number of COVID-19 cases increased exponentially before peaking in January 2021 (Figure 30.1). In the early months of the pandemic, nations closed borders and enacted various quarantine restrictions in desperate attempts to contain the virus, but COVID-19 was far too contagious. The only hope was to slow the spread, prevent healthcare systems from being completely overrun, and provide scientists with as much time as possible to develop a vaccine.

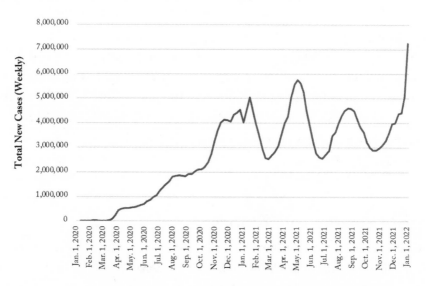

Figure 30.1: Total New Cases of COVID-19 (January 1, 2020–January 1, 2022)[4]

THE FINANCIAL EFFECTS OF A GLOBAL PANDEMIC

Most Americans believed that the COVID-19 pandemic, the subsequent financial panic, and the responses of policymakers were unprecedented, but multiple events in the past 230 years help explain what happened since December 2019. That said, like all previous financial crises there is no single event that explains everything. One way to understand the fundamental dynamics of the COVID-19 financial crisis is to isolate the distinct phases and map them to the most relevant historical events. Detailed explanations of each phase are throughout the remainder of this chapter.

Phase 1: A "Sudden Stop" Financial Panic

The financial panic in March 2020 seemed unusual because of the sheer magnitude of the impact and suddenness of the onset. Most market shocks arrive with at least some advance warning, providing people with time to prepare. COVID-19, however, was massively disruptive and arrived with almost no warning. In a matter of days, entire segments of the economy shut down, and Americans confronted the real prospect of a catastrophic economic collapse.

The financial effects of COVID-19 seemed unprecedented, but they were very similar to the ones following the sudden onset of World War I in late July 1914 (see chapter 14). Much like COVID-19, the outbreak of World War I was sudden, unexpected, and massively disruptive on a global scale. The primary difference was that U.S. policymakers in 1914 were less equipped to handle it. Foreign securities exchanges shut down and remained closed for years, which left U.S. securities markets as the only source of liquidity. The tidal wave of sell orders forced the New York Stock Exchange to close its doors on the morning of July 31, 1914.[5]

The impact of COVID-19 was less severe because policymakers had a more robust set of fiscal and monetary policy tools. In addition, having learned valuable lessons from the Great Depression in the 1930s and GFC in 2008 and 2009, they were willing to use them with little hesitation. This explains why the economy stopped far short of a Great Depression–level event and, instead, experienced only a mild and short-lived recession.

Phase 2: Emergency Response

The U.S. fiscal and monetary responses to the COVID-19 pandemic differed from those employed after the onset of World War I, but they were hardly unique. In fact, the policies looked a lot like the ones employed only twelve years earlier during the GFC (see

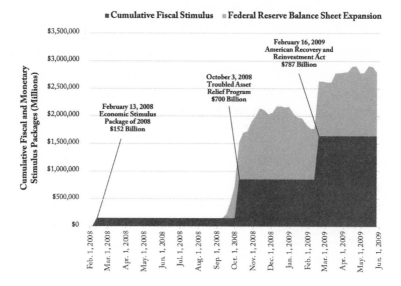

Figure 30.2: Cumulative Fiscal Stimulus and Federal Reserve Balance Sheet Expansion (Millions) (February 1, 2008–June 1, 2009)[6]

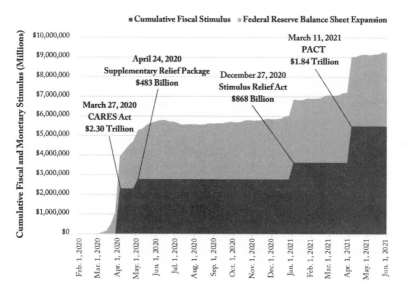

Figure 30.3: Cumulative Fiscal Stimulus and Federal Reserve Balance Sheet Expansion (Millions) (February 1, 2020–June 1, 2021)[7]

chapter 28). In October 2008, monetary and fiscal policymakers flooded the financial system with liquidity to reverse a self-reinforcing deflationary spiral. Had they failed to act aggressively, a Great Depression–level event was a virtual certainty. The Federal Reserve and Congress responded similarly in 2020. Showing the similarity of these two responses, the fiscal programs and Federal Reserve balance sheet expansions during the GFC and COVID-19 are depicted in Figure 30.2 and Figure 30.3, respectively.

The financial responses to COVID-19 were considerably larger and implemented much more rapidly than those employed during the GFC, but the fundamental tactics were similar. Because the GFC had occurred so recently, Americans were less resistant to actions that would have otherwise seemed unimaginable. In fact, the policy responses took effect so quickly that many Americans were stunned when the U.S. economy rebounded even though entire industries lay idle. This outcome is precisely what is expected, however, when monetary and fiscal stimulus immediately fills a deflationary void. In this respect, the quick and massive responses by policymakers were successful. On the other hand, stimulus of this magnitude comes with a cost. In addition to increasing U.S. debt levels substantially, the responses produced two unwanted side effects: reckless speculation and high levels of inflation.

Phase 3: Side Effects

It is important to emphasize that extreme monetary and fiscal policy responses were essential to prevent an economic catastrophe in 2020. The alternative was to allow the U.S. to suffer a Great Depression–level event, which is never a risk to take lightly. Chapters 16 and 19 reveal that the cost of major depressions involves far more than a loss of wealth. The U.S. monetary and fiscal policies enacted in 2020 and 2021 prevented this from happening. Many pundits later argued that the stimulus was excessive. In retrospect, some criticism was valid, but if given a choice between doing too little or too much, it is hard to fault the Fed and Congress for expressing a bias toward the latter. Nevertheless, when an economy is flooded with more money than is needed, unwanted side effects appear. These typically take the form of reckless speculation and high inflation. In early 2021, Americans were experiencing both. The excessive speculation resembled the dot-com bubble in the late 1990s, while elevated levels of inflation resembled the post–World War I/Great Influenza inflation of 1919–1920.

The Dot-com Bubble of 1999

The formation of speculative asset bubbles is almost inevitable when people have too much money. The post-COVID-19 bubbles formed soon after monetary and fiscal stimulus hit U.S. bank accounts. During the second half of 2020 and early 2021, Americans poured their newfound wealth into a variety of speculative assets, such as high-risk tech stocks, cryptocurrencies, and non-fungible tokens (NFTs). The bubbles were reminiscent of the dot-com bubble that formed in the late 1990s (see chapter 27).

Figure 30.4: Growth of $1 Invested in the ARK Innovation ETF (ARKK) and S&P 500 Index ETF (SPY) (January 2, 2020–March 31, 2023)[8]

When speculative manias end, the media searches for archetypical villains who best exemplify the delusion of the era. After the dot-com bust, two prominent villains were Henry Blodget, an overly optimistic sell-side analyst, and the company Pets. com, whose sock puppet mascot became an icon of the crash. A leading candidate for the archetypical villain of the COVID-19 era is Cathie Wood, CIO of the ARK Innovation ETF (ARKK). Wood invested the fund in an assortment of highly speculative tech and crypto stocks. As is often the case, the ARKK fund initially experienced breathtaking gains when the monetary floodwaters rose in 2020 and early 2021. The 290 percent gain from March 2, 2020, to February 12, 2021, made the respectable 27 percent gain of the S&P 500 seem tame. However, as is usually the case with overconfident speculation, ARKK's fall surpassed its rise. As of March 31, 2023, the ARK fund hovered at a mere 25 percent of its peak value, massively underperforming the S&P 500 Index. Figure 30.4 tracks the rise and fall of the ARK Innovation Fund. The final verdict on the ARKK fund was undetermined as of the completion of this manuscript, but history strongly suggests that it will not be good.

Inflation of 1919–1920

On April 13, 2021, the Bureau of Labor Statistics (BLS) reported an inflation rate of 4.2 percent for the twelve-month period ending March 31, 2021. Over the subsequent

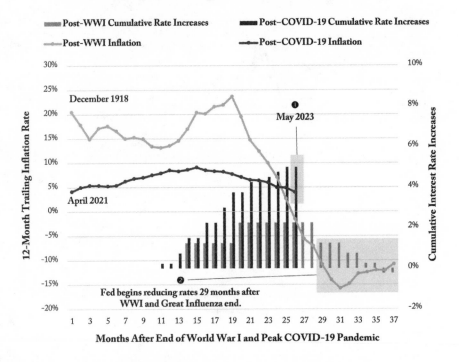

Figure 30.5: Comparison of COVID-19 Inflation and 1919 Inflation
(Months since End of World War I and Second Wave of COVID-19)[9]

fifteen months, inflation rose to even higher levels before starting to decline gradually. Unlike asset bubbles, persistently high inflation is relatively rare in U.S. history. The most comparable event occurred almost exactly one hundred years ago when World War I and the deadly second wave of the Great Influenza ended nearly simultaneously (see chapter 14). Within months, Americans began spending their pent-up savings, but goods and services were in short supply because the sudden shift from total war back to normalcy created severe supply chain disruptions. Figure 30.5 shows inflation rates in the aftermath of COVID-19 compared to those reported after the end of World War I and the deadly second wave of the Great Influenza.

Phase 4: Cleanup

The U.S. entered the final phase of the COVID-19 financial crisis in the winter of 2022/2023. Asset bubbles had already deflated just like the dot-com stocks had in 2000, but inflation persisted. By March 2022, the Federal Reserve had decisively shifted to a hawkish position and made it clear that taming inflation was the top priority. At the time, many investors underestimated the Fed's commitment because they assumed that the Fed's dovish bias over the prior decades was ideological rather than circumstantial. They failed to appreciate that the Fed could afford to be dovish when unemployment and deflationary pressures were the primary economic risks, but the situation in 2022 was much different. Unemployment was exceptionally low and inflationary pressures had persisted for too long. If the Fed allowed inflation to persist, high levels of *current inflation* could mutate into higher *inflation expectations*. The Federal Reserve's failure to appreciate the risk of higher inflation expectations in the late 1960s and 1970s was an important factor leading to the Great Inflation in 1965 to 1982 (see chapter 23).

As of the completion of this manuscript, the Great Inflation remained the event that the Federal Reserve feared most. Extinguishing inflation decisively still appeared likely to cause economic pain in the form of lower asset values, job losses, an overall contraction of the economy, and potential destabilization of the banking system. After inflation is tamed, it is likely that the concerns of secular stagnation, rise of economic rivals such as China, unsustainable fiscal deficits, and the general trend of increasing wealth disparity will return to the forefront. But this history has yet to be written.

Chapter 31

REFLECTIONS ON THE PAST AND SHADOWS OF AMERICA'S FUTURE

"I have thought it my duty to exhibit things as they are, not as they ought to be."[1]

—ALEXANDER HAMILTON

E ach chapter of this book shared multiple lessons that remain just as relevant today as they were decades or even hundreds of years ago. This is because human behavior changes little with the passage of time. Financial events that seem unprecedented on the surface are, in fact, driven by the same underlying economic currents and human behaviors. There are not enough pages remaining in this book to revisit every lesson, but it is worth highlighting a few.

LESSON #1: THE PRESENT IS MOSTLY A RECOMBINATION OF THE PAST

Edmund Burke once said that "those who don't know history are destined to repeat it." There is truth to this statement, but in the case of financial history, the same events never repeat exactly. Instead, each new iteration constitutes a unique combination of multiple events from the past. This often makes it difficult to understand what is happening in the moment because nothing in the past is an exact match. The COVID-19 crisis was an excellent example. Forecasting the financial consequences required an understanding of the Panic of 1914, the end of the Great Influenza and World War I in 1918–1919, the inflation of 1919–1920, and the Great Inflation of 1965–1982. This explains why it is essential to study history well beyond one's lifespan. To this end, my hope is that readers use this book as a tool to regularly travel back in time and contextualize what is happening in the present.

LESSON #2: THE NOISE OF SECURITIES MARKETS CONCEALS THE MOST IMPORTANT UNDERLYING CURRENTS

Peter Brown, CEO of Renaissance Technologies, once said, "Anytime you hear financial experts talking about how the market went up because of such and such—remember it's all nonsense." There are few investors who heed this advice. Instead, most spend their days fixated on stock market data and financial news feeds, struggling to make sense of information that has little meaning. These habits are harmful because they prevent people from noticing the most important currents that shape the future. Gaining knowledge of financial history is a remedy. By understanding the nature of the most powerful economic currents, it becomes easier to differentiate meaningful events from background noise. A recent example was the run on Silicon Valley Bank (SVB) in March 2023. Now that you have learned about the uncontrolled bank runs during the Panics in 1819, 1839, 1907, 1929, and 2008, you can appreciate why the Federal Reserve was forced to act quickly and aggressively. The problems at SVB may have been somewhat anomalous, but the vulnerability that it exposed was systemic. Had the Federal Reserve failed to remove the incentive of depositors with balances greater than $250,000 to liquidate their accounts, a full-blown run on the U.S. banking system was highly likely. History demonstrates that the media is highly prone to sensationalizing financial shocks that are not as threatening as they appear, but, in this case, understanding the history and dynamics of bank runs made the SVB situation stand out as a real threat.[2]

LESSON #3: OUTSMARTING SECURITIES MARKETS IS A FEAT THAT FEW SHOULD ATTEMPT

Soon after the signing of the Buttonwood Agreement in 1792, investors and speculators relentlessly sought ways to cheat or outsmart the market. Prior to the Securities Act of 1933 and Securities Exchange Act of 1934, cheating rather than outsmarting the market was by far the most lucrative strategy. But once market manipulation and insider trading were outlawed, outsmarting the market became the only remaining option. The problem, however, is that securities analysis is subjected to the unbending law of the wisdom of crowds, which dictates that the number of investors capable of profiting from securities mispricing will always be small. This is why most investors are better off streamlining their asset allocation (i.e., avoiding exotic asset classes) and relying predominantly (if not exclusively) on index funds. Few investors take this approach, but hopefully this book will change a few minds.

LESSON #4: PRESENT SOLUTIONS ARE OFTEN THE SEEDS OF FUTURE PROBLEMS

One of the most enduring principles of financial history is that the solutions to present problems plant the seeds of future ones. This principle is often hidden by the fact that it often takes decades for solutions to morph into problems. In the 1800s, the U.S. attracted enormous sums of capital to build out its railroad network, but the excesses led to price wars and waves of business failures. In the 1930s, the New Deal and World War II spending reduced unemployment to the low single digits. Yet the lingering scars of persistently high unemployment during the Great Depression led the Federal Reserve and federal government to prioritize full employment over price stability, which contributed to the onset of the Great Inflation in 1965. This cycle has been repeated multiple times in the past and will continue to repeat in the future. This does not mean that current solutions are unnecessary, but it does mean that we must be vigilant so that we can detect when they outlive their utility.

LESSON #5: THE AGONY AND THE ECSTASY OF AMERICA'S ECONOMIC EVOLUTION

The most difficult thing about studying U.S. financial history is witnessing how the American system creates extraordinary benefits while simultaneously inflicting pain. This is because, as Joseph Schumpeter observed, capitalism is a process of creative destruction. The creative element of capitalism has fueled more than 230 years of extraordinary economic progress that benefitted society as a whole. At the same time, progress was accompanied by the periodic destruction of companies, philosophies, and professions that no longer offered sufficient value. Such destruction was often essential for the good of the whole, but there were also instances in which destructive forces were applied in error and unfairly. The expansion of railroads in the late 1800s contributed to horrific crimes against Native Americans, yet also served as the backbone of the arsenal of democracy in World War II. Technological advancements over the past fifty years have improved the quality of life for many Americans, yet also led to the obsolescence of jobs that many hoped to hold for their entire lives.

The U.S. willingly submits itself to the often ruthless power of market forces more than most nations, and this has enabled it to advance at a faster pace, but the benefits and drawbacks are never evenly distributed. This is why there is and always will be battles between those burdened disproportionately by the costs of capitalism and those who enjoy more of the benefits. A critical challenge for the U.S. has and always will be where to draw the line. How much individual sacrifice and pain experienced by some Americans is tolerable for the advancement of society as a whole? A low tolerance of pain risks the squelching of innovation and sacrifices the nation's competitiveness, but a tolerance that is too high allows too many people to suffer, which eventually destabilizes the system. Finding the appropriate balance will always drive intense conflict in the U.S., and if the nation tilts too far in either direction, it risks ending its 230-year run of growing economic prosperity.

LESSON #6: THREATS TO U.S. ECONOMIC PROSPERITY ARE FORMIDABLE BUT NEED NOT BE FATAL

The United States of America has prospered for more than 230 years. It started as a frontier market that depended almost entirely on agricultural production. After World War II, the U.S. replaced the British Empire as the world's financial center and issuer of the world's reserve currency. Today, it remains the most powerful nation in the world financially and militarily; however, there are emerging threats that cannot be taken lightly. Several threats were revealed in part 6. At the top of the list is America's well-entrenched habit of spending beyond its means. After World War II ended, America's debt burden declined as a percentage of GDP because of strong economic growth that was driven by exceptional productivity gains and America's unique competitive position relative to a world that lay in ruins. While America maintains many of its competitive advantages, they are not as formidable as they once were. Absent a revolutionary acceleration of productivity, the U.S. cannot grow its way out of its spending problem—and competition from rising nations adds to this headwind. How the nation chooses to address this challenge will determine how long it can sustain its reign as the heir to the British Empire.

SHADOWS OF THE FUTURE

Over the past three and a half years, I buried myself so deep in books that I often lost sight of the present. I went into this process pessimistic about America's future, but I emerged confident. One reason is because I now realize that America's future has almost always appeared bleak to those living in the moment. Americans' ancestors wrestled constantly with existential threats to their system of government, economic well-being, personal freedoms, and often their very survival. They feared and experienced attacks from foreign nations, a civil war, battles in distant lands, discrimination, economic depressions, financial exploitation, political corruption, devastating pandemics, apocalyptic natural disasters, and periods of civil unrest that approached the brink of anarchy. It is undeniable that some races, genders, religious groups, socioeconomic classes, and other disadvantaged groups tended to suffer disproportionately during hard times. Those who deny this reality do so only by remaining willfully blind to the past.

On the other hand, the United States has prevailed over every challenge thrown in its path, and its citizens have emerged scarred but stronger for having endured them. During the immigration waves of the late 1800s, America was labeled a melting pot to describe the mix of nationalities and religions drawn to the economic opportunities and personal freedoms afforded to its citizens. These opportunities are real. But America is also a melting pot of conflicting values and behaviors, which sometimes weave and, at other times, unwind the fabric of society. Americans have shown that they can be both greedy and altruistic; prejudiced and welcoming; cruel and empathetic; foolish and ingenious; entitled and sacrificial; and cowardly and heroic. America is a nation populated by flawed human beings who, nonetheless, collectively aspire to move closer to perfection. It is this enduring attribute of the American spirit that has driven the nation's successes for more than two hundred years.

Shadows of America's future appear daunting in 2024. Debt levels are rising, the wealth gap is expanding, political polarization is intensifying, economic rivals are becoming more competitive, and climate change threatens the quality of life for humanity. Those who deny the existence of such challenges gamble with their children's futures, but those who believe the future is hopeless disregard the exceptional track record and selfless sacrifice of their ancestors. Ensuring the continuity of the American spirit and extending its exceptional track record will not be easy—nor has it ever been easy. It will require a healthy combination of wisdom to recognize shared challenges, grace to live peacefully with irreconcilable differences, resilience to sacrifice in ways that many believe are no longer necessary, and confidence that the nation still has the ability to prevail collectively.

There is now a contagious belief that the United States of America is in decline, but the nation's battle scars—acquired from more than two centuries of struggle—demonstrate that America is assuredly not out. Warren Buffett, America's best investor of the last one hundred years, has repeatedly stated that investors would be unwise to bet against America. Despite the nation's setbacks and imperfections, bets against America still seem unlikely to reward those who dare make them. My hope is that this book helps people understand how the U.S. financial system contributed to this nation's outstanding track record and helps its leaders build a better future for the nation's children.

NOTES

Introduction

1. Charles D. Ellis, *Figuring it Out: Sixty Years of Answering Investors' Most Important Questions* (Hoboken, NJ: John Wiley & Sons, 2022).

Part 1

1. Alexander Hamilton, *Report on a Plan for the Further Support of Public Credit*, January 16, 1795.

2. Creditworthiness refers to the confidence that lenders have in a borrower's ability to repay their debts; the First Bank of the United States was technically a central bank, but its powers were more limited in comparison to the modern Federal Reserve System. The mandates of the First Bank were to stabilize the currency, serve as the nation's fiscal agent, and provide a rudimentary form of monetary policy.

3. The New York Stock Exchange experienced several name changes since its initial formation. Purely for the purposes of avoiding confusion with the use of multiple names, it is only referred to as the New York Stock Exchange or NYSE throughout the entirety of this book.

Chapter 1

1. Alexander Hamilton *The Warning No. III*, February 21, 1797, https://founders.archives.gov/documents/Hamilton/01-20-02-0330#ARHN-01-20-02-0330-fn-0001.

2. Some veterans staged open revolts to force payment. Shays' Rebellion was the most notable of these revolts; William N. Goetzmann and K. Geert Rouwenhorst, eds. *The Origins of Value: The Financial Innovations That Created Modern Capital Markets* (New York: Oxford University Press, 2005).

3. Goetzmann and Roewenhorst, *The Origins of Value*.

4. Ron Chernow, *Alexander Hamilton* (New York: Penguin Books, 2004), 110.

5. Alexander Hamilton, *First Report on the Public Credit* (January 9, 1790), https://commons.wikimedia.org/wiki/File:P13_3Large.jpg; Goetzmann and Roewenhorst, *The Origins of Value*, 303-304; Payment in full was not entirely accurate, as the U.S. negotiated various repayment options, such as partial payment in land, with at least some creditors.

6. The core principle of a fractional reserve banking system is that only a "fraction" of deposits must be available for immediate withdrawal. This allows banks to invest customer deposits in assets (usually loans and safe fixed-income securities) that have a higher expected return than the rate of interest paid to depositors. The ever-present risk in a fractional reserve banking system is the occurrence of panics in which customers demand withdrawals that exceed the amount of cash on hand. Modern central banks address this by serving as a lender of last resort to banks that are faced with insolvency due only to temporarily elevated levels of withdrawals.

7. Private investors funded 80 percent of the First Bank's initial $10 million in capital, while the federal government funded the remaining 20 percent in the form of a loan from the First Bank. Private investors were permitted to fund 75 percent of their commitment with U.S. government bonds and 25 percent with specie.

8. Alexander Hamilton, *Second Report on the Further Provision Necessary for Establishing Public Credit*, December 13, 1790, https://founders.archives.gov/documents/Hamilton/01-07-02-0229-0003.

9. Andrew H. Browning, *The Panic of 1819: The First Great Depression* (Columbia, MO: University of Missouri Press, 2019).

10. Browning, *The Panic of 1819*; Mark Higgins, "A History of Central Banking in the United States," *Financial History* 144 (Winter 2023); Clifford F. Thies, "Not Worth a Continental." https://www.aier.org/article/not-worth-a-continental.

11. The capitalization of $10 million was an enormous sum in 1791. It exceeded the combined capital of all other U.S. banks and insurance companies at the time.

12. *Tariff of 1790*, United States House of Representatives, August 10, 1790.

13. Alexander Hamilton. *Reports of the Secretary of the Treasury of the United States, Volume 1*, 199.

14. P. Garber, "Alexander Hamilton's Market-Based Debt Reduction Plan" (working paper no. 3597, National Bureau of Economic Research, January 1991), 33, https://www.nber.org/system/files/working_papers/w3597/w3597.pdf.

15. Louis Johnston and Samuel H. Williamson, "What Was the U.S. GDP Then?" MeasuringWorth.com, accessed April 28, 2023, https://www.measuringworth.com/datasets/usgdp/.

16. Ron Chernow, *Alexander Hamilton* (New York: Penguin Books, 2004), 647.

17. Edmund Stedman, ed., *The New York Stock Exchange: Volume I* (New York: Stock Exchange Historical Company, 1905), 45. https://archive.org/details/cu31924030206506/page/n15/mode/2up.

18. Jeff Wilser, *Alexander Hamilton's Guide to Life* (New York: Three Rivers Press, 2016), 21, https://archive.org/details/alexanderhamilto0000wils/page/n5/mode/2up?q=genius&view=theater.

Chapter 2

1. Joseph Stancliffe Davis, *Essays in the Earlier History of American Corporations* (Cambridge, MA: Harvard University Press, 1917), 286.

2. Letter from Alexander Hamilton to Rufus King, August 17, 1791, https://founders.archives.gov/documents/Hamilton/01-09-02-0056.

3. The Federal Reserve employs similar tactics today, referring to them as "moral suasion."

4. Davis, *Essays in the Earlier History of American Corporations*, 202–203.

5. Walter Werner and Steven T. Smith, *Wall Street* (New York: Columbia University Press, 1991), 14–15.

6. Davis, *Essays in the Earlier History of American Corporations*, 208. Thomas Jefferson's estimate was exaggerated, but the financial crisis did present a major threat to the financial system. It is ironic, however, that Jefferson was the sole dissenting vote on the sinking fund commission when Alexander Hamilton sought more funds to stop the panic.

7. Davis, *Essays in the Earlier History of American Corporations*, 175–177. There were three separate issues of U.S. government bonds in circulation at the time. It is believed that Duer only intended to corner the market for one issue.

8. Davis, *Essays in the Earlier History of American Corporations*, 188.

9. Davis, *Essays in the Earlier History of American Corporations*, 175–177; Robert F. Jones, "William Duer and the Business of Government in the Era of the American Revolution," *The William and Mary Quarterly* 32, no. 3 (July 1975): 393–416.

10. "Bills discounted" is the term used at the time to describe loans issued by the First Bank; James O. Wettereau, *Statistical Records of the First Bank of the United States* (New York: Garland Publishing, 1985), 8.

11. Wettereau, *Statistical Records of the First Bank.*

12. Wettereau, *Statistical Records of the First Bank.*

13. Timothy F. Geithner, *Stress Test: Reflections on Financial Crises* (New York: Broadway Books, 2014), 262.

14. Geithner, *Stress Test*, 262.

15. Richard Sylla, Robert E. Wright, and David J. Cowen, "Alexander Hamilton, Central Banker: Crisis Management During the U.S. Financial Panic of 1792," *Business History Review* 83 (Spring 2009): 61–86.

16. Hamilton needed a majority vote to authorize use of the sinking fund. Initially, he was unable to obtain a majority because two commissioners, Edmund Randolph and Thomas Jefferson, rejected the request, and John Jay (the fifth commissioner) was unavailable to vote. Hamilton circumvented the rejection by using $50,000 that remained from the prior authorization granted in August 1791. On March 26, 1791, the sinking fund commissioners approved an additional $100,000 of open market purchases. Thomas Jefferson was the only dissenter.

17. It is questionable whether the actual signing took place beneath the buttonwood tree, but the pact has retained the name, nonetheless.

18. "Buttonwood Agreement," May 17, 1792, https://www.sechistorical.org/collection/papers/1790/1792_0517_NYSEButtonwood.pdf.

19. Sylla, Wright, and Cowen, "Alexander Hamilton, Central Banker."

Chapter 3

1. Browning, *The Panic of 1819.*

2. The most famous case of intellectual property theft was orchestrated by Samuel Slater. After memorizing the details of Arkwright's spinning wheel technology, Slater arrived in America in 1789 and partnered with a Rhode Island–based textile owner to create the first British-style textile mill in the United States. Francis Cabot Lowell also used stolen, British design specs to launch the Boston Manufacturing Company, which became the first large-scale textile manufacturer in the nation.

3. B. H. Beckhart, "Outline of Banking History," *The Annals of the American Academy of Political and Social Science* 99 (January 1922): 1–16.

4. Warren E. Weber, "Early State Banks in the United States: How Many Were There and When Did They Exist?" (working paper, Federal Reserve Bank of Minneapolis, Research Department, December 2005), https://doi.org/10.21034/wp.634. Weber defines "bank" as a financial institution that was chartered by a state or was established under a "free banking" law and was legally permitted to issue notes—bearer instruments (pieces of paper) that were liabilities of the issuer and redeemable in specie on demand.

5. William N. Goetzmann and K. Geert Rouwenhorst, eds. *The Origins of Value: The Financial Innovations That Created Modern Capital Markets* (New York: Oxford University Press, 2005), 302.

6. This is a simplified example. There are several measures of the money supply. The most important concept to understand is that "reserves" held by banks represent only a fraction of the total assets on a bank's balance sheet.

7. This practice was officially called "impressment." The British claimed that it was used only on British deserters, but, in truth, thousands of Americans were captured.

8. British forces were divided between the war with Napoleon and the U.S., but they still inflicted significant damage on the United States. The U.S. lost roughly 15,000 soldiers, and the White House was burned to the ground before the war ended.

9. Lisa R. Morales, "The Financial History of the War of 1812" (dissertation, University of North Texas, May 2009), https://digital.library.unt.edu/ark:/67531/metadc9922/m2/1/high_res_d/ dissertation.pdf; Hugh Rockoff, "War and Inflation in the United States from the Revolution to the First Iraq War" (working paper, National Bureau of Economic Research, May 2015), https:// doi.org/10.3386/w21221.

10. *Speeches of Henry Lord Brougham, Upon Questions Relating to Public Rights, Duties, and Interests* (Edinburgh, 1895).

11. Browning, *The Panic of 1819.*

12. Bureau of the Census, *Historical Statistics of the United States: Colonial Times to 1970* (Washington, DC: U.S. Bureau of the Census, 1975), 209, https://archive.org/details/ HistoricalStatisticsOfTheUnitedStatesColonialTimesTo1970.

13. Browning, *The Panic of 1819;* "This Day in History: Mount Tambora Explosively Erupts in 1815," National Oceanic and Atmospheric Administration, April 10, 2020, https://www.nesdis.noaa.gov/ news/day-history-mount-tambora-explosively-erupts-1815. Accessed February 5, 2023.

14. Malcolm J. Rohrbough, *The Land Office Business: The Settlement and Administration of American Public Lands, 1789–1837* (London: Oxford University Press, 1968), 115.

15. Rohrbough, *The Land Office Business,* 115.

16. Browning, *The Panic of 1819.*

17. Mississippi "stock" refers to banknotes issued at the time by state banks located in Mississippi.

18. Browning, *The Panic of 1819.*

19. Some of this was the fault of the bank's board of directors. One example was the failure of the bank to collect specie from investors. The bank's charter required an initial investment of $35 million, 25 percent of which was payable in specie and 75 percent payable in government bonds or specie. But these conditions were not enforced. After the three installment payments were completed at the end of twelve months, the Second Bank had an estimated $2 million in specie despite a charter that required $7 million.

20. John T. Holdsworth, and Davis R. Dewey, "The First and Second Banks of the United States," The National Monetary Commission (Washington, DC: Government Printing Office, 1910).

21. *Historical Statistics of the United States: Colonial Times to 1970,* 209.

22. *Historical Statistics of the United States: Colonial Times to 1970,* 201.

23. William H. Crawford, *Annual Report of the Secretary of the Treasury on the State of the Finances,* Secretary of the Treasury, February 1820, https://fraser.stlouisfed.org/files/docs/publications/ treasar/AR_TREASURY_1820.pdf.

24. There were an estimated 261 state banks in existence at the end of 1819, which would mean that roughly 30 percent of banks failed.

25. Browning, *The Panic of 1819.*

26. Browning, *The Panic of 1819.*

Chapter 4

1. Werner and Smith, *Wall Street,* 76.

2. Werner and Smith, *Wall Street, 158–159.*

3. Robert Sobel, *The Big Board: A History of the New York Stock Market* (New York: Free Press, 1965). The official name at the time was the New York Stock and Exchange Board.

4. Bernard F. Cataldo, "Limited Liability with One-Man Companies and Subsidiary Corporations," *Law and Contemporary Problems* 18, no. 4 (Fall 1953): 473–504, https://scholarship.law.duke.edu/ lcp/vol18/iss4/4.

5. Trading volume for 1822, 1823, 1827, 1828 was lost to history and is, therefore, not included in the calculation for 1820–1829; Werner and Smith, *Wall Street*, 162.

6. Yi Wen, *The Making of an Economic Superpower: Unlocking China's Secret of Rapid Industrialization* (Hackensack, NJ: World Scientific Press, 2016).

7. Richard E. Sylla and Robert E. Wright, "U.S. Corporate Development, 1801–1860," Cambridge, MA: National Bureau of Economic Research, SES Grant no. 0751577.

8. Edmund Clarence Stedman, ed. *The New York Stock Exchange: Volume I* (New York: Stock Exchange Historical Company, 1905), 407, https://archive.org/details/cu31924030206506/page/n15/mode/2up.

9. "A Century of Lawmaking for a New Nation: U.S. Congressional Documents and Debates, 1774–1875," American State Papers, House of Representatives, 16th Congress, 1st Session, *Finance: Volume 3*, https://memory.loc.gov/cgi-bin/ampage?collId=llsp&fileName=011/llsp011.db&recNum=517.

10. Ralph C. H. Catterall, *The Second Bank of the United States* (Chicago: University of Chicago Press, 1903).

11. Public opinion polls did not exist in the 1830s, but metrics such as the number of letters received by congressmen for or against the second bank clearly indicate the public opinion tilted in favor of its existence.

12. Robert V. Remini, *Andrew Jackson and the Bank War* (New York: W.W. Norton & Company, 1967).

13. Catterall, *The Second Bank of the United States*.

14. Alasdair Roberts, *America's First Great Depression: Economic Crisis and Political Disorder after the Panic of 1837* (Ithaca, NY: Cornell University Press, 2012).

15. Remini, *Andrew Jackson and the Bank War*, 125.

16. Holden Lewis, "Experts: No Real-Estate Bubble Burst," *Chicago Sun-Times*, September 10, 2004.

17. The data shows a massive increase in sales but still significantly underestimates the impact. Speculators often sold land at much higher prices soon after auctions, but this effect is not captured in the data.

18. *Report of the Secretary of the Treasury on the State of the Finances for the Year 1865* (Washington, DC: Government Printing Office, 1865), https://fraser.stlouisfed.org/title/annual-report-secretary-treasury-state-finances-194/report-secretary-treasury-state-finances-year-1865-5509.

19. The cause of the outflows was investment in higher yielding securities in the U.S. and increased wheat imports due to several years of poor harvests. In Great Britain, the 1840s were referred to as the Hungry Forties due to the shortage of wheat.

20. Peter Temin, *The Jacksonian Economy* (New York: W.W. Norton & Company, 1969); Sobel, *The Big Board*, 48.

21. Roberts, *America's First Great Depression*, 14.

22. Roberts, *America's First Great Depression*.

23. Sydney Smith, "The Reverend Sydney Smith on the American Debt," *The True Colonist*, March 8, 1844, https://trove.nla.gov.au/newspaper/article/202420517.

24. Roberts, *America's First Great Depression*.

25. Michigan was an especially sad case in that they never received the proceeds of their bond sale because a bank that bought them defaulted before paying the state.

26. Roberts, *America's First Great Depression*.

Chapter 5

1. Sidney George Fisher, "The Diary of Sidney George Fisher, 1844," *The Pennsylvania Magazine of History and Biography* 79, no. 4 (October 1995): 485–505.

2. Edmund Clarence Stedman, ed. *The New York Stock Exchange: Volume I* (New York: Stock Exchange Historical Company, 1905), 111, https://archive.org/details/cu31924030206506/page/n15/mode/2up.

3. Southerners were likely correct that the U.S. would eventually outlaw slavery entirely, but there is little evidence that Abraham Lincoln and the Republican Party sought anything more than the halt of westward expansion in 1860. Further, while there was a vocal abolitionist movement in the Northern states, it was a small minority. On the eve of the Civil War, estimates are that only 5 percent of Northerners advocated for eliminating slavery entirely in the South.

4. Gerald Gunderson, "The Origin of the American Civil War," *The Journal of Economic History* 34, no. 4 (December 1974): 915–950, https://doi.org/10.1017/S0022050700089361.

5. Both Missouri and Kentucky had internal conflicts between Confederate and Union sympathizers. Both received recognition as Confederate states, but their status was not universally recognized within the state.

6. Roger Ransom and Richard Sutch, "Capitalists without Capital: The Burden of Slavery and Impact of Emancipation," *Agricultural History* 62, no. 3 (Summer 1988): 133–160, https://www.jstor.org/stable/3743211.

7. The New York bankers requested suspension of the 1846 Independent Treasury Act, sale of bonds below par value, and heavier taxation. Secretary Chase believed that it was not politically feasible to satisfy these requests.

8. Patrick Newman, "The Origins of the National Banking System: The Chase-Cooke Connection and the New York City Banks," *The Independent Review* 22, no. 3 (Winter 2018): 383–401, https://www.independent.org/publications/tir/article.asp?id=1260.

9. H. R. 240, 37th Congress, 2nd Session (1862), https://www.govtrack.us/congress/bills/37/hr202400.

10. Henrietta M. Larson, *Jay Cooke, Private Banker* (Cambridge, MA: Harvard University Press, 1936).

11. Newman, "Origins of the National Banking System."; *Report of the Secretary of the Treasury on the State of the Finances for the Year Ending June 30, 1863* (Washington, DC: Government Printing Office, 1863), https://fraser.stlouisfed.org/files/docs/publications/treasar/AR_TREASURY_1863.pdf.

12. Newman, "Origins of the National Banking System."

13. Andrew McFarland Davis, *The Origin of the National Banking System*, The National Monetary Commission (Washington, DC: Government Printing Office, 1910), https://fraser.stlouisfed.org/title/origin-national-banking-system-645/origin-national-banking-system-21962.

14. *Report of the Secretary of the Treasury on the State of Finances for the Year 1866*, (Washington, DC: Government Printing Office, 1865), https://archive.org/details/reportofsecret00unit.

15. This was true in most but not all cases. Central Reserve City Banks located in New York were backed by specie.

16. Andrew McFarland Davis, *The Origin of the National Banking System*, The National Monetary Commission (Washington, DC: Government Printing Office, 1910), https://fraser.stlouisfed.org/title/origin-national-banking-system-645/origin-national-banking-system-21962.

17. One of the chief complaints of the New York banks is that the national banking system would result in an outflow of deposits. Prior to 1863, many state-chartered banks were allowed to count deposits held in New York banks as reserves, but this was not allowed under the National Currency Act. The National Bank of 1864 reduced the risk of outflows by allowing country banks to use

deposits held in Central Reserve City banks located in New York City to satisfy part of their reserve requirements.

18. U.S. Treasury Department, *Statistical Abstract of the United States: 1878* (Washington, DC: Government Printing Office, 1879), 14, https://www2.census.gov/library/publications/1879/compendia/1878statab.pdf.

19. J. David Hacker, "A Census-Based Count of the Civil War Dead," *Civil War History* 57, no. 4 (December 2011): 307–348, https://doi.org/10.1353/cwh.2011.0061; *Report of the Secretary of the Treasury on the State of the Finances for the Year Ending June 30, 1870* (Washington, DC: Government Printing Office, 1870), https://fraser.stlouisfed.org/files/docs/publications/treasar/AR_TREASURY_1870.pdf.

Part 2

1. Arthur T. Hadley, *Railroad Transportation: Its History and Its Laws* (New York: The Knickerbocker Press, 1886).

2. "Stock plunger" is a term that was often used to describe speculators during the late 1800s.

Chapter 6

1. Simon Newcomb, "The Organization of Labor," *History of Economic Thought* 2 (1880): 393–410, https://www.econbiz.de/Record/the-organisation-of-labor-i-the-organizer-as-a-producer-newcomb-simon/10005424269.

2. "It's All About Steam," The Transcontinental Railroad, accessed May 13, 2023, https://railroad.lindahall.org/essays/locomotives.html; Hadley, *Railroad Transportation*.

3. U.S. Treasury Department, *Statistical Abstract of the United States: 1880* (Washington, DC: Government Printing Office, 1881), https://www2.census.gov/library/publications/1881/compendia/1880statab.pdf.

4. Richard E. Sylla and Robert E. Wright, "U.S. Corporate Development, 1801–1860," Cambridge, MA: National Bureau of Economic Research, SES Grant no. 0751577.

5. *Statistical Abstract of the United States: 1880*. On June 30, 2022, total public debt (including intragovernmental holdings) was $30.6 trillion, and total nonfinancial corporate debt was $16.3 trillion. Stanley Lebergott, "Labor Force and Employment 1800–1960," National Bureau of Economic Research, 1966, https://www.nber.org/books-and-chapters/output-employment-and-productivity-united-states-after-1800/labor-force-and-employment-1800-1960.

6. Different start and end dates for these statistics are a function of the limited availability of data.

7. U.S. Treasury Department, *Statistical Abstract of the United States: 1900* (Washington, DC: Government Printing Office, 1901), https://www.census.gov/library/publications/1901/compendia/statab/23ed.html; *Statistical Abstract of the United States: 1880*. The end date for all graphs corresponds to the last data point on the graph, not necessarily the last axis label.

8. Richard E. Sylla and Robert E. Wright, "U.S. Corporate Development, 1801–1860," Cambridge, MA: National Bureau of Economic Research, SES Grant no. 0751577.

9. Bureau of the Census, *Historical Statistics of the United States, 1789–1945* (Washington, DC: U.S. Bureau of the Census, 1949), 32–46, https://www.census.gov/library/publications/1949/compendia/hist_stats_1789-1945.html.

10. Bureau of the Census, *Historical Statistics of the United States: Colonial Times to 1970* (Washington, DC: U.S. Bureau of the Census, 1975), https://archive.org/details/HistoricalStatisticsOfTheUnitedStatesColonialTimesTo1970.

11. *Historical Statistics of the United States, 1789–1945*, 302–330.

12. *Statistical Abstract of the United States: 1900*; *Statistical Abstract of the United States: 1880*.

13. Sidney Sherwood, "Influence of the Trust in the Development of Undertaking Genius," *Publications of the American Economic Association* 1 (February 1900): 163–176, https://archive.org/details/jstor-2485828.

14. Alfred D. Chandler Jr., *The Visible Hand: The Managerial Revolution in American Business* (Cambridge, MA: Harvard University Press, 1977).

Chapter 7

1. Arthur T. Hadley, *Railroad Transportation: Its History and Its Laws* (New York: The Knickerbocker Press, 1886).

2. Richard White, *Railroaded* (New York: W. W. Norton, 2011), 35.

3. "The Progress of Purification," *New York Times*, February 19, 1873.

4. "The Progress of Purification."

5. United States Congress, House, Select Committee On Credit Mobilier And Union Pacific Railroad, and Jeremiah M. Wilson, *Report of the Select Committee of the House of Representatives, appointed under the resolution of January 6, to make inquiry in relation to the affairs of the Union Pacific Railroad Company, the Credit Mobilier of America, and other matters specified in said resolution and in other resolutions referred to said Committee* (Washington, DC: Government Printing Office, 1873), https://www.loc.gov./item/08028576.

6. White, *Railroaded*.

7. Joseph H. Moore, *How Members of Congress are Bribed*, updated February 6, 2013, https://www.gutenberg.org/files/3316/3316-h/3316-h.htm.

8. "Buffalo Hunting," *Harper's Weekly*, December 14, 1867.

9. "Buffalo Hunting," *Harper's*; "Bison, Buffalo, Tatanka: Bovids of the Badlands," National Park Service, accessed May 13, 2023, https://www.nps.gov/articles/bison_badl.htm.

10. Letter from Lieutenant Joe A. Cramer to Major Ned Wynkoop, National Park Service, December 19, 1864, https://www.nps.gov/sand/learn/historyculture/joseph-cramer-biography.htm.

11. "The Sand Creek Massacre," National Park Service, accessed May 13, 2023, https://www.nps.gov/sand/index.htm.

12. John R. Cook, *The Border and the Buffalo* (Topeka, KS: Crane & Company, 1907), https://archive.org/details/GR_864.

13. Cook, *The Border and the Buffalo*.

14. Stephen E. Ambrose, *Nothing Like It in the World: The Men Who Built the Transcontinental Railroad, 1863–1869* (New York: Simon & Schuster, 2000).

15. The brutal conditions from which many Chinese laborers fled likely contributed to their exceptional resilience. Many Chinese immigrants fled during the Taiping Rebellion, which lasted from 1850 to 1864. An estimated twenty million Chinese were killed, countless villages were destroyed, and famine was rampant. As harsh as the conditions were on the transcontinental railroads, many Chinese immigrants likely viewed it as an improvement relative to those from which they had fled.

16. J. Piper. "The Great Railroad Strike of 1877: A Catalyst for the American Labor Movement," *The History Teacher* 47, no. 1 (November 2013): 93–110, https://www.jstor.org/stable/i40128742.

17. *Debates and Proceedings of the Constitutional Convention of the State of California: Volume I* (Sacramento: State Printing Office, 1880); David S. Terry had a legitimate point in this case, but his overall character is unworthy of praise. His speech at the California Constitutional Convention was laced with racist language against Chinese immigrants. He also killed a U.S. Senator in a duel in 1859.

Chapter 8

1. Joseph Whitworth, *New York Industrial Exhibition: Presented to Parliament by Command of Her Majesty* (London: Harrison and Sons, 1854).

2. "London During the Great Exhibition," *Illustrated London News*, May 17, 1851.

3. David A. Hounshell, *From the American System to Mass Production, 1800–1932: The Development of Manufacturing Technology in the United States* (Baltimore: Johns Hopkins University Press, 1984).

4. Ambrose, *Nothing Like It in the World*.

5. Hounshell, *From the American System to Mass Production*.

6. Hounshell, *From the American System to Mass Production*.

7. Hounshell, *From the American System to Mass Production*.

8. Some products, such as Cyrus McCormick's mechanical reaper, were later than others in adopting the American system. It was not until 1880 that McCormick embraced many of the principles.

9. *Historical Statistics of the United States, 1789–1945*.

10. The "robber baron" moniker may have been appropriate in some cases, but certainly not all. For example, John D. Rockefeller was generally well respected and known to treat competitors fairly. Jay Gould, on the other hand, likely earned his reputation for reasons that are revealed in chapter 9.

11. The companies founded by Andrew Carnegie and John D. Rockefeller underwent several name changes and multiple consolidations before taking on the names of Standard Oil and Carnegie Steel.

12. Descriptions of improvements in the manufacturing process were derived from Charles R. Morris, *The Tycoons* (New York: Henry Holt & Company, 2005), 36.

13. *Statistical Abstract of the United States: 1900*.

14. Estimates of GDP come from the Bureau of the Census; Thomas Berry, *Revised Annual Estimates of American Gross National Product* (Richmond, VA.: Bostwick Press, 1978); Robert E. Gallman and Stanley L. Engerman, eds., "Economic Growth and Structural Change in the Long Nineteenth Century," *The Cambridge Economic History of the United States, vol. 2, The Long Nineteenth Century* (Cambridge, England: Cambridge University Press, 2000), 1–55; Nathan S. Balke and Robert J. Gordon, "The Estimation of Prewar Gross National Product: Methodology and New Evidence," *Journal of Political Economy* 97, no. 1 (February 1989), 38–92; Bureau of Economic Analysis, U.S. Department of Commerce.

15. U.S. Treasury Department, *Statistical Abstract of the United States: 1901* (Washington, DC: Government Printing Office, 1902), https://www.census.gov/library/publications/1902/compendia/statab/24ed.html.

Chapter 9

1. Boyden Sparkes and Samuel Taylor Moore, *The Witch of Wall Street: Hetty Green* (New York: Doubleday, 1935), https://archive.org/details/witchofwallstree0000spar/page/n7/mode/2up.

2. New York Stock Exchange records from the 1860s and 1870s are incomplete, so the annual averages for these decades only include 1866–1868 and 1875–1879; *The Commercial & Financial Chronicle* 6, no. 132 (January 4, 1868), https://fraser.stlouisfed.org/title/commercial-financial-chronicle-1339/january-4-1868-558231; *The Commercial & Financial Chronicle* 8, no. 185 (January 9, 1869) https://fraser.stlouisfed.org/title/commercial-financial-chronicle-1339/january-9-1869-558286; Edmund Clarence Stedman, ed., *The New York Stock Exchange: Volume 1* (New York: Stock Exchange Historical Company, 1905), https://archive.org/details/cu31924030206506/page/n15/mode/2up.

3. "Market breadth" is another important term that refers to the diversity of securities listings. Market breadth remained narrow throughout the Gilded Age. The majority of securities traded on the NYSE consisted of government bonds and railroad securities. Market breadth began expanding at the end of the nineteenth century.

4. When securities markets reach Stage Three, index funds become the optimal investment strategy for most investors. This topic is covered in more detail in chapters 22 and 25.

5. Trumbull White, *Wizard of Wall Street and His Wealth: The Life and Deeds of Jay Gould* (Philadelphia: John C. Yorston & Company, 1893), https://archive.org/details/wizardofwallstre00whit/page/n7/mode/2up.

6. "Stock operator" was a common term used to describe speculators who engaged in various forms of market manipulation.

7. A peddler was the Gilded Age equivalent of a door-to-door salesperson. Peddlers traveled with wagons full of goods and sold them in villages throughout the countryside.

8. Edwin Lefevre, *Reminiscences of a Stock Operator* (New York: George H. Doran, 1923; Project Gutenberg 2019), x, https://www.gutenberg.org/ebooks/60979.

9. For simplicity, the tactics described only include buying or shorting shares. In reality, there are many ways to profit from insider trading using more complex techniques.

10. W. A. Swanberg, *Jim Fisk: The Career of an Improbable Rascal* (New York: Charles Scribner's Sons, 1959).

11. Swanberg, *Jim Fisk*.

12. Julius Grodinsky, *Jay Gould: His Business Career 1867–1892* (Philadelphia: University of Pennsylvania Press, 1957), https://archive.org/details/jaygould0000unse/page/n9/mode/2up.

13. "Railroad Slaughter," *New York Times*, April 16, 1868.

14. A wash sale occurs when buyers and sellers agree to buy and sell securities from each other at a consistent price to increase trading volume and create the perception of increased interest in the security. Securities exchanges frowned on this practice but usually tolerated it in all but the most egregious cases.

15. The term "corner artist" was created by the author for simplicity. This term was never used in the Gilded Age.

16. M. Hiltzik, *Iron Empires: Robber Barons, Railroads, and the Making of Modern America* (New York: Houghton Mifflin Harcourt, 2020), 317. Most corners ended with painful settlements between short sellers and the corner artist. Sometimes settlements entailed lending the shares to the short seller at a high rate of interest. Other times the two parties settled on a price that left the victim solvent but with few remaining assets.

17. Swanberg, *Jim Fisk*.

18. Swanberg, *Jim Fisk*.

19. Robert Sobel, *The Big Board: A History of the New York Stock Market* (New York: Free Press, 1965), 43; Stedman, *The New York Stock Exchange*, 168–181. Jim Fisk never blamed Jay Gould for his treachery. In Maury Klein's biography of Jay Gould he theorized that Fisk knew that if he and Gould abandoned the corner at the same time, they would have both suffered financial ruin. Instead, Gould sacrificed Fisk to save himself, but he likely assured Fisk that he would be taken care of in the aftermath.

20. Swanberg, *Jim Fisk*.

21. "Investigation into the Causes of the Gold Panic," *Report of the Majority of the Committee on Banking and Currency*. H. R. 31, 41st Congress, 2nd Session, 1869–1870, https://archive.org/details/cu31924032442679/page/n5/mode/2up.

22. This changed after the passage of the Resumption Act of 1875, which required the U.S. Treasury to redeem greenbacks with specie beginning on January 1, 1879.

23. Stedman, *The New York Stock Exchange*, 168–181.

24. Edward J. Renehan Jr., *Dark Genius of Wall Street: The Misunderstood Life of Jay Gould, King of the Robber Barons* (New York: Basic Books, 2005), 177.

25. "Denounced from the Pulpit," *New York Times*, December 5, 1892, https://www.nytimes.com/1892/12/05/archives/denounced-from-the-pulpit-a-boston-clergymans-estimate-of-go-old.html.

26. Grodinsky, *Jay Gould: His Business Career*; Renehan, *Dark Genius of Wall Street*, 260.

27. Maury Klein, *The Union Pacific: Volume I, 1862–1893* (Minneapolis: University of Minnesota Press, 1987).

28. Klein, *The Union Pacific*.

29. Sparkes and Moore, *The Witch of Wall Street*, 182.

30. Sparkes and Moore, *The Witch of Wall Street*.

31. Sparkes and Moore, *The Witch of Wall Street*.

32. Janet Wallach, *The Richest Woman on Wall Street: Hetty Green in the Gilded Age* (New York: Anchor Books: New York, 2012).

33. Mark Higgins, "The Story of Hetty Green: America's First Value Investor and Financial Grandmaster," *Financial History* 143 (Fall 2022): 11–15, https://doi.org/10.2139/ssrn.4054959.

34. Sobel, *The Big Board*, 105.

Chapter 10

1. Christopher P. Munden, "Jay Cooke: Banks, Railroads, and the Panic of 1873," *Pennsylvania Legacies* 11, no. 1(May 2011): 3–5, https://doi.org/10.5215/pennlega.11.1.0003.

2. Henrietta M. Larson, *Jay Cooke, Private Banker* (Cambridge, MA: Harvard University Press, 1936).

3. The term "investment banking" is used because it is more recognizable today. This profession was commonly referred to as "private banking" in the 1800s.

4. Many of these firms underwent several name changes and consolidations over the past 175 years. Also, Kuhn Loeb is unlikely a household name today, but it was among the most important investment banks in the late 1800s and early 1900s. "Excitement on the Vienna Bourse—The Exhibition—The Archduke Charles Disgusted," *New York Times*, May 10, 1873.

5. Larson, *Jay Cooke, Private Banker*.

6. Larson, *Jay Cooke, Private Banker*.

7. Larson, *Jay Cooke, Private Banker*.

8. "Excitement on the Vienna Bourse."

9. Bureau of the Census, *Historical Statistics of the United States: Colonial Times to 1957* (Washington, DC: Government Printing Office, 1961), 200–201.

10. Scott Mixon, "The Crisis of 1873: Perspectives from Multiple Asset Classes," *The Journal of Economic History* 68, no. 3 (2008): 722–757, https://doi.org/10.1017/S0022050708000624; O. M. W. Sprague, *History of Crises Under the National Banking System*, The National Monetary Commission (Washington, DC: Government Printing Office, 1910), https://fraser.stlouisfed.org/title/history-crises-national-banking-system-633.

Chapter 11

1. William Jennings Bryan, "Democratic National Convention Address," July 8, 1896, American Rhetoric Online Speech Bank, transcript and studio recording, https://www.americanrhetoric.com/speeches/williamjenningsbryan1896dnc.htm.

2. Hugh McCulloch, "Our Future Fiscal Policy," *North American Review* 132, no. 295 (June 1881): 513–532.

3. Maury Klein, *The Life and Legend of Jay Gould* (Baltimore: Johns Hopkins University Press, 1986).

4. Maury Klein, *Union Pacific: Volume 1, 1862–1893* (Minneapolis: University of Minnesota Press, 1987).

5. Backing the U.S. dollar with silver was inflationary because it enabled the Treasury to issue notes, referred to as "Treasury Notes of 1890," to purchase silver from U.S. mines. At the time, silver production substantially exceeded gold production, which allowed the money supply to increase at a much faster rate than it would have under the gold standard. Milton Friedman and Anna Jacobson Schwartz, *A Monetary History of the United States, 1867–1960* (Princeton, NJ: Princeton University Press, 1963), 106.

6. Bureau of the Census, *Historical Statistics of the United States: Colonial Times to 1970* (Washington, DC: U.S. Bureau of the Census, 1975), https://archive.org/details/ HistoricalStatisticsOfTheUnitedStatesColonialTimesTo1970.

7. *Annual Report of the Director of the Mint*, Treasury Department (Washington, DC: Government Printing Office, 1933), 29, https://nnp.wustl.edu/library/book/514137; Friedman and Schwartz, *A Monetary History*, 115.

8. F. W. Taussig, "The United States Treasury in 1894–1896," *The Quarterly Journal of Economics* 13, no. 2 (January 1899): 205, https://doi.org/10.1093/qje/13.2.203; National Monetary Commission, A. Piatt Andrew, ed., "Statistics for the United States, 1867–1909" (Washington, DC: Government Printing Office, 1910), 269, https://fraser.stlouisfed.org/title/ statistics-united-states-1867-1909-662.

9. In fairness, free silver advocates had a legitimate complaint with respect to deflation. In fact, the movement was largely a continuation of a long-standing opposition to the Resumption Act, which was also a key driver of deflation.

10. Friedman and Schwartz, *A Monetary History*, 131–132.

11. T. Cochran and W. Miller, *The Age of Enterprise: A Social History of Industrial America* (New York: Macmillan, 1942), 59, reprinted in *The Journal of Economic History* 4, no. 1 (May 1944), 92–93, https://doi.org/10.1017/S0022050700084126.

12. Albert C. Stevens, "Analysis of the Phenomena of the Panic in the United States in 1893," *The Quarterly Journal of Economics* 8, no. 2 (January 1894): 117–148.

13. "Index of All Common Stock Prices, Cowles Commission and Standard and Poor's Corporation for United States," Federal Reserve Bank of Saint Louis, updated August 15, 2012, https://fred. stlouisfed.org/series/M1125AUSM343NNBR.

14. Stevens, "Analysis of the Phenomena," 117–148.

15. David Teather and Graeme Wearden, "Markets Boosted as Warren Buffett Invests $5 Billion in Goldman Sachs," *Guardian*, September 24, 2008, https://www.theguardian.com/business/2008/ sep/24/warrenbuffett.goldmansachs.

16. Ron Chernow, *The House of Morgan: An American Banking Dynasty and the Rise of Modern Finance* (New York: Grove Press, 1990), 75.

17. Friedman and Schwartz, *A Monetary History*, 112.

Part 3

1. "*The Farmer Refuted*, &c., [23 February] 1775," *Founders Online*, National Archives, https:// founders.archives.gov/documents/Hamilton/01-01-02-0057, [Original source: Harold C. Syrett, ed., *The Papers of Alexander Hamilton, vol. 1, 1768–1778* (New York: Columbia University Press, 1961), 81–165]; Ron Chernow, *Alexander Hamilton* (New York: Penguin, 2004), 61.

2. The importance of the election of 1896 is reflected in L. Frank Baum's famous book *The Wonderful Wizard of Oz*. It was later discovered that the story was an allegory for the election.

3. Friedman and Schwartz, *A Monetary History*, 8; "Dave Leip's Atlas of U.S. Presidential Elections," www.uselectionatlas.org.

Chapter 12

1. *Wall Street Journal* (March 3, 1900).

2. Curt Schleier, "Entrepreneur Charles H. Dow: He Played to His Strengths to Give Financial Customers What They Wanted," *Investor's Business Daily*, January 19, 2001.

3. Cynthia Crossen, "It All Began in the Basement of a Candy Store," *Wall Street Journal*, August 1, 2007, https://www.wsj.com/articles/SB118591182345183718.

4. Steve Schaefer, "The First 12 Dow Components: Where Are They Now?" *Forbes*, July 15, 2011, https://www.forbes.com/sites/steveschaefer/2011/07/15/the-first-12-dow-components-where-are-they-now.

5. Crossen, "It All Began in the Basement."

6. Frank Vanderlip, *The American "Commercial Invasion" of Europe* (New York: Frank Vanderlip, 1902), https://archive.org/details/americancommerci00vandrich/page/n9/mode/2up.

7. Vicki A. Mack, *Frank A. Vanderlip: The Banker Who Changed America* (Palos Verdes Estates, CA: Pinale Press, 2013).

8. Vanderlip, *The American "Commercial Invasion."*

9. Bureau of the Census, *Historical Statistics of the United States: Colonial Times to 1970* (Washington, DC: U.S. Bureau of the Census, 1975), 589–590, https://archive.org/details/HistoricalStatisticsOfTheUnitedStatesColonialTimesTo1970.

10. *Historical Statistics of the United States: Colonial Times to 1970*, 593–594.

11. *Historical Statistics of the United States: Colonial Times to 1970*, 606.

12. *Historical Statistics of the United States: Colonial Times to 1970*, 606.

13. *Historical Statistics of the United States: Colonial Times to 1970*, 599.

14. *Historical Statistics of the United States: Colonial Times to 1970*, 693–694.

15. Vanderlip, *The American "Commercial Invasion."*

16. Charles R. Morris, *The Tycoons: How Andrew Carnegie, John D. Rockefeller, Jay Gould, and J. P. Morgan Invented the American Supereconomy* (New York: Henry Holt & Company, 2005), 243.

17. Vanderlip, *The American "Commercial Invasion."*

18. Vanderlip, *The American "Commercial Invasion."*

19. Mary O'Sullivan, "The Expansion of the U.S. Stock Market, 1885–1930: Historical Facts and Theoretical Fashions," *Enterprise and Society* 8, no. 3 (September 2007): 489–542.

20. Descriptions of improvements in the manufacturing process were derived from Morris, *The Tycoons*, 36.

21. Vanderlip, *The American "Commercial Invasion."*

22. The emphasis here is on *Continental* Europe, as the British financial system remained superior to the U.S. at the time.

23. Vanderlip, *The American "Commercial Invasion,"* 26.

24. Wayne Collins, "Trusts and the Origins of Antitrust Legislation," *Fordham Law Review*, April 1, 2013, https://fordhamlawreview.org/issues/trusts-and-the-origins-of-antitrust-legislation/.

25. Collins, "Trusts and the Origins."

26. This does not mean that consolidations were always benign or that abusive monopolies did not exist. It only asserts that ensuring a company's survival was the more common motive.

27. Naomi Lamoreaux, *The Great Merger Movement in American Business, 1895–1904* (Cambridge: Cambridge University Press, 1985), https://doi.org/10.1017/CBO9780511665042.

28. Lamoreaux, *The Great Merger Movement*, 2.

29. Theodore Roosevelt, "Seventh Annual Message," December 3, 1907, Miller Center, University of Virginia, transcript, https://millercenter.org/the-presidency/presidential-speeches/december-3-1907-seventh-annual-message.

30. Stephen Broadberry and Irwin Douglas, "Labor Productivity in the United States and the United Kingdom During the Nineteenth Century," *Explorations in Economic History* 43, no. 2 (April 2006): 257–279, https://doi.org/10.1016/j.eeh.2005.02.003. All else being equal, greater productivity enables a nation to produce more output per unit of effort. A ratio above 100 indicates a higher level of productivity in the U.S. relative to the U.K. Figure 12.9 reveals that U.S. and British productivity were roughly on par from 1869 to 1891. After the American Commercial Invasion, U.S. productivity far exceeded that of Britain. Historical data for the United States and U.K. are reported for slightly different time periods. Data for the United States was collected during the last year for each decade (i.e., 1869, 1879, etc.), while data for the U.K. was collected for the first year of the subsequent decade (i.e., 1871, 1881, etc.).

31. Matthew Simon and David E. Novack, "Some Dimensions of the American Commercial Invasion of Europe, 1871–1914: An Introductory Essay," *Journal of Economic History* 24, no. 4. (December 1964): 591–605, https://doi.org/10.1017/S0022050700061295.

32. A trade surplus (or deficit) captures the value of a nation's exports minus its imports. When a country runs a trade *surplus*, the total value of exports exceeds the total value of imports. When a country runs a trade *deficit*, the total value of imports exceeds the total value of its exports. A trade surplus indicates that a country has a net excess of capital from all trade activities. U.S. Treasury Department, *Statistical Abstract of the United States: 1901* (Washington, DC: Government Printing Office, 1902), https://www.census.gov/library/publications/1902/compendia/statab/24ed.html.; U.S. Department of Commerce, *Statistical Abstract of the United States: 1930* (Washington, DC: Government Printing Office, 1931), https://www.census.gov/library/publications/1930/compendia/statab/52ed.html.

33. "Index of All Common Stock Prices, Cowles Commission and Standard and Poor's Corporation for United States," Federal Reserve Bank of St. Louis, updated August 15, 2012, https://fred.stlouisfed.org/series/M1125AUSM343NNBR.

34. *Historical Statistics of the United States: Colonial Times to 1970*, 256.

35. Vanderlip, *The American "Commercial Invasion,"* 3.

Chapter 13

1. David Cowen, Richard Sylla, and Robert E. Wright, "The U.S. Panic of 1792: Financial Crisis Management and the Lender of Last Resort," (paper, National Bureau of Economic Research DAE Summer Institute, July 2006, and XIV International Economic History Congress, Session 20, "Capital Market Anomalies in Economic History"), https://users.nber.org/~confer/2006/si2006/dae/sylla.pdf.

2. National Monetary Commission, A. Piatt Andrew, ed., "Statistics for the United States, 1867–1909" (Washington, DC: Government Printing Office, 1910).

3. Edwin W. Kemmerer, *Seasonal Variations in the Relative Demand for Money and Capital in the United States: A Statistical Study*, National Monetary Commission (Washington, DC: Government Printing Office, 1910), https://fraser.stlouisfed.org/title/653.

4. National Monetary Commission, Andrew, "Statistics for the United States 1867–1909."

5. "A New Trust Company Up Town," *New York Times*, July 12, 1884.

6. Edward Ten Broeck Perine, *The Story of the Trust Companies* (New York: G.P. Putnam's Sons, 1916), https://archive.org/details/storyoftrustcomp01peri/page/n7/mode/2up.

7. Jon Moen and Ellis Tallman, "The Bank Panic of 1907: The Role of Trust Companies," *The Journal of Economic History* 52, no.3 (September 1992): 614, https://doi.org/10.1017/S0022050700011414.

8. Moen and Tallman, "Bank Panic of 1907."

9. Moen and Tallman, "Bank Panic of 1907."

10. Kerry A. Odell & Marc D. Weidenmier, "Real Shock, Monetary Aftershock: The 1906 San Francisco Earthquake and the Panic of 1907," *The Journal of Economic History* 64, no. 4 (December 2004), 1010, https://doi.org/10.1017/S0022050704043062.

11. O. M. W. Sprague, *History of Crises Under the National Banking System,* The National Monetary Commission (Washington, DC: Government Printing Office, 1910), https://fraser.stlouisfed.org/title/history-crises-national-banking-system-633.

12. *The Commercial & Financial Chronicle,* multiple issues from 1905 to 1907.

13. "Index of All Common Stock Prices, Cowles Commission and Standard and Poor's Corporation for United States," Federal Reserve Bank of Saint Louis, updated August 15, 2012, https://fred.stlouisfed.org/series/M1125AUSM343NNBR; National Monetary Commission, Andrew, "Statistics for the United States 1867–1909."

14. Donald Morgan and James Narron, "The Final Crisis Chronicle: The Panic of 1907 and the Birth of the Fed," Federal Reserve Bank of New York, November 18, 2016, https://libertystreeteconomics.newyorkfed.org/2016/11/the-final-crisis-chronicle-the-panic-of-1907-and-the-birth-of-the-fed/.

15. Morgan and Narron, "The Final Crisis Chronicle."

16. Edwin Lefevre, "The Game Got Them: How the Great Wall Street Gambling Syndicate Fell Into Its Own Trap," *Busy Man's Magazine,* February 1, 1908.

17. Robert F. Bruner and Sean D. Carr, *The Panic of 1907: Lessons Learned from the Market's Perfect Storm* (New York: John Wiley & Sons, 2007).

18. Bruner and Carr, *The Panic of 1907.*

19. Bruner and Carr, *The Panic of 1907.*

20. Bruner and Carr, *The Panic of 1907.* A short squeeze refers to a situation in which investors who hold shares in a security are forced to return the security to the lender. This forces the short seller to purchase the security for whatever price is offered in the market. If there are few sellers, the price of the security will increase rapidly.

21. *New York Times,* multiple issues from October 1907.

22. "Crash in Coppers; Heinze Quits Bank," *New York Times,* October 17, 1907, https://www.nytimes.com/1907/10/17/archives/crash-in-coppers-heinze-quits-bank-lets-go-mercantile-national.html; "Heinze Butte Bank Closed," *New York Times,* October 18, 1907, https://www.nytimes.com/1907/10/18/archives/heinze-butte-bank-closed-fearing-run-and-short-of-currency.html.

23. Jack W. Wilson and Charles P. Jones, "An Analysis of the S&P 500 Index and Cowles's Extensions: Price Indexes and Stock Returns, 1870–1999," *The Journal of Business* 75, no. 3 (July 2002), https://ssrn.com/abstract=313845.

24. This representation is intentionally simplified. The mechanics of running a bank today are more complex. The key point is that the fundamental structure of a bank prevents it from satisfying too many withdrawal requests simultaneously.

25. "Crash in Coppers; Heinze Quits Bank."; "Pays Out $8,000,000 and Then Suspends," *New York Times,* October 23, 1907, https://www.nytimes.com/1907/10/23/archives/pays-out-8000000-and-then-suspends-1500000-hanover-national-check.html.

26. Bruner and Carr, *The Panic of 1907;* Moen and Tallman, "Bank Panic of 1907," 611–630.

27. The values for 2019 are used because the level of M1 was distorted by the massive monetary and fiscal stimulus in response to the COVID-19 pandemic.

28. "US Total Net Worth—Balance Sheet of Households and Nonprofit Organizations," Y Charts, accessed May 14, 2023, https://ycharts.com/indicators/total_net_worth_balance_sheet_of_households_and_nonprofit_organizations_unadjusted.

29. The civil unrest that accompanies major depressions is not just theoretical. Later chapters reveal that if not for the Great Depression, it is likely that World War II would never have happened.

30. Bruner and Carr, *The Panic of 1907*; Moen and Tallman, "The Bank Panic of 1907."

31. Sprague, *History of Crises Under the National Banking System.*

32. Bruner and Carr, *The Panic of 1907.*

33. Boyden Sparkes and Samuel Taylor Moore, *The Witch of Wall Street: Hetty Green* (New York: Doubleday, Doran, and Company, 1935), https://archive.org/details/witchofwallstree0000spar/page/n7/mode/2up.

34. Niall Ferguson, *The Ascent of Money: A Financial History of the World* (New York: Penguin Books, 2008).

35. Bruner and Carr, *The Panic of 1907*; Moen and Tallman, "The Bank Panic of 1907."

36. Sparkes and Moore, *The Witch of Wall Street.*

37. Ron Chernow, *The House of Morgan: An American Banking Dynasty and the Rise of Modern Finance* (New York: Grove Press, 1990).

38. Sparkes and Moore, *The Witch of Wall Street.*

39. Bruner and Carr, *The Panic of 1907.*

40. The currency was not completely inelastic in 1907. The NYCH played a critical role in easing the panic by issuing clearinghouse certificates; however, the effectiveness of this technique was much more limited relative to those that could be employed by a central bank.

41. Gary Richardson and Jessie Romero, "The Meeting at Jekyll Island," Federal Reserve History, accessed May 14, 2023, https://www.federalreservehistory.org/essays/jekyll-island-conference.

42. Richardson and Romero, "Meeting at Jekyll Island."

43. The Aldrich-Vreeland Act proved invaluable only six years after its introduction. After World War I broke out in the summer of 1914, yet another panic threatened to sink the entire U.S. financial system. The Federal Reserve System was not yet in place, and if not for the Aldrich-Vreeland Act, the U.S. may not have weathered the storm.

44. James Neal Primm, "Banking Reform, 1907–1913," in *A Foregone Conclusion: The Founding of the Federal Reserve Bank of St. Louis*, Federal Reserve Bank of St. Louis, accessed May 14, 2023, https://www.stlouisfed.org/a-foregone-conclusion/chapter-two.

45. *Investigation of Financial and Monetary Conditions in the United States*, Subcommittee of the Committee on Banking and Currency (Washington, DC: Government Printing Office, 1912), 1,084, https://fraser.stlouisfed.org/files/docs/historical/house/money_trust/montru_pt12.pdf.

46. "Colossal Figure Is Gary's Tribute," *New York Times*, April 1, 1913, https://www.nytimes.com/1913/04/01/archives/colossal-figure-is-garys-tribute-mr-morgan-greatest-man-of-his-age.html.

Chapter 14

1. Alexander Dana Noyes, *The War Period of American Finance 1908–1925* (New York: Knickerbocker Press, 1926), https://www.google.com/books/edition/The_War_Period_of_American_Finance_1908/x9o9AQAAIAAJ?hl=en&gbpv=1.

2. Vladimir Dedijer, "Sarajevo Fifty Years After," *Foreign Affairs* 42, no. 4 (July 1, 1964), 569–584,

https://doi.org/10.2307/20029714.

3. Jesse Greenspan, "The Assassination of Archduke Franz Ferdinand," History, updated February 12, 2020, https://www.history.com/news/the-assassination-of-archduke-franz-ferdinand.

4. Greenspan, "The Assassination of Archduke Franz Ferdinand."

5. The country of Serbia was spelled "Servia" in 1914.

6. *The Commercial & Financial Chronicle* 99, no. 2562 (August 1, 1914): 293, https://archive.org/details/sim_commercial-and-financial-chronicle_1914-08-01_99_2562.

7. James Joll, *The Origins of the First World War* (New York, Routledge, 1984), 15.

8. Joll, *The Origins of the First World War*, 15.

9. Henry George Stebbins Noble, *The New York Stock Exchange in the Crisis of 1914* (New York: The Country Life Press, 1915), https://archive.org/details/cu31924032545851.

10. "Abrupt Recovery After Further Fall—Our Market Presents Striking Contrast to Those Abroad," *New York Times*, July 30, 1914, 12, https://www.nytimes.com/1914/07/30/archives/financial-markets-abrupt-recovery-after-further-fall-our-market.html; James Grant, *The Forgotten Depression: 1921: The Crash that Cured Itself* (New York: Simon & Schuster, 2014), 47.

11. Noble, *The New York Stock Exchange in the Crisis of 1914*.

12. John Kenneth Galbraith, *A Short History of Financial Euphoria*, 4th ed. (New York: Penguin, 1990).

13. "Rediscounting" is a term that describes the lending of bank assets to a monetary authority (the Treasury in this case) in exchange for currency (i.e., cash). The interest rate payable on these loans from the Treasury was determined by the "rediscount rate."

14. William Silber, "The Great Financial Crisis of 1914: What Can We Learn from Aldrich-Vreeland Emergency Currency?" (NYU working paper no. FIN-06-009, October 2006), 2–3, https://ssrn.com/abstract=1293641; Sean Fulmer, "United States: Aldrich-Vreeland Emergence Currency during the Crisis of 1914," *Journal of Financial Crises* 4, no. 2 (April 2022): 1156–1179, https://elischolar.library.yale.edu/cgi/viewcontent.cgi?article=1342&context=journal-of-financial-crises; Tim Sablik, "The Last Crisis Before the Fed," *Econ Focus* 4Q (2013): 6, https://www.richmondfed.org/publications/research/econ_focus/2013/q4/-/media/5CB182DD657E48DDABFDFFE57F5E1BE1.ashx.

15. U.S. Treasury Department, *Annual Report of the Comptroller of the Currency, December 6, 1915* (Washington, DC: Government Printing Office, 1916), https://fraser.stlouisfed.org/title/56/item/19131.

16. United States Department of Commerce, *Statistical Abstract of the United States: 1929* (Washington, DC: Government Printing Office, 1929), https://www2.census.gov/library/publications/1929/compendia/statab/51ed/1929-01.pdf.

17. Ron Chernow, *The House of Morgan : An American Banking Dynasty and the Rise of Modern Finance* (New York: Grove Press, 1990).

18. Chernow, *The House of Morgan*.

19. Memorandum from Admiral Henning vin Holtzendorff, December 16, 1916, http://www.gwpda.org/naval/holtzendorffmemo.htm.

20. Annette McDermott, "How the Sinking of Lusitania Changed World War I," History, updated November 21, 2022, https://www.history.com/news/how-the-sinking-of-lusitania-changed-wwi; Holger H. Herwig and David F. Trask, "The Failure of Imperial Germany's Undersea Offensive Against World Shipping, February 1917–October 1918," *The Historian* 33, no. 4 (1971), https://doi.org/10.1111/j.1540-6563.1971.tb01168.x.

21. From the German perspective, the U-boat campaign fell short of expectations. Admiral von Holtzendorff's goal was to sink 600,000 tons of shipping per month, which is a target that the

Germans never hit.

22. The convoy system refers to the practice of sending merchant ships in groups with naval escorts. The tactic was less efficient than allowing ships to travel independently, but it provided greater protection from German U-boats.

23. "Ship Losses by Month," uboat.net, accessed June 27, 2023, https://www.uboat.net/wwi/ships_hit/losses_year.html.

24. "Zimmerman Telegram (1917)," National Archives, accessed May 15, 2023, https://www.archives.gov/milestone-documents/zimmermann-telegram.

25. There is no evidence that the Mexican government would have even considered Germany's offer, but the fact that Germany was proposing it caused more than enough fear and anger to push the nation toward war.

26. M. Martin, V. Gazzaniga, N. L. Bragazzi, and I. Barberis, "The Spanish Influenza Pandemic: A Lesson from History 100 Years after 1918," *Journal of Preventive Medicine & Hygiene* 60, no. 1 (March 2019): E64–E67, https://doi.org/10.15167/2421-4248/jpmh2019.60.1.1205.

27. Jeffery K. Taubenberger and David M. Morens, "1918 Influenza: The Mother of All Pandemics," *Emerging Infectious Diseases* 12, no. 1 (January 2006): 19, https://doi.org/10.3201/eid1201.050979.

28. John Barry, *The Great Influenza: The Story of the Deadliest Pandemic in History* (New York: Penguin, 2005).

29. Barry, *The Great Influenza*.

30. Hugh Rockoff, "Until It's Over, Over There: The U.S. Economy in World War I" (working paper no. 10580, National Bureau of Economic Research, June 2004), 21, https://www.nber.org/system/files/working_papers/w10580/w10580.pdf.

31. Winthrop H. Smith Jr., *Catching Lightning in a Bottle: How Merrill Lynch Revolutionized the Financial World* (New York: John C. Wiley and Sons, 2014), 69.

32. *Annual Report of the Secretary of the Treasury on the State of the Finances for the Fiscal Year Ended June 30, 1920* (Washington, DC: Government Printing Office, 1920), https://fraser.stlouisfed.org/files/docs/publications/treasar/AR_TREASURY_1920.pdf.

33. *Annual Report of the Secretary of the Treasury, 1920*.

34. Richard Sutch, "Liberty Bonds: April 1917–September 1918," Federal Reserve History, accessed May 15, 2023, https://www.federalreservehistory.org/essays/liberty-bonds.

35. Rockoff, "Until It's Over, Over There," 6.

36. "Consumer Price Index, 1800-," Federal Reserve Bank of Minneapolis, accessed May 4, 2023, https://www.minneapolisfed.org/about-us/monetary-policy/inflation-calculator/consumer-price-index-1800-.

37. "Gold Reserves of Principal Banks of Issue, 1900–1919," *Federal Reserve Bulletin*, February 1920, https://fraser.stlouisfed.org/files/docs/publications/FRB/pages/1920-1924/23219_1920-1924.pdf; "Gold Held in the Treasury and Federal Reserve Banks for United States (1900–1949)," updated August 20, 2012, Federal Reserve Bank of St. Louis, https://fred.stlouisfed.org/series/M1437BUSM144NNBR (data for 1920 only).

38. The term "Federal Reserve" is used for simplicity even though each Federal Reserve regional bank had some flexibility to set their own rediscount rates. Sometimes rates differed, but the differences were usually modest.

39. Milton Friedman and Anna Jacobson Schwartz, *A Monetary History of the United States, 1867–1960* (Princeton, NJ: Princeton University Press, 1963), 223–224.

40. Rediscount rates were the rates of interest charged to member banks for securities offered as collateral to the Federal Reserve regional banks in exchange for currency.

41. The timing and amount of the increase in the discount rate is based on the New York Federal Reserve Bank.

42. Friedman and Schwartz, *A Monetary History*, 232.

43. "Banking and Monetary Statistics, 1914–1941," Board of Governors of the Federal Reserve System (November 1943): 439–441, https://fraser.stlouisfed.org/files/docs/publications/bms/1914-1941/BMS14-41_complete.pdf; Leland Crabbe, "The International Gold Standard and U.S. Monetary Policy from World War I to the New Deal," *Federal Reserve Bulletin* (June 1989): 427, https://fraser.stlouisfed.org/files/docs/meltzer/craint89.pdf; Friedman and Schwartz, *A Monetary History*, 222–224.

44. Friedman and Schwartz, *A Monetary History*, 222–224.

45. "Dow-Jones Industrial Stock Price Index for United States," Federal Reserve Bank of St. Louis, updated August 15, 2012, https://fred.stlouisfed.org/series/M1109BUSM293NNBR.

Chapter 15

1. "Ayres Sees New Era in Security Values," *New York Times*, August 16, 1929, https://www.nytimes.com/1929/08/16/archives/ayres-sees-new-era-in-security-values-former-accepted-standards-no.html.

2. "Credit History: The Evolution of Consumer Credit in America," Federal Reserve Bank of Boston, https://www.econlowdown.org/v3/public/credit-history-the-evolution-of-consumer-credit-in-america.

3. Charles E. Persons, "Credit Expansion, 1920 to 1929, and Its Lessons," *The Quarterly Journal of Economics* 45, no. 1 (November 1930): 94–130, https://doi.org/10.2307/1882528.

4. Persons, "Credit Expansion."

5. Robert Sobel, *The Big Board: A History of the New York Stock Market* (New York: Free Press, 1965), 230.

6. Interestingly, a second rarely mentioned result of these studies was the revelation that portfolios of stocks selected at random tended to outperform portfolios based on criteria intended to isolate the highest quality stocks. In other words, even data that dated as far back as the late 1800s supported the concept of an index fund. Over the course of the next one hundred years, a mountain of evidence continued to support the merits of index funds, but it was unheeded by many investors.

7. Edgar Lawrence Smith, "Common Stocks as Long Term Investments," *Journal of Political Economy* 33, no. 6 (December 1925), https://doi.org/10.1086/253729.

8. Raymond W. Goldsmith, *A Study of Saving in the United States* (Princeton, NJ: Princeton University Press, 1955), 279.

9. Gene Smiley and Richard H. Keehn, "Margin Purchases, Brokers' Loans and the Bull Market of the Twenties," *Business and Economic History* 17 (1988): 129–42, https://thebhc.org/sites/default/files/beh/BEHprint/v017/p0129-p0142.pdf.; "Financial Markets: Stocks Move Irregularly, Call Money 6%, Then 7–Sterling Unchanged," *New York Times*, August 23, 1929, https://www.nytimes.com/1929/08/23/archives/financial-markets-stocks-move-irregularly-call-money-6-then-7.html.

10. "Call loan" is a term used to describe twenty-four-hour loans used to purchase stocks. The loans were instantly callable by the lender but were usually rolled over on a daily basis.

11. Smiley and Keehn, "Margin Purchases."

12. Ron Chernow, *The House of Morgan: An American Banking Dynasty and the Rise of Modern Finance* (New York: Grove Press, 1990), 24.

13. *Money Trust Investigation: Investigation of Financial and Monetary Conditions in the United States*, Subcommittee of the Committee on Banking and Currency (Washington, DC: Government Printing Office, 1913), https://fraser.stlouisfed.org/files/docs/historical/house/money_trust/montru_pt12.pdf.

14. Joel Seligman, *The Transformation of Wall Street: A History of the Securities and Exchange Commission and Modern Corporate Finance* (Boston: Northeastern University Press, 1995), 24.

15. John Kenneth Galbraith, *The Great Crash 1929* (Boston: Houghton Mifflin, 2009).

16. The discipline of diversification is often marketed as a relatively recent innovation, but it was hardly a novel concept in the early 1900s.

17. The investment companies of the 1920s were roughly equivalent to mutual funds of today.

18. Hugh Bullock, *The Story of Investment Companies* (New York: Columbia University Press, 1959).

19. The Massachusetts Investors Trust is one of the few investment companies from the 1920s that still exists. It will celebrate its one-hundred-year anniversary on July 15, 2024.

20. Bullock, *The Story of Investment Companies*, 199–216.

21. This is a simplification of the different structures. There were also investment holding companies, semi-fixed trusts, installment trusts, and several other forms. This book focuses primarily on closed-ended trusts and open-ended trusts, as these played the most important role in U.S. financial history.

22. Bullock, *The Story of Investment Companies*, 199–216.

23. *Investment Trusts and Investment Companies: Part Three, Abuses and Deficiencies in the Organization and Operation of Investment Trusts and Investment Companies*, Securities and Exchange Commission (Washington, DC: Government Printing Office, 1940), 18, https://archive.org/details/investmenttrusts312unit/page/n9/mode/2up.

24. *Investment Trusts and Investment Companies: Part Two, Statistical Survey of Investment Trusts and Investment Companies*, Securities and Exchange Commission (Washington, DC: Government Printing Office, 1939), 205, https://babel.hathitrust.org/cgi/pt?id=msu.31293020955351&view=1up&seq=1; *Investment Trusts and Investment Companies: Part Three*, 22.

25. "Topics in Wall Street," *New York Times*, October 4, 1928, 39.

26. The term "call loans" is used as the standard terminology in this book, but other commonly used terms were "brokers' loans," "call money," and "margin debt."

27. *New York Times*, multiple issues from January 1, 1928, to October 31, 1929.

28. Smiley and Keehn, "Margin Purchases."

29. Smiley and Keehn, "Margin Purchases."

30. Galbraith, *The Great Crash 1929*, 124.

31. "Stabilization: Hearings Before the Committee on Banking and Currency, Part 1," H. R. 7895, 69th Congress, 1st Session (Washington, DC.: Government Printing Office, 1927), 518, https://fraser.stlouisfed.org/title/stabilization-108/part-i-1271/fulltext.

32. Frank C. Costigliola, "Anglo-American Financial Rivalry in the 1920s," *The Journal of Economic History* 37, no. 4 (December 1977): 927, https://doi.org/10.1017/S0022050700094742.

33. *The Commercial & Financial Chronicle* 126, no. 3268 (February 11, 1928), https://fraser.stlouisfed.org/title/1339/item/516995; *The Commercial & Financial Chronicle* 126, no. 3279 (April 28, 1928), https://fraser.stlouisfed.org/title/1339/item/517006; *The Commercial & Financial Chronicle* 127, no. 3292 (July 28, 1928), https://fraser.stlouisfed.org/title/1339/item/517019.

34. Maury Klein, "The Stock Market Crash of 1929: A Review Article," *The Business History Review* 75, no. 2 (June 2001), 325–351, https://doi.org/10.2307/3116648.

35. "The Financial Situation," *The Commercial & Financial Chronicle* 128, no. 3327 (March 30, 1929): 1, https://fraser.stlouisfed.org/title/1339/item/517041.

36. "Financial Situation," *The Commercial & Financial Chronicle*.

37. Galbraith, *The Great Crash 1929*; "Reserve Bank Keeps Rate at 5 Per Cent After Long Debate," *New York Times*, February 15, 1929, https://www.nytimes.com/1929/02/15/archives/reserve-bank-keeps-rate-at-5-per-cent-after-long-debate-brokers.html.

38. Galbraith, *The Great Crash 1929*.

39. Galbraith, *The Great Crash 1929*, 125.

40. U.S. Department of Commerce, *Statistical Abstract of the United States: 1935* (Washington, DC: Government Printing Office, 1935), 232, https://www2.census.gov/library/publications/1935/compendia/statab/57ed/1935-01.pdf.

41. *New York Times*, multiple issues.

42. Hyman P. Minsky, "The Financial Instability Hypothesis," The Jerome Levy Economics Institute working paper no. 72, May 1992, https://ssrn.com/abstract=161024.

43. Ray Dalio, *Principles for Navigating Big Debt Crises: Part 2: US Debt Crisis and Adjustment (1928–1937)* (Westport, CT: Bridgewater, 2018), 56.

44. Louis Johnston and Samuel H. Williamson, "What Was the U.S. GDP Then?" MeasuringWorth, http://www.measuringworth.org/usgdp12/.

45. The stock market decline is often reported in nominal terms, which overstates the actual impact of the decline in terms of purchasing power. The stock market losses were still dramatic when reported in real terms, but they were considerably less, as a dollar was worth considerably more in 1936 than it was in 1929 due to deflation.

46. Robert Sobel, *The Great Bull Market: Wall Street in the 1920s* (New York: W.W. Norton, 1968).

Part 4

1. Floyd Hamilton, *Bonnie & Clyde and Me!*, audio recorded by Floyd Hamilton, 1938.

Chapter 16

1. John Kenneth Galbraith, *The Great Crash 1929* (Boston: Houghton Mifflin, 2009), 108.

2. "Unemployment Rate for United States," Federal Reserve Bank of St. Louis, updated August 17, 2012, https://fred.stlouisfed.org/series/M0892AUSM156SNBR.

3. "U.S. Business Cycle Expansions and Contractions," National Bureau of Economic Research, https://www.nber.org/research/data/us-business-cycle-expansions-and-contractions.

4. Michael K. Salemi, "Hyperinflation," Econlib, https://www.econlib.org/library/Enc/Hyperinflation.html.

5. The Weimar hyperinflation will be revisited in a later chapter, as it contributed to the rise of Nazi Germany; The reason that printing money has no effect on paying debt denominated in a foreign currency is because the exchange rate immediately adjusts to reflect the additional money printing.

6. Ray Dalio, *Principles for Navigating Big Debt Crises* (New York: Avid Reader Press, 2018).

7. Herbert Hoover, *The Memoirs of Herbert Hoover: The Great Depression 1929–1941* (New York: The Macmillan Company, 1952), 30, https://hoover.archives.gov/sites/default/files/research/ebooks/b1v3_full.pdf.

8. The Reconstruction Finance Corporation (RFC) was a government program that provided emergency lending to financial institutions and corporations in need.

9. Dalio, *Principles for Navigating Big Debt Crises*.

10. *Eighteenth Annual Report of the Federal Reserve Board Covering Operations for the Year 1931*, Federal Reserve Board (Washington, DC: Government Printing Office, 1932), https://fraser.stlouisfed.org/files/docs/publications/arfr/1930s/arfr_1931.pdf.

11. *Historical Statistics of the United States: Colonial Times to 1970.*

12. Bureau of the Census, *Historical Statistics of the United States: Colonial Times to 1970* (Washington, DC: U.S. Bureau of the Census, 1975), https://archive.org/details/HistoricalStatisticsOfTheUnitedStatesColonialTimesTo1970.

13. Ben S. Bernanke, "On Milton Friedman's Ninetieth Birthday: Remarks by Ben S. Bernanke," Federal Reserve Board, November 8, 2002, https://www.federalreserve.gov/boarddocs/Speeches/2002/20021108/default.htm.

14. U.S. Department of Commerce, *Statistical Abstract of the United States: 1935* (Washington, DC: Government Printing Office, 1935), https://www2.census.gov/library/publications/1935/compendia/statab/57ed/1935-01.pdf; *Historical Statistics of the United States: Colonial Times to 1970*, Long-Term Economic Growth 1860–1965 (Kuznets Series); *Journal of Economic History* 43, no. 2 (June 1983)—Lebergott BLS Data.

15. Dalio, *Principles for Navigating Big Debt Crises*, 87.

16. Susan Estabrook Kennedy, *The Banking Crisis of 1933* (Lexington, KY: University of Kentucky Press, 1973), 59, https://archive.org/details/bankingcrisisof10000kenn/page/n7/mode/2up; Arthur Herman, *Freedom's Forge: How American Business Produced Victory in World War II* (New York: Random House, Inc., 2012), 12. Hoover argued that Roosevelt's refusal to explain his policies in advance made the banking crisis worse in the winter of 1933. There is likely truth to this statement, but there is little evidence that Roosevelt intentionally sabotaged Hoover's legacy. It is more likely that Roosevelt sought a fresh start to create safe distance from the Hoover administration's policies. Roosevelt believed that this would help him gain the confidence of the American people, which was desperately needed.

17. There was debate as to the legality of Roosevelt's executive order on March 6, 1933. The Emergency Banking Act of 1933 eliminated this debate by retroactively authorizing it by law.

18. Amity Shlaes, "Herbert Hoover Was Wrong," *Wall Street Journal*, November 18, 2016, https://www.wsj.com/articles/herbert-hoover-was-wrong-1479508055.

19. U.S. Department of Commerce, *Statistical Abstract of the United States: 1935*; *Historical Statistics of the United States: Colonial Times to 1970*; Gene Smiley, "Recent Unemployment Rate Estimates for the 1920s and 1930s," *Journal of Economic History* 43, no. 2 (June 1983): 487–493. Export values differ from values reported from 1927 to 1933 in Figure 16.4 due to the devaluation of the U.S. dollar relative to gold. Money stock includes commercial banks and currency held by public for the United States.

20. Benn Steil, *The Battle of Bretton Woods: John Maynard Keynes, Harry Dexter White, and the Making of a New World Order* (Princeton, NJ: Princeton University Press, 2013), 97.

21. It is important to note that competitive currency devaluations and protectionist trade policies initially benefited individual countries, but they eventually harmed all countries collectively by causing a collapse in international trade. Politicians would later refer to them as "beggar thy neighbor" policies, and undoing the damage was the fundamental objective of the Bretton Woods Agreement. This topic is covered more extensively in chapter 21.

22. U.S. Department of Commerce, *Statistical Abstract of the United States: 1934* (Washington, DC: Government Printing Office, 1934), https://www2.census.gov/library/publications/1934/compendia/statab/56ed/1934-01.pdf.

23. "Gold Ban Is Seen as Loss to US," *New York Times*, May 6, 1933, https://www.nytimes.com/1933/05/06/archives/gold-ban-is-seen-as-a-loss-to-us-embargo-works-two-ways-and-will.html; "President Signs Farm Bill, Making Inflation the Law," *New York Times*, May 13, 1933, https://www.nytimes.com/1933/05/13/archives/president-signs-farm-bill-making-inflation-the-law-but-he-is-silent.html.

Chapter 17

1. Robert Sobel, *The Big Board: A History of the New York Stock Market* (New York: Free Press, 1965).

2. Kennedy, *The Banking Crisis of 1933.*

3. "La Guardia Charges Pools Paid Writers to 'Ballyhoo' Stock," *New York Times*, April 27, 1932, https://www.nytimes.com/1932/04/27/archives/la-guardia-charges-pools-paid-writers-to-ballyhoo-stock-produces.html; Joel Seligman, *The Transformation of Wall Street: A History of the Securities and Exchange Commission and Modern Corporate Finance* (Boston: Northeastern University Press, 1995).

4. Seligman, *The Transformation of Wall Street.*

5. *Stock Exchange Practices: Hearings Before a Subcommittee of the Committee on Banking and Currency, Part 6* (Washington, DC: Government Printing Office, 1933), https://www.senate.gov/about/resources/pdf/pecora-e-brown-testimony.pdf.

6. Ferdinand Pecora, *Wall Street Under Oath: The Story of Our Modern Money Changers* (New York: Graymalkin Media, 1939).

7. Pecora, *Wall Street Under Oath.*

8. Bucket shops were pseudo securities-trading venues in which customers simply bet on the direction of securities. Functionally, they were little different than a modern-day casino.

9. For those interested in reviewing source documents, the Final Report of the Stock Exchange Practices provides an outstanding starting point. The document can be accessed for free in the Federal Reserve's FRASER database at https://fraser.stlouisfed.org/title/stock-exchange-practices-87?browse=1930s.

10. *Stock Exchange Practices.*

11. *Stock Exchange Practices.*

12. "The Financial Situation," *The Commercial & Financial Chronicle* 128, no. 3327 (March 30, 1929): 1, https://fraser.stlouisfed.org/title/1339/item/517041.

13. "Glass Assails Mitchell for Bank's Aid to Market; Stocks Up in Buying Rush," *New York Times*, March 29, 1929, https://www.nytimes.com/1929/03/29/archives/glass-assails-mitchell-for-banks-aid-to-market-stocks-up-in-buying.html.

14. *Stock Exchange Practices.*

15. *Stock Exchange Practices*, part 6.

16. Pecora, *Wall Street Under Oath.*

17. Matthew Field, James Titcomb, and Rozina Sabur, "How Redditors Propelled GameStop to $26 Billion in War with Wall Street," *Telegraph*, January 28, 2021, https://www.telegraph.co.uk/technology/2021/01/27/redditors-propelled-gamestop-26bn-war-wall-street/.

18. "Arthur W. Cutten, Grain Trader, Dies," *New York Times*, June 25, 1936, https://www.nytimes.com/1936/06/25/archives/arthur-w-cutten-grain-trade-ds-speculator-made-millionswon-when.html; "Cutten Left $350,000; Tax Claim is $644,469; Will Is Filed in Chicago and Federal Attorney Says Lien I will Be Placed on Estate," *New York Times*, July 23, 1936, https://www.nytimes.com/1936/07/23/archives/cutten-left-350000-tax-claim-is-644469-will-is-filed-in-chicago-and.html.

19. *Stock Exchange Practices*, part 2.

20. *Stock Exchange Practices*, part 2.

21. *Stock Exchange Practices*, part 2.

22. Seligman, *The Transformation of Wall Street*, 128.

23. Seligman, *The Transformation of Wall Street*, 127.

Chapter 18

1. Alexander Hamilton, *First Report on the Public Credit* (January 9, 1790), https://commons. wikimedia.org/wiki/File:P13_3Large.jpg.

2. Joel Seligman, *The Transformation of Wall Street: A History of the Securities and Exchange Commission and Modern Corporate Finance* (Boston: Northeastern University Press, 1995), 66; Matthew P. Fink, *The Unlikely Reformer: Carter Glass and Financial Regulation* (Fairfax, VA: George Mason University Press, 2019).

3. Fink, *The Unlikely Reformer.*

4. The four components highlighted in this chapter are not the only important provisions of the act. Other examples include Regulation Q and establishment of the Federal Open Markets Committee (FOMC).

5. Howard H. Preston, "The Banking Act of 1933," *The American Economic Review* 23, no. 4 (December 1933): 591, https://www.jstor.org/stable/1807513.

6. "Bank Suspensions, 1892–1935," Federal Reserve System Board of Governors (September 26, 1936), https://fraser.stlouisfed.org/title/403.

7. Preston, "The Banking Act of 1933."

8. Preston, "The Banking Act of 1933."

9. The study by the Federal Reserve does not show the percentage of bank suspensions for each category for the years 1930–1933, but it did state that 83 percent of failures during this period were banks with less than $500,000.

10. "Bank Suspensions, 1892–1935," 3.

11. "Bank Suspensions, 1892–1935," 27.

12. Seligman, *The Transformation of Wall Street.*

13. Seligman, *The Transformation of Wall Street*, 45.

14. W.D.S. "The Securities Act of 1933," *The Virginia Law Review* 20, no. 4 (February 1934): 459, https://doi.org/10.2307/1066403.

15. "Roosevelt Plan to Guard Selling of New Securities is Taken Up By Congress," *New York Times*, March 30, 1933, 1, https://timesmachine.nytimes.com/timesmachine/1933/03/30/issue.html.

16. *Securities and Exchange Act of 1934* (June 6, 1934, ch. 404, title I, Sec. 1, 48 Stat. 881), https:// www.nyse.com/publicdocs/nyse/regulation/nyse/sea34.pdf.

17. *Securities and Exchange Act of 1934.*

18. *Securities and Exchange Act of 1934.*

19. *Securities and Exchange Act of 1934.*

20. *Securities and Exchange Act of 1934.*

21. Seligman, *The Transformation of Wall Street*, 85.

22. "Speech of Joseph P. Kennedy chairman of the Securities and Exchange Commission, at the National Press Club," *New York Times*, July 26, 1934, 13, https://timesmachine.nytimes.com/ timesmachine/1934/07/26/94554648.html?pageNumber=1.

23. Seligman, *The Transformation of Wall Street.*

24. "Kennedy Is Reported Chosen by President," *New York Times*, June 30, 1934, https://www. nytimes.com/1934/06/30/archives/kennedy-is-reported-chosen-by-president-banker-here-said-to-have.html.

25. There is an urban legend that claims that Joe Kennedy sold out of the market after a shoeshine boy gave him stock tips. It is unclear whether this story is true, but the observation that the mania had reached a point at which few additional buyers remained was valid.

26. *Stock Exchange Practices: Report of the Committee on Banking and Currency.* (Washington, DC: Government Printing Office, 1934), https://archive.org/details/StockExchangePracticesReport1934.

27. Seligman, *The Transformation of Wall Street.*

28. Seligman, *The Transformation of Wall Street.*

29. Matthew Fink, *The Rise of Mutual Funds: An Insider's View* (New York: Oxford University Press, 2011).

30. "The Nation" *New York Times*, March 17, 1940, https://www.nytimes.com/1940/03/17/archives/the-nation-hatch-bill-battle.html.

31. Fink, *The Rise of Mutual Funds.*

32. Jeffrey M. Colon, "Oil and Water: Mixing Taxable and Tax-Exempt Shareholders in Mutual Funds," *Loyola University Chicago Law Journal* 45 (2013): 781, https://ir.lawnet.fordham.edu/faculty_scholarship/520/.

33. Colon, "Oil and Water."

Chapter 19

1. Hubert Humphrey, "Remarks," November 11, 1965, Veterans' Day Service, Arlington Memorial Cemetery, http://www2.mnhs.org/library/findaids/00442/pdfa/00442-01731.pdf.

2. Purges in the Soviet Union, China, and in many civil wars following the exit of the British, Dutch, and French empires from their colonial empires easily exceed the total casualties of World War II. The Nazis' systematic approach to genocide, rather than the scale of the genocide itself, is what most distinguished their behavior.

3. Press Release no. 29–37, The U.S. Department of the Treasury (January 4, 1942), 4, https://fraser.stlouisfed.org/files/docs/publications/treaspr/treasury_pressreleases_volume0039.pdf.

4. "The Paris Peace Conference and the Treaty of Versailles," U.S. State Department: Office of the Historian, https://history.state.gov/milestones/1914-1920/paris-peace.

5. William L. Shirer, *The Rise and Fall of the Third Reich: A History of Nazi Germany* (New York: Simon and Schuster, 1960).

6. Shirer, *The Rise and Fall of the Third Reich.*

7. Ray Dalio, *Principles for Navigating Big Debt Crises* (New York: Avid Reader Press, 2018).

8. Dalio, *Principles for Navigating Big Debt Crises.*

9. Shirer, *The Rise and Fall of the Third Reich.*

10. Shirer, *The Rise and Fall of the Third Reich.*

11. Shirer, *The Rise and Fall of the Third Reich.*

12. James K. Pollock, "The German Reichstag Elections of 1930," *American Political Science Review* 24, no. 4 (November 1930): 989–995, https://doi.org/10.2307/1946755.

13. Shirer, *Rise and Fall of the Third Reich.*

14. Pollock, "The German Reichstag Elections of 1930."

15. Shirer, *Rise and Fall of the Third Reich.*

16. Shirer, *Rise and Fall of the Third Reich.*

17. André François-Poncet, *The Fateful Years: Memoirs of a French Ambassador in Berlin, 1931–1938* (New York: Harcourt, Brace and Company, 1949), 43.

18. "Goering: Reichstag Fire," The Propagander, accessed July 26, 2023, https://gooring.tripod.com/goo06.html.

19. Shirer, *Rise and Fall of the Third Reich.*

20. "Georing: Reichstag Fire."

21. Shirer, *Rise and Fall of the Third Reich.*

22. Shirer, *Rise and Fall of the Third Reich.*

23. Shirer, *Rise and Fall of the Third Reich.*

24. Shirer, *Rise and Fall of the Third Reich.*

25. It is likely true that the world was too distracted with their own problems to make much of an effort to stop Germany's ethnic cleansing, but the argument that the world was unaware of the atrocities is not true. Reports of mass arrests and murders appeared regularly in the *New York Times* and international newspapers throughout the 1930s.

26. Shirer, *Rise and Fall of the Third Reich.*

27. Dwight D. Eisenhower, speech after inspecting Ohrdruf Nord concentration camp, April 12, 1945, https://www.shapell.org/manuscript/general-eisenhower-ohrdruf-concentration-camp/.

28. Winston Churchill, radio broadcast to London, January 20, 1940, https://winstonchurchill.org/resources/speeches/1940-the-finest-hour/the-war-situation-house-of-many-mansions/.

29. Shirer, *Rise and Fall of the Third Reich.*

30. "Nuremberg Trial Proceedings Volume 15: June 4, 1946, Morning Session," The Avalon Project, Lillian Goldman Law Library, Yale Law School, https://avalon.law.yale.edu/imt/06-04-46.asp.

31. "Speech of Adolf Hitler before the Reichstag: A reply to U.S. President F. D. Roosevelt, Berlin, April 28, 1939," https://archive.org/details/HitlerAdolfSpeechBeforeTheReichstagAReplyToU.S.PresidentF.D.RooseveltBerlinApril281939.

32. Terry Parssinen, *The Oster Conspiracy of 1938: The Unknown Story of the Military Plot to Kill Hitler and Avert World War II* (New York: HarperCollins, 2003), 172.

33. Shirer, *Rise and Fall of the Third Reich.*

34. Shirer, *Rise and Fall of the Third Reich.*

35. It would later emerge that German soldiers took Pervitin, which is a drug more commonly known as crystal meth. This enabled soldiers to fight around the clock for several days without sleeping.

36. A few days prior to the invasion, French reconnaissance detected a massive traffic jam of German armored vehicles on the eastern edge of the Ardennes Forest, but French military leaders dismissed the report because they thought passage through the Ardennes was impossible. Had they taken this intelligence seriously, British and French bombers could have decimated Nazi forces, which would have likely ended the war prior to the German invasion of France.

37. "What You Need to Know about the Dunkirk Evacuations," Imperial War Museums, United Kingdom, https://www.iwm.org.uk/history/what-you-need-to-know-about-the-dunkirk-evacuations.

38. Arthur Herman, *Freedom's Forge: How American Business Produced Victory in World War II* (New York: Random House, Inc., 2012). There is evidence that the British considered using mustard gas to repel a German amphibious assault. On the flip side, evidence also exists that the Nazis intended to deport all healthy British men and place them in slave labor camps. Given that Germans enslaved hundreds of thousands of French citizens, it is a safe bet that British citizens would have suffered a similar fate.

39. Nobutaka Ike, "Western Influences on the Meiji Restoration," *Pacific Historical Review* 17, no. 1 (February 1948): 1–10, https://doi.org/10.2307/3634763.

40. Richard Grabowski, "Early Japanese Development and the Role of Trade," *Quarterly Journal of Business and Economics* 27, no. 1 (Winter 1988): 126.

41. John Toland, *The Rising Sun: Decline and Fall of the Japanese Empire 1936–1945* (New York: Modern Library, 2003).

42. Grabowski, "Early Japanese Development and the Role of Trade."

43. Toland, *The Rising Sun.*

44. "The London Naval Conference, 1930," Office of the Historian, https://history.state.gov/milestones/1921-1936/london-naval-conf.

45. "London Naval Conference, 1930."

46. Toland, *The Rising Sun.*

47. U.S. Department of Commerce, *Statistical Abstract of the United States: 1935* (Washington, DC: Government Printing Office, 1935), 520, https://www2.census.gov/library/publications/1935/compendia/statab/57ed/1935-01.pdf.

48. Toland, *The Rising Sun.*

49. Toland, *The Rising Sun.*

50. The strategy was years in the making, but the Mukden Incident itself was hastily planned. The reason is that military leaders in Tokyo had caught wind of the Kwantung Army's plans, and a higher-ranking officer was enroute to Manchuria to stop it. This forced Ishiwara and Itigaki to improvise a military conflict before it was too late; Toland, *The Rising Sun.*

51. The U.S. was not a member of the League of Nations, but they adopted a similar policy known as the Stimson Doctrine.

52. Toland, *The Rising Sun.*

53. Sandra Wilson, "Containing the Crisis: Japan's Diplomatic Offensive in the West, 1931–33," *Modern Asian Studies* 29, no. 2 (May 1995): 337–372, https://doi.org/10.1017/S0026749X00012762.

54. Toland, *The Rising Sun.*

55. Toland, *The Rising Sun.*

56. Toland, *The Rising Sun*; Sue De Pasquale, "Nightmare in Nanking," *Johns Hopkins Magazine* (November 1997), https://pages.jh.edu/jhumag/1197web/nanking.html.

57. Johnson Chalmers, "The Looting of Asia," *London Review of Books* 25, no. 22 (November 20, 2003), https://www.lrb.co.uk/the-paper/v25/n22/chalmers-johnson/the-looting-of-asia.

58. Toland, *The Rising Sun*, 100–106.

59. "This Day in History, July 26, 1941: United States Freezes Japanese Assets," History, https://www.history.com/this-day-in-history/united-states-freezes-japanese-assets.

60. Toland, *The Rising Sun.*

61. Hiroyuki Agawa, *The Reluctant Admiral: Yamamoto and the Imperial Navy* (Tokyo: Kodansha International, 1979).

62. Toland, *The Rising Sun.*

63. In a letter written to an ultranationalist, Admiral Yamamoto revealed just how little faith he had in Japan's ability to win a war with the U.S., stating that anything short of invading the continental U.S. and marching all the way to Washington would be insufficient; Toland, *The Rising Sun.*

64. Toland, *The Rising Sun.*

65. Toland, *The Rising Sun.*

66. Harry Dexter White was a senior advisor to Secretary of the Treasury Henry Morgenthau. Operation Snow was a clumsy reference to White's last name. After World War II, intercepted communications revealed that White collaborated with Russia before and during World War II. There is also evidence that White used his influence to stiffen America's terms for a peaceful settlement with Japan. This was in Russia's interest, as a war between the U.S. and Japan would eliminate threats on Russia's southeastern border.

67. Benn Steil, *The Battle of Bretton Woods: John Maynard Keynes, Harry Dexter White, and the Making of a New World Order* (Princeton, NJ: Princeton University Press, 2013), 87; Toland, *The Rising Sun.*

68. Toland, *The Rising Sun.*

69. Toland, *The Rising Sun.*

70. Toland, *The Rising Sun.*

Chapter 20

1. John Toland, *The Rising Sun: Decline and Fall of the Japanese Empire 1936–1945* (New York: Modern Library, 2003), 354.

2. Arthur Herman, *Freedom's Forge: How American Business Produced Victory in World War II* (New York: Random House, Inc., 2012).

3. Herman, *Freedom's Forge.*

4. Herman, *Freedom's Forge.*

5. Herman, *Freedom's Forge.*

6. Herman, *Freedom's Forge.*

7. Herman, *Freedom's Forge.*

8. Herman, *Freedom's Forge.*

9. Herman, *Freedom's Forge.*

10. Herman, *Freedom's Forge.*

11. Herman, *Freedom's Forge.*

12. "Machine Tools Fight the Battle of Production," *American Machinist* 85 (November 26, 1941): 13.

13. Herman, *Freedom's Forge.*

14. "Machine Tools Fight the Battle of Production," 13.

15. Herman, *Freedom's Forge.*

16. Herman, *Freedom's Forge.*

17. "Military Production of Japan." WW2 Weapons, June 13, 2022, https://www.ww2-weapons.com/military-production-japan/.

18. "Military Production of Japan." N/A indicates that data was not available for this year.

19. "Executive Order 9024 Establishing the War Production Board," The American Presidency Project, January 16, 1942, https://www.presidency.ucsb.edu/documents/executive-order-9024-establishing-the-war-production-board; Herman, *Freedom's Forge.*

20. "Military Production of Japan." Germany did not produce any aircraft carriers, and Japan did not produce aircraft carriers, in 1940 and 1945.

21. Alexander Hamilton, *First Report on the Public Credit* (January 9, 1790), https://commons.wikimedia.org/wiki/File:P13_3Large.jpg.

22. Herman, *Freedom's Forge.*

23. U.S. Department of Commerce, *Statistical Abstract of the United States: 1946* (Washington, DC: Government Printing Office, 1946), https://www2.census.gov/library/publications/1946/compendia/statab/67ed/1946-01.pdf.

24. "Historical Highest Marginal Income Tax Rates," Tax Policy Center, February 9, 2022, https://www.taxpolicycenter.org/statistics/historical-highest-marginal-income-tax-rates; *Statistical Abstract of the United States: 1946.*

25. *Statistical Abstract of the United States: 1946.*

26. Kevin Madigan, "Battles of Wills," *Harvard Divinity Bulletin* (Winter 2008), https://bulletin.hds. harvard.edu/battles-of-wills/.

27. William L. Shirer, *The Rise and Fall of the Third Reich: A History of Nazi Germany* (New York: Simon and Schuster, 1960).

28. Francis Pike, "The Development of a Death Cult in 1930s Japan and the Decision to Drop the Atom Bomb," *Asian Affairs* 47, no. 1 (2016): 12, https://doi.org/10.1080/03068374.2015.1128682.

29. Pike, "Development of a Death Cult," 12.

30. Pike, "Development of a Death Cult," 12.

31. Total fatalities far exceed these initial estimates when the long-term effects of radiation exposure are considered.

32. Several military units defied the surrender order after the second atomic bomb, and U.S. and Japanese forces continued to engage in limited hostilities for several weeks.

33. The U.S. placed considerably less weight on Japanese lives as part of the calculation, but it is possible that fewer Japanese died from the atomic bombs than would have died in an invasion. We will never know the answer to this question conclusively, and this decision remains controversial. Regardless of which outcome was worse, it is important to acknowledge the tremendous suffering that the Japanese endured as a result of the atomic explosions.

34. As described in chapter 16, it is important to note that these tactics apply to a deflationary depression.

35. Ray Dalio, *Principles for Dealing with the Changing World Order: Why Nations Succeed and Fail* (New York: Avid Reader Press, 2021).

Part 5

1. George C. Marshall, Speech to Princeton University, February 22, 1947, https://paw.princeton. edu/sites/default/files/pdf/george_marshall_AlumniDay.pdf.

Chapter 21

1. Benn Steil, *The Battle of Bretton Woods: John Maynard Keynes, Harry Dexter White, and the Making of a New World Order* (Princeton, NJ: Princeton University Press, 2013).

2. Beggar-thy-neighbor policies varied by nation but generally included a combination of currency devaluations, tariffs, and capital controls. The intent was to support domestic production and reduce imports.

3. The trade blocs considered are the Sterling bloc (Australia, New Zealand, Denmark, Finland, Ireland, Norway, Portugal, Sweden, and the United Kingdom), Reichmark bloc (Australia, Germany, Greece, and Hungary), and Gold bloc (Belgium, France, the Netherlands, and Switzerland). Jakob B. Madsen, "Trade Barriers and the Collapse of World Trade During the Great Depression," *Southern Economic Journal* 67, no. 4 (April 2001): 851, https://doi. org/10.1002/j.2325-8012.2001.tb00377.x.

4. Comparative advantage is an economic concept that explains *quantitatively* why nations optimize their wealth by specializing in the production of goods and services in which they are most productive. Countries then trade surplus production with other nations to obtain goods and services that they lack.

5. The example is an adaptation of a case study provided in the Stanford Encyclopedia of Philosophy. "Game Theory," first published January 25, 1997; substantive revision March 8, 2019, https:// plato.stanford.edu/entries/game-theory/.

6. Increasing economic interdependence to minimize the probability of warfare was an important motive for the creation of the Eurozone. The theory was that if countries were more interdependent, they would be less likely to engage in hostilities.

7. Steil, *The Battle of Bretton Woods*.

8. John H. Crider, "Fund Established," *New York Times*, December 28, 1945, 1, https://www.nytimes.com/1945/12/28/archives/fund-established-8800000000-will-be-employed-to-stabilize-world.html.

9. Benn Steil, *The Marshall Plan: Dawn of the Cold War* (New York: Simon & Schuster, 2018).

10. Ray Dalio, *Principles for Dealing with a Changing World Order: Why Nations Succeed and Fail* (New York: Simon & Schuster, 2021).

11. Dalio, *Principles for Dealing with a Changing World Order*.

12. R. Bruce Craig,, "Treasonable Doubt: The Harry Dexter White Spy Case," *Studies in Intelligence* 49, no. 1 (2005), https://www.cia.gov/static/3513decb3cf464d706b6ec6c0132cfb0/Review-Treasonable-Doubt.pdf. It remains inconclusive whether White was guilty of espionage, but at a minimum, he shared sensitive information with the Soviet Union.

13. Steil, *The Marshall Plan*.

14. Odd Arne Westad, *The Cold War: A World History* (New York: Basic Books, 2017).

15. "The Aid Program Begins," *New York Times*, April 5, 1948, https://www.nytimes.com/1948/04/05/archives/the-aid-program-begins.html.

Chapter 22

1. Robert Sobel, *The Big Board: A History of the New York Stock Market* (New York: Free Press, 1965), 331.

2. Timothy C. Jacobson, *From Practice to Profession: A History of the Financial Analysts Federation and the Investment Profession* (Charlottesville, VA: AIMR, 1997).

3. Nancy Regan, *The Gold Standard: A Fifty Year History of the CFA Charter* (CFA Institute, 2012).

4. Jacobson, *From Practice to Profession*.

5. Jacobson, *From Practice to Profession*.

6. The evolution of the CFA® program also serves as a microcosm for the evolution of the entire investment industry, which now includes millions of professionals.

7. "CFA Society Chicago: Celebrating 90 Years 1925–2015," The CFA Society Chicago, 2015, https://cfachicago.org/wp-content/uploads/2020/10/CFA-Society-Chicago-90th-Anniversary-Book-Lo-Res.pdf.

8. For the purposes of simplicity, the term "financial analyst" is used throughout the remainder of the book. Other terms commonly used include "investment analyst," "securities analyst," "stock analyst," and several others.

9. Jacobson, *From Practice to Profession*.

10. T. R. Kennedy Jr., "Electronic Computer Flashes Answers, May Speed Engineering," *New York Times*, February 15, 1946, https://www.nytimes.com/1946/02/15/archives/electronic-computer-flashes-answers-may-speed-engineering-new.html.

11. Benjamin Graham, *The Memoirs of the Dean of Wall Street* (New York: McGraw Hill, 1996).

12. Graham, *Memoirs of the Dean of Wall Street*.

13. Graham, *Memoirs of the Dean of Wall Street*.

14. The website for the CFA Institute, www.cfainstitute.org.

15. Jacobson, *From Practice to Profession*.

16. Jacobson, *From Practice to Profession*.

17. The website for the CFA Institute.

18. Winthrop H. Smith Jr., *Catching Lightning in a Bottle: How Merrill Lynch Revolutionized the Financial World* (New York: John C. Wiley and Sons, 2014).

19. Smith, *Catching Lightning in a Bottle.*

20. Smith, *Catching Lightning in a Bottle.*

21. Smith, *Catching Lightning in a Bottle.*

22. Smith, *Catching Lightning in a Bottle.*

23. Smith, *Catching Lightning in a Bottle.*

24. Smith, *Catching Lightning in a Bottle.*

25. Smith, *Catching Lightning in a Bottle.*

26. Churning is the practice of intentionally trading stocks in client portfolios solely to generate commissions. When brokers are compensated primarily with commissions, they have a natural incentive to trade excessively.

27. Smith, *Catching Lightning in a Bottle.*

28. Smith, *Catching Lightning in a Bottle.*

29. Smith, *Catching Lightning in a Bottle.*

30. The language in bold was added by the author to capture the thematic content of each commandment; Merrill Lynch listed only nine actual commandments, but employees still referred to them as the "ten" commandments. Smith, *Catching Lightning in a Bottle.*

31. Smith, *Catching Lightning in a Bottle.*

32. Smith, *Catching Lightning in a Bottle.*

33. The Securities and Exchange Commission, *Securities and Exchange Commission Annual Report: 1970* (Washington, DC: Government Printing Office, 1970), https://www.sec.gov/files/1970.pdf.

34. "Dow-Jones Industrial Stock Price Index for United States," Federal Reserve Bank of St. Louis, updated August 15, 2012, https://fred.stlouisfed.org/series/M1109BUSM293NNBR.

35. "Stockholders," PBS, https://www.pbs.org/fmc/book/14business6.htm.

36. Total institutional ownership, which also included banks, investment advisors, and mutual funds, exceeded 30 percent of the total market in 1985.

37. Educational endowments are included in this chart even though the value of endowment holdings represented only a small fraction of the total. Despite their small footprint, endowment strategies would inspire a dramatic shift in the investment philosophies of all institutional investment plans at the turn of the twenty-first century. Paul Gompers and Andrew Metrick, "Institutional Investors and Equity Prices," *The Quarterly Journal of Economics* 116, no. 1(February 2001): 229–259, https://doi.org/10.1162/003355301556392.

38. "Private Pension Funds; Total Financial Assets, Level," Federal Reserve Bank of St. Louis, updated March 9, 2023, https://fred.stlouisfed.org/series/BOGZ1FL574090005Q; "Life Insurance Companies; Total Financial Assets, Level," Federal Reserve Bank of St. Louis, updated March 9, 2023, https://fred.stlouisfed.org/series/BOGZ1FL544090005Q; Digest of Educational Statistics, U.S. Department of Health, Education, and Welfare (various annual reports).

39. A funded pension plan uses a portfolio of assets to ensure that adequate resources are available to pay future benefits.

40. Robert L. Clark, Lee A. Craig, and Jack W. Wilson, "Early Pension Plans for State and Local Workers" (University of Pennsylvania, Wharton Pension Research Council working paper 661, 2003), https://repository.upenn.edu/prc_papers/661?utm_source=repository.upenn.edu.

41. Clark, Craig, and Wilson, "Early Pension Plans."

42. Clark, Craig, and Wilson, "Early Pension Plans"; *The Evolution of Public Pension Plans: Past, Present, and Future*, National Conference on Public Employee Retirement Systems, March 2008, https://www.ncpers.org/files/ncpers-evolution-of-public-pensions-2008.pdf.

43. American Express limited benefits to disabled retirees, which was consistent with most early pension plans.

44. Patrick W. Seburn, "Evolution of Employer Provided Pension Plans," *Monthly Labor Review* 114, no. 12 (December 1991): https://fraser.stlouisfed.org/title/6130/item/611062/toc/626516.

45. Seburn, "Evolution of Employer Provided Pension Plans."

46. Seburn, "Evolution of Employer Provided Pension Plans."

47. F. C Oviatt, "Historical Study of Fire Insurance in the United States," *The Annals of the American Academy of Political and Social Science* 26, no. 2 (September 1905), https://doi.org/10.1177/000271620502600212.

48. Prior to the allowance of multiline products, insurance companies specialized in a single line of business. As consumers demanded the packaging of multiple products, states eliminated these restrictions in the 1950s.

49. The term "mutual fund" is most familiar to investors; however, the term "investment company" was used for much of U.S. history. Technically speaking, investment company is often the more accurate description of these funds, but "mutual fund" is used in this book because it is more familiar.

50. Hugh Bullock, *The Story of Investment Companies* (New York: Columbia University Press, 1959).

51. Matthew Fink, *The Rise of Mutual Funds: An Insider's View* (New York: Oxford University Press, 2011).

52. Timothy C. Jacobson, *From Practice to Profession: A History of the Financial Analysts Federation and the Investment Profession* (Charlottesville, VA: AIMR, 1997).

53. *2007 Investment Company Fact Book*, Investment Company Institute, https://www.ici.org/system/files/attachments/pdf/2007_factbook.pdf.

54. *2007 Investment Company Fact Book*.

55. All funds employed active management until the first index fund was launched in 1970.

56. Benjamin Graham, "The Future of Financial Analysis," *Financial Analysts Journal* 19, no. 3 (May/June 1963): 66, https://doi.org/10.2469/faj.v19.n3.65.

57. Francis Galton, "Vox Populi," *Nature* 75, (1907): 450–451, https://www.nature.com/articles/075450a0.

58. Data collected from an experiment author conducted at Riverdale High School in Portland, Oregon, March 2023.

59. The Vanguard Group was the first fund company to commercialize the index fund at a large scale, but the firm did not invent the index fund. Rex Sinquefield, William Sharpe, Eugene Fama, and many others deserve credit for inventing the concept.

60. Mark Hebner, *Index Funds: The 12-Step Recovery Program for Active Investors* (IFA Publishing, 2018).

Chapter 23

1. Alexander Hamilton, *Second Report on the Further Provision Necessary for Establishing Public Credit*, December 13, 1790, https://founders.archives.gov/documents/Hamilton/01-07-02-0229-0003.

2. "Real Gross Domestic Product," Federal Reserve Bank of St. Louis, updated April 27, 2023, https://fred.stlouisfed.org/series/GDPC1/.

3. Milton Friedman, *Inflation: Causes and Consequences* (New York: Asia Publishing House, 1963).

4. Lyndon B. Johnson, "Annual Message to the Congress on the State of the Union, January 8, 1964," The American Presidency Project, January 8, 1964, https://www.presidency.ucsb.edu/documents/annual-message-the-congress-the-state-the-union-25.

5. Amity Shlaes, *Great Society: A New History* (New York: HarperCollins Publishers, 2019).

6. Shlaes, *Great Society*.

7. Guian A. McKee, "Lyndon B. Johnson and the War on Poverty," digital recording available online (Presidential Recordings Digital Edition at the University of Virginia Miller Center), 2010, https://rotunda.upress.virginia.edu/pdf/american-cent/WarOnPoverty-introduction-USletter.pdf.

8. Hunter Majorie, "Johnson Signs Bill to Fight Poverty; Pledges New Era," *New York Times*, August 30, 1964, https://www.nytimes.com/1964/08/21/archives/johnson-signs-bill-to-fight-poverty-pledges-new-era.html; "President Signs Medicare Bill; Praises Truman," *New York Times*, July 31, 1964, https://www.nytimes.com/1965/07/31/archives/president-signs-medicare-bill-praises-truman-he-flies-to.html.

9. Andrew T. Jebb, Louis Tay, Ed Diener, and Shigehiro Oishi, "Happiness, Income Satiation, and Turning Points," *Nature Human Behavior* 2, no. 1 (January 2018): 33–38, https://doi.org/10.1038/s41562-017-0277-0.

10. Ray Dalio, *Principles for Dealing with a Changing World Order: Why Nations Succeed and Fail* (New York: Simon & Schuster, 2021).

11. Guian A. McKee, "Lyndon B. Johnson and the War on Poverty," Miller Center, University of Virginia, https://prde.upress.virginia.edu/content/WarOnPoverty2.

12. Shlaes, *Great Society*.

13. Shlaes, *Great Society*.

14. Christopher Goscha, *The Road to Dien Bien Phu: A History of the First War for Vietnam* (New Jersey: Princton University Press, 2022), 135.

15. "Vietnam War U.S. Military Fatal Casualty Statistics," National Archives, https://www.archives.gov/research/military/vietnam-war/casualty-statistics; "Vietnam Statistics & War Costs: Complete Picture Impossible," *Congressional Quarterly*, https://library.cqpress.com/cqalmanac/document.php?id=cqal75-1213988.

16. Dwight D. Eisenhower, "The President's News Conference," The American Presidency Project, April 7, 1954, https://www.presidency.ucsb.edu/documents/the-presidents-news-conference-361.

17. Odd Arne Westad, *The Cold War: A World History* (New York: Basic Books, 2017).

18. The term "Viet Minh" is often used as a blanket term to describe the independence movement that later morphed into North Vietnam.

19. George C. Herring, *America's Longest War: The United States and Vietnam, 1950–1975* (New York: McGraw-Hill, 1996).

20. Herring, *America's Longest War*.

21. Sana Noor Haq, Kostan Nechyporenko, and Anna Chernova, "Without Gas or Without You? Without You: Zelensky's Words for Russia as Ukraine Sweeps Through Northeast," CNN, September 12, 2022, https://edition.cnn.com/2022/09/12/europe/zelensky-message-kharkiv-russia-ukraine-intl/index.html.

22. Pat Paterson, "The Truth About Tonkin," *Naval History Magazine* 22, no. 1 (February 2008), https://www.usni.org/magazines/naval-history-magazine/2008/february/truth-about-tonkin.

23. Herring, *America's Longest War*.

24. Ken Burns, *The Vietnam War*, PBS, film by Ken Burns and Lynn Novick, 2017, https://www.pbs.org/show/vietnam-war/.

25. "Wage Resistance War! An Appeal to the Vietnamese People," in Truong Nhu Tanh, *A Viet Cong Memoir: An Inside Account of the Vietnam War and Its Aftermath* (New York Vintage, 1946), https://www.marxists.org/reference/archive/ho-chi-minh/works/1946/december/19.htm.

26. Burns, *The Vietnam War*.

27. Herring, *America's Longest War*.

28. Charles Hirschman, Samuel Preston, and Vu Manh Loi, "Vietnamese Casualties During the American War," *Population and Development Review* 21, no. 4 (December 1995): 783–812, https://doi.org/10.2307/2137774; Hirschman, "Vietnamese Casualties."

29. Hirschman, "Vietnamese Casualties."

30. "Johnson Says He Won't Run; Halts North Vietnam Raids; Bids Hanoi Join Peace Moves," *New York Times*, April 1, 1968, https://archive.nytimes.com/www.nytimes.com/books/98/04/12/specials/johnson-run.html.

31. George Wallace's decision to run as an independent was probably even more damaging as he drew southern Democrats away from the Democratic party. It was also later revealed that Richard Nixon purposely disrupted a peace conference between the North and South Vietnamese to improve his election prospects. Recorded conversations proving this were obtained from a listening device placed in the South Vietnamese prime minister's office. Johnson reluctantly withheld this information from the public because it risked compromising sources and methods.

32. "Nixon Wins by a Thin Margin, Pleads for Reunited Nation," *New York Times*, November 7, 1968, https://archive.nytimes.com/www.nytimes.com/learning/general/onthisday/big/1105.html; Hirschman, "Vietnamese Casualties."

33. Arthur F. Burns, "The Anguish of Central Banking," The Per Jacobsson Foundation, September 30, 1979, https://fraser.stlouisfed.org/files/docs/publications/FRB/pages/1985-1989/32252_1985-1989.pdf.

34. "Consumer Price Index, 1800–," Federal Reserve Bank of Minneapolis, https://www.minneapolisfed.org/about-us/monetary-policy/inflation-calculator/consumer-price-index-1800-.

35. Milton Friedman, *Inflation: Causes and Consequences* (New York: Asia Publishing House, 1963).

36. This is not an exhaustive list, but it includes the most important factors. Other factors include Arthur Burns's bias toward price and wage controls. Burns also questioned the degree to which monetary policy was the most effective tool to combat inflation. He preferred using fiscal policy.

37. The act also stated that the federal government was responsible for promoting purchasing power as an important priority. Therefore, the bias toward full employment appears to be more of a legal interpretation rather than a fundamental flaw in the actual law.

38. Ben Bernanke, *21st Century Monetary Policy: The Federal Reserve from the Great Inflation to COVID-19* (New York: W.W. Norton & Company, 2022).

39. "The Employment Act of 1946," S. 380, 79th Congress, February 20, 1946, https://fraser.stlouisfed.org/files/docs/historical/trumanlibrary/srf_014_002_0002.pdf; Burns, "The Anguish of Central Banking."

40. Alexander Hamilton, *Second Report on the Public Credit* (December 13, 1790), https://founders.archives.gov/documents/Hamilton/01-07-02-0229-0003.

41. Shlaes, *Great Society*.

42. Shlaes, *Great Society*.

43. Allan H. Meltzer, "Origins of the Great Inflation," *Federal Reserve Bank of St. Louis Review* 87, no. 2, part 2 (March/April 2005): 145–175, https://files.stlouisfed.org/files/htdocs/publications/review/05/03/part2/Meltzer.pdf.

44. *Homeland*, season 5, episode 5, "Better Call Saul," Showtime, November 1, 2015; Meltzer, "Origins of the Great Inflation."

45. In 1972, inflation dipped to 3.3 percent, but this was an aberration during the Great Inflation.

46. "United States Misery Index," http://www.miseryindex.us/indexbyyear.aspx; "Measuring Misery," Federal Reserve Bank of St. Louis, July 6, 2015, https://fredblog.stlouisfed.org/2015/07/measuring-misery/.

47. "Monetary Gold Stock for United States," Federal Reserve Bank of St. Louis, updated August 20, 2012, https://fred.stlouisfed.org/series/M1476CUSM144NNBR.

48. Susan Strange, "The Dollar Crisis 1971," *International Affairs* 48, no. 2 (April 1972): 191–216, https://doi.org/10.2307/2613437.

49. The Shiller P/E ratio is calculated by taking the current stock price divided by the average real earnings of companies over the prior ten-year period. The ratio seeks to smooth the effects of earnings volatility that typically occur during the business cycle. "Shiller PE Ratio by Year," Multpl.com, accessed May 7, 2023, https://www.multpl.com/shiller-pe/table/by-year.

50. "Balance on Goods and Services (Discontinued)," Federal Reserve Bank of St. Louis, updated June 18, 2014, https://fred.stlouisfed.org/series/BOPBGSA.

51. Nhu Tanh, "Wage Resistance War!"

52. William Nordhaus, "Retrospective Analysis of the 1970s Productivity Slowdown," National Bureau of Economic Research working paper 10950, December 2004, https://doi.org/10.3386/w10950.

53. "Nation: Thoughts from Camp David," *Time* 114, no. 4 (July 23, 1979), https://content.time.com/time/magazine/0,9263,7601790723,00.html.

54. To this day, people often mistakenly believe that the oil shocks were the primary cause of 1970s stagflation, but the data clearly rejects this thesis. The oil shocks added to inflation, but they were not the primary cause.

55. Martin F. Seligman and Steven F. Maier, "Failure to Escape Traumatic Shock," *Journal of Experimental Psychology* 74, no. 1 (1967): 1–9, https://psycnet.apa.org/doi/10.1037/h0024514.

56. Seligman and Maier, "Failure to Escape Traumatic Shock."

57. Shlaes, *Great Society*.

58. "Inflation's Back," *Economist*, May 22, 2008, https://www.economist.com/leaders/2008/05/22/inflations-back.

59. Bernanke, *21st Century Monetary Policy*; Paul Volcker and Toyoo Gyohten, *Changing Fortunes: The World's Money and the Threat to American Leadership* (New York: Random House, 1992).

60. Milton Friedman, *Inflation: Causes and Consequences* (New York: Asia Publishing House, 1963).

61. Volcker and Gyohten, *Changing Fortunes*.

62. Robert J. Samuelson, *The Great Inflation and Its Aftermath: The Past and Future of American Affluence* (New York: Random House, 2010).

63. "Gallup Poll Finds Opposition to Tax Surcharge," *New York Times*, January 24, 1968, https://www.nytimes.com/1968/01/24/archives/gallup-poll-finds-opposition-to-tax-surcharge.html.

64. Volcker and Gyohten, *Changing Fortunes*.

65. Samuelson, *The Great Inflation and Its Aftermath*.

66. Sometimes Federal Reserve presidents voice dissent on monetary policy. Under normal circumstances Volcker did not discourage dissent, but to combat entrenched inflation expectations, he believed that a unified message was important.

67. Volcker and Gyohten, *Changing Fortunes*.

68. "Federal Funds Effective Rate," Federal Reserve Bank of St. Louis, updated May 1, 2023, https://fred.stlouisfed.org/series/fedfunds.

69. Volcker and Gyohten, *Changing Fortunes*.

70. Volcker and Gyohten, *Changing Fortunes*.

71. "Unemployment Rate," Federal Reserve Bank of St. Louis, updated May 5, 2023, https://fred. stlouisfed.org/series/UNRATE.

72. "Federal Funds Effective Rate."

73. Volcker and Gyohten, *Changing Fortunes*.

Part 6

1. Vannevar Bush, *Science: The Endless Frontier*, Office of Scientific Research and Development (Washington, DC: Government Printing Office, 1945), https://www.nsf.gov/od/lpa/nsf50/ vbush1945.htm.

Chapter 24

1. David Clark Scott, "Robert Noyce: Why Steve Jobs Idolized Noyce," *Christian Science Monitor*, December 12, 2011, https://www.csmonitor.com/Technology/2011/1212/ Robert-Noyce-Why-Steve-Jobs-idolized-Noyce.

2. Stanford and Silicon Valley are the focus of this chapter, but it is not intended to discount the contributions of Harvard, MIT, and many other leading academic institutions. Stanford may be the leader of high-tech innovation, but it is not the only contributor to America's exceptional track record of high-tech innovation.

3. This does not lessen the horrific human costs of war, nor does it assert that valuable commercial inventions justify the horrors of war. There is almost certainly a better way to promote innovation without resorting to armed conflict. Nevertheless, the objective of this book is to report financial history factually, and it would be inaccurate to ignore the fact that the demands of war contributed heavily to many important commercial inventions.

4. Paul N. Edwards, *The Closed World: Computers and the Politics of Discourse in Cold War America* (Cambridge, MA: MIT Press, 1997).

5. Edwards, *The Closed World*; T. R. Kennedy Jr., "Electronic Computer Flashes Answers, May Speed Engineering," *New York Times*, February 15, 1946, https://www.nytimes.com/1946/02/15/ archives/electronic-computer-flashes-answers-may-speed-engineering-new.html.

6. Tom Nicholas, *VC: An American Story* (Cambridge, MA: Harvard University Press, 2019).

7. Margaret O'Mara, *The Code: Silicon Valley and the Remaking of America* (New York: Penguin, 2019).

8. Leslie W. Stuart and Robert H. Kargon, "Selling Silicon Valley: Frederick Terman's Model for Regional Advantage," *Business History Review* 709, no. 4 (Winter 1996): 435–472, https://doi. org/10.2307/3117312.

9. Stuart and Kargon, "Selling Silicon Valley."

10. Hewlett Packard was founded in 1939, but the company expanded dramatically by selling critical electronic components during the war.

11. Stuart and Kargon, "Selling Silicon Valley."

12. Stuart and Kargon, "Selling Silicon Valley."

13. "Foundation for the Future," Stanford Research Park, https://stanfordresearchpark.com/about.

14. Nicholas, *VC: An American History*.

15. There is disagreement over who invented the silicon-based transistor. Shockley contributed heavily to the creation of transistors generally, but Gordon Teal, a scientist at Texas Instruments, was the first to commercialize them.

16. "Foundation for the Future."

17. The most notable members of the traitorous eight were Eugene Kleiner (cofounder of Kleiner-Perkins), Robert Noyce (cofounder of Intel), Gordon Moore (cofounder of Intel), and Jean Hoerni (inventor of the planar process).

18. David Burg and Jesse H. Ausubel, "Moore's Law Revisited through Intel Chip Density," *Public Library of Science* 16, no. 8 (August 18, 2021): e0256245, https://doi.org/10.1371/journal.pone.0256245.

19. There is disagreement over who invented the integrated circuit. Jack Kilby, an engineer at Texas Instruments, also claimed the invention.

20. O'Mara, *The Code.*

21. Ernest Braun and Stuart MacDonald, *Revolution in Miniature: The History and Impact of Semiconductor Electronics,* 2nd ed. (Cambridge: Cambridge University Press, 1982).

22. Braun and MacDonald, *Revolution in Miniature.*

23. Berlin Leslie, "Robert Noyce and Fairchild Semiconductor, 1957–1968," *Business History Review* 75, no. 1 (Spring, 2001): 63–101, https://doi.org/10.2307/3116557.

24. Braun and MacDonald, *Revolution in Miniature.*

25. Nicholas, *VC: An American History.*

26. There were other venture capital firms, such as one used to invest the Rockefeller fortune, but these were primarily vehicles for ultra-wealthy families.

27. Nicholas, *VC: An American History.*

28. Spencer E. Ante, *Creative Capital: Georges Doriot and the Birth of Venture Capital* (Cambridge, MA: Harvard University Press, 2008).

29. Ante, *Creative Capital.*

30. Ante, *Creative Capital.*

31. Alexander Starbuck, *History of the American Whale Fishery from its Earliest Inception to the Year 1876* (Waltham, MA: Alexander Starbuck, 1878), https://archive.org/details/historyofamerica00star/page/8/mode/2up.

32. Isaac Howland Jr., Hetty Green's great-grandfather, was ranked among the best whaling investors in the early 1800s. Several of Hetty's investing virtues likely derived from lessons taught to her by her ancestors and from her experience on the docks of New Bedford.

33. Internal rate of return (as opposed to time-weighted return) takes the timing of cash flows into account. It is the standard used to evaluate venture capital returns.

34. Nicholas, *VC: An American History.*

35. Nicholas, *VC: An American History.*

36. Ante, *Creative Capital.*

37. O'Mara, *The Code,* 90.

38. Nicholas, *VC: An American History.*

39. "Employee Retirement Income Security Act of 1974," U.S. Government, September 2, 1974, 877, https://www.govinfo.gov/content/pkg/STATUTE-88/pdf/STATUTE-88-Pg829.pdf.

40. O'Mara, *The Code.*

41. Eric S. Hintz, "The Mother of All Demos," Smithsonian, December 10, 2018, https://invention.si.edu/mother-all-demos.

42. O'Mara, *The Code.*

43. O'Mara, *The Code.*

44. The first meeting was actually held at a garage in Menlo Park, but all future meetings were held at Stanford.

45. Phone phreaks were an early type of hacker. Phreakers created devices that enabled users to get free phone calls. Wozniak and Jobs built these devices and sold them to dorm residents at the University of California at Berkeley in the early 1970s.

46. Ron Wayne was the third partner, but he reportedly sold his stake to Steve Jobs and Steve Wozniak for $800 in 1976; O'Mara, *The Code*.

47. Philip Shabecoff, "U.S. Eases Pension Investing," *New York Times*, June 21, 1979, https://www.nytimes.com/1979/06/21/archives/us-eases-pension-investing-pension-investments.html.

48. Personal interview with Ian Lanoff, September 14, 2022.

49. Venture capital firms were not the only beneficiaries of these changes. Institutional investors also began investing more heavily in buyout funds. In anticipation of the change, KKR raised the first institutional fund in 1978.

50. *Venture Capital Yearbook 1988* (Venture Economics, 1988); James M. Poterba, "Venture Capital and Capital Gains Taxation," *Tax Policy and the Economy* 3 (1989), https://doi.org/10.1086/tpe.3.20061783.

51. Jeremy Reimer, "Total Share: Personal Computer Market Share 1975–2010," *Jeremy's Blog*, December 7, 2012, https://jeremyreimer.com/rockets-item.lsp?p=137.

52. The fiscal year end for Microsoft and Oracle were June 30 and May 30, respectively. The combined annual sales are not precise given the one-month difference in the fiscal year end. "Microsoft Company 1975," https://www.landley.net/history/mirror/ms/microsoft_company.htm; "Microsoft Revenue (Annual)," https://ycharts.com/companies/MSFT/revenues_annual; Colin McLachlan, "Phenomenal Growth for Oracle Systems," *Australian Financial Review*, November 16, 1987, https://www.afr.com/politics/phenomenal-growth-for-oracle-system-19871116-k2ilq.

53. O'Mara, *The Code*.

54. The difference in real returns for each asset class were even wider in the 1980s, as inflation averaged 7.4 percent in the 1970s versus 5.0 percent in the 1980s.

55. "S&P 500 Historical Prices by Year," https://www.multpl.com/s-p-500-historical-prices/table/by-year.

56. "Data Update 1 for 2023: Setting the Table," updated January 5, 2023, https://www.stern.nyu.edu/~adamodar/New_Home_Page/data.html.

57. The real return represents the real increase in value of the investment after considering the impact of inflation.

58. "S&P 500 Historical Prices by Year."

59. Kaleb Nygaard, "The Federal Reserve's Response to the 1987 Market Crash," *Journal of Financial Crises* 2, no. 3 (2020), https://elischolar.library.yale.edu/cgi/viewcontent.cgi?article=1109&context=journal-of-financial-crises; Mark Carlson, "A Brief History of the 1987 Stock Market Crash with a Discussion of the Federal Reserve Response," Finance and Economics Discussion Series working paper no. 2007-13, April 26, 2007, https://dx.doi.org/10.2139/ssrn.982615.

60. Barrie A. Wigmore, "Revisiting the October 1987 Crash," *Financial Analysts Journal* 54, no.1 (1998): 36–48 https://doi.org/10.2469/faj.v54.n1.2143.

61. Jason Zweig, "Back to the Future: Lessons from the Forgotten 'Flash Crash' of 1962," *Jason Zweig*, blog, May 29, 2010, https://jasonzweig.com/back-to-the-future-lessons-from-the-forgotten-flash-crash-of-1962/; Tom Lauricella, "Dow Takes a Harrowing 1,010.14-Point Trip," *Wall Street Journal*, May 7, 2010, https://www.wsj.com/articles/SB10001424052748704370704575227754131412596.

62. Edwin Lefevre, *Reminiscences of a Stock Operator* (New York: George H. Doran, 1923), https://www.gutenberg.org/ebooks/60979.

Chapter 25

1. Charles D. Ellis, *Figuring it Out: Sixty Years of Answering Investors' Most Important Questions* (Hoboken, NJ: John Wiley & Sons, 2022).

2. The chapter does not address all alternative asset classes, but rather focuses on the largest sectors of private equity buyout funds and hedge funds.

3. Buyout funds are often referred to as "private equity" funds. In this book, buyout funds are considered a subset of the larger universe of private equity funds.

4. Carried interest is a share of the fund's profit. Carried interest rates can vary but tend to converge around 20 percent of the fund's profits over a specified return (known as the hurdle rate). There are methods used to calculate carried interest, but the important principle is that fund managers share in the profits of the fund.

5. Bryan Burrough and John Helyar, *Barbarians at the Gate: The Fall of RJR Nabisco* (New York: HarperCollins, 2009).

6. Burrough and Helyar, *Barbarians at the Gate*.

7. Steven N. Kaplan and Per Strömberg, "Leveraged Buyouts and Private Equity," *Journal of Economic Perspectives* 23, no. 1 (Winter 2009): 121–146, https://doi.org/10.1257/jep.23.1.121.

8. Every LBO had a unique capital structure, but this is a reasonable approximation of a particularly aggressive structure that was not unheard of in the 1980s. Junk bonds are now more commonly referred to as high-yield bonds.

9. Burrough and Helyar, *Barbarians at the Gate*.

10. Cynthia A. Montgomery, "Corporate Diversification," *The Journal of Economic Perspectives* 8, no. 3 (Summer 1994): 163–178, https://pubs.aeaweb.org/doi/pdfplus/10.1257/jep.8.3.163.

11. Burrough and Helyar, *Barbarians at the Gate*.

12. Burrough and Helyar, *Barbarians at the Gate*.

13. Burrough and Helyar, *Barbarians at the Gate*.

14. *Wall Street*, directed by Oliver Stone (American Entertainment Company, 1987).

15. Robert Sobel, *The Great Bull Market: Wall Street in the 1920s* (New York: W.W. Norton, 1968), 158.

16. Tim Melvin, "It's OK to Be a Pig," *RealMoney*, April 13, 2015, https://realmoney.thestreet.com/articles/04/13/2015/its-ok-be-pig.

17. Melvin, "It's OK to Be a Pig."

18. Kristin Aguilera, "What Was the Very First Hedge Fund? Ask Warren Buffett," Bloomberg, April 24, 2012, https://www.bloomberg.com/opinion/articles/2012-04-24/what-was-the-very-first-hedge-fund-ask-warren-buffett.

19. Gregory J. Millman, *The Vandal's Crown: How Rebel Currency Traders Overthrew the World's Central Banks* (New York: The Free Press, 1995).

20. *2021 Yale Endowment Report*, Yale Investments Office, https://static1.squarespace.com/static/55db7b87e4b0dca22fba2438/t/62507d42618fc8048d8eb50f/1649442120675/2021+Endowment+Report.pdf.

21. David Swensen, *Pioneering Portfolio Management*, 2009 ed. (New York: The Free Press, 2009).

22. *2021 Yale Endowment Report*; Swensen, *Pioneering Portfolio Management*.

23. David Swensen credits Dean Takahashi as much as himself for Yale's success. In *Pioneering Portfolio Management*, Swensen stated, "The ideas and influence of Dean Takahashi, my friend for twenty-three years and my colleague for twelve years, touch every page of this book."

24. "Yale University Endowment Reports," Yale Investments Office, https://investments.yale.edu/endowment-reports; "Historic Endowment Study Data," National Association of College University Business Offices (NACUBO), February 17, 2023, https://www.nacubo.org/Research/2022/Historic%20Endowment%20Study%20Data.

25. The analysis does not include returns for fiscal years 1986–1987 because median endowment returns were unavailable during these years.

26. *2021 Yale Endowment Report.*

27. Taken from Dean Takahashi's comments at the Swensen Memorial Celebration, 2022.

28. Chuck Jaffe, "Experts: Slow and Steady Still Wins Race," *The Star-Ledger*, February 6, 2012.

29. Timothy C. Jacobson, *From Practice to Profession: A History of the Financial Analysts Federation and the Investment Profession* (Charlottesville, VA: AIMR, 1997).

30. Swensen, *Pioneering Portfolio Management.*

31. "Total Assets of Pension Funds in the United States from 2010 to 2021," Statista Research Department, May 16, 2023, https://www.statista.com/statistics/421729/pension-funds-assets-usa.

32. An increasing number of plans outsource the entire portfolio to outsourced chief investment officers (OCIOs). These firms suffer many of the same challenges as investment consulting firms but charge higher fees and, depending on the strategy, can be difficult and costly to unwind due to large positions in illiquid, alternative assets; The term investment committee is used broadly. Other terms commonly used are finance committees and investment boards.

33. Most investment committees meet only once per quarter for a few hours.

34. Some plans also invested the entire portfolio with balanced fund managers, which offered diversified portfolio consisting primarily of stocks and bonds.

35. Richard Ennis, *Never Bullshit the Client: My Life in Investment Consulting* (Fort Myers, FL: The Carom Press, 2019).

36. Ennis, *Never Bullshit the Client.*

37. EnnisKnupp embraced portfolio simplicity and heavy use of index funds soon after the company's founding. Even in retirement, Richard Ennis remains a vocal advocate of this philosophy.

38. Charles D. Ellis, "Murder on the Orient Express: The Mystery of Underperformance," *Financial Analysts Journal* 68, no. 4 (July/August 2012): 13–19, https://doi.org/10.2469/faj.v68.n4.2.

39. Even if a firm does provide performance data voluntarily, trustees should remain skeptical. There are no performance reporting standards for investment consulting firms, making it difficult to determine whether self-reported performance is an accurate representation of their skill.

Chapter 26

1. Steven Hayward, *The Age of Reagan: The Fall of the Old Liberal Order: 1964–1980* (New York: Crown Forum, 2009).

2. Mark Skousen, "Milton Friedman's Last Lunch," *Forbes*, November 24, 2006, https://www.forbes.com/forbes/2006/1211/056a.html?sh=70faa04f6b6f.

3. The napkin displayed at the Smithsonian is unlikely to be the original, but the original expressed the same concept and with the same neglect of analysis.

4. Alexander Hamilton, *First Report on the Public Credit* (January 9, 1790), https://commons.wikimedia.org/wiki/File:P13_3Large.jpg.

5. The brief surpluses recorded in 1947–1948 and 1998–2001 were anomalies.

6. Bureau of the Census, *Historical Statistics of the United States, 1789–1945* (Washington, DC: U.S. Bureau of the Census, 1949), https://www.census.gov/library/publications/1949/compendia/hist_stats_1789-1945.html.

7. *Budget of the U.S. Government Fiscal Year 2023*, Office of Management and Budget (Washington D.C.: Government Printing Office, 2022), https://www.whitehouse.gov/wp-content/uploads/2022/03/budget_fy2023.pdf.

8. "Federal Receipts as Percent of Gross Domestic Product," Federal Reserve Bank of St. Louis, updated March 30, 2023, https://fred.stlouisfed.org/series/FYFRGDA188S.

9. Daron Acemoglu and Pasqual Restreop, "Tasks, Automation, and the Rise in US Wage Inequality," (National Bureau of Economic Research working paper 28920, June 2021), https://doi.org/10.3386/w28920.

10. Throughout this section, economic growth is assumed to be real economic growth. In other words, growth of output after accounting for the impact of inflation.

11. "Nonfarm Business Sector: Labor Productivity (Output per Hour) for All Workers," Federal Reserve Bank of St. Louis, updated May 4, 2023, https://fred.stlouisfed.org/series/PRS85006092.

12. Robert J. Gordon, *The Rise and Fall of American Growth: The U.S. Standard of Living since the Civil War* (Princeton, NJ: Princeton University Press, 2016); Robert J. Gordon and Hassan Sayed, "A New Interpretation of Productivity Growth Dynamics in the Pre-Pandemic and Pandemic Era U.S. Economy 1950–2022" (working paper 30267, National Bureau of Economic Research, July 2022), https://www.nber.org/system/files/working_papers/w30267/w30267.pdf.

13. "Real Gross Domestic Product," Federal Reserve Bank of St. Louis, updated April 27, 2023, https://fred.stlouisfed.org/series/GDPC1/.

14. Acemoglu and Restreop, "Tasks, Automation, and the Rise in US Wage Inequality"; Gordon, *The Rise and Fall of American Growth*.

15. "All Employees, Manufacturing," Federal Reserve Bank of St. Louis, updated May 5, 2023, https://fred.stlouisfed.org/series/MANEMP; "Civilian Labor Force Level," Federal Reserve Bank of St. Louis, updated May 5, 2023, https://fred.stlouisfed.org/series/CLF16OV.

16. Data for 1982 was not available. The data point is simply an average of the rate in 1981 and 1983, which is an approximation of the actual value. Barry T. Hirsch, David A. Macpherson, and Wayne G. Vroman, "Estimates of Union Density by State," *Monthly Labor Review* 124, no. 7 (July 2001): 51–55, https://www.jstor.org/stable/41861610.

17. "Nominal Broad Dollar Index," Federal Reserve Board, https://www.federalreserve.gov/releases/h10/summary/indexb_m.txt.

18. "Statistical Abstracts Series (1947–1969)," U.S. Census Bureau, multiple reports from various years, https://www.census.gov/library/publications/time-series/statistical_abstracts.html.

19. Ben S. Bernanke, "The Global Savings Glut and the U.S. Current Account Deficit," Federal Reserve Board, March 10, 2005, https://www.federalreserve.gov/boarddocs/speeches/2005/200503102/.

20. Joseph A. Schumpeter, *Socialism, Capitalism, Democracy* (New York: Harper & Row, 1975).

21. It is ironic that Schumpeter coined the phrase, as he believed that capitalism would be replaced by socialism.

22. Ichak Adizes, *Managing Corporate Lifecycles Updated* (Carpinteria, CA: Idizes Institute, 2004).

23. Adizes, *Managing Corporate Lifecycles Updated*.

24. *Budget of the U.S. Government Fiscal Year 2023*.

Chapter 27

1. John Kenneth Galbraith, *The Great Crash 1929* (Boston: Houghton Mifflin, 2009), 108.

2. Odd Arne Westad, *The Cold War: A World History* (New York: Basic Books, 2017).

3. Westad, *The Cold War.*

4. "Berlin Border Guards Stunned by the News," *New York Times,* November 10, 1989, https://www.nytimes.com/1989/11/10/world/clamor-in-the-east-berlin-border-guards-stunned-by-the-news.html.

5. Westad, *The Cold War.*

6. Westad, *The Cold War.*

7. Press Release no. 29-37, The U.S. Department of the Treasury (January 4, 1942), 4, https://fraser.stlouisfed.org/files/docs/publications/treaspr/treasury_pressreleases_volume0039.pdf.

8. Galbraith, *The Great Crash 1929,* 33.

9. Margaret O'Mara, *The Code: Silicon Valley and the Remaking of America* (New York: Penguin, 2019).

10. David Einstein, "Netscape Mania Ends Stock Soaring/Internet Software Firm's IPO Doubles in Price," *San Francisco Chronicle,* August 10, 1995.

11. The original name, Mosaic Communications, was soon changed to Netscape Communications due to a copyright dispute with the University of Illinois. Matt Blitz, "Later, Navigator: How Netscape Won and Then Lost the World Wide Web," *Popular Mechanics* (April 4, 2019), https://www.popularmechanics.com/culture/web/a27033147/netscape-navigator-history/.

12. Laurence Zuckerman, "With Internet Cachet, Not Profit, a New Stock is Wall Street's Darling," *New York Times,* August 10, 1995, https://www.nytimes.com/1995/08/10/style/chronicle-187595.html.

13. Prior to the acquisition by AOL, Andreesen publicly released the source code of Netscape Navigator. The software was used as the foundation for the Firefox browser, which remains in use today.

14. Laura Rich, "Investment Engines in Search of Their Next Move," *New York Times,* May 3, 2004, https://www.nytimes.com/2004/05/03/business/investment-engines-in-search-of-their-next-moves.html.

15. George Soros, "Bush Doctrine Incites an Angry, Allergic Reaction," *Irish Times,* March 14, 2003, https://www.irishtimes.com/business/bush-doctrine-incites-an-angry-allergic-reaction-1.352106.

16. Tom Nicholas, *VC: An American Story* (Cambridge, MA: Harvard University Press, 2019), 295.

17. *NVCA Yearbook 2015,* National Venture Capital Association.

18. NVC*A Yearbook 2015,* National Venture Capital Association.

19. Jay R. Ritter, "Initial Public Offerings: Updated Statistics," Warrington College of Business, University of Florida, April 13, 2023, https://site.warrington.ufl.edu/ritter/files/IPO-Statistics.pdf.

20. Laura M. Holson, "Still Feeding an Internet Frenzy," *New York Times,* June 6, 1999, https://www.nytimes.com/1999/06/06/business/investing-still-feeding-an-internet-frenzy.html.

21. Gretchen Morgenson, "Telecom's Pied Piper: Whose Side Was He On?" *New York Times,* November 18, 2001, https://www.nytimes.com/2001/11/18/business/telecom-s-pied-piper-whose-side-was-he-on.html.

22. The Associated Press, "Regulators Finalize $1.4 Billion Wall Street Settlement," *New York Times,* April 28, 2003, https://www.nytimes.com/2003/04/28/business/regulators-finalize-14-billion-wall-st-settlement.html.

23. Ian McDonald, "Fund Openings, Closings, Manager Moves: Bullish

Amerindo to Launch Two More Funds," TheStreet.com, May 25, 2000, https://www.thestreet.com/investing/funds/mutual-funds/fund-openings-closings-manager-moves-bullish-amerindo-to-launch-two-more-funds-947568.

24. "Victory Munder Multi-Cap Fund (MNNAX): Historical Data," Yahoo! Finance, https://finance.yahoo.com/quote/MNNAX/history?p=MNNAX.

25. Ian McDonald, "Mutual Funds Helped Puff Up the Tech Bubble," *Wall Street Journal*, March 11, 2003, https://www.wsj.com/articles/SB1047299436480816960.

26. Aaron Lucchetti, "Munder Plans to Close Off NetNet Fund to Newcomers," *Wall Street Journal*, March 24, 2000, https://www.wsj.com/articles/SB9538488469896350.

27. Amy C. Arnott, "Mind the Gap: A Report on Investor Returns in the United States," Morningstar, August 31, 2021, https://www.highview.com.au/wp/wp-content/uploads/2022/04/2021-mind-the-gap.pdf.

28. Jim Cramer, "The Winners of the New World," Speech at 6th Annual Internet and Electronic Commerce Conference and Exposition, TheStreet, February 29, 2000, https://www.thestreet.com/personal-finance/the-winners-of-the-new-world-891820.

29. This critique is not intended to diminish the importance of freedom of the press. The fact that the media can amplify asset bubbles is a disadvantage, but this fundamental right is critical to a well-functioning democracy.

30. *New York Times*, February 26, 2000, C1, https://timesmachine.nytimes.com/timesmachine/2000/02/26/issue.html.

31. Will Daniel, "Jim Cramer Says it's 'Almost Irresponsible' for Companies not to Own Bitcoin as the Cryptocurrency Soars to New Highs," *Business Insider*, February 9, 2021, https://www.businessinsider.in/stock-market/news/jim-cramer-says-its-almost-irresponsible-for-companies-not-to-own-bitcoin-as-the-cryptocurrency-soars-to-new-highs/articleshow/80775004.cms.

32. Robert Sobel, *The Big Board: A History of the New York Stock Market* (New York: Free Press, 1965).

33. Ritter, "Initial Public Offerings: Updated Statistics."

34. Ritter, "Initial Public Offerings: Updated Statistics."

35. Henry M. Paulson Jr., *On the Brink: Inside the Race to Stop the Collapse of the Global Financial System* (New York: Hatchett, 2010).

36. John Kenneth Galbraith, *A Short History of Financial Euphoria*, 4th ed. (New York: Penguin, 1990).

37. "NASDAQ Composite (^IXIC): Historical Data," Yahoo! Finance, https://finance.yahoo.com/quote/%5EIXIC/history?p=%5EIXIC.

Chapter 28

1. Galbraith, *A Short History of Financial Euphoria*.

2. In their extensive evaluation of financial crises throughout history, Kenneth Rogoff and Carmen Reinhardt refer to such events as banking crises; Carmen M. Reinhardt and Kenneth Rogoff, *This Time is Different: Eight Centuries of Financial Folly* (Princeton, NJ: Princeton University Press, 2009).

3. Former Chairman of the Federal Reserve Ben Bernanke raised an important point that several of these problems were mutually reinforcing. For example, the real estate bubble (problem #1) was reinforced by the deterioration of mortgage underwriting standards (problem #3). Each problem is explained independently in this chapter, but it is important to recognize the mutually reinforcing dynamics.

4. Robert J. Shiller, *Irrational Exuberance*, revised and expanded edition (Princeton, NJ: Princeton University Press, 2016).

5. "S&P CoreLogic Case-Shiller Home Price Indices," S&P Dow Jones Indices, https://www.spglobal.com/spdji/en/index-family/indicators/sp-corelogic-case-shiller/sp-corelogic-case-shiller-composite/#overview.

6. Hyman P. Minsky, "The Financial Instability Hypothesis," The Jerome Levy Economics Institute working paper no. 72, May 1992, https://ssrn.com/abstract=161024.

7. Holden Lewis, "Experts: No Real-Estate Bubble Burst," *Chicago Sun-Times*, September 10, 2004, accessed via LexisNexis search.

8. The term "GSEs" refers only to Fannie Mae and Freddie Mac, as these were the most problematic during the GFC. Other entities, such as Sallie Mae and FHL Banks, are also GSEs but were not material contributors to the GFC.

9. *The Financial Crisis Inquiry Report*, The Financial Crisis Inquiry Commission (Washington, DC: Government Printing Office, 2011), https://www.govinfo.gov/content/pkg/GPO-FCIC/pdf/GPO-FCIC.pdf.

10. *The Financial Crisis Inquiry Report.*

11. Mark Calabria, "Role of Fannie and Freddie in Driving Financial System Leverage," The Cato Institute, September 24, 2013, https://www.cato.org/speeches/role-fannie-freddie-driving-financial-system-leverage.

12. Board of Governors of the Federal Reserve, Federal Reserve Flow of Funds Accounts (1991–2007), data compiled from multiple reports.

13. "Expanded Guidance for Subprime Lending Programs," OCC Bulletin 2001-6, January 31, 2001, https://ots.gov/news-issuances/bulletins/2001/bulletin-2001-6.html.

14. Adam B. Ashcraft and Til Schuermann, *Understanding the Securitization of Subprime Mortgage Credit*, Federal Reserve Staff Report no. 318, March 2008, https://www.newyorkfed.org/medialibrary/media/research/staff_reports/sr318.pdf.

15. Stephen A. Holmes, "Fannie Mae Eases Credit to Aid Mortgage Lending," *New York Times*, September 30, 1999, https://www.nytimes.com/1999/09/30/business/fannie-mae-eases-credit-to-aid-mortgage-lending.html.

16. Ashcraft and Schuermann, *Understanding the Securitization.*

17. *The Financial Crisis Inquiry Report.*

18. Ben Bernanke, *21st Century Monetary Policy: The Federal Reserve from the Great Inflation to COVID-19* (New York: W.W. Norton & Company, 2022).

19. These are not the only regulatory changes that contributed to the GFC. Part 2 of the *Financial Crisis Inquiry Report* provides a more comprehensive inventory of problems and their sources.

20. *The Financial Crisis Inquiry Report.*

21. The *Financial Crisis Inquiry Report.*

22. "*Money Market Funds; Total Financial Assets, Level,*" The Federal Reserve Bank of St. Louis, updated March 9, 2023, https://fred.stlouisfed.org/series/MMMFFAQ027S.

23. "Money Market Funds."

24. "Asset-Backed Commercial Paper Outstanding," Federal Reserve Bank of St. Louis, updated May 11, 2023, https://fred.stlouisfed.org/series/ABCOM.

25. Moody's Investors Services Annual 10-K Reports, https://www.sec.gov/cgi-bin/browse-edgar?action=getcurrent.

26. International Swaps and Derivatives Association (2010), ISDA Market Survey.

27. *The Financial Crisis Inquiry Report.*

28. Henry M. Paulson Jr., *On the Brink: Inside the Race to Stop the Collapse of the Global Financial System* (New York: Hatchett, 2010).

29. Richard White, *Railroaded* (New York: W.H. Norton and Company, 2011), 78.

30. Paulson, *On the Brink*; *The Financial Crisis Inquiry Report*.

31. Bernanke, *21st Century Monetary Policy*, 109.

32. "Federal Funds Effective Rate," Federal Reserve Bank of St. Louis, updated May 1, 2023, https://fred.stlouisfed.org/series/fedfunds.

33. Bernanke, *21st Century Monetary Policy*.

34. Eric Arentsen et al., "Subprime Mortgage Defaults and Credit Default Swaps," *The Journal of Finance* 70, no. 2 (April 2015): 689–731, https://doi.org/10.1111/jofi.12221.

35. "S&P CoreLogic Case-Shiller Home Price Indices," S&P Dow Jones Indices, https://www.spglobal.com/spdji/en/index-family/indicators/sp-corelogic-case-shiller/sp-corelogic-case-shiller-composite/#overview.

36. Timothy F. Geithner, *Stress Test: Reflections on Financial Crises* (New York: Crown Publishers, 2014).

37. *The Financial Crisis Inquiry Report*.

38. John Gapper, "Wall Street's Bruising Musical Chairs," *Financial Times*, November 14, 2007. In fairness, Prince was referring to the lending practices in leveraged buyouts, but Citi behaved similarly in its approach to subprime mortgages.

39. Sudip Kar-Gupta and Yann Le Guernigou, "BNP Freezes $2.2 Billion of Funds Over Subprime," Reuters, August 8, 2007, https://www.reuters.com/article/us-bnpparibas-subprime-funds-idUSWEB612920070809.

40. Paulson, *On the Brink*.

41. "Asset-Backed Commercial Paper Outstanding," Federal Reserve Bank of St. Louis, updated May 10, 2023, https://fred.stlouisfed.org/series/ABCOMP.

42. The purchase price was later increased to $10 per share to ensure that the Bear Stearns board of directors would approve the deal. Paulson, *On the Brink*.

43. Manuel León Hoyos, "Term Securities Lending Facility," *Journal of Financial Crises* 2, no. 3 (2020), 202–228, https://ssrn.com/abstract=3717255; "Board Announces Initiatives to Provide Additional Support to Financial Markets," Federal Reserve Bank of New York, September 15, 2008, https://www.newyorkfed.org/banking/circulars/11985.html; Rosalind Z. Wiggins, "The Asset-Backed Commercial Paper Money Market Mutual Fund Liquidity Facility (AMLF) (U.S. GFC)," *Journal of Financial Crises* 2, no. 3 (2020): 229–255, https://elischolar.library.yale.edu/journal-of-financial-crises/vol2/iss3/10?utm_source=elischolar.library.yale.edu.

44. Washington Mutual was initially taken over by the FDIC after declaring bankruptcy; it was then almost immediately sold to J.P. Morgan for $1.9 billion.

45. Paulson, *On the Brink*.

46. Robert F. Bruner and Sean D. Carr, *The Panic of 1907: Lessons Learned from the Market's Perfect Storm* (New York: John Wiley & Sons, 2007).

47. *The Financial Crisis Inquiry Report*.

48. Unlike Lehman, the failure of Washington Mutual was an unforced error as the FDIC had the power to prevent it under the exception to the "least cost" solution requirement in the case of systemically important financial institutions. Sheila Bair would never repeat this mistake, and she played an important role in providing guarantees to the banking system as part of the stress tests in the spring of 2009.

49. *The Financial Crisis Inquiry Report.*

50. The *Financial Crisis Inquiry Report.*

51. Paulson, *On the Brink.*

52. John Kenneth Galbraith, *The Great Crash 1929* (Boston: Houghton Mifflin, 2009).

53. Paulson, *On the Brink.*

54. Paulson, *On the Brink.*

55. Paulson, *On the Brink.*

56. Paulson, *On the Brink.*

57. Paulson, *On the Brink.*

58. "Gross Domestic Product: Fourth Quarter 2008 (FINAL)," Bureau of Economic Analysis, March 26, 2009, https://www.bea.gov/news/2009/gross-domestic-product-fourth-quarter-2008-final-and-corporate-profits.

59. "S&P 500 Index (^SPX): Historical Data," Yahoo! Finance, https://finance.yahoo.com/quote/%5ESPX/history?p=%5ESPX.

60. Robert Sobel, *The Great Bull Market: Wall Street in the 1920s* (New York: W.W. Norton, 1968).

61. Geithner, *Stress Test.*

62. "Unemployment Rate," Federal Reserve Bank of St. Louis, updated May 5, 2023, https://fred.stlouisfed.org/series/UNRATE/.

63. Robert Jabaily, "The Bank Holiday of 1933," March 1933, https://www.federalreservehistory.org/essays/bank-holiday-of-1933.

64. Geithner, *Stress Test.*

65. Bernanke, *21st Century Monetary Policy.*

66. Franklin D. Roosevelt, "Fireside Chat 1: On the Banking Crisis," March 12, 1933, https://millercenter.org/the-presidency/presidential-speeches/march-12-1933-fireside-chat-1-banking-crisis.

67. Jabaily, "The Bank Holiday of 1933."

Chapter 29

1. Robert Solow, "We'd Better Watch Out," *New York Times Book Review* 36 (December 1986), https://typeset.io/papers/we-d-better-watch-out-1tycfktvqf.

2. Bernanke, *21st Century Monetary Policy.*

3. "Real Gross Domestic Product," Federal Reserve Bank of St. Louis, updated April 27, 2023, https://fred.stlouisfed.org/series/GDPC1/.

4. Robert J. Gordon, *The Rise and Fall of American Growth: The U.S. Standard of Living since the Civil War* (Princeton, NJ: Princeton University Press, 2016).

5. "Corporate Profits After Tax (without IVA and CCAdj)," Federal Reserve Bank of St. Louis, updated March 30, 2023, https://fred.stlouisfed.org/series/CP/.

6. "S&P 500 Index - 90 Year Historical Chart," Macrotrends, updated May 10, 2023, https://www.macrotrends.net/2324/sp-500-historical-chart-data.

7. "Unemployment Rate," Federal Reserve Bank of St. Louis, updated May 5, 2023, https://fred.stlouisfed.org/series/UNRATE/.

8. "S&P CoreLogic Case-Shiller Home Price Indices," S&P Dow Jones Indices, https://www.spglobal.com/spdji/en/index-family/indicators/sp-corelogic-case-shiller/sp-corelogic-case-shiller-composite/#overview.

9. The "natural employment rate" is calculated by subtracting the estimated "natural rate of unemployment" from 100 percent. The "natural employment rate" is not a traditional metric; it is used solely for the purpose of simplifying the formula.

10. It is assumed that inflation is excluded from this calculation.

11. The traditional formula for calculating GDP growth is expressed as $GDP = C + G + I + NX$. The four factors are: consumption (C), government spending (G), investment (I), and net exports (NX). This formula is not used in this section because it does not isolate the fundamental source of output that drives each of these four factors.

12. "Fast Facts," U.S. Census Bureau, https://www.census.gov/history/www/through_the_decades/ fast_facts/; Jonathan Vespa, Lauren Medina, and David M. Armstrong, "Demographic Turning Points for the United States: Population Projections for 2020 to 2060," U.S. Census Bureau, revised February 2020, https://www.census.gov/content/dam/Census/library/publications/2020/ demo/p25-1144.pdf.

13. Population growth is not expected to be spread evenly over the next forty years. Projections over the next decade are anticipated to be closer to 0.3 percent.

14. Data regarding the labor force participation rate is considerably less reliable prior to 1948.

15. "Labor Force Participation Rate," Federal Reserve Bank of St. Louis, updated May 5, 2023, https://fred.stlouisfed.org/series/CIVPART.

16. "Projections Overview and Highlights, 2021–2031," U.S. Bureau of Labor Statistics: Monthly Labor Review, November 2022, https://www.bls.gov/opub/mlr/2022/article/projections-overview- and-highlights-2021-31.htm.

17. Older and more experienced workers are generally less prone to experience unemployment than younger workers.

18. Bernanke, *21st Century Monetary Policy*.

19. The *Summary of Economic Projections* expresses these ranges as the natural rate of unemployment. The ranges in this table are calculated by subtracting the ranges provided by the FOMC from 100 percent. *Summary of Economic Projections*, Federal Reserve Board, June of each year, https://www. federalreserve.gov/monetarypolicy/fomc_historical_year.htm; Bernanke, *21st Century Monetary Policy*.

20. Data prior to 1940 was not uniformly reported by decade. The years 1910, 1920, and 1930 are roughly represented by data reported for 1909, 1919, and 1929. Data reported from 1830 to 1890 is based only on the manufacturing industry, and therefore may not paint an accurate picture of the average labor hours across all industries. Nevertheless, the general observation that the workweek shortened is still well supported; Robert Whaples, "Hours of Work in U.S. History," Economic History Association, 1966, https://eh.net/encyclopedia/hours-of-work-in- u-s-history/. (Data is the average of manufacturing survey data from Aldrich and Weeks for the years 1830 to 1890); "Labor Statistics from the Current Population Survey," U.S. Bureau of Labor Statistics, https://www.bls.gov/cps/data.htm (data for 1990 and 2000); "Average Weekly Hours of All Employees, Total Private," Federal Reserve of St. Louis, updated May 5, 2023, https://fred. stlouisfed.org/series/AWHAETP. (Data for December 1, 2010 and December 1, 2020 is used for the decades of 2010 and 2020, respectively.)

21. Gordon, *The Rise and Fall of American Growth*.

22. Gordon's projections were made in 2014. If the same projections were made today, there would likely be slight differences.

23. Gordon, *The Rise and Fall of American Growth*.

24. Data for debt from "Historical Debt Outstanding," TreasuryDirect, last updated October 2, 2022, https://fiscaldata.treasury.gov/datasets/historical-debt-outstanding/historical-debt-outstanding; Data for population from the Bureau of the Census, multiple reports.

25. Debt-to-GDP ratios are often expressed as "total debt held by the public," which excludes the debt that is held by the social security and Medicare trust funds. Total debt includes the holdings of the trust funds.

26. "The 2022 Long-Term Budget Outlook," Congressional Budget Office, July 27, 2022, https://www.cbo.gov/publication/57971.

27. The White House Office of Management and Budget; Federal Reserve Bank of St. Louis [GFDEGDQ188S]; Donald B. Marron, "The Budget and Economic Outlook: Fiscal Years 2007 to 2016," *CBO Testimony before the Committee on the Budget of the United States Senate*, February 2, 2006; Alexander Hamilton, *The First Report on the Public Credit*, January 9, 1790.

28. In fairness, the United States likely would have transitioned much more rapidly if the technological capabilities were invented earlier. Nevertheless, the advancement of the Chinese economy has occurred more rapidly than other emerging nations operating with the same access to technology; Yi Wen, *The Making of an Economic Superpower: Unlocking China's Secret of Rapid Industrialization* (Hackensack, NJ: World Scientific Press, 2016).

29. Estimates of GDP come from the Bureau of the Census; Thomas Berry, *Revised Annual Estimates of American Gross National Product* (Richmond, Va.: Bostwick Press, 1978); Robert E. Gallman, "Economic Growth and Structural Change in the Long Nineteenth Century," in Gallman and Stanley L. Engerman, eds., *The Cambridge Economic History of the United States, vol. 2, The Long Nineteenth Century* (Cambridge, England: Cambridge University Press, 2000), 1–55; Nathan S. Balke and Robert J. Gordon, "The Estimation of Prewar Gross National Product: Methodology and New Evidence," *Journal of Political Economy* 97, no. 1 (February 1989): 38–92; and the Department of Commerce, Bureau of Economic Analysis; Federal Reserve Bank of St. Louis [GDP] for years 2001 to 2021. World Bank Estimates for China from 1960 to 2020, https://data.worldbank.org/indicator/NY.GDP.MKTP.CD?locations=CN.

30. Wen, *The Making of an Economic Superpower*.

31. Odd Arne Westad, *The Cold War: A World History* (New York: Basic Books, 2017).

32. Wen, *The Making of an Economic Superpower*.

33. Wen, *The Making of an Economic Superpower*.

34. Wen, *The Making of an Economic Superpower*.

35. Wen, *The Making of an Economic Superpower*.

36. Wen, *The Making of an Economic Superpower*.

37. Enrico C. Perotti, Sun Laixiang, and Liang Zou, "State-Owned versus Township and Village Enterprises in China," in Josef C. Brada, Paul Wachtel, and Dennis Tao Yang, eds., *China's Economic Development* (London: Palgrave Readers in Economics, 2014), https://doi.org/10.1057/9781137469960. Mao's programs failed to spark the industrial revolution, but several programs provided Deng with a head start. Examples included the creation of industrial infrastructure (even though it was unprofitable at the time) and the initial experimentation with TVEs.

38. Wen, *The Making of an Economic Superpower*.

39. Wen, *The Making of an Economic Superpower*.

40. International Monetary Fund, Balance of Trade Statistics, https://www.imf.org/en/Publications/WEO/weo-database/2023/April/weo-report?c=924,&s=TM_RPCH,TMG_RPCH,TX_RPCH,TXG_RPCH,&sy=1980&ey=2028&ssm=0&scsm=1&scc=0&ssd=1&ssc=0&sic=0&sort=country&ds=.&br=1.

41. "China Statistical Yearbook 2010–2021," *China Daily News*, updated June 29, 2020, https://govt.chinadaily.com.cn/s/202006/29/WS5ef995fd498ed1e2f34075ef/china-statistical-yearbook-2010-2020.html.

42. Wen, *The Making of an Economic Superpower*.

43. Thomas Piketty, "World Inequality Database," https://wid.world/.

44. Piketty, "World Inequality Database."

45. Gordon, *The Rise and Fall of American Growth*.

Chapter 30

1. Paul Volcker and Toyoo Gyohten, *Changing Fortunes: The World's Money and the Threat to American Leadership* (New York: Times Books, 1992).

2. "Updated Assessment on COVID-19 Origins," Office of the Director of National Intelligence: National Intelligence Council—DECLASSIFIED, October 29, 2021, https://www.intelligence.gov/assets/documents/702%20Documents/declassified/Declassified-Assessment-on-COVID-19-Origins.pdf; Jon Cohen, "Evidence Suggests Pandemic Came From Nature, Not Lab, Panel Says," *Science* 378, no. 6616 (October 14, 2022), https://www.science.org/content/article/evidence-suggests-pandemic-came-nature-not-lab-panel-says.

3. CDC Museum COVID-19 Timeline, CDC, https://www.cdc.gov/museum/timeline/covid19.html#Late-2019.

4. "WHO Coronavirus (COVID-19) Dashboard," World Health Organization, https://covid19.who.int.

5. Mark, Higgins, "A Post-COVID Recovery Is Unlikely to Resemble the Roaring 20s; The Years 1919 and 1999 Serve as More Insightful Comparisons," SSRN, May 2, 2021, https://ssrn.com/abstract=3838380; James Grant, *The Forgotten Depression: 1921: The Crash that Cured Itself* (New York: Simon & Schuster, 2014); "War's Effect on Our Markets," *New York Times*, July 31, 1914, https://www.nytimes.com/1914/07/31/archives/bankers-here-confer-on-war-closing-of-stock-exchange-not-necessary.html.

6. The actual amount of several programs was later revised; the charts show the estimated values when the programs were first passed into law. Federal Reserve Bank of St. Louis, https://fred.stlouisfed.org/series/WALCL; "International Monetary Fund," U.S. Department of the Treasury, https://home.treasury.gov/policy-issues/international/international-monetary-fund.

7. Federal Reserve Bank of St. Louis; "International Monetary Fund," U.S. Department of the Treasury.

8. "ARK Innovation ETF (ARKK): Historical Data," Yahoo! Finance, https://finance.yahoo.com/quote/ARKK/; "SPDR S&P 500 ETF Trust (SPY): Historical Data," Yahoo! Finance, https://finance.yahoo.com/quote/SPY.

9. "Banking and Monetary Statistics, 1914–1941," Board of Governors of the Federal Reserve System (November 1943): 439–441, https://fraser.stlouisfed.org/files/docs/publications/bms/1914-1941/BMS14-41_complete.pdf; "Consumer Price Index," U.S. Bureau of Labor Statistics, https://www.bls.gov/cpi/; "Historical Inflation Rates: 1914–2023," US Inflation Calculator, https://www.usinflationcalculator.com/inflation/historical-inflation-rates/.

Chapter 31

1. Letter from Alexander Hamilton to Robert Morris, August 13, 1782, https://founders.archives.gov/documents/Hamilton/01-03-02-0057-0001.

2. Gregory Zuckerman, *The Man Who Solved the Market: How Jim Simons Launched the Quant Revolution* (New York: Penguin Books, 2019).

INDEX

O

P

Q

R

ABOUT THE AUTHOR

Mark J. Higgins, CFA, CFP® is a widely respected financial historian, author, and speaker. His works appear regularly in publications such as the Museum of American Finance's *Financial History* magazine and the CFA Institute's *Enterprising Investor*. Prior to writing *Investing in U.S. Financial History*, Mark served as a senior investment advisor for more than twelve years. In this role, he provided investment advice to large pension funds, endowments, foundations, and corporate plans with aggregate assets exceeding $60 billion. Mark is also a frequent speaker both domestically and internationally on topics relating to U.S. financial history and institutional investment management. Mark graduated Phi Beta Kappa from Georgetown University and holds a master's degree in business administration from the Darden School of Business at the University of Virginia.